EIGHTH EDITION

JUSTICE ADMINISTRATION

POLICE, COURTS, AND CORRECTIONS MANAGEMENT

Kenneth J. Peak

University of Nevada, Reno

PEARSON

Boston Columbus Indianapolis New York San Francisco Hoboken Amsterdam
Cape Town Dubai London Madrid Milan Munich Paris Montreal Toronto Delhi
Mexico City São Paulo Sydney Hong Kong Seoul Singapore Taipei Tokyo

Editorial Director: Andrew Gilfillan
Product Manager: Gary Bauer
Program Manager: Tara Horton
Editorial Assistant: Lynda Cramer
Director of Marketing: David Gessell
Senior Marketing Manager: Mary Salzman
Senior Marketing Coordinator: Alicia Wozniak
Senior Marketing Assistant: Les Roberts
Project Management Team Lead: JoEllen Gohr
Project Manager: Jessica H. Sykes
Procurement Specialist: Deidra Skahill
Senior Art Director: Diane Ernsberger
Text and Cover Designer: Cenveo
Media Project Manager: Leslie Brado
Full-Service Project Management: Munesh Kumar/Aptara®, Inc.
Composition: Aptara®, Inc.
Printer/Binder: Edwards Brothers Malloy
Cover Printer: Phoenix Color/Hagerstown
Text Font: Minion Pro

Photos by Kenneth J. Peak.

Library of Congress Cataloging-in-Publication Data

Peak, Kenneth J.,
    Justice administration : police, courts, and corrections management / Kenneth J. Peak,
University of Nevada, Reno. — Eighth Edition.
        pages cm
    ISBN 978-0-13-359119-4—ISBN 0-13-359119-0
    1. Criminal justice, Administration of—United States.   2. Law
enforcement—United States.   3. Prison administration—United States.
I. Title.
    HV9950.P43   2014
    364.973—dc23   2014032025

10 9 8 7 6 5 4 3 2 1

ISBN 10:   0-13-359119-0
ISBN 13: 978-0-13-359119-4

Dedication

*"[There] are . . . two points in the adventure of the diver: one—when a beggar,
he prepares to plunge. Two—when a prince, he rises with his pearl."*
—Robert Browning, *Paracelsus*, Part I: "Paracelsus Aspires" (1835)

*This eighth edition is dedicated to those who are willing to "plunge" into criminal justice
administration—which is surely, today more than ever, one of the most challenging and
difficult roles our society has to offer.*
—K. P.

THE CRIMINAL

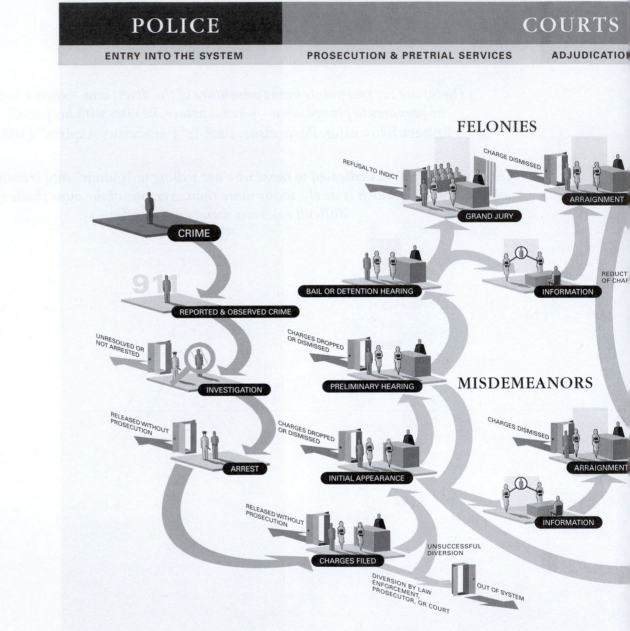

FELONIES

CHARGE DISMISSED

REFUSAL TO INDICT

ARRAIGNMENT

GRAND JURY

CRIME

911

BAIL OR DETENTION HEARING

INFORMATION

REDUCT
OF CHAR

REPORTED & OBSERVED CRIME

UNRESOLVED OR
NOT ARRESTED

CHARGES DROPPED
OR DISMISSED

INVESTIGATION

PRELIMINARY HEARING

MISDEMEANORS

RELEASED WITHOUT
PROSECUTION

CHARGES DROPPED
OR DISMISSED

CHARGES DISMISSED

ARRAIGNMENT

ARREST

INITIAL APPEARANCE

RELEASED WITHOUT
PROSECUTION

INFORMATION

UNSUCCESSFUL
DIVERSION

CHARGES FILED

OUT OF SYSTEM

DIVERSION BY LAW
ENFORCEMENT,
PROSECUTOR, OR COURT

JUSTICE SYSTEM

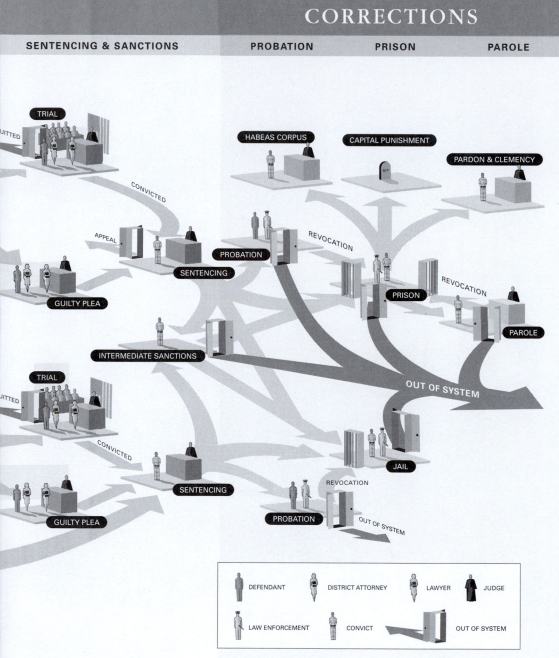

CORRECTIONS

SENTENCING & SANCTIONS   **PROBATION**   **PRISON**   **PAROLE**

TRIAL

UITTED

CONVICTED

APPEAL

GUILTY PLEA

PROBATION

SENTENCING

INTERMEDIATE SANCTIONS

TRIAL

UITTED

CONVICTED

SENTENCING

GUILTY PLEA

HABEAS CORPUS

CAPITAL PUNISHMENT

PARDON & CLEMENCY

REVOCATION

PRISON

REVOCATION

PAROLE

OUT OF SYSTEM

JAIL

REVOCATION

PROBATION

OUT OF SYSTEM

DEFENDANT   DISTRICT ATTORNEY   LAWYER   JUDGE

LAW ENFORCEMENT   CONVICT   OUT OF SYSTEM

Brief Contents

Contents

PART **2**
The Police 77

PART 3
The Courts   159

Chapter 12 **Corrections Issues and Practices 280**

PART 5

Issues Spanning the Justice System: Administrative Challenges and Practices 303

Chapter 13 **Ethical Considerations 304**

New Topics in This Eighth Edition

In addition to the general updated information provided throughout the book, as well as dozens of new examples of various aspects of criminal justice administration, following are other substantively new additions to this revised eighth edition:

Chapter 1: Two *"Deliberate and Decide"* problems.

Chapter 2: New materials on the "Generation Y" employees; the learning organization; a *"Deliberate and Decide"* problem

Chapter 3: This chapter—formerly Chapter 13, concerning rights of criminal justice employees—is relocated to this point for better fit and to set forth many legal aspects and administrative concepts discussed in later chapters; two *"Deliberate and Decide"* employee problems

Chapter 4: Pros and cons of having a single, national police organization; possible shifts in emphases in police organization and operation since 9/11: in mission and emphasis, changing economies and practices, and toward federalization and militarization (moved here from Chapter 6); smart policing (discussions of intelligence-led policing and predictive policing were also moved here, from Chapter 6); a *"Deliberate and Decide"* problem

Chapter 5: Machiavellian advice for chief executives; police chief candidate interviewing and psychological testing; police hiring process as per Kansas City, Missouri; a career profile (county sheriff); a *"Deliberate and Decide"* problem

Chapter 6: Listing of terrorist attacks in the United States; types of officers predisposed to using force; use of force with people having mental disorders; new approaches to "active shooters"; pros and cons of police use of social media; dealing with sexual harassment; updated material on contract/consolidated policing; a *"Deliberate and Decide"* problem

Chapter 7: A century's attempts to streamline the courts; a discussion of the District of Columbia Circuit Court of Appeals; a *"Deliberate and Decide"* problem

Chapter 8: New examples and guidelines on judges' use of electronic social media; what is meant by the appearance of impropriety; examples of judicial misconduct; establishing the office of, and educational requirements for state court administrators; a *"Deliberate and Decide"* problem

Chapter 9: New material and exhibits on the CSI effect; new material and exhibits on problem-solving (drug, mental health, veterans) courts; courts' use of dogs for victims; controversy concerning, effects of federal prosecutors using 21 U.S.C. Sec. 851 to enhance punishments of drug offenders; material and exhibit on juvenile waivers; four steps in conducting a threat assessment; a *"Deliberate and Decide"* problem

Chapter 10: How California's prison population affects that of the nation; the world's worst prisons; warrantless collection of DNA swabs from pre-trial arrestees; adult and juvenile probation and parole agencies' organization, arming of officers, and peace officer status; Hawaii's Project HOPE (for probation); *"Deliberate and Decide"* problem

Chapter 11: Career profile, director of corrections; evolving role of correctional officers; addressing stress and burnout for COs; parole decision making for Charles Manson; federal executions and the Boston Marathon bomber case; *"Deliberate and Decide"* problem

Chapter 12: Supreme Court ban on life without parole sentences for juveniles; programs and treatment for geriatric inmates; updated information on condoms for inmates and use of intermediate sanctions; a "therapeutic community" approach to drug offenders; new and updated information/examples concerning private prisons and day reporting centers; a *"Deliberate and Decide"* problem

Chapter 13: Dealing with *Brady* materials and officers; expanded sections on ethics in policing and corrections; examples of judicial misconduct; a *"Deliberate and Decide"* problem

Chapter 14: Use of a discipline matrix; examining internal complaints against officers; a *"Deliberate and Decide"* problem

Chapter 15: Effects of the Great Recession in the United States, generally; effects of the recession on criminal justice agencies in specific; several responses by police, courts, and corrections agencies to the budget shortfalls; career profile by a budget analyst; a *"Deliberate and Decide"* problem

Chapter 16: This technologies chapter has been completely revised to include recently implemented databases for criminal justice agencies; advances in existing technologies; security, privacy, and/or policy issues concerning cloud computing, unmanned aerial vehicles (drones), and "bring your own device"; use of telemedicine; a *"Deliberate and Decide"* problem

Appendix   New case studies

Famed educator John Dewey advocated the "learn by doing" approach to education, or problem-based learning. Another contemporary, popular learning method, espoused by Benjamin Bloom and known as "Bloom's Taxonomy," called for "higher-order thinking skills"—critical and creative thinking that involves analysis, synthesis, and evaluation.

This eighth edition of *Justice Administration: Police, Courts, and Corrections Management* attempts, to the extent possible, to adhere to such philosophy and practice from start to finish, while continuing to examine all facets of the criminal justice system as well as several related matters of interest to prospective and current administrators. The author has held several administrative and academic positions in a criminal justice career spanning more than 35 years; thus, this book's 16 chapters contain a palpable real-world flavor not found in most textbooks.

Hopefully readers will put into use this eighth edition's new "Deliberate and Decide" and the "In Their Own Words: Administrative Advice from the Field" features that have been added to each chapter. Those additions, along with the continuation of the "Learn by Doing" and the 28 Appendix case-study exercises, should greatly enhance the text's applied nature as well as the reader's problem-solving capabilities and the practical application of information provided in the chapters. These combined chapter and appendix scenarios and activities place the reader in hypothetical—yet typically real-world—situations, moving the emphasis to student-centered projects. These activities also create opportunities to practice skills in communication and examining and addressing current community issues. Again, readers are encouraged to become engaged in some or all of these scenarios and activities.

In addition to the chapters concerning police, courts, and corrections administration, the book includes chapters on personnel and financial administration, rights of criminal justice employees, discipline and liability, ethics, and technologies. A practice continued in this edition is the listing of key terms and concepts and chapter learning objectives, which appear at the beginning of each chapter.

As indicated above, there are two appendices at the book's end. The first appendix includes a total of 28 case studies that apply to most of the book's chapters; they are listed by the number of the chapter to which they apply. Appendix II provides some writings of three noted early philosophers: Confucius, Machiavelli, and Lao-Tzu.

Criminal justice is a people business. This book reflects that fact as it looks at human foibles and some of the problems of personnel and policy in justice administration. Thanks to many innovators in the field, a number of exciting and positive changes are occurring. The general goal of the book is to inform the reader of the primary people, practices, and terms that are utilized in justice administration.

Finally, there may well be activities, policies, actions, and my own views with which the reader will disagree. This is not at all bad, because in the management of people and agencies, there are few absolutes, only ideas and endeavors to make the system better. From the beginning to the end of the book, the reader is provided with a comprehensive and penetrating view of what is certainly one of the most difficult and challenging positions that one can occupy in the United States: the administration of a criminal justice agency. I solicit your input concerning any facet of this textbook; feel free to contact me if you have ideas for improving it.

▶ Instructor Supplements

Instructor's Manual with Test Bank. Includes content outlines for classroom discussion, teaching suggestions, and answers to selected end-of-chapter questions from the text. This also contains a Word document version of the test bank.

TestGen. This computerized test generation system gives you maximum flexibility in creating and administering tests on paper, electronically, or online. It provides state-of-the-art features for viewing and editing test bank questions, dragging a selected question into a test you are creating, and printing sleek, formatted tests in a variety of layouts. Select test items from test banks included with TestGen for quick test creation, or write your own questions from scratch. TestGen's random generator provides the option to display different text or calculated number values each time questions are used.

PowerPoint Presentations. Our presentations offer clear, straightforward outlines and notes to use for class lectures or study materials. Photos, illustrations, charts, and tables from the book are included in the presentations when applicable.

To access supplementary materials online, instructors need to request an instructor access code. Go to **www.pearsonhighered.com/irc,** where you can register for an instructor access code. Within 48 hours after registering, you will receive a confirming e-mail, including an instructor access code. Once you have received your code, go to the site and log on for full instructions on downloading the materials you wish to use.

▶ Pearson Online Course Solutions

Justice Administration is supported by online course solutions that include interactive learning modules, a variety of assessment tools, videos, simulations, and current event features. Go to www.pearsonhighered.com or contact your local representative for the latest information.

▶ Alternate Versions

eBooks. This text is also available in multiple eBook formats, including Adobe Reader and CourseSmart. *CourseSmart* is an exciting new choice for students looking to save money. As an alternative to purchasing the printed textbook, students can purchase an electronic version of the same content. With a *CourseSmart* eTextbook, students can search the text, make notes online, print out reading assignments that incorporate lecture notes, and bookmark important passages for later review. For more information, or to purchase access to the *CourseSmart* eTextbook, visit **www.coursesmart.com.**

▶ Acknowledgments

This edition, like its seven predecessors, is the result of the professional assistance of several people. First, I continue to benefit by the guidance of the staff at Pearson Education. This effort involved: Gary Bauer, Product Manager; Jessica Sykes, Project Manager; and Megan Moffo, Program Manager. Copyediting was masterfully accomplished by

Seilesh Singh. I also wish to acknowledge the invaluable assistance of William Kelly, Auburn University; David Legere, New England College and River Valley Community College; Todd Lough, Western Illinois University; Suzanne Montiel, Nash Community College; Arkil Starke, Keiser University; and Susan Whitstone, Blackhawk Technical College, whose reviews of this edition resulted in many beneficial additions and modifications.

—Ken Peak
peak_k@unr.edu

About the Author

Kenneth J. Peak is a full professor and former Chairman of the Department of Criminal Justice, University of Nevada, Reno, where he was named "Teacher of the Year" by the university's Honor Society. After serving for several years as a municipal police officer in Kansas, Ken subsequently held positions as a nine-county criminal justice planner for southeast Kansas, Director of a four-state Technical Assistance Institute for the Law Enforcement Assistance Administration, Director of University Police at Pittsburg State University (and, later, as Acting Director of Police Services, University of Nevada, Reno), and Assistant Professor of Criminal Justice at Wichita State University. He has authored or coauthored 28 textbooks and 2 historical books on bootlegging and temperance. His other recent books include *Policing America: Methods, Issues, Challenges*, 8th ed.; *Community Policing and Problem Solving: Strategies and Practices*, 6th ed. (with R. W. Glensor); *Police Supervision and Management*, 3rd ed. (with L. K. Gaines and R. W. Glensor); and *Women in Law Enforcement Careers* (with V. B. Lord). He also has published more than 60 monographs, journal articles, and invited chapters on a variety of policing topics. His teaching and research interests include general and community policing, planned change, administration, victimology, and comparative justice systems. Ken has served as chairman of the Police Section of the Academy of Criminal Justice Sciences (ACJS); president of the Western and Pacific Association of Criminal Justice Educators; and Deputy Chair, Academic Review Committee for ACJS. He holds a doctorate from the University of Kansas, and received two gubernatorial appointments to statewide committees while residing in Kansas.

PART 1

Justice Administration
An Introduction

This part, consisting of three chapters, sets the stage for the later analysis of criminal justice agencies and their issues, problems, functions, and challenges in Parts 2 through 5. Chapter 1 examines the scope of justice administration and why we study it. Chapter 2 discusses organization and administration in general, looking at both how organizations are managed and how people are motivated. The rights of criminal justice employees are reviewed in Chapter 3. The introductory section of each chapter previews the specific chapter content.

Telesniuk/shutterstock

1 The Study and Scope of Justice Administration

LEARNING OBJECTIVES

After reading this chapter, the student will be able to:

1. *explain and distinguish between the concepts of* administration, manager, *and* supervisor

2. *understand and distinguish among criminal justice process, network, and nonsystem*

3. *understand system fragmentation and how it affects the amount and type of crime*

4. *understand consensus and conflict theorists and their theories*

5. *understand the two goals of the U.S. criminal justice system (CJS)*

6. *distinguish between extrinsic and intrinsic rewards and how they relate to the CJS*

7. *explain the differences between planned change and unplanned change in an organization*

► Introduction

The overarching theme of this book is that administration is far too important than to be left to on-the-job training or to one's personal idiosyncrasies and ideals. Concisely put, today's leaders must know their people, the current trends and issues of the day, how to deal with related challenges (e.g., financial administration), and the legal underpinnings of their work. Unfortunately, many readers of this book have had to suffer an administrator, manager, or supervisor who was not educated, trained, or well-prepared in these daunting tasks.

This first chapter explains in more detail this book's purposes and general approach, and why it is important and essential to study criminal justice administration. Included are discussions of the criminal justice system itself—whether or not there is a true "system" of justice, how and why the U.S. justice system was founded, and some differences between public and private administration. After a review of planned change and policymaking in justice administration, the chapter concludes with review questions, "deliberate and decide" problems, and "learn by doing" exercises.

► Why Study Justice Administration?

Many of us may find it difficult when we are young to imagine ourselves assuming a leadership role in later life. As one person quipped, we may even have difficulty envisioning ourselves serving as captain of our neighborhood block watch program. The fact is, however, that the organizations increasingly seek people with a high level of education and experience as prospective administrators. The college experience, in addition to transmitting knowledge, is believed to make people more tolerant and secure and less susceptible to debilitating stress and anxiety than those who do not have this experience. We also assume that administration is a science that can be taught; it is not a talent that one must be born with. Unfortunately, however, administrative skills are often learned through on-the-job training; many of us who have worked for a boss with inadequate administrative skills can attest to the inadequacy of this training.

Purpose of the Book and Key Terms

As indicated in the Preface, this textbook attempts to follow, to the extent possible, an applied, practical approach as espoused by famed educator John Dewey, who advocated the "learn by doing" approach to education, or problem-based learning. Another contemporary, popular learning method is also followed, which was espoused by Benjamin Bloom and known as "Bloom's Taxonomy," which called for "higher-order thinking skills"— critical and creative thinking that involves analysis, synthesis, and evaluation.

This book alone, as is true for any other single work on the subject of administration, cannot instantly transform the reader into a bona fide expert in organizational behavior and administrative techniques. It alone cannot prepare someone to accept the reins of administration, supervision, or leadership; formal education, training, and experience are also necessary for such undertakings.

Many good basic books about administration exist; they discuss general aspects of leadership, the use of power and authority, and a number of specialized subjects that are beyond the reach of this book. Instead, here I simply consider some of the major theories, aspects, and issues of administration, laying the foundation for the reader's future study and experience.

Many textbooks have been written about *police* administration; a few have addressed administering courts and corrections agencies. Even fewer have analyzed justice administration from a *systems* perspective, considering all of the components of the justice system and their administration, issues, and practices. This book takes that perspective. Furthermore, most books on administration are immersed in pure administrative theory and concepts; in this way, the *practical* criminal justice perspective is often lost on many college and university students. Conversely, many books dwell on minute concepts, thereby obscuring the administrative principles involved. This book, which necessarily delves into some theory and specialized subject matter, focuses on the practical aspects of justice administration.

Justice Administration is not written as a guidebook for a major sweeping reform of the U.S. justice system. Rather, its primary intent is to familiarize the reader with the methods and challenges of criminal justice administrators. It also challenges the reader, however, to consider what reform is desirable or even necessary and to be open-minded and visualize where changes might be implemented.

Although the terms *administration*, *manager*, and *supervisor* are often used synonymously, each is a unique concept that is related to the others. Administration encompasses both management and supervision; it is the process by which a group of people is organized and directed toward achieving the group's objective. The exact nature of the organization will vary among the different types and sizes of agencies, but the general principles and the form of administration are similar. **Administrators** focus on the overall organization, its mission, and its relationship with other organizations and groups external to it. In a hierarchical organization, they typically hold such ranks as police chief/sheriff, and assistant chief or undersheriff, warden and associate warden, and so on, and include those persons who are in a policymaking position.

Managers, often termed middle management or mid-level managers, are typically the intermediate level of leadership in a hierarchical organization, reporting to the higher echelon of administrators and responsible for carrying out their policies and the agency's mission, while also supervising subordinate managers and employees to ensure a smooth functioning organization; they are typically the ranks of captains and lieutenants. **Supervisors** (also sometimes termed *first-line supervisors*) occupy the lowest position of leadership in an organizational hierarchy, and typically plan, organize, and direct staff members in their daily activities. They are typically sergeants in a hierarchical organization.

In policing (or in prisons, or wherever there is a paramilitary rank structure), for example, although we tend to think of the chief executive as the administrator, the bureau chiefs or commanders as managers, and the sergeants as supervisors, it is important to note that on occasion all three of these roles are required of one administrator; such may be the case when a critical situation occurs, such as a hostage or barricaded-subject incident, and a single person is responsible for all of these levels of decision making.

The terms *police* and *law enforcement* are generally used interchangeably. Many people in the police field believe, however, that the police do more than merely enforce laws; they prefer to use the term *police*.

administrator the person whose focus is on the overall organization, its mission, acquisition and use of resources, and agency relationship with external organizations and groups.

manager a person in the intermediate level of management, responsible for carrying out the policies and directives of upper-level administrators and supervising subordinate managers and employees.

supervisor typically the lowest position of leadership in an organization, one who plans, organizes, and directs staff members in their daily activities.

Organization of the Book

To understand the challenges that administrators of justice organizations face, we first need to place justice administration within the big picture; thus, in Part 1, Justice Administration: An Introduction, I discuss the organization, administration, and general nature of the U.S. justice system; the state of our country with respect to crime and government control; the evolution of justice organization and administration in all of its three components: police, courts, and corrections; and the rights of criminal justice employees,

Parts 2, 3, and 4, which discuss contemporary police, courts, and corrections administration, respectively, follow the same organizational theme: The first chapter of each part deals with the *organization and operation* of the component, followed in the next chapter by an examination of the component's *personnel roles and functions*, and in the third chapter by a discussion of *issues and practices* (including future considerations).

Part 5 examines administrative problems and factors that influence the entire justice system, including ethical considerations, financial administration, and technology for today and the future.

This initial chapter sets the stage for later discussions of the criminal justice system (CJS) and its administration. I first consider whether the justice system comprises a process, a network, a nonsystem, or a true system. A discussion of the legal and historical bases for justice and administration follows (an examination of what some great thinkers have said about governance in general is provided at the end of the book, in Appendix II). The differences between public and private sector administration are reviewed next, and the chapter concludes with a discussion of policymaking in justice administration. After completing this chapter, the reader will have a better grasp of the structure, purpose, and foundation of our CJS.

▶ A True *System* of Justice?

What do justice administrators—police, courts, and corrections officials—actually *administer*? Do they provide leadership over a system that has succeeded in accomplishing its mission? Do individuals within the system work amiably and communicate well with one another? Do they all share the same goals? Do their efforts result in crime reduction? In short, do they compose a *system*? I now turn to these questions, taking a fundamental yet expansive view of justice administration.

The U.S. CJS attempts to decrease criminal behavior through a wide variety of uncoordinated and sometimes uncomplementary efforts. Each system component—police, courts, and corrections—has varying degrees of responsibility and discretion for dealing with crime. Often a federal, state, or local system component fails, however, to engage in any coordinated planning effort; hence, relations among and between these components are often characterized by friction, conflict, and deficient communication. Role conflicts also serve to ensure that planning and communication are stifled.

For example, one role of the police is to arrest suspected offenders. Police typically are not judged by the public on the quality (e.g., having probable cause) of arrests but on their number. Prosecutors often complain that police provide case reports of poor quality. Prosecutors, for their part, are partially judged by their success in obtaining convictions; a public defender or defense attorney is judged by success in getting suspected offenders' charges dropped. The courts are very independent in their operation, largely sentencing offenders as they see fit. Corrections agencies are torn between the philosophies of punishment and rehabilitation and, in the view of many, wind up performing neither function with a large degree of success. These agencies are further burdened with overcrowded conditions, high caseloads, and antiquated facilities.[1] Unfortunately, this situation has existed for several decades and continues today.

This criticism of the justice system or process—that it is fragmented and rife with role conflicts and other problems—is a common refrain. Following are several views of the CJS as it currently operates: the process, network, and nonsystem points of view. Following the discussion of those three points of view, I consider whether criminal justice truly represents a system.

A Criminal Justice Process?

What is readily seen in the foregoing discussion is that our CJS may not be a system at all. Given its current operation and fragmentation, it might be better described as a **criminal justice process**. As a process, it involves the decisions and actions taken by an institution, offender, victim, or society that influence the offender's movement into, through, or out of the justice system.[2] In its purest form, the criminal justice process occurs as shown in

> **criminal justice process** the decisions and actions by an institution, offender, victim, or society that influence the offender's movement into, through, or out of the justice system.

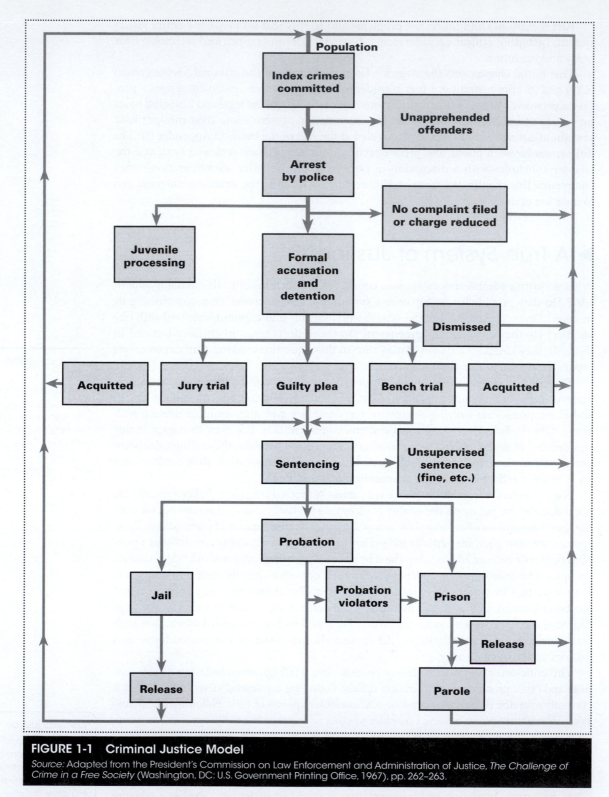

FIGURE 1-1   Criminal Justice Model

Source: Adapted from the President's Commission on Law Enforcement and Administration of Justice, *The Challenge of Crime in a Free Society* (Washington, DC: U.S. Government Printing Office, 1967), pp. 262–263.

Figure 1-1 ■. Note that the horizontal effects result from factors, such as the amount of crime, the number of prosecutions, and the type of court disposition affecting the population in correctional facilities and rehabilitative programs. Vertical effects represent the primary system steps or procedures.[3]

At one end of this process are the police who understandably may view their primary role as getting lawbreakers off the street. At the other end of the process are the corrections officials who may see their role as being primarily custodial in nature. Somewhere in between are the courts that try to ensure a fair application of the law to each case coming to the bar.

As a process, the justice system cannot reduce crime by itself nor can any of the component parts afford to be insensitive to the needs and problems of the other parts. In criminal justice planning jargon, "You can't rock one end of the boat." In other words, every action has a reaction, especially in the justice process. If, say, a bond issue for funds to provide 10 percent more police officers on the streets is passed in a community, the additional arrests made by those added police personnel will have a decided impact on the courts and correction components. Obviously, although each component operates largely on its own, the actions and reactions of each with respect to crime will send ripples throughout the process.

Much of the failure to deal effectively with crime may be attributed to organizational and administrative fragmentation of the justice process. Fragmentation exists among the components of the process, within the individual components, among political jurisdictions, and among persons.

A Criminal Justice Network?

Other observers contend that U.S. justice systems constitute a **criminal justice network**.[4] According to Steven Cox and John Wade, the justice system functions much like a television or radio network whose stations share many programs but in which each station also presents programs that the network does not air on other stations. The network appears as a three-dimensional model in which the public, legislators, police, prosecutors, judges, and correctional officials interact with one another and with others who are outside the traditionally conceived CJS.[5]

> **criminal justice network** a view that the justice system's components cooperate and share similar goals but operate independently and competing for funding.

Furthermore, the criminal justice network is said to be based on several key yet erroneous assumptions, including the following:

1. The components of the network cooperate and share similar goals.

2. The network operates according to a set of formal procedural rules to ensure uniform treatment of all persons, the outcome of which constitutes justice.

3. Each person accused of a crime receives due process and is presumed innocent until proven guilty.

4. Each person receives a speedy public trial before an impartial jury of his or her peers and is represented by competent legal counsel.[6]

Cox and Wade asserted that these key assumptions are erroneous for the following reasons:

1. The three components have incompatible goals and are continually competing with one another for budgetary dollars.

2. Evidence indicates that blacks and whites, males and females, and middle- and lower-class citizens receive differential treatment in the criminal justice network.

3. Some persons are prosecuted, some are not; some are involved in plea bargaining, others are not; some are convicted and sent to prison, whereas others convicted of the same type of offense are not. A great deal of the plea negotiation process remains largely invisible, such as "unofficial probation" with juveniles. In addition, Cox and Wade argued, considerable evidence points to the fact that criminal justice employees do not presume their clients or arrestees to be innocent.

4. Finally, these proponents of a network view of the justice process argued that the current backlog of cases does not ensure a speedy trial, even though a vast majority (at least 90%) of all arrestees plead guilty prior to trial.[7]

Adherents of this position, therefore, believe that our CJS is probably not a just network in the eyes of the poor, minority groups, or individual victims. Citizens, they also assert, may not know what to expect from such a network. Some believe that the system does not work as a network at all and that this conception is not worth their support.[8]

A Criminal Justice Nonsystem?

Many observers argue that the three components of the CJS actually comprise a **criminal justice nonsystem**. They maintain that the three segments of the U.S. CJS that deal with criminal behavior do not always function in harmony and that the system is neither efficient enough to create a credible fear of punishment nor fair enough to command respect for its values.

Indeed, these theorists are given considerable support by the President's Commission on Law Enforcement and the Administration of Justice (commonly known as the *Crime Commission*), which made the following comment:

> The system of criminal justice used in America to deal with those crimes it cannot prevent and those criminals it cannot deter is not a monolithic, or even a consistent, system. It was not designed or built in one piece at one time. Its philosophic core is that a person may be punished by the Government, if, and only if, it has been proven by an impartial and deliberate process that he has violated a specific law. Around that core, layer upon layer of institutions and procedures, some carefully constructed and some improvised, some inspired by principle and some by expediency, have accumulated. Parts of the system—magistrates, courts, trial by jury, bail—are of great antiquity. Other parts—juvenile courts, probation and parole, professional policemen—are relatively new. Every village, town, county, city, and State has its own criminal justice system, and there is a Federal one as well. All of them operate somewhat alike, no two of them operate precisely alike.[9]

Alfred Cohn and Roy Udolf stated that criminal justice "is not a system, and it has little to do with justice as that term is ordinarily understood."[10] Also, in this school of thought are Burton Wright and Vernon Fox, who asserted that "the criminal justice system—is frequently criticized because it is not a coordinated structure—not really a system. In many ways this is true."[11]

These writers would probably agree that little has changed since 1971, when *Newsweek* stated in a special report entitled "Justice on Trial" that:

> America's system of criminal justice is too swamped to deliver more than the roughest justice—and too ragged really to be called a system. "What we have," says one former government hand, "is a non-system in which the police don't catch criminals, the courts don't try them, and the prisons don't reform them. The system, in a word, is in trouble. The trouble has been neglect. The paralysis of the civil courts, where it takes five years to get a judgment in a damage suit—the courts—badly managed, woefully undermanned and so inundated with cases that they have to run fast just to stand still."[12]

Unfortunately, in many jurisdictions, those words still ring true. Too often, today's justice administrators cannot be innovators or reformers but rather simply "make do." As one law professor stated, "Oliver Wendell Holmes could not survive in our criminal court. How can you be an eminent jurist when you have to deal with this mess?"[13]

Those who hold that the justice system is in reality no system at all can also point to the fact that many practitioners in the field (police, judges, prosecutors, correctional workers, and private attorneys) and academicians concede that the entire justice system is in crisis, even rapidly approaching a major breakdown. They can cite problems everywhere—large numbers of police calls for service, overcrowded court dockets, and increasing prison populations. In short, they contend that the system is in a state of dysfunction, largely as a result of its fragmentation and lack of cohesion.[14]

System fragmentation is largely believed to directly affect the amount and type of crime that exists. Contributing to this fragmentation are the wide discretionary powers possessed by actors in the justice system. For example, police officers (primarily those having the least experience, education, and training) have great discretion over whom they arrest and are effectively able to dictate policy as they go about performing their duties. Here again, the Crime Commission was moved to comment as follows, realizing that how the police officer moves around his or her territory depends largely on this discretion:

> Crime does not look the same on the street as it does in a legislative chamber. How much noise or profanity makes conduct "disorderly" within the meaning of the law? When must a quarrel be treated as a criminal assault: at the first threat, or at the first shove, or at the first blow, or after blood is drawn, or when a serious injury is inflicted? How suspicious must conduct be before there is "probable cause," the constitutional basis for an arrest? Every [officer], however sketchy or incomplete his education, is an interpreter of the law.[15]

Judicial officers also possess great discretionary latitude. State statutes require judges to provide deterrence, retribution, rehabilitation, and incapacitation—all in the same sentence. Well-publicized studies of the sentencing tendencies of judges—in which participants were given identical facts in cases and were to impose sentences based on the offender's violation of the law—have demonstrated considerable discretion and unevenness in the judges' sentences. The nonsystem advocates believe this to be further evidence that a basic inequality exists—an inequality in justice that is communicated to the offender.[16]

Finally, fragmentation also occurs in corrections—the part of the criminal justice process that the U.S. public sees the least of and knows the least about. Indeed, as the Crime Commission noted, the federal government, all 50 states, the District of Columbia, and most of the country's 3,047 counties now engage in correctional activities of some form. Each level of government acts independently of the others, and the responsibility for the administration of corrections is divided within the given jurisdictions as well.[17]

With this fragmentation comes polarity in identifying and establishing the primary goals of the system. The police, enforcing the laws, emphasize community protection; the courts weigh both sides of the issue—individual rights and community needs; and corrections facilities work with the individual. Each of these groups has its own perception of the offender, creating goal conflict; that is, the goal of the police and the prosecutor is to get the transgressor off the street, which is antithetical to the caretaker role of the corrections worker who often wants to rehabilitate and return the offender to the community. The criminal justice process does not allow many alternative means of dealing with offenders. The nonsystem adherent believes that eventually the offender will become a mere statistic, more important on paper than as a human being.[18]

Because the justice process lacks sufficient program and procedural flexibility, these adherents argue, its workers either can circumvent policies, rules, and regulations or adhere to organizational practices they know are, at times, dysfunctional. (As evidence of the former, they point to instances of *informal* treatment of criminal cases; e.g., a police officer "bends" someone's constitutional rights in order to return stolen property to its rightful owner, or a juvenile probation officer, without a solid case but with strong suspicion, warns a youth that any further infractions will result in formal court-involved proceedings.)

system fragmentation the view that members of police, courts, and corrections agencies have tremendous discretion and their own perception of the offender, resulting in goal conflict.

Or, Is It a True Criminal Justice System?

That all of the foregoing perspectives on the justice system are grounded in truth is probably evident by now. In many ways, the police, courts, and corrections components work and interact to function like a process, a network, or even a nonsystem. However, the justice system may still constitute a true system. As Willa Dawson stated, "Administration of justice can be regarded as a system by most standards. It may be a poorly functioning system but it does meet the criteria nonetheless. The systems approach is still in its infancy."[19] J. W. La Patra added, "I do believe that a criminal justice system [CJS] does exist, but that it functions very poorly. The CJS is a loosely connected, nonharmonious, group of social entities."[20]

To be fair, however, perhaps this method of dealing with offenders is best after all; it may be that having a well-oiled machine—in which all activities are coordinated, goals and objectives are unified, and communication between participants is maximized, all serving to grind out justice in a highly efficacious manner—may not be what we truly want or need in a democracy.

I hope that I have not belabored the subject; however, it is important to establish early in this book the type of system and the components that you, as a potential criminal justice administrator, may encounter. You can reconcile for yourself the differences of opinion described earlier. In this book, I adhere to the notion that even with all of its disunity and lack of fluidity, what criminal justice officials administer in the United States is a system. Nonetheless, it is good to look at its operation and shortcomings and, as stated earlier, confront the CJS's problems and possible areas for improvement.

Now that we have a systemic view of what it is that criminal justice managers actually administer, it would be good to look briefly at how they go about doing it. I first consider the legal and historical bases that created the United States as a democracy regulated by a government and by a system of justice; I include the consensus–conflict continuum, with the social contract on one end and the maintenance of the status quo/repression on the other. Next, I distinguish between administration and work in the public and private sectors because the styles, incentives, and rewards of each are, by their very nature, quite different. This provides the foundation for the final point of discussion, a brief look at the policymaking process in criminal justice agencies.

▶ The Foundations of Justice and Administration: Legal and Historical Bases

Given that our system of justice is founded on a large, powerful system of government, the following questions must be addressed: From where is that power derived? How can governments presume to maintain a system of laws that effectively governs its people and, furthermore, a legal system that exists to punish persons who willfully suborn those laws? We now consider the answers to those questions.

The Consensus versus Conflict Debate

U.S. society has innumerable lawbreakers. Most of them are easily handled by the police and do not challenge the legitimacy of the law while being arrested and incarcerated for violating it. Nor do they challenge the system of government that enacts the laws or the justice agencies that carry them out. The stability of our government for more than 200 years is a testimony to the existence of a fair degree of consensus as to its legitimacy.[21] Thomas Jefferson's statements in the *Declaration of Independence* are as true today as the day when he wrote them and are accepted as common sense:

We hold these truths to be self-evident, that all men are created equal, that they are endowed by their Creator with certain inalienable Rights, that among these are Life, Liberty, and the pursuit of Happiness—That to secure these rights, Governments are instituted among Men, deriving their just powers from the consent of the governed. That whenever any Form of Government becomes destructive of these ends, it is the Right of the People to alter or abolish it.

The principles of the Declaration are almost a paraphrase of John Locke's *Second Treatise on Civil Government*, which justifies the acts of government on the basis of Locke's theory of social contract. In the state of nature, people, according to Locke, were created by God to be free, equal, independent, and with inherent inalienable rights to life, liberty, and property. Each person had the right of self-protection against those who would infringe on these liberties. In Locke's view, although most people were good, some would be likely to prey on their fellows, who in turn would constantly have to be on guard against such evildoers. To avoid this brutish existence, people joined together, forming governments to which they surrendered their right of self-protection. In return, they received governmental protection of their lives, property, and liberty. As with any contract, each side has benefits and considerations; people give up their right to protect themselves and receive protection in return. Governments give protection and receive loyalty and obedience in return.[22]

Locke believed that the chief purpose of government was the protection of property. Properties would be joined together to form the commonwealth. Once the people unite into a commonwealth, they cannot withdraw from it nor can their lands be removed from it. Property holders become members of that commonwealth only with their express consent to submit to the government of the commonwealth. This is Locke's famous theory of *tacit consent*: "Every Man . . . doth hereby give his *tacit Consent*, and is as far forth obliged to Obedience to the Laws of the Government."[23] Locke's theory essentially describes an association of landowners.[24]

Another theorist connected with the **social contract** theory is Thomas Hobbes, who argued that all people were essentially irrational and selfish. He maintained that people had just enough rationality to recognize their situation and to come together to form governments for self-protection, agreeing "amongst themselves to submit to some Man, or Assembly of men, voluntarily, on confidence to be protected by him against all others."[25] Therefore, they existed in a state of consensus with their governments.

Jean-Jacques Rousseau, a conflict theorist, differed substantively from both Hobbes and Locke, arguing that "Man is born free, but everywhere he is in chains."[26] Like Plato, Rousseau associated the loss of freedom and the creation of conflict in modern societies with the development of private property and the unequal distribution of resources. Rousseau described conflict between the ruling group and the other groups in society, whereas Locke described consensus within the ruling group and the need to use force and other means to ensure the compliance of the other groups.[27]

Thus, the primary difference between the consensus and conflict theorists with respect to their view of government vis-à-vis the governed concerns their evaluation of the legitimacy of the actions of ruling groups in contemporary societies. Locke saw those actions as consistent with natural law, describing societies as consensual and arguing that any conflict was illegitimate and could be repressed by force and other means. Rousseau evaluated the actions of ruling groups as irrational and selfish, creating conflicts among the various groups in society.[28]

This debate is important because it plays out the competing views of humankind toward its ruling group; it also has relevance with respect to the kind of justice system (or process) we have. The system's model has been criticized for implying a greater level of organization and cooperation among the various agencies of justice than actually exists. The word *system* conjures an idea of machinelike precision in which wasted effort, redundancy, and

social contract a belief that people are essentially irrational and selfish, but have enough rationality to come together to form governments for self-protection.

conflicting actions are nearly nonexistent; our current justice system does not possess such a level of perfection. As mentioned earlier, conflicts among and within agencies are rife, goals are not shared by the system's three components, and the system may move in different directions. Therefore, the systems approach is part of the **consensus model** point of view, which assumes that all parts of the system work toward a common goal.[29] The **conflict model**, holding that agency interests tend to make actors within the system self-serving, provides the other approach. This view notes the pressures for success, promotion, and general accountability, which together result in fragmented efforts of the system as a whole, leading to a criminal justice nonsystem.[30]

This debate also has relevance for criminal justice administrators. Assume a consensus–conflict continuum, with social contract (the people totally allow government to use its means to protect them) on one end and class repression on the other. That our administrators *do not* allow their agencies to drift too far to one end of the continuum or the other is of paramount importance. Americans cannot allow the compliance or conflict that would result at either end; the safer point is toward the middle of the continuum, where people are not totally dependent on their government for protection and maintain enough control to prevent totalitarianism.

Crime Control through Due Process

In 1968, Herbert Packer described two now-classic models of the criminal justice process (See Figure 1-2 ■) in terms of two competing value systems: crime control and due process.[31] The **due process model**—likened to an "obstacle course" by some authors—essentially holds that criminal defendants should be presumed innocent, that the courts' first priority is protecting the constitutional rights of the accused, and that granting too much freedom to law enforcement officials will result in the loss of freedom and civil liberties for all Americans; therefore, each court case must involve formal factfinding to uncover mistakes by the police and prosecutors. This view also stresses that crime is not a result of individual moral failure, but is the result of social influences (such as unemployment, racial discrimination, and other factors that disadvantage the poor); thus, courts that do not follow this philosophy are fundamentally unfair to these defendants. Furthermore, rehabilitation will prevent further crime.

Crime Control Model

1. The repression of crime is of utmost importance, to provide order.
2. CJ focus should be on helping victims rather than on defendants' rights.
3. Police powers should be expanded, legal technicalities eliminated, for ease of arrest, search and seizure, conviction.
4. The CJ process should operate like an assembly-line, moving cases through swiftly.
5. There should generally be a presumption of guilt of the accused (and police/prosecutors' views trusted).

Due Process Model

1. CJ must provide due process, fairness, and a focus on defendants' rights, as provided in the Bill of Rights.
2. Police powers should be limited to prevent oppression.
3. Constitutional rights aren't "technicalities," so hold police/prosecutors accountable to ensure fairness.
4. The CJ process should resemble an obstacle course, w/impediments/safeguards to protect the innocent & convict the guilty.

FIGURE 1-2   Herbert Packer's Crime Control/Due Process Models of Criminal Justice: A Synopsis

Note: No city will be wholly in one or the other; also, the political climate determines which model shapes criminal justice policy at a specific point in time.

In contrast is the **crime control model**, which is a much more traditional philosophy and which Packer likened to an "assembly line." This model views crime as a breakdown of individual responsibility. It places the highest importance on repressing criminal conduct and thus protecting society. Persons who are charged are presumed guilty, and the courts should not hinder effective enforcement of the laws; rather, legal loopholes should be eliminated and offenders swiftly punished. Under this philosophy, the police and prosecutors should have a high degree of discretion. Punishment will deter crime, so there must be speed and finality in the courts to ensure crime suppression.

Although Packer indicated that neither of these models would be found to completely dominate a particular community or control U.S. crime policy,[32] even to say that one of these models is superior to the other requires an individual to make a value judgment. How much leeway should be given to the police? Should they be allowed to "bend" the laws just a little bit in order to get criminals off the streets? Does the end justify the means? These are important questions; note that these questions will be revisited in discussions of ethics in Chapter 4 and police discretion in Chapter 6.

> ## Public versus Private Sector Administration

The fact that people derive positive personal experiences from their work has long been recognized.[33] Because work is a vital part of our lives and carries tremendous meaning in terms of our personal identity and happiness, the right match of person to job has long been recognized as a determinant of job satisfaction.[34] Factors such as job importance, accomplishment, challenge, teamwork, management fairness, and rewards become very important.

People in both the public (i.e., government) and private (e.g., retail business) sectors derive personal satisfaction from their work. The means by which they arrive at those positive feelings and are rewarded for their efforts, however, are often quite different. Basically, whereas private businesses and corporations can use a panoply of *extrinsic* (external) rewards to motivate and reward their employees, people working in the public sector must achieve job satisfaction primarily through *intrinsic* (internal) rewards.

Extrinsic rewards include perquisites such as financial compensation (salary and a benefits package), a private office, a key to the executive washroom, bonuses, trips, a company car, awards (including designations such as the employee of the month or the insurance industry's "million-dollar roundtable"), an expense account, membership in country clubs and organizations, and a prestigious job title. The title assigned to a job can affect one's general perceptions of the job regardless of the actual job content. For example, the role once known disparagingly as "grease monkey" in a gasoline service station has commonly become known as "lubrication technician," garbage collectors have become "sanitation engineers," and so on. Enhancement of job titles is done to add job satisfaction and extrinsic rewards to what may often be lackluster positions.

Corporations often devote tremendous amounts of time and money to bestowing extrinsic rewards, incentives, and job titles on employees to enhance their job satisfaction. These rewards, of course, cannot and do not exist in the public sector anywhere near the extent that they do in the private sector.

As indicated earlier, public sector workers must seek and obtain job satisfaction primarily from within—through intrinsic means. These workers, unable to become wealthy through their salaries and to be in a position that is filled with perks, need jobs that are gratifying and that intrinsically make them feel good about themselves and what they accomplish. Practitioners often characterize criminal justice work as intrinsically rewarding, providing a sense of worth in making the world a little better place in which to live. These employees also seek appreciation from their supervisors and coworkers and generally enjoy challenges.

crime control model
a philosophy that states crime must be repressed, the accused presumed guilty, legal loopholes eliminated, offenders swiftly punished, and police and prosecutors given a high degree of discretion.

To be successful, administrators should attempt to understand the personalities, needs, and motivations of their employees and attempt to meet those needs and provide motivation to the extent possible. The late Sam Walton, the multibillionaire founder of Wal-Mart stores, provided a unique example of the attempt to do this. One night, Walton could not sleep, so he went to a nearby all-night bakery in Bentonville, Arkansas, bought four dozen doughnuts, and took them to a distribution center where he chatted with graveyard-shift Wal-Mart employees. From that chat, he discovered that two more shower stalls were needed at that location.[35] Walton obviously solicited—and valued—employees' input and was concerned about their morale and working conditions. Although Walton was known to be unique in his business sense, these are elements of administration that can be applied by all public administrators.

▶ Planned Change and Policymaking in Justice Administration

Planning Interventions

In past decades and simpler times, change in criminal justice agencies typically occurred slowly and incrementally. Continuous change is now a constant rather than an exception, however, and the pace and frequency of change have increased. While change is not bad in itself, if unplanned, programs will often fail and even result in negative consequences in the workplace—absences, tardiness, medical or stress leaves, high turnover rates, and even sabotage. Remember, too, that a major change occurring in one component of the justice system can have severe repercussions on the others if not anticipated and planned for. Often times, major changes are enacted without due consideration given to planning, design, implementation, and evaluation; a good example is the initial "three-strikes" laws, initiated in California in 1994, which had a very different structure and outcome than originally intended.

Obviously, then, change in criminal justice should not and typically does not occur accidentally or haphazardly. Justice administrators must know how to plan, implement, and evaluate interventions that address problems in their organizations and systems while taking into account components such as time frame, target population, outcomes, and normative values—guiding assumptions about how the CJS *ought* to function. **Planned change**, therefore, involves problem analysis, setting goals and objectives, program and policy design, developing an action plan, and monitoring and evaluation.

As examples, specific programs and policies have been developed to address domestic violence; prostitution; drug abuse; gang activities; repeat offenders; the availability of handguns; prison overcrowding; and the efficacy of statutory enactments, such as the "three-strikes" law.

The most complex and comprehensive approach to effecting planned change in criminal justice is to create a *policy*. Policies vary in the complexity of the rule or guidelines being implemented and the amount of discretion given to those who apply them. For example, police officers are required to read *Miranda* warnings to suspects before they begin questioning them if the information might later be used in court against the defendant. This is an example where discretion is relatively constrained, although the Supreme Court has formulated specific exceptions to the rule. Sometimes policies are more complex, such as "the social policy" of President Lyndon Johnson's War on Poverty in the 1960s. Organizations, too, create policies specifying how they are going to accomplish their mission, expend their resources, and so on.[36]

Imagine the following scenario. Someone in criminal justice operations (e.g., a city, or county manager, or a municipal, or criminal justice planner) is charged with formulating

planned change
rational approach to criminal justice planning that involves problem analysis, setting goals and objectives, program and policy design, developing an action plan, and monitoring and evaluation.

an omnibus policy with respect to crime reduction. He or she might begin by trying to list all the related variables that contribute to the crime problem: poverty; employment; demographics of people residing within the jurisdiction; environmental conditions (such as housing density and conditions and slum areas); mortality, morbidity, and suicide rates; educational levels of the populace; and so on.

The administrator would request more specific information from each justice administrator within the jurisdiction to determine where problems might exist in the practitioners' view of the police, courts, and corrections subsystems. For example, a police executive would contribute information concerning calls for service, arrests, and crime data (including offender information and crime information—time of day, day of week, methods, locations, targets, and so on). The status of existing programs, such as community policing and crime prevention, would also be provided. From the courts, information would be sought concerning the sizes of civil and criminal court dockets and backlogs ("justice delayed is justice denied"). Included in this report would be input from the prosecutor's office concerning the quality and quantity of police reports and arrests, as well as data on case dismissals and conviction rates at trial. From corrections administrators would come the average officer caseload and the recidivism and revocation rates. Budgetary information would certainly be solicited from all subsystems, as well as miscellaneous data regarding personnel levels, training levels, and so on. Finally, the administrator would attempt to formulate a crime policy, setting forth goals and objectives for addressing the jurisdiction's needs.

As an alternative, the policymaker could approach this task in a far less complex manner, simply setting, either explicitly or without conscious thought, the relatively simple goal of "keeping crime down." This goal might be compromised or complicated by other factors, such as an economic recession. This administrator could in fact disregard most of the other variables discussed earlier as being beyond his or her current needs and interest and would not even attempt to consider them as immediately relevant. The criminal justice practitioners would not be pressed to attempt to provide information and critical analyses. If pressed for time (as is often the case in these real-life scenarios), the planner would readily admit that these variables were being ignored.[37]

Because executives and planners of the alternative approach expect to achieve their goals only partially, they anticipate repeating endlessly the sequence just described as conditions and aspirations change and as accuracy of prediction improves. Realistically, however, the first of these two approaches assumes intellectual capacities and sources of information that people often do not possess; furthermore, the time and money that can be allocated to a policy problem are limited. Public agencies are in effect usually too hamstrung to practice the first method; it is the second method that is followed. Curiously, however, the literature on decision making, planning, policy formulation, and public administration formalizes and preaches the first approach.[38] The second method is much neglected in this literature.

In the United States, probably no part of government has attempted a comprehensive analysis and overview of policy on crime (the first method just described). Thus, making crime policy is at best a rough process. Without a more comprehensive process, we cannot possibly understand, for example, how a variety of problems—education, housing, recreation, employment, race, and policing methods—might encourage or discourage juvenile delinquency. What we normally engage in is a comparative analysis of the results of similar past policy decisions. This explains why justice administrators often believe that outside experts or academics are not helpful to them—why it is safer to "fly by the seat of one's pants." Theorists often urge the administrator to go the long way to the solution of his or her problems, following the scientific method, when the administrator knows that the best available theory will not work. Theorists, for their part, do not realize that the administrator is often in fact practicing a systematic method.[39] So, what may appear to be mere

policymaking
(1) developing plans that are then used by an organization or government as a basis for making decisions; (2) establishing rules, principles, or guidelines to govern actions by ordinary citizens and persons in positions of authority.

muddling through is both highly praised as a sophisticated form of **policymaking**—the formal development of ideas or plans that are then used by an organization or government to guide decision making—and soundly denounced as no method at all. What society needs to bear in mind is that justice administrators possess an intimate knowledge of past consequences of actions that outsiders do not. Although seemingly less effective and rational, this method, according to policymaking experts, has merit. Indeed, this method is commonly used for problem solving in which the means and ends are often impossible to separate, aspirations or objectives undergo constant development, and drastic simplification of the complexity of the real world is urgent if problems are to be solved in reasonable periods of time.[40]

Force-Field Analysis

force-field analysis
a process of identifying forces in support of change, those resisting change.

There will always be barriers and resistance to change in criminal justice organizations. Such barriers may be physical, social, financial, legal, political, and/or technological in nature. One useful technique for identifying sources of resistance (and support) is called **force-field analysis**. This technique, developed by Kurt Lewin, is based on an analogy to physics: A body will remain at rest when the sum of forces operating on it is zero. When the forces pushing or pulling it in one direction exceed the forces pushing or pulling it in the opposite one, the body will move in the direction of the greater forces. (Note, however, that in criminal justice administration, change involves *social* forces rather than *physical* ones.) Generally, we focus on reducing rather than overcoming resistance.

Three steps are involved in a force-field analysis:

1. Identifying driving forces (those supporting change) and restraining forces (those resisting change)
2. Analyzing the forces identified in Step 1
3. Identifying alternative strategies for changing each force identified in step 1; focus on reducing forces of resistance[41]

Take, for example, the forces at work concerning whether or not one will attend a university that is some distance away. Forces favoring the decision might be parents' and friends' encouragement to attend, the opportunity to meet new people and to experience new places and cultures, the prospect of attaining a desirable career with higher income, and the acquisition of far greater knowledge. Forces in opposition might be the costs of tuition, books, and living expenses; the financial loss while attending school and not working; unexceptional high school grades; the number of years required to graduate; and perhaps going to a strange locale and leaving friends, family, and other support groups behind. To reduce the opposing pressures, the student might obtain financial aid or scholarships, plan to call family and friends often, visit the school and community first to try to become more comfortable with them, and so on.

Summary

This chapter presented the foundation for the study of justice administration. It also established the legal existence of governments, laws, and the justice agencies that administer them. It demonstrated that the three components of the justice system are independent and fragmented and often work at odds with one another toward the accomplishment of the system's overall mission.

Key Terms and Concepts

Administrator *04*

Conflict model *12*

Consensus model *12*

Crime control model *13*

Criminal justice network *07*

Criminal justice nonsystem *08*

Criminal justice process *05*

Due process model *12*

Force-field analysis *16*

Manager *04*

Planned change *14*

Policymaking *16*

Social contract *11*

Supervisor *04*

System fragmentation *09*

Questions for Review

1. Do the three justice components (police, courts, and corrections) constitute a true system, or are they more appropriately described as a process or a true nonsystem? Defend your response.

2. What are the legal and historical bases for a justice system and its administration in the United States? Why is the conflict versus consensus debate important?

3. What are some of the substantive ways in which public and private sector administration are similar? How are they dissimilar?

4. What elements of planned change must the justice administrator be familiar with in order to ensure that change is effected rationally and successfully?

5. Which method, a rational process or just muddling through, appears to be used in criminal justice policymaking today? Which method is probably best, given real-world realities? Explain your response.

Deliberate and Decide 1

Is Our Justice System Always "Just"?[42]

Nancy Black, a California marine biologist, also captains a whale watching ship. She was with some watchers in 2005 when a member of her crew whistled at a nearby humpback whale, hoping the whale would linger. Meanwhile, on land one of Black's employees contacted a national oceanographic organization to see if the whistling was in fact harassment of a marine mammal—an environmental crime. Black provided a videotape of the incident, slightly edited to show the whistling; for the editing, she was charged with a felony under the 1863 False Claims Act. She was also charged with a federal crime involving the feeding of killer whales (orcas)—having rigged an apparatus that would stabilize a slab of blubber to better photograph the orca while feeding on a dead gray whale. Since the charges were filed, Black has spent more than $100,000 in legal fees and could be sentenced to 20 years in prison.

Questions for Discussion

1. Does this case represent the conflict or consensus model of justice?

2. Assume Black were to be convicted: Would the end justify the means? Conversely, would the means justify the end result (i.e., having such federal laws, compelling such exorbitant legal fees)?

3. Do you believe politics played a part in this case?

4. Should the prosecutor have the discretion to drop all charges in this case?

Deliberate and Decide 2

The Sovereign Citizen Movement[43]

Recently a 50-year-old Arizona man who rejects government authority as a member of the "sovereign movement" was sentenced to more than 8 years in a federal prison and ordered to forfeit more than $1.29 million in assets. He was convicted on 1 count of conspiracy to commit money laundering, 13 counts of money laundering, and 4 counts of failure to appear, and ordered to pay $98,782 in restitution once he leaves prison.

This man is heavily involved in the sovereign movement, whose members believe that the U.S. government is illegitimate and that they should not have to pay taxes or be subject to federal laws. Most of them have their own constitution, bill of rights, and government officials. Sovereign citizens can be dangerous and violent, and have been tied with a number of shootouts with, and killings of police officers. Furthermore, members often commit financial fraud crimes, are extremely dangerous and violent, and have been tied to a number of shootouts with, and killings of police officers.

It is estimated that hundreds of thousands of sovereign citizens currently live throughout the United States. They are such a threat that the FBI maintains a website on these citizens.

Questions for Discussion

1. Based on this chapter's discussions of the foundations of governments and their criminal justice systems, what

determination would you make concerning such a movement's legitimacy and legality?

2. Looking at their beliefs, are such people truly American "citizens"?

3. Do you believe any of their beliefs have any redeemable merit?

4. What types and amounts of punishment, if any, do you believe are justified for members of such movements?

Learn by Doing

1. Your criminal justice professor asks you to consider the CJS flowchart displayed on the inside cover of the text. Then, after reading this chapter, you are asked to prepare a paper concerning how this chart implies that criminal justice agencies constitute both a *system* and a *nonsystem*. What will be your response? Alternatively, do you believe that the CJS most closely resembles a *network* or *process*? Explain.

2. It is announced that because of financial shortfalls, your local police department must eliminate 10 percent of its officer positions through layoffs and retirements.
   a. Given the criminal justice planning adage that "you cannot rock one end of the boat," what might be the effects of such position reductions on your local criminal justice system?
   b. Assume instead that local revenues have *increased* in your jurisdiction, and your local police department is told it can add 10 percent more officers' positions. What possible impacts on your local CJS might result?

3. Your criminal justice professor is working on a journal article concerning the social compact or contract

theory of the origin of government. As her research assistant, you are assigned to summarize John Locke's theory of the same, including its significance and application to the U.S. CJS. What will be contained in your report?

4. The head of your state department of corrections wants to close the state's oldest prison, now located in the state capitol; constructed in the 1920s, it is now extremely dangerous as well as very expensive to operate. Although the new location would be in a community that is 50 miles away, the new location would be nearer the state capitol and offer a considerably larger labor pool of prospective prison employees as well as a much better public transportation system. Being politically astute, the director asks you and several of your fellow staff members to conduct a force-field analysis, looking at *both* communities to determine opposition and support for the move. Identify at least three forces or factors that are likely to *support* the decision to relocate the prison and three that are likely to *oppose* it.

Notes

1. Michael E. O'Neill, Ronald F. Bykowski, and Robert S. Blair, *Criminal Justice Planning: A Practical Approach* (San Jose, CA: Justice Systems Development, 1976), p. 5.
2. Ibid., p. 12.
3. Ibid.
4. Steven M. Cox and John E. Wade, *The Criminal Justice Network: An Introduction,* 2nd ed. (Dubuque, IA: Wm. C. Brown, 1989), p. 1.
5. Ibid., p. 4.
6. Ibid., p. 12.
7. Ibid., pp. 13–14.
8. Philip H. Ennis, "Crime, Victims, and the Police," *Transaction* 4 (1967):36–44.
9. The President's Commission on Law Enforcement and the Administration of Justice, *The Challenge of Crime in a Free Society* (Washington, DC: U.S. Government Printing Office, 1967), p. 7.
10. Alfred Cohn and Roy Udolf, *The Criminal Justice System and Its Psychology* (New York: Van Nostrand Reinhold, 1979), p. 152.
11. Burton Wright and Vernon Fox, *Criminal Justice and the Social Sciences* (Philadelphia, PA: W. B. Saunders, 1978).

12. "Justice on Trial: A Special Report," *Newsweek* (March 8, 1971):16.

13. Ibid., p. 18.

14. Alan R. Coffey and Edward Eldefonso, *Process and Impact of Justice* (Beverly Hills, CA: Glencoe Press, 1975), p. 32.

15. The President's Commission, *Challenge of Crime in a Free Society*, p. 5.

16. Alan R. Coffey and Edward Eldefonso, *Process and Impact of Justice*, p. 35.

17. Ibid., p. 39.

18. Ibid., p. 41.

19. Willa Dawson, "The Need for a System Approach to Criminal Justice," in Donald T. Shanahan (ed.), *The Administration of Justice System—An Introduction* (Boston, MA: Holbrook, 1977), p. 141.

20. J. W. La Patra, *Analyzing the Criminal Justice System* (Lexington, MA: Lexington Books, 1978), p. 75.

21. Alexander B. Smith and Harriet Pollack, *Criminal Justice: An Overview* (New York: Holt, Rinehart and Winston, 1980), p. 9.

22. Ibid., p. 10.

23. Ibid., p. 366.

24. Thomas J. Bernard, *The Consensus–Conflict Debate: Form and Content in Social Theories* (New York: Columbia University Press, 1983), p. 78.

25. Thomas Hobbes, *Leviathan* (New York: E. P. Dutton, 1950), pp. 290–291.

26. Jean-Jacques Rousseau, "A Discourse on the Origin of Inequality," in G. D. H. Cole (ed.), *The Social Contract and Discourses* (New York: E. P. Dutton, 1946), p. 240.

27. Bernard, *Consensus–Conflict Debate*, pp. 83, 85.

28. Ibid., p. 86.

29. Frank Schmalleger, *Criminal Justice Today*, 10th ed. (Upper Saddle River, NJ: Prentice Hall, 2009), pp. 16–17.

30. One of the first publications to express the nonsystems approach was the American Bar Association, *New Perspective on Urban Crime* (Washington, DC: ABA Special Committee on Crime Prevention and Control, 1972).

31. Herbert L. Packer, *The Limits of the Criminal Sanction* (Stanford, CA: Stanford University Press, 1968).

32. Herbert L. Packer, *Two Models of the Criminal Process*, 113 U. PA. L. REV. 1, 2 (1964).

33. Fernando Bartolome and Paul A. Lee Evans, "Professional Lives versus Private Lives: Shifting Patterns of Managerial Commitment," *Organizational Dynamics* 7 (1982):2–29; Ronald C. Kessler and James A. McRae, Jr., "The Effect of Wives' Employment on the Mental Health of Married Men and Women," *American Sociological Review* 47 (1979): 216–227.

34. Robert V. Presthus, *The Organizational Society* (New York: Alfred A. Knopf, 1962).

35. Joseph A. Petrick and George E. Manning, "How to Manage Morale," *Personnel Journal* 69 (1990):87.

36. Wayne N. Welsh and Philip W. Harris, *Criminal Justice Policy and Planning*, 2nd ed. (Cincinnati, OH: LexisNexis Anderson, 2004), p. 5.

37. This scenario is modeled on one set out by Harvard economist Charles E. Lindblom, "The Science of 'Muddling Through,'" *Public Administration Review* 19 (Spring 1959):79–89.

38. Ibid., p. 80.

39. Ibid., p. 87.

40. Ibid., p. 88.

41. Kurt Lewin, *Field Theory in Social Science* (New York: Harper and Row, 1951).

42. For more information, see: "Nancy Black, Indicted Marine Biologist, Denies Feeding Orcas," *Huffington Post*, February 1, 2012, http://www.huffingtonpost.com/2012/02/01/indicted-marine-biologist-nancy-black_n_1247284.html (accessed October 14, 2013).

43. See William D'Urso, "Sovereign citizen' gets 8 years in money laundering case," *Las Vegas Sun*, March 20, 2013, http://www.lasvegassun.com/news/2013/mar/20/sovereign-citizen-gets-8-years-money-laundering-ca/ (accessed September 20, 2013); also see Nadine Maeser, "Special report: A closer look at sovereign citizens," WECT, http://www.wect.com/story/21237082/special-report-sovereign-citizens (accessed September 26, 2014).

Micha Klootwijk/shutterstock

2 Organization and Administration
Principles and Practices

LEARNING OBJECTIVES

After reading this chapter, the student will be able to:

1. *define organizations and the types of organizations*
2. *understand the evolution of organizational theory, including scientific, human relations, systems, and bureaucratic management*
3. *understand the major components of organizational structure, such as span of control and unity of command*
4. *explain the uniqueness of communication within police organizations*
5. *describe the primary components of communication, such as its process, barriers, cultural cues, and upward/downward/horizontal forms*
6. *comprehend the primary leadership theories and skills, including the characteristics and skills of America's best leaders*
7. *describe the challenges and implications of new generations of workers who will soon be entering the workplace*
8. *describe the rights and interests—and legal aspects—concerning both employees and employers regarding employees' personal appearance at the workplace*

▶ Introduction

It is no surprise that *Dilbert*—a popular cartoon strip character—portrays downtrodden workers, inconsiderate bosses, and dysfunctional organizations. Scott Adams's cartoon "hero," a mouthless engineer with a perpetually bent necktie, is believed by many Americans to be representative of today's workers. Although a sizable majority of U.S. workers routinely indicate that their workplace is a pleasant environment, more than 70 percent also experience stress at work because of red tape, unnecessary rules, poor communication with management, and other causes. Indeed, what gives Adams grist for the Dilbert mill is the way managers mishandle their employees and carry out downsizing.[1] But, as we will see, it does not have to be so.

This chapter—one of the lengthiest in this book and certainly one of the most essential chapters in terms of providing the foundation of administration—examines organizations and the employees within them and how they should be managed and motivated. The underlying theme is that *administrators must know their* people, and the chapter offers a general discussion of organizations, focusing on their definition, theory and function, and structure. Included are several approaches to managing and communicating within organizations.

Also, as indicated in Chapter 1, the initial chapters of Parts 2, 3, and 4 of this book discuss the organization and operation of police, courts, and corrections agencies, respectively. Similarly, countless books and articles have been written about organization and administration in general (many of them in the business and human resources disciplines); therefore, in this chapter, I will attempt to discuss the major elements of organization and administration that apply to the field of criminal justice administration. Then, we review the evolution of organizational theory, including scientific, human relations, systems, and bureaucratic management.

Next, we consider the structure of organizations (including concepts such as span of control and unity of command). We then focus on one of the most important aspects of organizations: communications; after defining what constitutes communication, we consider its process, barriers, role, some cultural cues, and the uniqueness of communication within police organizations. Next is a discussion of leadership and primary theories of how to lead the organization; included is an overview of the characteristics and skills of America's best leaders. Following is a discussion of several classical motivational techniques that are used with employees; here, we include major theorists in the field such as McGregor, Maslow, Katz, and Herzberg.

Then, I look at some of the unique challenges posed by the coming generation of criminal justice employees—the so-called Generations X (or millennial) employees—including the world into which they were born, the influences of technologies on their worldview, their penchant for bodily adornment, and the implications for the criminal justice workplace. The chapter concludes with review questions, "deliberate and decide" problems, and "learn by doing" exercises.

▶ Defining Organizations

Like *supervision* and *management,* the word *organization* has a number of meanings and interpretations that have evolved over the years. We think of organizations as entities of two or more people who cooperate to achieve an objective(s); it can therefore be a company, business, club, and so forth, which engages in planning and arranging the different parts of the group toward accomplishing a fundamental mission. In that sense, certainly, the concept of organization is not new. Undoubtedly, the first organizations were primitive hunting parties. Organization and a high degree of coordination were required to bring down huge animals, as revealed in fossils from as early as 40,000 years ago.[2]

An **organization** may be formally defined as "a consciously coordinated social entity, with a relative identifiable boundary, that functions on a relatively continuous basis to achieve a common goal or set of goals."[3] The term *consciously coordinated* implies management. **Social entity** refers to the fact that organizations are composed of people who interact with one another and with people in other organizations. **Relatively identifiable boundary** alludes to the organization's goals and the public served.[4] Using this definition, we can consider many types of formal groups as full-blown organizations. Four different types of formal organizations have been identified by asking the question "Who benefits?" Answers include (1) mutual benefit associations, such as police labor unions; (2) business concerns, such as General Motors; (3) service organizations, such as community mental health centers, where the client group is the prime beneficiary; and (4) commonweal (e.g., those that exist for the public good or welfare) organizations, such as the Department of Defense and criminal justice agencies, where the beneficiaries are the public at large.[5] The following analogy is designed to help the reader understand organizations.

An organization corresponds to the bones that structure or give form to the body. Imagine that the hand is a single mass of bone rather than four separate fingers and a thumb made up of bones joined by cartilage to be flexible. The single mass of bones could not, due to its structure, play musical instruments, hold a pencil, or grip a baseball bat. A criminal justice organization is analogous. It must be structured properly if it is to be effective in fulfilling its many diverse goals.[6]

It is important to note that no two organizations are structured or function exactly alike, nor is there one best way to run an organization.

▶ The Evolution of Organizational Theory

Next, we discuss the evolution of **organizational theory**, which is the study of organizational designs and structures, the relationship of organizations with their external environment, and the behavior of administrators and managers within organizations.

According to Ronald Lynch,[7] the history of management can be divided into three approaches and time periods: (1) scientific management (1900–1940), (2) human relations management (1930–1970), and (3) systems management (1965–present). To this, I would add another important element to the concept of organizations: bureaucratic management, which is also discussed in this section.

Scientific Management

Frederick W. Taylor, who first emphasized time and motion studies, is known today as the father of **scientific management**—a school of management thought that is concerned primarily with the efficiency and output of the individual worker. Spending his early years in the steel mills of Pennsylvania, Taylor became chief engineer and later discovered a new method of making steel; this allowed him to retire at the age of 45 years to write and lecture. He became interested in methods for getting greater productivity from workers and was hired in 1898 by Bethlehem Steel, where he measured the time it took workers to shovel and carry pig iron. Taylor recommended giving workers hourly breaks and going to a piecework system, among other adjustments. Worker productivity soared; the total number of shovelers needed dropped from about 600 to 140, and worker earnings increased from $1.15 to $1.88 per day. The average cost of handling a long ton (2,240 pounds) dropped from $0.072 to $0.033.[8]

---

organization entities of two or more people who cooperate to achieve an objective(s).

social entity an organization composed of people who interact with one another and with other people.

relatively identifiable boundary an organization's goals and the public it is intended to serve.

organizational theory the study of organizational designs and structures that includes the behavior of administrators and managers within organizations.

scientific management a school of management thought that is concerned primarily with the efficiency and output of an individual worker.

Taylor, who was highly criticized by unions for his management-oriented views, proved that administrators must know their employees. He published the book *The Principles of Scientific Management* in 1911. His views caught on, and soon emphasis was placed entirely on the formal administrative structure; terms such as *authority, chain of command, span of control*, and *division of labor* were coined.

In 1935, Luther Gulick formulated the theory of **POSDCORB**, an acronym for planning, organizing, staffing, directing, coordinating, reporting, and budgeting (Figure 2-1 ■); this philosophy was emphasized in police management for many years. Gulick stressed the technical and engineering side of management, virtually ignoring the human side.

The application of scientific management to criminal justice agencies was heavily criticized. It viewed employees as passive instruments whose feelings were completely disregarded. In addition, employees were considered to be motivated by money alone.

POSDCORB an acronym for planning, organizing, staffing, directing, coordinating, reporting, and budgeting; this philosophy was emphasized in police management for many years.

Human Relations Management

Beginning in the 1930s, people began to realize the negative effects of scientific management on the worker. A view arose in policing that management should instill pride and dignity in officers. The movement toward human relations management began with the famous studies conducted during the late 1920s through the mid-1930s by the Harvard Business School at the Hawthorne plant of the Western Electric Company.[9] These studies, which are discussed in more detail later in this chapter, found that worker productivity is more closely related to *social* capacity than to physical capacity, noneconomic rewards play a prominent part in motivating and satisfying employees, and employees do not react to management and its rewards as individuals but as members of groups.[10]

In the 1940s and 1950s, police departments began to recognize the strong effect of the informal structure on the organization; agencies began using techniques such as job

PLANNING: working out in broad outline what needs to be done and the methods for doing it to accomplish the purpose set for the enterprise

ORGANIZING: the establishment of a formal structure of authority through which work subdivisions are arranged, defined, and coordinated for the defined objective

STAFFING: the whole personnel function of bringing in and training the staff and maintaining favorable conditions of work

DIRECTING: the continuous task of making decisions, embodying them in specific and general orders and instructions, and serving as the leader of the enterprise

COORDINATING: the all-important duty of interrelating the various parts of the organization

REPORTING: informing the executive and his or her assistants as to what is going on, through records, research, and inspection

BUDGETING: all that is related to budgeting in the form of fiscal planning, accounting, and control

FIGURE 2-1   Gulick's POSDCORB
Source: Luther Gulick and Lyndall Urwick, *Papers on the Science of Administration* (New York: Institute of Public Administration, 1937).

enlargement and job enrichment to generate interest in policing as a career. Studies indicated that the supervisor who was "employee centered" was more effective than one who was "production centered." Democratic or participatory management began to appear in police agencies. The human relations approach had its limitations, however. With the emphasis placed on the employee, the role of the organizational structure became secondary; the primary goal seemed to many to be social rewards, with little attention given to task accomplishment. Many police managers saw this trend as unrealistic. Employees began to give less and expect more in return.[11]

Systems Management

In the mid-1960s, features of the human relations and scientific management approaches were combined in the *systems management* approach. Designed to bring the individual and the organization together, it attempted to help managers use employees to reach desired production goals. The systems approach recognized that it was still necessary to have some hierarchical arrangement to bring about coordination, that authority and responsibility were essential, and that overall organization was required.

The systems management approach combined the work of Abraham Maslow,[12] who developed a hierarchy of needs; Douglas McGregor,[13] who stressed the general theory of human motivation; and Robert Blake and Jane Mouton,[14] who developed the "managerial grid," which emphasized two concerns—for task and for people—that managers must have. In effect, the systems management approach holds that to be effective, and the manager must be interdependent with other individuals and groups and have the ability to recognize and deal with conflict and change. More than mere technical skills are required; managers require knowledge of several major resources: people, money, time, and equipment.[15] Team cooperation is required to achieve organizational goals.

Several theories of leadership and means of motivating employees have also evolved over the past several decades; we discuss several of them in the following sections.

Bureaucratic Management

Criminal justice agencies certainly fit the description of an organization. First, they are managed by being organized into a number of specialized units. Administrators, managers, and supervisors exist to ensure that these units work together toward a common goal (each unit working independently would lead to fragmentation, conflict, and competition). Second, these agencies consist of people who interact within the organization and with external organizations, and they exist to serve the public. Through a mission statement, policies and procedures, a proper management style, and direction, criminal justice administrators attempt to ensure that the organization maintains its overall goals of crime treatment and suppression, and that it works amicably with other organizations and people. As the organization becomes larger, the need becomes greater for people to cooperate to achieve organizational goals.

Criminal justice organizations are *bureaucracies,* as are virtually all large organizations in modern society. The idea of a pure **bureaucracy** was developed by Max Weber, the German sociologist and the "father of sociology," who argued that if a bureaucratic structure is to function efficiently, it must have the following elements:

bureaucracy structuring of an organization so as to function efficiently; it includes rules, division of labor, hierarchy of authority, and expertise among its members.

1. *Rulification and routinization.* Organizations stress continuity. Rules save effort by eliminating the need for deriving a new solution for every problem. They also facilitate standard and equal treatment of similar situations.

2. **Division of labor.** This involves the performance of functions by various parts of an organization along with providing the necessary authority to carry out these functions.

3. **Hierarchy of authority.** Each lower office is under the control and supervision of a higher one.

4. **Expertise.** Specialized training is necessary. Only a person who has demonstrated adequate technical training is qualified to be a member of the administrative staff.

5. **Written rules.** Administrative acts, decisions, and rules are formulated and recorded in writing.[16]

Today, many people view bureaucracies in negative terms, believing that all too often, officials tell clients "That's not my job," or appear to be "going by the book"—relying heavily on rules and regulations, and policies and procedures ("red tape"). Second, they are said to stifle the individual freedom, spontaneity, and self-realization of their employees.[17] James Q. Wilson referred to this widespread discontent with modern organizations as the "bureaucracy problem," where the key issue is "getting the frontline worker . . . to do 'the right thing.'"[18]

Weber's ideal bureaucracy, however, as described earlier, was designed to eliminate inefficiency and waste in organizations. As shown for each of the earlier principles, many of the characteristics that he proposed many years ago are found in today's criminal justice agencies as well as in other bureaucracies (e.g., political parties, churches, educational institutions, and private businesses).

The administration of most police and prison organizations is based on the traditional, pyramidal, quasi-military organizational structure containing the elements of a bureaucracy: specialized functions, adherence to fixed rules, and a hierarchy of authority. (This pyramidal organizational environment is undergoing increasing challenges, especially as a result of departments implementing community policing, as will be seen in Chapter 4.)

Organizational Inputs/Outputs

Another way to view organizations is as systems that take **inputs** (e.g., committing resources as funds, personnel/labor, and equipment needed for accomplishing a goal or mission), process them, and thus produce **outputs** (the desired outcome, goods, or services). A police agency, for example, processes reports of criminal activity and, like other systems, attempts to satisfy the customer (crime victim). Figure 2-2 ■ demonstrates the input/output model for the police and private business. There are other types of inputs by police agencies; for example, a robbery problem might result in an input of newly created robbery surveillance teams, the processing would be their stakeouts, and the output would be the number of subsequent arrests by the team. Feedback would occur in the form of conviction rates at trial.

inputs an organization's committing such resources as funds, personnel/labor, and equipment toward accomplishing a goal or mission.

outputs an organization's desired outcome, goods, or services.

▶ Organizational Structure

Primary Principles

All organizations have an organizational structure or table of organization, be it written or unwritten, very basic or highly complex. An experienced manager uses this organizational chart or table as a blueprint for action. The size of the organization depends on the demands placed on it and the resources available to it. Growth precipitates the need for more personnel, greater division of labor, specialization, written rules, and other such elements.

In building the organizational structure, the following principles should be kept in mind:

1. *Principle of the objective.* Every part of every organization must be an expression of the purpose of the undertaking. You cannot organize in a vacuum; you must organize for something.

2. *Principle of specialization.* The activities of every member of any organized group should be confined, as far as possible, to the performance of a single function.

BUSINESS ORGANIZATION

Inputs	**Processes**	**Outputs**
Customer takes photos to shop to be developed.	Photos are developed and packaged for customer to pick up.	Customer picks up photos and pays for them.

Feedback
Analysis is made of expenses/revenues and customer satisfaction.

LAW ENFORCEMENT AGENCY

Inputs	**Processes**	**Outputs**
A crime prevention unit is initiated.	Citizens contact unit for advice.	Police provide spot checks and lectures.

Feedback
Target hardening results; property crimes decrease.

COURT

Inputs	**Processes**	**Outputs**
A house arrest program is initiated.	Certain people in pre- and post-trial status are screened and offered the option.	Decrease in number of people in jail, speeding up court process.

Feedback
Violation rates are analyzed for success; some offenders are mainstreamed back into the community more smoothly.

FIGURE 2-2 The Organization as an Input–Output Model

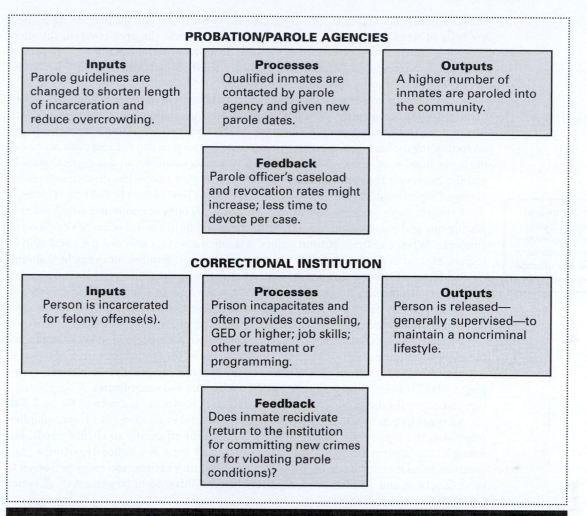

PROBATION/PAROLE AGENCIES

Inputs	Processes	Outputs
Parole guidelines are changed to shorten length of incarceration and reduce overcrowding.	Qualified inmates are contacted by parole agency and given new parole dates.	A higher number of inmates are paroled into the community.

Feedback
Parole officer's caseload and revocation rates might increase; less time to devote per case.

CORRECTIONAL INSTITUTION

Inputs	Processes	Outputs
Person is incarcerated for felony offense(s).	Prison incapacitates and often provides counseling, GED or higher; job skills; other treatment or programming.	Person is released—generally supervised—to maintain a noncriminal lifestyle.

Feedback
Does inmate recidivate (return to the institution for committing new crimes or for violating parole conditions)?

FIGURE 2-2 *(continued)*

3. *Principle of authority.* In every organized group, the supreme authority must rest somewhere. There should be a clear line of authority to every person in the group.

4. *Principle of responsibility.* The responsibility of the superior for the acts of his or her subordinates is absolute.

5. *Principle of definition.* The content of each position, the duties involved, the authority and responsibility contemplated, and the relationships with other positions should be clearly defined in writing and published for all concerned.

6. *Principle of correspondence.* In every position, the responsibility and the authority to carry out the responsibility should correspond.

7. *Span of control.* No person should supervise more than six direct subordinates whose work interlocks.[19]

Span of Control and Unity of Command

The last concept in the preceding list, **span of control**, has recently been revisited in the literature and deserves additional commentary. How many subordinates can a chief executive, manager, or supervisor in a criminal justice organization effectively supervise? The

> **span of control** the number of subordinates a chief executive, manager, or supervisor in a criminal justice organization can effectively supervise.

answer will depend on factors such as the capacity of the leader and the persons supervised, the type of work performed, the complexity of the work, the area covered, distances between elements, the time needed to perform the tasks, and the types of persons served. Normally, a police patrol sergeant will supervise 6–10 officers, while a patrol lieutenant may have 4 or 5 sergeants reporting to him or her.[20]

Several authors now argue for even higher spans of control, however, to afford reductions in the distortion of information as it flows through the organization; less slow, ineffective decision making and action; fewer functional roadblocks and "turf protection"; greater emphasis on controlling the bureaucracy rather than on customer service; and reduced costs because of the lower number of managers and management support staff. Some also argue that rank-and-file employees favor high spans of control because they receive less detailed and micromanaged supervision, greater responsibility, and a higher level of trust by their supervisors.[21]

unity of command
the principle holding that only one person should be in command or control of a situation or an employee.

A related, major principle of hierarchy of authority is **unity of command**, which refers to placing one and only one superior officer in command or in control of every situation and employee. When a critical situation occurs, it is imperative that only one person should be responsible and in charge. The unity of command principle ensures, for example, that multiple and/or conflicting orders are not issued to the same police officers by several superior officers. For example, a patrol sergeant might arrive at a hostage situation, deploy personnel, and give all appropriate orders, only to have a shift lieutenant or captain come to the scene and countermand the sergeant's orders with his or her own orders. This type of situation would obviously be counterproductive for all concerned. All officers must know and follow the chain of command at such incidents. Every person in the organization should report to one and only one superior officer. When the unity of command principle is followed, everyone involved is aware of the actions initiated by superiors and subordinates. A simple structure indicating the direct line of authority in a chain of command is shown in Figure 2-3 ■.

An organization should be developed through careful evaluation of its responsibilities; otherwise, the agency may become unable to respond efficiently to clients' needs. For example, the implementation of too many specialized units in a police department (e.g., community relations, crime analysis, media relations) may obligate too many personnel to these functions and result in too few patrol officers. Today, 56 to 90 percent of all sworn personnel are assigned to patrol.[22]

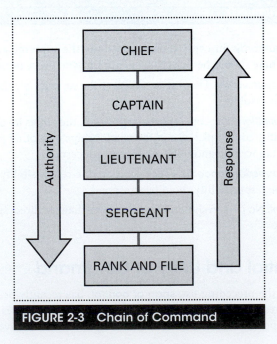

FIGURE 2-3 Chain of Command

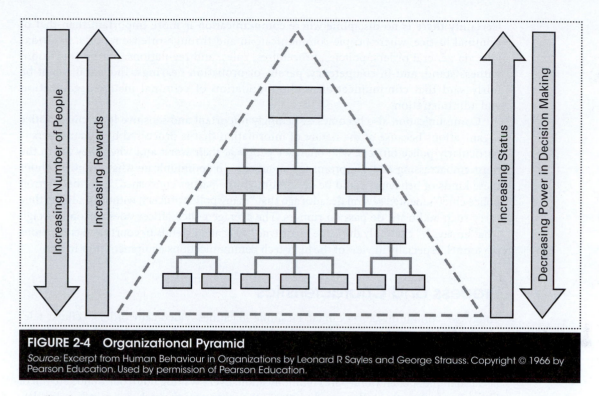

FIGURE 2-4 Organizational Pyramid

Source: Excerpt from Human Behaviour in Organizations by Leonard R Sayles and George Strauss. Copyright © 1966 by Pearson Education. Used by permission of Pearson Education.

The classic pyramidal design is shown in Figure 2-4 ■. The pyramidal structure has the following characteristics:

1. Nearly all contacts take the form of orders going *down* and reports of results going *up* the pyramid.

2. Each subordinate must receive instructions and orders from only one boss.

3. Important decisions are made at the top of the pyramid.

4. Superiors have a specific span of control, supervising only a limited number of people.

5. Personnel at all levels, except at the top and bottom, have contact only with their boss above them and their subordinates below them.[23]

▶ Communication within the Organization

Import and Consequence

Communication (generally, the use of words, sounds, signs, bodily cues, or other actions to convey or exchange information, or to express ideas, to another person or group) is obviously important in every segment of our society. As Mark Twain put it, "The difference between the right word and the almost right word is the difference between lightning and lightning bug."[24]

And to that we might add one more quote, by the noted Italian-American linguist Mario Pei,[25] who wrote about the essential nature of proper communication in general:

> Rightly or wrongly, most people consider language as an index of culture, breeding, upbringing, personality, sometimes even of intelligence, decency, and integrity. Under the circumstances, it is unwise, not to say harmful, to pay no heed to your language. Ignorance or improper use of language can easily interfere with your success and advancement. It can take money out of your pocket.

> **communication** use of words, sounds, signs, bodily cues, or other actions to convey or exchange information, or to express ideas, to another person or group.

Certainly there is no discipline where communication is more important than that of criminal justice, where people communicate in and through offense reports; in affidavits; via general orders, policies, procedures, rules, and regulations; on the courtroom witness stand; and in competency, parole, or probation hearings. Indeed, it might be fairly said that communication is the foundation of criminal justice organization and administration.

Communication also becomes exceedingly important and sensitive in criminal justice organizations because of the nature of information that is processed by practitioners—particularly police officers, who often see people at their worst and when they are in the most embarrassing and compromising situations. To communicate what is known about these kinds of behaviors could be devastating to the parties concerned. A former Detroit police chief lamented several decades ago that "many police officers, without realizing they carry such authority, do pass on rumors. The average police officer doesn't stop to weigh what he says."[26] Certainly the same holds true today and extends to courts and corrections personnel, especially in view of the high-tech communications equipment now in use.

Process and Characteristics

Today, we communicate via e-mail, facsimile machines, video camcorders, cellular telephones and text messages, satellite dishes, and many other forms. We converse orally, in written letters and memos, through our body language, via television and radio programs, and through newspapers and meetings. Even private thoughts—which occur four times faster than the spoken word—are communication. Every waking hour, our minds are full of ideas. Psychologists say that nearly 100,000 thoughts pass through our minds every day, conveyed by a multitude of media.[27]

Studies have long shown that communication is the primary problem in administration and lack of communication is employees' primary complaint about their immediate supervisors.[28] Indeed, managers are in the communications business. It has been said that

> [o]f all skills needed to be an effective manager/leader/supervisor, skill in communicating is *the* most vital. In fact, research has shown that 93 percent of police work is one-on-one communication. Estimates vary, but all studies emphasize the importance of communications in everyday law enforcement operations.[29]

Several elements compose the communication process: encoding, transmission, medium, reception, decoding, and feedback.[30]

Encoding. To convey an experience or idea, we translate, or encode, that experience into symbols. We use words or other verbal behaviors or nonverbal behaviors such as gestures to convey the experience or idea.

Transmission. This element involves the translation of the encoded symbols into some behavior that another person can observe. The actual articulation (moving our lips, tongue, and so on) of the symbol into verbal or nonverbal observable behavior is transmission.

Medium. Communication must be conveyed through some channel or medium. Media for communication include sight, hearing, taste, touch, and smell. Some other media are television, telephone, paper and pencil, and radio. The choice of the medium is important; for example, a message that is transmitted via a formal letter from the CEO will carry more weight than the same message conveyed via a secretary's memo.

Reception. The stimuli, the verbal and nonverbal symbols, reach the senses of the receiver and are conveyed to the brain for interpretation.

Decoding. The individual who receives the stimuli develops some meaning for the verbal and nonverbal symbols and decodes the stimuli. These symbols are translated into some concept or experience for the receiver. Whether or not the receiver is familiar with the symbols, or whether or not interference such as noise or a physiological problem occurs, determines how closely the message that the receiver has decoded approximates the message that the sender has encoded.

Feedback. After decoding the transmitted symbols, the receiver usually provides some response or feedback to the sender. If someone appears puzzled, we repeat the message or we encode the concept differently and transmit some different symbols to express that concept. Feedback that we receive acts as a guide or steering device and lets us know whether the receiver has interpreted our symbols as we intended. Feedback is obviously a crucial element in guaranteeing that the sender's intended meaning was in fact conveyed to the receiver.

An organization's systems of communication are usually created by establishing formal areas of responsibility and explicit delegations of duties, including statements of the nature, content, and direction of the communications that are necessary for the group's performance. Most criminal justice administrators prefer a formal system, regardless of how cumbersome it may be, because they can control it and because it tends to create a record for future reference. Several human factors, however, affect the flow of communication. Employees typically communicate with those persons who can help them to achieve their aims; they avoid communicating with those who do not assist, or may retard, their accomplishing those goals; and they tend to avoid communicating with people who threaten them and make them feel anxious.[31] Other barriers to effective communication are discussed later.

Communication within a criminal justice organization may be downward, upward, or horizontal. There are five types of downward communication within a criminal justice organization:

1. ***Job instruction.*** Communication relating to the performance of a certain task
2. ***Job rationale.*** Communication relating a certain task to organizational tasks
3. ***Procedures and practice.*** Communication about organizational policies, procedures, rules, and regulations (discussed as they relate to police, in Chapter 4)
4. ***Feedback.*** Communication appraising how an individual performs the assigned task
5. ***Indoctrination.*** Communication designed to motivate the employee[32]

Other reasons for communicating downward—implicit in this list—are opportunities for administrators to spell out objectives, to change attitudes and mold opinions, to prevent misunderstandings from lack of information, and to prepare employees for change.[33]

Upward communication in a criminal justice organization may be likened to a trout trying to swim upstream: With its many currents of resistance, it is a much harder task than to float downstream. Several deterrents restrict upward communication. The physical distance between superior and subordinate impedes upward communication. Communication is often difficult and infrequent when superiors are isolated and seldom seen or spoken to. In large criminal justice organizations, administrators may be located in headquarters that are removed from the operations personnel. The complexity of the organization may also cause prolonged delays of communication. For example, if a corrections officer or a patrol officer observes a problem that needs to be taken to the highest level, normally this information must first be taken to the sergeant, then to the lieutenant, captain, deputy warden or chief, and so on. At each level, these higher-level individuals will reflect on the problem, put their own interpretation on it (possibly including how the problem might affect them professionally or even personally), and possibly even dilute or distort the problem. Thus, delays in communication are inherent in a bureaucracy. Delays could mean that problems are not brought to the attention of the CEO for a long time. The more levels the communication passes through, the more it is filtered and diluted in its accuracy.

There is also the danger that administrators have a "no news is good news" or "slay the messenger" attitude, thereby discouraging the reception of information. Unless the superior does in fact maintain an open-door atmosphere, subordinates are often reluctant to bring, or will temper, bad news, unfavorable opinions, and mistakes or failures to the superior.[34] Administrators may also believe that they know and understand what their subordinates want and think, and that complaints from subordinates are an indication of disloyalty.

For all of these reasons, administrators may fail to take action on undesirable conditions brought to their attention; this will cause subordinates to lose faith in their leaders. Many time-consuming problems could be minimized or eliminated if superiors took the time to listen to their employees.

Horizontal communication thrives in an organization when formal communication channels are not open.[35] The disadvantage of horizontal communication is that it is much easier and more natural to achieve than vertical communication and therefore it often replaces vertical channels. The horizontal channels are usually informal in nature and include the grapevine, discussed next. The advantage is that horizontal communication is essential if the subsystems within a criminal justice organization are to function in an effective and coordinated manner. Horizontal communication among peers may also provide emotional and social bonds that build morale and feelings of teamwork among employees.

Communicating in Police Organizations: Consequence, Jargon, and the Grapevine

Because of their 24/7 work schedules, decentralized nature, unique jargon, and the gravity of what they encounter on the streets, let's briefly consider communications in policing. Police officers must possess the ability to communicate internally and externally regarding policies and procedures that affect daily operations. The ability of the police to communicate effectively using both oral and written means is also paramount because of the damage that can be done by, say, not completing an offense report properly or failing to convey accurately to one's supervisors, to the district attorney, or in court what actually happened in a criminal matter. Officers must also be prepared to converse with highly educated people in their day-to-day work.

Like people in other occupations and the professions, the police have their own jargon, dialect, and/or slang that they use on a daily basis. To the police, an offender might be a "perp" (perpetrator); a "subject" is simply someone of interest whom they are talking with, while a "suspect" is someone suspected of having committed a crime. In an "interview," the officer attempts to obtain basic information about a person (name, address, date of birth, and so forth), while an "interrogation" involves questioning an individual about his or her knowledge of, or involvement in, a crime. Such jargon and slang help officers to communicate among themselves.

The police also communicate with one another by listening and talking on the squad car radio. Agencies generally have detailed instructions and do's and don'ts in their policies and procedures regarding the use of radio. Supervisors must ensure that officers' radio transmissions are as concise, complete, and accurate as possible; officers are to refrain from making unprofessional, rude, sarcastic, or unnecessary remarks while on their radio; and those who fail to abide by these rules will quickly be admonished or even disciplined.

Police communicate on their radios using codes and have done so since the 1920s. The police also communicate with the use of a phonetic alphabet, which was designed to avoid confusion between letters that sound alike, say, when radioing in the name of a person or a license plate number to the dispatcher. For example, a *d* might easily be confused with a *b* or an *m* with an *n*. So, if radioing in a license plate number that is "DOM-123," the officer would say "David Ocean Mary 1-2-3." This eliminates any possible confusion on the receiver's part.

In addition to the several barriers to effective communication just discussed, the so-called **grapevine**—an informal means of circulating and communicating information or gossip, and so called because it zigzags back and forth across organizations—can also hinder communication. Communication includes rumors, and probably *no* type of organization in our society has more grapevine "scuttlebutt" than police agencies. Departments even establish *rumor control* centers during major crisis situations. Increasing the usual barriers to communication is the fact that policing, prisons, and jails are 24-hour, 7-day operations, so that rumors are easily carried from one shift to the next.

grapevine an informal means of circulating and communicating information or gossip.

The grapevine's most effective characteristics are that it is fast, it operates mostly at the place of work, and it supplements regular, formal communication. On the positive side, it can be a tool for management to gauge employees' attitudes, to spread useful information, and to help employees vent their frustrations. However, the grapevine can also carry untruths and be malicious. Without a doubt, the grapevine is a force for administrators to reckon with on a daily basis.

Oral and Written Communication

Our society tends to place considerable confidence in the written word within complex organizations. Writing establishes a permanent record, but transmitting information this way does not necessarily ensure that the message will be clear to the receiver. Often, in spite of the writer's best efforts, information is not conveyed clearly. This may be due in large measure to shortcomings with the writer's skills. Nonetheless, criminal justice organizations seem to rely increasingly on written communication, as evidenced by the proliferation of written directives found in most agencies.

This tendency for organizations to promulgate written rules, policies, and procedures has been caused by three contemporary developments. First is the *requirement for administrative due process* in employee disciplinary matters, encouraged by federal court rulings, police officer bill of rights legislation, and labor contracts. Another development is *civil liability*. Lawsuits against local governments and their criminal justice agencies and administrators have become commonplace; written agency guidelines prohibiting certain acts provide a hedge against successful civil litigation.[36] Written communication is preferred as a medium for dealing with citizens or groups outside the criminal justice agency. This means of communication provides the greatest protection against the growing number of legal actions taken against agencies by activists, citizens, and interest groups.

Finally, a third stimulus is the *accreditation movement*. Agencies that are either pursuing accreditation or have become accredited must possess a wealth of written policies and procedures.[37]

In recent years, electronic mail (e-mail) and text messaging have proliferated as a communication medium in criminal justice organizations. Such messages are easy-to-use and almost instantaneous communication—in upward, downward, or horizontal directions. For all their advantages, however, such messages can lack security and can be ambiguous—not only with respect to content meaning but also with regard to what they represent. Are such messages, in fact, mail, to be given the full weight of an office letter or memo, or should they be treated more as offhand comments?[38]

Other Barriers to Effective Communication

In addition to the barriers just discussed, several other potential barriers to effective communication exist. Some people, for example, are not good listeners. Unfortunately, listening is one of the most neglected and the least understood of the communication arts.[39] We allow other things to obstruct our communication, including time constraints, inadequate or excessive information, the tendency to say what we think others want to hear, failure to select the best word, prejudices, and strained sender–receiver relationships.[40] In addition, subordinates do not always have the same "big picture" viewpoint that superiors possess and do not always communicate well with someone in a higher position who is perhaps more fluent and persuasive than they are.

Cultural Cues

It is important to note that at least 90 percent of communication is *nonverbal* in nature, involving posture, facial expressions, gestures, tone of voice ("it's not what you say but how you say it"), and so on.[41] People learn to interpret these nonverbal messages by growing up in a particular culture, but not every culture interprets nonverbal cues in the same way.

For example, in some cultures, avoiding eye contact by looking at the ground is meant to convey respect and humility. Making what to some people are exaggerated hand gestures may be a normal means of communication in some cultures, and social distance for conversation in some societies may be much closer than it is in the United States. Someone from Nigeria, for example, may stand less than 15 inches from someone while conversing, whereas about 2 feet is a comfortable conversation zone for Americans. These few examples demonstrate why criminal justice practitioners must possess cultural empathy and understand the cultural cues of citizens from other nations.

Over 20 years ago, Peter Drucker, often referred to as the *business guru*,[42] conducted a study of the Los Angeles Police Department; among Drucker's findings was: "You police are so concerned with doing things right that you fail to do the right things." Drucker added, "Managers do things right; leaders do the right thing." Another leadership guru, Warren Bennis, has said essentially the same thing. In other words, administrators cannot be so concerned with managing that they fail to lead.[43]

We now look at theories underlying leadership and what leaders can do to motivate their subordinates.

▶ Primary Leadership Theories

What Is Leadership?

Probably since the dawn of time, when cave dwellers clustered into hunting groups and some particularly dominant person assumed a leadership role over the party, administrators have received advice on how to do their jobs from those around them. Even today, manuals for leaders and upwardly mobile executives abound, offering quick studies in how to govern others. Although many have doubtlessly been profitable for their authors, most of these how-to primers on leading others enjoy only a brief, ephemeral existence.

> **leadership** influencing and working with and through individuals or a group to generate activities that will accomplish organizational goals.

To understand **leadership**, we must first define the term. This is an important and fairly complex undertaking, however. Perhaps the simplest definition is to say that leading is "getting things done through people." In general, it may be said that a manager operates in the status quo, but a leader takes risks. Managers are conformers; leaders are reformers. Managers control; leaders empower. Managers supervise; leaders coach. Managers are efficient; leaders are effective. Managers are position oriented; leaders are people oriented. In sum, police administrators must be both skilled managers and effective leaders.[44]

Other definitions of leadership include the following:

- "The process of influencing the activities of an individual or a group in efforts toward goal achievement in a given situation"[45]
- "Working with and through individuals and groups to accomplish organizational goals"[46]
- "The activity of influencing people to strive willingly for group objectives"[47]
- "The exercise of influence"[48]

Conversely, it has been said that the manager may be viewed as a team captain, parent, steward, battle commander, fountain of wisdom, poker player, group spokesperson, gatekeeper, minister, drill instructor, facilitator, initiator, mediator, navigator, candy-store keeper, linchpin, umbrella-holder, and everything else between nurse and Attila-the-Hun.[49]

In criminal justice organizations, leaders take the macro view; their role might best be defined as "the process of influencing organizational members to use their energies willingly and appropriately to facilitate the achievement of the [agency's] goals."[50] I discuss leaders and managers in greater length later in this chapter and in Chapter 5 (the Mintzberg model of CEOs).

Next, we discuss what kinds of activities and philosophies constitute leadership.

Trait Theory

Trait theory was popular until the 1950s, but it raises important questions for us today. This theory was based on the contention that good leaders possessed certain character traits that poor leaders did not. Those who developed this theory, Stogdill and Goode, believed that a leader could be identified through a two-step process. The first step involved studying leaders and comparing them to nonleaders to determine which traits only the leaders possessed. The second step sought people who possessed these traits to be promoted to managerial positions.[51]

A study of 468 administrators in 13 companies found certain traits in successful administrators. They were more intelligent and better educated; had a stronger need for power; preferred independent activity, intense thought, and some risk; enjoyed relationships with people; and disliked detail work more than their subordinates.[52] Figure 2-5 ■ shows traits and skills commonly associated with leader effectiveness, according to Gary Yuki. Following this study, a review of the literature on trait theory revealed the traits most identified with leadership ability: intelligence, initiative, extroversion, a sense of humor, enthusiasm, fairness, sympathy, and self-confidence.[53]

Trait theory has lost much of its support since the 1950s, partly because of the basic assumption of the theory that leadership cannot be taught. A more important reason, however, is simply the growth of new, more sophisticated approaches to the study of leadership. Quantifiable means to test trait theory were limited. What does it mean to say that a leader must be intelligent? By whose standards? Compared with persons within the organization

> **trait theory** a theory based on the notion that good leaders possess certain character traits that poor leaders do not.

Traits	Skills
Adaptable to situations	Clever (intelligent)
Alert to social environment	Conceptually skilled
Ambitious and achievement oriented	Creative
Assertive	Diplomatic and tactful
Cooperative	Fluent in speaking
Decisive	Knowledgeable about group task
Dependable	Organized (administrative ability)
Dominant (desire to influence others)	Persuasive
Energetic (high activity level)	Socially skilled
Persistent	
Self-confident	
Tolerant of stress	
Willing to assume responsibility	

FIGURE 2-5 Traits and Skills Commonly Associated with Leader Effectiveness

Source: Excerpt from Leadership in Organizations by Gary A Yukl. Copyright © 1966 by Pearson Education. Used by permission of Pearson Education.

or within society? How can traits such as a sense of humor, enthusiasm, fairness, and the others listed earlier be measured or tested? The inability to measure these factors was the real flaw in and the reason for the decline of trait theory.

Style Theory

A study at Michigan State University investigated how leaders motivated individuals or groups to achieve organizational goals. The study determined that leaders must have a sense of the task to be accomplished as well as the environment in which their subordinates work. Three principles of leadership behavior emerged from the Michigan study:

1. Leaders must give task direction to their followers.

2. Closeness of supervision directly affects employee production. High-producing units had less direct supervision; highly supervised units had lower production. Conclusion: Employees need some area of freedom to make choices. Given this, they produce at a higher rate.

3. Leaders must be employee oriented. It is the leader's responsibility to facilitate employees' accomplishment of goals.[54]

style theory a theory that focuses on what leaders do, and arguing that leaders engage in two distinct types of behaviors: those relating to task and relationships.

In the 1950s, Edwin Fleishman began studies of leadership at Ohio State University. After focusing on leader behavior rather than personality traits, he identified two dimensions or basic principles of leadership that could be taught: *initiating structure* and *consideration* (Figure 2-6 ■).[55] Initiating structure referred to supervisory behavior that focused on the achievement of organizational goals, and consideration was directed toward a supervisor's openness to subordinates' ideas and respect for their feelings as persons. High consideration and moderate initiating structure were assumed to yield higher job satisfaction and productivity than high initiating structure and low consideration.[56]

The major focus of **style theory** is the adoption of a single managerial style by a manager based on his or her position in regard to initiating structure and consideration. Three pure leadership styles were thought to be the basis for all managers: autocratic, democratic, and laissez-faire.

autocratic leader leaders who are primarily authoritarian in nature and prefer to give orders rather than invite group participation.

The autocratic style is leader centered and has a high initiating structure. An **autocratic leader** is primarily authoritarian in nature and prefers to give orders rather than invite group participation. Such a leader has a tendency to be personal with criticism. This style

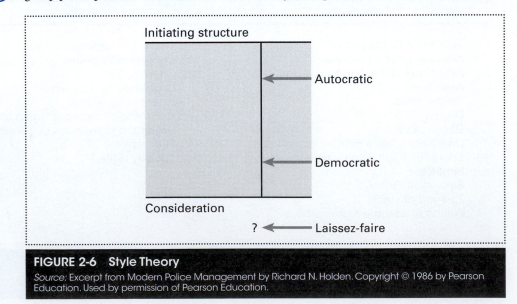

FIGURE 2-6   Style Theory
Source: Excerpt from Modern Police Management by Richard N. Holden. Copyright © 1986 by Pearson Education. Used by permission of Pearson Education.

works best in emergency situations in which strict control and rapid decision making are needed. The problem with autocratic leadership is the organization's inability to function when the leader is absent. It also stifles individual development and initiative because subordinates are rarely allowed to make an independent decision.[57]

In the democratic style, the **democratic leader** tends to focus on working within the group and strives to attain cooperation from group members by eliciting their ideas and support. Democratic managers tend to be viewed as consideration oriented and strive to attain mutual respect with subordinates. These leaders operate within an atmosphere of trust and delegate much authority. The democratic style is useful in organizations in which the course of action is uncertain and problems are relatively unstructured. It often taps the decision-making ability of subordinates. In emergency situations requiring a highly structured response, however, democratic leadership may prove too time-consuming and awkward to be effective. Thus, although the worker may appreciate the strengths of this style, its weaknesses must be recognized as well.[58]

In the laissez-faire style, the **laissez-faire leader** has a hands-off approach in which the leader is actually a nonleader. The organization in effect runs itself, with no input or control from the manager. This style has no positive aspects, as the entire organization is soon placed in jeopardy. In truth, this may not be a leadership style at all; instead, it may be an abdication of administrative duties.

> **democratic leader** leaders who stress working within the group and strive to attain cooperation from group members by eliciting their ideas and support.

> **laissez-faire leader** a hands-off approach to leadership, in which the organization essentially runs itself.

▶ Characteristics and Skills of America's Best Leaders

"Good in Their Skin"

Given today's deep-seated skepticism and distrust of leaders—often justified by public- and private-sector leaders' ethical violations, fraud, and cover-ups—it may seem that there is a complete dearth of leadership. To assess that view, recently, a weekly news magazine, *U.S. News & World Report*, teamed with Harvard University's Center for Public Leadership to identify leaders who are making a difference. A national panel sifted through nominations and agreed on a small group of men and women who embody the more important traits of leadership. The survey determined that there is not a lack of leadership, but rather a "wrong-headed notion of what a leader is," causing leaders to be hired for their style rather than substance and their image instead of integrity. It was also learned that there is no shortage of people with the capacity to lead who are just waiting for the opportunity.[59]

The survey found that twenty-first-century authentic leaders know who they are; they are "good in their skin," so they do not feel a need to impress or please others. They inspire those around them and bring people together around a shared purpose and a common set of values. They know the "true north" of their moral compass and are prepared to stay the course despite challenges and disappointments. They are more concerned about serving others than about their own success or recognition. By acknowledging their weaknesses, failings, and errors, they connect with people and empower them to take risks. Usually authentic leaders demonstrate the following five traits: pursuing their purpose with passion, practicing solid values, leading with their hearts as well as their heads, establishing connected relationships, and demonstrating self-discipline.[60]

For a less contemporary, classical view of what skills leaders need to possess, we consider the views of Robert Katz.

Katz's Three Skills

Robert Katz, in 1975, identified three essential skills that leaders should possess: technical, human, and conceptual. Katz defined a *skill* as the capacity to translate knowledge into action in such a way that a task is accomplished successfully.[61] Each of these skills (when performed effectively) results in the achievement of objectives and goals, which is the primary task of management.

Technical skills are those a manager needs to ensure that specific tasks are performed correctly. They are based on proven knowledge, procedures, or techniques. A police detective, a court administrator, and a probation officer have all developed technical skills directly related to the work they perform. Katz wrote that a technical skill "involves specialized knowledge, analytical ability within that specialty, and facility in the use of the tools and techniques of the specific discipline."[62] This is the skill most easily trained for. A court administrator, for example, has to be knowledgeable in areas such as computer applications, budgeting, caseload management, space utilization, public relations, and personnel administration; a police detective must possess technical skills in interviewing, fingerprinting, and surveillance techniques.[63]

Human skills involve working with people, including being thoroughly familiar with what motivates employees and how to utilize group processes. Katz visualized human skills as including "the executive's ability to work effectively as a group member and to build cooperative effort within the team he leads."[64] Katz added that the human relations skill involves tolerance of ambiguity and empathy. *Tolerance of ambiguity* means that the manager is able to handle problems when insufficient information precludes making a totally informed decision. *Empathy* is the ability to put oneself in another's place. An awareness of human skills allows a manager to provide the necessary leadership and direction, ensuring that tasks are accomplished in a timely fashion and with the least expenditure of resources.[65]

Conceptual skills, Katz said, involve "coordinating and integrating all the activities and interests of the organization toward a common objective."[66] Katz considered such skills to include "an ability to translate knowledge into action." For example, in a criminal justice setting, a court decision concerning the admissibility of evidence would need to be examined in terms of how it affects detectives, other court cases, the forensic laboratory, the property room, and the work of the street officer.

Katz emphasized that these skills can be taught to actual and prospective administrators; thus, good administrators are not simply born but can be trained in the classroom. Furthermore, all three of these skills are present in varying degrees at each management level. As one moves up the hierarchy, conceptual skills become more important and technical skills less important. The common denominator for all levels of management is *human* skills. In today's litigious environment, it is inconceivable that a manager could neglect the human skills.

▶ Motivating Employees

One of the most fascinating subjects throughout history has been how to motivate people. Some have sought to do so through justice (Plato), others through psychoanalysis (Freud), some through conditioning (Pavlov), some through incentives (Taylor), and still others through fear (any number of dictators and despots). From the Industrial Revolution to the present, managers have been trying to get a full day's work from their subordinates. The controversy in the early 1990s caused by Japanese businessmen who stated that American workers were lazy certainly raised our collective ire; many U.S. businesspeople and managers would probably agree that better worker motivation is needed. As Donald Favreau and Joseph Gillespie stated, "Getting people to work, the way you want them to work, when you want them to work, is indeed a challenge."[67]

Many theories have attempted to explain motivation. Some of the best known are those resulting from the Hawthorne studies and those developed by Abraham Maslow, Douglas

McGregor, and Frederick Herzberg, all of which are discussed here along with the expectancy and contingency theories.

The Hawthorne Studies

Another important theory that criminal justice leaders must comprehend is that of the **Hawthorne effect**, which essentially means that employees' behavior may be altered if they believe they are being studied—and that management *cares*; this was demonstrated in the following research project.

As mentioned earlier, one of the most important studies of worker motivation and behavior, launching intense interest and research in those areas, was the Western Electric Company's study in the 1920s. In 1927, engineers at the Hawthorne plant of Western Electric near Chicago conducted an experiment with several groups of workers to determine the effect of illumination on production. The engineers found that when illumination was increased in stages, production increased. To verify their finding, they reduced illumination to its previous level; again, production increased. Confused by their findings, they contacted Elton Mayo and his colleague Fritz Roethlisberger from Harvard to investigate.[68] First, the researchers selected several experienced female assemblers for an experiment. Management removed the women from their formal group and isolated them in a room. The women were compensated on the basis of the output of their group. Next, researchers began a series of environmental changes, each discussed with the women in advance of its implementation. For example, breaks were introduced and light refreshments were served. The normal 6-day workweek was reduced to 5 days, and the workday was cut by 1 hour. *Each* of these changes resulted in increased output.[69] To verify these findings, researchers returned the women to their original working conditions; breaks were eliminated, the 6-day workweek was reinstituted, and all other work conditions were reinstated. The results were that production again increased!

Mayo and his team then performed a second study at the Hawthorne plant. A new group of 14 workers—all men who performed simple, repetitive telephone coil-winding tasks—were given variations in rest periods and workweeks.[70] The men were also put on a reasonable piece rate—i.e., the more they produced, the more money they would earn. The assumption was that the workers would strive to produce more because it was in their own economic interest to do so.

The workers soon split into two informal groups on their own, each group setting its own standards of output and conduct. The workers' output did not increase. Neither too little nor too much production was permitted, and peers exerted pressure to keep members in line. The values of the informal group appeared to be more powerful than the allure of bigger incomes:

1. Don't be a "rate buster" and produce too much work.
2. If you turn out too little work, you are a "chiseler."
3. Don't be a "squealer" to supervisors.
4. Don't be officious; if you aren't a supervisor, don't act like one.[71]

Taken together, the Hawthorne studies revealed that people work for a variety of reasons, not just for money and subsistence. They seek satisfaction for more than their physical needs at work and from their coworkers. For the first time, clear evidence was gathered to support workers' social and esteem needs. As a result, this collision between the human relations school, begun in the Hawthorne studies, and traditional organizational theory sent researchers and theorists off in new and different directions. At least three major new areas of inquiry evolved: (1) what motivates workers (leading to the work of Maslow and Herzberg), (2) leadership (discussed earlier), and (3) organizations as behavioral systems.

Maslow's Hierarchy of Needs

Abraham H. Maslow (1908–1970), who argued for the application of the **humanistic school** of psychology—which basically stressed the importance of growth and self-actualization and argued that people are innately good—conducted research on human behavior at the Air University, Maxwell Air Force Base, Alabama, during the 1940s. His approach to motivation was unique in that the behavior patterns analyzed were those of motivated, happy, and production-oriented people—achievers, not underachievers. He studied biographies of historical and public figures, including Abraham Lincoln, Albert Einstein, and Eleanor Roosevelt; he also observed and interviewed some of his contemporaries—all of whom showed no psychological problems or signs of neurotic behavior.

Maslow hypothesized that if he could understand what made these people function, it would be possible to apply the same techniques to others, thus achieving a high state of motivation. His observations were coalesced into a **hierarchy of needs**.[72]

Maslow concluded that because human beings are part of the animal kingdom, their basic and primary needs or drives are physiological: air, food, water, sex, and shelter. These needs are related to survival. Next in order of importance are needs related to safety or security; protection against danger: murder, criminal assault, threat, deprivation, and tyranny. At the middle of the hierarchy is belonging, or social needs: being accepted by one's peers and associating with members of groups. At the next level of the hierarchy are the needs or drives related to ego: self-esteem, self-respect, power, prestige, recognition, and status. At the top of the hierarchy is self-realization or actualization: self-fulfillment, creativity, becoming all that one is capable of becoming.[73] Figure 2-7 ■ depicts this hierarchy.

Unlike the lower needs, the higher needs are rarely satisfied. Maslow suggested that to prevent frustration, needs should be filled in sequential order. A satisfied need is no longer a motivator. Maslow's research also indicated that once a person reaches a high state of motivation (i.e., esteem or self-realization levels), he or she will remain highly motivated, will have a positive attitude toward the organization, and will adopt a "pitch in and help" philosophy.

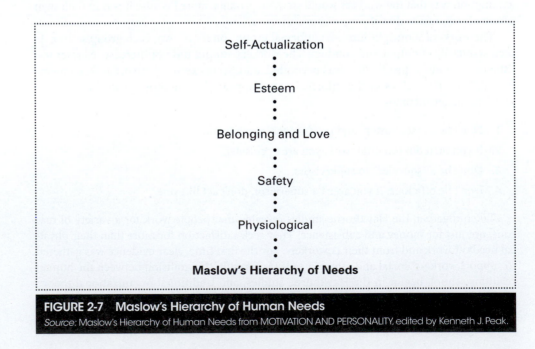

FIGURE 2-7 Maslow's Hierarchy of Human Needs
Source: Maslow's Hierarchy of Human Needs from MOTIVATION AND PERSONALITY, edited by Kenneth J. Peak.

McGregor's Theory X/Theory Y

Douglas McGregor (1906–1967), who served as president of Antioch College and then on the faculty of the Massachusetts Institute of Technology, was one of the great advocates of humane and democratic management. At Antioch, McGregor tested his theories of democratic management. He noted that behind every managerial decision or action are assumptions about human behavior. He chose the simplest terms possible with which to express them, designating one set of assumptions as **Theory X** and the other as **Theory Y**.[74]

Theory X managers hold traditional views of direction and control, such as the following:

- The average human being has an inherent dislike of work and will avoid it if possible. This assumption has deep roots, beginning with the punishment of Adam and Eve and their banishment into a world where they had to work for a living. Management's use of negative reinforcement and the emphasis on "a fair day's work" reflect an underlying belief that management must counter an inherent dislike for work.[75]

- Because of their dislike of work, most people must be coerced, controlled, directed, or threatened with punishment to get them to put forth adequate effort to achieve organizational objectives. Their dislike of work is so strong that even the promise of rewards is not generally enough to overcome it. People will accept the rewards and demand greater ones. Only the threat of punishment will work.[76]

- The average human being prefers to be directed, wishes to avoid responsibility, has relatively little ambition, and wants security above all. This assumption of the "mediocrity of the masses" is rarely expressed so bluntly. Although much lip service is paid to the "sanctity" of the worker and of human beings in general, many managers reflect this assumption in practice and policy.

Theory Y managers take the opposite view of the worker:

- The expenditure of physical and mental effort in work is as natural as play or rest. The average human being does not inherently dislike work; it may even be a source of satisfaction, to be performed voluntarily.

- External control and the threat of punishment are not the only means for producing effort to achieve organizational objectives.

- Commitment to objectives is a function of the rewards associated with their achievement. The most significant rewards—satisfaction of ego and self-actualization needs—can be direct products of effort directed to organizational objectives.

- Under proper conditions, the average human being learns not only to accept but also to seek responsibility. In this view, the avoidance of responsibility, lack of ambition, and emphasis on security are general consequences of experience, not inherent human characteristics.

- The capacity to exercise a high degree of imagination, ingenuity, and creativity in the solution of organizational problems is widely, not narrowly, distributed in the population.

- Under the conditions of modern industrial life, the intellectual potential of the average human being is only partially utilized.

Herzberg's Motivation-Hygiene Theory

During the 1950s, Frederick Herzberg conducted a series of studies in which he asked workers, primarily engineers, to describe the times when they felt particularly good and particularly bad about their jobs. The respondents identified several sources of satisfaction

theory X the management view holding that people inherently dislike work and will avoid it, and thus negative reinforcements (punishments) and other "drivers" must be used as motivators.

theory Y the management view holding that people inherently like to work, seek greater responsibility, and are inherently motivated rather than by punishment.

and dissatisfaction in their work. Then, from these findings, Herzberg isolated two vital factors found in all jobs: maintenance or hygiene factors and motivational factors.

Maintenance and hygiene factors are those elements in the work environment that meet an employee's hedonistic need to avoid pain. These factors include the necessities of any job (e.g., adequate pay, benefits, job security, decent working conditions, supervision, interpersonal relations). Hygiene factors do not satisfy or motivate; they set the stage for motivation. They are, however, a major source of dissatisfaction when they are inadequate.[77]

Motivational factors are those psychosocial factors that provide intrinsic satisfaction and serve as an incentive for people to invest more of their time, talent, energy, and expertise in productive behavior. Examples include achievement, recognition, responsibility, the work itself, advancement, and potential for growth. The absence of motivators does not necessarily produce job dissatisfaction.[78]

Although these needs are obviously related, they represent totally different dimensions of satisfaction.

Expectancy and Contingency Theories

In the 1960s, **expectancy theory** was developed, focusing on certain beliefs that can influence effort and performance. As examples, if an employee believes that his or her efforts will result in a certain level of performance leading to a desired reward, then that employee will likely take action accordingly. Of course, the opposite is true as well: If an employee perceives a low correlation between effort or performance and reward, then the result may well be inaction. Essentially, expectancy theory holds that employees will do what their managers or organizations want them to do if the following are true:

1. The task appears to be possible (employees believe that they possess the necessary competence).

2. The reward (outcome) offered is seen as desirable by the employees (intrinsic rewards come from the job itself; extrinsic rewards are supplied by others).

3. Employees believe that performing the required behavior or task will bring the desired outcome.

4. There is a good chance that better performance will bring greater rewards.[79]

Expectancy theory will work for an organization that specifies what behaviors it expects from people and what the rewards or outcomes will be for those who exhibit such behaviors. Rewards may be pay increases, time off, chances for advancement, a sense of achievement, or other benefits. Managers and organizations can find out what their employees want and see to it that they are provided with the rewards they seek. Walter Newsom[80] said that the reality of the expectancy theory can be summarized by the "nine C's": (1) capability (does a person have the capability to perform well?), (2) confidence (does a person believe that he or she can perform the job well?), (3) challenge (does a person have to work hard to perform the job well?), (4) criteria (does a person know the difference between good and poor performance?), (5) credibility (does a person believe the manager will deliver on promises?), (6) consistency (do subordinates believe that all employees receive similar preferred outcomes for good performance, and vice versa?), (7) compensation (do the outcomes associated with good performance reward the employee with money and other types of rewards?), (8) cost (what does it cost a person, in effort and outcomes foregone, to perform well?), and (9) communication (does the manager communicate with the subordinate?).

Later, in the 1970s, Morse and Lorsch built on McGregor's and Herzberg's theories with their theory of motivation called **contingency theory**. This theory sought to determine the fit between the organization's characteristics and its tasks and the motivations of individuals. The basic components of the contingency theory are that (1) among people's needs is a central need to achieve a sense of competence, (2) the ways in which people fulfill this need will vary from person to person, (3) competence motivation is most likely to be achieved when there is a fit between task and organization, and (4) a sense of competence continues to motivate people even after competence is achieved. In essence, we all want to be competent in our work. Contingency theory contends that people performing highly structured and organized tasks perform better in Theory X organizations and that those who perform unstructured and uncertain tasks perform better under a Theory Y approach. This theory tells managers to tailor jobs to fit people or to give people the skills, knowledge, and attitudes they will need to become competent.[81]

▶ Preparing for Employees of the Future: Generation Y

Changing Demographics and Mindset

American workers, although working longer, are aging and approaching retirement. In fact, over the next 20 years, 10,000 people will turn age 65 each day; 75 million baby boomers (people born between 1946 and 1964) are poised to retire and will leave large gaps in the workforce.[82] Certain administrators of the criminal justice system—particularly those in police and corrections (i.e., jails, prisons, probation and parole) agencies—must be prepared for the literal "changing of the guard" that is imminent.[83] They are already being replaced by persons born in what is termed Generation X, or Gen Xers (those born between 1965 and 1979), and in the near future will see the arrival of members of another generation—the so-called **Generation Y** (sometimes termed the millennials, or those born between 1980 to 2000).[84]

> **Generation Y**
> sometimes termed the millennials, persons born between 1980 to 2000.

People from Generation Y were raised in an environment where they received awards just for showing up. Their parents have emphasized self-esteem building and feelings of success rather than keeping score of winners and losers. Generation Y will probably be more team-oriented and the most technically literate workers ever to hit the job market; they will likely also prefer to work to live, rather than live to work. Gen Yers will probably think nothing of leaving their job for a year to work as a volunteer in Africa. They already give signs of viewing the workplace as a means to an end and do not allow their career and job title to define them. Gen Y employees will want to be find immediate fulfillment and respect at the workplace, and not be willing to wait 20 years to pay their dues. They expect educational opportunities both in and outside the job, a balanced work and play life, and recognition on the job.

Coming Challenges

How must justice administrators adapt their views and organizational cultures in order to meet these new employees of the future? Should they attempt to mold the Gen Y police officer or prison correction officer so as to fit the traditional, "correct" attitude and ways of behaving at the work site? Or should the administrator change his or her approach to leadership in order to attract and keep these coming employees? Kelly Sharp offered five challenges for administrators in finding, training, and keeping these employees, as well as some recommendations for their body art and technological skills.[85]

Challenge 1: Finding Them—Think electronically. The agency must attract Gen Yers via a presence on Facebook, My Space, or some type of police blog if recruitment is to be seen. The agency must have an up-to-date, attractive website.

Challenge 2: Training Them—The agency's training program must also be designed to keep Gen Yers, who were raised on video games and television and thus expect rapid access to information and will quickly become bored. Training should be interactive and entertaining as well as educational, and include the ability to brainstorm with each other and to engage in problem-solving.

Challenge 3: Keeping Them—The workplace should be a fun, flexible environment. The days of "do it my way or hit the highway" management style will not suffice. While pay is important to the Gen Y employee, he or she is seeking an environment in which to learn and grow—and one that includes volunteerism and educational opportunities. Gen Yers also prefer feedback that is informal and immediate, so agencies may wish to adjust their evaluation process accordingly.

Challenge 4: Body Art—Gen Y employees will likely display a very casual attitude toward unusual body art and piercing among their coworkers—a normal form of expression. Therefore, the traditional militaristic, standardized look (and dress code) may be jeopardized when every applicant comes decorated with body art. Dress codes may thus have to be rewritten at some point, or at least allow the option of softening the more stringent requirements.

Challenge 5: Technology—Gen Y employees, being surrounded by technology since birth, cannot imagine life without it. Indeed, their approaching any task without technologies to use may well baffle them. They were also raised online and inundated with reality TV, so it is natural for them to wish to record and broadcast their lives. The Internet, their cell phones, and their I-pods are viewed in the same manner as earlier generations viewed pen and pencil or typewriters. As a result, administrators may need to rethink policies that prohibit "surfing the Web at work."

Becoming a Learning Organization

In sum, the criminal justice workplace is about to change in dramatic ways. Understanding the millennials is important not only for developing future leaders, but also for basic workplace effectiveness and employee retention.

Agency administrators must promote what is termed a "**learning organization**" culture, where communication and collaboration are promoted so that everyone is engaged in identifying and solving problems. This culture will enable organizations of the future to continually experiment, improve, adapt to generational differences, and meet the challenges of a more complex role. The learning organization will prize equity, open information, reduced hierarchy, and a culture that encourages adaptability and participation toward seizing opportunities and handling crises.[86]

> **learning organization**
> an organizational culture that is looks to the future to continually experiment, improve, and adapt so as to meet the challenges of a more complex role.

Summary

Most young people entering the labor force would probably like to retain their individuality, feel free to express themselves, have a sense of being an important part of the team, and realize both extrinsic and intrinsic rewards from their work. The reality is, however, that a majority of people entering the job market will work within the structure of an organization that will not meet all of their personal needs.

We have seen that many organizations have a highly refined bureaucracy. Whether an organization will meet an employee's needs depends largely on its administrative philosophy. Therefore, the discussions in this chapter covered the structure and function of organizations and, just as important, how administrators and subordinates function within them. Also shown to be of major importance are the need for effective communication and the ability to work effectively with future generations who will soon enter the workforce.

The point to be made above all else is that administrators *must know their people.* In addition to covering several prominent theories that have withstood the test of time, I pointed out some approaches that have not succeeded. One can learn much from a failed approach or even from a poor boss who failed to appreciate and understand subordinates and used improper or no motivational techniques.

Key Terms and Concepts

Autocratic leader *36*

Bureaucracy *24*

Communication *29*

Contingency theory *42*

Democratic leader *37*

Expectancy theory *42*

Generation Y *43*

Grapevine *33*

Hawthorne effect *39*

Hierarchy of needs *40*

Humanistic school *40*

Inputs *25*

Laissez-faire leader *37*

Leadership *34*

Learning organization *44*

Maintenance and hygiene factors *42*

Motivational factors *42*

Organization *22*

Organizational theory *22*

Outputs *25*

POSDCORB *23*

Relatively identifiable boundary *22*

Scientific management *22*

Social entity *22*

Span of control *27*

Style theory *36*

Theory X *41*

Theory Y *41*

Trait theory *35*

Unity of command *28*

Questions for Review

1. Define *organization.* What is its function and structure?
2. Explain the evolution of organizational theory, including scientific, human relations, systems, and bureaucratic management theories.
3. Define *span of control* and *unity of command.*
4. Explain the characteristics and skills of America's best leaders.
5. What did Katz say are the three most important general qualities in leaders?
6. What does *communication* mean? What is its importance in organizations? Explain cultural cues, the nature and uniqueness of police communications, and some of the major barriers to effective communication.
7. Objectively assess what kind of leader you would likely be. Is it an effective style? What are some of the possible advantages and disadvantages of that style?
8. What kind of world did the Generation X grow up in, and what advantages and challenges do those persons pose in the criminal justice workplace? In criminal justice, what are the policy and legal implications of the younger generations' penchant for tattoos and body art—a generally nontraditional appearance?

Deliberate and Decide

A Communication Conundrum

Communication and budgetary problems have beset your state's Secretary of Corrections and the area's prison warden. First, costs for your county's new prison far exceeded the budget, and the warden never sought or obtained the corrections or budget director's authorization for cost overruns. The warden added a second prison drug dog program and sent the dog and a correctional officer for training without the director's authorization. And, despite his assertions to the contrary, it appears that a new program for geriatric inmates would not be covered entirely by grants and instead cost the state $75,000; the warden also hired a personal acquaintance to run this program—an employee from another prison. The warden also bought a van with personal funds and registered it to the state without authorization.

Questions for Discussion

1. What are the issues involved in this situation?
2. What should the secretary do about them?
3. What must the secretary do to prevent such situations from occurring in the future?

Learn by Doing

1. As part of a criminal justice class project concerning government careers, you are assigned to examine bureaucracies. What would you say are some of the specific characteristics and criticisms of bureaucracies? What could happen in criminal justice if these characteristics were applied in the extreme?

2. You are contacted by a friend who belongs to a local civic club that is planning a Labor Day luncheon to recognize all workers in the community. Knowing of your background and prior study of organizational theory, she asks you to speak at this luncheon concerning the scientific management approach to organizational theory—particularly the career of Frederick W. Taylor and his contributions and primary motivations regarding management. What will you report?

3. Your prison duty shift's middle manager (a lieutenant) comes to you saying he has personally observed a number of problems concerning the manner in which communication is occurring from one duty shift to another. These problems appear to primarily involve inaccurate information being disseminated, a grapevine that seems bent on carrying incorrect, malicious information, and a diverse group of employees with language and cultural barriers. You are assigned to look at the problem as well as recommend means by which communications could be improved. How would you proceed, and what kinds of ideas might you put forth?

Notes

1. Steven Levy, "Working in Dilbert's World," *Newsweek* (August 12, 1996):52–57.
2. David A. Tansik and James F. Elliott, *Managing Police Organizations* (Monterey, CA: Duxbury Press, 1981), p. 1.
3. Stephen P. Robbins, *Organizational Theory: Structure, Design and Applications* (Upper Saddle River, NJ: Prentice Hall, 1987).
4. Larry K. Gaines, John L. Worrall, Mittie D. Southerland, and John E. Angell, *Police Administration*, 2nd ed. (New York: McGraw-Hill, 2002), p. 8.
5. Peter W. Blau and W. Richard Scott, *Formal Organizations* (Scranton, PA: Chandler, 1962), p. 43.
6. Gaines et al., *Police Administration*, p. 12.
7. Ronald G. Lynch, *The Police Manager: Professional Leadership Skills,* 3rd ed. (New York: Random House, 1986), p. 4.
8. Samuel C. Certo, *Principles of Modern Management: Functions and Systems,* 4th ed. (Boston: Allyn and Bacon, 1989), p. 35.
9. See Elton Mayo, *The Human Problems of an Industrial Civilization* (New York: Macmillan, 1933).
10. Paul M. Whisenand and Fred Ferguson, *The Managing of Police Organizations,* 3rd ed. (Upper Saddle River, NJ: Prentice Hall, 1989), pp. 218–219.
11. Lynch, *Police Manager,* pp. 5–6.
12. Abraham H. Maslow, *Motivation and Personality* (New York: Harper & Row, 1954).
13. Douglas McGregor, *The Human Side of Enterprise* (New York: McGraw-Hill, 1960).
14. Robert R. Blake and Jane S. Mouton, *The Managerial Grid* (Houston, TX: Gulf, 1964).
15. Lynch, *Police Manager,* pp. 7–8.
16. Max Weber, *The Theory of Social and Economic Organization,* trans. A. M. Henderson and Talcott Parsons (New York: Oxford University Press, 1947), pp. 329–330.
17. James Q. Wilson, *Varieties of Police Behavior* (Cambridge, MA: Harvard University Press, 1968), pp. 2–3.
18. Ibid., p. 3.
19. Lyndall F. Urwick, *Notes on the Theory of Organization* (New York: American Management Association, 1952).
20. Troy Lane, "Span of Control for Law Enforcement Agencies," *The Associate* (March–April 2006):19–31.
21. Ibid.
22. Gaines et al., *Police Administration*, p. 12.
23. Leonard R. Sayles and George Strauss, *Human Behavior in Organizations* (Upper Saddle River, NJ: Prentice Hall, 1966), p. 349.
24. Charles R. Swanson, Leonard Territo, and Robert W. Taylor, *Police Administration,* 2nd ed. (New York: Macmillan, 1988), p. 308.
25. Mario Pei, *Language for Everybody: What It Is and How to Master It* (Greenwich, CT: Devin-Adair Co., 1961), pp. 4–5.

26. Louis A. Radelet, *The Police and the Community: Studies* (Beverly Hills, CA: Glencoe, 1973), p. 92.

27. Swanson et al., *Police Administration*, p. 86.

28. Institute of Government, University of Georgia, *Interpersonal Communication: A Guide for Staff Development* (Athens: Author, 1974), p. 15.

29. Wayne W. Bennett and Karen Hess, *Management and Supervision in Law Enforcement* (St. Paul, MN: West, 1992), p. 72.

30. See R. C. Huseman, quoted in ibid., pp. 21–27. Material for this section was also drawn from Swanson et al., *Police Administration*, pp. 309–311.

31. Swanson et al., *Police Administration*, pp. 312–313.

32. D. Katz and R. L. Kahn, *The Social Psychology of Organizations* (New York: Wiley, 1966), p. 239. As cited in P. V. Lewis, *Organizational Communication: The Essence of Effective Management* (Columbus, OH: Grid, 1975), p. 36.

33. Lewis, *Organizational Communication*, p. 38.

34. Swanson et al., *Police Administration*, p. 315.

35. See R. K. Allen, *Organizational Management Through Communication* (New York: Harper & Row, 1977), pp. 77–79.

36. Swanson et al., *Police Administration*, p. 343.

37. Stephen W. Mastrofski, "Police Agency Accreditation: The Prospects of Reform," *American Journal of Police* 5(3) (1986):45–81.

38. Alex Markels, "Managers Aren't Always Able to Get the Right Message across with E-mail," *The Wall Street Journal* (August 6, 1996), p. 2.

39. Robert L. Montgomery, "Are You a Good Listener?" *Nation's Business* (October 1981):65–68.

40. Bennett and Hess, *Management and Supervision in Law Enforcement*, p. 82.

41. G. Weaver, "Law Enforcement in a Culturally Diverse Society," *FBI Law Enforcement Bulletin* (September 1992):1–10.

42. Certo, *Principles of Modern Management*, p. 103.

43. Wayne W. Bennett and Karen M. Hess, *Management and Supervision in Law Enforcement,* 4th ed. (Belmont, CA: Wadsworth, 2004), p. 52; Warren Bennis and Burt Nanus, *Leaders* (New York: Harper & Row, 1985).

44. Bennett and Hess, *Management and Supervision in Law Enforcement*, 4th ed., pp. 53–54.

45. Paul Hersey and Kenneth H. Blanchard, *Management of Organizational Behavior*, 3rd ed. (Upper Saddle River, NJ: Prentice Hall, 1977), p. 12.

46. Ibid.

47. Bennett and Hess, *Management and Supervision in Law Enforcement*, 4th ed., p. 52.

48. Ibid.

49. Roger D. Evered and James C. Selman, "Coaching and the Art of Management," *Organizational Dynamics* 18 (Autumn 1989):16.

50. Charles R. Swanson, Leonard Territo, and Robert W. Taylor, *Police Administration: Structures, Processes, and Behavior*, 6th ed. (Upper Saddle River, NJ: Prentice Hall, 2005), p. 272.

51. Richard Holden, *Modern Police Management,* 2nd ed. (Upper Saddle River, NJ: Prentice Hall, 1994), p. 47.

52. Thomas A. Mahoney, Thomas H. Jerdee, and Alan N. Nash, "Predicting Managerial Effectiveness," *Personnel Psychology* 13(2) (Summer 1960):147–163.

53. Joe Kelly, *Organizational Behavior: An Existential Systems Approach,* rev. ed. (Homewood, IL: Richard D. Irwin, 1974), p. 363.

54. Bennett and Hess, *Management and Supervision in Law Enforcement*, 4th ed., p. 57.

55. Edwin Fleishman, "Leadership Climate, Human Relations Training and Supervisory Behavior," *Personnel Psychology* 6 (1953):208–222.

56. Stephen M. Sales, "Supervisory Style and Productivity: Review and Theory," in Larry Cummings and William E. Scott (eds.), *Readings in Organizational Behavior and Human Performance* (Homewood, IL: Richard D. Irwin, 1969), p. 122.

57. Holden, *Modern Police Management*, pp. 39–40.

58. Ibid., pp. 41–42.

59. Bill George, "Truly Authentic Leadership," *U.S. News & World Report* (October 30, 2006):52.

60. Ibid.

61. Robert L. Katz, "Skills of an Effective Administrator," *Harvard Business Review* 52 (1975):23.

62. Ibid., p. 23.

63. Dan L. Costley and Ralph Todd, *Human Relations in Organizations* (St. Paul, MN: West, 1978).

64. Ibid., p. 24.

65. James M. Higgins, *Human Relations: Concepts and Skills* (New York: Random House, 1982).

66. Ibid., p. 27.

67. Favreau and Gillespie, *Modern Police Administration*, p. 85.

68. Warren Richard Plunkett, *Supervision: The Direction of People at Work* (Dubuque, IA: Wm. C. Brown, 1983), p. 121.

69. Elton Mayo, *The Social Problems of an Industrial Civilization* (Boston: Division of Research, Graduate School of Business Administration, Harvard University, 1945), pp. 68–86.

70. Favreau and Gillespie, *Modern Police Administration*, pp. 100–101.

71. Frederick J. Roethlisberger and William J. Dickson, *Management and the Worker* (Cambridge, MA: Harvard University Press, 1939), p. 522.

72. Favreau and Gillespie, *Modern Police Administration*, p. 87.

73. Ibid.

74. Ibid., p. 88.

75. Ibid., p. 89.

76. Ibid.

77. Harry W. More and W. Fred Wegener, *Behavioral Police Management* (New York: Macmillan, 1992), pp. 163–164.

78. Frederick Herzberg, "One More Time: How Do You Motivate Employees?" in *Harvard Business Review Classic,* September–October 1987, http://hbr.org/2003/01/one-more-time-how-do-you-motivate-employees/ (accessed September 26, 2014).

79. Randall S. Schuler, *Personnel and Human Resources Management* (St. Paul, MN: West, 1981), pp. 41–43.

80. Walter B. Newsom, "Motivate, Now!" *Personnel Journal* 14 (February 1990):51–55.

81. Plunkett, *Supervision*, pp. 131–132.

82. Dave Bernard, "The Baby Boomer Number Game," *U.S. News and World Report*, http://money.usnews.com/money/blogs/On-Retirement/2012/03/23/the-baby-boomer-number-game (accessed September 26, 2014).

83. Kelly Sharp, "Recruiting Generation Y," *Law and Order* 60 (8) (August 2012):58–60.

84. Matt Rosenberg, "Names of Generations," About.com: Geography, http://geography.about.com/od/population-geography/qt/generations.htm (accessed October 15, 2013).

85. Sharp, "Recruiting Generation Y," pp. 59–60.

86. Tommy York, Andy Whitford, and Brian Williams, "Command and Control Meets the Millennials," *American Jails* 26(2) (May/June 2012):23–24, 26–31.

Uneasy lies the head that wears the crown.

—*William Shakespeare*

Good orders make evil men good and bad orders make good men evil.

—*James Harrington*

3 Rights of Criminal Justice Employees

LEARNING OBJECTIVES

After reading this chapter, the student will be able to:

1 *describe laws and rights affecting criminal justice employees*

2 *delineate and describe several aspects and rights of the employment relationship, such as proper recruitment and hiring, disparate treatment, affirmative action, property rights, pay and benefits, and providing a safe workplace*

3 *explain the elements of a due process claim under U.S. Section 1983*

4 *define the impact of the Fair Labor Standards Act on criminal justice employees*

5 *delineate the nature and impact of workplace harassment in criminal justice*

6 *review the eligibility requirements for Family and Medical Leave Act benefits*

7 *describe the Americans with Disabilities Act*

▶ Introduction

In the last few decades, the rights and obligations of criminal justice employees, like those of workers in the private sector, have changed dramatically. Changes in values, demographics, law, and technology have blurred the line dividing the manager and the managed in enforcement, judicial, and correctional agencies. Today's criminal justice employee is far more sophisticated about employee rights.[1] For that reason, and because of attendant liability considerations (discussed in Chapter 14), contemporary criminal justice managers must be more aware of employees' legal rights.

After an overview of the relevant employment laws, we discuss recruitment and hiring issues, age discrimination, affirmative action, discipline and discharge, pay and benefits, and safe workplace issues. Then we examine constitutional rights of criminal justice employees as determined by the courts regarding free speech, searches and seizures, self-incrimination, religious practices, sexual misconduct, residency requirements, moonlighting, misuse of firearms, alcohol and drugs in the workplace, workplace harassment, and the Americans with Disabilities Act. The chapter concludes with review questions, "deliberate and decide" problems, and "learn by doing" exercises.

▶ Overview

Law and litigation affecting criminal justice employees can arise out of federal and state constitutions, statutes, administrative regulations, and judicial interpretations and rulings. Even poorly written employee handbooks or long-standing agency customs or practices may create vested rights. The ripple effect begun by improper or illegal hiring, training, discipline, or discharge can lead not only to poor agency performance and morale but also to substantial legal and economic liability. It should become apparent in the following overview and the court decisions that follow that utilizing good common sense as well as a sense of fairness will go a long way toward preventing legal problems in the employment relationship.[2]

It should also be noted that the Civil Rights Act of 1991, like its predecessors, may result in further amended versions and changes in public and private sector employment; however, it will take several years for significant decisions to wind their way through the courts for a final determination by the Supreme Court of the intent and reach of the Act. Therefore, this section focuses on presenting the issues rather than on attempting to settle the law in these areas.

- *Fair Labor Standards Act (FLSA; at 29 U.S.C. 203 et seq.).* This Act provides minimum salary and overtime provisions covering both public and private sector employees. Part 7(a) contains special provisions for firefighters and police officers. I discuss the FLSA more fully later.

- *Title VII of the Civil Rights Act of 1964 and its amendments (42 U.S.C. 2000e).* This broadly based Act establishes a federal policy requiring fair employment practices in both the public and private sectors. It prohibits unlawful employment discrimination in the hiring process, discharge, discipline, and working conditions and the unlawful provision of benefits based on race, color, religion, sex, and national origin. Its provisions extend to "hostile work environment" claims based on sexual, racial, or religious harassment.

- *Equal Pay Act [29 U.S.C. 206(d)].* This legislation provides an alternative remedy to Title VII for sex-based discrimination in wages and benefits when men and women do similar work. It applies the simpler Fair Labor Standards Act procedures to claims. Note that the Equal Pay Act does not mean "comparable worth"—an attempt to determine wages by requiring equal pay for employees whose work is of comparable worth even if the job content is totally different.

- ***The Pregnancy Discrimination Act of 1978 [42 U.S.C. Section 2000e(k)].*** This Act is an amendment to the scope of sexual discrimination under Title VII. It prohibits unequal treatment of women because of pregnancy or related medical conditions (e.g., nausea). The Act requires that employers treat pregnant women like other temporarily disabled employees. The U.S. Supreme Court decided a major case in 1991 that limited employers' ability in excluding women who are pregnant or of childbearing years from certain jobs under a fetal protection policy.[3]

- ***Age Discrimination in Employment Act (29 U.S.C. 623).*** This Act generally prohibits the unequal treatment of applicants or employees based on their age, if they are age 40 years or older, in regard to hiring, firing, receiving benefits, and other conditions of employment.

- ***Americans with Disabilities Act of 1990 (ADA) (42 U.S.C. 12112).*** The goal of this legislation is to remove barriers that might prevent otherwise qualified individuals with disabilities from enjoying the same employment opportunities as persons without disabilities. Before the ADA, the Rehabilitation Act of 1973 (see 29 U.S.C. 701) and its amendments prevented similar disability discrimination among public agencies receiving federal funds. The ADA is discussed more fully later.

- ***Section 1983 (codified as Title 42, U.S. Code Section 1983).*** This major piece of legislation is the instrument by which an employee may sue an employer for civil rights violations based on the deprivation of constitutional rights. It is the most versatile civil rights action and is also the most often used against criminal justice agencies. Section 1983 is discussed more in Chapter 14.

In addition to the legislative enactments and state statutes that prohibit various acts of discrimination in employment, there are remedies that have tremendous impact on public sector employees. Tort actions (a tort is the infliction of a civil injury) may be brought by public sector employees against their employer for a wide variety of claims, ranging from assault and battery to defamation. Contractual claims may grow out of collective bargaining agreements, which may include procedures for assignments, seniority, due process protections (such as in the Peace Officers' Bill of Rights, discussed later), and grievance procedures. Often the source of the right defines the remedy and the procedure for obtaining that remedy; for example, statutes or legal precedents often provide for an aggrieved employee to receive back pay, compensatory damages, injunctive relief, or punitive damages.

▶ The Employment Relationship

Recruitment and Hiring

Numerous selection methods for hiring police and corrections officers have been tried over the years. Issues in recruitment, selection, and hiring also often involve internal promotions and assignments to special units, such as a special weapons team in a police agency. Requirements concerning age (e.g., the FBI will hire no one older than 37 years), height, weight, vision, education, and possession of a valid driver's license have all been utilized over the years in criminal justice. In addition, tests are commonly used to determine intelligence, emotional suitability and stability (using psychological examinations and oral interviews), physical agility, and character (using polygraph examinations and extensive background checks).[4] More recently, drug tests have become frequently used as well (discussed more fully later).

The critical question for such tests is whether they validly test the types of skills needed for the job. A companion concern is whether the tests are used for discriminatory purposes or have an unequal impact on protected groups (e.g., minorities, the physically challenged). As a result of these considerations, a number of private companies provide valid, reliable examinations for use by the public sector.

Disparate Treatment

disparate treatment treating people differently because of their age, gender, sex, or other protected status.

It should be emphasized that there is nothing in the law that states that an employer must hire or retain incompetent personnel. In effect, the law does not prohibit discrimination; thus, for positions that require driving, it is not unlawful to refuse to hire people who have a record of driving while intoxicated. What is illegal is to treat people differently because of their age, gender, sex, or other protected status, that is, **disparate treatment**. It is also illegal to deny equal employment opportunities to such persons; that is disparate impact.[5] Federal equal opportunity law prohibits the use of selection procedures for hiring or promotion that have a discriminatory impact on the employment opportunities of women, Hispanics, blacks, or other protected classes. An example of overt discriminatory hiring is reflected in a court decision in 1987 arising out of a situation in a sparsely populated county in Virginia. Four women sued because they were denied positions as courtroom security officer, deputy, and civil process server because of their gender. Sheriffs had refused to hire the women, justifying their decision by contending that being male was a **bona fide occupational qualifier (BFOQ)** (i.e., in certain situations it is lawful and reasonable to discriminate because of a business necessity, such as a female corrections facility maintaining at least one female staff member on duty at all times to assist inmates in toileting, showering, and disrobing) for the positions and that because the positions were within the "personal staff" of the sheriff, they were exempt from the coverage of Title VII. The Fourth Circuit overturned a lower court decision, finding that the sheriff did not establish that gender was a BFOQ for the positions and that the positions were not part of the sheriff's personal staff (the positions were not high level, policymaking, or advisory in nature). Thus, the refusal to hire the women violated Title VII.[6] There may, however, be a "business justification" for a hiring policy even though it has a disparate impact. For example, in one case an employer required airline attendants to cease flying immediately on discovering they were pregnant. The court upheld the policy on the ground that pregnancy could affect one's ability to perform routine duties in an aircraft, thereby jeopardizing the safety of passengers.[7]

bona fide occupational qualifier (BFOQ) in certain situations, a rationale for discriminating on the basis of a business necessity.

A classic example of an apparent neutral employment requirement that actually had a disparate impact on gender, race, and ethnicity was the once-prevalent height requirement used by most public safety agencies. Minimum height requirements of 5 feet, 10 inches or above were often advertised and effectively operated to exclude most women and many Asians and Hispanics from employment.[8] Such a requirement has gradually been superseded by a "height in proportion to weight" requirement.

Nonetheless, other existing physical agility tests serve to discriminate against women and small men with less upper-body strength. One wonders how many pushups a police officer must do on the job or be able to do to perform his or her duties adequately, or how many 6-foot walls, ditches, and attics officers must negotiate. (Occasionally, preemployment physical abilities testing becomes ludicrous. For example, I once allowed a recruiter from a major western city to recruit students in an upper-level criminal justice course. The recruiter said the city's physical test included scaling a 6-foot wall; however, he quickly pointed out that testing staff would boost all female applicants over it.)

Litigation is blossoming in this area. In a western city, a woman challenged the police department's physical abilities test as discriminatory and not job related, prompting the agency to hire a Canadian consultant who developed a job-related preemployment agility test (currently used by the Royal Canadian Mounted Police and other agencies across Canada) based on data provided by officers and later computer analyzed for incorporation into the test. In other words, recruits were soon tested in terms of the physical demands placed on police officers in that specific community. (No pushups or 6-foot walls are included.)[9]

Discrimination may also exist in promotions and job assignments. As an example of the former, a Nebraska female correctional center worker brought suit alleging that her employer violated her Title VII and equal protection rights by denying her a promotion. The woman was qualified for the higher-level position (assistant center manager for programming), and she also alleged that the center treated women inequitably and unprofessionally, that assertiveness in women was viewed negatively, and that women were assigned clerical duties not assigned to men. The court found that she was indeed denied a promotion because of her sex, in violation of Title VII and the equal protection clause of the Fourteenth Amendment; she was awarded back pay and front pay biweekly until a comparable position became available, general damages, and court costs.[10]

With respect to litigation in the area of job assignments, four female jail matrons who were refused assignments to correctional officer positions in Florida even though they had been trained and certified as jail officers were awarded damages. It was ruled that a state regulation prohibiting females in male areas of the jail was discriminatory without proof that gender was a BFOQ.[11] However, a particular assignment may validly exclude one gender. An assignment to work as a decoy female prostitute demonstrates a business necessity for women.[12]

How Old Is "Too Old" in Criminal Justice?

State and public agencies are not immune from age discrimination suits in which arbitrary age restrictions have been found to violate the law. In Florida, a police lieutenant with the state highway patrol with 29 years of service was forced by statute to retire at age 62. The Equal Employment Opportunity Commission (EEOC) brought suit, alleging that Florida's statute violated the Age Discrimination in Employment Act (ADEA). The court held that age should not be a BFOQ because youthfulness is not a guarantee of public safety. Rather, a physical fitness standard would better serve the purpose of ensuring the ability to perform the tasks of the position.[13]

Indeed, the U.S. Supreme Court rejected mandatory retirement plans for municipal firefighters and police officers.[14] Until 1985, the city of Baltimore had relied on a federal police officer and firefighter statute (5 U.S.C. 8335b), an exemption to the ADEA, to establish age limits for appointing and retiring its fire and police officers; the city also contended that age was a BFOQ for doing so. The U.S. Supreme Court said that although Congress had exempted federal employees from application of the ADEA, another agency cannot just adopt the same standards without showing an agency-specific need. Age is not a BFOQ for nonfederal firefighters (or, by extension, police officers). The Court also established a "reasonable federal standard" in its 1984 decision in *EEOC v. Wyoming*,[15] in which it overturned a state statute providing for the mandatory retirement of state game wardens at age 55; it held that the ADEA did not require employers to retain unfit employees, only to make individualized determinations about fitness.

Criminal Justice and Affirmative Action

Probably no single employment practice has caused as much controversy as **affirmative action**—actions or policies favoring persons or groups who have suffered from discrimination, particularly in employment or education. The very words bring to mind visions of quotas and of unqualified people being given preferential hiring treatment.[16]

affirmative action
actions or policies that favor persons or groups who have suffered from discrimination, particularly in employment or education.

Indeed, quotas have been at the center of legal, social, scientific, and political controversy for more than four decades.[17] However, the reality of affirmative action is substantially different from the myth; as a general rule, affirmative action plans give preferred treatment only to affected groups when all other criteria (e.g., education, skills) are equal.[18]

The legal question (and to many persons, a moral one) that arises from affirmative action is, When does preferential hiring become **reverse discrimination** (where, it is argued, the aforementioned affirmative action policies have resulted in unfair treatment for members of majority groups)? The leading case here is *Bakke v. Regents of the University of California*[19] in 1978, in which Allan Bakke was passed over for medical school admission at the University of California, Davis, partly because the school annually set aside a number of its 100 medical school admissions slots for "disadvantaged" applicants. The Supreme Court held, among other things, that race could be used as a criterion in selection decisions, but it could not be the only criterion.

In a series of cases beginning in 1986,[20] the Supreme Court considered the development and application of affirmative action plans, establishing a two-step inquiry that must be satisfied before an affirmative action plan can be put in place. A plan must have (1) a remedial purpose, to correct past inequities, and (2) there must be a manifest imbalance or significant disparity to justify the plan. The Court, however, emphasized that such plans cannot completely foreclose employment opportunities to nonminority or male candidates.

The validity of such plans is generally determined on a case-by-case basis. For example, the District of Columbia Circuit Court held in 1987 that an affirmative action plan covering the promotion of blacks to management positions in the police department was justified because only 174 of the 807 positions (22%) above the rank of sergeant were filled by blacks in a city where 60 percent of the labor market was black.[21] Twenty-one past and present nonminority male detectives of the Metropolitan Police Department who were passed over for promotion challenged the department's voluntary affirmative actions plan designed to place "special emphasis" on the hiring and advancement of females and minorities in those employment areas where an "obvious imbalance" in their numbers existed.[22]

The plaintiffs believed that their failure to be promoted was attributable to illegal preferential treatment of blacks and women (reverse discrimination) that violated their rights under Title VII and the due process clause of the Fifth Amendment. The court held that the nonminority and male employees of the department failed to prove that the plan was invalid; a considerable body of evidence showed racial and sexual imbalance at the time the plan was adopted. Also, the plan did not unnecessarily trammel any legitimate interests of the nonminority or male employees because it did not call for displacement or layoff and did not totally exclude them from promotion opportunities.[23]

In summary, then, whenever a criminal justice employer wishes to implement and maintain job requirements, they must be job related. Furthermore, whenever a job requirement discriminates against a protected class, it should have a strong legitimate purpose and be the least restrictive alternative. Finally, attempts to remedy past hiring inequities by such means as affirmative action programs need substantial justification to avoid reverse discrimination.[24]

Property Rights in Employment

The Fourteenth Amendment to the U.S. Constitution provides in part that

> No state shall make or enforce any law which shall abridge the privileges or immunities of citizens of the United States; nor shall any State deprive any person of life, liberty, or property without due process of law; nor deny to any person within its jurisdiction the equal protection of the law.

Furthermore, the Supreme Court has set forth four elements of a due process claim under Section 1983: (1) A person acting under color of state law (2) deprived an individual (3) of constitutionally protected property (4) without due process of law.[25]

A long line of court cases has established the legal view that public employees have a property interest in their employment. This flies in the face of the old view that employees served "at will" or until their employer, for whatever reason, no longer needed their services. The Supreme Court has provided some general guidance on how the question of a constitutionally protected property interest is to be resolved:

> To have a property interest in a benefit, a person clearly must have more than an abstract need or desire for it. He must have more than a unilateral expectation of it. He must, instead, have a *legitimate claim of entitlement to it*. It is a purpose of the ancient institution of property to protect those claims *upon which people rely in their daily lives, reliance that must not be arbitrarily undermined* [emphasis added].[26]

The Court has also held that employees are entitled to both a pretermination hearing (setting forth the reasons and supporting evidence prompting the proposal to terminate the employee) and a posttermination notice,[27] as well as an opportunity to respond, and that state legislators are free to choose not to confer a property interest in public employment.

The development of a property interest in employment has an important ramification: It means that due process must be exercised by a public entity before terminating or interfering with an employee's property right. What has been established, however, is that a probationary employee has little or no property interest in employment; for example, the Ninth Circuit held that a probationary civil service employee ordinarily has no property interest and could be discharged without a hearing or even "good cause." In that same decision, however, the court held that a woman who had passed her 6-month probationary period and who had then been promoted to a new position for which there was a probationary period had the legitimate expectation of continued employment.[28]

To the contrary, an Indiana police captain was deemed to have a property interest in his position even though a state statute allowed the city manager to demote without notice. There, a captain of detectives, a Democrat, was demoted by a newly elected Republican mayor. The court determined that the dismissal of even a policymaking public employee for politically motivated reasons is forbidden unless the position inherently encompasses tasks that render political affiliation an appropriate prerequisite for effective performance.[29]

Normally, however, policymaking employees (often called exempt appointments) possess an automatic exception to the contemporary property interest view. These personnel, often elected agency heads, are generally free to hire and fire those employees who are involved in the making of important decisions and policy. Examples of this area include new sheriffs who appoint undersheriffs and wardens who appoint deputy wardens. These subordinate employees have no property interest in their positions and may be asked at any time to leave the agency or revert back to an earlier rank.

This property interest in employment is, of course, generally implied. An example of this implication is found in a Utah case in which a property interest was found to exist based on an implied contract founded on an employment manual. Due process standards were therefore violated when the police department fired an officer without showing good cause or giving him a chance to respond to the charges against him.[30] In a Pennsylvania case, a patrol officer was suspended for 30 days without pay for alleged violations of personnel policies and was not given an opportunity to file a written response to the charges. The court held that the officer's suspension resulted in a deprivation of property.[31]

The property right in one's employment does not have to involve discipline or discharge to afford an employee protections. The claim of a parole officer that he was harassed, humiliated, and interfered with in a deliberate attempt to remove him from his position established a civil rights action for deprivation of property.[32] This decision, against the Illinois Department of Corrections, resulted from allegations that the department engaged in "a deliberate and calculated effort to remove the plaintiff from his position by forcing him to resign, thereby making the protections of the personnel code unavailable to him." As a result, the plaintiff suffered anxiety and stress and eventually went on disability status at substantially reduced pay.[33]

The key questions, then, once a property right is established, are: (1) What constitutes adequate grounds for interference with that right and (2) what is adequate process to sustain that interference?[34]

Pay and Benefits

The **Fair Labor Standards Act (FLSA)** has had a major impact on criminal justice agencies. One observer referred to the FLSA as the criminal justice administrator's "worst nightmare come true."[35] Enacted in 1938 to establish minimum wages and to require overtime compensation in the private sector, amendments were added in 1974 extending its coverage to state and local governmental employees and including special work period provisions for police and fire employees. In 1976, however, the U.S. Supreme Court ruled that the extension of the Act into traditional local and state governmental functions was unconstitutional.[36] In 1985, the Court reversed itself, bringing local police employees under the coverage of the FLSA. In this major (and costly) decision, *Garcia v. San Antonio Transit Authority,*[37] the Court held, 5 to 4, that Congress could impose the requirements of the FLSA on state and local governments.

Criminal justice operations take place 24 hours per day, 7 days per week, and often require overtime and participation in off-duty activities such as court appearances and training sessions. The FLSA comes into play when overtime salaries must be paid. It provides that an employer must pay employees time and a half for all hours worked over 40 per week. Overtime must also be paid to personnel for all work in excess of 43 hours in a 7-day cycle or 171 hours in a 28-day period. Public safety employees may accrue a maximum of 240 hours of compensatory or "comp" time, which, if not utilized as leave, must be paid on separation from employment at the employee's final rate of pay or at the average pay over the last 3 years, whichever is greater.[38] Furthermore, employers usually cannot require employees to take compensatory time in lieu of cash.

A recent decision by the U.S. Supreme Court favored administrators in this regard, however. A county in Texas became concerned that after employees reached their cap on comp time accrued, it would be unable to afford to pay them for overtime worked. So, the county sought to reduce accrued comp time and implemented a policy under which the employees' supervisor set a maximum number of compensatory hours that could be accumulated. When an employee's accrued amount of comp time approached that maximum, the employee would be asked to take some compensatory time off so as to reduce his or her number of comp hours. If the employee did not do so voluntarily, the supervisor would order the employee to use his or her comp time at specified times. This policy was challenged in the Court by 127 deputy sheriffs. The Court held that nothing in the FLSA prohibited employers from instituting such a policy.[39]

An officer who works in the night shift must now receive pay for attending training or testifying in court during the day. Furthermore, officers who are ordered to remain at home in anticipation of emergency actions must be compensated. Notably, however, the FLSA's overtime provisions do not apply to persons employed in a bona fide executive, administrative, or professional capacity. In criminal justice, the Act has generally been held to apply to detectives and sergeants but not to those of the rank of lieutenant and above.

A companion issue with respect to criminal justice pay and benefits is that of equal pay for equal work. Disparate treatment in pay and benefits can be litigated under Title VII or statutes such as the Equal Pay Act or the equal protection clause. An Ohio case involved matron/dispatchers who performed essentially the same job as jailers but were paid less. This was found to be in violation of the Equal Pay Act and, because discriminatory intent was found, Title VII.[40]

Other criminal justice employee benefits are addressed in Title VII, the ADEA, and the Pregnancy Discrimination Act (PDA). For example, it is illegal to provide less insurance coverage for a female employee who is more likely to use maternity leave or for an older employee who is more liable to use more coverage. In addition, an older person or a woman could not be forced to pay higher pension contributions because he or she might be paying in for a shorter period of time or would be expected to live longer. Regarding pregnancy, the PDA does not require an employer to discriminate in favor of a pregnancy-related condition. It demands only that the employer not treat pregnancy differently from any other temporary medical condition. For example, if an agency has a 6-month leave policy for officers who are injured or ill from off-duty circumstances (on-duty circumstances would probably be covered by workers' compensation), that agency would have to provide 6 months' leave (if needed) for a pregnancy-related condition.[41]

Criminal Justice and a Safe Workplace

It is unclear what duties are owed by public employers to their employees in providing a safe workplace. Federal, state, and local governments are exempted from the coverage of the Occupational Safety and Health Act (OSHA), in 29 U.S.C. 652. Nonetheless, criminal justice work is often dangerous, involving the use of force and often occurring in locations outside governmental control. Therefore, workplace safety issues in criminal justice are more likely to revolve around adequacy of training and supervision than physical plants.[42]

The Supreme Court has noted the unique nature and danger of public service employment. In one case, the Court specifically stated that an employee could not bring a Section 1983 civil rights action alleging a workplace so unsafe that it violated the Fourteenth Amendment's due process clause. In this matter, a sewer worker was asphyxiated while clearing a sewer line. His widow alleged that the city knew the sewer was dangerous and that the city had failed to train or supervise the decedent properly.[43]

Other federal courts, especially the federal circuits, however, have ruled inconsistently on the safe workplace issue. One federal circuit held that a constitutional violation could be brought if it was proven that the city actively engaged in conduct that was "deliberately indifferent" to the employee's constitutional rights.[44]

However, the Fifth Circuit held differently in a Louisiana case, based on a failure to comply with a court order to have three officers on duty at all times in a prison disciplinary unit.[45] Here, a prison correctional officer in Baton Rouge was the only guard on a dangerous cellblock. While attempting to transfer a handcuffed inmate, the guard got into a scuffle with the inmate and was injured, although not severely. However, he claimed that he received insufficient medical attention and that as a result he became permanently disabled and that the institution "consciously" and with wanton disregard for his personal safety conspired to have him work alone on the cellblock. He invoked 42 U.S.C. 1983 in his charges, claiming that the institution acted in an indifferent, malicious, and reckless manner toward him, and that he suffered "class-based discrimination." The court held that the guard had no cause of action (no federal or constitutional grounds for litigation).

Liability for an employee's injury, disability, or death is a critical concern for criminal justice agencies. In particular, police and correctional officers often work in circumstances involving violent actions. Although state workers' compensation coverage, disability

▼

pensions, life insurance, and survivor pensions are designed to cover such tragedies, such coverage is typically limited and only intended to be remedial. On the other hand, civil tort actions in such cases can have a devastating impact on governmental budgets. Clearly, this is a difficult and costly problem to resolve. It is also an area with moral dilemmas as well. For example, what should be done with a prison intelligence unit that has knowledge of an impending disturbance but fails to alert its officers (who are subsequently injured)? And might a police department with knowledge that its new police vehicles have defective brakes fail to take immediate action for fear that its officers will refuse to drive the vehicles, thus reducing available personnel?[46]

▶ Constitutional Rights of Criminal Justice Employees

Freedom of Speech and Association

Many criminal justice executives have attempted to regulate what their employees say to the public; executives develop and rely on policies and procedures designed to govern employee speech. On occasion those restrictions will be challenged; a number of court decisions have attempted to define the limits of criminal justice employees' exercise of free speech.

Although the right of freedom of speech is one of the most fundamental of all rights of Americans, the Supreme Court has indicated that "the State has interests as an employer in regulating the speech of its employees that differ significantly from those it possesses in connection with regulation of the speech of the citizenry in general."[47] Thus, the state may impose restrictions on its employees that it would not be able to impose on the citizenry at large; however, these restrictions must be reasonable.[48]

There are two basic situations in which a police regulation may be found to be an unreasonable infringement on the free speech interests of officers.[49] The first occurs when the action is overly broad. A Chicago Police Department rule prohibiting "any activity, conversation, deliberation, or discussion which is derogatory to the Department" is a good example, because such a rule obviously prohibits all criticism of the agency by its officers, even in private conversation.[50] A similar situation arose in New Orleans, where the police department had a regulation that prohibited a police officer from making statements that "unjustly criticize or ridicule, or express hatred or contempt toward, or which may be detrimental to, or cast suspicion on the reputation of, or otherwise defame, any person."[51] The regulation was revised and later ruled constitutional.[52]

The second situation in which free speech limitations may be found to be unreasonable is in the way in which the governmental action is applied. Specifically, a police department may be unable to demonstrate that the statements by an officer being disciplined actually adversely affected the operation of the department. A Baltimore regulation prohibiting public criticism of police department action was held to have been unconstitutionally applied to a police officer who was president of the police union and had stated in a television interview that the police commissioner was not leading the department effectively[53] and that "the bottom is going to fall out of this city."[54]

A related area is that of political activity. The most protected type of speech is political speech. However, governmental agencies may restrict the political behavior of their employees—and the U.S. Supreme Court has upheld the constitutionality of laws that do so.[55] Exhibit 3.1 discusses how the Hatch Act operates at the federal, state, and local levels.

EXHIBIT 3.1

NOT "POLITICS AS USUAL": THE HATCH ACTS

All federal executive branch and civil service employees (except the president and vice president) are subject to the Hatch Act, which limits partisan political activities of governmental employees. Federal employees who are "further restricted"—working in several key federal law enforcement agencies—cannot run for office in a partisan election, solicit, or encourage political activity of those doing business with their agency, or use their official authority to affect the outcome of an election. In addition, political contributions may not be received from subordinates, and covered employees may not participate in political fundraising, canvass for votes, or endorse or oppose a candidate in political literature. They may, however, vote in all partisan elections and express opinions on political topics, work in nonpartisan campaigns, attend political meetings, donate money to political parties and candidates, and sign nominating petitions.

State and local agency employees are also covered by the law, often known as "Little Hatch Acts," if they perform duties connected to programs financed totally or in part by federal funds—i.e., in programs funding homeland security, training, employment, overtime, community development, emergency preparedness. Such employees may, however, run for public office in nonpartisan elections, hold office in political organizations, and actively campaign for candidates for public office (as well as engage in drafting speeches, write letters, contribute money to political organizations, and attend political fundraisers).

The Office of Special Counsel investigates alleged Hatch Act violations by federal employees, and the state or local levels of government will investigate those of their employees.

Source: Based on Michael Bulzomi, "Casting More Than Your Vote: The Hatch Act and Political Involvement for Law Enforcement Personnel," *FBI Law Enforcement Bulletin* 77(12) (2008):16–25.

Although it may appear that Supreme Court decisions have lain to rest all controversy in this area, such has not been the case. Two recent cases show lower courts opting to limit the authority of the state to restrict political activities of their employees. In Pawtucket, Rhode Island, two firefighters ran for public office (mayor and city council member), despite a city charter provision prohibiting all political activity by employees (except voting and privately expressing their opinions). The Rhode Island Supreme Court issued an injunction against enforcing the charter provision, on the ground that the provision applied only to partisan political activities.[56] In a similar Boston case, however, the court upheld the police department rule on the basis that whether the partisan–nonpartisan distinction was crucial was a matter for legislative or administrative determination.[57]

In a Michigan case, a court declared unconstitutional, for being overly broad, two city charter provisions that prohibited contributions to or solicitations for any political purpose by city employees.[58] Clearly, although the Supreme Court seems to be supportive of governmental attempts to limit the political activities of its employees, lower courts seem just as intent to limit the Supreme Court decisions to the facts of those cases.

Could a police officer be disciplined, even discharged, because of his or her political affiliations? The Supreme Court ruled on that question in a case arising out of the Sheriff's Department in Cook County, Illinois.[59] The newly elected sheriff, a Democrat, fired the chief deputy of the process division and a bailiff of the juvenile court because they were Republicans. The Court ruled that it was a violation of the employees' First Amendment rights to discharge them from nonpolicymaking positions solely on the basis of their political party affiliation.[60]

Nonpolitical associations are also protected by the First Amendment; however, it is common for police departments to prohibit officers from associating with known felons or

> **Hatch Acts** legislation that limits partisan political activities by governmental employees.

others of questionable reputation, on the ground that "such associations may expose an officer to irresistible temptations to yield in his obligation to impartially enforce the law, and . . . may give the appearance that the police are not themselves honest and impartial enforcers of the law."[61]

However, rules against association, as with other First Amendment rights, must not be overly broad. A Detroit Police Department regulation prohibiting associating with known criminals or persons charged with crimes, except in connection with regular duties, was declared unconstitutional. The court held that it prohibited some associations that had no bearing on the officers' integrity or public confidence in the officer (e.g., an association with a fellow church member who had been arrested on one occasion years ago, or the befriending of a recently convicted person who wanted to become a productive citizen).[62]

Occasionally, a criminal justice employee will be disciplined for improper association even though it was not demonstrated that the association had a detrimental effect on the employee or the agency. For example, a Maryland court held that a fully qualified police officer who was a nudist could not be fired simply on that basis.[63] On the other hand, a court upheld the discharge of an officer who had had sexual intercourse at a party with a woman he knew to be a nude model at a local "adult theater of known disrepute."[64]

An individual has a fundamental interest in being free to enter into certain intimate or private relationships; nevertheless, freedom of association is not an absolute right. For example, a federal district court held that the dismissal of a married police officer for living with another man's wife was a violation of the officer's privacy and associational rights.[65] Other courts, however, have found that off-duty sexual activity can affect job performance. When a married city police officer allegedly had consensual, private, non-duty, heterosexual relations with single adult women other than his wife in violation of state law criminalizing adultery, the adultery was not a fundamental right. Thus, the officer's extramarital affairs were not protected and the intimate relationship affected the public's perception of the agency.[66]

In another case, a police officer became involved with a city dispatcher who was the wife of a sergeant in the same department. The adulterous officer became eligible for promotion and scored high on the exam. The chief, confirming via an investigation that the officer had in fact been involved in an adulterous relationship with the dispatcher, refused on that basis to promote the officer, as he "would not command respect and trust" from rank-and-file officers and would adversely affect the efficiency and morale of the department. The Texas Supreme Court held that the officer's private, adulterous sexual conduct was not protected by state or federal law; the U.S. Supreme Court denied the appeal.[67]

Finally, the U.S. Court of Appeals for the Sixth Circuit held that a police department could conduct an investigation into the marital sexual relations of a police officer accused of sexual harassment.[68] In this case, there were allegations that the married officer had sexually harassed coworkers and had dated a gang member's mother. The department investigated the accusations, and the officer and his wife brought a Section 1983 action, alleging that the investigation violated their constitutional rights to privacy and freedom of association. The court held that the agency's investigation was reasonable, and, furthermore, that the police department would have been derelict in not investigating the matter.

In summary, police administrators have the constitutional authority to regulate employees' off-duty associational activities, including off-duty sexual conduct that involves a supervisory/subordinate relationship and associations that impact adversely employees' ability to do their jobs or impair the effectiveness and efficiency of the organization.[69]

The First Amendment's reach also includes means of expression other than verbal utterances. The Supreme Court upheld the constitutionality of a regulation of the Suffolk County, New York, Police Department that established several grooming standards (regarding hair, sideburn, and moustache length) for its male officers. In this case, *Kelley v. Johnson*,[70] the Court believed that to make officers easily recognizable to the public and to maintain the esprit de corps within the department, the agency justified the regulations and did not violate any right guaranteed by the First Amendment.

Searches and Seizures

The Fourth Amendment to the U.S. Constitution protects "the right of the people to be secure in their persons, houses, papers, and effects, against unreasonable searches and seizures." In an important case in 1967, the Supreme Court held that the amendment also protected individuals' reasonable expectations of privacy, not just property interests.[71]

The Fourth Amendment usually applies to police officers when they are at home or off duty in the same manner as it applies to all citizens. Because of the nature of their work, however, police officers can be compelled to cooperate with investigations of their behavior when ordinary citizens would not. Examples include searches of equipment and lockers provided by the department to the officers. There, the officers have no expectation of privacy that affords or merits protection.[72] Lower courts have established limitations on searches of employees themselves. The rights of prison authorities to search their employees arose in a 1985 Iowa case in which employees were forced to sign a consent form for searches as a condition of hire; the court disagreed with such a broad policy, ruling that the consent form did not constitute a blanket waiver of all Fourth Amendment rights.[73]

Police officers may also be forced to appear in a lineup, a clear "seizure" of his or her person. Appearance in a lineup normally requires probable cause, but a federal appeals court upheld a police commissioner's ordering of 62 officers to appear in a lineup during an investigation of police brutality, holding that "the governmental interest in the particular intrusion [should be weighed] against the offense to personal dignity and integrity." Again, the court cited the nature of the work, noting that police officers do "not have the full privacy and liberty from police officials that [they] would otherwise enjoy."[74]

Self-Incrimination

The Supreme Court has also addressed questions concerning the Fifth Amendment as it applies to police officers who are under investigation. In *Garrity v. New Jersey*,[75] a police officer was ordered by the attorney general to answer questions or be discharged. The officer testified that information obtained as a result of his answers was later used to convict him of criminal charges. The Supreme Court held that the information obtained from the officer could not be used against him at his criminal trial because the Fifth Amendment forbids the use of coerced confessions.

In *Gardner v. Broderick*,[76] a police officer refused to answer questions asked by a grand jury investigating police misconduct because he believed his answers might tend to incriminate him. The officer was terminated from his position as the result. The Supreme Court ruled that the officer could not be fired for his refusal to waive his constitutional right to remain silent. The Court added, however, that the grand jury could have forced the officer to answer or be terminated for his refusal provided that the officer was informed that his answers would not be used against him later in a criminal case.

As a result of these decisions, it is proper to fire a police officer who refuses to answer questions that are related directly to the performance of his or her duties provided that the officer has been informed that any answers may not be used later in a criminal proceeding. Although there is some diversity of opinion among lower courts on the question of whether an officer may be compelled to submit to a polygraph examination, the majority of courts that have considered the question have held that an officer can be required to take the examination.[77]

Religious Practices

Criminal justice work requires that employees of police, corrections, and even some courts organizations be available and on duty 24 hours per day, 7 days a week. Although it is not always convenient or pleasant, such shift configurations require that many criminal justice employees work weekends, nights, and holidays. It is generally assumed that one who takes such a position agrees to work such hours and to abide by other such conditions (e.g., carrying a weapon, as in a policing position); it is usually the personnel with the least seniority on the job who must work the most undesirable shifts.

There are occasions when one's religious beliefs are in direct conflict with the requirements of the job. Conflicts can occur between work assignments and attendance at religious services or periods of religious observance. In these situations, the employee may be forced to choose between his or her job and religion. The author is acquainted with a midwestern state trooper whose religion posed another related cause of job–religion conflict: His religion (with which he became affiliated after being hired as a trooper) banned the carrying or use of firearms. The officer chose to give up his weapon, and thus his job. A number of people have chosen to litigate the work–religion conflict rather than accept agency demands.

Title VII of the Civil Rights Act of 1964 prohibits religious discrimination in employment. The Act defines religion as including "all aspects of religious . . . practice, as well as belief, unless an employer . . . is unable to reasonably accommodate to an employee's . . . religious . . . practice without undue hardship on the conduct of the employer's business."[78] Thus, Title VII requires reasonable accommodation of religious beliefs, but not to the extent that the employee has complete freedom of religious expression.[79] For example, an Albuquerque firefighter was a Seventh Day Adventist and refused to work Friday or Saturday nights because such shifts interrupted his honoring the Sabbath. He refused to trade shifts or take leave with (as vacation) or without pay, even though existing policy permitted his doing so. Instead, he said that the *department* should make such arrangements for coverage or simply excuse him from his shifts. The department refused to do either, discharging him. The court ruled that the department's accommodations were reasonable and that no further accommodation could be made without causing an undue hardship to the department. His firing was upheld. The court emphasized, however, that future decisions would depend on the facts of the individual case.[80]

Religious practices can also conflict with state law. For example, a circuit court held that the termination of a Mormon police officer for practicing plural marriage (polygamy) in violation of state law was not a violation of his right to freely exercise his religious beliefs.[81]

Another issue relating to religious expression concerns the display of religious items on one's uniform. In a Texas case, a police veteran wished to wear a small gold cross pin on his uniform as well as on plainclothes attire "as a symbol of his evangelical Christianity." The agency forbade officers doing so unless approved by the police chief; the chief offered the plaintiff several other accommodations, such as wearing a cross ring or bracelet instead of the pin, or wearing the pin under his uniform shirt or collar. Refusing such accommodations, the plaintiff was fired for insubordination. The Fifth Circuit Court of Appeals upheld his firing, agreeing that a police uniform "is not a forum for . . . expressing one's personal beliefs," that the constitution is not violated when a department bars religious symbols, and that the plaintiff had "myriad alternative ways to manifest this tenet of his religion."[82]

Finally, policies prohibiting the wearing of beards have also been challenged on First Amendment grounds. Two devout Sunni Muslim police officers challenged the Newark, New Jersey, Police Department's banning of beards, arguing that in their religion the lack of a beard is a "major sin"; they also noted that the department had made several medical exemptions to the policy (some officers were allowed to grow beards because of a skin condition called *folliculitis barbae*, which affects up to 60% of African American men; this condition is exacerbated by shaving). The Third Circuit Court of Appeals accepted the plaintiff's arguments and struck down the no-beards provision as it applied to the Muslim officers. The court determined that because the department granted exemptions for nonreligious reasons, closer scrutiny was warranted; the court concluded that the policy simply could not stand up under that scrutiny.[83]

Sexual Misconduct

To be blunt, criminal justice employees have ample opportunity to become engaged in sexual affairs, incidents, trysts, dalliances, or other behavior that is clearly sexual in nature. History and news accounts have shown that wearing a uniform, occupying a high or extremely sensitive position, or being sworn to maintain an unblemished and unsullied lifestyle does not mean that all people will do so for all time. Some people are not bashful about their intentions: Several officers have told me they aspired to police work because they assumed that wearing a uniform made them sexually irresistible. On the civilian side, there are police "groupies" who chase police officers and others in uniform.

Instances of sexual impropriety in criminal justice work can range from casual flirting while on the job to becoming romantically involved with a foreign agent whose principal aim is to learn delicate matters of national security. There have been all manner of incidents between those extremes, including the discipline of female police officers who posed nude in magazines. Some major police departments have even been compelled by their mayors to recruit officers for their sexual preference (i.e., homosexuality).

This is a delicate area, one in which discipline can be and has been meted out as police managers attempt to maintain high standards of officer conduct. It has also resulted in litigation because some officers believe that their right to privacy has been intruded on.

Officers may be disciplined for impropriety involving adultery and homosexuality. Most court decisions of the 1960s and 1970s agreed that adultery, even when involving an off-duty police officer and occurring in private, could result in disciplinary action[84] because such behavior brought debilitating criticism on the agency and undermined public confidence in the police. The views of the courts in this area, however, seem to be moderating with the times. A case involving an Internal Revenue Service agent suggested that to uphold disciplinary action for adultery, the government would have to prove that the employing agency was actually discredited.[85] The U.S. Supreme Court more recently appeared to be divided on the issue of extramarital sexual activity in public employment. In 1984, the Sixth Circuit held that a Michigan police officer could not be fired simply because he was living with a woman to whom he was not married (a felony under Michigan law).[86]

The issue of homosexual activity as a ground for termination of public employees arose in an Oklahoma case in which a state law permitted the discharge of schoolteachers for engaging in "public homosexual activity."[87] A lower court held the law to be unconstitutionally restrictive, and the Supreme Court agreed.[88] Another federal court held that the firing of a bisexual guidance counselor did not deprive the counselor of her First or Fourteenth Amendment rights. The counselor's discussion of her sexual preferences with teachers was not protected by the First Amendment.[89]

Residency Requirements

In the 1970s and 1980s, interest in residency requirements for governmental employees heightened, especially in communities experiencing economic difficulties.[90] Many governmental agencies now specify that all or certain members in their employ must live within the geographical limits of their employing jurisdiction. In other words, employees must reside within the county or city of employment. Such residency requirements have often been justified by employing agencies, particularly in criminal justice, on the grounds that employees should become familiar with and be visible in the jurisdiction of employment and that they should reside where they are paid by the taxpayers to work. Perhaps the strongest rationale given by employing agencies is that criminal justice employees must live within a certain proximity of their work in order to respond quickly in the event of an emergency.

Prior to 1976, numerous challenges to residency requirements were raised, even after the Michigan Supreme Court ruled that Detroit's residency requirement for police officers was not irrational (see Exhibit 3.2).[91] In 1976, when the U.S. Supreme Court held that Philadelphia's law requiring firefighters to live in the city did not violate the Constitution, the challenges subsided. The cases now seem to revolve around the question of what constitutes residency. Generally, the police officer must demonstrate that he or she spends a substantial amount of time at the in-city residence.[92] Strong arguments have been made, however, that in areas where housing is unavailable or is exceptionally expensive, a residency requirement is unreasonable.[93]

EXHIBIT 3.2

RESIDENCY RULE IS A YAWNER: NEW ORLEANS RESIDENTS DON'T SEEM TO CARE WHERE COPS LIVE

Opponents of a New Orleans residency rule that has been on the books since the 1950s, but largely ignored until now, contend they have proof that a majority of residents do not care if their police officers live outside the city limits.

This month the New Orleans Police Foundation released a study which showed that nearly three-quarters of residents oppose the requirement. The poll of 400 city residents was conducted in September by a political analyst and assistant sociology professor at Xavier University, Silas Lee. His findings showed 73 percent agreeing that "it's OK for police officers to live in other parishes," and 55 percent who somewhat or strongly disagreed with the residency rule.

"I think the study tells us that the people of New Orleans want their city safe and they're willing to have police officers live anywhere as long as they can help achieve that goal," said Bob Stellingworth, the foundation's president. "That's their primary concern, making the city safe to live in," he told the publication New Orleans City Business.

Until 1995, when then-Mayor Marc Morial led the charge to enforce a new and more stringent residency requirement passed by the City Council, New Orleans' domicile rule was not at the top of anyone's agenda, according to local press reports. It requires anyone seeking to work for the municipal government to live within city limits. While a grandfather clause covers those who lived outside of New Orleans at the time it was enacted, they must move to the city if they want to be promoted....

Opponents of the residency rule claim that it has made recruitment difficult. The police force is currently 1,600 officers strong, but officials would like to see that figure rise to 2,000. Just 6 percent of the 52 recruits as of August 25, 2004, qualified for employment on the basis of residency. In 2003, that figure was 8 percent, and in 2002, it was 13 percent . . .

Some black supporters, however, believe that the rule will curtail incidents of profiling, harassment and police brutality...

According to the findings of the police foundation's poll, 55 percent said they disagreed with the domicile policy, 41 percent said they agreed. A slim majority of 52 percent of blacks agreed with it, but just 1 in 4 white people did so...

Source: Excerpt from Residency Rule Is a Yawner: New Orleans Residents Don't Seem to Care Where Cops Live from Law Enforcement News, Vol XXX, no. 626. Copyright © 2004 by John Jay College of Criminal Justice. Used by permission of John Jay College of Criminal Justice.

Moonlighting

The courts have traditionally supported criminal justice agencies placing limitations on the amount and kind of outside work their employees can perform.[94] For example, police department restrictions on moonlighting range from a complete ban on outside employment to permission to engage in certain forms of work, such as investment counseling, private security, teaching police science courses, and so on. The rationale for agency limitations is that "outside employment seriously interferes with keeping the [police and fire] departments fit and ready for action at all times."[95]

In a Louisiana case, however, firefighters successfully provided evidence that moonlighting had been a common practice for 16 years before the city banned it. No firefighters had ever needed sick leave as a result of injuries acquired while moonlighting, there had never been a problem locating off-duty firefighters to respond to an emergency, and moonlighting had never caused a level of fatigue that was serious enough to impair a firefighter's work. With this evidence, the court invalidated the city ordinance that had sought to prohibit moonlighting.[96]

Misuse of Firearms

Because of the need to defend themselves or others and be prepared for any exigency, police officers are empowered to use lethal force when justified. Although restricted by the Supreme Court's 1985 decision in *Tennessee v. Garner*[97] (deeming the killing of unarmed, nondangerous suspects as unconstitutional), the possession of, and familiarity with, firearms remains a central aspect of the contemporary officer's role and function. Some officers take this responsibility to the extreme, however, becoming overly reliant on and consumed with their firepower.

Thus, police agencies typically attempt to restrain the use of firearms through written policies and frequent training in "Shoot/Don't Shoot" scenarios. Still, a broad range of potential and actual problems remains with respect to the use and possible misuse of firearms, as the following shows.

In the face of extremely serious potential and real problems and the omnipresent specter of liability suits, police agencies generally have policies regulating the use of handguns and other firearms by their officers, both on and off duty. The courts have held that such regulations need only be reasonable and that the burden rests with the disciplined police officer to show that the regulation was arbitrary and unreasonable.[98] The courts also grant considerable latitude to administrators in determining when their firearms regulations have been violated.[99] Police firearms regulations tend to address three basic issues: (1) requirements for the safeguarding of the weapon, (2) guidelines for carrying the weapon while off duty, and (3) limitations on when the weapon may be fired.[100]

Courts and juries are becoming increasingly harsher in dealing with police officers who misuse their firearms. The current tendency is to "look behind" police shootings to determine whether the officer acted negligently or the employing agency inadequately trained and supervised the officer/employee. In one case, a federal appeals court approved a $500,000 judgment against the District of Columbia when a police officer who was not in adequate physical shape shot a man in the course of an arrest. The court noted that the District officer had received no fitness training in 4 years and was physically incapable of subduing the victim. The court also noted that had the officer been physically fit and adequately trained in disarmament techniques, a gun would not have been necessary. In his condition, however, the officer posed a "foreseeable risk of harm to others."[101]

Courts have awarded damages against police officers and/or their employers for other acts involving misuse of firearms: An officer shot a person while intoxicated and off duty in a bar,[102] an officer accidentally killed an arrestee with a shotgun while handcuffing him,[103] an unstable officer shot his wife five times and then committed suicide with an off-duty weapon the department required him to carry,[104] and an officer accidentally shot and killed an innocent bystander while pursuing another man at night (the officer had had no instruction on shooting at a moving target, night shooting, or shooting in residential areas).[105]

Alcohol and Drugs in the Workplace

Alcoholism and drug abuse problems have taken on a life of their own in contemporary criminal justice; employees must be increasingly wary of the tendency to succumb to these problems, and administrative personnel must be able to recognize and attempt to counsel and treat these problems.

Indeed, in the aftermath of the early 1990s beating death of Malice Green by a group of Detroit police officers, it was reported that the Detroit Police Department had "high alcoholism rates and pervasive psychological problems connected with the stress of policing a city mired in poverty, drugs, and crime."[106] It was further revealed that although the Detroit Police Department had paid $850,000 to two drug-testing facilities, the department did not have the counseling programs many other cities offer their officers. A psychologist asserted, "There are many, many potential time bombs in that department."[107]

It is obvious, given the extant law of most jurisdictions and the nature of their work, that criminal justice employees must be able to perform their work with a clear head, unaffected by alcohol or drugs.[108] Police departments and prisons will often specify in their manual of policy and procedures that no alcoholic beverages be consumed within a specified period prior to reporting for duty.

Such regulations have been upheld uniformly because of the hazards of the work. A Louisiana court went further, upholding a regulation that prohibited police officers from consuming alcoholic beverages on or off duty to the extent that it caused the officer's behavior to become obnoxious, disruptive, or disorderly.[109] Enforcing such regulations will occasionally result in criminal justice employees being ordered to submit to drug or alcohol tests, discussed next.

Drug Testing

The courts have had several occasions to review criminal justice agency policies requiring employees to submit to urinalysis to determine the presence of drugs or alcohol. It was held as early as 1969 that a firefighter could be ordered to submit to a blood test when the agency had reasonable grounds to believe he was intoxicated, and that it was appropriate for the firefighter to be terminated from employment if he refused to submit to the test.[110]

In March 1989, the U.S. Supreme Court issued two major decisions on drug testing of public employees in the workplace. *Skinner v. Railway Labor Executives Association*[111] and *National Treasury Employees Union v. Von Raab*[112] dealt with drug-testing plans for railroad and U.S. Customs workers, respectively. Under the Fourth Amendment, governmental workers are protected from unreasonable search and seizure, including how drug testing can be conducted. The Fifth Amendment protects federal, state, and local workers from illegal governmental conduct.

In 1983, the Federal Railway Administration promulgated regulations that required railroads to conduct urine and blood tests on their workers following major train accidents. The regulations were challenged, one side arguing that because railroads were privately owned, governmental action, including applying the Fourth Amendment, could not legally be imposed. The Supreme Court disagreed in *Skinner,* ruling that railroads must be viewed as an instrument or agent of the government.

Three of the most controversial drug-testing issues have been whether testing should be permitted when there is no indication of a drug problem in the workplace, whether the testing methods are reliable, and whether a positive test proves on-the-job impairment.[113]

The *Von Raab* case addressed all three issues. The U.S. Customs Service implemented a drug-screening program that required urinalysis for employees desiring transfer or promotion to positions that were directly involved in drug interdiction, where carrying a firearm was necessary, or where classified material was handled. Only 5 of 3,600 employees tested positive. The Treasury Employees Union argued that such an insignificant number of positives created a "suspicionless search" argument; in other words, drug testing was unnecessary and unwarranted. The Supreme Court disagreed, ruling that although only a few employees tested positive, drug use is such a serious problem that the program could continue.

Furthermore, the Court found nothing wrong with the testing protocol. An independent contractor was used. The worker, after discarding outer garments, produced a urine specimen while being observed by a member of the same sex; the sample was signed by the employee, labeled, placed in a plastic bag, sealed and delivered to a lab for testing. The Court found no "grave potential for arbitrary and oppressive interference with the privacy and personal security of the individuals" in this method.

Proving the connection between drug testing and on-the-job impairment has been an ongoing issue. Urinalysis cannot prove when a person testing positive actually used the drug. Therefore, tests may punish and stigmatize a person for extracurricular drug use that may have no effect on the worker's on-the-job performance.[114] In *Von Raab,* the Court indicated that this dilemma is still no impediment to testing. It stated that the Customs Service had a compelling interest in having a "physically fit" employee with "unimpeachable integrity and judgment."

Together, these two cases may set a new standard for determining the reasonableness of drug testing in the criminal justice workplace. They may legalize many testing programs that formerly would have been risky. *Von Raab* presented three compelling governmental interests that could be weighed against the employee's privacy expectations: the integrity of the work force, public safety, and protection of sensitive information. *Skinner* stated that railroad workers also have diminished expectations of privacy because they are in an industry that is widely regulated to ensure safety.[115]

▶ Rights of Police Officers

Delineated earlier were several areas (e.g., place of residence, religious practice, freedom of speech, search, and seizure) in which criminal justice employees, particularly the police, may encounter treatment by their administrators and the federal courts that is quite different from that received by other citizens. One does give up certain constitutional rights and privileges by virtue of wearing a justice system uniform. This section looks at how, for the police at least, the pendulum has swung more in the direction of the rank and file.

In the last decade, police officers have insisted on greater procedural safeguards to protect themselves against what they perceive as arbitrary infringement on their rights. These demands have been reflected in statutes enacted in many states, generally known as the **Peace Officers' Bill of Rights (POBR)**. This legislation mandates due process rights for peace officers who are the subject of internal investigations that could lead to disciplinary action. These statutes identify the type of information that must be provided to the accused officer, the officer's responsibility to cooperate during the investigation, the officer's right to representation during the process, and the rules and procedures concerning the collection of certain types of evidence. Following are some common provisions of state POBR legislation:

Peace Officers Bill of Rights (POBR) legislation mandating due process rights for peace officers who are the subject of internal investigations that could lead to disciplinary action.

Written notice: The department must provide the officer with written notice of the nature of the investigation, summary of alleged misconduct, and name of the investigating officer.

Right to representation: The officer may have an attorney or a representative of his or her choosing present during any phase of questioning or hearing.

Polygraph examination: The officer may refuse to take a polygraph examination unless the complainant submits to an examination and is determined to be telling the truth. In this case, the officer may be ordered to take a polygraph examination or be subject to disciplinary action.

Officers expect to be treated fairly, honestly, and respectfully during the course of an internal investigation. In turn, the public expects that the agency will develop sound disciplinary policies and conduct thorough inquiries into allegations of misconduct.

It is imperative that administrators become thoroughly familiar with statutes, contract provisions, and existing rules between employer and employee so that procedural due process requirements can be met, particularly in disciplinary cases in which an employee's property interest might be affected.

Police officers today are also more likely to file a grievance when they believe their rights have been violated. Grievances may cover a broad range of issues, including salaries, overtime, leave, hours of work, allowances, retirement, opportunity for advancement, performance evaluations, workplace conditions, tenure, disciplinary actions, supervisory methods, and administrative practices. The preferred method for settling officers' grievances is through informal discussion: The employee explains his or her grievance to the immediate supervisor. Most complaints can be handled in this way. Those complaints that cannot be dealt with informally are usually handled through a more formal grievance process, which may involve several different levels of action.

▶ Workplace Harassment

Although sexual harassment has been a major concern in the nation for several decades—and is even outlawed in the Code of Federal Regulations (see, 29 C.F.R. 1604.11[a])—the more contemporary approach is for agencies to have a broader policy that applies to all forms of **workplace harassment**. All such harassment is a form of discrimination that violates Title VII of the Civil Rights Act of 1964 and other federal laws.

Unwelcome verbal or physical conduct based on race, color, religion, sex (whether or not of a sexual nature), national origin, age (40 years and older), disability (mental or physical), sexual orientation, or retaliation constitutes harassment when:

1. The conduct is sufficiently severe to create a hostile work environment, or
2. A supervisor's harassing conduct results in a change in an employment status or benefits (such as demotion, termination, failure to promote, and so on).[116]

Hostile work environment occurs when unwelcome comments or conduct based on sex, race, or other legally protected characteristics unreasonably interferes with an employee's work performance or creates an offensive work environment. Examples of such actions can include:

- Leering in a sexually suggestive manner
- Making offensive remarks about looks, clothing, body parts
- Touching in a way that makes an employee uncomfortable, such as patting, pinching, brushing against another's body
- Sending or telling suggestive letters or notes, or telling sexual or lewd jokes
- Using racially derogatory words, phrases, epithets

workplace harassment unwelcome verbal or physical conduct (whether or not of a sexual nature) that creates a hostile work environment, or a change in an employment status or benefits.

A claim of harassment generally requires that the complaining party be a member of a statutorily protected class and was subjected to unwelcome verbal or physical conduct, that the unwelcome conduct complaint is based on his or her membership in that protected class, and that the unwelcome conduct affected a term or condition of employment and unreasonably interfered with his or her work performance. Any employee wishing to initiate an Equal Employment Complaint (EEO) arising out of the prohibited conduct described earlier must contact an EEO official within 45 days of the incident.

Still, however, sexually related improprieties can and do occur; police supervisors and managers must be vigilant of such inappropriate behaviors, seven types of which have been identified[117]:

1. *Nonsexual contacts that are sexually motivated.* An officer will stop another citizen without legal justification to obtain information or get a closer look at the citizen.

2. *Voyeuristic contacts.* Police officers attempt to observe partially clad or nude citizens. They observe apartment buildings or college dormitories. In other cases, they roust citizens parked on lovers' lanes.

3. *Contacts with crime victims.* Crime victims generally are emotionally distraught or upset and particularly vulnerable to sexual overtures from officers. In these instances, officers may make several return visits and calls with the intention of seducing the victim.

4. *Contacts with offenders.* In these cases, officers may conduct body searches, frisks, and patdown searches. In some cases, officers may demand sexual favors. Offenders' complaints of sexual harassment will not be investigated by a department without corroborating evidence, which seldom exists.

5. *Contacts with juvenile offenders.* In some cases, officers have exhibited some of the same behaviors with juveniles that they have with adults, such as patdowns, frisks, and sexual favors. There have also been cases in which officers assigned as juvenile or school liaison officers have taken advantage of their assignment to seduce juveniles.

6. *Sexual shakedowns.* Police officers demand sexual services from prostitutes, homosexuals, and others engaged in criminal activity as a form of protection.

7. *Citizen-Initiated sexual contacts.* Some citizens are attracted to police officers and attempt to seduce them. They may be attracted to the uniform, authority, or the prospect of a "safe" sexual encounter. In other cases, the citizen may be lonely or may want a "break" when caught violating the law.

▶ Family and Medical Leave Act

Eligibility Requirements

The **Family and Medical Leave Act (FMLA)**, enacted by Public Law 103-3, became effective in August 1993 and is administered and enforced by the U.S. Department of Labor's Wage and Hour Division. FMLA applies to all public agencies, including state, local, and federal employers; local schools; and private sector employers with 50 or more employees in 20 or more workweeks and who are engaged in commerce. FMLA entitles eligible employees to take up to 12 weeks of unpaid, job-protected leave in a 12-month period for specified family and medical reasons.

To be eligible for FMLA benefits, an employee must:

- work for a covered employer
- have worked for a covered employer for at least 12 months (and have worked at least 1,250 hours during that time)

> **Family and Medical Leave Act (FMLA)**
> legislation that entitles eligible employees to take unpaid, job-protected leave for specified family and medical reasons.

A covered employer must grant an eligible employee unpaid leave for one or more of the following reasons:

- For the birth and care of a newborn child of the employee
- For placement with the employee of a child for adoption or child care
- To care for an immediate family member with a serious health condition
- To take medical leave when the employee is unable to work because of a serious health condition

A serious health condition means an illness, injury, impairment, or physical or mental condition that involves either any period of incapacitation or treatment, or continuing treatment by a health care provider; this can include any period of inability to work, attend school, or perform regular daily activities.

Recent Amendments

The 2009 and 2010 amendments to the FMLA[118] addressed hardships being placed on military families. Two new categories of leave were created in the amendments—qualifying exigency leave and military caregiver leave—which are designed to ease the strains.

Qualifying exigency leave is designed to allow family members of deployed regular Armed Forces personnel to take time away from work to provide for the exigencies that arise out of a military deployment (the 2008 NDAA only allowed exigency leave to members of the National Guard or Reserves). Such leave is triggered only when the deployed military member is the employee's spouse, son, daughter, or parent. Military caregiver leave is triggered when a family member must help a wounded soldier on his return home; it also imposes new obligations on employers. An eligible employee—including a spouse, son, daughter, parent, or next-of-kin of a covered service member—is entitled to this type of leave in order to care for a member of the Armed Forces as well as National Guard or Reserves who has a serious injury or illness that was incurred in the line of duty on active duty and requires ongoing medical treatment, recuperation, or therapy.[119]

Also, in June 2010, President Obama expanded the rights of gay workers by allowing them to take family and medical leave to care for sick or newborn children of same-sex partners. The policy was set forth in a ruling issued by the Department of Labor. The new ruling indicates that an employee in a same-sex relationship can qualify for leave to care for the child of his or her partner, even if the worker has not legally adopted the child.[120]

▶ The Americans with Disabilities Act (ADA)

Americans with Disabilities Act legislation making it illegal to discriminate against persons with disabilities in their recruitment, hiring, and promotion practices.

The **Americans with Disabilities Act (ADA)** was signed into law in 1990. Although certain agencies in the federal government, such as the Federal Bureau of Investigation, are exempt from the ADA, state and local governments and their agencies are covered by the law. It is critical for administrators to develop written policies and procedures consistent with the ADA and have them in place before a problem arises.[121]

Under the law, criminal justice agencies may not discriminate against qualified individuals with disabilities. A person has a disability under the law if he or she has a mental or physical impairment that substantially limits a major life activity, such as walking, talking, breathing, sitting, standing, or learning.[122] Title I of the ADA makes it illegal to discriminate against persons with disabilities. This mandate applies to the agency's recruitment, hiring, and promotion practices. ADA is not an affirmative action law, so persons with disabilities are not entitled to preference in hiring.

Employers are to provide reasonable accommodation to disabled persons. A reasonable accommodation can include modifying existing facilities to make them accessible, job restructuring, part-time or modified work schedules, acquiring or modifying equipment, and changing policies.[123] Hiring decisions must be based on whether an applicant meets the established prerequisites of the position (e.g., experience or education) and is able to perform the essential functions of the job. Under the law, blanket exclusions of individuals with a particular disability (such as diabetes) are, in most cases, impermissible.

Corrections agencies—jails, prisons, and detention facilities—are also covered by the ADA; programs offered to inmates must be accessible. For example, if a hearing-impaired inmate wished to attend Alcoholics Anonymous meetings, the corrections facility would need to make reasonable accommodation to allow him or her to do so, through such means as providing a sign language interpreter or writing notes as needed.[124]

Summary

After providing an overview of related legislation, this chapter examined several areas of criminal justice employee rights, including the issues of drug testing, privacy, hiring and firing, sexual harassment, disabilities, and peace officers' rights. Criminal justice employers' responsibilities were also discussed.

Being an administrator in the field of criminal justice has never been easy. Unfortunately, the issues facing today's justice administrators have probably never been more difficult or complex.

This chapter clearly demonstrated that these are challenging and, occasionally, litigious times for the justice system; one act of negligence can mean financial disaster for an individual or a supervisor.

Key Terms and Concepts

Americans with Disabilities Act (ADA) *70*

Affirmative action *53*

Bona fide occupational qualifier (BFOQ) *52*

Disparate treatment *52*

Fair Labor Standards Act (FLSA) *56*

Family and Medical Leave Act (FMLA) *69*

Hatch Acts *59*

Peace Officers' Bill of Rights (POBR) *67*

Reverse discrimination *54*

Workplace harassment *68*

Questions for Review

1. What are criminal justice employees' rights in the workplace according to federal statutes?
2. What is the general employee–employer relationship in criminal justice regarding recruitment and hiring and affirmative action?
3. It has been stated that criminal justice employees have a "property interest" in their jobs as well as a right to a safe workplace. What does this mean?
4. What constitutional rights are implicated for criminal justice employees on the job? (In your response, address whether rights are held regarding freedom of speech, searches and seizures, self-incrimination, and religion.)
5. In what regard is a greater standard of conduct expected of criminal justice employees? (In your response, include discussions of sexual behavior, residency, moonlighting, use of firearms, and alcohol/drug abuse.)
6. What kinds of behaviors can lead to charges of workplace harassment in a criminal justice agency?
7. What are the protections afforded criminal justice employees under the Family and Medical Leave Act (including its amendments) and the Americans with Disabilities Act.

Deliberate and Decide 1

When to Dole out Discipline

Officer Seymour is a 9-year veteran of your police agency, experienced in both the patrol and detective divisions. He takes pride in being "old school," but his hard-nosed style alienates a lot of officers. At times he responds to calls for service without requesting cover units or backup, has had several complaints of brutality lodged during the last 3 years, and is borderline insubordinate when dealing with supervisors, leading to some of past and present supervisors even commenting that he is a "walking time bomb" who is unpredictable.

One day while on patrol, Seymour responds to a shooting in a home just outside of his city's jurisdiction, where county sheriff, fire, and medical personnel are working on a man with a head wound who is lying on the floor. He informs the dispatcher that he is out "assisting." Nearby on a wall divider is a large, unique, foreign-made handgun; awed by it, he picks it up and examines it. A fire department captain yells at him, "Hey! Put that down, this might become a homicide case!" so he places the revolver back on the shelf. Later, the fire captain informs you, Seymour's supervisor, of his actions, and so you require that he write a report of his actions. He denies both verbally and in writing that he touched or picked up the handgun. Looking at his personnel file, you find his performance evaluations for the past 9 years have been "standard" or above—average to above average; he has never been suspended from duty. Although verbally expressing concerns and general unhappiness with his work and attitude, his former supervisors never expressed such in writing.

Questions for Discussion

1. What are the primary issues in this situation?
2. Do sufficient grounds exist for bringing disciplinary action against Seymour? If so, what would be the specific charges, and the type/level of punishment?
3. Do grounds exist for termination even though his past supervisors have rated him as standard for 9 years?

Deliberate and Decide 2

At the Heart of the Matter

A police sergeant suffers a heart attack and undergoes a triple bypass operation. Now 4 years later, he takes and passes the written and oral examinations for lieutenant but is denied promotion solely because of his heart attack. The agency claims that because lieutenants can be assigned as shift commanders, they must be able to apprehend suspects and engage in high-speed pursuits. In truth, middle managers in the agency are rarely involved in situations requiring high levels of physical stress. The officer has exercised regularly and has had a strong performance record prior to and after his heart attack. Medical opinion is that his health is normal for someone of his age. The agency has adopted community policing, providing the opportunity for a manager to be assigned to one of several lieutenant positions that do not entail physical exertion. The sergeant sues the agency for violating provisions of the ADA.

Questions for Discussion

1. Is the sergeant "handicapped" within the meaning of the law?
2. Is the sergeant otherwise qualified for the position of lieutenant?
3. Was the sergeant excluded from the position solely on the basis of a handicap? Explain your answer.
4. Should the sergeant prevail in the suit? If so, on what grounds?[125] (the outcome of this matter is provided in the Notes section)

Learn by Doing

1. As an administrator in your probation and parole office, you have long been supportive of your subordinates and appreciate their hard work. Lately, however, the effects of budget cutbacks have taken a serious toll on your organization, with no new hiring occurring and positions being frozen when someone retires or resigns. Your officers have sent you a letter stating that they are very upset with the work environment now that there are too fewer employees, resulting in their having to be on-call for prolonged amounts of time, caseloads being extremely high, their paperwork being excessive, and their home visits with clients now seemingly much more dangerous—particularly when someone's probation or parole is revoked and he or she must be arrested and taken to jail. Clearly they perceive that the workplace is unsafe and their morale is low. How will you attempt to address their concerns?

2. You are a mid-manager in a campus police organization. During the fall semester, you and your personnel

are quite challenged with special events—students returning to campus, football games, concerts, and other activities—that require officers to work a lot of overtime. A sergeant comes to you with a problem: Two of his day-shift officers are refusing to work overtime for evening and weekend events. Their reason is that they are very busy (and making a lot of extra money) moonlighting, one for a private security firm and the other installing fencing for a home developer. This is causing a major problem in terms of filling required overtime needs at special events on campus. How will you address this problem?

Notes

1. Robert H. Chaires and Susan A. Lentz, "Criminal Justice Employee Rights: An Overview," *American Journal of Criminal Justice* 13 (April 1995):259.
2. Ibid.
3. *United Autoworkers v. Johnson Controls,* 111 S.Ct. 1196 (1991).
4. Kenneth J. Peak, *Policing America: Challenges and Best Practices,* 7th ed. (Upper Saddle River, NJ: Prentice Hall, 2012), Chapter 4, generally.
5. Chaires and Lentz, "Criminal Justice Employee Rights," p. 260.
6. *U.S. v. Gregory,* 818 F.2d 114 (4th Cir. 1987).
7. *Harris v. Pan American,* 649 F.2d 670 (9th Cir. 1988).
8. Chaires and Lentz, "Criminal Justice Employee Rights," p. 267.
9. Ken Peak, Douglas W. Farenholtz, and George Coxey, "Physical Abilities Testing for Police Officers: A Flexible, Job-Related Approach," *The Police Chief* 59 (January 1992):52–56.
10. *Shaw v. Nebraska Department of Corrections,* 666 F.Supp. 1330 (ND Feb. 1987).
11. *Garrett v. Oskaloosa County,* 734 F.2d 621 (11th Cir. 1984).
12. Chaires and Lentz, "Criminal Justice Employee Rights," p. 268.
13. *EEOC v. State Department of Highway Safety,* 660 F.Supp. 1104 (ND Fla.: 1986).
14. *Johnson v. Mayor and City Council of Baltimore* (105 S.Ct. 2717, 1985).
15. 460 U.S. 226, 103 S.Ct. 1054, 75 L.Ed.2d 18 (1983).
16. Chaires and Lentz, "Criminal Justice Employee Rights," p. 269.
17. Paul J. Spiegelman, "Court-Ordered Hiring Quotas after *Stotts*: A Narrative on the Role of the Moralities of the Web and the Ladder in Employment Discrimination Doctrine," *Harvard Civil Rights–Civil Liberties Law Review* 20 (1985):72.
18. Chaires and Lentz, "Criminal Justice Employee Rights," p. 269.
19. *Regents of the University of California v. Bakke,* 98 S.Ct. 2733, 438 U.S. 265, 57 L.Ed.2d (1978).
20. *Wygant v. Jackson Board of Education,* 106 S.Ct. 1842 (1986).
21. Chaires and Lentz, "Criminal Justice Employee Rights," p. 269.
22. *Ledoux v. District of Columbia,* 820 F.2d 1293 (D.C. Cir. 1987), at 1294.
23. Ibid.
24. Chaires and Lentz, "Criminal Justice Employee Rights," p. 270.
25. *Parratt v. Taylor,* 451 U.S. 527, 536–537, 101 S.Ct. 1908, 1913–1914, 68 L.Ed.2d 420 (1981).
26. *Board of Regents v. Roth,* 408 U.S. at 577, 92 S.Ct. at 2709.
27. *Cleveland Board of Education v. Loudermill,* 470 U.S. 532, 541 (1985).
28. *McGraw v. City of Huntington Beach,* 882 F.2d 384 (9th Cir. 1989).
29. *Lohorn v. Michael,* 913 F.2d 327 (7th Cir. 1990).
30. *Palmer v. City of Monticello,* 731 F.Supp. 1503 (D. Utah, 1990).
31. *Young v. Municipality of Bethel Park,* 646 F.Supp. 539 (WD Pa.: 1986).
32. *McAdoo v. Lane,* 564 F.Supp. 1215 (ND Ill., 1983).
33. Ibid., at 1217.
34. Chaires and Lentz, "Criminal Justice Employee Rights," p. 273.
35. Lynn Lund, "The' Ten Commandments' of Risk Management for Jail Administrators," *Detention Reporter* 4 (June 1991):4.
36. *National League of Cities v. Usery,* 426 U.S. 833 (1976).
37. 105 S.Ct. 1005 (1985).
38. Charles R. Swanson, Leonard Territo, and Robert W. Taylor, *Police Administration: Structures, Processes, and Behavior,* 6th ed. (Upper Saddle River, NJ: Prentice Hall, 2005), p. 599
39. *Christiansen v. Harris County,* 529 U.S. 576, 120 S. Ct. 1655, 146 L.Ed.2d 621 (2000).
40. *Jurich v. Mahoning County,* 31 Fair Emp. Prac. 1275 (BNA) (ND Ohio,1983).
41. Chaires and Lentz, "Criminal Justice Employee Rights," p. 280.
42. Ibid.
43. *Collins v. City of Harker Heights,* 112 S.Ct. 1061 (1992).
44. *Ruge v. City of Bellevue,* 892 F.2d 738 (1989).
45. *Galloway v. State of Louisiana,* 817 F.2d 1154 (5th Cir. 1987).
46. Chaires and Lentz, "Criminal Justice Employee Rights," pp. 280–283.
47. *Pickering v. Board of Education,* 391 U.S. 563 (1968), p. 568.
48. *Keyishian v. Board of Regents,* 385 U.S. 589 (1967).

49. Swanson, Territo, and Taylor, *Police Administration,* p. 394.
50. *Muller v. Conlisk,* 429 F.2d 901 (7th Cir. 1970).
51. *Flynn v. Giarusso,* 321 F.Supp. 1295 (ED La.: 1971), at p. 1299.
52. *Magri v. Giarusso,* 379 F.Supp. 353 (ED La.: 1974).
53. Swanson, Territo, and Taylor, *Police Administration,* p. 395.
54. *Brukiewa v. Police Commissioner of Baltimore,* 263 A.2d 210 (MD: 1970).
55. See Hatch Reform Act Amendments of 1993, Pub. L. No. 103-94, 107 Stat. 1001 (1993) (codified at 5 U.S.C. Secs. 1501-1503); also see *United Public Workers v. Mitchell,* 330 U.S. 75 (1947).
56. *Magill v. Lynch,* 400 F.Supp. 84 (R.I. 1975).
57. *Boston Police Patrolmen's Association, Inc. v. City of Boston,* 326 N.E.2d 314 (MA: 1975).
58. *Phillips v. City of Flint,* 225 N.W.2d 780 (MI: 1975).
59. *Elrod v. Burns,* 427 U.S. 347 (1976); see also *Ramey v. Harber,* 431 F.Supp 657 (WD Va., 1977) and *Branti v. Finkel,* 445 U.S. 507 (1980).
60. *Connick v. Myers,* 461 U.S. 138 (1983); *Jones v. Dodson,* 727 F.2d 1329 (4th Cir. 1984).
61. Swanson, Territo, and Taylor, *Police Administration,* p. 397.
62. *Sponick v. City of Detroit Police Department,* 211 N.W.2d 674 (MI: 1973), p. 681; but see *Wilson v. Taylor,* 733 F.2d 1539 (11th Cir. 1984).
63. *Bruns v. Pomerleau,* 319 F.Supp. 58 (D. Md. 1970); see also *McMullen v. Carson,* 754 F.2d 936 (11th Cir. 1985), where it was held that a Ku Klux Klansman could not be fired from his position as a records clerk in the sheriff's department simply because he was a Klansman. The court did uphold the dismissal because his active KKK participation threatened to negatively affect the agency's ability to perform its public duties.
64. *Civil Service Commission of Tucson v. Livingston,* 525 P.2d 949 (Ariz. 1974).
65. *Briggs v. North Muskegon Police Department,* 563 F.Supp. 585 (WD Mich., 1983), affd. 746 F.2d 1475 (6th Cir. 1984).
66. *Oliverson v. West Valley City,* 875 F.Supp. 1465 (D. Utah, 1995).
67. *Henery v. City of Sherman,* 116 S.Ct. 1098 (1997).
68. *Hughes v. City of North Olmsted,* 93 F.3d 238 (6th Cir., 1996).
69. Michael J. Bulzomi, "Constitutional Authority to Regulate Off-Duty Relationships: Recent Court Decisions," *FBI Law Enforcement Bulletin* (April 1999):26–32.
70. 425 U.S. 238 (1976).
71. *Katz v. United States,* 389 U.S. 347 (1967).
72. *People v. Tidwell,* 266 N.E.2d 787 (IL: 1971).
73. *McDonell v. Hunter,* 611 F.Supp. 1122 (SD Iowa, 1985), affd. as mod., 809 F.2d 1302 (8th Cir., 1987).
74. *Biehunik v. Felicetta,* 441 F.2d 228 (1971), p. 230.
75. 385 U.S. 483 (1967).
76. 392 U.S. 273 (1968).
77. *Gabrilowitz v. Newman,* 582 F.2d 100 (1st Cir. 1978). Cases upholding the department's authority to order a polygraph examination for police officers include *Eshelman v. Blubaum,* 560 P.2d 1283 (Ariz.: 1977); *Dolan v. Kelly,* 348 N.Y.S.2d 478 (1973); *Richardson v. City of Pasadena,* 500 S.W.2d 175 (Tex.: 1973); *Seattle Police Officer's Guild v. City of Seattle,* 494 P.2d 485 (Wash.: 1972); *Roux v. New Orleans Police Department,* 223 So.2d 905 (La.: 1969); and *Farmer v. City of Fort Lauderdale,* 427 So.2d 187 (Fla.: 1983), cert. den., 104 S.Ct. 74 (1984).
78. 42 U.S.C. 200e(j).
79. *United States v. City of Albuquerque,* 12 EPD 11, 244 (10th Cir. 1976); see also *Trans World Airlines v. Hardison,* 97 S.Ct. 2264 (1977).
80. *United States v. Albuquerque,* 545 F.2d 110 (10th Cir. 1977).
81. *Potter v. Murray City,* 760 F.2d 1065 (10th Cir. 1985).
82. *Daniels v. City of Arlington, Texas,* 246 F.3d 500 (5th Cir. 2001), cert. denied, 122 S. Ct. 347 (2001).
83. *Fraternal Order of Police Newark Lodge No. 12 v. City of Newark,* 170 F.3d 359 (3rd Cir. 1999), cert. denied, 120 S. Ct. 56 (1999).
84. *Faust v. Police Civil Service Commission,* 347 A.2d 765 (Pa. 1975); *Stewart v. Leary,* 293 N.Y.S.2d 573 (1968); *Brewer v. City of Ashland,* 86 S.W.2d 669 (Ky. 1935); *Fabio v. Civil Service Commission of Philadelphia,* 373 A.2d 751 (Penn.: 1977).
85. *Major v. Hampton,* 413 F.Supp. 66 (1976).
86. *Briggs v. City of North Muskegon Police Department,* 563 F.Supp. 585 (6th Cir. 1984).
87. *National Gay Task Force v. Bd. of Ed. of Oklahoma City,* 729 F.2d 1270 (10th Cir. 1984).
88. *Board of Education v. National Gay Task Force,* 53 U.S.L.W. 4408, No. 83-2030 (1985).
89. *Rowland v. Mad. River Sch. Dist.,* 730 F.2d 444 (6th Cir. 1984).
90. David J. Schall, *An Investigation into the Relationship between Municipal Police Residency Requirements, Professionalism, Economic Conditions, and Equal Employment Goals,* Unpublished dissertation, University of Wisconsin–Milwaukee, 1996.
91. *Detroit Police Officers Association v. City of Detroit,* 190 N.W.2d 97 (1971), appeal denied, 405 U.S. 950 (1972).
92. *Miller v. Police Board of City of Chicago,* 349 N.E.2d 544 (Ill.: 1976); *Williamson v. Village of Baskin,* 339 So.2d 474 (La.: 1976); *Nigro v. Board of Trustees of Alden,* 395 N.Y.S.2d 544 (1977).
93. *State, County, and Municipal Employees Local 339 v. City of Highland Park,* 108 N.W.2d 898 (1961).
94. See, for example, *Cox v. McNamara,* 493 P.2d 54 (Ore.: 1972); *Brenckle v. Township of Shaler,* 281 A.2d 920 (Penn.: 1972); *Hopwood v. City of Paducah,* 424 S.W.2d 134 (Ken.: 1968); *Flood v. Kennedy,* 239 N.Y.S.2d 665 (1963).
95. Richard N. Williams, *Legal Aspects of Discipline by Police Administrators* (Traffic Institute Publication 2705) (Evanston, IL: Northwestern University, 1975), p. 4.
96. *City of Crowley Firemen v. City of Crowley,* 264 So.2d 368 (La.: 1972).
97. 471 U.S. 1, 105 S.Ct. 1694, 85 L.Ed.2d 1 (1985).
98. *Lally v. Department of Police,* 306 So.2d 65 (La. 1974).
99. See, for example, *Peters v. Civil Service Commission of Tucson,* 539 P.2d 698 (Ariz. 1977); *Abeyta v. Town of Taos,* 499 F.2d 323 (10th Cir. 1974); *Baumgartner v. Leary,* 311 N.Y.S.2d 468 (1970); *City of Vancouver v. Jarvis,* 455 P.2d 591 (Wash.: 1969).

100. Swanson, Territo, and Taylor, *Police Administration,* p. 433.
101. *Parker v. District of Columbia,* 850 F.2d 708 (1988), at 713, 714.
102. *Marusa v. District of Columbia,* 484 F.2d 828 (1973).
103. *Sager v. City of Woodlawn Park,* 543 F.Supp. 282 (D. Colo.: 1982).
104. *Bonsignore v. City of New York,* 521 F.Supp. 394 (1981).
105. *Popow v. City of Margate,* 476 F.Supp. 1237 (1979).
106. Eloise Salholz and Frank Washington, "Detroit's Brutal Lessons," *Newsweek* (November 30, 1992):45.
107. Ibid.
108. *Krolick v. Lowery,* 302 N.Y.S.2d 109 (1969), p. 115; *Hester v. Milledgeville,* 598 F.Supp. 1456, 1457 (MD Ga.: 1984).
109. *McCracken v. Department of Police,* 337 So.2d 595 (La.: 1976).
110. *Krolick v. Lowery.*
111. 489 U.S. 602 (1989).
112. 489 U.S. 656 (1989).
113. Robert J. Alberts and Harvey W. Rubin, "Court's Rulings on Testing Crack Down on Drug Abuse," *Risk Management* 38 (March 1991):36–41
114. Ibid., p. 38.
115. Ibid., p. 40.
116. Federal Communications Commission, "Understanding Workplace Harassment," http://www.fcc.gov/encyclopedia/understanding-workplace-harassment-fcc-staff (accessed August 21, 2014).
117. Allen D. Sapp, "Sexual Misconduct by Police Officers," in T. Barker and D. Carter (eds.), *Police Deviance* (Cincinnati: Anderson, 1994), pp. 187–200.
118. The amendments were contained in the National Defense Authorization Act for Fiscal Year 2008 (2008 NDAA), which became effective on January 16, 2009; the 2009 amendments were expanded again by amendments contained in the National Defense Authorization Act for Fiscal Year 2010 (2010 NDAA); see Public Law 110-181 and Public Law 111-84, respectively.
119. See Richard G. Schott, "Family and Medical Leave Act Amendments: New Military Leave Entitlements," *FBI law Enforcement Bulletin* 79(6) (June 2010), http://www.fbi.gov/stats-services/-publications/law-enforcement-bulletin/june-2010/family-and-medical-leave-act-amendments (accessed August 21, 2014).
120. Robert Pear, "Gay Workers Will Get Time to Care for Partner's Sick Child," *The New York Times,* June 21, 2010, http://www.nytimes.com/2010/06/22/us/politics/22rights.html (accessed August 21, 2014).
121. Paula N. Rubin and Susan W. McCampbell, "The Americans with Disabilities Act and Criminal Justice: Providing Inmate Services," *U.S. Department of Justice, National Institute of Justice Research in Action* (July 1994):2.
122. Paula N. Rubin, "The Americans with Disabilities Act and Criminal Justice: An Overview," *U.S. Department of Justice, National Institute of Justice Research in Action* (September 1993):1.
123. "Health and Criminal Justice: Strengthening the Relationship," *U.S. Department of Justice, National Institute of Justice Journal, Research in Action,* (November 1994):40.
124. Ibid., p. 41
125. This case study is based on *Kuntz v. City of New Haven,* No. N-90–480 (JGM), March 3, 1993. Kuntz prevailed, was promoted, and won back pay, demonstrating to the court that his possible assignment to field duties would not be dangerous to him, to other officers, or to the public.

PART 2

The Police

This part consists of three chapters. Chapter 4 examines the organization and operation of police departments, Chapter 5 covers police personnel roles and functions, and Chapter 6 discusses police issues and practices. The introductory section of each chapter previews the specific chapter content, and case studies in police administration appear in Appendix I.

Good order is the
foundation of all
things.
—*Edmund Burke*

4 Police Organization and Operation

LEARNING OBJECTIVES

After reading this chapter, the student will be able to:

1. *understand why police agencies are arranged into organizations*

2. *understand the division of labor in an organization*

3. *describe the seven elements of police organizational structure*

4. *define the purposes of policies, procedures, rules, and regulations in police organizations*

5. *explain how the military model can both help and hinder policing*

6. *explain community policing and its problem-solving S.A.R.A. process*

7. *review how police organization and operation appear to have changed since 9/11, particularly in areas as mission and emphasis, economies and practices, and the debate about whether or not this had led to too much federalization and militarization*

8. *define how three emerging management tools—smart policing, intelligence-led policing, and predictive policing—are being put to use in crime fighting*

9. *describe what experts say is needed to transform a good police organization into a great one*

10. *relate how a police organization can become accredited and the benefits of doing so*

▶ Introduction

To perform smoothly (at least as smoothly as society, resources, politics, and other influences permit), police agencies must be organized to enhance the accomplishment of their basic mission and goals. This chapter generally examines the elements of contemporary police organization, how policing has changed since 9/11, and how organizations have been modified over time to adapt to the community-oriented policing and problem-solving (COPPS) strategy. First, we consider how law enforcement agencies constitute and operate as bona fide organizations; included here are the seven elements of police organizational structure, examples of basic as well as more specialized organizational structures for police agencies, the need for grouping of activities and the division of labor, and a comment on their quasi-military nature. Next, after an overview of policies, procedures, rules, and regulations that provide guidelines for organizations, we examine what is now the dominant concept in police philosophy and operations: COPPS; this approach has caused many changes in the organization and administration of police agencies. Next are considerations of how—and whether—police organization and operation have changed since 9/11 in several areas: mission and emphasis, and economies and practices. In this connection, we will also contemplate whether or not, as some people now argue, there has been too much accompanying federalization and militarization of police. We then examine three emerging paradigms that are a direct result of these aforementioned shifts: smart policing, intelligence-led policing (ILD), and predictive policing. Following is a look at what experts say is needed in order to transform a good police organization into a great one. Following that is a discussion of how a police organization may become accredited and the benefits of doing so. Examples of COPPS and crime prevention are provided throughout the chapter as well. The chapter concludes with review questions, "deliberate and decide" problems, and "learn by doing" exercises.

▶ Police Agencies as Organizations

Today the policing of America is a very labor-intensive and costly undertaking, employing about 875,000 full-time personnel at state and local (city and county) levels (about 775,000 of whom are employed in local agencies) at a cost of about $95.5 billion.[1] In this chapter section, we will look at how all of these personnel—and their collective functions—are organized for greater efficiency.

The Grouping of Activities

As stated in Chapter 2, an organization is an artificial structure created to coordinate either people or groups and resources to achieve a mission or goal.[2] Certainly, police agencies fit this definition. First, the organization of these agencies includes a number of specialized units (e.g., patrol, traffic, investigation, records). The role of chief executives, middle managers, and first-line supervisors is to ensure that these units work together to reach a common goal; allowing each unit to work independently would lead to fragmentation, conflict, and competition and would subvert the entire organization's goals and purposes. Second, police agencies consist of people who interact within the organization and with external organizations.

Through mission statements, policies and procedures (discussed later), and management style, among other factors, police administrators attempt to ensure that the organization meets its overall goals of investigating and suppressing crime and that the organization works amicably with similar organizations. As the organization becomes larger, the need for people to cooperate to achieve the organizational goals increases. Formal organization charts assist in this endeavor by spelling out areas of responsibility and lines of communication and by defining the chain of command.

Police administrators modify or design the structure of their organization to fulfill their mission. An organizational structure reflects the formal organization of task and authority relationships determined to be best suited to accomplishing the police mission (organizational structures are discussed and shown later in this chapter).

The Division of Labor

The larger an agency, the greater the need for specialization and the more vertical (taller) its organizational chart becomes. Some 2,300 years ago, Plato observed that "each thing becomes . . . easier when one man, exempt from other tasks, does one thing."[3]

division of labor
a basic feature of traditional organizational theory, where specialization produces different groups of functional responsibilities.

Specialization, or the **division of labor**, is one of the basic features of traditional organizational theory.[4] Specialization produces different groups of functional responsibilities, and the jobs allocated to meet these different responsibilities are held by people who are considered to be especially well qualified to perform those jobs. Thus, specialization is crucial to effectiveness and efficiency in large organizations.[5]

Specialization makes the organization more complex, however, by complicating communication, increasing the number of units from which cooperation must be obtained, and creating conflict among different units. Specialization creates an increased need for coordination because it adds to the hierarchy, which can lead to narrowly defined jobs that stifle the creativity and energy of those who hold them. Police administrators are aware of these potential shortcomings of specialization and attempt, through various means, to inspire their employees to the extent possible. For example, personnel can be rotated to various jobs and given additional responsibilities that challenge them. In addition, in a medium-sized department—e.g., one serving a community of 100,000 or more—a police officer with 10 years of experience may have had the responsibilities of dog handler, motorcycle officer, detective, and/or traffic officer while being a member of special weapons or hostage negotiation teams.

In sum, the advantages to specialization in large police departments include the following:

- *Placement of responsibility.* The responsibility for performing given tasks can be placed on specific units or individuals. For example, the traffic division investigates all accidents, and the patrol division handles all calls for service.

- *Development of expertise.* Those who have specialized responsibilities receive specialized training. Homicide investigators can be sent to forensic pathology classes; special weapons and tactics teams train regularly to deal with terrorists or hostage situations.

- *Group esprit de corps.* Groups of specially trained persons share camaraderie and depend on one another for success; this leads to cohesion and high morale.

- *Increased efficiency and effectiveness.* Specialized units have a high degree of proficiency in performing job tasks. For example, a specially trained financial crimes unit normally is more successful in handling complex fraud cases than a general detective division.[6]

organizational structure how an organization divides up its work and establishes lines of authority and communication.

▶ Elements of Police Organizational Structure

According to Henry Mintzberg, an **organizational structure** can be defined simply as the sum total of the ways in which the organization divides its labor into distinct tasks and then achieves coordination among them.[7] This definition translates into measures that are relatively easy to compute.

Supported in part by a grant from the National Institute of Justice, Maguire et al. accomplished an excellent analysis of organizations and structural change in large police agencies. Essentially, they determined that there are seven specific elements of law enforcement organizational structure; the first four are types of structural differentiation, or methods of dividing labor. These elements are (1) functional, (2) occupational, (3) spatial, and (4) vertical differentiation, and (5) centralization, (6) formalization, and (7) administrative intensity[8]:

1. **Functional differentiation** is the degree to which tasks are broken down into functionally distinct units. A police agency with a homicide unit, an accident reconstruction unit, and a juvenile division is more functionally differentiated than one that only employs patrol officers. Law enforcement organizations became more functionally differentiated throughout the twentieth century, adding new bureaus, divisions, and specialized units to perform separate functions as the need arose.[9]

2. **Occupational differentiation** measures distinctions within the staff (job titles) and the extent to which an organization relies on specially trained workers from distinct occupational groups. Civilianization has increased in policing, and today, civilian police employees represent a separate occupational group.[10]

3. **Spatial differentiation** is the extent to which an organization is spread geographically. A police agency with a headquarters and several precinct stations is more spatially differentiated than a department that operates out of a single police facility. Police agencies with a single patrol beat and a single facility are the least spatially differentiated. Those agencies that carve the jurisdiction into a large number of small beats, with functioning ministations scattered throughout the jurisdiction and district stations in different areas of the community, are the most spatially differentiated.[11]

4. **Vertical differentiation** focuses on the hierarchical nature of an organization's command structure, including its (a) segmentation, (b) concentration, and (c) height. Organizations with elaborate chains of command are more vertically differentiated than those with flatter command structures. *Segmentation* is the number of command levels in an organization, from the lowest ranking to the highest. Some agencies maintain "status" ranks that carry greater prestige and/or pay but no supervisory or command authority other than in very limited circumstances. Examples are master police officers and corporals in some agencies, who are given supervisory authority on rare occasion, such as when a sergeant is unavailable. Other rank structures are a mix of functional and hierarchical differentiation; for example, sometimes detectives may receive greater pay and prestige than other officers but have no greater supervisory or command authority. *Concentration* is the percentage of personnel located at various levels, and *height* is the social distance between the lowest- and the highest-ranking employees in the organization. Police agencies in which patrol officers can drop in routinely to chat with the chief of police or sheriff are less vertically differentiated than those in which there is significant social distance between the chief and the lowest-ranking employees.[12]

5. **Centralization** is the extent to which the decision-making capacity within an organization is concentrated in a single individual or a small, select group. Organizations in which lower-ranking employees are given the autonomy to make decisions are less centralized than those in which senior administrators make most decisions.

6. **Formalization** is the extent to which employees are governed by specific rules and policies. Some factors in law enforcement, including liability issues and accreditation, are likely to encourage increase in formalization.

7. **Administrative intensity** refers to the proportion of organizational resources committed to administration. Organizations with high levels of administrative intensity are often thought of as being more bureaucratic.[13]

▶ Examples of Police Organization

The Basic Organizational Structure

As noted previously, an organizational structure helps departments carry out the many complex responsibilities of policing. It should be noted, however, that organizational structures vary from one jurisdiction to another and are fluid in nature. The highly decentralized nature and the different sizes of police departments in the United States, as well as the turnover in the chief executive officer (chief of police or sheriff) position, cause these structures to change. It is possible, however, to make certain general statements about all agencies to characterize a typical police organization.

The police traditionally organize along military lines, with a rank structure that normally includes the patrol officer, sergeant, lieutenant, captain, and chief. Many departments, particularly larger ones, employ additional ranks, such as corporal, major, and deputy chief, but there is a legitimate concern that these departments will become top-heavy. The military rank hierarchy allows the organization to designate authority and responsibility at each level and to maintain a chain of command. The military model also allows the organization to emphasize supervisor–subordinate relationships and to maintain discipline and control. The quasi-military style of policing is discussed later.

Every police agency, regardless of size, has a basic plan of organization. In addition, every such agency, no matter how large or small, has an organizational structure. A visitor to the police station or sheriff's office may even see this organizational structure displayed prominently on a wall. Even if it is not on paper, such a structure exists. A basic organizational structure for a small agency is shown in Figure 4-1 ■.

Operational or line elements involve policing functions in the field and may be subdivided into primary and secondary line elements. The patrol function—often called the "backbone" of policing—is the primary line element because it is the major law enforcement responsibility within the police organization. Most small police agencies, in fact, can be described as patrol agencies, with the patrol forces responsible for all line activities. Such agencies provide routine patrols, conduct criminal and traffic investigations, and make arrests. These agencies are basically generalists. In a community that has only one

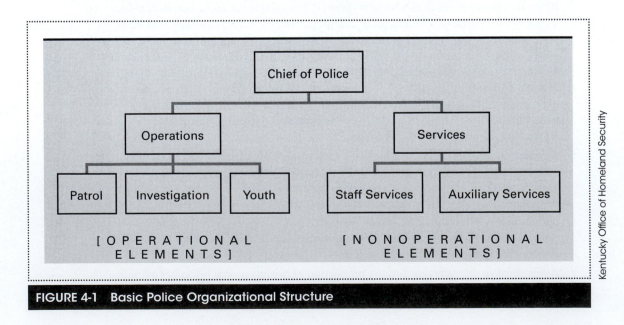

FIGURE 4-1 Basic Police Organizational Structure

Kentucky Office of Homeland Security

Portland Police Bureau
Organizational Chart

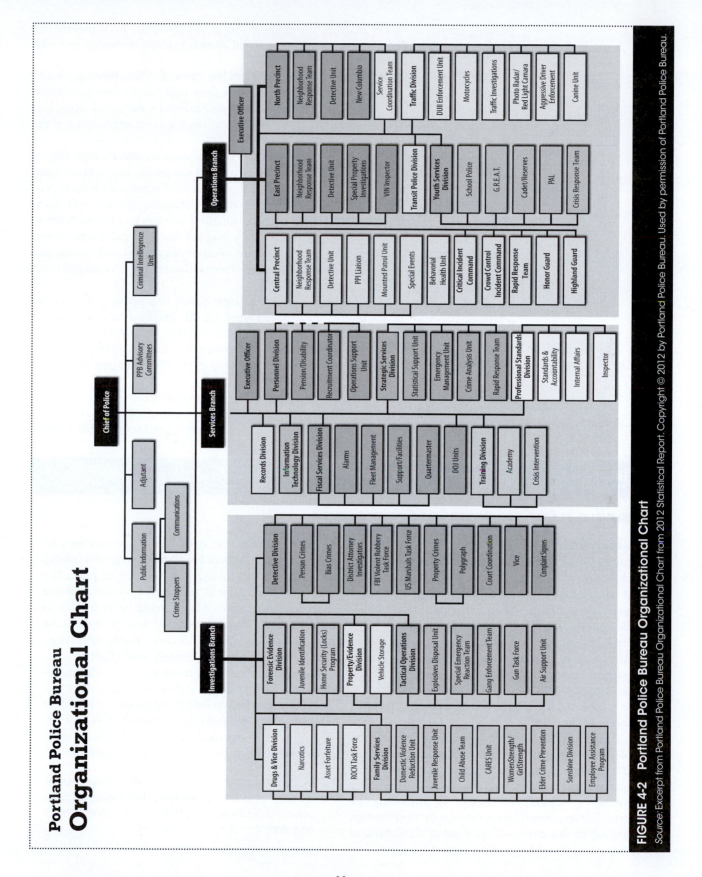

FIGURE 4-2 Portland Police Bureau Organizational Chart

Source: Excerpt from Portland Police Bureau Organizational Chart from 2012 Statistical Report. Copyright © 2012 by Portland Police Bureau. Used by permission of Portland Police Bureau.

83

policing employee—a city marshal, for example—he or she obviously must perform all the functions just listed. This agency's organizational chart is a simple horizontal one with little or no specialization.

Investigative and youth activities are the secondary line elements. These functions would not be needed if the police were totally successful in their patrol and crime prevention efforts—an obviously impossible goal. Time and area restrictions on the patrol officers, as well as the need for specialized training and experience, require some augmenting of the patrol activity.

The nonoperational functions and activities can become quite numerous, especially in a large community. These functions fall within two broad categories: *staff services* (also known as *administrative*) and *auxiliary* (or *technical*) *services*. Staff services are usually people oriented and include recruitment, training, promotion, planning and research, community relations, and public information services. Auxiliary services involve the types of functions that a nonpolice person rarely sees, including jail management, property and evidence handling, crime laboratory services, communications (dispatch), and records and identification. Many career opportunities exist for persons interested in police-related work who cannot or do not want to be a field officer.

Consider the organizational structure for a larger police organization, that of the Portland (Oregon) Police Bureau (PPB) (See Figure 4-2 ■). Portland has a population of about 600,000, but the metropolitan area (consisting of five counties) has about 2.2 million people.[14] The PPB has about 1,000 sworn personnel.[15] As with all organizations, especially those that are medium or large in size, some of the PPB functions are unique to that organization.[16]

Portland's and other cities' police department organizational structures are designed to fulfill five functions: (1) apportioning the workload among members and units according to a logical plan; (2) ensuring that lines of authority and responsibility are as

---

EXHIBIT 4.1

A SINGLE, NATIONAL POLICE ORGANIZATION?

Traditionally, American policing has been highly fragmented and localized, governed, and controlled largely by local governing boards; however, most European and many Asian countries have historically had police organizations that are centralized into one national police force. On a smaller scale, centralizing or combining some police functions is not new in the United States. Since the 1960s, many local police and sheriff's departments located in the same county have consolidated their units into one, thus avoiding the duplication of several expensive functions (e.g., records, communications, and jail).

The idea of a national police force is attractive to some Americans who believe that the nation is already drifting in that direction given the creation of the Department of Homeland Security and local police devoting more and more energy to protecting the nation's borders, scanning the Internet for cybercrimes, engaging in searches and seizures at seaports, and enforcing immigration laws. They argue that the current decentralization of law enforcement into federal, state, municipal, county, and even private police (or security) entities is inefficient and fragmented, and that a single, national police force would be better able to train their personnel, have fewer laws to uphold, be more accountable, and realize considerable cost savings if eliminating the current duplication of effort.

In the other camp are those who see such centralization as a huge danger to democracy as well as personal freedom. They believe that a national force would be more disengaged from the community, involve a loss of local control and oversight over the police, and be vulnerable to being abused by the central government.

1. What do you think? Would implementing a single, national police force such as that found in many other countries work in the United States? Why or why not?

definite and direct as possible; (3) specifying unity of command throughout so that there is no question as to which orders should be followed; (4) placing responsibility and authority, and if responsibility is delegated, holding the delegator responsible; and (5) coordinating the efforts of members so that all will work harmoniously to accomplish the mission.[17] In sum, this structure establishes the chain of command and determines lines of communication and responsibility. Exhibit 4.1 explores the possibility of a national police organization.

Commentary on the Quasi-Military Style of Policing

Police experts have long written about the quasi-military style of policing.[18] Egon Bittner, for example, felt that the adoption of the **military model** by the police—wearing uniforms, using rank designations, adopting a hierarchical command structure, acquiring legal authority (use of weapons and force)—was a reaction to the political influences over the police in the late nineteenth century that contributed to corruption[19] (e.g., payoffs for underenforcement of laws, political activity to get out the vote).

> **military model**
> where, for example, police and many correctional officers wear uniforms, use rank designations, and have a hierarchical command structure much as the military services.

Proponents of the military style of policing uphold the model's tradition, its imposition of control and commanding authority with strict discipline,[20] respect for chain of command and rigid rank differences, the "elite warrior" self-image, and centralized command. Critics of the model, however, note that it is excessively rigid (controlled by micromanaging bureaucrats), autocratic, secretive, intellectually and creatively constraining, and highly resistant to any initiative that will allow employee participation in the decision-making processes. In other words, it is said to often discourage creativity; cultivate the "us-versus-them" and "war on crime" mentalities[21]; eschew scientific or academic approaches in favor of an "applied" focus; rely heavily on tradition, or the "we've always done it this way" approach, causing a commitment to outmoded methods of operation; and have a distinct tendency to mismatch talent with job positions.

With today's emphasis on COPPS, discussed later, in the "Community-Oriented Policing and Problem Solving" section, many COPPS advocates believe that the quasi-military model is incompatible with this philosophy. As one police chief executive put it:

> Whereas community policing requires a policing approach that demonstrates openness, a service orientation, innovative/creative thinking, and problem solving, these characteristics are not likely to be developed in a militaristic managerial model. This is a style which at worst will tend to give rise to an operational police culture which is action oriented, cynical, suspicious, reactive and, most importantly in the context of community policing, insular and isolated from the general community.[22]

Some types of situations, such as critical incidents, will likely compel the retention of command and control in police training and tactical application. But in nonemergency situations involving a focus on crime and disorder, problem-solving policing requires personal and intellectual reasoning skills, skills that must be trained if a COPPS culture is to be developed.

▶ Organizational Guidelines: Policies, Procedures, Rules, and Regulations

Policies, procedures, rules, and regulations are important for defining role expectations for all police officers. The officers are granted unusually strong power in a democratic society; because they possess such extraordinary powers, police officers pose a potential threat to individual freedom. Thus, because police agencies are service oriented in nature, they must work within well-defined, specific guidelines designed to ensure that all officers conform to behavior that will enhance public protection.[23]

Related to this need for policies, procedures, rules, and regulations is the fact that police officers possess a broad spectrum of discretionary authority in performing their duties. This fact, coupled with the danger posed by their work and the opportunities to settle problems informally, works against having narrow, inflexible job requirements.

Thus, the task for the organization's chief executive is to find the middle ground between unlimited discretion and total standardization. The police role is much too ambiguous to become totally standardized, but it is also much too serious and important to be left completely to the discretion of the patrol officer. As Robert Sheehan and Gary Cordner put it, the idea is for chief executives to "harness, but not choke, their employees."[24]

Organizational **policies** are more general than procedures, rules, or regulations; they serve as basic guides to the organization's philosophy and mission and help in interpreting their elements to the officers.[25] Policies should be committed to writing, then modified according to the changing times and circumstances of the department and community. An example would be a police or prison policy stating that employees are prohibited from "posting or transmitting any photographs or video or audio recordings that specifically identifies (name of agency) on any personal or social networking website or web page, without the express written permission of the (police chief/sheriff/warden)." Some policies are dictated by federal or state law or court decisions, such as the prohibition against police officers placing juveniles in any form of institutional confinement without a specific order from a juvenile judge in the jurisdiction. Another example is the Supreme Court's 1985 decision in *Tennessee v. Garner*, which allows officers to use deadly force only when a "suspect threatens the officer with a weapon or there is probable cause to believe that [the suspect] has committed a crime involving the infliction or threatened infliction of serious physical harm."[26] Thus, the "policy" governing the use of deadly force provides that it only be used when the officer's or citizen's life is threatened.

Procedures are more specific than policies; they serve as guides to action. A procedure is "more specific than a policy but less restrictive than a rule or regulation. It describes a method of operation while still allowing some flexibility within limits."[27] Many organizations are awash in procedures; examples are written directives that inform employees how to conduct investigations, patrol, arrests, and suspect bookings; engage in radio communications; prepare reports; arrive at roll call or start-of-shift briefings; the proper use of sick leave; and many other related activities. Such procedures are not totally inflexible, but they do describe in rather detailed terms the preferred methods for carrying out policy.

Some police executives have attempted to run their departments via flurries of memos containing new procedures. This method is often fraught with difficulty. An abundance of standardized procedures can stifle initiative and imagination, as well as complicate jobs.[28] On the positive side, procedures can decrease the time wasted in figuring out how to accomplish tasks and thereby increase productivity. As they do with policies, chief executives must seek the middle ground in drafting procedures and remember that it is next to impossible to have procedures that cover all possible exigencies.

Rules and regulations are specific managerial guidelines that leave little or no latitude for individual discretion; they require action (or, in some cases, inaction). Some require officers to wear their hats when outside their patrol vehicle, check the patrol vehicle's oil and emergency lights before going on patrol, not consume alcoholic beverages within 4 hours of going on duty, and arrive in court 30 minutes before sessions open or at roll call 15 minutes before scheduled duty time. Rules and regulations are not always popular, especially if perceived as unfair or unrelated to the job. Nonetheless, they contribute to the total police mission of community service.

policies written guidelines that are general in nature and serve to further the organization's philosophy and mission and help in interpreting their elements to the officers.

procedures specific guidelines that serve to direct employee actions, such as how to prepare investigations and conduct patrol, bookings, radio communications, and prepare reports.

rules and regulations specific managerial guidelines for officers, such not smoking in public, types of weapons to be carried on duty, and so on.

Rules and regulations should obviously be kept to a minimum because of their coercive nature. If they become too numerous, they can hinder action and send the message that management believes that it cannot trust the rank and file to act responsibly on their own. Once again, the middle ground is the best. As Thomas Reddin, former Los Angeles police chief, stated:

> Certainly we must have rules, regulations and procedures, and they should be followed. But they are no substitutes for initiative and intelligence. The more a [person] is given an opportunity to make decisions and, in the process, to learn, the more rules and regulations will be followed.[29]

Next, we discuss COPPS, including some evaluation and research efforts.

▶ Community-Oriented Policing and Problem Solving (COPPS)

Rationale and Definition

Community-oriented policing and problem solving—**COPPS**—has emerged as the dominant philosophy and strategy of policing—*a form of police operation*. It is an approach to crime detection and prevention that provides police officers and supervisors with new tools for addressing recurrent problems that plague communities and consume a majority of police agency time and resources. The California Department of Justice provided the following definition of COPPS:

> Community-oriented policing and problem solving is a philosophy, management style, and organizational strategy that promotes proactive problem solving and police–community partnerships to address the causes of crime and fear as well as other community issues.[30]

Two principal and interrelated components emerge from this definition: community engagement (partnerships) and problem solving. With its focus on collaborative problem solving, COPPS seeks to improve the quality of policing.

The S.A.R.A. process discussed next provides the police with the tools necessary to accomplish these tasks.

COPPS community-oriented policing and problem solving, which has emerged as the dominant philosophy and strategy of policing.

The S.A.R.A. Process

S.A.R.A. (*Scanning, Analysis, Response, Assessment*) (See Figure 4-3 ■) provides officers with a logical, step-by-step framework in which to identify, analyze, respond to, and evaluate crime, fear of crime, and neighborhood disorder. This approach, with its emphasis on in-depth analysis and collaboration, replaces officers' short-term, reactive responses with a process vested in longer-term outcomes.

S.A.R.A. for scanning, analysis, response, assessment—the logical framework for officers to respond to crime and neighborhood disorder.

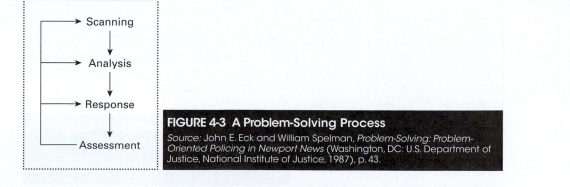

FIGURE 4-3 A Problem-Solving Process
Source: John E. Eck and William Spelman, *Problem-Solving: Problem-Oriented Policing in Newport News* (Washington, DC: U.S. Department of Justice, National Institute of Justice, 1987), p. 43.

Scanning: Problem Identification

Scanning involves problem identification. The police officer initiates the problem-solving process by conducting a preliminary inquiry to determine whether a problem really exists and whether further analysis is needed. A problem may be defined as a cluster of two or more similar or related incidents that are of substantive concern to the community and to the police. If the incidents to which the police respond do not fall within the definition of a problem, then the problem-solving process is not applicable.

Numerous resources are available to the police for identifying problems, including calls for service data (especially repeat calls), crime analysis information, police reports, and officers' experiences. Scanning helps the officer to determine whether a problem really exists before moving on to more in-depth analysis.

Analysis: Determining the Extent of the Problem

Analysis is the heart of the problem-solving process. It is the most difficult and important step in the S.A.R.A. process. Without analysis, long-term solutions are unlikely and the problem will persist.

Here, officers gather as much information as possible from a variety of sources. A complete and thorough analysis consists of identifying the seriousness of the problem, all persons affected, and the underlying causes. Officers should also assess the effectiveness of current responses.

Many tools are available to assist analysis. Crime analysis may be useful in collecting, collating, analyzing, and disseminating data relating to crime, incidents not requiring a report, criminal offenders, victims, and locations. Mapping and geographic information systems (GIS) can identify patterns of crime and "hot spots." Police offense reports can also be analyzed for suspect characteristics, victim characteristics, and information about high-crime areas and addresses. Computer-aided dispatch (CAD) is also a reliable source of information, as it collects data on all incidents and specific locations from which an unusual number of incidents require a police response.

Generally, three elements are needed for a problem to occur: an *offender*, a *victim*, and a *location*. The problem analysis triangle, shown in Figure 4-4 ■, helps officers to visualize the problem and understand the relationship among the three elements. The three elements must be present for a crime or harmful event to occur; removing one or more of these elements will remove the problem. Strategies for removing one of these elements are limited only by an officer's ability to develop responses and the available resources.

Response: Formulating Tailor-Made Strategies

Once a problem has been clearly defined, officers may seek the most effective responses. Developing long-term solutions to problems is of paramount importance in COPPS;

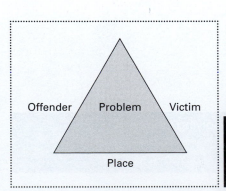

FIGURE 4-4   Problem Analysis Triangle
Source: Bureau of Justice Assistance, U.S. Department of Justice, *Comprehensive Gang Initiative: Operations Manual for Implementing Local Gang Prevention and Control Programs* (Draft, October 1993), pp. 3–10.

however, officers cannot ignore the fact that more serious situations may require immediate action. For example, in the case of an open-air drug market involving rival gang violence, police may initially increase the number of patrols in the area to arrest offenders, gain control of public space, and secure the safety of residents and officers. Once this is accomplished, long-term responses, which include the collaborative efforts of officers, residents, and other agencies, may be considered.

Administrators must bear in mind that responses to substantive problems rarely involve a single agency or tactic or a quick fix. Arrest is often viewed as the only response to a problem even though it is rarely sufficient to provide permanent solutions. More appropriate responses often involve the police and public and other appropriate actors, including businesses, private and social service organizations, and other government agencies.

Patrol officers have many options to use in responding to problems, but they should not expect to eliminate every problem they take on. With some social problems, such as gangs and homelessness, elimination is impractical and improbable.

Assessment: Evaluating Overall Effectiveness

The final stage of the S.A.R.A. process is assessment. Here, officers evaluate the effectiveness of their actions and may use the results to revise their responses, collect more data, or even redefine the problem. A COPPS initiative that is not reinforced by an evaluation process may have difficulty establishing whether it succeeded and thus should continue to receive resources; therefore, rigorous evaluation is an essential component of the COPPS initiative. Evaluations provide knowledge; key decision makers in the jurisdiction need a gauge of the strategy's impact and cost-effectiveness. Exhibit 4.2 provides an example of the S.A.R.A. process in action, in Oakland, California.

EXHIBIT 4.2

A WINNING EXAMPLE OF S.A.R.A.: THE OAKLAND AIRPORT MOTEL PROGRAM

The Oakland Police Department (OPD) addressed a serious motel problem near its local airport; for the following efforts, the OPD won the coveted Herman Goldstein Award for Excellence in Problem-Oriented Policing, conferred at the Annual International Problem Oriented Policing Conference.

- **Scanning:** Located along a major gateway to the city of Oakland, the Oakland Airport Motel is situated within a commercial area comprising lodging, restaurants, and fast food outlets; it is also situated about 2 miles from Oakland's professional baseball, football, and basketball franchises. A complainant informed an Oakland officer that, while he had been working at the motel for several weeks, prostitutes soliciting sex had approached him nightly, prostitutes "had the run of the place", there were loud parties and disturbances each night around the clock, junked vehicles littered the parking lot, and the smell of marijuana came through his window nightly.

- **Analysis:** After consulting with the city zoning and attorneys' offices concerning applicable laws, an officer reviewed the property owner information and determined that a large corporation owned the motel, there was no policy of limiting the duration of guest stays, and a disproportionately high number of narcotics arrests had occurred over the previous 2 years. The officer made a site visit, photographing and documenting his observations, and interviewing tenants and the motel staff. He noted that a corner of the motel parking lot was used as a freelance and illegal auto repair business, that rooms were routinely rented to minors, and that prostitution activity was rampant. A review of police incidents over the past 3 years revealed that the motel had an astounding 900 percent higher number of police incidents than other comparable lodging facilities in the area.

- **Response:** A response plan was developed. Phase One involved working with the motel manager to

(Continued)

clean up the property and deal with problem tenants. A policy was implemented to rent rooms only to persons 21 years of age or older, to evict problem tenants in a timely manner, to monitor the parking lot to prevent junked vehicles from being dumped there, and to fire employees caught renting out rooms "under the table" and using their passkeys. Corporate officials balked at several of these initiatives, however, so the officer sent a drug nuisance abatement notification letter to the motel. Police surveillance revealed that motel security guards were not taking steps to keep nuisances out of the parking lot, and frequent prostitution and open drug transactions continued to occur. An undercover officer rented rooms at the motel; on two occasions, motel managers changed the room locks and took the officer's property left in the rooms in order to double-rent the rooms. Given this lack of improvement, Phase Two involved meeting with the motel's corporate officials. A document was prepared covering the criminal activity at the motel over a 3-year period, descriptions and photographs of the prostitution and violent crimes occurring at the site, and the legal consequences and costs of not complying with relevant legal, health, and safety codes. It was requested that the motel be closed for 90 days to improve its physical aspects and to retrain motel staff in their proper duties, post a $250,000 performance bond, and repay OPD for its investigative costs. Corporate officials promised swift change; again, however, there was little improvement in the conditions at the motel after 2 weeks had passed. Phase Three of the project was then launched: preparation of lawsuits and negotiations. Police continued surveillance of activities at the motel, and a drug nuisance abatement lawsuit was prepared for filing and sent to the CEO at his home in France. Finally, after 7 hours of negotiations, corporate officials agreed to post the performance bond and to pay the city $35,000 in fees and expenses incurred to date. Furthermore, barbed wire was installed along all fence lines to discourage fence climbing, area lighting was upgraded, room rates were increased by 50 percent to improve the quality of the motel's clientele, room rentals for more than 30 days were prohibited, foot and vehicle traffic was stopped for identification by security guards, a "no-rent" list was developed for banned guests, the property was cleaned and painted, rigorous background checks were performed on new employees, and problem employees were fired.

- **Assessment:** Seven months after these activities were launched, calls for service to the motel dropped by 59 percent. Two years later, there had been only one call for police service. Overall, crime and nuisance activity was also on par with the other five adjacent motels.

Source: Based on "The Oakland Airport Motel Program: Eliminating Criminal and Nuisance Behavior at a Motel," 2003, http://www.popcenter.org/library/awards/goldstein/2003/03-26(W).pdf (accessed November 4, 2014).

Desired Organizational Elements Under COPPS

Part of the analysis of police organizations by Maguire et al. included the extent to which these organizations changed during the 1990s, when COPPS was in full bloom. To accomplish its goals, COPPS relies on some form of structural innovation for its implementation efforts: reducing levels of vertical and functional differentiation (officers being "uniformed generalists," responsible for developing customized responses to a wide variety of situations), increasing levels of occupational differentiation (discussed earlier, to include greater use of civilians in police agencies, thereby freeing up officers' time and allowing them to patrol the streets) and spatial differentiation (using more ministations and precincts to extend officers into their communities) and decreasing formalization (less reliance on and enforcement of formal written rules, policies, and procedures), centralization (shared decision making), and administrative intensity (smaller administrative components and less bureaucracy, concentrating police on the streets and not at desks).[31]

Maguire et al. determined that most large municipal organizations in the United States experienced significant decreases in centralization and administrative intensity, together with significant increases in occupational differentiation. These changes are consistent with the structural reform agendas of community policing (which call for law enforcement administrators to decrease the levels of centralization and administrative intensity within their organizations). On the other hand, the flattening of the police hierarchy did not occur, and segmentation, or the number of command levels, did not change significantly during the 1990s.[32] Hierarchy height increased significantly, and there was no change in formalization. With regard to spatial differentiation, although there was a significant increase in the number of police stations, there was also a significant increase in the use of ministations.[33]

Overall, Maguire et al. found room for optimism for community policing reformers, with police agencies being less centralized, employing a greater proportion of civilian employees, and having leaner administrative components. Spatially, they have more ministations and police stations, but their beat coverage has remained about the same. Police organizations are capable of changing in many dimensions: in culture, leadership, management, programs, and operations, although many of these changes were not reflected in Maguire et al.'s analysis.[34]

Most community policing reformers felt that it was essential for law enforcement agencies to move from the traditional organizational structures to accommodate COPPS' philosophy and operations. Although policing has been in the community policing era for a relatively short period of time, much has been written about how agencies have modified their structures, as well as their implementation and evaluation of COPPS. There are also countless examples of the resulting successes they have achieved through COPPS in dealing with crime and disorder.[35] The reader is encouraged to explore some of these resources to better understand the current era of policing.

▶ Changes in Police Organization and Operation Post-9/11

There is no question that policing has changed dramatically since the terrorist attacks of September 11, 2001. Some of those changes brought significant changes in agencies' organizational structure and operations. Indeed, major changes have occurred in two broad areas: (1) a shift in emphasis from community policing to homeland security (to include what some believe has been a concerning militarization and federalization of police) and (2) the economic downturn beginning in the late-2000s, leading to changes in personnel recruitment and hiring; greater collaboration and multijurisdictional sharing of resources; and less face-to-face contact with the public.

Next we focus on these distinct yet quite intertwined changes as they have affected police organization and administration.

A "Paradigm Shift" in Mission and Emphasis?

Recently MoonSun Kim and Melchor C. de Guzman[36] set out to empirically test whether or not community policing was, in effect, supplanted by homeland security in the aftermath of the 9/11 terrorist attacks. To do so, they compared the 1999 Law Enforcement Management and Administrative Statistics (LEMAS) data before the 9/11 attacks with two sets of LEMAS data following the attacks (for 2003 and 2007). Their analysis also covered a period of time when information technologies were making rapid strides in U.S. policing, which facilitated the rapid transfer of information and thus marked the beginning of a new era of community policing and problem solving.

MoonSun and de Guzman did in fact report a "paradigm shift" in policing since 9/11— that most police agencies de-emphasized their community policing efforts after the 9/11 terrorist attacks and shifted their attention and resources to homeland security policing

(HSP).[37] Interestingly, however, they also found that the agencies' *problem-solving* efforts (using the SARA model, discussed earlier), increased somewhat. This finding also suggested that relatively new policing practices such as intelligence-led and smart policing (both of which are discussed below in the "Emerging Paradigms" section) shared common ground with problem-solving policing, emphasizing crime data, evidence, and scientific analyses. It was also found that problem-solving partnerships and citizen training significantly improved and remained valuable practices for police departments.

MoonSun and de Guzman thus concluded that a new "era" of innovations in policing has arrived, even though police problem solving has remained an area of emphasis because of its core value to intelligence-based policing. These innovations are felt to be based in part on the extreme national shock and distress of the attacks, which they believe demonstrated that police agencies might be influenced more by their environment rather than by factors intrinsic to the culture of the organization. Or, the police may have felt compelled to act more aggressively against terrorism realizing that something had to be done immediately, so as to "confront the enemy," leading to a temporary shift in their philosophies and strategies away from community policing strategies. Another possible explanation for this shift in emphasis may be due to reduced funding and support from federal agencies that local police had come to rely on in their community policing efforts.

Kim and deGuzman also believe that these findings bode well for the society that the US police serve, as the police could be relied upon to protect and serve during extreme circumstances of heightened threats. They note, moreover, that perhaps community policing and HSP are not really competing theories but are, rather, overlapping or complementary.[38]

Changing Economies and Practices

Following a quarter century of steady increases in the number of both sworn and civilian police personnel in the United States, beginning in the late 2000s things have begun to change due to what has been termed a "perfect storm"—the emerging demands placed on law enforcement by globalization (to include persistent threats of terrorism), multinational criminal networks, and evolving cyberthreats and cybercrimes[39]—that require collective actions, collaboration, and flexibility. During 2011, approximately 12,000 police officers and sheriffs' deputies were laid off and 30,000 federal, state, and local law enforcement positions went unfilled; another 28,000 sworn personnel faced work furloughs of at least one week or more, and similar cutbacks were made for civilian personnel serving in police agencies.[40]

Agencies had to undergo a broad array of belt-tightening measures: A "triage" approach was used for responding to calls for service, with some severely limiting the types of calls that result in direct face-to-face responses by officers; alternative methods for handling certain reports, greater utilization of closed-circuit television cameras, and greater utilization of civilian volunteers were also employed.[41]

A survey by the Major Cities Chiefs Association found that about one-fourth of police agencies had reduced their investigative follow-ups, fugitive tracking, non-felony domestic assaults, financial crimes, computer crimes, narcotics, and traffic cases.[42] While forcing agencies to become much more resourceful and do more with less, these changes also combined to greatly reduce the direct face-to-face contacts between citizens and police personnel.

Meanwhile, there were trends toward much greater civilianization and the use of volunteers, and many departments began using technology to enhance efficiency (see Chapter 16). There also came to pass expanded collaboration among agencies and a willingness to look at regionalization to increase efficiencies and promote cost-effectiveness. More and more, fusion centers (discussed in Chapter 6) became used to promote partnerships and cross-jurisdictional collaboration not only for homeland security but also in the sharing of intelligence and information integration for all crimes and hazards.[43]

Multijurisdictional sharing of resources also grew in such areas as dispatch services, special weapons and tactics (SWAT), hazardous materials (HAZMAT), use of crime technicians and laboratories, and training. Some agencies even opted for complete consolidation and to contract for services with other agencies—often county sheriffs[44] (contract and consolidated policing are discussed in Chapter 6).

And, as police executives were becoming more concerned about avoiding layoffs and other cutbacks, hiring became an employer's market, and those agencies that were fortunate enough to be able to hire new personnel could be relatively selective given the supply-demand forces of the marketplace (many people looking for fewer job openings).

Too Much Federalization and Militarization?

Concurrent with a perceived shift from community policing to homeland security since 9/11, some observers also see the local police being increasingly co-opted by federal law enforcement agencies, seeing more and more effort on the part of local police being directed toward protecting the nation's borders, scanning the Internet for cybercrimes, engaging in searches and seizures at seaports, and enforcing immigration laws. In sum, they see a greater **federalization**, centralization, loss of local political control, and municipal and county police becoming the eyes and ears of federal enforcement agencies. This perceived shift is most disturbing, it is argued, because it leads to a concentration of police power at the national level that is democratically unhealthy and undermines the most basic principles under which the nation was founded. According to the American Bar Association, Congress should not bring into play the federal government's investigative power, prosecutorial discretion, judicial authority, and sentencing sanctions unless there is a strong reason for making wrongful conduct a federal crime and there is a distinct federal interest of some sort that is involved.[45]

Closely related to the perceived trend of federalization is what many see as the concurrent **militarization** of the local police; they cite as evidence the use of military-style weapons, tactics, training, uniforms, and even heavy equipment by civilian police departments. They also point to millions of pieces of surplus military equipment being given to local police departments across the country, including military-grade semi-automatic weapons, armored personnel vehicles, tanks, helicopters, and airplanes.[46]

Of course, it should be emphasized that neither all police personnel in the United States nor the civilian population perceives any problem or a threat of harm posed by this increased collaboration between the civilian police and the military. Indeed, the research and development, and eventual application, of police technologies began in the military arena, and, for their part, the police will no doubt welcome military assistance, equipment, and funding that can be rendered to combat terrorism, generally promote homeland security, and even be used during such crises as hurricanes.

The topic of police militarization is also discussed briefly in Chapter 6, relating to the August 2014 protests and riots occurring in the aftermath of the police killing of a young African American in Ferguson, Missouri.

federalization the notion that local police are being overly co-opted by federal law enforcement agencies, directing too many resources toward protecting the nation's borders and other federal duties.

militarization a belief held by some that local police—using military-style weapons, tactics, training, uniforms, and even heavy equipment—are becoming too militaristic in nature.

▶ Emerging Paradigms in Policing

In keeping with the previous discussion of how police organization and operation have changed since 9/11 and even more recently, next we will discuss three relatively new and intertwined administrative tools for crime fighting paradigms that can complement COPPS and appear to have strong merit and enduring presence in the field: smart policing, intelligence-led policing, and predictive policing. They may be fairly said to greatly enhance the analysis phase of the SARA problem-solving model, discussed earlier.

Smart Policing: Pairing Practitioners and Academics for Crime Fighting

smart policing a policing approach that emphasizes the use of data and analytics as well as improved crime analysis, performance measurement, and evaluation research.

Smart policing emphasizes the use of data and analytics as well as improved crime analysis, performance measurement, and evaluation research. As discussed earlier, in the late 2000s local police agencies throughout the United States were hard-hit with budget reductions and other problems (hiring stoppages, employee layoffs, deferred technology, and equipment purchases) and were forced to adjust their responses to reports to crimes and even their community policing and problem-solving activities. Against this backdrop of fiscal gloom, the police were also forced to be more resourceful and inventive regarding crime-fighting. In June 2009 the federal Bureau of Justice Assistance (BJA) began soliciting grant proposals for "smart policing" initiatives (SPI), seeking proposals that would identify or confirm effective, crime-reduction techniques that were effective and efficient (i.e., reasonably affordable) for most agencies to replicate.[47] Perhaps the most important element of SPI was to be research partnerships, which BJA emphasized in the call for proposals, with police and academics working together to test solutions that were informed by crime science theories and assessed with sound evaluation. Since BJA made its first 10 SPI awards to police agencies in 2009, to date, more than $12.4 million has been awarded to 33 local law enforcement agencies conducting 36 SPI projects.

Because the initial SPI did not prescribe any particular policing model or approach, but instead stressed the importance of in-depth problem analysis and definition to guide their later efforts, an impressive array of strategies and tactics were developed and implemented by the local SPI sites. For example, while some sites focused primarily on hot spot and place-based policing strategies, others focus primarily on offender-based approaches (e.g., focused deterrence through identification of prolific offenders and strategic application of suppression and social support strategies). Some first identified hot spots and then pinpointed the prolific offenders within them. Some sites begin with a distinct problem-oriented policing approach (e.g., application of the SARA), and others adopted a distinctly community-oriented policing approach (e.g., strong emphasis on community and victim engagement); again, some sites combine these two approaches. Several sites have implemented initiatives with a strong predictive-analytic approach, others have incorporated elements of intelligence-led policing or have implemented strategies to move their entire agency toward an intelligence-led policing model, and others have adopted technological approaches to improving police operations (e.g., strategic use of surveillance cameras, enhanced crime analysis capabilities, enhancements to "real-time crime centers," or enhanced predictive analytic capabilities).

The Philadelphia SPI employed an experimental design in its testing of foot patrol, problem-oriented policing, and offender-focused strategies. The Boston SPI employed a quasi-experimental design using propensity score matching techniques to evaluate the implementation of SPI in 13 hot spots. The Los Angeles SPI employed an interrupted time-series analysis methodology to evaluate the effectiveness of its SPI in one historically violent police district. The research results from these and other initiatives report significant crime decreases in the targeted areas and, after accounting for crime levels in the control or comparison areas, for the targeted offenses. In some instances, SPI materials have been incorporated into police academy training and departmental (e.g., roll call) training. Other sites have reported the incorporation of SPI in police officer performance assessment, and the integration of SPI into CompStat meetings.

Findings thus far also suggest that smart policing programs can significantly reduce violent crime (Philadelphia); creative use of crime analytics and crime analysis resources, coupled with targeted problem-solving approaches, can also reduce violent crime in historically violent police districts (Los Angeles); and problem-solving teams can prevent violence in stubborn chronic hot spots (Boston) and reduce service calls and property

EXHIBIT 4.3

SMART POLICING IN LOS ANGELES: A CASE STUDY[48]

The Los Angeles Police Department Smart Policing Initiative (SPI) sought to reduce gun violence in the Newton Division, 1 of 21 areas the LAPD serves. The SARA problem-solving process—scanning, analysis, response, and assessment—was first applied. During scanning, the LAPD and its research partner examined gun-related crimes by the Newton Division for 2011, determining it was ranked third in gun violence among the 21 Divisions. Next the Los Angeles SPI team sought to identify specific areas for intervention in the division, employing a geographic analysis of data on gun-related crimes, arrests, and calls for service over a 6-year period (2006–2011). The location-based analysis resulted in the identification of five large hot spots. Once the target areas were identified, the SPI team developed their intervention strategy, which it termed the Los Angeles Strategic Extraction and Restoration Program (or Operation LASER). Established in September 2011, LASER's overall goal was to target the violent repeat offenders and gang members who committed crimes in the target areas. LASER involved both location- and offender-based strategies, most notably the creation of a Crime Intelligence Detail (CID). CID's primary mission centered on the development of proactive, real-time intelligence briefs called *Chronic Offender Bulletins*. The bulletins assist officers in identifying crime trends and solving current investigations, and gave officers a tool for proactive police work. The SPI team also assessed the impact of LASER using interrupted time-series analysis, looking at monthly crime data for the Newton Division and 18 other divisions from January 2006 to June 2012. Results show that Part I violent crimes, homicide, and robbery all decreased significantly in the Newton Division after Operation LASER began. After the program was implemented, Part I violent crimes in the Newton Division dropped by an average of 5.4 crimes per month, and homicides dropped by 22.6 percent per month. Meanwhile, the crime declines did not occur in the other LAPD divisions, which provided strong evidence that LASER caused the declines in the Newton Division.

crime at troubled high-traffic convenience stores (Glendale, Arizona). Other SPI projects now underway seek to examine patrol officer body-worn camera testing (Phoenix, AZ), explore the links between traffic violations/vehicle crashes and other criminal activity (Shawnee, Kansas, and York, Maine) and video camera surveillance of high-density, order-maintenance areas (Pullman, Washington), and test intelligence-led policing (Columbia, South Carolina) and predictive policing (in Cambridge, Massachusetts, and Indio, California).

Certainly technology was an essential piece of these early SPI projects, as will be seen in Exhibit 4.3. The Los Angeles SPI experience described offers a number of lessons learned for both police managers and line officers. First, the value of the SARA problem-solving process is underscored, when used as an evidence-based framework for crime control, and it highlights the central role of both crime analysis and technology in data-driven decision making. LASER strongly involved a close working relationship between line officers and crime analysts, and the investment paid off in the target areas.

Intelligence-Led Policing: Knowing the "Who" of Crime

Intelligence-led policing originated in Great Britain, where police believed that a relatively small number of people were responsible for a comparatively large percentage of crimes; they believed that officers would have the best effect on crime by focusing on the most prevalent offenses occurring in their jurisdiction.[49]

The word *intelligence* is often misused; the most common mistake is to consider intelligence as secretly collected data that were analyzed. Intelligence is information; furthermore, "information plus analysis equals intelligence," and without analysis, there is no

> **intelligence-led policing** a style of policing that combines crime analysis (where the "who, what, when, and where" of crime is analyzed) with intelligence analysis (which looks at the "who" of crime—the crime networks and individuals).

intelligence. Intelligence is what is produced after the collected data were evaluated and analyzed by a trained intelligence professional.[50]

To better comprehend intelligence-led policing, let's break it down into its core components. For example, many police agencies have both crime analysts and intelligence analysts. Crime analysts keep their fingers on the pulse of crime in the jurisdiction: which crime trends are up, which ones are down, where the hot spots are, what type of property is being stolen, and so on. Intelligence analysts, on the other hand, are likely to be more aware of the specific *people* responsible for crime in the jurisdiction—who they are, where they live, what they do, who they associate with, and so on. Integrating these two functions—crime analysis and intelligence analysis—is essential for obtaining a comprehensive grasp of the crime picture. *Crime analysis* allows police to understand the "who, what, when, and where," while *intelligence analysis* provides an understanding of the "who"—the crime networks and individuals.

As shown in Figure 4-5 ■, the National Criminal Intelligence Sharing Plan (NCISP)[51] categorizes the intelligence gathering process into six steps: planning and direction, collection, processing/collation, analysis, dissemination, and reevaluation.

Levels of Intelligence

In general, law enforcement agencies can be categorized according to four levels of intelligence operations.[52]

Level 1 intelligence is the highest level, wherein agencies produce tactical and strategic intelligence products that benefit their own department as well as other law enforcement agencies. The law enforcement agency at this level employs an intelligence manager, intelligence officers, and professional intelligence analysts. Examples of level 1 intelligence agencies include Intelligence Support Centers, and the National Drug Intelligence Center.

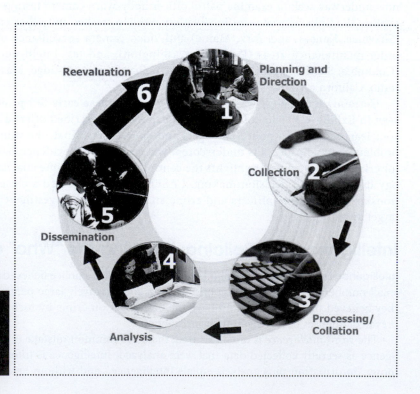

FIGURE 4-5 The Intelligence Gathering Process

Source: U.S. Department of Justice, Office of Justice Programs, *National Criminal Intelligence Sharing Plan,* p. 6; http://www.fas.org/irp/agency/doj/ncisp.pdf (accessed December 1, 2010).

Level 2 intelligence includes police agencies that produce tactical and strategic intelligence for internal consumption, generally to support investigations rather than to direct operations. These departments may have intelligence units and intelligence officers, analysts, and an intelligence manager. Some examples are state police agencies, large city police departments, and some investigating commissions, where intelligence supports investigations into complex crimes, such as organized crime, insurance fraud, and environmental crime.

Level 3 intelligence is the most common level of intelligence function in the United States. It includes law enforcement agencies with anywhere from dozens to hundreds of sworn employees, and they do not normally employ analysts or intelligence managers; however, they may have named one or more sworn individuals as their "intelligence officers" and may have sent them to intelligence and/or analytic training. These agencies may be capable of developing intelligence products internally, but they are more likely to rely on products developed by partner agencies, to include federal and state intelligence centers.

Level 4 intelligence is the category that comprises most agencies in the United States. These agencies, often with a few dozen employees or less, do not employ intelligence personnel. Officers may be involved in a limited information-sharing network made up of county or regional databases. Some departments have received intelligence awareness training and may be able to interpret analytic products.

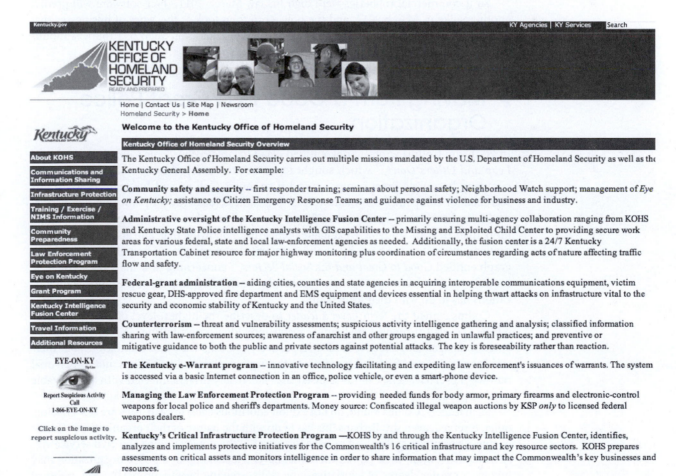

Kentucky Homeland Security web page

Intelligence operations have led to the creation of the fusion center (discussed below) and are compatible with the community-oriented policing and problem concepts (discussed in Chapter 6).[53]

Predictive Policing: Knowing the "Where" of Crime

The term **predictive policing**, according to the U.S. Department of Justice (DOJ), is a relatively new law enforcement concept that "integrates approaches such as cutting-edge crime analysis, crime-fighting technology, intelligence-led policing, and more to inform forward thinking crime prevention strategies and tactics." The DOJ states that, ultimately, predictive policing is intended as a framework to advance strategies like community policing, problem-oriented policing, intelligence-led policing, and hot spots policing.[54]

The police have always known that robberies surge near check-cashing businesses, that crime spikes on hot days and plummets during the rain, that residential burglaries often occur on Sunday mornings (while people are attending church services), and that Super Bowl Sunday is usually the slowest crime day of the year.[55] But officers' minds can store and remember only so much data. So when the police monitor crime data and query a computer system for historical and real-time patterns, they can predict, more systematically, over a bigger area, and across shifts and time spans, where crimes are likely to occur. More important, the crime-analysis software does not forget details, get sick, take vacation, or transfer to a different precinct.

So if commercial robberies were high in, say, March 2011, their software will predict another spike in March 2012, and the police can then look at the types of businesses that were hit, their locations, and time of day. The system can even analyze a robber's modus operandi—what was said, type of weapon used, and so on.[56]

▶ Moving from a Good to a Great Police Organization

In 2001, Jim Collins wrote a book entitled *Good to Great: Why Some Companies Make the Leap and Others Don't*,[57] which sought to answer the compelling question: Can a good company become a great company, and if so, how? Collins and his team of assistants searched for companies that made a "leap to greatness," as defined by stock market performance and long-term success; they found 11 companies that met their criteria and spent more than 10 years studying what made them great. Following that, and acknowledging the growing interest in his book by nonbusiness entities, 4 years later, he published a monograph entitled *Good to Great and the Social Sectors*,[58] concerning how his lessons could be modified to fit government agencies. Certainly, much of the success of great police organizations has to do with their leadership.

Collins coined the term *Level 5 leader* to describe the highest level of executive capabilities (Levels 1 through 4 are highly capable individual, contributing team member, competent manager, and effective leader, respectively). Level 5 leaders are ambitious, but their ambition is directed first and foremost to the organization and its success, not to personal renown. Level 5 leaders, Collins stressed, are "fanatically driven, infected with an incurable need to produce results."[59]

Such leaders, Collins found, do not exhibit enormous egos; instead, they are self-effacing, quiet, reserved, even shy. Perhaps this has to do with the nature of their organizations. Unlike business executives, police leaders have to answer to the public; unions and civil service systems further inhibit their power, therefore, Level 5 leadership in a police organization may involve a greater degree of legislative-type skills—relying heavily on persuasion, political currency, and shared interests to create the conditions for the right decisions to happen.[60]

Collins also likes to use a bus metaphor when talking about igniting the transformation from good to great:

> The executives who ignited the transformations . . . did not first figure out where to drive the bus and then get people to take it there. No, they *first* got the right people on the bus (and the wrong people off the bus) and *then* figured out where to drive it. (emphasis in the original)[61]

In fact, Collins wrote, "The main point is not about assembling the right team—that's nothing new." Rather, the main point is that great leaders assemble their teams *before* they decide where to go. The executive who hires the right people does not need to waste time looking for ways to manage and motivate them; the right people will be self-motivated. Good-to-great organizations, Collins found, also have a "culture of discipline" in which employees show extreme diligence and intensity in their thoughts and actions, always focusing on implementing the organization's mission, purpose, and goals.[62]

People are not an organization's most important asset; rather, the *right* people are. When police executives are appointed or promoted, they inherit nearly all of their personnel, including poor performers who are unenthusiastic about the organization's vision and philosophy. Some of these people may be near retirement (about ready to "get off the bus"). Collins states that picking the right people and getting the wrong people off the bus are critical: "By whatever means possible, personnel problems have to be confronted in an organization that aspires to greatness."[63]

This is why performance evaluations are so critical. Unfortunately, however, many police departments still have not created evaluation tools that adequately reflect the work police do. The tendency is to measure what is easy to measure: orderliness (neatness, attendance, punctuality) and conformity to organizational rules and regulations. A consultant to a Texas police agency asked how employees could be expected to act like supervisors, managers, and leaders when everyone in the organization was evaluated by an instrument that was "designed to control a 20-year-old, high-testosterone male who was armed with a gun and given a fast car to drive."[64] Until police agencies invest in valid and reliable instruments for measuring the real work of policing, it will remain very difficult to move the nonperformers out of the organization.

As an illustration, when William Bratton became Police Commissioner of the New York City, he decided that he had to reach down at least two generations to get leaders who were motivated to improve the organization. Overnight, he wiped out several generations of command staff, which was unheard of in New York. He promoted Jack Maple, then a lieutenant in the Transit Police, to Deputy Commissioner for Crime Control; Maple designed CompStat (see Chapter 16). The message from a Level 5 leader is clear: It is no longer business as usual.

Perhaps the most difficult part of achieving greatness is *sustaining* that greatness. Police chiefs have notoriously short tenure in office, therefore, in their world, some of Collins' principles may be particularly important—e.g., finding Level 5 leaders who pay close attention to preparing for the next generation of leaders, giving managers authority to make key decisions, sending them to leadership academies and conferences, and encouraging them to think on their own and ask questions. This process is termed *succession planning*. This major aspect of police leadership and motivation is discussed more fully in Chapter 5.

▶ Agency Accreditation

In 1979, the **accreditation** of police agencies began slowly with the creation of the Commission on Accreditation for Law Enforcement Agencies (CALEA), located in Fairfax, Virginia. CALEA is a nonprofit organization that has developed and administers

accreditation a voluntary effort by a criminal justice agency where it seeks to meet national standards in its field and thus be officially designated as accredited

459 voluntary standards for law enforcement agencies to meet. These standards cover the role and responsibilities of the agency; its organization and administration; law enforcement, traffic, and operational support; prisoner- and court-related services; and auxiliary and technical services. Accreditation, a voluntary process, is quite expensive, both in dollars and in human resources; it often takes 12–18 months for an agency to prepare for the assessment.[65] Today, there are nearly 600 agencies accredited or recognized in one of the Commission's various programs, with several hundred others working toward their first award.[66]

Once an agency believes it is ready to be accredited, an application is filed and the agency receives a self-evaluation questionnaire to determine its current status. If the self-evaluation indicates that the agency is ready to attempt accreditation, an on-site team appointed by CALEA conducts an assessment and writes a report on its findings. After becoming accredited, the agency must apply for reaccreditation after 5 years.[67]

Several unanticipated consequences of the accreditation process have emerged. First, a number of states have formed coalitions to assist police agencies in the process of accreditation. Second, some departments report decreased insurance costs as a result of accreditation. Finally, the accreditation self-assessment process provides many opportunities to institutionalize community policing. Not only do the accreditation standards help to weave community policing into an agency's internal fabric, but they also provide a way to integrate such objectives into external service delivery, such as:

* enhancing the role and authority of patrol officers,
* improving analysis and information management, and
* managing CFS.[68]

In comparing accredited and nonaccredited police agencies, Kimberly A. McCabe and Robin G. Fajardo found that accredited police agencies (1) provided more training for their officers and required higher minimum educational requirements for new officers, (2) were nearly twice as likely to require drug testing for sworn applicants, and (3) were more likely to operate special units for the enforcement of drug laws and laws against child abuse.[69]

Summary

This chapter explored the importance and elements of police organizational structure, including the bureaucratic nature of such organizations; division of labor; and the policies, procedures, rules, and regulations that are a part of such organizations. Included was an examination of the current era and the organizational paradigm of policing, community-oriented policing, and problem solving. In considering this topic, we examined two related aspects of its crime prevention function: crime prevention through environmental design and situational crime prevention. We also considered how a police organization may become great rather than merely being good, and in a related vein, we looked

at how police agencies become accredited and the benefits of doing so.

Perhaps what was most clearly demonstrated in this chapter is the extent to which modern policing is changing, and how its organizational elements must also be viewed as fluid in nature and must be modified in order to adapt to and provide the foundation for today's demands on the police.

Clearly, the traditional reactive, unilateral approach to addressing crime and disorder is not suited for today's police organization and administration. The manner in which the organization remains fluid as needs arise and its structures and functions are of paramount concern to police administrators.

Key Terms and Concepts

Accreditation 99

COPPS 87

Division of labor *80*

Federalization *93*

Intelligence-led policing *95*

Militarization *93*

Military model *85*

Organizational structure *80*

Policies *86*

Predictive policing *98*

Procedures *86*

Rules and regulations *86*

S.A.R.A. *87*

Smart policing *94*

Questions for Review

1. What is an organization, and how does a typical police agency constitute an organization? What are the key components of a basic police organizational structure, and how would it look if graphically illustrated?

2. What is a bureaucracy, and which aspects of police organizations make them bureaucracies?

3. What are the definitions of a policy, a procedure, and rules and regulations? Why are they necessary in police agencies? What are their relationship and role vis-à-vis police discretion?

4. What is meant by *community-oriented policing and problem solving,* and what are the components of the problem-solving process?

5. What major changes have occurred in police organization and operation since 9/11, particularly in the areas of mission, emphasis, and economies?

6. What do some observers point to so as to justify claims that since 9/11 the police have become too federalized and militarized?

7. How are smart policing, intelligence-led policing, and predictive policing being applied toward crime fighting?

8. What is needed to transform a good police organization into a great one?

9. How does a police organization become accredited, and what are the benefits of doing so?

Deliberate and Decide

Changing Agency Organization and Culture

Your local police department is in a rapidly growing city of close to 250,000 residents, lying 30 miles to the east of a large Midwestern city. With 350 officers and another 120 civilians, the department is among the largest in the region and was once viewed as the premier law enforcement agency in the state. At the beginning of the 2000s, the city began undergoing major changes in its local government, including the appointment of a new, reform-minded city manager, and greater openness and emphasis on accountability on the part of its city council. These changes, however, also brought to light many problems that existed in the local police department.

The former police chief—who was promoted from within—sought to meet these challenges in the early 2000s but left behind a complicated legacy. On the one hand, she was able to revamp the agency's technologies, modernizing the communications and budgeting systems; however, she refused to lay the foundation for community policing and problem solving. Officers thus have little dialogue with citizens outside of individual calls for service, and there is not much in the way of an informative departmental website; a recent university survey found that while 65 percent of white citizens rated the agency's performance in a positive manner, "fair" or "poor" ratings were given by 54 percent of African Americans and 31 percent of Latinos.

Retiring officers often tell the Human Resources office that the department has become too top-heavy and loosely administered, while lacking direction. Indeed, several problems indicate communications and accountability issues. Regarding agency operations, some in the city also worry that the department has become overly specialized, with far too many persons out of patrol and working in various types of offices, in investigations and special assignments. Furthermore, patrol beats are not divided in a meaningful fashion according to workload or demands for service, so while some officers are backlogged on calls during their shifts, others have little to do. The patrol lieutenants and sergeants have little inclination to change the aforementioned; nor do they appear to support officers engaged in problem-solving projects.

The basic problems, then, are that the department is loosely organized and has weak leaders, operating in an informal manner where employees see rules, policies, and procedures as an unnecessary infringement on their freedom, intelligence, and traditions. Many of these problems may be traced to the department's long-established philosophy of management, which is one of "high trust, low control." Indeed, about half of the agency's middle managers and first-line supervisors are nearing retirement and appear to be "retired on the job." The policies and procedures manual has not been revised for 20 years; no one even knows what the department's disciplinary process consists of. Finally, while the department's mandatory recruit training meets state standards, its in-service training programs are poor and more than one-third of the force is close to being out of compliance with state training requirements.

The police union membership voted "no confidence" in the former police chief, indicating its frustration with the agency's lack of direction. The city manager is trying to decide whether to open up the search for the chief's position to outside applicants or to promote again from within. In the latter case, there appears to be a dearth of qualified people to promote up to the first-line supervisor and middle manager ranks, much less the chief's position.

Questions for Discussion

1. What are the major issues that exist within this department?
2. What needs to be done to move the agency from where it is to where it can become a "great" organization?
3. What changes in the agency's organization seem warranted?
4. What must it do to become nationally accredited?[70]

Learn by Doing

1. Your chief law enforcement executive has become increasingly concerned about the potential for problems with employee dress and appearance, particularly with their wanting to sport beards and tattoos. You are directed to write a new policy that prohibits beards, arm or otherwise visible tattoos, and branding and intentional scarring on the face, head, neck, hands, and exposed arms and legs. Employees who already have tattoos are to be exempt. How will your policy read?

2. A new low-income housing development in your community consists of 58 apartments and has become a popular hangout for selling drugs, drinking liquor, and intimidating residents until early morning hours. Gunshots are an occasional occurrence, with 5–10 calls for service in every 24-hour period. Criminals hide guns in the thick overgrowth around the complex, and when approached, they flee through a large open field behind the complex. An adjacent convenience store has become a problem as well, particularly as a magnet for drug dealers. A nearby drug house also contributes to the problem, and a T-shaped alley behind the store provides easy ingress and egress for buyers, both on foot and in vehicles. The lighting is poor (with people frequently shooting out street lights), and pay telephones in the store's front are used constantly by traffickers. Street people in the area also engage in theft-, drug-, prostitution-, and vandalism-related activities. Additionally, these people sleep on private property; defecate and urinate on public streets; and engage in public drunkenness, graffiti, and littering. You are assigned to launch a problem-oriented policing (POP)/SARA initiative at the location to effect long-term results. What kinds of information would you collect concerning the area and its drug problem? What kinds of responses might be considered? What type of assessment would you perform?

3. Your chief executive has assigned you, as head of the agency's research, planning, and analysis unit, the task of developing a comprehensive report containing recommendations for establishing intelligence-led policing. Explain what your report would contain.

Notes

1. Bureau of Justice Statistics, *Justice Expenditure and Employment Extracts, 2010—Preliminary* (July 1, 2013, Tables 4 and 5), http://www.bjs.gov/index.cfm?ty=pbdetail&iid=4679 (accessed October 18, 2014).
2. Wayne W. Bennett and Karen M. Hess, *Management and Supervision in Law Enforcement*, 4th ed. (Belmont, CA: Wadsworth, 2004), p. 2.
3. *The Republic of Plato*, trans. Allen Bloom (New York: Basic Books, 1968), p. 7.
4. Luther Gulick and L. Urwick (eds.), *Papers on the Science of Administration* (New York: Augustus M. Kelley, 1969).
5. Charles R. Swanson, Leonard Territo, and Robert W. Taylor, *Police Administration: Structures, Processes, and Behavior*, 6th ed. (Upper Saddle River, NJ: Prentice Hall, 2005), pp. 232–233.

6. Ibid., p. 233.

7. Henry Mintzberg, *The Structure of Organizations* (Upper Saddle River, NJ: Prentice Hall, 1979), p. 253.

8. Edward R. Maguire, Heunhee Shin, Zihong Zhao, and Kimberly D. Hassell, "Structural Change in Large Police Agencies during the 1990s," *Policing: An International Journal of Police Strategies & Management* 26(2) (2003):251–275.

9. Ibid., p. 255.

10. Ibid., p. 259.

11. Ibid., p. 261.

12. Ibid., pp. 266–267.

13. Ibid., pp. 268–270.

14. Portland, Oregon, population statistics from Metro Regional Government, http://library.oregonmetro.gov/files//msa_popdata1990_2010.pdf (accessed August 1, 2014).

15. "Portland Police Bureau Statistical Report 2012," http://www.portlandoregon.gov/police/article/454721 (accessed August1, 2014), p. 10.

16. In the Portland Police Bureau (PPB) organizational structure shown in Figure 4.2, the Sunshine Division includes personnel who work to provide food, clothing, and toys to needy families, and WomenStrength/GirlsStrength is a program that teaches women and girls self-defense tactics.

17. President's Commission on Law Enforcement and Administration of Justice, *Task Force Report: The Police* (Washington, DC: U.S. Government Printing Office, 1967), p. 46.

18. See, for example, Egon Bittner, "The Quasi-Military Organization of the Police," in Victor Kappeler (ed.), *Police and Society: Touchstone Readings*, 2nd ed. (Long Grove, IL: Waveland, 2003), pp. 170–181.

19. Ibid.

20. Thomas J. Cowper, "The Myth of the 'Military Model' of Leadership in Law Enforcement," in Quint C. Thurman and Jihong Zhao (eds.), *Contemporary Policing: Controversies, Challenges, and Solutions* (Los Angeles, CA: Roxbury, 2004), pp. 113–125.

21. Samuel Walker and Charles M. Katz, *The Police in America*, 5th ed. (Columbus, OH: McGraw-Hill, 2005).

22. John Murray, "Developing the 'Right' Police for Community Policing," *Platypus Magazine* 74 (March 2002): 7–13.

23. Robert Sheehan and Gary W. Cordner, *Introduction to Police Administration*, 2nd ed. (Cincinnati, OH: Anderson, 1989), pp. 446–447.

24. Ibid., p. 449.

25. Ibid.

26. 471 U.S. 1 (1985).

27. O. W. Wilson and Roy C. McLaren, *Police Administration*, 3rd ed. (New York: McGraw-Hill, 1972), p. 79.

28. Raymond O. Loen, *Manage More by Doing Less* (New York: McGraw-Hill, 1971), pp. 86–89.

29. Thomas Reddin, "Are You Oriented to Hold Them? A Searching Look at Police Management," *The Police Chief* (March 1966): 17.

30. California Department of Justice, *COPPS: Community-Oriented Policing and Problem Solving. Office of the Attorney General, Crime Violence Prevention Center* (Sacramento, CA: Author, 1995).

31. Maguire et al., "Structural Change in Large Police Agencies during the 1990s," pp. 254–255.

32. Ibid., p. 270.

33. Ibid., p. 271.

34. Ibid., p. 272.

35. For a fundamental view of community-oriented policing and problem solving, see, for example, Herman Goldstein, *Problem-Oriented Policing* (New York: McGraw-Hill, 1990); Kenneth J. Peak and Ronald W. Glensor, *Community Policing and Problem Solving: Strategies and Practices*, 6th ed. (Upper Saddle River, NJ: Prentice Hall, 2012); and Robert Trojanowicz and Bonnie Bucqueroux, *Community Policing: A Contemporary Perspective* (Cincinnati, OH: Anderson, 1990). Also note that each year, the National Institute of Justice, U.S. Department of Justice, publishes the *Best Practices in Problem-Oriented Policing: Winners of the Herman Goldstein Award for Excellence in Problem-Oriented Policing.*

36. MoonSun Kim and Melchor de Guzman, "Police Paradigm Shift: The Impact of the 911 Attack on Police Practices among United States Municipal Police Departments," *Criminal Justice Studies: A Critical Journal of Crime, Law and Society* 25(4) (2012): 323–342.

37. Ibid.

38. Ibid.

39. Bernard K. Melekian, "Policing in the New Economy: A New Report on the Emerging Trends from the Office of Community Oriented Policing Services," *The Police Chief* 79 (January 2012): 16–19, http://www.policechiefmagazine.org/magazine/index.cfm?fuseaction=display_arch&article_id=2576&issue_id=12012 (accessed March 18, 2014).

40. Ibid.

41. Ibid.

42. Major Cities Chiefs Association, "Police Economic Challenges Survey Results" (unpublished survey, Sun Valley, Idaho, 2011).

43. Melekian, "Policing in the New Economy," p. 1.

44. Ibid.

45. American Bar Association, *Task Force on the Federalization of Criminal Law 1998* (Washington, DC: Author, 1998), http://www.americanbar.org/content/dam/aba/publications/criminaljustice/Federalization_of_Criminal_Law.authcheckdam.pdf (accessed March 18, 2014); also see Samson Habte, "Guest Speaker Warns of Dangers of Federalization of Criminal Law," *Virginia Law Weekly* (March 21, 2008), http://www.lawweekly.org/?module=displaystory&story_id=2004&edition_id=86&format=html (accessed March 18, 2014).

46. Peter B. Kraska, "Militarization and Policing: Its Relevance to 21st Century Police," *Policing* 1(4): 501–513.

47. Information concerning the origins and initial grant funded test sites for SPI was obtained from the following sources: James R. Coldren Jr., Alissa Huntoon, and Michael Medaris, "Introducing Smart Policing: Foundations, Principles, and Practice," *Police Quarterly* 16(3) (September 2014): 275–286; and Nola M. Joyce, Charles H. Ramsey, and James K. Stewart, "Commentary on Smart Policing," *Police Quarterly* 16(3) (September 2014): 358–368. This special issue of

Police Quarterly contains a number of other, site-specific articles that discuss SPI.

48. Adapted from: U.S. Department of Justice, Bureau of Justice Assistance, *Los Angeles, California Smart Policing Initiative Reducing Gun-Related Violence through Operation LASER*, October 2012, p. 2, http://www.smartpolicinginitiative.com/sites/all/files/spotlights/LA%20Site%20Spotlight%20FINAL%202012.pdf (accessed August 21, 2014).

49. U.S. Department of Justice, Office of Justice Programs, Bureau of Justice Statistics, *Intelligence-Led Policing: The New Intelligence Architecture* (Washington, DC: Author, 2005), p. 9.

50. Ibid., p. 3.

51. See U.S. Department of Justice, Office of Justice Programs, *National Criminal Intelligence Sharing Plan*, p. 6; www.fas.org/irp/agency/doj/ncisp.pdf (accessed March 5, 2014).

52. Ibid., pp. 12–13.

53. Ibid., pp. 10–11.

54. U.S. Department of Justice, National Institute of Justice, "Predictive Policing Symposium: The Future of Prediction in Criminal Justice," http://www.nij.gov/topics/law-enforcement/strategies/predictive-policing/symposium/future.htm (accessed March 5, 2014).

55. Ellen Perlman, "Policing by the Odds," *Governing*, December 1, 2008, www.governing.com/article/policing-odds (accessed March 5, 2014).

56. Ibid.

57. Jim Collins, *Good to Great and the Social Sectors: A Monograph to Accompany Good to Great* (New York: HarperCollins, 2005).

58. Ibid.

59. Chuck Wexler, Mary Ann Wycoff, and Craig Fischer, *Good to Great: Application of Business Management Principles in the Public Sector* (Washington, DC: Office of Community Oriented Policing Services and the Police Executive Research Forum, 2007), p. 5.

60. Ibid., p. 7.

61. Ibid., p. 6.

62. Ibid.

63. Ibid., p. 22.

64. Ibid., p. 24.

65. Steven M. Cox, *Police: Practices, Perspectives, Problems* (Boston, MA: Allyn & Bacon, 1996), p. 90.

66. CALEA, personal communication, October 25, 2006; also see the CALEA website, http://www.calea.org.

67. Cox, *Police: Practices, Perspectives, Problems*, p. 90.

68. Fulton County, Georgia, Sheriff's Office, "CALEA Law Enforcement Accreditation," p. 2.

69. Kimberly A. McCabe and Robin G. Fajardo, "Law Enforcement Accreditation: A National Comparison of Accredited versus Nonaccredited Agencies," *Journal of Criminal Justice* 29 (2001):127–131.

70. This case study is loosely adapted from David Thatcher, National COPS Evaluation Organizational Change Case Study: Riverside, California, Program in Criminal Justice Policy and Management, John F. Kennedy School of Government, Harvard University, https://www.ncjrs.gov/nij/cops_casestudy/riversid.html (accessed August 23, 2014). Case Study Prepared for the Urban Institute.

The police
are the public
and the public
are the police.
—*Robert Peel*

Washoe County Sheriff's Office

5 Police Personnel Roles and Functions

LEARNING OBJECTIVES

After reading this chapter, the student will be able to:

1 *describe each of Mintzberg's three main roles of the chief executive officer (CEO)*

2 *review the kinds of activities that can be included in an assessment center to obtain the most capable chief executive, as well as the skills the executive must possess*

3 *explain some of Machiavelli's tenets and how they might be applied by today's police administrators*

4 *review the duties and qualifications (including interviewing and psychological testing) for chiefs of police, and their job status in the political arena*

5 *define the duties performed by the sheriff's office*

6 *review the tasks performed by middle managers (captains and lieutenants)*

7 *describe the roles and tasks of a first-line supervisor (patrol sergeant)*

8 *relate the tasks of patrol officers and name the 12 qualities imperative for entry-level officers*

9 *describe some innovative strategies for recruiting and hiring the best police personnel, as well as training them after the academy under the field training officer (FTO) and police training officer (PTO) concepts*

10 *review the roles and functions performed by all leadership personnel in COPPS*

▶ Introduction

Some of the most important and challenging positions in our society are those of a police administrator, manager, or supervisor. This chapter examines the roles and functions of law enforcement chief executives (chiefs of police and county sheriffs), middle managers (typically including captains and lieutenants), first-line supervisors (sergeants), and patrol officers.

First, we examine, in general terms, the roles of law enforcement executives, adapting Mintzberg's model of chief executive officers to policing in order to better understand what roles police executives play and what they actually do. Next, we review other aspects of police administration, including the use of the assessment center process to hire chief executives and the "Ten Commandments" of good police leadership. We then consider what might be Machiavelli's advice for contemporary police executives, some protocols for interviewing and testing police chief candidates, and chiefs in the political arena.

Next, we explore more specifically the functions of chiefs of police and sheriffs, and then consider the roles and functions of middle managers (captains and lieutenants), supervisors (sergeants), and patrol officers. Regarding the latter, we will consider the traits that executives should look for and methods used when trying to hire quality personnel and a new training model that has been developed to assist new recruits as they make the transition from the academy to the street. We then look at the roles of each of these four levels under the community-oriented policing and problem-solving strategy. The chapter concludes with review questions, "deliberate and decide" problems, and "learn by doing" exercises.

▶ Roles of the Police Executive: The Mintzberg Model for CEOs

> **chief executive officer (CEO)** the highest-ranking executive or administrator in an organization, who is in charge of its overall operation.

A **chief executive officer (CEO)**, as the highest-ranking executive or administrator in charge of the organization's overall operation, fills many roles. Henry Mintzberg[1] described a model that serves to delineate and define those roles. And, while the **Mintzberg model for CEOs** could therefore be applied to courts and corrections administrators as well as to the police, it is most easily applied and understood when used with the latter; therefore, following is an examination of the three primary roles of the police chief executive—the chief of police or sheriff—according to Mintzberg: the interpersonal, the informational, and the decision-maker roles.

> **Mintzberg model for CEOs** a model that delineates and defines the primary roles of a chief executive officer.

The Interpersonal Role

The *interpersonal* role has three components: (1) the figurehead, (2) leadership, and (3) liaison duties.

In the figurehead role, the CEO performs various ceremonial functions. He or she rides in parades and attends civic events; speaks to school and university classes and civic organizations; meets visiting officials and dignitaries; attends academy graduations, swearing-in ceremonies, and certain weddings and funerals; and visits injured officers. Like a city's mayor, whose public responsibilities include cutting ribbons and kissing babies, the police CEO performs these duties simply because of his or her title and position within the organization. Although the chiefs or sheriffs are not expected to attend the grand opening of every retail or commercial business and other such events to which they are invited, they are certainly obligated from a professional standpoint to attend many civic functions and ceremonies.

The leadership role requires the CEO to motivate and coordinate workers while achieving the mission, goals, and needs within the department and the community. A chief or sheriff may have to urge the governing board to enact a code or ordinance that, whether or not popular, is in the best interest of the jurisdiction. For example, a chief in a western state recently led a drive to pass an ordinance that prohibited parking by university students in residential neighborhoods surrounding the campus. This was a highly unpopular undertaking, but the chief was prompted by the complaints of hardships suffered by the area residents. The CEO also may provide leadership by taking stands on bond issues (seeking funds to hire more officers or build new buildings, for example) and by advising the governing body on the effects of proposed ordinances.

The liaison role is undertaken when the CEO of a police organization interacts with other organizations and coordinates work assignments. It is not uncommon for executives from a geographical area—the police chief, sheriff, ranking officer of the local highway patrol office, district attorney, campus police chief, and so on—to meet informally each month to discuss common problems and strategies. The chief executive also serves as liaison to regional law enforcement councils, narcotics units, crime labs, dispatching centers, and so on. He or she also meets with the representatives of the courts, the juvenile system, and other criminal justice agencies.

The Informational Role

Another role identified by Mintzberg's model is the *informational* one. In this capacity, the CEO engages in tasks relating to (1) monitoring/inspecting, (2) dissemination, and (3) spokesperson duties.

In the monitoring/inspecting function, the CEO constantly reviews the department's operations to ensure that it is operating smoothly (or as smoothly as police operations can be expected to be). This function is often referred to as "roaming the ship"; many CEOs who isolated themselves from their personnel and the daily operations of the agency can speak from sad experience of the need to be involved and present. Many police executives use daily staff meetings to acquire information about their jurisdictions, especially criminal and other activities during the previous 24 hours.

Dissemination tasks involve distributing information to members of the department via memoranda, special orders, general orders, and policies and procedures as described in Chapter 3. The spokesperson function is related to the dissemination task but is focused more on providing information to the news media. This is a difficult task for the chief executive; news organizations, especially television and the print media, are competitive businesses that seek to obtain the most complete news in the shortest amount of time, which often translates into wider viewership and therefore greater advertising revenues for them. From one perspective, the media must appreciate that a criminal investigation can be seriously compromised by premature or excessive coverage. From the other perspective, the public has a right to know what is occurring in the community, especially matters relating to crime; therefore, the prudent police executive attempts to have an open and professional relationship with the media in which each side knows and understands its responsibilities. The prudent chief executive also remembers the power of the media and does not alienate them; as an old saying goes, "Never argue with someone who buys his ink by the barrel." Unfortunately, many police executives (a good number of whom left office involuntarily) can speak of the results of failing to develop an appropriate relationship with the media.

An example of the good–bad relationship that often exists between the police and the media is the Washington, DC-area "Beltway sniper" investigation of late 2002. Although Montgomery County, Maryland, Police Chief Charles Moose was at times very frustrated by leaks of confidential information to the media, he also used the media to communicate with the snipers, who eventually were captured after the suspects' photographs and a vehicle description were broadcast.

The Decision-Maker Role

In the decision-maker role, the CEO of a police organization serves as (1) an entrepreneur, (2) a disturbance handler, (3) a resource allocator, and (4) a negotiator.

In the capacity of entrepreneur, the CEO must sell ideas to the members of the governing board or the department—perhaps helping them to understand a new computer or communications system, the implementation of a policing strategy, or different work methods, all of which are intended to improve the organization. Sometimes roles blend, as when several police executives band together (in their entrepreneurial and liaison functions) to lobby the state attorney general and the legislature for new crime-fighting laws.

As a disturbance handler, the executive's tasks range from resolving minor disputes between staff members to dealing with major events, such as riots, continued muggings in a local park, or the cleanup of the downtown area. Sometimes, the executive must solve intradepartmental disputes, which can reach major proportions. For example, the executive must intervene when friction develops between different units, as when the patrol commanders' instruction to street officers to increase arrests for public drunkenness causes a strain on the resources of the jail division's commander.

As a resource allocator, the CEO must clearly understand the agency's budget and its priorities. The resource allocator must consider requests for funds from various groups. Personnel, for example, will ask for higher salaries, additional officers, and better equipment. Citizens may complain about speeding motorists in a specific area, which would require the allocation of additional resources to that neighborhood. In the resource allocator role, the CEO must be able to prioritize requests and to defend his or her choices.

As a negotiator, the CEO resolves employee grievances and, through an appointed representative at the bargaining table, tries to represent the best interests of both the city and labor during collective bargaining. In this role, the CEO must consider the rank and file's request for raises and increased benefits as part of budget administration. If funds available to the jurisdiction are limited, the CEO must negotiate with the collective bargaining unit to reach an agreement. At times, contract negotiations reach an impasse or a deadlock.

I will elaborate on some of these chief executive functions later in the chapter; labor relations—including unionism and collective bargaining—are discussed more fully in Chapter 14.

▶ Law Enforcement Executives, Generally

Prior to examining the role and functions of contemporary police executives, I consider how such persons are selected for these positions. Given the responsibilities placed on those who occupy such positions, the means employed to test applicants for or to promote individuals to them becomes important.

Obtaining the Best: The Assessment Center

To obtain the most capable people for chief executive positions (and also for middle-management and even supervisory positions) in policing, the **assessment center** method has proved to be an efficacious means of hiring and promoting personnel. (*Note:* Sheriffs are normally elected, not hired or promoted into their position; thus, the assessment center is of little use for that position.) The assessment center method is now increasingly utilized to select people for all management or supervisory ranks. The process may include interviews; psychological tests; in-basket exercises; management tasks; group discussions; role-playing exercises, such as simulations of interviews with subordinates, the public, and news media; fact-finding exercises; oral presentation exercises; and written communications exercises.[2]

The first step is to identify behaviors important to successful performance in the position. Job descriptions listing responsibilities and skills should exist for all executive, middle management, and supervisory positions (such as chief, captain, lieutenant, sergeant, and so on). Then, each candidate's abilities and skill levels should be evaluated using several of the techniques mentioned.

Individual and group role playing are valuable hands-on exercises during the selection process. Candidates may be required to help solve simulated police–community problems (they conduct a "meeting" to hear the concerns of local minority groups), to react to a major incident (explaining what they would do and in what order in a simulated shooting or riot situation), to hold a news briefing, or to participate in other such exercises. They may be given an in-basket situation in which they receive an abundance of paperwork, policies, and problems to be prioritized and dealt with in a prescribed amount of time. Writing abilities may also be evaluated: Candidates may be given 30 minutes to develop a use-of-force policy for a hypothetical or real police agency. This type of exercise not only demonstrates candidates' written communications skills and understanding of the technical side of police work but also shows how they think cognitively and build a case.

During each exercise, several assessors or raters analyze each candidate's performance and record some type of evaluation; when the assessment center process ends, each rater submits his or her rating information to the person making the hiring or promotion decision. Typically selected because they have held the position for which candidates are now vying, assessors must not only know the types of problems and duties incumbent in the position but also should be keen observers of human behavior.

Assessment center procedures are logistically more difficult to conduct, as well as more labor-intensive and costly, than traditional interviews, but they are well worth the extra investment. Monies invested at the early stages of a hiring or promotional process can help avoid selecting the wrong person and can prevent untold problems for years to come. Good executives, middle managers, and supervisors make fewer mistakes and are probably sued less often.

> **assessment center**
> a process used for promoting and hiring personnel that may include oral interviews, psychological tests, group and in-basket exercises, and writing and role-playing exercises.

Skills of Good Managers

To expand on the discussion of leadership skills in Chapter 2, note the basic management skills that the police executive must develop. First is *technical skill,* which involves specialized knowledge, analytical ability, and facility in the use of the tools and techniques of the specific discipline. This is the skill most easily trained for. Examples in policing include budgeting, computer use, and fundamental knowledge of some specialized equipment, such as radar or breathalyzer machines.

Second is *human skill,* which is the executive's ability to work effectively as a group member and build cooperation; this includes being sensitive to the needs and feelings of others, tolerating ambiguity, and being able to empathize with persons with different views and those from different cultures.

Last is *conceptual skill*, which involves coordinating and integrating all the activities and interests of the organization in pursuit of a common objective; in other words, being able to translate knowledge into action.[3]

These skills can be taught, just as other skills can, which proves that good administrators are not simply born. They can be trained in the classroom and by practicing the skills on the job.

The "Ten Commandments"

Following is an adaptation of the "Ten Commandments" of being a police executive—rules of personal and professional conduct that are vital to one's success—developed by Jurkanin et al.[4]

1. *Practice what you preach:* You must lead by example, remembering that actions speak louder than words. The chief executive must be a person of morality, integrity, and honor.

2. *A day's pay for a day-and-a-half of work:* The chief must put in long hours to accomplish all that needs to be done, at the expense of personal freedom. Staff meetings, phone conversations, luncheon meetings, press conferences, interviews, report reading, and labor negotiations all take place during the day, leaving the evenings for writing letters and reports; reviewing budgets; reading professional journals; attending governing board meetings; and meeting with civic, church, or other groups.

3. *Maintain and promote integrity:* See the First Commandment.

4. *Develop a positive image:* The chief executive is also responsible for the morale of the employees; although law enforcement can be filled with bad news, disappointment, and failures, the chief must work to accentuate the positive. Recognition of employees' contributions and valiant actions is one way to do so, with awards ceremonies, memorandums, and so forth.

5. *Remain committed:* The chief must be committed to implementing the agency's goals, mission, and values; this might mean taking risks, which can have its dangers.

   Failure must be faced immediately, and one must learn from mistakes. The chief executive can normally weather the storm by taking responsibility and being responsive.

6. *Be respectful:* Be prepared to stand up for employees who have performed admirably well while being fair, firm, concerned, and sincere. When possible, criticize in private and praise in public. Remember that there will always be some people who will vigorously oppose your views. Do not compromise yourself to try to obtain everyone's support.

7. *Accept assistance from others:* This will build a teamwork approach, although the chief remains the final authority in the agency. Two (or more) heads are always better than one. The chief also needs a confidante with whom to share thoughts, ideas, and concerns.

8. *Be eager for knowledge:* Stay abreast of technology, current events, topics that impact the community, and current management, leadership, and administration trends and issues. Be familiar with the history of the agency and the community to avoid repeating past mistakes. Know the financial aspects of the jurisdiction. Employ both formal (workshops) and informal (networking with other executives) means of training and education. Encourage employees to do likewise.

9. *Maintain a healthy lifestyle:* One who is physically fit is better able to perform and react to demands of the position. Obviously, wise choices in diet, exercise, annual checkups, and avoidance of all things harmful to one's health are keys to healthy living.

10. *Set personal goals:* Having reached the helm, one should still review short-, medium-, and long-term objectives and skills that need development, to assist in establishing a future direction for oneself as well as for the organization. Along with career goals, personal goals should be examined.

▶ Machiavelli's Just Deserts and Advice

Appendix II of this textbook contains advice to a leader—"The Prince"—as offered in the 1500s by Italian philosopher Niccolo Machiavelli, to whom history has not been kind. Although his writings are widely read in college and university administration and management courses, he is nevertheless widely known and criticized for a statement he never wrote: "The end justifies the means." [Nor did he suggest that being brutal and cunning were intrinsically good; rather, he meant that when there are no other acceptable standards, that "In the actions of all men, and especially of princes, where there is no court of appeal, one judges by the result. So let a prince set about the task of conquering and maintaining his state; his methods will always be judged honorable and will be universally praised. The common people are always impressed by appearances and results."[5]]

However, his views of leadership nearly 500 years ago can be very instructive for today's police chief executives. Machiavelli focused on those who have a newly acquired leadership role, and (for current purposes) both promoted from within their agency as well as hired from without. This is particularly apropos today, when job tenure for police chief executives is typically quite brief.

In fact, much depends on whether the chief was promoted from within the agency or brought in from without. If promoted up the ranks—the chief "inherited the kingdom"—in rather easy, uncontested fashion, Machiavelli would likely advise the leader to merely avoid stupid mistakes. In such cases, unless the organization is in shambles and its people are in upheaval, being the leader is relatively easy, and to go about initiating radical or unpopular policy changes would be unwise. The leader should remember the organization's culture and traditions, and focus on keeping the organization on a well-run, status-quo basis, and not attempt to fix what is not broken. Any substantive changes being considered (such as the implementation of problem-solving, smart policing, and acquisition of new technologies) should have been raised and approved during the interviews for the position.

Assume, on the other hand, the chief executive had to compete with others for the position—perhaps insiders who were more highly qualified, and was brought in from outside the organization where the previous agency's culture, geography, crime rates, agency size and structure, and everything else were different. Here, a different tact is required, and the chief executive may have to adapt. The first order of business, per Machiavelli, would be to build alliances. Learn who has been doing well under the previous "order" or leadership, and will thus be wary of the new regime; also learn who was disgruntled or perhaps stifled under the old administration, and might expect to do better under the new one. There will be those who are both pleased and disgruntled; the new leader must forge alliances with people of both temperaments in order to gain their loyalty and legitimacy. Some people expecting to fare better under the new order will be disappointed and oppose everything. Still, the new leader should enjoy the benefits and opportunities that exist during this "honeymoon period" and use the good will of the employees and legislative figures to make sound changes.

Gaining support from the rank-and-file during this time will also be crucial; as Sanow[6] put it, "the priority is to gain the confidence and legitimacy from the worker bees." These people have important work to do, and they mostly just want to be allowed to do it. One way to gain the favor of the rank-and-file is to have, to the extent possible, an open-door/ good listener policy that allows access and input—both of which are of extreme importance (see the discussion of Generation Y in Chapter 2). Are the officers clamoring for four 10-hour work shifts per week? If so, attempt to obtain it for them. Did the previous chief hoard money to the extent of allowing such things as uniforms and training to go by the wayside? Again, if feasible and not wasteful, one might try to take an "early Christmas" approach and provide these essentials (the author has been in just such a position). Such changes can gain everlasting allies.

The command staff may be harder to win, but Machiavelli—a political realist—would argue that they too need to be on the side of, and loyal to the leader. Seek and listen to their opinions (suggestion box?). Where absolutely necessary, judiciously try to get the wrong people off of the bus, while moving others into the proper seats on the bus (a reference to the discussion in Chapter 4 of Jim Collins' moving a "good" organization to a "great" one). One must be able to say no and make the tough decisions—and to do so in quick fashion, rather than drag them out over time.

Machiavelli would argue, however, that the leader will be judged by his or her results—so yes, the means and ends are related, and the actions leading to the end result must be well thought out; therefore, in today's administrative climate, options must be discussed honestly with subordinates prior to major decisions being made. It is also wise to obtain a reputation of being willing to accept criticism and bad news (don't "kill the messenger").[7]

▶ Chiefs of Police

What do law enforcement executives do? In contrast to Mintzberg's rather sophisticated model described earlier, Ronald Lynch stated the primary tasks of these executives in simple terms:

> They listen, talk, write, confer, think, decide—about [personnel], money, materials, methods, facilities—in order to plan, organize, direct, coordinate, and control their research service, production, public relations, employee relations, and all other activities so that they may more effectively serve the citizens to whom they are responsible.[8]

Next, I look at what city officials and the community expect of police chiefs, as well as how individuals ascend to this position.

Expectations of Government and the Community

chief of police the title given to the top official in the chain of command of a municipal police department.

The **chief of police** (the title typically given to the top official in the chain of command of a municipal police department; can also be given the title of *commissioner* or *superintendent*) is generally considered to be one of the most influential and prestigious persons in local government. Indeed, people at this position often amass considerable power and influence in their jurisdiction. Mayors, city managers and administrators, members of the agency, labor organizations, citizens, special-interest groups, and the media all have differing role expectations of the chief of police that often conflict.

The mayor or city manager likely wants the chief of police to promote departmental efficiency, reduce crime, improve service, and so on. Others appreciate the chief who simply keeps morale high and citizens' complaints low.

ADMINISTRATIVE ADVICE FROM THE FIELD

Kenneth J. Peak

Name: Debora Black

Current Position/City/State: Police Chief, Glendale Police Department, Glendale, Arizona

College attended/academic major/degree(s): Bachelor of Science and Master in Public Administration, Arizona State University; Certificate in Legal Studies, Phoenix College; Senior Executives in State and Local Government Program, Kennedy School of Government at Harvard.

My primary duties and responsibilities in this position include: responsibility for leading all 540 sworn and civilian members of the department to achieve our mission of protecting the lives and property of the people we serve. Internal and external communications are incredibly important in my position. Administrative responsibilities also include planning, establishing policy, budget management, procurement, and managing complex radio communication and technology systems. Staffing and hiring are critical responsibilities, as well as maintaining high levels of accountability and integrity throughout the organization. Community outreach is essential to accomplishing our mission, so cultivating relationships and feedback mechanisms require continuous attention.

Personal attributes/characteristics that have proven to be most helpful to me in this position are: perseverance, creativity, and humility.

My three greatest challenges in this administrative role include: severe budget reductions spanning several years. Although public safety is considered an essential service provided by municipal government, the impact of the Great Recession has required organizational restructuring and realignment of existing staff to absorb additional duties as the employee base is reduced. The resulting instability and decline in employee morale has required contentious communication and the identification of non-monetary rewards to maintain employee engagement. Due to the ongoing nature of our reductions, retention of highly skilled workers has been an ongoing challenge.

Personal accomplishments during my administrative career about which I am most proud are: formalizing leadership development and mentoring programs within my organization, which has encouraged incredibly talented individuals to assume new roles and take on additional responsibility in the organization. Identifying creative solutions such as alternative funding sources, establishing new partnerships, and advancing technology efficiencies have been the cornerstone of my tenure as police chief. My goal of inspiring individual employees is to focus on service to others while connecting to our mission and values defines the organizational culture I am creating today and the leadership legacy I hope will remain long after I leave.

Advice for someone who is interested in occupying an administrative position such as mine would be: Know your individual strengths and those of your team; fill gaps as soon as you identify them. Develop people and invest in systems that support their work, not the other way around. Establish high expectations for individual and organizational excellence. Treat people with dignity and respect, and never stop growing.

The mayor also expects the chief to communicate with city management about police-related issues and to be part of the city management team; to communicate city management's policies to police personnel; to establish agency policies, goals, and objectives and put them in writing; to develop an administrative system for managing people, equipment, and the budget in a professional and businesslike manner; to set a good example, both personally and professionally; to administer disciplinary action consistently and fairly when required; and to select personnel whose performance will ably and professionally promote the organization's objectives.

Members of the agency also have expectations of the chief executive: to be their advocate, supporting them when necessary, and representing the agency's interests when dealing with judges and prosecutors who may be indifferent or hostile. Citizens tend to expect the chief of police to provide efficient and cost-effective police services while keeping crime and tax rates down (often an area of built-in conflict) and preventing corruption and illegal use of force. Special-interest groups expect the chief to advocate policy positions that they favor. For example, Mothers Against Drunk Driving (MADD) would desire strong anti-DUI measures by the police. Finally, the media expect the chief to cooperate fully with their efforts to obtain fast and complete information on crime.

Qualifications

Qualifications for the position of police chief vary widely, depending on the size of the agency and the region of the country. Small agencies, especially those in rural areas, may not have a minimum educational requirement for the job. In the early 1970s, the National Advisory Commission on Criminal Justice Standards and Goals surveyed police chiefs and their superiors to determine the essential qualities for the job.

Education was found to be an important consideration; today, many agencies require a college education along with several years of progressively responsible police management experience. A survey by the Police Executive Research Forum (PERF) of 358 police chiefs in jurisdictions of 50,000 or more residents found that chiefs were generally highly educated—87 percent held a bachelor's degree and 47 percent had a master's degree—and were more likely to be chosen from outside the agencies they headed, but they spent less than 5 years in the position.[9]

Police chief executives also need several important management skills. In 1998, the National Advisory Commission asked police chiefs and their superiors to rate, on a scale of 1 to 10, the importance of 14 desirable management skills. The ability to motivate and control personnel and to relate to the community was considered most important. A survey today would probably yield similar results.[10]

Many cities finding themselves in need of a police chief have to consider whether it would be better to promote someone from within the ranks or hire from outside (perhaps using the assessment center process described earlier). Although it is perhaps more economical and certainly less trouble to select a police chief from within the organization than to use an assessment center, both methods have advantages and disadvantages. One study of police chiefs promoted from within or hired from outside indicated only one significant difference in qualification: educational attainment. The outsiders were more highly educated. No differences were found with respect to other aspects of their background, attitudes, salary, tenure in their current position or in policing, the size of the agency or community, and their current budget.[11] Some states, however, have made it nearly impossible for an outsider to come in. California has mandated that the chief should be a graduate of its own Peace Officers Standards and Training (POST) academy; New Jersey and New York also encourage "homegrown" chiefs.[12] Exhibit 5.1 provides tips for interviewing a police chief.

EXHIBIT 5.1

HIRING THE BEST: THE POLICE CHIEF'S INTERVIEW

Whether for a large, medium, or small agency, the interviews conducted toward hiring a permanent police chief are among the most important roles of an outgoing chief or an assessment center/oral board. Given the many roles they occupy and the large impact they bring to bear on police employees' lives, the chief's interview should be conducted in a structured and thorough manner. It is an optimal time to determine if the applicant is the right fit and possesses the right values and abilities for the agency, and to impart the agency's mission, values, and expectations.

John Gray, who possesses 12 years as a police chief, recommends that the following sequence of questions be used for these purposes.[13]

The first phase might begin by saying something other than "Tell me about you." Rather, say, "I have your application and resume. So, tell me in about two minutes, what is the most important thing I should know about you." This open-ended, "ice-breaker" question allows applicants to talk about themselves and affords an opportunity to judge their communication style under the stress of time. As follow-up questions, applicants might be asked to describe their work experience, their three most important accomplishments in policing, hobbies, interests, and so on. During this time, the interviewer(s) is also observing the applicants' verbal and nonverbal communication skill and style.

Next, Gray recommends discussing the agency's mission, values, and culture, to include a summary of the challenges and accomplishments of the agency. Included here might be any nonnegotiable job behaviors, such as performance levels, service and integrity, and what specific behaviors will lead to termination.

Next, applicants might be asked questions that can reveal any character flaws. For example, ask candidates what is in their background that they would not want others to know about, what other agencies or supervisors might say about them, and the kinds of things they publicly display (profiles, statements and photos on a social networking site, a blog, bumper stickers on their car, and so on).

Last are questions that are geared toward learning the applicant's real motivation for, and degree of commitment to the position, as well as true passions. "Why do you want this job?" "Assume that policing had never happened for you. What would have been your Plan B?" It is also appropriate to ask candidates if they are applying or testing for other agencies; applicants who are applying at a number of other agencies are probably not highly committed to this particular one—and possibly not a strong candidate in general, as the best applicants often get hired quickly.

The interview might conclude with a question such as, "What questions do you have of me/us?" If the applicant offers none, he or she is missing a golden opportunity to demonstrate knowledge of the organization and jurisdiction, as well as interest in and enthusiasm for the position.

An Objective Chief's Testing Protocol

Given that the selection of a chief of police is one of the most serious and complex decisions a city can make, it is unfortunate that so little is known about them, what they do, and the competencies required to perform the job vis-à-vis the unique needs of the community. Much of the research has focused on their leadership style, political acumen, handling financial exigencies, challenges posed by homeland security, and so on, so the ability to determine and test for specific, appropriate, and objective selection procedures for the police chief is warranted.

It is possible, and highly desirable, for cities to use a hiring process that includes a systematic job analysis within the given jurisdiction, to include the use of a reliable and well-validated instrument to perform a psychological assessment of job candidates' leadership potential and skills. Private, for-profit concerns have such testing instruments that can: (1) perform a job analysis to determine the competencies and skills that are needed, as indicated by the community's size, needs, problems, and so on; then, once the competencies for the position have been established, (2) use a web-based instrument to evaluate job applicants to determine the degree to which they possess these necessary competencies.[14]

Using such an objective process can accomplish two important aims: First, it allows the final applicant pool for the police chief's search to be efficiently reduced by eliminating applicants who are not viable candidates or a good fit—and thus reducing the labor, time requirements, and expense of interviews and background checks; second, in doing so, the city is much more able to select a new police chief executive whose competencies appeared to be in line with the qualifications deemed as essential for successful performance in the position.[15]

▼

Job Protection, Termination, and the Political Arena

Traditionally, the job tenure of police chiefs has been short. A federal study in the mid-1970s found that the average length in office of chiefs of police was 5.4 years.[16] Another PERF study in the mid-1980s found the average to be practically unchanged: 5.5 years. That figure has not varied much in recent times.[17] This short tenure of police chiefs has several negative consequences. It prevents long-range planning, results in frequent new policies and administrative styles, and prohibits the development of the chief's political power base and local influence.

Police chiefs would, of course, prefer to possess some type of protection against their arbitrary and unjustified removal from office by an elected or political officeholder.[18] In fact, some police chiefs have resigned and reverted to their former position of assistant or deputy chief simply to have some job protection until retirement.

In some states, statutory protections against such actions exist, or special boards or commissions have been created for the sole purpose of establishing recruitment, selection, and retention policies for chiefs of police. Other states require written notice of the basis for the proposed termination, a hearing on the charges, and a finding of cause before the dismissal can be effected. Still, police chiefs across the country are looking for job protection in local civil service codes, municipal ordinances, and such individual employment contracts as they can negotiate.[19]

Losing the job of police chief is not difficult. Although some, of course, lose their positions because of their shortcomings, others leave their post as a result of situations and conflicts outside their control. These conflicts have been termed political arenas and can be divided into three types based on their duration, intensity, and pervasiveness: (1) confrontation, (2) shaky alliance, and (3) a politicized organization.[20]

The first type of political arena, *confrontation*, occurs when the situational conflict is intense but brief and confined. One obvious example is the termination of a police chief in the aftermath of a major incident (e.g., a scandal or acts of racial profiling by officers).

The second type of political arena is the *shaky alliance* in which conflict is less intense but still pervasive. An example involves a former Los Angeles police chief Willie Williams—Daryl Gates's successor and the first outsider appointed as chief in that city in more than 40 years. Williams had to deal with both external pressures (the impact of the 1991 Rodney King incident on the public) and internal pressures (the resentment of his own officers). This was a shaky alliance, and Williams's contract was not renewed.

The third type of political arena, *politicized organization,* features pervasive but muted conflict that is tolerable for a time. This kind of conflict is commonplace in American policing, and in this situation, the chief's survival depends on external support. Examples would be the resignation of the U.S. Secret Service director in October, 2014, following a security breach at the White House and other high-profile incidents, or a lengthy, unsuccessful, and possibly botched homicide investigation.

The history of policing is so replete with politics that it even experienced a political "era" in the United States, roughly from the 1840s to the 1930s. Still, this is an aspect of policing that is often overlooked and has had both good and bad elements. Politics colors nearly everything, and political influence can range from major policy, personnel, and budgetary decisions to the overzealous governing board member who wishes to micromanage the police agency and even appears unexpectedly at night at a crime scene (overheard on the police scanner) to "assist" the officers.

Norm Stamper, former chief of police in Seattle, Washington, described quite well the power and influence of politics in policing. Stamper wrote that "*everything* about policing is ultimately political. Who gets which office: political. Which services are cut when there's a budget freeze: political. Who gets hired, fired, promoted: political, political, political."[21] Stamper also observed that there is both good and bad politics: "I hire my brother-in-law's cousin, a certifiable doofus, because he's got a bass boat I wouldn't mind borrowing—bad politics. I promote a drinking buddy—bad politics. I pick an individual because he or she will add value to the organization and will serve the community honorably—good politics."[22]

▶ The Sheriff

The position of **sheriff** has a long tradition, rooted in the time of the Norman conquest of England (in 1066), and it played an important part in the early law enforcement activities of colonial America. Unfortunately, because of television and movie depictions, many people today view the county sheriff as a bumbling, cruel, overweight, or corrupt individual wearing a cowboy hat and sunglasses while talking with a Southern drawl (see, e.g., reruns of movies such as *Smoky and the Bandit, Mississippi Burning, The Dukes of Hazzard*, and *Walking Tall*). This image is both unfair and highly inaccurate. Next, we examine the role of today's county sheriffs.

> **sheriff** the title given to the top official in the chain of command of a county law enforcement agency.

Because of the diversity of sheriff's offices throughout the country, it is difficult to describe a typical sheriff's department; these offices run the gamut from the traditional, highly political, limited-service office to the modern, fairly nonpolitical, full-service police organization. It is possible, however, to list functions commonly associated with the sheriff's office:

1. Serving and/or implementing civil processes (divorce papers, liens, evictions, garnishments and attachments, and other civil duties, such as extradition and transportation of prisoners)

2. Collecting certain taxes and conducting real estate sales (usually for nonpayment of taxes) for the county

3. Performing routine order-maintenance duties by enforcing state statutes and county ordinances, arresting offenders, and performing traffic and criminal investigations

4. Serving as bailiff of the courts

5. Maintaining and operating the county correctional institutions[23]

Sheriffs, therefore, have a unique role in that they typically serve all three components of the justice system: (1) law enforcement (with patrol, traffic, and investigative functions), (2) the courts (as civil process servers and bailiffs), and (3) corrections (in the county jails). In many urban areas, civil process duties consume more time and resources than those involving law enforcement.[24]

Sheriffs are elected in all but two states (Rhode Island and Hawaii; note, however, that in some consolidated jurisdictions, such as Miami–Dade County, Florida, sheriffs are also appointed); thus, they tend to be aligned with a political party. As elected officials, sheriffs are important political figures and, in many rural areas, represent the most powerful political force in the county. As a result, sheriffs are far more independent than appointed municipal police chiefs, who can be removed from office by the mayors or city managers who appoint them; however, because they are elected, sheriffs receive considerable media scrutiny and are subject to state accountability processes.

Because of this electoral system, it is possible that the only qualification for the office is the ability to get votes. In some areas of the country, the sheriff's term of office is limited to one 2-year term at a time (a sheriff cannot succeed himself or herself); thus, the office has been known to be rotated between the sheriff and undersheriff. In most counties, however, the sheriff has a 4-year term of office and can be reelected.

The sheriff enjoys no tenure guarantee, although one study found that sheriffs (averaging 6.7 years in office) had longer tenure in office than chiefs of police (5.4 years). The politicization of the office of sheriff can result in high turnover rates of personnel who do not have civil service protection. The uncertainty concerning tenure is not conducive to long-range (strategic) planning. Largely as a result of the political nature of the office, sheriffs tend to be older, less likely to have been promoted through the ranks of the agency, and less likely to be college graduates and to have specialized training than police chiefs. Research has also found that sheriffs in small agencies have more difficulty with organizational problems (field activities, budget management) and that sheriffs in large agencies find dealing with local officials and planning and evaluation to be more troublesome.[25]

IN THEIR OWN WORDS

ADMINISTRATIVE ADVICE FROM THE FIELD

Sheriff Scott R. Jones

Name: Scott R. Jones

Current Position/City/State: Sheriff, Sacramento County, California

College attended/academic major/degree(s): Bachelor of Science, Criminal Justice, California State University, Sacramento; Juris Doctor (JD), Lincoln Law School, Sacramento

My primary duties and responsibilities in this position include: overseeing a very large Sheriff's Department with nearly 1,300 sworn officers, 2,000 total employees, and an annual budget over $400 million; providing not only first-responder public safety to over 580,000 persons, but also overseeing corrections and other countywide services for the entire county of 1.4 million people.

Personal attributes/characteristics that have proven to be most helpful to me in this position are: the ability to seek input on decisions when possible, but make decisions quickly and decisively when necessary; having a diminished ego; recognizing as a personal mantra that "there is no best, only better"; having a vision and drive for innovation and NOT the status quo.

My three greatest challenges in this administrative role include: (1) trying to effectuate change in a large, decentralized, diverse workforce, (2) creating "growth" without additional resources; looking inward for growth solutions through better technologies, strategies,

deployment of resources, and partnerships; and (3) trying to be available to all the myriad of stakeholders in the community, with limited time to do so.

Personal accomplishments during my administrative career about which I am most proud are: creating the first dedicated youth services unit in our history, to better foster early relationships with our youth; creating an annual strategic planning process that establishes our priorities year by year, becoming an engine that drives our department forward despite external challenges; creating a multijurisdictional team to combat youth and gang violence that is truly intelligence-led and one-of-a-kind in the nation; protecting our employees from layoffs and re-hiring all those personnel that were laid off during our downsizing; and creating and maintaining an air of transparency and trust for our department with the public and the media.

Advice for someone who is interested in occupying an administrative position such as mine would be: don't be too concerned with where you want to be; instead focus on where you are and make your decisions and guide your actions on how best to accomplish your current role, not some future role. Never be satisfied that anything you do or see is the best it can be; once you open yourself to the paradigm that ANYTHING can be improved, you'll be surprised at the vision that comes from yourself AND others. Never have an ego about who or what you are; you are the same person you were before you became "important." And always be human; you are dealing not with gears in a machine, but rather human beings with their own limitations, challenges, motivations, priorities, etc.

---

middle manager
typically a captain or lieutenant, one who coordinates agency units' activities and sees that the administrative strategies and overall mission are carried out.

▶ Middle Managers: Captains and Lieutenants

Few police administration books contain information about the **middle managers** of a police department: the captains and lieutenants. This is unfortunate because they are too numerous and powerful within police and other paramilitary organizations to ignore. Opinions concerning these middle-management personnel vary, however, as will be seen in the following discussion.

Leonhard Fuld, one of the early progressive police administration researchers, said in 1909 that the captain is one of the most important officers in the organization. Fuld believed that the position had two broad duties—policing and administration. The captain was held responsible for preserving the public peace and protecting life and property within the precinct. Fuld defined the captain's administrative duties as being of three kinds: clerical, janitorial, and supervisory.[26]

Middle managers are generally (as mentioned in Chapter 1) the intermediate level of leadership in a hierarchical organization, reporting to the higher eschelon of administrators and responsible for carrying out their policies and the agency's mission, while also supervising subordinate managers and employees to ensure a smooth functioning organization. In a mid-sized or large police agency, a patrol shift or watch may be commanded by a captain who will have several lieutenants reporting to him or her. The lieutenants may assist the captain in running the shift, but when there is a shortage of sergeants as a result of vacations or retirements, the lieutenant may assume the duties of a first-line supervisor. In some respects, the lieutenant's position in some departments is a training ground for future unit commanders (the rank of captain or higher).

Perhaps the best way to understand what these shift commanders do is to examine the tasks they perform in a medium-sized police department. First, I examine the tasks generally performed by the captain, using the Lexington, Kentucky, Police Department as an example. The 15 most important tasks performed by captains are as follows[27]:

1. Issuing assignments to individuals and units within the section
2. Receiving assignments for the section/unit
3. Reviewing incoming written complaints and reports
4. Preparing routine reports
5. Reviewing the final disposition of assignments
6. Ensuring that subordinates comply with general and special orders
7. Monitoring crime and other activity statistics
8. Evaluating the work of individuals and units within the section
9. Maintaining sector facilities
10. Discussing concerns and problems with people
11. Attending various staff meetings
12. Maintaining working contacts and responding to inquiries from other sections of the division
13. Reviewing and approving overtime in the section/unit
14. Monitoring section/unit operations to evaluate performance
15. Fielding and responding to complaints against subordinates

A review of these tasks shows that captains have more administrative responsibilities than lieutenants or sergeants, with 9 of the 15 tasks being administrative in nature. Captains spend a substantial amount of time coordinating their units' activities with those of other units and overseeing the operation of their units. As an officer progresses up the chain of command, his or her responsibilities become more administrative. At the same time, captains also have supervisory responsibilities (tasks 1, 3, 5, 6, 8, and 15). Whereas a sergeant or lieutenant may be supervising individual officers, a captain is more concerned with individual tasks, unit activities, and the overall performance of the officers under his or her command.

Every commander and administrator in the department, including the police chief, possesses administrative and supervisory responsibilities to some extent. As can be seen from the previous list, the unit commander functions to some extent like a police chief. The unit commander has many of the same responsibilities as the chief but on a smaller scale. The chief performs these functions for the total department, while the unit commander is concerned with only one unit.

Next, we examine the tasks generally performed by the lieutenant, again using the Lexington Police Department as an example. The 15 most important responsibilities for lieutenants include the following (this list is based on the frequency with which they are performed and their urgency)[28]:

1. Assisting in supervising or directing the activities of the unit
2. Performing the duties of a police officer
3. Ensuring that departmental and governmental policies are followed
4. Preparing the duty roster
5. Reviewing the work of individuals or groups in the section
6. Responding to field calls requiring an on-scene commander
7. Holding the roll call
8. Preparing various reports
9. Reviewing various reports
10. Coordinating the activities of subordinates on major investigations
11. Meeting with superiors concerning unit operations
12. Maintaining time sheets
13. Notifying the captain/bureau commander of significant calls
14. Answering inquiries from other sections/units, divisions, and outside agencies
15. Serving as the captain/bureau commander in the latter's absence

Notice that some of the tasks performed by the lieutenants are purely administrative in nature (tasks 4, 7, 8, and 12). These are administrative activities that occur in every operational unit in the police department. The lieutenants in Lexington also perform supervisory functions (tasks 1, 3, 5, 6, and 9). These functions include overseeing officers and sergeants to ensure that different tasks are completed. Here, direct supervision generally focuses on the most critical tasks or those tasks that, when performed incorrectly, can result in dire consequences. Tasks 11 and 13 through 15 are managerial in nature. These responsibilities are generally vested within a unit commander, but many lieutenants perform them, especially in the absence of the captain. Finally, lieutenants perform the duties of a police officer (task 2). With their supervisory and managerial responsibilities, they engage in a limited amount of police work. The list shows that lieutenants have a wide range of supervisory, managerial, and police duties.

One potential problem of police organizations is that they may become top-heavy, with too many administrative, management, and supervisory personnel in general or too many who are working in offices and not on the streets. Such structures can hinder the accomplishment of goals and objectives. Too often, middle managers become glorified paper pushers, especially in the present climate that requires myriad reports, budgets, grants, and so on.

The agency should determine what administrative, management, and supervisory functions are essential and how many captains, lieutenants, and sergeants are needed to perform them. Some communities, such as Kansas City, Missouri, have eliminated the rank of lieutenant; they found that this move had no negative consequences.[29]

▶ First-Line Supervisors: The Patrol Sergeant

Seeking the Gold Badge

Sometime during the career of a patrol officer (provided that he or she acquires the minimal number of years of experience), the opportunity for career advancement is presented—the chance to wear the sergeant's "gold badge." This is a difficult position to occupy because at this lowest leadership level, **first-line supervisors** are caught between upper management and the rank-and-file officers.

This initial opportunity to attain the rank of sergeant is normally quite attractive. It is not uncommon for 60–65 percent or more of those who are eligible to take the test for promotion; thus, competition for the sergeant openings in most departments is quite keen.

Becoming a sergeant often involves an assessment center process, discussed earlier, and departmental and civil service procedures that are intended to guarantee legitimacy and impartiality in the process. Officers are often told that it is best to rotate into different assignments before testing for sergeant to gain exposure to a variety of police functions and supervisors. The promotional system, then, favors well-rounded officers; furthermore, being skilled at test taking is often of tremendous assistance, so even if one fails the first or several tests, going through the testing process can be invaluable. As with the chief executives' hiring process, an assessment center, which includes critical-incident, problem-solving, in-basket, disciplinary problems, role-playing exercises, and/or other components, will provide candidates with valuable training and testing experience. Other factors that might come into play as part of the promotional process include education and training, years of experience, supervisory ratings, psychological evaluations, and departmental commendations.

> **first-line supervisor**
> the lowest yet a very important level of leadership, the supervisor directs, controls, and evaluates the work of field personnel, ensures that agency policies and procedures are followed, counsels and places employees where resources are most needed, resolves employee conflicts, and performs related duties.

Assuming the Position: General Roles and Functions

Administrative personnel know that a good patrol officer is not automatically a good supervisor. Because supervisors are promoted from within the ranks, they are often placed in charge of their friends and peers. Longstanding relationships are put under stress when a new sergeant suddenly has official authority over former equals. Leniency or preferential treatment is often expected of new sergeants by their former peers.

When new supervisors attempt to correct deficient behavior, their previous performance may be recalled as a means of challenging the reasonableness or legitimacy of their supervisory action. Supervisors with any skeletons in their closets can expect to hear those skeletons rattling as they begin to use their new-found authority. This places a great deal of pressure on the supervisor. A new supervisor, therefore, must go through a transitional phase to learn how to exercise command and get cooperation from subordinates.

The new supervisor is no longer responsible solely for her or his behavior but also for the behavior of several other employees. The step from officer to supervisor is a big one and calls for a new set of skills and knowledge largely separate from those learned at lower levels in the organization.

Supervision is challenging not only in policing but also in corrections, where supervisors must follow federal and state laws and court decisions that concern the custody, care, and treatment of inmates. Their subordinates, however, expect them to be understanding, to protect them from prison management's potentially unreasonable expectations and arbitrary decisions, and to represent their interests.

The supervisor's role, put simply, is to get his or her subordinates to do their very best. This task involves a host of actions, including communicating, motivating, leading, team building, training, appraising, counseling, and disciplining. Getting them to do their very best includes figuring out each subordinate's strengths and weaknesses; defining good and bad performance; measuring performance; providing feedback; and making sure that subordinates' efforts coincide with the organization's mission, values, goals, and objectives.

Supervising a group of subordinates is made more difficult because of the so-called human element. People are complex and sometimes unpredictable. Rules and principles for communicating, leading, and other supervisory tasks are rarely hard and fast because different people react differently. What works for a supervisor in one situation may not work for that supervisor in another situation, much less for some other supervisor. Thus, supervisors have to learn to "read" subordinates and diagnose situations before choosing how to respond. Supervisors have to become students of human behavior and of behavioral science disciplines, such as psychology and sociology.

Effective supervision is also difficult because the job is dynamic, not static. One's subordinates change over time as they age, grow, mature, and experience satisfaction and dissatisfaction in their personal and work lives. In addition, attrition is common, as personnel retire, promote, and transfer into other units within the department. When new subordinates come under the supervisor's wing, the supervisor must learn the best way to handle them and also be attuned to the new officers' effects on other subordinates and on the work group as a whole.

It is not only one's subordinates who change; the organization and its environment change over time. The organization's rules and expectations may change. The public may make new demands. Societal values evolve and change. Effective supervision over the long haul requires continuous monitoring and adaptation. The department expects the supervisor to keep up with such changes to better supervise subordinates. Subordinates, on the other hand, expect the supervisor to help them to interpret and adapt successfully to this changing environment. Table 5-1 ■ shows the expectations that both managers and rank-and-file officers have of first-line supervisors.

TABLE 5-1 Management's and Officers' Expectations of Supervisors

MANAGEMENT'S EXPECTATIONS

- Interpret departmental policies, procedures, and rules and ensure that officers follow them
- Initiate disciplinary action when officers fail to follow policies
- Ensure that officers' paperwork and reports are accurate and filed on a timely basis
- Train officers when they are deficient or unskilled
- Complete performance evaluations
- Ensure that officers treat citizens respectfully, professionally, and impartially
- Ensure that officers' equipment and appearance are in order
- Back up officers and review their performance when officers answer calls for service
- Take charge of high-risk or potential critical-incident situations
- Make assignments to ensure that the objectives of the unit are met

OFFICERS' EXPECTATIONS

- Interpret departmental policies, procedures, and rules to meet the needs of the officers
- Handle disciplinary actions informally rather than taking direct action, especially regarding minor infractions
- Advocate for officers when they request a vacation or time off
- Support them when there is a conflict with citizens
- Provide them with support and backup at high-risk calls
- Assist them in getting better assignments and shifts
- Emphasize law enforcement activities over other activities such as providing services, community policing activities, or mundane assignments such as traffic control
- Understand that officers need to take breaks and sometimes attend to personal needs while on duty

Basic Tasks

The following nine tasks are most important for police supervisors; they are listed with the most important first[30]:

1. Supervise subordinate officers in the performance of their duties
2. Disseminate information to subordinates
3. Ensure that general and special orders are followed
4. Review and approve various reports
5. Listen to problems voiced by officers
6. Answer calls
7. Keep superiors apprised of ongoing situations
8. Provide direct supervision for potential high-risk calls or situations
9. Interpret policies and inform subordinates

Tasks 1 and 8 on this list are global supervisory tasks that incorporate both direction and control. Tasks 2 and 9 are aspects of the directing function, whereas tasks 3 through 5 are elements of control. Thus, six of these top nine sergeant's tasks involve directing and controlling. The remaining three tasks provide interesting glimpses into some of the other duties and responsibilities of police supervisors: listening to subordinates' problems, notifying superiors of problems, and directly assisting subordinates in performing their work. Police supervisors provide an important communications link in the hierarchy between workers and management, as well as a sounding board for problems and grievances. They also get involved in performing street police work from time to time.

Supervisory tasks can range from the mundane (such as typing and filing reports, operating dictation equipment) to the challenging tasks (assigning priorities to investigations, training personnel in forced-entry procedures and barricaded person situations). Tasks may be administrative (preparing monthly activity reports, scheduling vacation leave), operational (securing major crime scenes, assisting stranded motorists), general (maintaining an inventory of equipment, training subordinates), or specialized (conducting stakeouts, training animals for use in specialized units).

Types of Supervisors

Robin S. Engel[31] studied police supervisors and found four distinct types: traditional, innovative, supportive, and active. Each of these types can be found in any police department. A particular supervisor's style is largely dependent on his or her experiences on the job, his or her training, and the department's organizational climate.

The first type, *traditional,* is law enforcement oriented. Traditional supervisors expect their subordinates to produce high levels of measurable activities, such as traffic citations and arrests. They expect officers to respond to calls for service efficiently, place a great deal of emphasis on reports and other paperwork, and provide officers with a substantial amount of instruction and oversight. To a great extent, traditional supervisors are task oriented. They tend to place greater emphasis on punishment than rewards and often believe that they do not have a great deal of power in the department. These supervisors see their primary role as controlling subordinates. Traditional supervisors often have morale and motivation problems with their subordinates.

The second type is the *innovative* supervisor, who is most closely associated with community policing. To some extent, innovative supervisors are the opposite of traditional supervisors. Innovative supervisors generally do not place a great deal of emphasis on citations or arrests. They also depend more on developing relationships with subordinates than on using power to control or motivate. Innovative supervisors usually are good mentors, and they tend to coach rather than order. They are open to new ideas and innovations. Their ultimate goal is to develop officers who can solve problems and have good relations with citizens. Innovative supervisors sometimes have problems with officers who are task oriented or who emphasize enforcement and neglect community relations.

The third type of supervisor is the *supportive* supervisor, who, like the innovative supervisor, is concerned with developing good relations with subordinates. The primary difference is that supportive supervisors are concerned with protecting officers from what are viewed as unfair management practices. They see themselves as a buffer between management and officers. They attempt to develop strong work teams and motivate officers by inspiring them. Their shortcoming is that they tend to see themselves as "one of the boys," and they sometimes neglect emphasizing departmental goals and responsibilities.

The final category of supervisors, according to Engel, is the *active* supervisor, who tends to work in the field. Active supervisors sometimes are police officers with stripes or rank. They often take charge of field situations rather than supervise them, although they are active supervisors in most situations. They are able to develop good relations with subordinates because they are perceived as being hardworking and competent. Their shortcoming is that, by being overly involved in some field situations, they do not give their subordinates the opportunity to develop.

Engel[32] found that the four types of supervision were fairly evenly distributed in the departments. The most effective supervisor was the active supervisor. Subordinates working for active supervisors performed better in a number of areas, including problem solving and community policing. This led Engel to conclude that active supervisors were able to develop a more productive work unit because of their ability to lead by example. It seems that working supervisors inspire subordinates to work and be productive.

Engel did identify one problem with active police supervisors: a higher incidence of the use of force relative to the other types. Because active supervisors are very involved in the provision of police services, efforts should be made to ensure that they follow policies and that their subordinates adhere to policies and procedures. Supervisors must not only be well trained and selected carefully but they must also receive a measure of supervision from their superiors. If the supervisor fails to make sure that employees perform correctly, the unit will not be successful, causing difficulties for the manager, the lieutenant, or the captain.

A police department is really nothing more than the sum total of all its units, and one problem unit can adversely affect other units and reduce the department's total effectiveness. This is particularly true for police organizations because there is substantial interdependence among the various units in a police department. For example, if patrol officers do a poor job of writing reports when they respond to crimes, the workload of detectives who later complete the case's follow-up investigation will increase.

▶ The Patrol Officer

Countless books and articles have been written about, and other chapters in this book deal, in part, with the beat officer. Here, we briefly discuss the nature of this position. Included is a review of their basic tasks, some traits of good officers, hiring the best personnel possible, and some basic training methods.

Basic Tasks

Many people believe that the police officer has the most difficult job in the United States. In fundamental terms, the police perform four basic functions: (1) enforcing the laws, (2) performing services (such as maintaining or assisting animal control units, reporting burned-out street lights or stolen traffic lights and signs, delivering death messages, checking the welfare of people in their homes, delivering blood), (3) preventing crime (patrolling, providing the public with information on locks and lighting to reduce the opportunity for crime), and (4) protecting the innocent (by investigating crimes, police systematically remove innocent people from consideration as crime suspects).[33]

Because police officers are solitary workers, spending much of their time on the job unsupervised, and because those officers who are hired today will become the supervisors of the future, police administrators must attempt to attract the best individuals possible. A major problem of police administration today involves personnel recruitment.

What Traits Make a Good Officer?

Although it may be difficult for the average police administrator to describe the qualities he or she looks for when recruiting, training, and generally creating a good officer, some psychological characteristics can be identified. According to psychologist Lawrence Wrightsman,[34] it is important that good officers be *incorruptible*, of high moral character. They should be *well adjusted* and able to carry out the hazardous and stressful tasks of policing without cracking up, and thick-skinned enough to operate without defensiveness. They should also be *people oriented* and able to respond to situations without becoming overly emotional, impulsive, or aggressive; they need to exercise restraint. They also need *cognitive skills* to assist in their investigative work.

Dennis Nowicki[35] compiled 12 qualities that he believes are imperative for entry-level police officers:

1. *Enthusiasm.* Believes in what he or she is doing and goes about it with a vigor that is almost contagious

2. *Good communications skills.* Highly developed speaking and listening skills; ability to interact equally well with people from all socioeconomic levels

3. *Good judgment.* Wisdom and analytical ability to make good decisions based on an understanding of the problem

4. *Sense of humor.* Ability to laugh and smile, to help officers cope with the regular exposure to human pain and suffering

5. *Creativity.* Ability to use creative techniques by placing themselves in the mind of the criminal and legally accomplishing arrests

6. *Self-motivation.* Making things happen, proactively solving difficult cases, creating their own luck

7. *Knowing the job and the system.* Understanding the role of a police officer, the intricacies of the justice system, what the administration requires, and using both formal and informal channels to be effective

8. *Ego.* Believing they are good officers, having the self-confidence that enables them to solve difficult crimes

9. *Courage.* Ability to meet physical and psychological challenges, thinking clearly during times of high stress, admitting when they are wrong, and standing up for what is difficult and right

10. *Understanding discretion.* Enforcing the spirit, not the letter, of the law; not being hardnosed, hardheaded, or hardhearted; giving people a break and showing empathy

11. *Tenacity.* Staying focused; seeing challenges, not obstacles; viewing failure not as a setback but as an experience

12. *Thirst for knowledge.* Staying current on new laws and court decisions, always learning (not only from the classroom but also via informal discussions with other officers)

Addressing a Front-End Problem: Recruiting Quality Officers

Certainly, the recruitment of quality police officers is the key to the success, values, and culture of any police organization. The current "cop crunch" is exacerbated in many cities by exploding growth, a competitive job market, natural catastrophes (e.g., Hurricane Katrina in New Orleans), and struggles to retain diversity.[36] Furthermore, this crunch comes at a time when today's police need a stronger focus on problem-solving skills, ability to collaborate with the community, and a greater capacity to use technology.[37] Adding to the problems are today's higher incidence of obesity, major debt, drug use, and criminal records that are found among potential recruits.[38]

Police recruitment issues are such a concern at present that a national meeting was recently convened to discuss these issues by the U.S. Department of Justice, the National Institute of Justice, and the RAND Corporation. This national meeting produced several recruiting measures that can be adopted, however, toward generating a satisfactory applicant pool:

- Have one leader in charge of the entire recruiting process, from marketing to testing to background investigation through academy training.

- Consider the academy dropout rate: Are recruiters signing up the most promising candidates for the academy?[39]

- Publicize hiring campaigns on business cards, use department vehicles as billboards, and make the agency websites more effective by emphasizing the positive reasons for joining (rather than focusing on the challenges faced by police officers).

- Limit recruiting trips to those locations where candidates are likely to be found, such as areas with economic difficulties; out-of-town recruiting trips are generally not effective.[40]

- Look at the academy program to see if something is hindering diversity and in effect "washing out" candidates, particularly those whose native language is not English.[41]

- Make the department's recruiting efforts focus on the positives of police work, such as job security, the satisfaction of public service, and superior pay and benefits; too often they emphasize the challenges involved in becoming a police officer.[42]

- Use bonuses for officers who refer candidates to the academy.

- Include an online sample test on the agency website to give recruits an idea of the types of questions they will be facing.

- Allow other standardized tests, such as the Armed Services Vocational Aptitude Battery, to substitute for the police department's own written test; this will speed the acceptance process.[43]

The Kansas City, Missouri, Police Department attempts to recruit and hire the best personnel using the process described in Exhibit 5.2; then, Exhibit 5.3 demonstrates how police agencies are using social networking sites to perform background checks on recruits.

EXHIBIT 5.2

THE POLICE HIRING PROCESS IN KANSAS CITY, MISSOURI[44]

Following are the types of examinations and activities involved in the hiring process for the Kansas City, Missouri, Police Department (KCPD) (as well as many other police agencies). The entire process, which includes a substance abuse questionnaire (not shown), may require several months to complete.

- **Written Examination:** All applicants begin with and must take the Police Officer Selection Test (P.O.S.T.). A review for this examination is generally given within 1 month prior to the written examination, and a sample test is available upon request.

- **Physical Abilities Test:** This is an obstacle course designed to simulate challenges that could be encountered during an officer's tour of duty. Applicants must demonstrate their ability to maneuver through the course with minimal errors.

- **Pre-Employment Polygraph Examination:** The polygraph examination is administered by a qualified polygraph examiner and covers criminal activity, drug usage, integrity, truthfulness, and employment history.

- **Background Investigation:** The background investigation will cover pertinent facts regarding the applicant's character, work history, and any criminal or traffic records.

- **Ride-Along:** To expose applicants to the actual duties performed by KCPD officers, during the background investigation, the applicant will be required to ride with an officer on a weekend for a full tour of duty during the evening or night shift.

- **Oral Board:** This interview consists of questions designed to allow the KCPD to assess an applicant's overall abilities, which are related to the field of law enforcement.

- **Psychological Examination:** This interview is conducted by a certified psychologist, after a job offer has been made.

- **Physical Examination:** Applicants undergo a complete medical and eye examination performed by a licensed physician, after a job offer has been made.

EXHIBIT 5.3

USING SOCIAL NETWORKING SITES FOR BACKGROUND CHECKS[45]

Police agencies are using social networking sites to perform background checks, requesting that candidates sign waivers allowing investigators access to their Facebook, MySpace, YouTube, Twitter, and other personal Internet accounts. Some agencies also demand that applicants provide private passwords, Internet pseudonyms, text messages, and e-mail logs to allow the agency even greater access to information for the hiring process. Indeed, more than one-third of police agencies now review applicants' social media activity during background checks, according to the International Association of Chiefs of Police (IACP) in a recent survey of about 100 police chiefs.

In addition to inherent privacy concerns, there are also concerns that defense attorneys could use officers' posts to undercut their credibility in court, according to the National Fraternal Order of Police.

Among the findings on social networking sites are the following:

- In Massachusetts, an agency requested electronic message logs and found a recruit's text messages revealed past threats of suicide, resulting in disqualification.

- A New Jersey agency disqualified a candidate for posting racy photographs of himself with scantily clad women.

- Inappropriate officers' postings have been found that range from sexually explicit photographs to racially charged commentary.

▼

From Field Training Officer to Police Training Officer

A new aspect of policing that concerns rank-and-file officers and with which all police chiefs and sheriffs should be acquainted is a new method of officer training. This training concept is known as the **police training officer (PTO)** program.

The basic recruit academy is certainly a major phase of the neophyte officers' career—the starting point for their occupational socialization into the police role, providing them with essential formal training, shaping their attitudes, and developing technical occupational skills. However, once the recruits leave the academy, where their training was primarily academic, their training is still incomplete. They must then undergo a field training process while under the tutelage and supervision of a qualified **field training officer (FTO)**. The FTO program was developed in the late 1960s in San Jose, California,[46] to provide new officers and deputies with a smooth, supervised, and educational transition from the academy to the field at their respective agencies. FTO programs remain in wide use today and generally consist of several identifiable phases: introduction (with the recruit learning agency policies and local laws), training and evaluation (the recruit is introduced to more complicated tasks performed by patrol officers), and the final portion (wherein the FTO trainer may act as an observer and evaluator while the recruit performs all the functions of a patrol officer). The length of time a recruit is assigned to an FTO will vary, but normally the range is from 1 to 12 weeks.[47]

However, the FTO approach has changed very little in the past 40-plus years and is devoid of contemporary approaches to training that include adult- and problem-based learning and leadership principles. The newer approach departs from traditional police training methods that emphasize mechanical repetition skills and rote memory capabilities; rather, the focus is on developing an officer's learning capacity, leadership, and problem-solving skills. Its theoretical underpinnings include adult and problem-based learning. Regarding the former, Malcolm Knowles[48] believed in self-directed learning and thought that the adults should acquire the skills necessary to live up to their potential, understand their society, and be skilled in directing social change. Furthermore, adults should learn to react to the causes, not the symptoms, of behavior; therefore, many police executives have come to believe that the FTO approach is not relevant to the methods and challenges of community-oriented policing and problem solving (COPPS, discussed in Chapter 4). PTO was developed to better meet the needs of those agencies.

PTO seeks to take the traditional FTO program to a higher level—one that embraces and evaluates new officers based on their understanding and application of COPPS. With $500,000 in federal assistance, a new PTO program was recently developed and initiated at six national sites, including adult- and problem-based learning principles. PTO covers two primary training areas: substantive topics (the most common activities in policing) and core competencies (the common skills that officers are required to utilize in the daily performance of their duties). New officers must master 15 core competencies, which are specific skills, knowledge, and abilities that have been identified as essential for good policing. There is a learning matrix that serves as a guide for trainees and trainers during the training period, and demonstrates the interrelationships between the core competencies and daily policing activities during the eight phases of the PTO program.[49]

It is believed that PTO provides a foundation for lifelong learning that prepares new officers for the complexities of policing today and in the future. This approach is very different from traditional police training methods that emphasize mechanical repetition skills and rote memory capabilities; rather, the PTO focus is on developing an officer's learning capacity, leadership, and problem-solving skills. While applied skills (e.g., weaponless defense, shooting, and defensive tactics) are essential, they constitute only one set of skills for contemporary policing. This approach is also highly flexible, able to be tailored to each agency's needs; furthermore, because of its flexibility, it may be adjusted to meet future police training challenges.

police training officer (PTO) a relatively new program where new officer are evaluated on their application of community policing and problem-solving principles, using adult- and problem-based learning principles.

field training officer (FTO) a program designed to help new officers to transition smoothly from the recruit academy phase of their career, with a veteran officer observing and evaluating their performance in the field.

Summary

This chapter has described the traits and duties of today's law enforcement executives, middle-managers, first-line supervisors, and patrol officers. Clearly, these individuals occupy positions of tremendous responsibility. Police executives, managers, and supervisors must decide what the best leadership method is, both inside and outside their organizations. They must be concerned with their agency's performance and standing with the community, governing board, and rank and file. Their abilities will be challenged in additional ways if the COPPS strategy is being contemplated or is already being implemented.

Key Terms and Concepts

Assessment center *109*

Chief executive officer (CEO) *106*

Chief of police *112*

Field training officer (FTO) *128*

First-line supervisor *121*

Middle manager *118*

Mintzberg model for CEOs *106*

Police training officer (PTO) *128*

Sheriff *117*

Questions for Review

1. What are some of a police executive's primary roles? (Use the three major categories of the Mintzberg model of CEOs in developing your response.)
2. What are the components and advantages of using the assessment center process for hiring and promoting police personnel?
3. What are some elements of the police chief's and sheriff's positions that make them attractive and unattractive? Do you think that contemporary qualifications for the positions are adequate? How do chiefs and sheriffs differ in role and background?
4. What are the "Ten Commandments" of good executive leadership?
5. How might some of Machiavelli's views of leadership apply to today's police chief executives?
6. What are some recommended interviewing and psychological testing protocols for police chief candidates?
7. How do the role and function of sergeants differ from those of upper or middle managers?
8. What are the three types of political arena conflicts that can cause police chiefs to lose their jobs? What are examples of "good politics" and "bad politics?"
9. What are some of the 12 qualities said to make a good police officer, and what are some of the innovative means now in use for recruiting and hiring quality officers?
10. How would you describe the various parts of the "hurdle" (recruitment and hiring) process used by the Kansas City, Missouri, Police Department?
11. What are some similarities and differences between the FTO and PTO concepts?
12. What are the primary responsibilities of executive, management, and supervisory personnel under COPPS?

Deliberate and Decide

Applying the Mintzberg Model for CEOs

You have been the Park City police chief for 6 months, overseeing an agency of 60 sworn officers in a community of 80,000 people; your city abuts another, larger city, with a population of 160,000. These populations are deceptive, however, soaring during the summertime, because your area is a tourist-based gaming destination. Today is July 3, and at 8:00 A.M. you briefly attend a staff meeting of detectives, led by a deputy chief of operations, to learn the latest information concerning a highly publicized kidnap- ping. In the afternoon, you plan to deliver a news release concerning the case status. Then you will give the gradua- tion speech at the area police academy, which is followed by your attending a meeting of the Tri-County Regional Major Case Squad, where you will discuss the latest intel- ligence information concerning a ring of circulating slot machine cheaters in your jurisdiction. You then learn from Dispatch that one of your motorcycle officers has gone down, and you speed to the hospital emergency room to wish him well. You then meet with your events staff and other city officials to finalize security and traffic plans for tomorrow's huge fireworks display because last year's event resulted in huge numbers of alcohol-related traffic and fighting arrests. You are also scheduled to ride in a car in the holiday parade. At day's end, you make final preparations for your July 5 presentation to the City Council concerning the need for a modern, 800-megahertz communications system, which you hope to convince the council to purchase. You also will be attending a special ceremony at a city park that honors area law enforcement officers who have been killed in the line of duty.

1. Using Mintzberg's model for CEOs, classify each of the functions mentioned in the case study into the interpersonal, informational, and decision-maker roles.

2. More specifically, which of this chief executive's tasks or activities would fall within the figurehead, leadership, liaison, monitoring/inspecting, dissemination, spokesperson, entrepreneur, disturbance-handler, resource-allocator, and negotiator functions? Explain.

Learn by Doing

1. Your criminal justice professor has been hired as a consultant with an area police agency to develop and help conduct an assessment center for a sergeant's promotional examination. You are asked to assist him in doing so. What kinds of testing activities would you believe should be included at minimum, and how will you arrange to have the candidates' performance evaluated?

2. You are guest lecturing before a group of university students in a criminal justice organization and administration class. One of the students indicates confusion about the use of organizational structures in general as well as the roles of middle managers (captains and lieutenants) in specific. Provide an explanation.

Notes

1. Henry Mintzberg, "The Manager's Job: Folklore and Fact," *Harvard Business Review* 53 (July–August 1975):49–61.

2. For a comprehensive look at the assessment center process and tips for how to participate as a candidate, see John L. Coleman, *Police Assessment Testing: An Assessment Center Handbook for Law Enforcement Personnel* (Springfield, IL: Charles C Thomas, 2002).

3. Robert Katz, "Skills of an Effective Administrator," *Harvard Business Review,* http://hbr.org/1974/09/skills-of-an-effective-administrator/ar/1 (accessed August16, 2014).

4. Thomas J. Jurkanin, Larry T. Hoover, Jerry L. Dowling, and Janice Ahmad, *Enduring, Surviving, and Thriving as a Law Enforcement Executive* (Springfield, IL: Charles C Thomas, 2001), pp. 12–29.

5. See Thomas Lynch and Todd Dicker (eds.), *Handbook of Organizational Theory and Management: The Philosophical Approach* (New York: Marcel Dekker, Inc., 1998), p. 83.

6. Ed Sanow, "Solid Advice for New Chiefs from Machiavelli," *Law & Order* 60 (4)(April 2012):42–45, http://0-search.proquest.com.innopac.library.unr.edu/docview/1035368674 (accessed August 16, 2014).

7. Some of this material was adapted from Ed Sanow, "Solid Advice for New Chiefs from Machiavelli," *Law & Order* (April 2012):42–45, http://0-search.proquest.com.innopac.library.unr.edu/docview/1035368674 (accessed August16, 2014); also see, generally, Niccolo Machiavelli, *The Prince,* Robert M. Adams (trans.) (New York: W.W. Norton, 1992).

8. Ronald G. Lynch, *The Police Manager,* 3rd ed. (New York: Random House, 1986), p. 1.

9. "Survey Says Big-City Chiefs Are Better-Educated Outsiders," *Law Enforcement News* (April 30, 1998): 7.

10. Ibid.

11. Janice K. Penegor and Ken Peak, "Police Chief Acquisitions: A Comparison of Internal and External Selections," *American Journal of Police* 11 (1992):17–32.

12. Richard B. Weinblatt, "The Shifting Landscape of Chiefs' Jobs," *Law and Order* 47(10) (1999):50.

13. John Gray, "The Chief's Interview," *Law and Order* 59 (10) (October 2011):82–85; much of this discussion and several interview items are also based on the author's experiences with assessment centers and oral boards.

14. For an excellent case study describing the use of this testing protocol, see Michael R. Cunningham, John W. Jones, and Gary M. Behrens, "Psychological Assessment of Chief of Police Candidates: Scientific and Practice Issues," *Journal of Police & Criminal Psychology* 26 (2011):77–86, DOI 10.1007/s11896-011-9084-0.

15. Ibid.

16. National Advisory Commission on Criminal Justice Standards and Goals, *Police Chief Executive* (Washington, DC: U.S. Government Printing Office, 1976), p. 7.

17. Weinblatt, "The Shifting Landscape of Chiefs' Jobs," p. 51.

18. For an excellent compilation of articles concerning the chief's role, see William Geller (ed.), *Police Leadership in America: Crisis and Opportunity* (New York: Praeger, 1985).

19. Janet Ferris, "Present and Potential Legal Job Protections Available to Heads of Agencies," *Florida Police Chief* 14 (1994):43–45.

20. Henry Mintzberg, *Power in and around Organizations* (Upper Saddle River, NJ: Prentice Hall, 1983).

21. Norm Stamper, *Breaking Rank: A Top Cop's Exposé of the Dark Side of American Policing* (New York: Nation Books, 2005), p. 185.

22. Ibid.

23. Clemens Bartollas, Stuart J. Miller, and Paul B. Wice, *Participants in American Criminal Justice: The Promise and the Performance* (Englewood Cliffs, NJ: Prentice Hall, 1983), p. 35.

24. Charles R. Swanson, Leonard Territo, and Robert W. Taylor, *Police Administration: Structures, Processes, and Behavior,* 6th ed. (Upper Saddle River, NJ: Prentice Hall, 2005), pp. 129–130.

25. Colin Hayes, "The Office of Sheriff in the United States," *The Prison Journal* 74(2001):50–54.

26. Leonhard F. Fuld, *Police Administration* (New York: G. P. Putnam's Sons, 1909), pp. 59–60.

27. See Kenneth J. Peak, Larry K. Gaines, and Ronald W. Glensor, *Police Supervision and Management: In an Era of Community Policing,* 2nd ed. (Upper Saddle River, NJ: Prentice Hall, 2004), pp. 33–34.

28. Ibid., p. 33.

29. Richard N. Holden, *Modern Police Management,* 2nd ed. (Upper Saddle River, NJ: Prentice Hall, 1994), pp. 294–295.

30. Peak et al., *Police Supervision and Management,* Chapter 2 generally.

31. Robin S. Engel, "Patrol Officer Supervision in the Community Policing Era," *Journal of Criminal Justice* 30(2002):51–64.

32. Robin S. Engel, "Supervisory Styles of Patrol Sergeants and Lieutenants," *Journal of Criminal Justice* 29(2001):341–355.

33. Kenneth J. Peak, *Policing America: Challenges and Best Practices,* 8th ed., (Columbus, OH: Pearson Education, Inc., 2015), p. 71.

34. Lawrence S. Wrightsman, *Psychology and the Legal System* (Monterey, CA: Brooks/Cole, 1987), pp. 85–86.

35. Based on Dennis Nowicki, "Twelve Traits of Highly Effective Police Officers," *Law and Order* (October 1999): 45–46.

36. Jeremy M. Wilson and Clifford A. Grammich, *Police Recruitment and Retention in the Contemporary Urban Environment: A National Discussion of Personnel Experiences and Promising Practices from the Front Lines* (Santa Monica, CA: RAND Corporation, 2009), p. 5; also available at: http://www.rand.org/pubs/conf_proceedings/2009/RAND_CF261.pdf (accessed August 16, 2014).

37. Ibid., p. 2.

38. Stephanie Slahor, "RAND Study Suggests Strategies to Address Recruiting Shortage," *Law and Order* (December 8, 2008):32.

39. Ibid., p. 18.

40. Ibid., pp. 18–19.

41. Ibid.

42. Slahor, "RAND Study Suggests Strategies to Address Recruiting Shortage," pp. 32–38.

43. Wilson and Grammich, *Police Recruitment and Retention in the Contemporary Urban Environment,* p. 33.

44. Excerpt from Careers: Law Enforcement Hiring Process. Copyright by Kansas City MissouriI Police Department. Used by permission of Kansas City MissouriI Police Department.

45. Based on Kevin Johnson, "Cops get screened for digital dirt," *USA TODAY,* November 12, 2010, http://www.usatoday.com/tech/news/2010-11-12-1Afacebookcops12_ST_N.htm (accessed October 16, 2014); also see Martha Stonebrook and Rick Stubbs, "Social Networking in Law Enforcement," International Association of Chiefs of Police 2010 Annual Conference, Orlando, Florida, http://www.aele.org/los2010s&s.pdf (accessed August 16, 2014).

46. G. Kaminsky, *San Jose Field Training Model* (San Jose, CA: San Jose Police Department, 1970).

47. Roger G. Dunham and Geoffrey P. Alpert, *Critical Issues in Policing: Contemporary Readings* (Prospect Heights, IL: Waveland Press, 1989), pp. 111–115.

48. Malcolm Knowles, *Andragogy in Action* (San Francisco: Jossey-Bass, 1981).

49. Kenneth J. Peak, Steven Pitts, and Ronald W. Glensor, "From 'FTO' to 'PTO': A Contemporary Approach to Post-Academy Recruit Training," paper presented at the annual conference of the Academy of Criminal Justice Sciences, Seattle, Washington, March 22, 2007.

Semper paratus—

—Latin Phrase, Meaning "Always Prepared"; official motto of the U.S. CoastGuard

6 Police Issues and Practices

LEARNING OBJECTIVES

After reading this chapter, the student will be able to:

1. *explain the definition and nature of terrorism and the several practical and legislative responses to it*

2. *describe how to better manage use of force, including the types of officers and situations that tend to foster it, using force with persons having mental disorders, responding to active shooters, vehicular pursuits, and use-of-force continuums*

3. *describe some contemporary uses—and problems—involved with police uses of social media*

4. *list issues involved with bringing women into policing and the ongoing problem of sexual harassment*

5. *explain why succession planning is needed in order to prepare police leaders of the future*

6. *review the legal and psychological aspects of today's police uniforms and dress codes*

► Introduction

Other chapters of this book focused, or will focus, on some of the pressing issues and contemporary practices of law enforcement executives, specifically issues relating to police organization, operations, and personnel; later chapters, for example, will focus on ethics, liability, financial administration, and the application of new technologies.

This chapter looks at some equally challenging issues. Many years ago someone said, with tongue in cheek, that to be a police officer one needed "a size 3 hat and a size 43 jacket." Given the kinds of topics that are discussed in this chapter, this description could not be further from the truth today. In several ways, the police have increasingly been placed under the microscope with regard to how they deal with the public, exercise their force prerogative, guard our borders from uninvited intruders, and offer employment opportunity to all qualified Americans.

The chapter begins with an examination of terrorism, including definition, types, and some available practical and legislative means available for responding to this omnipresent threat. Then we consider several facets of how law enforcement executives must manage the use of force, including a relatively new area, the "active shooter." Following that, we look at issues concerning police use of social media as well as challenges involved with bringing more women into law enforcement ranks, including the continuing problem of sexual harassment. We then consider contract and consolidated policing services, and whether or not they are efficient and cost-effective.

Then a looming "crisis stage" is discussed: the need to begin identifying, grooming, and promoting future police executives as the baby boomer generation nears retirement. Finally, after an examination of the legal and psychological aspects of today's police uniforms and dress codes, we conclude the chapter with review questions, two "deliberate and decide" problems, and "learn by doing" exercises.

► Terrorism

As shown in Figure 6-1 ■, a number of attacks on American soil have demonstrated this nation's vulnerability to both foreign and domestic terrorists. These attacks also demonstrated the need for the nation's law enforcement agencies to become much more knowledgeable about terrorists' methods and how to respond in the event of an attack, adopting a long-term view of protecting the homeland.

This chapter section defines types of terrorism, some law enforcement and legislative responses to it, cyberterrorism, and a related issue: the use of unmanned aerial vehicles (or drones). In Chapter 4, a related discussion was provided concerning how police organization has changed since 9/11, and three relatively new policing paradigms that can also be applied to combatting terrorism—smart policing, intelligence-led policing, and predictive policing—that are being applied to crime fighting.

Definition and Types

The Federal Bureau of Investigation (FBI) defines **terrorism** as the "unlawful use of force against persons or property to intimidate or coerce a government, the civilian population, or any segment thereof, in furtherance of political or social objectives."[1] Furthermore, international terrorist threats are divided into the following three categories:

1. *Foreign sponsors of international terrorism.* This includes countries that have been designated as such sponsors and view terrorism as a tool of foreign policy. They fund, organize, network, and provide other support to formal terrorist groups and extremists.

terrorism the unlawful use of force against persons or property to intimidate or coerce a government or its population, so as to further political or social objectives.

2. *Formalized terrorist groups.* Autonomous organizations (such as bin Laden's Al-Qaeda, Afghanistan's Taliban, Iranian-backed Hezbollah, and Palestinian HAMAS) have their own infrastructures, personnel, finances, and training facilities.

3. *Loosely affiliated international radical extremists.* Examples are the persons who bombed the World Trade Center in 1993. They do not represent a particular nation but may pose the most urgent threat to the United States because they remain relatively unknown to law enforcement agencies.

Date	Perpetrator (if known)	Location of attack	Number of people injured (approx)	Number of people killed	Description of attack
9/11/2001		New York, NY	8,700	2,759	Two hijacked airplanes crash into the World Trade Center towers
9/11/2001		Alexandria, VA	200	189	A single airplane is hijacked and crashes into the Pentagon
9/11/2001		Somerset County, PA	0	45	A single airplane is hijacked and crashes into a rural area
9/18/2001		West Palm Beach, FL; New York, NY	10	1	Letters laced with anthrax are sent through the mail
10/9/2001		Washington, DC	7	4	Letters laced with anthrax are sent through the mail
12/2001	Richard Reid	Flight from Paris to Miami, FL	0	0	A man boards a flight with explosives inside his shoes; failing to light them with a match, he is apprehended and arrested
3/19/2002		Tucson, AZ	0	1	Muslim snipers shoot a 60-year-old man on a golf course
5/27/2002		Denton, TX	0	1	Muslim snipers shoot a man in his yard
7/4/2002		Los Angeles, CA	4	2	Two Israelis are killed by an Egyptian gunman at the airport
9/5/2002		Clinton, MD	0	1	Several Muslims shoot an owner of a pizza shop
9/21/2002		Montgomery, AL	1	1	Muslim snipers shoot two women (one dies)
9/23/2002		Baton Rouge, LA	0	1	A Muslim sniper shoots a Korean woman
10/2/2002 and 10/23/2002		Maryland, Virginia, and Washington, DC	1	10	Attempting to extort money and gain new recruits, 2 snipers kill at least 10 people
6/2003		Alexandria, VA	0	0	Eleven men, in support of several terrorist organizations, are arrested for weapons charges and violating the Neutrality Acts
8/6/2003		Houston, TX	0	1	A Saudi college student slashes the throat of a Jewish student
4/13/2004		Raleigh, NC	4	1	A Muslim man runs over five people with his car
11/29/2005		Santa Cruz, CA	4	0	Suspected animals rights activists commit several Incendiary attacks
3/5/2006	Mohammed Reza Taheri-azar	University of North Carolina, Chapel Hill, NC	6–9	0	A man drives his SUV into a group of students, seeking "retribution for the treatment of Muslims around the world"

FIGURE 6-1 **Terrorist Attacks Committed in the United States since September, 2001**

Source: Excerpt from Terrorist Attacks and Related Incidents in the United States by Wm. Robert Johnston. Copyright by Wm. Robert Johnston. Used by permission of Wm. Robert Johnston.

Date	Name	Location	Injured	Killed	Description
6/25/2006		Denver, CO	5	1	A Muslim man shoots a police officer and four of his coworkers because it is "Allah's choice"
7/28/2006		Seattle, WA	5	1	A Muslim man fires at a group of women at the Jewish Federation of Greater Seattle
12/2006	Derrick Shareef	Rockford, IL	0	0	A man attempts to detonate hand grenades inside a shopping mall
2/13/2007		Salt Lake City, UT	4	5	A shooting spree by a Muslim immigrant at a mall leaves five dead and four wounded
2/24/2008		Los Angeles, CA	1	0	In an attempted burglary of a biomedical researcher, animal rights activists injure the researcher's husband
7/27/2008		Knoxville, TN	7	2	A church congregation is fired upon by a male assailant
5/2009	James Cromitie, David Williams, Onta Williams, and Laguerre Payen	Newburgh, NY, and Riverdale, NY	0	0	Using Stinger missiles, four men attempt to shoot down planes at a national guard base and to blow up Jewish synagogues
5/31/2009		Wichita, KS	0	1	An attack on a Reformation Lutheran Church kills one patron
6/1/2009	Abdulhakim Mujahid Muhammad, formerly known as Carlos Bledsoe	Little Rock, AR	1	1	A shooting attack at an Army Navy Career Center kills one Army private and injures another
6/10/2009		Washington, DC	1	1	A shooting at the Holocaust Museum kills one person and wounds another
9/2009	Maher Husein Smadi	Dallas, TX	0	0	A man is arrested while attempting to plant a bomb in a skyscraper
9/11/2009		Owosso, MI	0	2	An abortion protester and a local businessman are shot and killed near a school
11/5/2009	Nidal Malik Hasan	Foot Hood, TX	32–44	13	A U.S. Army officer/psychiatrist goes on a shooting rampage
12/4/2009		Binghamton, NY	0	1	A Muslim graduate student stabs his non-Muslim Islamic Studies professor to death in the name of "persecuted Muslims"
12/25/2009	Umar Farouk Abdulmutallab	Detroit, MI	3	0	During a flight from Amsterdam, a Yemeni terrorist attempts to detonate a bomb hidden in his underwear; the passengers and crew subdue the terrorist
2/18/2010		Austin, TX	13	2	A small plane crashes into a federal office building in a suicide attack
3/4/2010		Alexandria, VA	2	1	A shootout occurs at a gate near the Pentagon; the gunman is killed, and two officers are wounded
9/1/2010		Silver Spring, MD	0	1	A gunman at Discovery Communications headquarters takes three persons hostage
12/2010	Antonio Martinez	Baltimore, MD	0	0	A would-be jihadist bomber attempts to purchase a bomb from undercover FBI agents for use at a military recruiting center

FIGURE 6-1   (*continued*)

Date	Perpetrator (if known)	Location of attack	Number of people injured (approx)	Number of people killed	Description of attack
1/8/2011		Tucson, AZ	13	6	At a political event, a federal judge is killed and a U.S. Congresswoman injured by a gunman
9/11/2011		Waltham, MA	0	3	A Muslim terrorist slits the throats of three Jewish men
8/5/2012		Oak Creek, WI	4	7	A shooting attack at a Sikh temple leaves seven dead and four injured
8/14/2012		LaPlace, LA	4	2	Shooters with ties to the sovereign citizen movement kill two police officers
8/15/2012		Washington, DC	1	0	At the Family Research Council offices, one guard is shot while subduing a gunman
4/15/2013	Tamerlan Tsarnaev, Dzhokhar Tsarnaev	Boston, MA	264	3	Two bombs are detonated at the Boston Marathon, killing 3 and injuring 183
4/17/2013		Washington, DC	0	0	Two letters, both containing Ricin, are mailed to a Mississippi state senator and to President Obama; they are discovered at mail screening facilities
4/18–19/2013		Watertown, MA	2	2	During the manhunt for the Boston Marathon bombers, one police officer is killed and one is injured

FIGURE 6-1   (continued)

A Companion Threat: Bioterrorism

The United States is also vulnerable to biological weapons and bioterrorism—terrorist acts that involve the use of biological agents, to produce sickness, disease, or death. Smallpox, botulism, and plague also constitute major threats, and many experts feel that it is only a matter of time before biological weapons get into the wrong hands and are used like explosives were in the past.

This form of terrorism is capable of eradicating an entire civilization. All that required is a toxin that can be cultured and put into a spray form that can be weaponized and disseminated into the population. Fortunately, they *are* extremely difficult for all but specially trained individuals to make in large quantities and in the correct dosage, tricky to transport because live organisms are delicate, and must be dispersed in a proper molecule size to infect the lungs of the target. Like chemical weapons, they are also dependent on the wind and the weather and are difficult to control.[2]

Practical and Legislative Responses

Several means exist for attempting to address domestic terrorism, both practical and legislative in nature or origin. Next, we discuss several of them.

Posse Comitatus

First is military support of law enforcement. The Posse Comitatus Act of 1878 prohibits using the military to execute the laws domestically; the military may be called on, however, to provide personnel and equipment for certain special support activities such as domestic terrorist events involving weapons of mass destruction.[3]

National Incident Management System

In Department of Homeland Security (DHS) Presidential Directive 5, *Management of Domestic Incidents*, President George W. Bush directed the DHS secretary to develop and administer a **National Incident Management System** (NIMS). This nationwide system provides a consistent approach for federal, state, and local governments to work effectively together to prepare for, prevent, respond to, and recover from domestic incidents. This directive requires all federal departments and agencies to adopt the NIMS and to use it—and to make its adoption and use by state and local agencies a condition for federal preparedness assistance beginning in fiscal year 2005.[4] The NIMS is a lengthy document that cannot be duplicated here in its entirety; interested persons may find the document at: http://www.fema.gov/pdf/emergency/nims/NIMS_core.pdf.

> **National Incident Management System** a nationwide system providing for levels of governments to work together to address domestic incidents.

USA Patriot Act

Enacted shortly after the 9/11 attacks, this Act dramatically expanded the federal government's ability to investigate Americans without establishing probable cause for "intelligence purposes," and to conduct searches if there are "reasonable grounds to believe" that there may be national security threats. Federal agencies such as the FBI and others are given access to financial, mental health, medical, library, and other records. The Act was reauthorized in March 2006, providing additional tools for protecting mass transportation systems and seaports from attack, taking steps to combat the methamphetamine epidemic, closing loopholes in our ability to prevent terrorist financing, and creating a National Security Division at the Department of Justice.[5]

Military Commissions Act of 2006

The fight against terrorism was also aided and expanded in October 2006 with the enactment of Public Law 109-366, the Military Commissions Act (MCA) of 2006, which President George W. Bush hailed as "one of the most important pieces of legislation in the War on Terror."[6] Under the MCA, the president is authorized to establish military commissions to try unlawful enemy combatants, the commissions are authorized to sentence defendants to death, and defendants are prevented from invoking the Geneva Conventions as a source of rights during commission proceedings. The law contains a provision stripping detainees of the right to file *habeas corpus* petitions in federal court and also allows hearsay evidence to be admitted during proceedings, so long as the presiding officer determines it to be reliable.[7]

Fusion centers have been formed by a number of cities and counties in partnership with the FBI as early warning groups for terrorism.[8] The fusion center coordinates all response and counter-terrorism elements within a community or metropolitan area. As information or intelligence is gathered by local and federal agencies, it is fed into the center and analyzed. Once analyzed, terrorist threat or activity information is generated and supplied to affected constituents. The fusion centers include medical personnel and fire department personnel as well as law enforcement personnel. The medical personnel can provide the fusion center with information about suspicious illnesses—an early warning system for a biological attack—and the firefighter personnel can provide information about suspicious fires or chemical problems. The fusion center also allows for more comprehensive planning and a better coordinated response should a terrorist event occur.

> **fusion center** coordination of all counter-terrorism elements within a jurisdiction by receiving and analyzing terrorist threat or activity information.

Cyberterrorism—and the Asian Threat

Cybercrime or cyberterrorism includes such activities as identity theft, attacks against computer data and systems, the distribution of child sexual abuse images, Internet auction fraud, and the penetration of online financial services, as well as the deployment of viruses, botnets, and various e-mail scams such as phishing.[9] According to Interpol, cybercrime is one of the fastest growing areas of crime, with increasing numbers of criminals now exploiting the anonymity, speed, and convenience that modern technologies provide. The Internet also allows such criminals to commit almost any illegal activity anywhere in the world, making it essential for all countries to adapt their domestic offline controls to cover crimes carried out in cyberspace.

Without question the most challenging and potentially disastrous type of cybercrime—actually, cyberespionage—now being perpetrated against the United States is by Chinese hackers, who are estimated to be responsible for the theft of 50 to 80 percent of all American intellectual property and have compromised many of the nation's most sensitive advanced weapons systems, including missile defense technology and combat aircraft.[10] It is believed that Chinese hackers have accessed designs for more than two dozen of the U.S. military's most important and expensive weapon systems. Doing so enables China to understand those systems and be able to jam or otherwise disable them. The Pentagon recently concluded that another country's computer sabotage can constitute an act of war, which could eventually lead to United States use of military force.[11]

Of course, China's computer hacking does not stop with the U.S. military complex; corporate and business secrets are also prime targets of hackers. Estimates are that hundreds of private companies, research institutions, and Internet service providers have already been hacked, and there are also concerns about threats posed to U.S. nuclear reactors, banks, subways, and pipeline companies.[12] The specter of electricity going out for days and perhaps weeks, the gates of a major dam opening suddenly and flooding complete cities, or pipes in a chemical plant rupturing and releasing deadly gas are nightmare scenarios that keep homeland security professionals awake at night.

How to Balance Security and Privacy—and the Unmanned Aerial Vehicles (Drones)

Americans have been willing to give up much of their privacy since 9/11, but when will they begin to balk at government's having access to their telephone, computer, travel, financial, and other personal information (now available through social media, smartphones, the automatic license plate recognition system, and other technologies)? There is a delicate balance between security and privacy, and the potential widespread police use of **unmanned aerial vehicles** (UAVs), or drones, has elevated this concern for many people.

unmanned aerial vehicles ground-operated, powered aerial vehicles that are designed to carry non-lethal payloads for reconnaissance, command and control, and deception.

Drones are powered aerial vehicles that are directed by a ground or airborne controller; do not carry human operators; and are designed to carry nonlethal payloads for reconnaissance, command and control, and deception. UAVs have rapidly become available in a variety of shapes, sizes, and capabilities, from one that is about the size and appearance of a hummingbird and carrying a tiny camera to another the size of a jumbo airplane.[13] Drones would seem to be tailor-made for seeking out and surveilling persons who are planning or involved in terroristic activities.

However, the issue concerning use of drones came to the forefront in early 2013 during Senate confirmation hearings for President Obama's nominee to head the CIA, John Brennan.[14] What is evident from the hearings is that Americans are very suspicious of—and may demand that legal criteria be established for—the overflights of drones in this country as we have deployed them over Pakistan and other countries. Clearly these are vexing security and privacy policy issues that our government and society must resolve, and each day the U.S. criminal justice system is closer and closer to the day when it will likewise be embroiled in those same issues.

A "Determine and Decide" problem concerning the use of drones is provided at chapter's end.

► Managing the Use of Force: Issues and Practices

The International Association of Chiefs of Police (IACP) has defined force as "that amount of effort required by police to compel compliance from an unwilling subject."[15] Next we discuss police **use of force** in several contexts: its lawful application; types; the characteristics of officers and situations in which force is more heavily involved; use with persons who have mental disorders, new responses to active shooters, vehicular pursuits, use-of-force continuums, and reporting and investigating occurrences.

use of force the amount of effort required by police or other criminal justice functionary to compel compliance by an unwilling subject.

Power to Be Used Judiciously

Certainly the events (riots, looting, protests, and shootings) that ensued following the August 2014 police killing of Michael Brown—a young, unarmed African American—in Ferguson, Missouri, underscored the ongoing volatility and controversial nature of police shootings and use of force. There, police reactions to the community's unrest, which included activating the state's national guard, also revived the debate about whether the police are becoming too militarized (discussed in Chapter 4).[16] The Ferguson shooting's aftermath—reminiscent of the rage and disorder occurring in the United States during the 1960s and 1970s—also laid bare the fact that much work remains to be done with respect to policing-minority relations in many cities of this nation.

Americans bestow a tremendous amount of authority on their police officers. Indeed, the police are the only element of our society (except for the military, under certain circumstances) that is allowed to use force against its citizens, up to and including lethal force. The *quid pro quo*, however, is that the police are given this power and authority with the expectation that they will use it judiciously, only when necessary, and as a last resort. A serious problem arises when officers deploy this force improperly.

Regardless of the type of force used, police officers must use it in a legally acceptable manner. The U.S. Supreme Court ruled that the use of force at arrest must be:

> [o]bjectively reasonable in view of all the facts and circumstances of each particular case, including the severity of the crime at issue, whether the suspect poses an immediate threat to the safety of the officers or others, and whether he is actively resisting arrest or attempting to evade arrest by flight.[17]

However, determining what constitutes "objectively reasonable" is not an easy task.

Police officers are allowed to use only that force necessary to affect an arrest. Thus, the amount of force that a police officer uses is dependent on the amount of resistance demonstrated by the person being arrested. This concept has traditionally been taught to police officers in training academies through a use-of-force continuum, the applicability of which is now being questioned and which is discussed more later.

A Typology of Abuse of Authority

The use-of-force continuum (discussed below in the "Managing the Use of Force" section), shows the range of force that officers can employ. David Carter[18] looked at officers' conduct and provided a typology of abuse of authority, which includes (1) physical abuse/excessive force, (2) verbal/psychological abuse, and (3) legal abuse/violations of civil rights.

- *Physical Abuse and Excessive Force:* Police use of physical force often results in substantial public scrutiny. Local incidents may not receive national media coverage, but they often have the same dramatic, chilling effect in a community. The application of deadly force can be a form of excessive force. When a police officer deliberately kills someone, a determination is made as to whether the homicide was justified to prevent imminent death or serious bodily injury to the officer or another person. In 1985, the U.S. Supreme Court ruled that the shooting of any unarmed, nonviolent fleeing felony suspect violates the Fourth Amendment to the Constitution.[19] As a result, almost all major urban police departments enacted restrictive policies regarding deadly force.

- *Verbal and Psychological Abuse:* Police officers sometimes inflict verbal and psychological abuse on citizens by berating or belittling them. One of the most common methods used by police officers to verbally abuse citizens is through the use of profanity. Unfortunately, profanity has become a part of the police culture and of many officers' everyday speech. When profanity is used liberally in the work setting, it increases the likelihood that it will be used inappropriately.

- *Legal Abuse and Violations of Civil Rights:* Legal abuse and civil rights violations consist of police actions that violate citizens' constitutional or statutory rights. This abuse usually involves false arrest, false imprisonment, and harassment. Supervisors and managers play a key role in preventing legal abuse and violations of citizens' civil rights. Supervisors frequently back up officers when responding to calls and observe situations that lead to an arrest. They should ensure that officers' decisions to arrest are based on probable cause, not some lesser standard. They should also review arrest reports and question officers when arrests are not observed to ensure that the arrests meet the probable cause standard.

Does a Particular "Type" of Officer Use More Force?

Do certain characteristics—"types"—of officers predispose them to be more (or less) likely to engage in the use of force? Are there differences in terms of officer gender, race, type and place of assignment, length of service, and so on? These are important policy questions that can, if answered, certainly affect how agencies recruit, hire, train, and assign their officers.

A 2013 study by Steven Brandl and Meghan Stroshine[20] conducted an analysis of more than 1,000 police officers and nearly 500 use-of-force reports to find the answers to these questions. Their findings were instructive:

1. Arrest activity is the strongest predictor of use of force. High-rate officers make over twice as many arrests as low-rate officers, and are significantly more likely to be involved in more force incidents, specifically those incidents that involve a weapon and/or bodily force that result in an injury or a complaint of an injury.

2. Consistent with prior studies, it was found that a few officers account for a large proportion of all the force incidents (officers who use a high rate of force—5.4% of all officers—accounted for about 32% of all recorded use-of-force situations).

3. Officers who use more force are more likely to work certain shifts—evenings and nights (or graveyard).

4. Male officers are more likely to be involved in force situations than female officers (however, male officers make more arrests).

5. There was no significant difference among officers in the type of force used; however, high-rate officers tended to use an electronic control device more often (however, it may be that officers who volunteer for Taser certification are more willing to use any type of force compared with the low-rate officers who do not desire such training).

6. White officers are more likely than minority officers to be involved in force incidents; however, Brandl and Stroshine suggest this may have to do with other factors; for example, minority officers are more likely to be female (and female officers are less

likely to be involved in force incidents) or older (older officers are less likely to be involved in force incidents), or because minority officers tend to make fewer arrests, they might have less likelihood of being involved in force situations.

Previous research also indicates that the location/type of patrol assignment may be related to use of force, as high-crime areas may foster conditions where use of force is more frequently necessary. There are also indications that time of day may be correlated with use-of-force incidents: serious crime and arrests are more likely to occur during the late evening/early morning hours. Finally, it is indicated that officers who are more active (in terms of the number of arrests made) may be more often involved in use-of-force situations.[21]

Policy implications for police administrators that are suggested from these findings include the following:

1. Because a small group of officers is responsible for the highest proportion of use-of-force incidents and complaints, they should consider (if one does not exist) adopting an Early Warning System, to more rapidly identify violence-prone or problem-prone officers, monitor citizen complaints, and identify officer performance problems; they will then be able to take corrective action.

2. Because more use-of-force incidents occur on the evening and night shifts, police administrators may want to reconsider the timeworn habit of assigning the newest, least experienced officers to those shifts; or alternatively, if they are so assigned, then they should at least ensure that close supervision is provided over them.

3. Because women are implicated much less than men in use-of-force situations, this indicates that there is either a difference in their actual performance or that women are less likely to need to employ force. Whatever the case, this seems to imply that greater integration of women into police ranks can reduce the incidence of police violence (see the discussion of women in policing, earlier).

Use of Force on Persons with Mental Disorders

A topic that has recently gained considerable attention concerns police treatment of persons suffering from mental disorders. Several studies have attempted to determine the extent to which officers encounter such persons, and if force is used by, and against the police in such encounters. First, findings suggest that many police believe that dealing with persons having mental disorders is dangerous, because such individuals are more likely to use violence (although this belief is not borne out by the existing research; rather, studies show that it is primarily when people are under the influence of drugs—rather than mental illness or alcohol—that police must use force). Police have also reported that they use more severe levels of force on suspects who appear to be mentally unstable—force which is justified because of the suspects' more aggressive behavior. It has also been suggested that police disproportionately use pepper spray against such individuals.[22]

It is clear that, although the proportion of incidents of use of force with persons having actual mental disorders is relatively small, it remains that dealing with such persons is a significant portion of the police workload; therefore, because such persons may seem irrational and unstable, and threaten to use (and may actually use) weapons on the police, officers need to be trained in communicating and verbally deescalating incidents with people who are mentally disordered, to minimize the likelihood of either party being injured. It is suggested that such training be standardized, focusing on risk assessment and management, while emphasizing the importance of cordoning and managing such situations and thus avoid situations where force must be deployed.[23] This training and overall policy development can be developed through partnering with mental health agencies.

New Approaches to "Active Shooters"

Mass Killings: Extent and Nature

Certainly a topic that is related to police use of force is the concern with shootings, particularly those occurring in the nation's schools. The horrific killings of 26 children and teachers at Sandy Hook Elementary School in Newtown, Connecticut, in December 2012, brought calls for a review of mass killings in the United States. Although one study found that such mass killings—defined as incidents in which four or more people are killed by the attacker—only account for about 1 percent of all murders, they do occur about every 2 weeks on average. In fact, a review of mass killings from 2006 through 2010—thus excluding such high-profile shootings as that in Newtown, a rampage in early 2012 in a movie theater in Aurora, Colorado (which left 12 dead and 57 injured), as well as an attack on a Sikh temple in Wisconsin that killed six—found that about one-fourth of mass murders involve two or more killers, that one-third of such killings do not involve guns (they can involve fire, a knife or a blunt instrument), and that children (ages 12 and below) are frequently victims, representing about one-fifth of all victims.[24]

Changes in Police Responses

Much has changed in the decade since the April 1999 mass murders by two shooters at Columbine High School in Golden, Colorado, where 13 people were killed while on-scene officers waited 45 minutes for an elite SWAT team to arrive. As seen in the aforementioned Sandy Hook Elementary School shootings, police have greatly modified their protocols for dealing with such critical incidents. The most immediate change in protocol calls for police across the country to react swiftly to an **active shooter** situation, where an individual is actively engaged in killing or attempting to kill people in a confined and populated area, is that responding officers are being trained to rush toward gunfire and, if necessary, even step over victims in order to stop the active shooter before more lives are lost. Such training is train police grounded on the assumption that a gunman, in a mass shooting, kills a person every 15 seconds. The old approach, prior to Columbine, was for police to take a contain-and-wait strategy, intended to prevent officers and bystanders from getting killed; first responders would establish a perimeter to contain the situation and then wait for the special-weapons team to go in and neutralize the shooters(s). Now, however, police typically employ so-called contact teams, where officers from any jurisdiction quickly band together to enter a building in formation and confront the shooters. Thus, officers shift the shooter's focus *from* persons in the building *to* the officers. Then the SWAT teams enter to search for any remaining shooters or to attempt to rescue any hostages.

Another change wrought by Columbine is that special-weapons teams now typically have armed medics and rescue teams trained to remove wounded persons under fire.[25]

> **active shooter**
> an individual who is actively engaged in killing or attempting to kill people in a confined and populated area.

Vehicular Pursuits

A High-Stakes Operation

Another policing matter that is at the heart of police use of force concerns **vehicular pursuits** where police attempt to apprehend someone in a fleeing vehicle who has indicated he or she does not intend to stop or yield. Civil litigation arising out of collisions involving police pursuits reveals it to be a high-stakes undertaking with serious and sometimes tragic results. Several hundred people are killed each year during police pursuits[26]; many of the resulting deaths and injuries involve innocent third parties or stem from minor traffic violations. The U.S. Supreme Court, as discussed in the next section, has strengthened most

> **vehicular pursuit**
> police attempts to apprehend someone in a fleeing vehicle who has indicated he or she does not intend to stop or yield.

progressive chase policies, but the Court has also conferred responsibility on the police. The responsibility for ensuring that proper policies and procedures exist rests squarely with the chief executive officer (CEO) of the agency.

Vehicular pursuits involve a delicate balancing act. On the one hand is the need to show that flight from the law is no way to freedom. If a police agency completely bans high-speed pursuits, its credibility with both law-abiding citizens and law violators may suffer; public knowledge that the agency has a no-pursuit policy may encourage people to flee, decreasing the probability of apprehension.[27]

On the other hand, the high-speed chase threatens everyone within range of the pursuit, including suspects, their passengers, and other drivers or bystanders. One police trainer tells officers to ask themselves a simple question to determine whether to continue a pursuit: "Is this person a threat to the public safety other than the fact that the police are chasing him?" If the officer cannot objectively answer "yes," the pursuit should be terminated.[28]

The following incidents demonstrate the dangerous nature of police pursuits:

- In Omaha, Nebraska, a 70-mile-per-hour pursuit through a residential neighborhood of a motorcyclist for expired license plates ended when the motorcyclist ran a stop sign, crashing into another vehicle and killing the female passenger on the motorcycle.

- A sheriff's deputy in Florida intentionally rammed a vehicle during a pursuit for an outstanding misdemeanor warrant, causing a collision and killing a backseat passenger.

- A police officer pursuing a shoplifter in Mobile, Alabama, crashed into a mall security vehicle, seriously injuring the guard.

The Supreme Court's View

In May 1990, two Sacramento County, California, deputies responded to a fight call. At the scene, they observed a motorcycle with two riders approaching their vehicle at high speed; turning on their red lights, they ordered the driver to stop. The motorcycle operator began to elude the officers, who initiated a pursuit reaching speeds of more than 100 miles per hour over about 1.3 miles. The pursuit ended when the motorcycle crashed; the deputies' vehicle could not stop in time and struck the bike's passenger, killing him; his family brought suit, claiming that the pursuit had violated the crash victim's due process rights under the Fourteenth Amendment.

In May 1998, the U.S. Supreme Court, in *County of Sacramento v. Lewis*,[29] ruled that the proper standard to be employed in these cases is whether the officer's conduct during the pursuit was conscience shocking; it further determined that high-speed chases with no intent to harm suspects do not give rise to liability under the Fourteenth Amendment.[30] The Court left unanswered many important questions such as whether an innocent third party can file a claim against the police for damages or whether a municipality can be held liable for its failure to train officers in pursuit issues.

The field supervisor is responsible for ensuring that proper methods are employed by patrol officers during pursuits, whether the pursuit involves simply a primary pursuing officer and a backup or a more elaborate scenario.

It is the responsibility of command personnel and supervisors to ensure that officers thoroughly understand and comply with pursuit policies. Factors to be considered by the courts in evaluating pursuit liability include the following:

- *The reason for the pursuit.* Does it justify the actions taken by the officer?

- *Driving conditions.* Any factor that could hinder an officer's ability to safely conduct a pursuit should be considered sufficient reason to terminate it.

- *The use of police warning devices.* Typically, lights and siren are required by state statutes.

- **Excessive speed.** This often depends on the conditions of the environment. For example, a 30-mile-per-hour pursuit in a school zone may be considered excessive and dangerous.

- **Demonstrations of due regard in officers' actions.** Officers who choose the course of safety will create the least danger to all parties affected and maintain the highest degree of protection from liability.

- **The use of deadly force.** There are few instances in which officers can justify driving tactics that result in the death of a fleeing driver; such situations include roadblocks, boxing in (which involves police pursuit vehicles surrounding a violator's moving vehicle, and then slowing the violator's vehicle to a stop), and ramming.

- **Departmental policies and state law.** These must be obeyed; to do otherwise greatly increases the potential liability of both the officer and the department.

- **Appropriate supervision and training.** In the absence of such measures, the department will be subject to a finding of negligence, and liability will attach.[31]

Use-of-Force Continuums

Use-of-force continuums have been evolving for over three decades; they serve as a guideline that officers can use to determine the type of force that is appropriate for certain types of citizen resistance they encounter. Graphically, continuums can be depicted as a simple staircase or ladder to a more elaborate wheel or matrix. A simple linear use-of-force continuum might contain the following five escalating steps: officer presence/verbal direction, touch control, empty-hand tactics and chemical agents, hand-held impact weapons, and lethal force.[32]

William Terrill and Eugene Paoline surveyed more than 600 police agencies to determine the extent to which they rely on a use-of-force continuum as part of their less-lethal policy. They found that more than 80 percent of the agencies use a continuum; furthermore, the most prevalent type of continuum was the linear design (sort of a staircase or ladder used by 47%), followed by a matrix/box or a circular/wheel approach, both used in about 10 percent of agencies.[33]

Today, however, many police executives and researchers are uncomfortable with the more simplistic, sequential depiction of the force continuum. They feel that police use of force is not and cannot always be employed in such a sequential, stair-step fashion as this continuum implies. So the question remains: How much force is reasonable for a police officer to use against a suspect? Even when agency policies accompany the continuum (as they always should), such continuums have always been confusing to most police officers. "How far and when do I 'climb the next rung' of the ladder" sort of confusion could and did exist. Force continuums also fail to represent properly the dynamic encounter between the officer and a resistant suspect and to take into account the wide array of tools that are available to officers today; it is too difficult for a department to dictate by a continuum in what situations, say, a baton or pepper spray or Taser or other, less lethal weapons, should be used.

Instead, many agencies now require their officers to be "objectively reasonable" in their use of force and have adopted the following definition of *objectively reasonable* as developed by the International Association of Chiefs of Police: "An officer's use of force on a free person shall be objectively reasonable based upon the totality of the circumstances known or perceived by him or her at the time force was used."[34]

A new approach to determine proper use of force has recently been developed by two special agents of the FBI. It is designed to "more accurately reflect the intent of the law and the changing expectations of society" and to provide officers with "simple, clear, unambiguous, and consistent guidelines in the use of force."[35]

Known as the DRRM, this approach combines a use-of-force continuum with the behaviors of suspects. *Dynamic* indicates that the model is fluid, and *resistance* demonstrates

use-of-force continuum a graphic depiction of levels of force used by police to determine the type of force that is appropriate for certain types of citizen resistance.

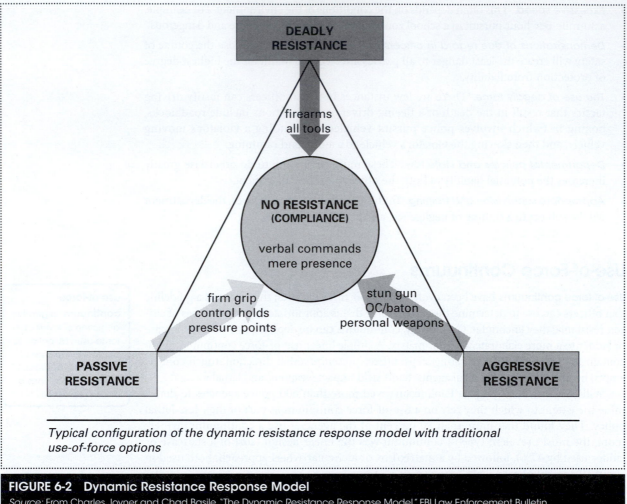

Typical configuration of the dynamic resistance response model with traditional use-of-force options

FIGURE 6-2   Dynamic Resistance Response Model
Source: From Charles Joyner and Chad Basile, "The Dynamic Resistance Response Model," FBI Law Enforcement Bulletin, September 2007, p. 19.

that the suspect controls the interaction. In this view, a major failing of past continuums has been that the emphasis was on the officer and the amount of force used. DRRM instead emphasizes that the suspect's level of resistance determines the officer's response. The model also divides suspects into one of four categories (See Figure 6-2 ■).

As shown in Figure 6-2, if a passively resistant suspect fails to follow commands and perhaps attempts to move away from the officer or escape, appropriate responses include using a firm grip, control holds, and pressure points to gain compliance. An aggressively resistant suspect—one who is taking offensive action by attempting to push, throw, strike, tackle, or physically harm the officer—on the contrary, would call for such responses as the use of personal weapons (hands, fists, and feet), batons, pepper spray, and a stun gun. Finally, because a deadly resistant (i.e., lethal force is being or is about to be utilized) suspect can seriously injure or kill the officer or another person, the officer is justified in using force, including deadly force, as is *objectively reasonable* to overcome the offender.

In the DRRM model, a suspect's lack of resistance (compliance) is in the center of the triangle, which is emphasized as the goal of every encounter. If a suspect's resistance level places him or her on one of the three corners of the triangle, the officer's response is intended to move the suspect's behavior to the center of the triangle and compliance. The sole purpose of the application of force is to gain compliance.

Reporting and Examining Use-of-Force Occurrences

To identify and monitor officers' use of force, law enforcement agencies need a comprehensive data collection strategy. At a minimum, departments should utilize use-of-force reports completed by officers involved in forceful incidents. Traditionally, agencies required reports when officers used force that was likely to cause death or serious bodily harm (e.g., firing a weapon); in recent years, however, a growing number of agencies have begun documenting *all* instances involving force, regardless of the potential for deadly force or injuries.[36]

Administrators should implement supervisors' control-of-persons reports, requiring supervisors to go to the scene of all incidents when officers use force in order to interview the officers, suspects, and witnesses and record their responses. Supervisors should also take photographs of any injuries or record complaints of injuries. These forms can also require information on demographics, level and type of force, resistance, weapons, and other information (some agencies go further, wanting information on suspects' race, ethnicity, health status, nature of treatment, impairment, and observed behavior). This kind of information should be supplemented by a detailed narrative explaining each of the parties' perspectives, allowing the supervisor to write a sequential account of all relevant actions: the original call or observation, officer's and suspect's behaviors, why suspects resisted, and levels and types of resistance.[37]

▶ Social Media and the Police: The Good and the Bad

A 2013 study of police use of **social media**—forms of electronic communication for social networking to share information, ideas, personal messages—found that the police typically post crimes occurring in the community or public relations announcements, as a "police blotter" (to indicate the arrest of a suspect), and announce crimes that have occurred in the previous 24 hours. Conversely, it was found that police tend not to seek the public's help through "be on the lookout" (BOLO) or other requests for information. Furthermore, agencies rarely use Facebook to warn citizens of specific crimes occurring in their community, and to alert the public about potential danger or traffic problems in the area, crime prevention tips, DUI check-points, missing persons, and police recruitment efforts.[38]

> **social media** forms of electronic communication for social networking, to share information, ideas, personal messages.

The power and usefulness of social networking sites has become quite evident (see Exhibit 6.1); during the recent devastation of Hurricane Sandy on the northeastern coast in October 2012, police and other emergency services relied on such sites to warn citizens and constantly update citizens on evacuations, street closures, flooding, and storm conditions almost as they occurred. The same social media value became evident after a mid-2012 shooting near the Oakland airport; using Nixle—a public notification service deployed for crimes in progress, traffic problems, and missing children—police quickly sent text alerts to thousands of nearby residents informing them to stay out of the area.[39]

EXHIBIT 6.1

THE POWER OF FACEBOOK

On a cold November night in New York City, a police officer observed an older, barefooted homeless man on the street. The officer left his post, but soon returned with a new pair of boots; he then knelt to help the man put them on. This act of kindness happened to be photographed by a tourist from Arizona, which she then posted to the NYPD's Facebook page, making the officer an overnight hero.[40] The picture produced more than 612,000 "likes" and 48,000 comments. Although a unique instance, this example clearly demonstrates the power of social media to strengthen a police agency's connection with the community, when used as a public relations tool.[41]

Some critics, however, question the use of social media, saying it releases too much information without adequate filtering. Furthermore, some authors caution police about their own personal use of social media. First, with social media, officers' community exposure is increased and the usual methods used in the past to protect their identity—post office boxes, license plate confidentiality, and so on—are ineffective. Social media sites offer easy access to an unlimited pool of potential "friends," and constraints do not exist for social media; anyone can post anything online with little fear of repercussions. Through social media, people can easily attack a police officer's character (and, if an officers' integrity is compromised, so is their courtroom testimony and investigations; see discussion of *Brady* material, Chapter 14).

Cases have arisen where comments posted online have led to disciplinary actions, and people can post questionable videos of police officers on such sites in hopes of their profiting financially from them by filing claims or lawsuits. Finally, some people even engage in "cop-baiting," intentionally creating confrontational situations with officers to exploit them for personal or political motives.[42]

However, such potential drawbacks have not stopped the police from employing social media sites. In fact, dozens of police agencies now post surveillance videos on YouTube to communicate with the public and catch criminals.[43] Philadelphia's police officers recently began using Twitter for crime-fighting, with officers at all levels to engage in greater use of tweeting to issue public safety alerts and crimes in the area. The social networking community is a "force multiplier," allowing the police to share data, photos, and videos as they solicit help in catching crooks.[44] As Camden, New Jersey, Police Chief Scott Thomson put it, social media makes police "appear bigger than we are."[45]

▶ Wanted: More Diversity in Policing and Less Sexual Harassment

Targeted efforts by local police agencies to recruit and hire racial/ethnic minorities have resulted in twice as many minorities being hired as women. Obviously much work remains to be done. During the 1970s, some formal barriers to hiring women, such as height requirements, were eliminated; in addition, subjective physical agility tests and oral interviews were modified.[46] Some job discrimination suits further expanded women's opportunities.

Key Issues with Hiring Women

Today women represent about 12 percent of sworn personnel in local police departments.[47] Although the representation of women officers is low compared with their overall proportion in the total population, the discrepancy is even more evident in the leadership ranks, where women number only 1 percent of the police chiefs in the United States.[48,49]

Peter Horne identified several key issues that need to be addressed[50]:

1. *Recruitment.* Literature such as flyers, posters, and brochures should feature female officers working in all areas of policing and be widely disseminated (at local colleges, women's groups, female community leaders, gyms, and martial arts schools) and use all types of media to attract qualified applicants.[51]

2. *Preemployment physical testing.* Historically, women have been screened out disproportionately in the preemployment screening physical testing used by many agencies, so agencies should examine their physical tests to determine the reasons for this occurrence.

3. *Academy training.* Recruits must be trained in sexually integrated academy classes to ensure full integration between female and male officers. Involving female instructors

in firearms and physical/self-defense training will send the message that trained, veteran female officers can effectively handle the physical aspects of policing.

4. *Field training.* Field training officers (FTOs) should be both supportive of female rookies and effective evaluators of their competence. Women should also serve as FTOs.

5. *Assignments.* Agencies should routinely review the daily assignments of all probationary officers to ensure that they have an equal opportunity to become effective patrol officers. The majority of supervisory positions exist in the patrol division, and departments generally believe that field supervisors must have adequate field experience to be effective and respected by subordinates.

6. *Promotions.* Performance evaluations and the overall promotional system utilized by agencies should be scrutinized for gender bias. To provide more objectivity (in terms of ability to measure aptitude), the process may include more hands-on (practical, applied) tasks and the selection of board members of both genders.

7. *Harassment and discrimination.* A Police Foundation study found that "most women officers have experienced both sex discrimination and harassment on the job"[52] (see discussion below in the diversity section). Departments need to have policies in place concerning sexual harassment and gender discrimination—and they need to enforce them.

8. *Mentoring.* Formal mentoring programs—which can begin even before the rookie enters the academy—have helped some agencies raise their retention rates for women; such programs can include having a veteran employee provide new hires with information concerning what to expect at the academy and beyond, during field training, and in the probationary period.

9. *Career and family.* Police agencies should have a leave policy covering pregnancy and maternity leave. Light- or limited-duty assignments (e.g., desk, communications, and records) can be made available to female officers when reassignment is necessary. Other issues include the availability of quality childcare and shift rotation (which can more heavily burden single parents), as well as uniforms, body armor, and firearms that fit women.

Sexual Harassment: Enigma Wrapped in Anachronism

In Chapter 3 we briefly defined and discussed workplace harassment in general; here, it is discussed more in terms of its occurrence in police agencies.

It is almost impossible to fathom that, in this century, sexual harassment still exists in our society, particularly in an occupation as tightly controlled with policies and procedures as policing. Yet it does occur, and is in fact "alive and well." A 2013 study by Lonsway et al.[53] estimated that between one-half to three-fourths of all women working in law enforcement have experienced some form of sexually harassing behavior in their workplace, and about 84 percent of their respondents indicated that had experienced such behavior in the past year. Lonsway et al.[54] found that most of these behaviors involved "dirty stories or jokes," statements that "put women down," were typically performed by a coworker, and were most likely unreported (only about 5% filing a formal complaint). More disturbingly, unwanted sexual attention that was physical in nature and *quid pro quo* harassment (where one offers another person a condition of employment or job-related benefits such as promotion, salary increases, shift or work assignments, in exchange for sexual favors), although less frequently experienced by the respondents, was more likely to be committed by a supervisor. Furthermore, about half of the respondents who had filed a formal complaint experienced retaliation as a result.[55]

Clearly, supervisors and administrators in policing (and, where it occurs, in courts and in prisons) should be aware that this study demonstrates a "high incidence" of such behaviors still occurs, which is cause for alarm. Such administrators must, as Lonsway et al. conclude, "ensure that sexually harassing behaviors are not committed or tolerated within their organizations and, when they do occur, that retaliation does not result."[56]

▶ Contract and Consolidated Policing

Following World War II, cities began contracting—primarily with sheriff's offices—for police services. Probably the first such instance was Lakewood, California, in Los Angeles County, in 1954. Since then, many smaller cities have contracted for police services, and with the recent recession, interest in contracting appears to be increasing.[57] Indeed, the National Sheriff's Association devotes special attention to contracting on its website.[58] Nearly one-third of California's cities contract with their county sheriff.

contract policing, where a (usually smaller) community contracts with an outside unit of government to provide its policing services, can be said to operate under public choice theory, which states that policing works best in small units that are more responsive than large organizations to residents' needs. Generally, this theory argues that smaller organizations are more efficient and effective overall by being close to their consumers, competing for their support and approval.[59] Some examples of contracted services include personnel wages and benefits, patrol vehicle and maintenance costs, uniforms, dispatchers, communications equipment, jails, forensic laboratories, mobile crime scene units, consolidated narcotics units, and even airplanes for extraditing arrestees.

Does contracting actually succeed, however, in being cost-effective while also providing quality police service? Those questions were the subject of a recent research project by Nelligan and Bourns, who compared more than 100 cities that contract with sheriff's offices in California with nearly 300 departments that do not. They found, first, that cities that contract with their sheriff's office, on average, spend far less per capita on police services than those cities that operate their own police departments. Furthermore, contract cities also appear to do substantially better than the department cities in clearing violent crimes. Nelligan and Bourns speculate that this may be due to the fact that the larger units (sheriff's office) can utilize specialized investigative units and specially trained personnel to solve such crimes.[60]

In sum, then, this study suggests that contracting is cost-effective and appears to carry no sacrifice of police effectiveness. The policy implications are not so clear; however, dissolving a city's police department in favor of contracting can carry considerable benefits—but at the same time may be politically unpalatable to, and solidly opposed by many people in policing as well as in municipal government. As suggested earlier by public choice theory, many people want their "own" police department that is smaller and perceived as more responsive to their community's needs; Nelligan and Bourns thus suggest that contracting may come about more as a result of a "no choice" situation, based on financial exigency, more than a political desire.[61]

Another means of unifying agencies and possibly achieving cost savings is through **consolidation**, which is the merging of two or more city and/or county law enforcement agencies into a single entity. The primary goal is to avoid duplication of costly services and thus realize cost savings, while streamlining operations (with the single agency's sworn personnel enforcing a single set of statutes or ordinances, wearing the same uniform, driving the same type of patrol vehicle, and so on).

Research has indicated that through consolidation, the more resource-intensive police functions such as crime labs, communications, and training are subject to economies of scale; conversely, however, the more labor-intensive functions, such as investigation and patrol, do not normally afford such savings. In general, then, it is probably more efficient to consolidate the training, communications, and laboratory functions, but to leave investigative and patrol functions remain in small- or moderately sized units.[62]

contract policing where a (usually smaller) community contracts with an outside unit of government to provide its policing services.

consolidation the merging of two or more city and/or county law-enforcement agencies into a single entity.

▶ Succession Planning for Future Leaders

Soon the administration, management, and supervision of police agencies could be in a crisis stage unless measures are taken in the near future to prepare for what is coming: the current aging, turnover, and retirement of baby boomers and other generational employees. Today an essential part of every chief's job is to prepare colleagues in the organization for the next advancement in their careers; indeed, today the mark of a good leader is the ability to ensure a ready supply of capable leaders for the future. Thorough preparation of successors can help a chief executive establish an important legacy—one that will sustain the improvements and progress that have been made, offer opportunities for mentoring, and instill the importance of the organization's history.

Police chief executives need to take a long view and implement **succession planning**— i.e., begin identifying and developing employees who have the potential to fill key leadership positions in the organization—and provide leadership development as a continuous process. To provide the ongoing supply of talent needed to meet organizational needs, chief executives should use recruitment, development tools (such as job coaching, mentoring, understudy, job rotation, lateral moves, higher-level exposure, acting assignments, and instructing), and career planning.[63]

Organizations may already have a sufficient pipeline of strong leaders—people who are competent in handling the ground-level, tactical operations but who are not trained in how to look at the big picture; efforts must be made to help such prospective leaders to develop a broader vision—as one author put it, prepare employees to take on broader roles and "escape the silos."[64]

A number of excellent police promotional academies and management institutes exist for developing chief executives, as well as middle managers and supervisors, in the kinds of skills described earlier as well as in the "Succession Planning" section below. One of these training programs is described in Exhibit 6.2.

> **succession planning**
> identifying and developing employees who have the potential to fill key leadership positions in the organization.

EXHIBIT 6.2

SENIOR MANAGEMENT INSTITUTE FOR POLICE: A TESTIMONIAL

One of the experiences that helped shape my career was my attendance at the Police Executive Research Forum's Senior Management Institute for Police (SMIP), which provided the best executive leadership program for me personally. This program excels because superb instructors provide an excellent forum during the 3-week period. They use an applied, case-based curriculum and rigorously demand thinking in ways one might not be accustomed to. The combination of the intensive curriculum and spending 3 weeks working with, and learning from, a group of peers presented an excellent learning environment. As a course graduate and chief, I have witnessed others return from that program better able to accomplish tasks with higher levels of responsibility.

Source: Based on Robert McNeilly, "SMIP Builds Leaders," in Chuck Wexler, Mary Ann Wycoff, and Craig Fischer (eds.), *Good to Great Policing: Application of Business Management Principles in the Public Sector* (Washington, DC: Office of Community Oriented Policing Services and Police Executive Research Forum, 2007), p. 28.

In addition, *agencies* can provide skill development opportunities by having those persons with leadership potential do things, such as plan an event, write a training bulletin, update policies or procedures, conduct training and research, write a proposal or grant, counsel peers, become a mentor, and write contingency plans. Meanwhile, the *individual* can lay plans for the future through activities, such as doing academic coursework, participating in and leading civic events, attending voluntary conferences and training sessions, reading the relevant literature, studying national and local reports, guest lecturing in college or academy classes, and engaging in research.[65]

▶ Officer Uniforms and Appearance: Legal and Psychological Challenges

As with the newer generations of people who are now, or will soon be entering the labor market (discussed in Chapter 2), times are also changing with regard to workers' appearance, at least as policing is concerned. Concurrently, changes may also be indicated for police agency **dress codes**—a set of rules, usually set forth in the agency's policy and procedure manual, specifying the required manner of dress and appearance for employees in an organization—and what should be permitted concerning one's body adornments? These are questions that are now causing police administrators to reconsider their view of the workplace.

From the moment a neophyte officer puts on a uniform, his or her world changes; the officer is immediately and uniquely set apart from society. For some, the uniform seems to be a target for all kinds of verbal abuse and even fists or bullets; for others, it is welcomed as a symbol of their legal authority. In either case, the uniform along with overall appearance of police officers has several psychological and legal aspects. For these previously mentioned reasons, police chief executives need to understand the legal and psychological aspects of their officers' uniforms. Succinctly stated, police administrators have long been able to regulate the appearance of their officers. In *Kelley v. Johnson*,[66] 1976, the U.S. Supreme Court held that police agencies have a legitimate, "rational" interest in establishing such rules and regulations. There, the Suffolk County (New York) Police Department's hair-grooming standards applicable to male members of the police force (governing the style and length of hair, sideburns, and mustaches; also, beards and goatees were prohibited) were attacked as violating officers' First and Fourteenth Amendment rights of expression and liberty. The Supreme Court upheld such regulations, on the grounds they:

> may be based on a desire to make police officers readily recognizable to the members of the public, or a desire for the esprit de corps, which such similarity is felt to inculcate within the police force itself. Either one is a sufficiently rational justification for regulations. . . .[67]

Certainly, the uniform conveys power and authority; it also identifies a person with powers to arrest and use force and establishes order, as well as conformity within the ranks of those who wear it by suppressing individuality.[68]

Many, if not most, police agencies have general orders or policies constituting a dress code—how their officers will dress and their general appearance—so as to:

> promote a professional image to the community served; have uniformed officers be consistently attired to reflect their authority, respective assignment, and rank within the agency; require the wearing of agency approved uniforms; have officers be properly groomed and his/her uniform clean, pressed, and in proper condition.[69]

Such dress codes might address matters such as the length of hair and sideburns, beards and goatees (whether or not they are permitted), types of sunglasses to be worn (mirrored, for example, are often banned), and tattoos (whether or not any body art is to be permitted for officers, and if they are to be covered while on duty). Regulations might also spell out prohibitions against the wearing of items of clothing with an identifying logo, so the jurisdiction is not viewed as endorsing a particular name (brand).

Imposing the will of the police administration concerning officers' appearance and attire is not always as easy as it might appear; however, today officers show little reluctance to file lawsuits if feeling that such codes violate their rights to freedom of expression:

• A northeastern Pennsylvania man sued in late 2009, claiming his rights were violated when he was not hired with the state police because he would not have his arm tattoo removed. Applicants' tattoos are subject to review by the Tattoo and Replica Review Committee, which can insist they be removed before a job will be offered. The lawsuit seeks to determine whether "the government can require you to physically alter your body in exchange for employment," and infringes on the applicant's "freedom of choice in personal matters."[70]

- The Houston City Council voted in late 2009 to spend up to $150,000 to hire outside lawyers to defend the city's no-beard policy for police. Four black officers filed a federal civil rights lawsuit against the city, claiming discrimination because shaving exacerbates a skin condition that disproportionately affects black men; officers with beards are barred from wearing the Houston Police Department uniform.[71]

- Des Moines, Iowa, police policy states that any tattoos, branding and intentional scarring on the face, head, neck, hands, and exposed arms and legs are prohibited. Employees who already have tattoos are exempted. The police union said the policy is unreasonable and filed a grievance.[72]

- Other agencies have implemented or are considering policies that would require officers to either not be tattooed or to cover the tattoos completely when on duty.[73]

Research is generally lacking on the psychological and legal aspects of police uniforms, but what has been done is extremely fruitful. For example, a 2013 study examined data for a 10-year period and 250 cases of assaults against police officers, citizens killed by police officers, and citizen complaints for use of excessive force for differences between officers with black-colored and non-black-colored uniforms. It was predicted, based on previous studies, that officers wearing black uniforms would experience more assaults on officers, citizens killed by police, and excessive force complaints; however, while it was found that agencies with officers wearing dark uniforms were "more likely" to act aggressively toward citizens than departments with lighter uniforms, the data did not indicate a statistically significant difference—which, as indicated earlier, contradicted previous studies showing that people are perceived as more aggressive, and act more aggressively, when wearing dark clothes.[74]

Summary

This chapter examined a number of issues that have challenged and will continue to challenge law enforcement administrators for years: managing the use of force; social media; biased policing; women and minorities in law enforcement; contract, consolidated, and civilianized services; police–media relations; succession planning; and police uniforms and dress codes.

Perhaps just as important as having administrators today who understand and deal with these problems are the subordinates of tomorrow; those who will wear the mantle of leadership in the future must likewise attempt to understand how to address these issues.

Key Terms and Concepts

Active shooter *143*
Consolidation *150*
Contract policing *150*
Dress code *152*
Fusion center *137*

National Incident Management
  System *137*
Social media *147*
Succession planning *151*
Terrorism *133*

Use of force *140*
Use-of-force continuum *145*
Unmanned aerial vehicles *138*
Vehicular pursuits *143*

Questions for Review

1. What is terrorism, and why is the prospect of bioterrorism particularly frightening?
2. What practical and legislative mechanisms have been devised to deal with terrorism?
3. Regarding police use of force, what are some of the "types" of officer characteristics that seem to promote it? What are some problems and considerations involving use of force with people who have mental disorders? While in vehicular pursuits? Policy implications for all of them?
4. What new approaches are now espoused with active shooters?
5. What is a use-of-force continuum, and how would you explain the DRRM?
6. What are some uses of social media by the police? What are some concerns and abuses?
7. What can be done to get more women into policing?
8. How would you define and describe sexual harassment, the extent of the problem in policing, and some possible solutions?
9. What are contract and consolidated policing, and some advantages (and concerns) with each?
10. What is succession planning, and why should it begin immediately in policing?
11. What are today's legal and psychological effects of police uniforms? How are times changing in these areas?

Deliberate and Decide 1

Biased Policing or Good Police Work?

Regarding physical, verbal, and legal abuse of citizens, consider the following: Few if any people believe the police should be stopping, questioning, searching, frisking, or otherwise impeding people of color purely on the basis of race or nationality. But where should the line be drawn between what some might perceive as biased policing on the one hand and solid, proactive police work on the other? Noted columnist Richard Cohen, writing in *The Washington Post* about controversial—and legal—stop-and-frisk actions by New York City police in 2013, observed that because young minorities are known to commit a disproportionate amount of crimes in NYC, those ought to be the people who are stopped and frisked: "It would be senseless for the cops to be stopping Danish tourists in Times Square just to make the statistics look good."[75] Similarly, Bernard Parks, former chief of Los Angeles Police Department and an African American, said this: "We have an issue of violent crime against jewelry salespeople. The predominant suspects are Colombians. We don't find Mexican-Americans, or blacks or other immigrants. It's a collection of several hundred Colombians who commit this crime. If you see six in a car in front of the Jewelry Mart, and they're waiting and watching people with briefcases, should we play the percentages and follow them? It's common sense."[76]

Questions for Discussion

1. Do you believe such police actions are racist in nature, or do they represent good police work?
2. Where does proactive policing such as that described earlier "cross the line" and become biased in nature, or racial profiling?

Deliberate and Decide 2

Police Use of Drones

Assume you are an advisor to a statewide panel that is to make recommendations to the governor concerning police use of UAVs/drones. Respond to the following questions:

Questions for Discussion

1. Would you support police use of drones for surveillance purposes involving serious offenses? If so, for what crime-related purposes?
2. Would you allow the police to use drones for Fourth Amendment (searches and seizures) types of operations, if legal conditions have been met?
3. Do you endorse using drones for lower-level functions, such as catching traffic speeders?
4. Would your panel be in favor of arming the drones with bullets or tear gas?
5. Do you believe drones should be used, without prior consent from any courts or other oversight body, for killing persons whose "profile" indicates they are a dangerous threat to security?

Learn by Doing

1. An investigative report by the local media has revealed an unusually high number of incidents involving inappropriate use of force by the police during the past few years. One aspect of the public reaction to this revelation is that the agency's training, policies, and procedures are now being questioned. What training topics as well as policies and procedures (refer to Chapter 4) concerning use of force do you believe should be examined (or, as necessary, added, clarified, or expanded) for the department? Defend your answers.

2. Your county sheriff has recently come out publicly in favor of contracting with all police agencies in your county having fewer than 10,000 population. Having caught your new city manager off-guard, you—the assistant city manager—are tasked with investigating and reporting on the pros and cons of such contracting, as well as the feasibility of complete consolidation into a single, county-wide police agency. How would you respond?

3. You are a new university police chief in a medium-sized city, and today is a huge football game at your university. You have just received information from a patrol sergeant that one of your male officers, Spicer, is at the football stadium working overtime and wearing an earring and sporting a new, visible (and rather risqué) tattoo on his arm. The sergeant says both are highly visible, and that a rudimentary dress code exists in your agency but does not cover earrings. You are aware that the other officers are anxiously watching the situation to see what you do. Spicer, the recipient of many letters of reprimand and filer of many grievances, is fully aware of what he can and cannot do, and no doubt aware that there is no specific prohibition against either earrings or tattoos under the agency's dress code, and that he is merely "expressing" himself under the First Amendment. What, if any, action will you take regarding the earring? Can you legally regulate the appearance of the employees in the workplace and require a "professional" appearance? Can you use to advantage any U.S. Supreme Court decisions in response to this matter?

Notes

1. Quoted in M. K. Rehm and W. R. Rehm, "Terrorism Preparedness Calls for Proactive Approach," *Police Chief* (December 2000):38–43.

2. D. Rogers, "A Nation Tested: What Is the Terrorist Threat We Face and How Can We Train for It?" *Law Enforcement Technology* (November 2001):16–21.

3. D. G. Bolgiano, "Military Support of Domestic Law Enforcement Operations: Working within Posse Comitatus," *FBI Law Enforcement Bulletin* (December 2001):16–24.

4. U.S. Department of Homeland Security, *National Incident Management System* (Washington, DC: Author, March 2004), pp. 8–9.

5. "House Approves Patriot Act Renewal," http://www.cnn.com/2006/POLITICS/03/07/patriot.act/(accessed October 6, 2014).

6. Jurist: Legal News and Research, "Bush Signs Military Commissions Act," http://jurist.org/thisday/2010/10/president-bush-signed-military-commissions-act.php (accessed October 6, 2014).

7. Ibid.

8. J. Sullivan, "Terrorism Early Warning Groups: Regional Intelligence to Combat Terrorism." In R. Howard, J. Forest, and J. Moore (eds.), *Homeland Security and Terrorism* (New York: McGraw-Hill, 2006), pp. 235–245.

9. Interpol, "Cybercrime," http://www.interpol.int/Crime-areas/Cybercrime/Cybercrime (accessed May 29, 2014).

10. "Admit Nothing and Deny Everything," *The Economist*, June 8, 2014, http://www.economist.com/news/china/21579044-barack-obama-says-he-ready-talk-xi-jinping-about-chinese-cyber-attacks-makes-one (accessed June 13, 2014).

11. Siobhan Gorman and Julian E. Barnes, "Cyber Combat: Act of War," *The Wall Street Journal*, May 30, 2011, http://online.wsj.com/article/SB10001424052702304563104576355623135782718.html (accessed June 13, 2014).

12. Michael Riley and John Walcott, "China-Based Hacking of 760 Companies Shows Cyber Cold War," December 14, 2011, http://www.bloomberg.com/news/2011-12-13/china-based-hacking-of-760-companies-reflects-undeclared-global-cyber-war.html (accessed June 11, 2014).

13. Lev Grossman, "Drone Home," *Time*, February 11, 2014, pp. 26–33.

14. See "White House, Justice Officials Defend Drone Program after Release of Memo," *Associated Press* and *Fox News*, February 5, 2014, http://www.foxnews.com/politics/2014/02/05/senators-threaten-confrontation-with-obama-nominees-over-drone-concerns/ (accessed February 17, 2014).

15. International Association of Chiefs of Police, *Police Use of Force in America 2001*, p. 1, http://www.theiacp.org/Portals/0/pdfs/Publications/2001useofforce.pdf (accessed August 23, 2014).

16. See, for example, Marisol Bello and Yamiche Alcindor, "Police in Ferguson Ignite Debate about Military Tactics," *USA Today*, August 19, 2014, http://feedblitz.com/f/?fblike=http%3a%2f%2fwww.usatoday.com%2fstory%2fnews%2fnation%2f2014%2f08%2f14%2fferguson-militarized-police%2f14064675%2f; also see Yamiche Alcindor and Brandi Piper, "National Guard Ordered to Ferguson after Curfew Brings More Clashes," *USA Today*, August 18, 2014, http://www.krem.com/video/featured-videos/Clashes-on-second-night-of-Ferguson-curfew-271632291.html (accessed August 21, 2014).

17. *Graham v. Connor*, 490 U.S. 386 (1989), p. 397.

18. David Carter, "Theoretical Dimensions in the Abuse of Authority," in T. Barker and D. Carter (eds.), *Police Deviance* (Cincinnati: Anderson, 1994), pp. 269–290.

19. *Tennessee v. Garner*, 471 U.S. 1, 105 S.Ct. 1694, 85 L.Ed.2d 1 (1985).

20. Steven G. Brandl and Meghan S. Stroshine, "The Role of Officer Attributes, Job Characteristics, and Arrest Activity in Explaining Police Use of Force," *Criminal Justice Policy Review* 24(5) (September 2014):551–572.

21. Kenneth Adams, "Measuring the prevalence of police abuse of force," in William A. Geller and Hans Toch (eds.), *And Justice for All: Understanding and Controlling Police Abuse of Force* (Washington, DC: Police Executive Research Forum, 1995), pp. 61–98; Hans Toch, "The 'Violence-Prone' Police Officer," in ibid., pp. 99–112; also see Kenneth Adams, "What We Know about Police Use of Force," in Kenneth Adams (ed.), *Use of Force by Police: Overview of National and Local Data* (Washington, DC: National Institute of Justice, 1995), pp. 1–14.

22. Dragana Kesic, Stuart D. M. Thomas, and James R. P. Ogloff, "Use of Nonfatal Force on and by Persons with Apparent Mental Disorder in Encounters with Police," *Criminal Justice & Behavior* 40(3) (March 2014):321–337.

23. Ibid.

24. Meghan Hoyer and Brad Heath, "Mass killings Occur in USA Once Every Two Weeks," *USA TODAY*, December 19, 2012, http://www.usatoday.com/story/news/nation/2012/12/18/mass-killings-common/1778303/ (accessed August 23, 2014).

25. "Shoot First: Columbine Tragedy Transformed Police Tactics," *USA Today*, April 19, 2009, http://usatoday30.usatoday.com/news/nation/2009-04-19-columbine-police-tactics_N.htm (accessed August 21, 2014).

26. National Highway Traffic Safety Administration, *National Highway Traffic Safety Administration Statistics* (Washington, DC: Author, 1995).

27. C. B. Eisenberg, "Pursuit Management," *Law and Order* (March 1999):73–77; also see A. Belotto, "Supervisors Govern Pursuits," *Law and Order* (January 1999):86.

28. G. T. Williams, "When Do We Keep Pursuing? Justifying High-Speed Pursuits," *The Police Chief* (March 1997):24–27.

29. 118 S.Ct. 1708.

30. Ibid. at p. 1720.

31. D. N. Falcone, M. T. Charles, and E. Wells, "A Study of Pursuits in Illinois," *The Police Chief* (March 1994):59–64.

32. Based on Lorie A. Fridell, "Improving Use-of-Force Policy: Policy Enforcement and Training," in Joshua A. Ederheimer and Lorie A. Fridell (eds.), *Chief Concerns: Exploring the Challenges of Police Use of Force* (Washington, DC: Police Executive Research Form, April 2005), p. 48.

33. William Terrill and Eugene A. Paoline, "Examining Less Lethal Force Policy and the Force Continuum: Results from a National Use-of-Force Study," *Police Quarterly* 16(1) (March 2014):38–65.

34. International Association of Chiefs of Police, "Force Continuums: Three Questions," *The Police Chief*, October 2010, http://www.policechiefmagazine.org/magazine/index.cfm?fuseaction=display_arch&article_id=791&issue_id=12006 (accessed October 6, 2014).

35. Charles Joyner and Chad Basile, "The Dynamic Resistance Response Model," *FBI Law Enforcement Bulletin* (September 2007):17.

36. William Terrill, Geoffrey P. Alpert, Roger G. Dunham, and Michael R. Smith, "A Management Tool for Evaluating Police Use of Force: An Application of the Force Factor," *Police Quarterly* 6(2) (June 2003):150–171.

37. Ibid., p. 152.

38. Joel D. Lieberman, Deborah Koetzle, and Mari Sakiyama, "Police Departments' Use of Facebook: Patterns and Policy Issues," *Policy Quarterly* 16(4) 438–462 (accessed November 26, 2014).

39. Facebook, "Delaware State Police Prepare for Hurricane Sandy," http://www.facebook.com/notes/delaware-state-police-news-room/delaware-state-police-prepare-for-hurricane-sandy/461858043855465 (accessed November 26, 2014); also see Terry Collins, "Police Embrace Emerging Social Media Tool," *Associated Press*, August 11, 2012, http://news.yahoo.com/police-embrace-emerging-social-media-tool-150141734.html (accessed November 26, 2014).

40. J. David Goodman, "Photo of Officer Giving Boots to Barefoot Man Warms Hearts Online," http://www.nytimes.com/2012/11/29/nyregion/photo-of-officer-giving-boots-to-barefoot-man-warms-hearts-online.html?_r=0 (accessed November 26, 2014).

41. Joel D. Lieberman, Deborah Koetzle, and Mari Sakiyama, "Police Departments' Use of Facebook: Patterns and Policy Issues," *Policy Quarterly* 16(4) 438–462.

42. Gwendolyn Waters, "Social Media and Law Enforcement: Potential Risks," *FBI Law Enforcement Bulletin* 81 (11), November 2012, http://www.fbi.gov/stats-services/publications/law-enforcement-bulletin/november-2012/social-media-and-law-enforcement (accessed October 6, 2014).

43. Natalie DiBlasio, "YouTube: The Latest Crime Solver," *USA Today*, July 5, 2012, http://m.lawofficer.com/article/news/youtube-latest-crime-solver (accessed October 6, 2014).

44. Jim McKay, "Cops on the Tweet to Solve Crimes and Educate the Public," *Government Technology* (August 31, 2009), http://www.govtech.com/pcio/Cops-on-the-Tweet-to-Solve.html (accessed October 6, 2014).

45. Kevin Johnson, "Police Tap Technology to Compensate for Fewer Officers," *USA Today* (April 25, 2012), http://usatoday30.usatoday.com/news/nation/2011-04-24-police-crime-technology-facebook.htm (accessed October 6, 2014).

46. Barbara Raffel Price, "Sexual Integration in American Law Enforcement," in William C. Heffernan and Timothy Stroup (eds.), *Police Ethics: Hard Choices in Law Enforcement,* (New York: John Jay Press, 1985), pp. 205–214; see also Vivian B. Lord and Kenneth J. Peak, *Women in Law Enforcement Careers: A Guide for Preparing and Succeeding* (Upper Saddle River, NJ: Prentice Hall, 2005).

47. U.S. Department of Justice, Bureau of Justice Statistics, *Local Police Departments, 2007* (Washington, DC: Author, 2010), p. 14, http://www.bjs.gov/content/pub/pdf/lpd07.pdf (accessed August 24, 2014).

48. Dorothy Moses Schulz, "Women Police Chiefs: A Statistical Profile," *Police Quarterly* 6(3) (September 2003):330–345.

49. Peg Tyre, "Ms. Top Cop," *Newsweek* (April 12, 2004):49.

50. Peter Horne, "Policewomen: 2000 A.D. Redux," *Law and Order* (November 1999):53.

51. For information about successful recruiting efforts as well as the diverse kinds of assignments women now occupy in law enforcement, see Vivian B. Lord and Kenneth J. Peak, *Women in Law Enforcement Careers: A Guide for Preparing and Succeeding* (Upper Saddle River, NJ: Prentice Hall, 2005).

52. Quoted in Horne, "Policewomen," p. 59.

53. Kimberly A. Lonsway, Rebecca Paynich, and Jennifer N. Hall, "Sexual Harassment in Law Enforcement: Incidence, Impact, and Perception," *Police Quarterly* 16(2) (June 2014): 177–210.

54. Ibid.

55. Ibid.

56. Ibid.

57. Peter J. Nelligan and William Bourns, "Municipal Contracting With County Sheriffs for Police Services in California: Comparison of Cost and Effectiveness," *Police Quarterly* 14(1) (March 2011):70–95.

58. See National Sheriffs Association, "Information Repository," http://www.sheriffs.org/content/information-repository (accessed August 23, 2014).

59. Vincent Ostrom and Elinor Ostrom, "Public Choice: A Different Approach to the Study of Public Administration." *Public Administration Review* 31(2) (March/April 1971):203–216.

60. Ibid.

61. Ibid.

62. See Nelligan and Bourns, "Municipal Contracting with County Sheriffs for Police Services in California: Comparison of Cost and Effectiveness," pp. 90–95.

63. Edward Davis and Ellen Hanson, *Succession Planning: Mentoring Future Leaders* (Washington, DC: Police Executive Research Forum, 2006), p. 5.

64. Douglas A. Ready, "How to Grow Leaders," *Harvard Business Review* (December 2004):93–100.

65. Rick Michelson, "Succession Planning for Police Leadership," *The Police Chief* (June 2006):16–22.

66. 425 U.S. 238 (1976).

67. Ibid., at pp. 247–248.

68. Richard R. Johnson, "The Psychological Influence of the Police Uniform," *FBI Law Enforcement Bulletin*, March 2001, pp. 27–32; Tinsley and Plecas, "Studying Public Perceptions of Police Grooming Standards," p. 2.

69. Based on the Watertown, South Dakota, Police Department General Order A-170, http://www.watertownpd.com/images/pdf_files/a-170%20personnel%20dress%20code%20and%20uniform%20regulations.pdf (accessed October 6, 2014).

70. "Tattooed State Police Job Applicant Sues over Policy," http://www.wpxi.com/news/20567045/detail.html (accessed October 6, 2014).

71. Gene Park, "HPD Weighs Tattoo Cover-up," http://www.starbulletin.com/news/20090126_hpd_weighs_tattoo_cover_up.html (accessed October 6, 2014);

72. "Des Moines Police Ban New Tattoos," http://www.foxnews.com/story/0,2933,379203,00.html (accessed October 6, 2014).

73. Park, "HPD Weighs Tattoo Cover-up," p. 1.

74. Richard R. Johnson, "An Examination of Police Department Uniform Color and Police–Citizen Aggression," *Criminal Justice and Behavior* 40(2) (February 2014):228–244, doi: 10.1177/0093854812456644 (accessed August 21, 2014).

75. Richard Cohen, "Racism vs. reality," *The Washington Post*, July 15, 2014, http://articles.washingtonpost.com/2014-07-15/opinions/40588296_1_george-zimmerman-trayvon-martin-males (accessed August 2, 2014).

76. Jeffrey Goldberg, "The Color of Suspicion," *The New York Times Magazine*, June 20, 1999, http://www.nytimes.com/1999/06/20/magazine/the-color-of-suspicion.html?pagewanted=all&src=pm (accessed August 2, 2014).

PART 3

The Courts

This part consists of three chapters. Chapter 7 examines court organization and operation, Chapter 8 covers personnel roles and functions, and Chapter 9 discusses court issues and practices. The introductory section of each chapter previews the specific chapter content. Case studies in court administration appear in Appendix I.

Henryk Sadura/shutterstock

> The place of justice is a hallowed place.
> —*Francis Bacon*

> Courts and camps are the only places to learn the world in.
> —*Earl of Chesterfield*

7 Court Organization and Operation

LEARNING OBJECTIVES

After reading this chapter, the student will be able to:

1. *understand the meaning and importance of court decor and decorum*
2. *describe the ramifications of the adversarial system*
3. *review the organization and administration of our dual (federal and state) court systems*
4. *delineate the roles and functions of the Judicial Conference of the United States and the Administrative Office of the U.S. Courts*
5. *list the four components of court unification, how a unified court is organized, and the functional and financial advantages of court unification*
6. *explain state courts and trial courts of general and limited jurisdictions*
7. *describe why the courts' caseloads have increased*
8. *review historical attempts to streamline the court systems in both England and the United States, as well as some reasons for and examples of doing so*
9. *describe the influence of courts on policymaking*

► Introduction

Courts have existed in some form for thousands of years. Indeed, the ancient trial court of Israel, and the most common tribunal throughout its biblical history, was the "court at the gate," where elders of each clan resolved controversies within the kin group. In the fourth century B.C.E., courts in Athens, Greece, dealt with all premeditated homicides and heard cases. The court system has survived the dark eras of the Inquisition and the Star Chamber (which, in England during the 1500s and 1600s, without a jury, enforced unpopular political policies and meted out severe punishment, including whipping, branding, and mutilation). The U.S. court system developed rapidly after the American Revolution and led to the establishment of law and justice on the western frontier.

This chapter opens by going inside the courts, considering their special nature in our country, as well as typical courtroom decor and decorum. Then I discuss how the courts attempt to get at the truth within the controversial adversary system of justice. The nature of our dual court system, comprising federal and state-level courts, is examined next; included are discussions of two entities (the Judicial Conference of the United States and the Administrative Office of the U.S. Courts [AO]) that administer those at the federal level. The discussion of the federal court system focuses on the U.S. Supreme Court, appeals courts (with emphasis on the District of Columbia Circuit Court of Appeals), and district courts; the overview of state courts includes their courts of last resort, appeals courts, and trial courts (including the major trial courts having general jurisdiction and limited-jurisdiction lower courts). Included in the discussion of state court systems is a look at the historical, functional, and financial advantages of statewide court unification/centralization. An underlying theme is that caseloads are generally burgeoning, and we consider some reasons for that trend. After discussing the role of courts as policymaking bodies, the chapter concludes with review questions, "deliberate and decide" problems, and "learn by doing" exercises.

► Inside the Courts: Decor, Decorum, Citizens

Hallowed Places

Practically everything one sees and hears in an American courtroom is intended to convey the sense that the courtroom is a hallowed place in our society. Alexis de Tocqueville, in his study of the United States more than a century ago, observed the extent to which our legal system permeates our lives:

> Scarcely any political question arises in the United States that is not resolved, sooner or later, into a judicial question. Hence all parties are obliged to borrow, in their daily controversies, the ideas, and even the language, peculiar to judicial proceedings. [T]he spirit of the law, which is produced in the schools and courts of justice, gradually penetrates beyond their walls into the bosom of society, where it descends to the lowest classes, so that at last the whole people contract the habits and the tastes of the judicial magistrate.[1]

The physical **décor**—the physical or decorative style of a setting—one finds in the courts conveys this sense of importance. On their first visit, citizens often are struck by the court's high ceilings, ornate marble walls, and comparatively expensive furnishings.

An appropriate degree of **decorum**—correct or proper behavior indicating respect and politeness—is accorded to this institution. All people must stand up when the judge enters the courtroom, permission must be granted before a person can approach the elevated bench, and a general attitude of deference is granted to the judge. A vitriolic utterance that

décor the physical or decorative style of a setting.

decorum correct or proper behavior indicating respect and politeness.

could lawfully be directed to the president of the United States could result in the individuals being jailed for contempt of court when directed to a judge.

The design of the courtroom, although generally dignified in nature, also provides a safe, functional space that is conducive to efficient and effective court proceedings. The formal arrangement of the participants and furnishings reflects society's view of the appropriate relationships between the defendant and judicial authority. The courtroom must accommodate judges, court reporters, clerks, bailiffs, witnesses, plaintiffs, defendants, attorneys, juries, and spectators, as well as police officers, social workers, probation officers, guardians ad litem, interpreters, and the press. Space must also be allotted for evidence, exhibits, recording equipment, and computers.

Judges and court staff now may require high-technology audiovisual equipment and computer terminals to access automated information systems. Chapter 16 discusses the kinds of technologies that are now commonly used in the nation's courtrooms.

Justice in the Eye of the Beholder

Whether or not justice is obtained in the courtrooms depends on the interests or viewpoints of the affected or interested parties. A victim may not agree with a jury's verdict; a winner in a civil case may not believe that he or she received an adequate sum of money for the suffering or damages involved. Thus, because the definition of *justice* is not always agreed on, the courts must *appear* to provide justice. The court's responsibility is to provide a fair hearing, with rights accorded to all parties to speak or not to speak, to have the assistance of counsel, to cross-examine the other side, to produce witnesses and relevant documents, and to argue their viewpoint. This process, embodied in the due process clause, must appear to result in justice.[2]

Seeking Truth in an Adversarial Atmosphere

Ralph Waldo Emerson stated that "every violation of truth is a stab at the health of human society."[3] Certainly, most people would agree that the traditional, primary purpose of our courts is to provide a forum for seeking and—through the adversarial system of justice—obtaining the truth. Indeed, the U.S. Supreme Court declared in 1966 in *Tehan v. United States ex rel. Shott*[4] that "the basic purpose of a trial is the determination of truth."

Today, however, increasing numbers of Americans have the impression that truth is being compromised and even violated with regularity in the trial, plea bargaining, and appellate apparatus of our justice system, thereby "stabbing at the health of human society."

High on their list of impediments is the **adversarial system** itself—the legal system whereby two opposing sides present their arguments in court—because of cases that included jury nullification (acquitting a defendant because the jury disagrees with a law or the evidence), lawyer grandstanding, improper and racist police procedures, and a general circus atmosphere allowed by the judge and engaged in by the media. Although many people would argue that such a system is vital to a free democratic society, under this system the courtroom becomes a battleground where participants often have little regard for guilt or innocence; rather, concern centers on whether the state is able to prove guilt beyond a reasonable doubt. To many people, this philosophy contradicts what courts were intended to accomplish. In the adversary system, the desire to win can become overpowering. As one state supreme court justice put it, prosecutors "are proud of the notches on their gun."[5] The defense counsel enjoys winning equally. The attention can shift from the goal of finding the truth to being effective game players.

Should this system be modified or replaced? That is an important and difficult question. As one law professor observed, "Lawyers are simply not appropriate to correct the

adversarial system the legal system whereby two opposing sides present their arguments in court.

defects of our adversary system. Their hearts will never be in it; it is unfair to both their clients and themselves to require them to serve two masters."[6]

It would appear, however, that the adversarial system is here to stay. Indeed, several safeguards have been put in place to enable this system to reach the truth. First, evidence is tested under this approach through cross-examination of witnesses. Second, power is lodged with several different people; each courtroom actor is granted limited powers to counteract those of the others. If, for example, the judge is biased or unfair, the jury can disregard the judge and reach a fair verdict. If the judge believes the jury has acted improperly, he or she can set aside the jury's verdict and order a new trial. Furthermore, both the prosecuting and defense attorneys have certain rights and authority under each state's constitution. This series of checks and balances is aimed at curbing misuse of the criminal courts.

A Dual Court System

In order to better understand the court system of the United States, it is important to know that this country has a **dual court system**: essentially, an organizational distinction between courts, with one federal court system and a state court system (composed of 50 individual state court systems plus the system of the District of Columbia). First, we will examine the federal court system; included are discussions of the entities responsible for overseeing the federal courts' operations: the Judicial Conference of the United States and the AO. Following that, we examine the state and local trial courts.

> **dual court system**
> an organizational distinction between courts, with a federal court system and 50 individual state court systems.

▶ Federal Courts: Organization and Administration

The U.S. Supreme Court: Its Jurists, Traditions, and Work

Judges and Advocacy

The U.S. Supreme Court is the highest and one of the oldest courts in the nation—formed in 1790. It is composed of nine justices: one chief justice and eight associate justices. Like other federal judges appointed under Article III of the Constitution, they are nominated to their post by the president and confirmed by the Senate, and they serve for life.[7] Each new term of the Supreme Court begins, by statute, on the first Monday in October.

Not just any lawyer may advocate a cause before the high court; all who wish to do so must first secure admission to the Supreme Court bar. Applicants must submit an application form that requires, under Supreme Court Rule 5, that applicants have been admitted to practice in the highest court of their state for a period of at least 3 years (during which time they must not have been the subject of any adverse disciplinary action), and they must appear to the Court to be of good moral and professional character. Each applicant must file with the clerk a certificate from the presiding judge or clerk of that court attesting that the applicant practices there and is in good standing, as well as the statements of two sponsors affirming that he or she is of good moral and professional character. Finally, applicants must swear or affirm to act "uprightly and according to law, and support the Constitution of the United States."[8]

Inside the Court: Revered Traditions and Practices

The Supreme Court Building, constructed in 1935, has 16 marble columns at the main west entrance that support the portico; on the architrave above is incised the words "Equal Justice Under Law." The building's chamber measures 82 feet wide by 99 feet long, rising

44 feet above the dark African marble floor. Gold leaf and red adorn the ceiling recesses. Twenty-four massive columns of silver gray Italian marble line walls of ivory mined in Spain. High on the walls, four 36-foot-long marble friezes depict the great classical and Christian lawgivers. A large clock is suspended high above the bench to remind the sometimes too verbose advocate that time marches on. Behind the bench are nine high-backed chairs and a flag. The clerk's desk is at the left end of the bench, and counsel tables are in front of and below the bench. Squarely in the middle, facing the chief justice, is the lectern used by attorneys while addressing the Court. On the lectern are two lights—a white one comes on when the speaker has 5 minutes remaining and a red one is the signal to stop.[9] Millions of visitors to the U.S. Supreme Court have been struck by the sight and the power of the building and its primary occupants. Justice Robert Jackson once described the Court's uniqueness, saying, "We are not final because we are infallible, but we are infallible because we are final."[10]

In many respects, the Court is the same institution that first met in 1790. Since at least 1800, it has been traditional for justices to wear black robes while in session. White quills are placed on counsel tables each day that the Court sits, as was done at the earliest sessions of the Court. The "Conference handshake" has been a tradition since the late nineteenth century. When the justices assemble to go on the bench each day and at the beginning of the private conferences at which they discuss decisions, each justice shakes hands with each of the other eight—a reminder that differences of opinion on the Court do not preclude the overall harmony of purpose. When the Court is in session, the following seating arrangement exists for each justice: The chief justice always sits in the middle, with four associate justices on either side. The justice who is senior in terms of service sits on the chief's immediate right as the justices face out; the justice who is second in seniority sits on the chief's left; thereafter, the justices are seated alternately right and left according to the amount of time served. The junior justice is always on the chief justice's extreme left.[11]

Exhibit 7.1 shows the current seating arrangement of the sitting justices of the U.S. Supreme Court.

EXHIBIT 7.1

TRADITIONS: SEATING CHART OF THE CURRENT SUPREME COURT OF THE UNITED STATES

1. Chief Justice Roberts
2. Justice Scalia
3. Justice Kennedy
4. Justice Thomas
5. Justice Ginsburg
6. Justice Breyer
7. Justice Alito
8. Justice Sotomayor
9. Justice Kagan
10. Clerk of the Court
11. Marshal of the Court
12. Counsel

Source: Supreme Court of the United States, "Visitor's Guide to Oral Arguments," p. 1, http://www.supremecourt.gov/visiting/visitorsguidetooralargument.aspx (accessed October 28, 2013).

Caseload and Conferences

The Court does not meet continuously in formal sessions during its nine-month term. Instead, the Court divides its time into four separate but related activities. First, some period of time is allocated to reading through the thousands of petitions for review of cases that come annually to the Court—usually during the summer and when the Court is not sitting to hear cases. Second, the Court allocates blocks of time for oral arguments— the live discussion in which lawyers for both sides present their clients' positions to the justices. During the weeks of oral arguments, the Court sets aside its third allotment of time, for private discussions of how each justice will vote on the cases they have just heard. Time is also allowed for the justices to discuss which additional cases to hear. These private discussions are usually held on Wednesday afternoons and Fridays during the weeks of oral arguments. The justices set aside a fourth block of time to work on writing their opinions.[12]

The Court has complete discretion to control the nature and number of the cases it reviews by means of the writ (order) of *certiorari*—an order from a higher court directing a lower court to send the record of a case for review. The Court considers requests for writs of certiorari according to the *rule of four*; if four justices decide to "grant cert," the Court will agree to hear the case. Several criteria are used to decide whether a case requires action: First, does the case concern an issue of constitutional or legal importance? Does it fall within the Court's **jurisdiction**—which is, simply put, the power or authority given to a court by law to hear certain kinds of cases (the Supreme Court can only hear cases that are mandated by Congress or the Constitution)? Does the party bringing the case has *standing*—a strong vested interest in the issues raised in the case and in its outcome?[13]

> **jurisdiction** the power or authority given to a court by law to hear certain kinds of cases.

The Court hears only a tiny fraction of the thousands of cases it is petitioned to consider. When it declines to hear a case, the decision of the lower court stands as the final word on the case. Adding to the Court's workload is a steady growth in congressional and state legislation that requires judicial interpretation and an increasing number of constitutional and other issues that can be reviewed in the federal courts.[14]

Administration

The chief justice orders the business of the Supreme Court and administers the oath of office to the president and vice president upon their inauguration. According to Article 1, Section 3, of the Constitution of the United States, the chief justice is also empowered to preside over the Senate in the event that it sits as a court to try an impeachment of the president. The duties of the chief justice are described more fully in Chapter 8.

The clerk of the Court serves as the Supreme Court's chief administrative officer, supervising a staff of 30 under the guidance of the chief justice. The marshal of the Court supervises all building operations. The reporter of decisions oversees the printing and publication of the Court's decisions. Other key personnel are the librarian and the public information officer. In addition, each justice is entitled to hire four law clerks, almost always recent top graduates of law schools, many of whom have served clerkships in a lower court in the previous year.[15]

U. S. Courts of Appeals

Judges, Jurisdiction, Caseloads

The courts of appeals are the intermediate courts of appeals (ICAs) for the federal court system. Eleven of the circuits are identified by number, and another is called the D.C. Circuit (See Figure 7-1 ■). A court of appeals hears appeals from the district courts located within its circuit, as well as appeals from decisions of federal administrative agencies.

The courts of appeals are staffed with 179 judges nominated by the president and confirmed by the Senate. As with the U.S. district courts, discussed below, the number of judges in each circuit varies, from 6 in the First Circuit to 28 in the Ninth, depending on the volume and complexity of the caseload. Each circuit has a chief judge (chosen by seniority) who has supervisory responsibilities. Several staffers aid the judges in conducting the work of the

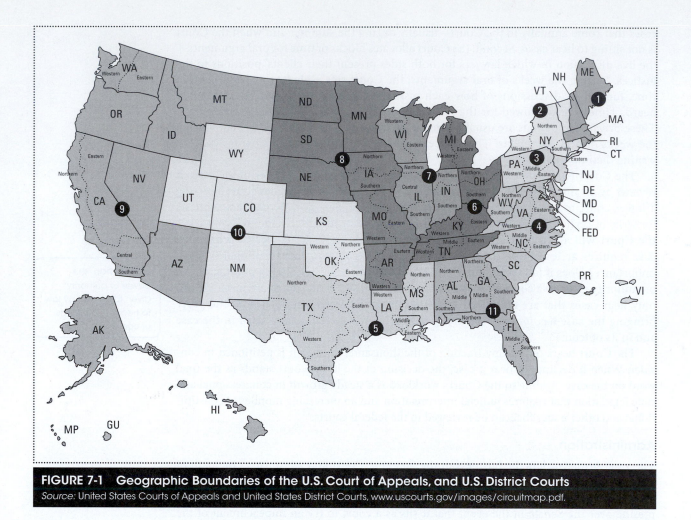

FIGURE 7-1   Geographic Boundaries of the U.S. Court of Appeals, and U.S. District Courts
Source: United States Courts of Appeals and United States District Courts, www.uscourts.gov/images/circuitmap.pdf.

courts of appeals. A circuit executive assists the chief judge in administering the circuit. The clerk's office maintains the records. Each judge is also allowed to hire three law clerks. In deciding cases, the courts of appeals may use rotating three-judge panels. Or, by majority vote, all the judges in the circuit may sit together to decide a case or reconsider a panel's decision; however, such *en banc* hearings are rare.[16] The caseload of the courts of appeals is about 57,500 per year[17]—about half being civil in nature, one-fourth being criminal, and the remainder originating from administrative agencies.[18] See Exhibit 7.2 for a description of the D.C. Circuit.

U.S. District Courts

Judges, Jurisdiction, Caseloads

Congress created 94 U.S. district courts, of which 89 are located within the 50 states. There is at least one district court in each state (some states have more, such as California, New York, and Texas, all of which have four). Congress has created 678 district court judgeships for the 94 districts. As with the other federal court judges discussed previously, the president nominates district judges, who must then be confirmed by the Senate; they then serve for life unless removed for cause. In the federal system, the U.S. district courts are the

EXHIBIT 7.2

D.C. CIRCUIT: THE SECOND MOST POWERFUL COURT IN THE LAND

Any discussion of the federal court system would probably be incomplete without elaborating somewhat on the District of Columbia Circuit Court of Appeals (known as the D.C. Circuit). Often described (and widely regarded) as the second most powerful court in the United States (after the U.S. Supreme Court), the D.C. Circuit's reputation is well earned because it often decides cases having national implications, ranging from environmental regulations and national security policy to drinking water standards and clean air. It even has jurisdiction over the federal government's bureaucracy; indeed, a number of federal and administrative statutes and agencies designate the D.C. Circuit as the appropriate forum for challenging federal agency orders and rules. Trade associations, labor unions, and other such organizations often appear before this court's distinguished panel of one chief judge and eight associate judges.[19]

Finally, the D.C. Circuit is viewed as a springboard for one to be appointed to the highest court in the nation. Indeed, the bench of the D.C. Circuit once was the locus for Chief Justice John Roberts and Justices Ruth Bader Ginsburg, Antonin Scalia, and Clarence Thomas.[20]

federal trial courts of original jurisdiction for all major violations of federal criminal law (some 500 full-time magistrate judges hear minor violations).[21]

District court judges are assisted by an elaborate supporting cast of clerks, secretaries, law clerks, court reporters, probation officers, pretrial services officers, and U.S. marshals. The larger districts also have a public defender. Another important actor at the district court level is the U.S. attorney; there is one U.S. attorney in each district. The work of district judges is significantly assisted by 352 bankruptcy judges, who are appointed for 14-year terms by the court of appeals in the district it is located.[22] There are about 80,000 criminal cases filed per year in the U.S. district courts.[23]

Judicial Conference of the United States

The **Judicial Conference of the United States** is the administrative policymaking organization of the federal judicial system. Its membership consists of the chief justice, the chief judges of each of the courts of appeals, one district judge from each circuit, and the chief judge of the Court of International Trade. The conference meets semiannually for only 2-day sessions, but most of the work is done by about 25 committees. The Judicial Conference directs the AO, (discussed in the following section), in administering the judiciary budget and makes recommendations to Congress, concerning the creation of new judgeships, increase in judicial salaries, revising federal rules of procedure, and budgets for court operations. The Judicial Conference also plays a major role in the impeachment of federal judges.[24]

> **Judicial Conference of the United States** the administrative policymaking organization of the federal judicial system.

Administrative Office of the U.S. Courts

Since 1939, the day-to-day administrative tasks of the federal courts have been handled by the AO, a judicial agency. The director of the AO is appointed by the chief justice of the Supreme Court and reports to the Judicial Conference. The AO's lobbying and liaison responsibilities include presenting the annual budget request for the federal judiciary, arguing for the need for additional judgeships, and transmitting proposed changes in court rules. The AO is also the housekeeping agency of the judiciary, responsible for allotting authorized funds and supervising expenditures.[25]

▶ State Courts of Last Resort and Appeals

Courts of Last Resort

A **court of last resort**—that court in a given state that has its highest and final appellate authority—is usually referred to as the state supreme court; however, the specific names differ from state to state, as do their number of judges (from as few as five to as many as nine—see Figure 7-2 ■). Unlike the intermediate appellate courts (discussed in the "Intermediate Courts of Appeals" section below), these courts do not use panels in making decisions; rather, the entire court sits to decide each case. All state supreme courts have a limited amount of original jurisdiction in dealing with matters such as disciplining lawyers and judges.[26]

	Court of last resort		Intermediate appellate court	
	Court name	Place of session	Court name	# of chief judges
Alabama	Supreme Court	Montgomery	Court of Civil Appeals	1
			Court of Criminal Appeals	1
Alaska	Supreme Court	Anchorage, Fairbanks, and Juneau	Court of Appeals	1
Arizona	Supreme Court	Phoenix	Court of Appeals	1
Arkansas	Supreme Court	Little Rock	Court of Appeals	1
California	Supreme Court	Los Angeles, Sacramento, and San Francisco	Courts of Appeals	9
Colorado	Supreme Court	Denvero	Court of Appeals	1
Connecticut	Supreme Court	Hartford	Appellate Court	1
Delaware	Supreme Court	Dover	~	~
District of Columbia	Court of Appeals	Washington, D.C.	~	~
Florida	Supreme Court	Tallahassee	District Courts of Appeal	5
Georgia	Supreme Court	Atlanta	Court of Appeals	1
Hawaii	Supreme Court	Honolulu	Intermediate Court of Appeals	1
Idaho	Supreme Court	7 locations	Court of Appeals	1
Illinois	Supreme Court	Springfield	Appellate Court	5
Indiana	Supreme Court	Indianapolis	Court of Appeals	1
			Tax Court	~
Iowa	Supreme Court	Des Moines	Court of Appeals	1
Kansas	Supreme Court	Topeka	Court of Appeals	1
Kentucky	Supreme Court	Frankfort	Court of Appeals	1
Louisiana	Supreme Court	New Orleans	Courts of Appeal	5
Maine	Supreme Judicial Court	Portland	~	~
Maryland	Court of Appeals	Annapolis	Court of Special Appeals	1
Massachusetts	Supreme Judicial Court	Boston	Appeals Court	1

FIGURE 7-2 Appellate Courts in the United States

	Court of last resort		Intermediate appellate court	
	Court name	Place of session	Court name	# of chief judges
Michigan	Supreme Court	Lansing	Court of Appeals	1
Minnesota	Supreme Court	St. Paul	Court of Appeals	1
Mississippi	Supreme Court	Jackson	Court of Appeals	1
Missouri	Supreme Court	Jefferson City Supreme	Court of Appeals	3
Montana	Supreme Court	Helena	~	~
Nebraska	Supreme Court	Lincoln	Court of Appeals	1
Nevada	Supreme Court	Carson City	~	~
New Hampshire	Supreme Court	Concord	~	~
New Jersey	Supreme Court	Trenton	Superior Court, Appellate Div.	1
New Mexico	Supreme Court	Santa Fe	Court of Appeals	1
New York	Court of Appeals	Albany	Supreme Court, Appellate Div.	4
North Carolina	Supreme Court	Raleigh	Court of Appeals	1
North Dakota	Supreme Court	Bismar	~	~
Ohio	Supreme Court	Columbus	Courts of Appeal	12
Oklahoma	Supreme Court	Oklahoma City	Court of Civil Appeals	1
	Court of Criminal Appeals	Oklahoma City		
Oregon	Supreme Court	Salem	Court of Appeals	1
Pennsylvania	Supreme Court	Harrisburg, Philadelphia, and Pittsburgh	Superior Court	1
			Commonwealth Court	1
Puerto Rico	Supreme Court	San Juan	Court of Appeals	1
Rhode Island	Supreme Court	Providence	~	~
South Carolina	Supreme Court	Columbia	Court of Appeals	1
South Dakota	Supreme Court	Pierre	~	~
Tennessee	Supreme Court	Jackson, Knoxville, and Nashville	Court of Criminal Appeals	1
			Court of Appeals	
Texas	Supreme Court	Austin	Courts of Appeal	14
	Court of Criminal Appeals	Austin		
Utah	Supreme Court	Salt Lake City	Court of Appeals	1
Vermont	Supreme Court	Montpelier	~	~
Virginia	Supreme Court	Richmond	Court of Appeals	1
Washington	Supreme Court	Olympia	Courts of Appeal	3
West Virginia	Supreme Court of Appeals	Charleston	~	~
Wisconsin	Supreme Court	Madison	Court of Appeals	1
Wyoming	Supreme Court	Cheyenne	~	~

FIGURE 7-2   (continued)

▼

In those 10 states that do not have an intermediate court of appeals, the state supreme court has no power to choose which cases will be placed on its docket; however, the ability of most state supreme courts to choose which cases to hear makes them important policy-making bodies. Although intermediate appellate courts review thousands of cases each year, looking for errors, state supreme courts handle 100 or so cases that present the most challenging legal issues arising in that state.

Nowhere is the policymaking role of state supreme courts more apparent than in deciding death penalty cases—which, in most states, are automatically appealed to the state's highest court, thus bypassing the ICAs. The state supreme courts are also the ultimate review board for matters involving interpretation of state law.[27]

Intermediate Courts of Appeals

Like their federal counterparts, state courts have experienced a significant growth in appellate cases that threatens to overwhelm the state supreme court; therefore, to alleviate the caseload burden on courts of last resort, state officials in 40 states have responded by creating an **intermediate court of appeals (ICA)**[28]—courts in both the federal and state court systems that hear appeals and are organizationally intermediate between the trial courts and the court of last resort. The states not having an ICA, such as New Hampshire, Vermont, Rhode Island, Delaware, and Maine, are typically sparsely populated and have low volumes of appeals. There are about 1,000 such judges in the nation today. The ICAs must hear all properly filed appeals.[29]

The structure of the ICA varies; in most states, these bodies hear both civil and criminal appeals; and like their federal counterparts, these courts typically use rotating three-judge panels. Also, like the federal appellate courts, the state ICAs' workload is demanding: According to the National Center for State Courts, state ICAs hear about 280,000 cases annually.[30] ICAs engage primarily in error corrections; they review trials to make sure that the law was followed; the overall standard is one of fairness. The ICAs represent the final stage of the process for most litigants; very few cases make it to the appellate court in the first place, and of those cases, only a small proportion will be heard by the state's court of last resort.[31]

State appellate court systems—both courts of last resort and ICAs—are shown in Figure 7-2. It was shown earlier that there is a widespread variation in terms of these courts' names and the number of judges for each.

▶ Trial Courts

General Jurisdiction: Major Trial Courts

Trial courts are courts of original jurisdiction (or "first instance") where evidence and testimony are first introduced and findings of fact and law are made. There are an estimated 2,000 major trial courts in the 50 states and Washington, D.C., staffed with more than 11,500 general-jurisdiction judges. The term *general jurisdiction* means that these courts have the legal authority to decide all matters not specifically delegated to lower courts; this division of jurisdiction is specified in law. The most common names for these courts are *district, circuit,* and *superior.*[32]

Each court has its own support staff consisting of a clerk of court, a sheriff, and others. In most states, the trial courts of general jurisdiction are also grouped into judicial districts or circuits. In rural areas, these districts or circuits encompass several adjoining counties, and the judges are true generalists who hear a wide variety of cases and literally ride the circuit; conversely, larger counties have only one circuit or district for the area, and the judges are often specialists assigned to hear only certain types of cases.[33]

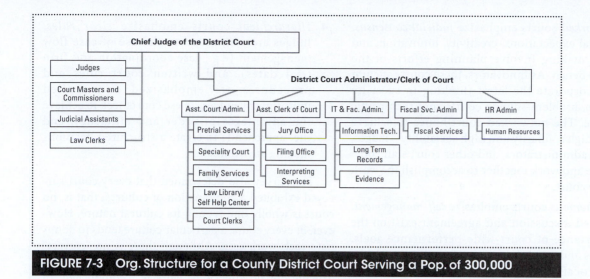

FIGURE 7-3 Org. Structure for a County District Court Serving a Pop. of 300,000

The great majority of the nation's judicial business occurs at the state, not the federal, level. State courts decide primarily street crimes. The more serious criminal violations are heard in the trial courts of general jurisdiction. State courts must also process a rising volume of drug-related offenses. Over the past 15 years, the number of criminal cases filed in general jurisdiction courts has increased by 25 percent; most criminal cases do not go to trial; thus, the dominant issue in the trial courts of general jurisdiction is not guilt or innocence, but what penalty to apply to the guilty.[34]

Figure 7-3 ■ shows the organizational structure of a county district court serving a population of 300,000. Note the variety of functions and programs that exist in addition to the basic court role of hearing trials and rendering dispositions.

It should also be noted that within the trial courts, a number of problem-solving or specialty courts—helping offenders with drug and mental health issues, as well as military veterans experiencing problems (all of which is discussed in Chapter 8)—have also become more common.[35] Exhibit 7.3 speaks to those courts and several other

EXHIBIT 7.3

IS THERE A LEGAL CULTURE WITHIN THE TRIAL COURTS?

Do criminal trial courts have a legal culture, with distinctive norms, values, beliefs, and expectations? The National Institute of Justice funded a study that set out to answer that question. Data were obtained by surveying judges, senior court administrators, and prosecuting/defense attorneys to gauge their views concerning how their courts handled cases, managed relationships between judges and court staff, and exercised courthouse leadership.

The study determined that there were four cultural orientations that can shape the conduct and performance of U.S. state trial courts: communal, networked, autonomous, and hierarchical.

1. *Communal* courts emphasize *flexibility;* general agreement on performance goals exists, but centralized judicial and administrative staff leadership is downplayed and creativity is encouraged. As a result, alternative and acceptable ways exist for individual judges to apply court rules, policies, and procedures. Here, judges and administrators emphasize the importance of getting along and acting collectively; group involvement, mutually agreed upon goals, teamwork, and developing a humane work environment are emphasized.

(Continued)

2. *Networked* courts emphasize *judicial consensus.* Judicial expectations, creativity, innovation, and policymaking involve planning efforts of the entire bench. As innovators, these courts attempt to incorporate the latest thinking in specialty courts, problem-solving courts, and therapeutic justice. The networked court hopes to achieve both high solidarity and high sociability—judges, court administrators, and other court staff coordinate and work together to accomplish the work of the court.

3. *Autonomous* courts emphasize *self-management.* Limited discussion and agreement exist on the importance of court-wide performance goals. Judges and administrators emphasize the importance of allowing each judge to conduct business as he or she sees fit. Many judges in this type of court are most comfortable with the traditional adversarial model of dispute resolution, wherein the judge is relatively passive and essentially referees the cases presented by attorneys.

4. *Hierarchical* courts emphasize *clear rules.* Judges are committed to the use of case flow management (e.g., case coordination and firm trial dates), and written court rules and procedures are emphasized and applied uniformly by judges. These courts seek to achieve the advantages of order and efficiency, and the approach is to create a structured decision-making environment.

The survey also determined that every court surveyed exhibited a combination of cultures; that is, no court is wholly one type in its cultural nature. However, in every court, a particular culture tends to dominate each work area. Although there is no "correct" culture for a particular area of work, different cultural orientations do affect how work is accomplished. In sum, the conventional wisdom that U.S. courts are generally loosely run organizations dominated by autonomous judges who resist administrative controls is not supported.

Source: Based on Brian J. Ostrom, Charles W. Ostrom, Roger A. Hanson, and Matthew Kleiman, *The Mosaic of Institutional Culture and Performance: Trial Courts as Organizations,* November 2005, pp. 51–52, http://www.ncjrs.gov/pdffiles1/nij/grants/212083.pdf (accessed October 25, 2013).

aspects of court administration, looking at whether or not these courts have a culture of their own.

Limited Jurisdiction: Lower Courts

inferior courts the lowest level of state courts, normally trial courts of limited jurisdiction.

At the lowest level of state courts are trial courts of limited jurisdiction, also known as **inferior courts** or *lower courts*. There are more than 13,500 trial courts of limited jurisdiction in the United States, staffed with about 18,000 judicial officers. The lower courts constitute 85 percent of all judicial bodies in the United States. Exhibit 7.4 provides an insider's view of a lower court.

Variously called *district, justice, justice of the peace, city, magistrate,* or *municipal courts,* the lower courts decide a restricted range of cases. These courts are created and maintained by city or county governments and, therefore, are not part of the state judiciary. The caseload of the lower courts is staggering—more than 34 million criminal and civil cases filed per year, the overwhelming number of which are traffic cases (more than 41 million in any given year)—more than half of which is traffic related.[36]

The workload of the lower courts can be divided into felony criminal cases, non-felony criminal cases, and civil cases. In the felony arena, lower court jurisdiction typically includes the preliminary stages of felony cases; therefore, after an arrest, a judge in a trial court of limited jurisdiction will hold the initial appearance, appoint counsel for indigents, and conduct the preliminary hearing. Later, the case is transferred to a trial court of general jurisdiction (discussed previously) for trial (or plea) and sentencing.[37] Note: Appendix I contains a quiz, consisting of five questions, which checks your knowledge concerning the actions and jurisdiction of federal and state courts.

AN INSIDER'S VIEW OF A LOWER COURT

A lower court judge provided compelling realism and insight—as well as a bit of humor—on his court's website concerning the proper decorum and performance of lawyers who are about to litigate cases therein:

We tend to be the fast-food operators of the court system—high volumes of traffic for short visits with a base of loyal repeat customers. Don't plan on having a private conversation with your client or a witness amid the throngs of other people trying to do the same thing. Prepared attorneys can be in and out in short order. Meeting your client for the first time after calling out his name in the lobby can take longer.

Patience is a virtue and communication with the bailiffs and court staff will keep everyone happy. We coordinate the court's calendar, your calendar, and opposing counsel's calendar with the availability of the witnesses. Here are a few other "do's" and "don'ts" for successfully navigating this Court:

- Everyone goes through the metal detector. Having to go back to your car to stow your Leatherman, linoleum cutting knife, stun gun, giant padlock, or sword-cane (all items caught by security) can be annoying.
- I once ruled against a very sweet elderly lady who reminded me of my own grandmother. She simply didn't have a case and I thought I had ruled fairly and gently. As she slowly walked by the front of the bench on the way out of the courtroom, she looked up and said, "Aw, go—yourself," and walked out the door. My mouth was hanging open; I just didn't know what to do. I'm fairly sure that this is the first and last time someone will get away with this, so even if the judge rules against you, smile on the way out. You can mutter to yourself all you want on the way back to the office rather than the holding cell in the back of the courthouse.
- I once watched a gentleman in the back row feed his parrot peanuts while it was sitting on his shoulder. I assumed I had a parrot case in the pile somewhere, but after the last case was called, the parrot left without testifying. I asked the security officer why he let the man with the parrot come into court. I was told that the man had been there to watch a friend's case and that his sick parrot needed to be fed every 15 minutes. While admiring the logic of his decision, I have advised our new court security officers that unless an animal is actually a service animal, various beasts, fish, and fowl are not allowed in simply to watch court.
- Expect the unexpected. Recent interesting events include a live pipe bomb being left at the front door by a concerned citizen; a gentleman dancing on top of his motor home in the parking lot while his laundry hung from the trees and his morning coffee perked on the propane stove he had set up in the next space; and the occasional ammonia discharges into the holding cell by one of the neighboring businesses.

Source: Excerpt from An Insider's View of a Lower Court by Kevin Higgins. Copyright © 2008 by Kevin Higgins. Used by permission of Kevin Higgins.

▶ "Unification," "Consolidation," "Reform": by any Name, a Century's Attempts to Streamline the Courts

Imagine being a student of criminal justice—or one who has received a traffic citation—and finding yourself in a position of having to navigate your state and local court systems. You discover that you live in an area where the highest court of appeal is the Court of Appeals (not, as is commonly used, a "Supreme Court"), but the primary felony trial courts are called Supreme Courts and the County Courts handle crimes occurring outside the city. There might also be City Courts, County Courts, Municipal Courts, and Justice of the

Peace Courts (still found in many states) that handle a variety of matters, such as traffic, small claims, and even some preliminary hearings.

Although this scenario might be a bit far-fetched, it really is not too different from what one might find in some states in the United States—a situation that has its roots in the early court systems of England. This chapter section discusses how the courts became so confusing and convoluted over time, and what has been done through **court unification** to try to rectify the matter.

Court unification can be defined in several ways, but it typically includes an attempt to simplify a state trial court's structure, procedures, funding, and administration so as to eliminate or reduce overlapping and fragmented jurisdiction, better deploy and use judges and support staff, and streamline and expedite trial and appellate processes.[38]

> **court unification**
> reorganizing a trial court's structure, procedures, funding, and administration so streamline operations, better deploy personnel, and improve trial and appellate processes.

Courts in Early England: A Desire to Unify

Beginning with the courts of the late 1800s in England, the need was demonstrated for "unified" state judicial systems, where the court system of any jurisdiction could be efficient, effective, and well understood by the people. But from their early beginnings, since the reign of Edward I in the late 1200s, this has been an elusive goal. Throughout most of the nineteenth century, according to William Raftery,[39] England's court system was a confusing patchwork, with courts for criminal proceedings, petty causes, and general civil matters. Towns, villages, and cities created their own courts or had them created for them by the legislature. Atop this myriad of courts sat, effectively, a jumble. State courts of last resort were just as convoluted as the trial courts. Legislators and governors were also invested with judicial authority, able to issue writs, grant divorces, and sit as appellate courts.

The United States: An Historical Hodgepodge

Although by the mid-1800s England had begun to discard this system of a-court-for-every-type-of-case,[40] the American states were continuing or expanding England's old system, and by 1900 the United States would see, in larger cities, numerous courts with various jurisdictions, overseen by a multitude of higher courts, and so the die was cast. Noted legal scholar and reformer Roscoe Pound was moved to comment on this situation in 1906, in what has become a classic essay entitled *The Causes of Population Dissatisfaction with the Administration of Justice*,[41] that this "multiplicity of courts" needed to come to an end.

In 1914 the American Judicature Society (AJS) began publishing bulletins spelling out what court systems should look like, arguing for a "single Court of Justice" composed of three divisions: a court of appeal, a superior court, and a county court. It also took the position that one chief justice in each state should be given the same power as a governor and the "executive head" and administer the state's courts so as to reduce confusion and enhance cooperation.[42] A much more controversial recommendation by the AJS was that the judiciary be removed from any involvement from the other two branches of government in the selection of judges and clerks. Finally, the AJS recommended that, to be truly unified, state courts had to cease their legislatures' rule-making authority over the courts,[43] so that the state supreme court has the power to adopt uniform rules to be followed by all courts in the state, including procedures for disciplining attorneys and setting time standards for disposing of cases.

It would not be until the late 1930s that success in these areas was realized, with some state legislatures beginning to turn over rule-making authority to the state supreme courts and creating judicial councils to oversee the state systems. World War II intervened and halted progress, however, but in 1949 the American Bar Association reprised the idea with its publication of *Minimum Standards of Judicial Administration*,[44] setting forth what each individual state needed to do to implement a more effective procedural system. Thus began a movement focusing on centralization and unification that would last for three decades; between 1959 and 1978, 33 states amended their constitutions or statutes to provide that the chief justice was the administrative head of the court system; today 46 states have such provisions.[45]

As It Stands Today

In sum, today, more than a century after the need was recognized to unify the courts in order to avoid duplication and waste of resources, the goal remains largely unmet. In order to be truly centralized or consolidated, a state's court system should have, at minimum: (1) consolidation into a single-tier trial court, (2) rule-making authority, and (3) centralization of administration. With unification would also come centralized budgeting by the state judicial administrator, a single budget would be prepared for the entire state judiciary and sent to the state legislature, the governor's power to recommend a judicial budget would be eliminated, and lower courts would be dependent on the Supreme Court for their monies. Today many states claim to be "unified" and assert in their constitutions and statutes that they are so, but to this day such courts maintain up to 8 or 10 trial courts whose judges are not interchangeable.[46]

Two Examples at the Extremes

Looking at two systems—one that is unified on a statewide basis and one that is not—may assist in better comprehending the concept of unification; to do so, we look at the states of Illinois and New York (Figure 7-4 ■). In 1964, Illinois became the first state to become unified. All of its trial courts were consolidated into a unified circuit court with one chief judge overseeing the operations and procedures in each division. Today, Illinois's state court system includes 1 court of last resort, 1 intermediate appellate court divided into 5 districts, and 1 court of general jurisdiction sectioned into 22 trial court divisions.[47]

In contrast, New York's state court system, as depicted in Figure 7-4, included 1 court of last resort, 2 intermediate appellate courts, 2 types of general jurisdiction trial courts divided into 69 divisions, and 8 types of limited jurisdiction trial courts separated into 1,695 divisions.[48]

In February 2002, a governmental body examined the budgetary impact of trial court restructuring in New York State; first, it was observed that "no state in the nation has a more complex court system structure than New York's, which consists of 11 separate courts—the Supreme Court, the Court of Claims, the County Court, the Family Court, the

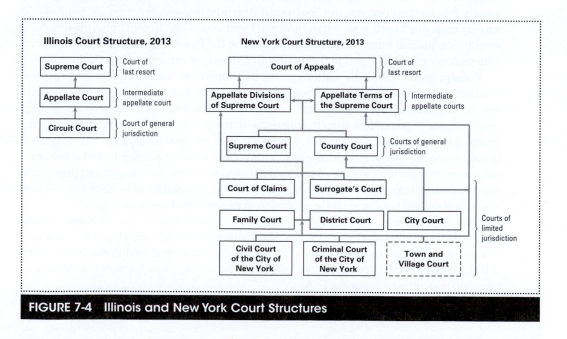

FIGURE 7-4 **Illinois and New York Court Structures**

Surrogate's Court, the New York City Civil and Criminal Courts, the District Courts on Long Island, the City Courts outside of New York City, and the Town and Village Justice Courts." The study noted the "numerous inefficiencies" of the arcane court structure while listing a number of benefits that would accrue to court unification—including an annual estimated net savings of $131.4 million over a 5-year period.[49]

▶ The Influence of Courts in Policymaking

The judicial branch has the responsibility to determine the legislative intent of the law and to provide public forums—the courts—for resolving disputes. This is accomplished by determining the facts and their legal significance in each case. If the court determines the legal significance of the facts by applying an existing rule of law, it is engaging in pure dispute resolution.[50] On the contrary, "if to resolve the dispute the court must create a new rule or modify an old one that is law creation."[51]

Determining what the law says and providing a public forum involve the courts in policymaking. **Policymaking** can be defined simply as "establishing rules, principles, or guidelines that govern actions by ordinary citizens as well as persons in positions of authority."[52] The policy decisions of the courts affect virtually all of us in our daily lives. In recent decades, the courts have been asked to deal with issues that previously were within the purview of the legislative and judicial branches. Because many of the Constitution's limitations on government are couched in vague language, the judicial branch must eventually deal with potentially volatile social issues, such as those involving prisons, abortion, and schools.[53]

U.S. Supreme Court decisions have dramatically changed race relations, resulted in the overhaul of juvenile courts, increased the rights of the accused, prohibited prayer and segregation in public schools, legalized abortion, and allowed for destruction of the U.S. flag. State and federal courts have together overturned minimum residency requirements for welfare recipients, equalized school expenditures, and prevented road and highway construction from damaging the environment. They have eliminated the requirement of a high school diploma for a firefighter's job and ordered increased property taxes to desegregate public schools. The only governmental area that has not witnessed judicial policymaking since the Civil War is foreign affairs. Cases in which courts make policy determinations usually involve government, the Fourteenth Amendment, and the need for equity—the remedy most often used against governmental violations of law. Recent policymaking decisions by the judicial branch have not been based on the Constitution, but rather on federal statutes concerning the rights of the disadvantaged and consumers and the environment.[54]

Perhaps nowhere have the nation's courts had more of an impact than in the prisons—from which nearly 60,000 prisoner petitions are filed each year in the U.S. district courts.[55] Among the accomplishments of judicial intervention have been extending recognized constitutional rights of free speech, religion, and due process to prisoners; abolishing the South's plantation model of prisons; accelerating the professionalization of U.S. correctional managers; encouraging a new generation of correctional administrators more amenable to reform; reinforcing the adoption of national standards for prisons; and promoting increased accountability and efficiency of prisons. The only failure of judicial intervention has been its inability to prevent the explosion in prison populations and costs.[56]

The courts have become particularly involved in administrative policy because of public interest group litigation. For example, legislation was enacted allowing citizen lawsuits when certain federal regulatory agencies, such as the Environmental Protection Agency (EPA), failed to perform certain duties as required by statute. Thus, a citizens' environmental group was allowed to sue the EPA.

It may appear that the courts are too broad in their review of issues; however, it should be remembered that judges "cannot impose their views until someone brings a case to court,

policymaking establishing rules, principles, or guidelines to govern actions by ordinary citizens and persons in positions of authority.

often as a last resort after complaints to unresponsive legislators and executives."[57] Plaintiffs must be truly aggrieved or have *standing*. The independence of the judicial branch, particularly at the federal court level, at which judges enjoy lifetime appointments, allows the courts to champion the causes of the underclasses: those with fewer financial resources or votes (by virtue of, say, being a minority group) or without a positive public profile.[58] It is also important to note that the judiciary is the "least dangerous branch," having no enforcement powers. Moreover, the decisions of the courts can be overturned by legislative action. Even decisions based on the Constitution can be overruled by subsequent constitutional amendment. Thus, the judicial branch depends on a perception of legitimacy surrounding its decisions.[59]

Note: the "Deliberate and Decide" problem at this chapter's end concerns recent public policy areas where many people believe the courts have become too involved; you are invited to voice your opinion concerning the handling and treatment of detainees at Guantanamo Bay, a U.S. naval base located at the southeast tip of Cuba.

Summary

This chapter reviewed the distinctive nature of the courts and their organization and some of their administration. Several areas were highlighted, including the nature of the courts in terms of the status they are accorded and their use of the adversarial system in trying to arrive at the truth; the dual system of courts in our country—the courts of last resort, appeals courts, and trial courts at the federal and state levels; and how the federal courts are administered and the growing movement toward court unification. We also discussed the role of courts in policymaking.

With regard to court unification, a need and an issue that is indicated in this chapter is that of court reform because of the often confusing way in which courts and judges are organized and utilized; many notable authorities believe changes are necessary to improve court efficiency and possibly to save large amounts of public money. It is clear, however, that until a number of political and tradition-based impediments are overcome, widespread court reform is unlikely.

Another issue raised in this chapter is the burgeoning caseloads of the courts; alternative dispute resolution, discussed in Chapter 9, is proposed as a means of helping in this area of court operation.

Key Terms and Concepts

Adversarial system *162*

Court of last resort *168*

Court unification *174*

Décor *161*

Decorum *161*

Dual court system *163*

Inferior courts *172*

Intermediate courts of appeals
  (ICAs) *170*

Judicial Conference of the United
  States *167*

Jurisdiction *165*

Policymaking *176*

Trial courts *170*

Questions for Review

1. In what ways are courts "hallowed" and unique in our society in terms of their décor and required decorum?

2. How is the adversarial system of justice related to the truth-seeking function of the courts?

3. What is the organization of our dual court system, and what are the primary functions of each of the major types of courts that exist within the federal and state court systems?

4. What are some of the traditions of the U.S. Supreme Court, and what functions do they provide?

5. How is the federal court system structured, and how would you describe the significance of the District of Columbia Circuit Court of Appeals?

6. What are some perceived benefits of streamlining a state court system, and how would such a system be organized? What are examples of a highly unified system and a poorly unified state system?

7. What are the types of, and reasons for, court jurisdiction?

8. How do the courts influence public policymaking?

Deliberate and Decide

Courts, Policymaking, and the Guantanamo Detainees

What is the appropriate role for the judiciary in policymaking? While some people favor judicial restraint and believe the courts should have little or no role in policymaking—where judges play minimal policymaking roles and leave policy decisions to the legislatures—others argue for judicial activism, believing judges can make policy decisions that help those who are politically or economically disadvantaged. One of the U.S. Supreme Court's own justices, Antonin Scalia, believes the Court needs to stay out of areas that would be best left to Congress or the people, citing the court's rulings in such areas as surveillance of phone records, a national health program (the Affordable Care Act), the right to bear arms, and "inventing" new classes of minorities such as the areas of gay marriage and benefits for same-sex couples.[60]

As another example, consider where the line should be drawn between protecting U.S. citizens from terrorists and individual rights and liberties. More specifically, what role should the courts play in determining how individuals be treated—both in terms of the rule of law and their confinement—when suspected of being "enemy combatants?" Furthermore, to what extent should the courts be involved in terms of crafting policy regarding law-of-war detention?

A specific example of policymaking in this arena is the detention of suspected enemy combatants at Guantanamo Bay, a 45-square-mile American naval base located at the southeast tip of Cuba. After the terrorist attacks of 9/11 and the war in Afghanistan, the United States moved about 600 captured prisoners to Guantanamo Bay, most of whom remained there for years without being charged with crimes or being given hearings.

In the wake of the September 11, 2001, attacks on the United States, the government authorized the use of "enhanced interrogation" techniques that were previously recognized as torture. The Bush Administration contended that certain persons were dangerous enemy combatants who could be detained and interrogated legally and humanely during the ongoing war on terrorism. The detainees eventually challenged this policy, filing suits in federal courts and triggering policy discussions at the national level. In addition, the detainees engaged in hunger strikes (with many of them being force-fed); the Supreme Court issued several major decisions: first, the government should have the power to recognize and detain enemy combatants, including U.S. citizens, but the latter must be afforded due process rights[61]; the president could not create military commissions to try Guantánamo detainees, thereby invalidating the system established to try accused war criminals (this case was widely seen as the most important ruling on executive power in decades, or perhaps ever)[62]; and foreign nationals who are held at Guantánamo Bay have a right to *habeus corpus*.[63]

Questions for Discussion

Should the court have remained detached from this entire matter—using restraint, as Justice Scalia suggested, and leaving it to Congress or the people to resolve?

1. Regarding the dilemma of protecting the public against terrorism versus individual rights, what do you believe are the major arguments for and against releasing the Guantanamo detainees? Should they ever be completely released, or at the very least committed to federal and state prisons?

2. What legal rights should these detainees possess? How do/should those rights differ from those of U.S. citizens who are accused of crimes?

3. Should such detainees who commit hunger strikes be force-fed, or left to either die or accept food on their own?[64]

Learn by Doing

1. You are a court administrator and have been invited to appear at a luncheon meeting of a local civic group of community and business leaders. While discussing your duties within the state court system, you are asked to explain the overall functions and interrelationship between the federal and state courts. How do you reply?

2. A county historical society has invited your criminal justice professor to speak at a meeting concerning the history and importance of the traditions within the U.S. Supreme Court. Your professor asks you, the graduate assistant, to draft an overview for this purpose. What will you write?

3. You are a teaching assistant in your university's criminal justice department and your instructor has fallen ill at the outset of the semester. As your instructor is a J.D./Ph.D., she often instructs courts courses. You are tasked to develop a 1-hour lecture on how state trial courts of general jurisdiction (i.e., the major trial courts) differ in scope and function from the higher state courts of last resort as well as appellate courts. What will you include in your lecture?

Notes

1. Alexis de Tocqueville, *Democracy in America,* Vol. 1, trans. H. Reeve (New York: D. Appleton, 1904), pp. 283–284.

2. H. Ted Rubin, *The Courts: Fulcrum of the Justice System* (Santa Monica, CA: Goodyear, 1976), p. 3.

3. Stephen Whicher and R. Spiller (eds.), *The Early Lectures of Ralph Waldo Emerson* (Philadelphia: University of Pennsylvania Press, 1953), p. 112.

4. 382 U.S. 406 (1966), 416.

5. Thomas L. Steffen, "Truth as Second Fiddle: Reevaluating the Place of Truth in the Adversarial Trial Ensemble," *Utah Law Review* 4 (1988):821.

6. W. Alschuler, "The Preservation of a Client's Confidences: One Value among Many or a Categorical Imperative?" *University of Colorado Law Review* 52 (1981):349.

7. David W. Neubauer, *America's Courts and the Criminal Justice System*, 9th ed. (Belmont, CA: Thomson Wadsworth, 2008), p. 63.

8. Supreme Court of the United States, "Instructions for Admission to the Bar," http://www.supremecourt.gov/bar/barinstructions.pdf (accessed October 28, 2014).

9. Ibid., "Visitor's Guide to Oral Arguments," p. 1, http://www.supremecourt.gov/visiting/visitorsguidetooralargument.aspx (accessed October 28, 2014).

10. Robert H. Jackson Center, "The Flags at Nuremberg," http://www.roberthjackson.org/the-man/speeches-articles/speeches/speeches-related-to-robert-h-jackson/the-flags-at-nuremberg/ (accessed October 28, 2014).

11. Supreme Court of the United States, "The Court and Its Traditions," http://www.supremecourt.gov/about/traditions.aspx (accessed October 28, 2013).

12. United States Courts, "U.S. Supreme Court Procedures," http://www.uscourts.gov/EducationalResources/ConstitutionResources/SeparationOfPowers/USSupremeCourtProcedures.aspx (accessed October 28, 2014).

13. Ibid., "Writs of Certiorari," http://www.uscourts.gov/educational-resources/get-informed/supreme-court/supreme-court-procedures.aspx (accessed October 28, 2014).

14. See University of Missouri—Kansas City Law School, "Exploring Constitutional Conflict: The Supreme Court in the American System of Government," http://law2.umkc.edu/faculty/projects/ftrials/conlaw/supremecourtintro.html (accessed October 28, 2014).

15. Supreme Court of the United States, "Members," http://www.supremecourt.gov/about/about_us.aspx (accessed October 28, 2014).

16. Federal Judicial Center, "The U.S. Courts of Appeals and the Federal Judiciary," http://www.fjc.gov/history/home.nsf/page/courts_of_appeals.html (accessed October 28, 2014).

17. U.S. Courts, "U.S. Courts of Appeals—Appeals Commenced, Terminated, and Pending—During the 12-Month Periods Ending September 30, 2011 and 2012," Table B, http://www.uscourts.gov/uscourts/Statistics/JudicialBusiness/2012/appendices/B00Sep12.pdf (accessed October 28, 2014).

18. Ibid., Table B1A. http://www.uscourts.gov/uscourts/Statistics/JudicialBusiness/2012/appendices/B01ASep12.pdf (accessed October 28, 2013).

19. For more discussion about the court, see Eric Andreas, "Key Role of the DC Circuit," Wiley Rein (Winter 2007), http://www.wileyrein.com/publications.cfm?sp=articles&newsletter=13&id=4074; also see Richard Wolf, "Senate Fights over Appeals Court Key to Obama Agenda," *USA Today*, November 21, 2013, http://www.usatoday.com/story/news/politics/2013/11/21/dc-circuit-judges-senate-obama-filibuster-nuclear/3663817/ (accessed October 6, 2014).

20. More information about this court may be found at its websites, at: http://www.cadc.uscourts.gov/internet/home.nsf and http://www.dccourts.gov/internet/appellate/main.jsf (accessed January 14, 2014).

21. United States Courts, "Federal Judgeships," http://www.uscourts.gov/JudgesAndJudgeships/FederalJudgeships.aspx (accessed October 28, 2014).

22. Ibid.

23. "United States Courts, U.S. District Courts—Criminal Cases Commenced, Terminated, and Pending (Including Transfers) during the 12-Month Periods Ending March 31, 2011 and 2012," Table D, http://www.uscourts.gov/Viewer.aspx?doc=/uscourts/Statistics/FederalJudicialCaseloadStatistics/2012/tables/D00CMar12.pdf (accessed October 28, 2014).

24. Neubauer, *America's Courts and the Criminal Justice System,* p. 68.

25. U.S. Courts, "The Federal Judiciary," http://www.uscourts.gov/adminoff.html (accessed October 6, 2014).

26. Neubauer, *America's Courts and the Criminal Justice System,* p. 85.

27. Ibid., p. 87.

28. See National Center for State Courts, *The Role of State Intermediate Appellate Courts: Principles for Adapting to Change* (November 2012), p. 3.

29. U.S. Department of Justice, Bureau of Justice Statistics, *State Court Organization, 1987–2004.* (Washington, DC: Author, October 2007), p. 3.

30. National Center for State Courts, "Appellate Caseloads," http://www.courtstatistics.org/Appellate/20121Appellate.aspx (accessed October 28, 2014).

31. Neubauer, *America's Courts and the Criminal Justice System,* p. 85.

32. National Center for State Courts, "Court Statistics Project," http://www.courtstatistics.org/ (accessed October 6, 2014).

33. Neubauer, *America's Courts and the Criminal Justice System,* p. 82.

34. Ibid., pp. 82–83.

35. U.S. Department of Justice, Bureau of Justice Statistics, *State Court Organization,* p. 3.

36. See National Center for State Courts, generally, "Court Statistics Project," http://www.courtstatistics.org/Court-Statistics-Project-Constrained-Search-Page.aspx?q=trial%20court%20cases&site=prod_csp (accessed October 6, 2014).

37. Ibid., pp. 402–403.

38. See, generally, William Raftery, "Unification and 'Bragency': A Century of Court Organization and Reorganization," *Judicature* 96(6) (May/June 2014): 338; also see National Center for State Courts, "Court Unification Resource Guide," http://www.ncsc.org/Topics/Court-Management/Court-Unification/Resource-Guide.aspx (accessed October 30, 2014).

39. Ibid.

40. Ibid.

41. Roscoe Pound, "The Causes of Population Dissatisfaction with the Administration of Justice," 40 *American Law Review* 729 (1926)

42. American Judicature Society, "Model Judiciary Article," 6 *Journal of the American Judicature Society* 48–58 (1922).

43. Silas A. Harris, "The Extent and Use of Rule-making Authority," 22 *Journal of the American Judicature Society* 30 (1938).

44. See Louden L. Bomberger, "Minimum Standards of Judicial Administration, by Arthur T. Vanderbilt," *Indiana Law Journal* 26 (1) (1950), http://www.repository.law.indiana.edu/ilj/vol26/iss1/13 (accessed October 30, 2014).

45. Raftery, "Unification and 'Bragency,'" p. 342.

46. Ibid.

47. State of Illinois, "Illinois Court System," http://19thcircuitcourt.state.il.us/Organization/Pages/il_crts.aspx (accessed October 29, 2014); also see Illinois State Courts, "The Illinois Judiciary," http://www.courts.us/state/il/courts.php (accessed October 30, 2014).

48. NYCourts.gov, "Structure of the New York State Unified Court System," http://www.nycourts.gov/courts/8jd/structure.shtml (accessed October 3, 2014).

49. New York State Unified Court System, "The Budgetary Impact of Trial Court Restructuring," http://www.nycourts.gov/reports/trialcourtrestructuring/ctmerger2802.pdf (accessed October 28, 2014).

50. Howard Abadinsky, *Law and Justice: An Introduction to the American Legal System,* 4th ed. (Chicago: Nelson-Hall, 1999), p. 33.

51. Richard A. Posner, *The Federal Courts: Crisis and Reform* (Cambridge, MA: Harvard University Press, 1985), p. 3.

52. Wayne N. Welsh and Philip W. Harris, *Criminal Justice Policy & Planning,* 4th ed. (Boston: Elsevier, 2013) p. 108; also see: Harold J. Spaeth, *Supreme Court Policy Making: Explanation and Prediction* (San Francisco, CA: W. H. Freeman, 1979), p. 19.

53. Abadinsky, *Law and Justice,* p. 174.

54. Ibid., p. 170.

55. U.S. Department of Justice, *Sourcebook of Criminal Justice Statistics 2000* (Washington, DC: U.S. Government Printing Office, 2001), p. 467.

56. Malcolm M. Feeley and Edward L. Rubin, *Judicial Policy Making and the Modern State: How the Courts Reformed America's Prisons* (New York: Cambridge University Press, 1998).

57. Stephen L. Wasby, *The Supreme Court in the Federal System,* 3rd ed. (Chicago: Nelson-Hall, 1989), p. 5.

58. Abadinsky, *Law and Justice,* p. 171.

59. Ibid., p. 166.

60. Matt Volz, "Antonin Scalia: Supreme Court Should Not Be Policymakers," *Huffington Post,* August 13, 2014, http://www.huffingtonpost.com/2014/08/19/antonin-scalia-supreme-court_n_3782297.html (accessed October 29, 2014).

61. See *Hamdi v. Rumsfeld,* 542 U.S. 507 (2004).

62. See *Hamdan v. Rumsfeld,* 548 U.S. 557 (2006).

63. See *Boumediene v. Bush*, 553 U.S. 723 (2008).

64. George C. Edwards, III, Martin P. Wattenberg, and Robert L. Lineberry, "Government in America: People, Politics, and Policy," http://wps.ablongman.com/long_edwards_ga_12/33/8517/2180538.cw/ (accessed September 23, 2014); Susan Seligson, "The Legal Mess behind the Ethical Mess," Boston University "BU Today," May 28, 2014, http://www.bu.edu/today/2014/gitmo-the-legal-mess-behind-the-ethical-mess/ (accessed September 23, 2014); Dante Gatmaytan, "Crafting Policies for the Guantánamo Bay Detainees: An Interbranch Perspective," *DePaul Rule of Law Journal* (Fall 2010), http://www.academia.edu/3412061/Crafting_Policies_for_the_Guantanamo_Bay_Detainees_An_Interbranch_Perspective; see the U.S. Department of Defense Guantanamo website at: http://www.defense.gov/home/features/gitmo/ (all URLs accessed on September 23, 2014).

In the span of 7 years, the Supreme Court issued four decisions and Congress enacted two laws that together shaped the rights of the detainees, resulting in an interbranch perspective—policy making not from a single branch of government, but from the interaction of its branches.

Four things belong to a Judge: To hear courteously, To answer wisely, To consider soberly, and To decide impartially.

—*Socrates*

8 Court Personnel Roles and Functions

LEARNING OBJECTIVES

After reading this chapter, the student will be able to:

 define and understand judicial administration and court administration

❷ understand the methods of judicial selection: partisan elections, nonpartisan elections, merit selection, and appointment

❸ discuss the benefits and problems encountered by judges, including the problems faced by newly appointed judges

❹ describe how civility is maintained in the courtroom, the meaning of good judging, and a new model code of conduct for state and local judges

❺ explain some issues surrounding judges' personal and professional use of electronic social media/networking sites

❻ provide a description of the "appearance of impropriety" concept as it applies to judges (and other criminal justice employees), as well as its importance and how it functions

❼ delineate the duties of judges who serve as court managers, including the Chief Justice of the United States Supreme Court

❽ relate the importance of court clerks

⑨ *define the six major duties of court administrators*

⑩ *review several strategies that judges follow in determining the quality of administrators' work*

⑪ *delineate the components of jury administration, including special considerations during notorious cases*

▶ Introduction

Chapter 7 looked at the "hallowed" nature of the courts and at how the courts and judges—with gavels, flowing robes, ornate surroundings, and other aspects of décor and decorum that are accorded their office—are enveloped in a mystique of importance and authority. This chapter expands that discussion, focusing more on judges and other key personnel who are involved in court administration.

The administration of the judicial process is probably the least understood area of justice administration and possibly all of criminal justice. This lack of understanding is compounded by the fact that, very often, even judges and court administrators are not formally trained in their roles. Furthermore, few judges would probably "like to spend all day or most of the day handling union grievances or making sure that employees know what their benefits are."[1] Opportunities to receive training and education are expanding, however, and this chapter addresses some of the means by which that can be accomplished.

This chapter opens by defining and distinguishing the terms *judicial administration* and *court administration* and then considering judges: how they ascend to the bench, benefits and problems of the position, and some thoughts on good judging and courtroom civility; included here are discussions of a revised code of conduct for state and local judges, some ethical considerations concerning judges' use of social networking sites, and a definition and some examples of what is meant by the "appearance of impropriety." Then, we specifically examine the judge's role as the ultimate judicial administrator. The historically important role of court clerks is then reviewed, and next, we examine the relatively new position of the specially trained court administrator, including training and duties, judges' evaluation criteria, and conflict among judicial administrators. This is followed by an overview of the problems court administrators might confront in creating and maintaining juries, especially during sequestration and notorious trials. The chapter concludes with review questions, "deliberate and decide" problems, and "learn by doing" exercises.

Note that Chapter 15, concerning financial administration, discusses a role of court administration that took on new significance with the onset of the recent recession: grant writing.

▶ Defining Judicial Administration

The purpose of judicial independence is to mitigate arbitrariness in judging. But what is the definition and purpose of **judicial (or court) administration**. This relatively new criminal justice concept can be difficult to define. Consequently, as Russell Wheeler noted, "many court administrators today find themselves under the inevitable strain of not knowing for certain what their purpose is."[2]

Most works on judicial administration point to Roscoe Pound as the founder of the study of judicial administration because of his 1906 essay "The Causes of Popular Dissatisfaction with Administration of Justice."[3] Pound issued a call to improve judicial administration, by efficient and equitable practices. Pound contended that the courts were

> **judicial (court) administration** the day-to-day and long-range activities of those persons who are responsible for the activities and functions of a court.

archaic and did indeed need to be administered more effectively. He also noted that the adversary system often turned litigation into a game, irritating parties, jurors, and witnesses and giving the public a false notion of the purpose and end of law. Pound's lecture remains a treasure trove of ideas concerning the management of courts and has also led some states to unify their trial courts (discussed in Chapter 7).[4]

However, another major essay that influenced court administration was written by Woodrow Wilson 19 years earlier, in 1887, entitled "The Study of Administration." Wilson stressed that the vocation of administration was a noble calling and not a task for which every person was competent.[5] He emphasized that policy and administration are two different matters, and that judges are responsible for "establishing fundamental court policy," and that a "trained executive officer, working under the chief judge or presiding judge, [was needed to] relieve judges generally [of] the function of handling the numerous business and administrative affairs of the courts."[6]

Wilson's essay certainly gives intellectual respectability to the field of administration; however, almost every administrator and policymaker knows that a court's policy decisions inevitably intertwine with administrative decisions. For example, today's court administrator must often set policy for dealing with issues, such as celebrity cases, evidence, case scheduling, and the use of cameras in the courtroom—the kinds of issues discussed here and in Chapter 9.

The difficulty of defining judicial administration became even more obvious during the 1970s when it became an attractive vocation. Various people and commissions tried to define it but seemed capable only of listing the duties of the office. For example, the National Advisory Commission on Criminal Justice Standards and Goals stated succinctly in 1973 that "the basic purpose of court administration is to relieve judges of some administrative chores and to help them perform those they retain."[7] Furthermore, in 1974, the American Bar Association (ABA) specified a variety of functions for the court administrator to perform "under the authority of the judicial council and the supervision of the chief justice."[8]

To help and provide more clarity, a good working definition of judicial administration was advanced by Russell Wheeler and Howard Whitcomb:

> The direction of and influences on the activities of those who are expected to contribute to just and efficient case processing—except legal doctrinal considerations, insofar as they dispose of the particular factual and legal claims presented in a case.[9]

This definition also separates the judicial and nonjudicial functions of the court, and it implies that a *set* of people share a role norm and that judicial administration constitutes *all* of the factors that direct and influence those people.[10]

In sum, the term *court administration* might be conceived of as the day-to-day and long-range activities of those persons who are responsible for the activities and functions of the court system. This term is more commonly used in this chapter because I focus on the development of the role and functions of the *individual trial court administrator*. This will become clearer as the chapter unfolds and the relationship between judge and court administrator is discussed.

▶ The Jurists

There are many facets involved with serving as a judge: getting educated and trained for the position, getting elected or appointed, overseeing the proper conduct of court proceedings, and administering the full range of services and resources pertaining to the court. This chapter section discusses those elements.

ADMINISTRATIVE ADVICE FROM THE FIELD

Kenneth J. Peak

Name: Jennifer P. Togliatti

Current Position/City/State: Chief Judge, Eighth Judicial District Court (EJDC), Las Vegas, NV

College attended/academic major/degree(s): Undergraduate: UNLV, Bachelor's Degree in Business Administration

Graduate: California Western School of Law, Juris Doctorate Degree

My primary duties and responsibilities in this position include: responsibility for performing duties as both an administrator well as a judge. As an administrator, I conduct monthly meetings for all of the judges of the EJDC and attend meetings of the civil and criminal judges. I also lead a legislative committee that works with the judiciary statewide to monitor legislation for Nevada courts. I decide the vast majority of motions to disqualify judges filed in the EJDC, conduct settlement conferences, and handle criminal matters. I manage labor issues and deal with litigation matters for the court. I conduct several monthly meetings with community partners in justice. I oversee the Court Executive Officer and meet with him regularly to manage budgetary issues and all issues associated with the EJDC's functions. Finally, I am responsible for overseeing the management of 600 court employees, including the marshal force, 51 judges, and 17 hearing masters and commissioners, all while keeping costs within the Court's $54 million budget.

Personal attributes/characteristics that have proven to be most helpful to me in this position are: patience, diplomacy, and willingness to compromise.

My three greatest challenges in this administrative role include: providing consistent level of service in the face of historic budget cuts, managing the growth of the EJDC (namely the addition of 10 judges and 8 courtrooms), and dealing with problems regarding the separation of powers, which arise because the EJDC is funded by the legislative and executive branches.

Personal accomplishments during my administrative career about which I am most proud are: during my term as Chief, focusing on major advances in technology. In order to expand the Court and provide greater access to justice, I instituted a new system of electronic filing, which resulted in a paperless filing system. This efficiency has aided the environment and has saved space at the courthouse. My administration also launched the EJDC's own app, CourtFinder (at: https://play.google.com/store/apps/details?id=gov.clarkcountynv.courts.docket.android). Next, I take pride in my work with the court's marshal force. At this incredible time in our history, when we face threats ranging from basic criminal acts to domestic terrorism, our court system absolutely must focus on security while adhering to recent budget cuts. Our marshal force (consisting of 98 marshals and the head of court security, as well as 11 marshal support staff and court security administrators) has exploded in growth since I was sworn in as Chief. Previously, the court employed one marshal for each judge. As the court grew, we became responsible for the security of a building that houses the municipal, district, and justice courts, as well as the Nevada Supreme Court. As Chief, I am responsible for a marshal force that polices the facilities and keeps the building and its occupants safe. To accomplish this, I improved the EJDC's marshal training, developed new policies and procedures to manage a large administrative marshal pool, implemented an internal affairs bureau to increase integrity, and reorganized the Court to provide high-level management.

Advice for someone who is interested in occupying an administrative position such as mine would be: particularly in a large court, commit 100 percent of your time and attention to the duties of administration. While you may have the sense that you are first a judge, and therefore would enjoy maintaining a regular caseload, the policy matters, budgetary issues, personnel decisions, litigation, and necessary meetings with partners in the justice community require full attention at all times. Most importantly, start your term with several goals in mind, including the three to five most important changes to the policy or operations of your court you wish to make. Don't lose sight of these overarching goals, even when bogged down with daily problems and minutiae that seem to take up all your time.

Those Who Would Be Judges: Methods of Selection

To a large extent, the quality of justice Americans receive depends on the quality of the judges who dispense it. Many factors have a bearing on the quality of judicial personnel: salary, length of term, prestige, independence, and personal satisfaction with the job. The most important factor considered by court reformers is judicial selection.[11]

As noted in Chapter 7, all federal judges are nominated by the president and confirmed by the Senate; they then serve for life (unless they resign or are impeached). **Judicial selection,** or the method used to nominate, select, or elect and install judges into office, is very different in the state courts, however, with a variety of means (involving partisan elections, nonpartisan elections, merit selection, or appointment) being used to select for a full term of office using (See Figure 8-1 ■), to fill an unexpired term upon the death, retirement, or resignation of a judge, and at the end of a special term.[12]

Figure 8-1 demonstrates regional patterns in the methods of judicial selection. It shows that partisan elections are concentrated in the South, nonpartisan elections in the West and upper Midwest, legislative elections and executive appointments in the East, and merit selection in the west of the Mississippi River.[13]

Following are brief discussions of the partisan election, nonpartisan election, and merit selection methods of judicial selection (only four states use the executive [gubernatorial/legislative] appointment method, whereby a vacancy is filled by the governor or legislature; also, some states use a combination of methods). In some states, judges are selected using partisan elections (the nominee's party is listed on the ballot). In other states, judges are

> **judicial selection**
> the method used to nominate, select, or elect and install judges into office.

Merit Selection (17)	Partisan Election (9)	Non-Partisan Election (17)	Gubernatorial (2) or Legislative (2) Appointment	Combined Methods (4)[1]
Alaska	Alabama	Arkansas	California (G)	Arizona
Colorado	Illinois	Georgia	New Jersey (G)	Florida
Connecticut	Louisiana	Idaho	South Carolina (L)	Indiana
Delaware[2]	New Mexico	Kentucky	Virginia (L)	Kansas
District of columbia	Ohio[3]	Michigan		Missouri
Hawaii[4]	Pennsylvania	Minnesota		New York
Iowa	Texas	Mississippi		Oklahoma
Maine	West Virginia	Montana		South Dakota
Maryland[2]		Nevada		Tennessee
Massachusetts[2]		North Carolina		
Nebraska		North Dakota		
New Hampshire[2]		Oregon		
New Mexico		Washington		
Rhode Island		Wisconsin		
Utah				
Vermont				
Wyoming				

1. In these states, some judges are chosen through merit selection and some are chosen in competitive elections.
2. Merit selection is established by executive order.
3. Candidates appear on the general election ballot without party affiliation but are nominated in partisan primaries.
4. The chief justice makes appointments to the district court and family court.

FIGURE 8-1   Initial Selection Methods of State Judges

Source: Excerpt from Judicial Selection In The States: Appellate And General Jurisdiction Courts. Copyright © 2004 by American Judicature Society. Used by permisssion of American Judicature Society.

selected using nonpartisan elections (no party affiliations are listed on the ballot). Nevertheless, even in these elections, partisan influences are often present: Judicial candidates are endorsed or nominated by parties, receive party support during campaigns, and are identified with party labels. In either case, although campaigns for judgeships are normally low key and low visibility, in recent years, some contests—particularly for state supreme court seats—have been contentious and costly election battles involving millions of dollars.

The general lack of information about judges and the low levels of voter interest, however, give incumbent judges important advantages in running for reelection. The prestigious title of "judge" is often listed on the ballot in front of the judge's name or on political signs and billboards. Few sitting judges are even opposed for reelection.[14]

Merit selection has been favored by court reformers wanting to "remove the courts from politics!" They point to three problems with popular elections of judges: (1) Elections fail to encourage the ablest lawyers to seek judicial posts and discourage qualified persons who want to avoid the rigors (if not the ordeal) of a campaign, (2) elections may provide an incentive for judges to decide cases in a popular manner, and (3) the elective system is a contest in which the electorate is likely to be uninformed about the merits of the candidates. To solve these problems, reformers advocate merit selection, also known as the **Missouri Bar Plan**. Thirty-four states and the District of Columbia use the merit system, and a number of other states have considered it. Merit selection involves the creation of a nominating commission whenever a vacancy occurs for any reason; the commission is composed of lawyers and laypersons; this group suggests a list of qualified nominees (usually three) to the governor, who chooses one person as the judge. After serving a period on the bench, the new judge stands uncontested before the voters. The sole question on the ballot is: "Should Judge X be retained in office?" If the incumbent wins a majority of the votes, then he or she earns a full term of office, and each subsequent term is secured through another uncontested *retention ballot*. Most judges are returned to office by a healthy margin.[15]

Note, however, that while the 1970s and 1980s marked the rise of merit selection for judges, the last 8 years has seen a trend whereby states either eliminate merit selection, modify its components, or return judicial selection "to its roots." Several states seem to favor going to a quasi-federal systems, where the executive appoints, the legislature (senate or house and senate) confirms, and the judges are then subject to retention elections thereafter.[16]

However, many experts—both individuals and groups—strongly believe that candidates for judgeships should not have to run for election to that office. For instance, retired U.S. Supreme Court Justice Sandra Day O'Connor said in November 2007 that she would do away with such partisan elections because candidates for judgeships risk being compromised by the growing amount of campaign funds they must raise; she stated, "If I could wave a magic wand, I would wave it to secure some kind of merit selection of judges across the country."[17] After O'Connor's home state of Arizona switched from partisan elections of judges to an appointed system in the 1970s, she "watched the improvement of the judiciary in the state."[18]

Similarly, the American Judicature Society has supported limiting the role of politics in the selection of state judges, compiling comprehensive information on judicial selection processes in each of the 50 states and the District of Columbia and providing a website on the subject (at http://www.judicialselection.us/; topics covered include methods of selecting, retaining, and removing judges; successful and unsuccessful reform efforts; the roles of parties, interest groups, and professional organizations in selecting judges; and the diversity of the bench).[19]

Judicial Benefits and Problems

Judges enjoy several benefits of office, including life terms for federal positions and in some states. Ascending to the bench can be the capstone of a successful legal career for a lawyer, even though a judge's salary can be less than that of a lawyer in private practice. Judges certainly warrant a high degree of respect and prestige as well; from arrest to final disposition, the accused face judges at every juncture involving important decisions about their future: bail, pretrial motions, evidence presentation, trial, and punishment.

Although it would seem that judges are the primary decision makers in the court, such is not always the case. Judges often accept recommendations from others who are more familiar with the case—e.g., bail recommendations from prosecutors, plea agreements struck by prosecuting and defense counsels, and sentence recommendations from the probation officer. These kinds of input are frequently accepted by judges in the informal courtroom network that exists. Although judges run the court, if they deviate from the consensus of the courtroom work group, they may be sanctioned: Attorneys can make court dockets go awry by requesting continuances or by not having witnesses appear on time.

Other problems can await a new jurist-elect or appointee. Judges who are new to the bench commonly face three general problems:

1. ***Mastering the breadth of law they must know and apply.*** New judges would be wise, at least early in their career, to depend on other court staff, lawyers who appear before them, and experienced judges for invaluable information on procedural and substantive aspects of the law and local court procedures. Through informal discussions and formal meetings, judges learn how to deal with common problems. Judicial training schools and seminars have also been developed to ease the transition into the judiciary. For example, the **National Judicial College (NJC)**, located on the campus of the University of Nevada, Reno, is a full-time institution offering nearly 100 educational sessions per year—including a number that are offered on the Web as well as in 10 cities across the country—for more than 3,300 state judges, including judges from around the world (see Exhibit 8.1).

2. ***Administering the court and the docket while supervising court staff.*** One of the most frustrating aspects of being a judge is the heavy caseload and corresponding administrative problems. Instead of having time to reflect on challenging legal questions or to consider the proper sentence for a convicted felon, trial judges must move cases. They can seldom act like a judge in the "grand tradition." As Abraham Blumberg noted several years ago, the working judge must be a politician, administrator, bureaucrat, and lawyer in order to cope with the crushing calendar of cases.[20] Judges are required to be competent administrators, a fact of judicial life that comes as a surprise to many new judges. One survey of 30 federal judges found that 23 (77%) acknowledged having major administrative difficulties on first assuming the bench. Half complained of heavy caseloads, stating that their judgeship had accumulated backlogs and that other adverse conditions compounded the problem. A federal judge maintained that it takes about 4 years to "get a full feel of a docket."[21]

The NJC offers several courses that can assist judges in better administering their courts. The following 1-week courses are available:

- Court Management for Judges and Court Administrators (covering topics such as managing human resources, conflict resolution, team building, budgeting, data collection, public relations)
- Management Skills for Presiding Judges
- Judges as Change Agents: Problem-Solving Courts

The National Center for State Courts in Williamsburg, Virginia, also has a program designed specifically for management and leadership in the courts: the Institute for Court Management's Court Executive Development Program (CEDP).[22]

National Judicial College an institute of learning in Reno, Nevada, that trains lawyers on how to be judges as well as veteran judges how to be better arbiters of justice.

ADVANCING JUDICIAL EDUCATION AND JUSTICE FOR MORE THAN 50 YEARS: THE NATIONAL JUDICIAL COLLEGE

For over 50 years, the National Judicial College (NJC) has provided judicial education to judges around the nation and the world, being the first to offer programs toward improving the delivery of justice and the rule of law. After opening its doors in 1963 at the University of Colorado at Boulder, in 1964, the NJC moved its permanent academic home to the University of Nevada, Reno campus. With U.S. Supreme Court Justice Tom C. Clark serving as one of its founders, since its inception the NJC has attracted a number of other Supreme Court justices as speakers and conference attendees. The American Bar Association, State of Nevada, U.S. Department of Justice, the University of Nevada, Reno, and a variety of corporations and foundations provide ongoing financial support for the not-for-profit educational corporation.

The NJC offers an average of 90 courses/programs per year, with more than 4,000 judges attending from all 50 states and more than 150 countries. The NJC's technologically enhanced facilities include 90,000 square feet of space, housing an auditorium, classrooms, a model courtroom, computer lab, multimedia room, judge's resource center, and discussion areas. All classrooms are equipped with "SMART" classroom technologies, integrating computers, audio/visual equipment, and sound systems that serve to enhance the classroom learning experience.

The NJC also provides customized programs and technical assistance to judges, offering a broad range of specialized, practical, and advanced programs in administrative law, military and tribal justice systems, as well as for international countries seeking to enhance the rule of law. A Professional Certificate program allows judges to specialize in five areas: Administrative Law Adjudication Skills, Dispute Resolution Skills, General Jurisdiction Trial Skills, Special Court Trial Skills, and Tribal Judicial Skills. Furthermore, since 1986 the NJC has offered judges the opportunity to obtain advanced degrees, to include master's and doctoral degrees in judicial studies.

Source: Adapted from the National Judicial College, "A Legacy of Learning," http://www.judges.org/about/history.html (accessed May 5, 2014).

3. *Coping with the psychological discomfort that accompanies the new position.* Most trial judges experience psychological discomfort on assuming the bench. Seventy-seven percent of new federal judges acknowledged having psychological problems in at least one of five areas: maintaining a judicial bearing both on and off the bench, the loneliness of the judicial office, sentencing criminals, forgetting the adversary role, and local pressure. One aspect of the judicial role is that of assuming a proper mien, or "learning to act like a judge." One judge remembers his first day in court: "I'll never forget going into my courtroom for the first time with the robes and all, and the crier tells everyone to rise. You sit down and realize that it's all different, that everyone is looking at you and you're supposed to do something."[23] Like police officers and probation and parole workers, judges complain that they "can't go to the places you used to. You always have to be careful about what you talk about. When you go to a party, you have to be careful not to drink too much so you won't make a fool of yourself."[24] And the position can be a lonely one:

> After you become a . . . judge some people tend to avoid you. For instance, you lose all your lawyer friends and generally have to begin to make new friends. I guess the lawyers are afraid that they will some day have a case before you and it would be awkward for them if they were on too close terms with you.[25]

Judges frequently describe sentencing criminals as the most difficult aspect of their job: "This is the hardest part of being a judge. You see so many pathetic people and you're never sure of what is a right or a fair sentence."[26]

▶ Courtroom Civility and Judicial Misconduct

"Good Judging"

What traits make for good judging? Obviously, judges should treat each case and all parties before them in court with absolute impartiality and dignity while providing leadership as the steward of their organization in all of the court management areas described in the following section. In addition to those official duties, however, other issues and suggestions have been put forth.

For example, a retired jurist with 20 years on the Wisconsin Supreme Court maintained that the following qualities define the art and craft of judging:

- Judges are keenly aware that they occupy a special place in a democratic society. They exercise their power in the most undemocratic of institutions with great restraint.

- They are aware of the necessity for intellectual humility—an awareness that what they think they know might well be incorrect.

- They do not allow the law to become their entire life; they get out of the courtroom, mingle with the public, and remain knowledgeable about current events.[27]

Other writers believe that judges should remember that the robe does not confer omniscience or omnipotence; as one trial attorney put it, "Your name is now 'Your Honor,' but you are still the same person you used to be, warts and all."[28] As if it weren't difficult enough to strive for and maintain humility and balance in their personal lives, judges must also enforce **courtroom civility**—i.e., a courtroom environment where litigants and all other court actors conduct themselves appropriately so that all parties are afforded a fair opportunity to present their case. Many persons have observed that we are becoming an increasingly uncivil society; the courts are certainly not immune to acts involving misconduct (see the discussion of courthouse violence in Chapter 9).

Personal character attacks by lawyers, directed at judges, attorneys, interested parties, clerks, jurors, and witnesses, both inside and outside the courtroom, in criminal and civil actions have increased at an alarming rate in the past 15 years.[29]

Following are some examples of the kinds of conduct involved:

- An attorney stated that opposing counsel and other attorneys were "a bunch of starving slobs," "incompetents," and "stooges."[30]

- A prosecutor argued to a jury that defense witnesses were "egg-sucking, chicken-stealing gutter trash."[31]

- The prosecutor called defense counsel "maggots" and "poor excuses for human beings." Defense counsel implied that the prosecutor was a "scumbag."[32]

- Counsel in trial and argument before a jury referred to parties as "cowardly, dirty, low-down dogs."[33]

Such invective clearly does not enhance the dignity or appearance of justice and propriety that is so important to the courts' public image and function. The Code of Judicial Conduct addresses these kinds of behaviors; Canon 3B(4) requires judges to be "patient, dignified, and courteous to litigants, jurors, witnesses, lawyers, and others with whom the judge deals in an official capacity" and requires judges to demand "similar conduct of lawyers, and of staff, court officials, and others subject to the judge's direction and control."[34]

At a minimum, judges need to attempt to prevent such vitriol and discipline offenders when it occurs. Some means that judges have at their disposal to control errant counsel include attorney disqualifications, new trials, and reporting of attorneys to disciplinary boards.[35]

courtroom civility
judges, litigants, and court actors conducting themselves appropriately so that all parties are afforded a fair opportunity to present their case.

Problems of Their Own: Types of Judicial Misconduct

What types of misconduct among judges themselves must the judiciary confront? Sometimes, medications may affect a judge's cognitive process or emotional temperament, causing him or her to treat parties, witnesses, jurors, lawyers, and staff poorly. Some stay on the bench too long; such judges will ideally have colleagues who can approach them, suggest retirement, and explain why this would be to their benefit. And sometimes, according to one author, judicial arrogance (sometimes termed "black robe disease" or "robe-itis") is the primary problem. This is seen when judges "do not know when to close their mouths, do not treat people with dignity and compassion, do not arrive on time, or do not issue timely decisions."[36]

Some bar associations or judicial circuits perform an anonymous survey of a sample of local attorneys who have recently argued a case before a particular judge and then share the results with the judge. Sometimes, these surveys are popularity contests, but a pattern of negative responses can have a sobering effect on the judge and encourage him or her to correct bad habits. Many judges will be reluctant to acknowledge that they have problems such as those described earlier. In such cases, the chief judge may have to scold or correct a subordinate judge. Although this is difficult, it may be imperative to do so in trying to maintain good relations with bar associations, individual lawyers, and the public. A single judge's blunders and behaviors can affect the reputation of the entire judiciary as well as the workloads of the other judges in his or her judicial district. Chief judges must therefore step forward to address such problems formally or informally.[37]

The reader's attention is directed to the "Deliberate and Decide" segment at this chapter's end, discussing a New Jersey jurist's having a part-time job as a stand-up comedian; this situation certainly raised questions of judicial propriety, conflict of interest, and the *appearance* of justice (discussed in the "Appearance of Impropriety" section below) on the part of this and other judicial officers. Related questions are included in this case study for your consideration.

Then, Chapter 9 includes discussion of a related matter, gender bias in the courts, while Chapter 13 includes a broader discussion of ethics in the courts. Next, we discuss what is being done formally to address problems of sexual harassment within the judiciary.

A Revised Model Code of Conduct for State and Local Judges

Model Code of Judicial Conduct standards written by the ABA to assist judges in maintaining the highest standards of judicial and personal conduct.

The ABA adopted a **Model Code of Judicial Conduct** in 2007 that provides written standards concerning the ethical conduct of judges so as to guide and assist judges in maintaining the highest standards of judicial and personal conduct. It spelled out, for the first time, that they are to avoid "sexual advances," requests for sexual favors, and other such unwelcome behavior. The code is not binding, but it has long served as a model that individual states use in adopting rules for disciplining their judges. It covers a range of conduct, including ethical behavior for judicial candidates, when judges might accept gifts, and in what instances they should disqualify themselves from hearing cases. The ABA commission that prepared the revised code said that it adopted the language on sexual harassment after hearing from witnesses who were "emphatic about the need to single out sexual harassment for special mention, given the nature, extent, and history of the problem."[38]

A Thorny Issue: Judges' Use of Electronic Social Media Sites

An appellate court in Florida was recently compelled to confront the following question: Where the presiding judge in a criminal case has accepted the prosecutor assigned to the case as a Facebook "friend," would a reasonably prudent person fear that he could not get a fair and impartial trial, so that the defendant's motion for disqualification should be granted? (The trial judge had denied the motion to be disqualified, as "legally insufficient.")

Using the test "whether or not the facts alleged . . . would prompt a reasonably prudent person to fear that he could not get a fair and impartial trial," the appellate court answered "yes" to the question, saying the judge should have disqualified himself and noting that:

> Judges do not have the unfettered social freedom of teenagers. Central to the public's confidence in the courts is the belief that fair decisions are rendered by an impartial tribunal. Maintenance of the appearance of impartiality requires the avoidance of entanglements and relationships that compromise that appearance. Unlike face to face social interaction, an electronic blip on a social media site can become eternal in the electronic ether of the internet. Posts on a Facebook page might be of a type that a judge should not consider in a given case. The existence of a judge's Facebook page might exert pressure on lawyers or litigants to take direct or indirect action to curry favor with the judge.[39]

A number of other states have attempted to address the question concerning judges' use of electronic social media (ESM) sites. For example, Tennessee, citing the cautions of several other states (e.g., California, Maryland, Oklahoma), notes on its courts website that:

> Because of constant changes in social media, this committee cannot be specific as to allowable or prohibited activity, but our review, as set out in this opinion, of the various approaches taken by other states to this area makes clear that judges must be constantly aware of ethical implications as they participate in social media and whether disclosure must be made. In short, judges must decide whether the benefit and utility of participating in social media justify the attendant risks.[40]

The ABA has also been moved to offer guidelines on the matter. In February 2013 the ABA's Standing Committee on Ethics and Professional Responsibility stated that "a judge may participate in electronic social networking, but as with all social relationships and contacts, a judge must comply with relevant provisions of the Code of Judicial Conduct and avoid any conduct that would undermine the judge's independence, integrity, or impartiality, or create an **appearance of impropriety**."[41] The committee noted that judges should assume that comments posted using ESM "may be disseminated to thousands of people without the consent or knowledge of the original poster" and "have long, perhaps permanent, digital lives." The committee also cautioned judges to keep in mind the requirement that a judge act in a manner that promotes public confidence in the judiciary and stated that a judge should not form relationships with persons or organizations that may convey an impression that the persons or organizations are in a position to influence the judge.

Certainly not all judges see problems with their use of ESM, however. A 2012 survey by the Conference of Court Public Information Officer found that nearly half (46.1%) of judges use social media sites. About the same amount (44%) indicated a belief that judges can use social media sites in their personal lives without compromising professional conduct codes of ethics.

Nevertheless, accounts such as those mentioned earlier in the Florida case indicate that problems can and do arise. Another issue needing to be addressed, perhaps, concerns the basic definition of being "friends" on such websites—which in ESM terms does not necessarily mean being personal friends and is merely a means of connecting with other people. What about judges who "friend" attorneys who appear before them in court—or a related situation where a judge declines to be "friends" with an attorney on a social website?

These are key questions that go to the heart of the appearance of impropriety and impartiality; however, the "appearance of propriety" is not easily defined, there are not as yet any uniform, definitive rules in place, and the ABA and state bar associations can only offer general guidelines.[42]

appearance of impropriety where someone creates a circumstance or situation that appears to raise questions of ethics.

▶ What Does "Appearance of Impropriety" Mean? An Example

As indicated earlier, the appearance of impropriety—where someone creates a circumstance or situation that appears to raise questions of ethics—as a general concept may not be well understood; however, it takes on a much more significance where judges, police officers, corrections personnel, and other criminal justice functionaries are concerned. Indeed, it is a concept that wise public officials typically learn early in their career. As Abraham Lincoln stated, in order to maintain credibility in his personal and professional lives, he had to "not only be chaste but above suspicion."[43] Lincoln even alluded to the appearance of propriety in his political appointments, saying, "Any man whom I may appoint to a [Cabinet] position, must be, as far as possible, like Caesar's wife, pure and above suspicion.").[44]

This concept is perhaps both shrouded in controversy and a lack of public awareness due to the roles of the people involved, as illustrated in the following example:

> Assume that a judge happens to be attending a public luncheon where new attorneys are being admitted to the county bar association. Upon entering, the judge observes that the room is nearly full, and takes the only vacant seat—which happens to be at a table occupied by an attorney who represents the plaintiff in a highly publicized trial currently before the judge. The judge mentions, and the attorney agrees, that they will not discuss the case during the luncheon festivities, and no such discussion takes place.

Now consider the other guests who observe these two sitting together. How will they perceive this situation? The answer depends on how much information the observers possess. One group of observers will be those who are unaware of the case involving the judge and attorney and probably think nothing of their sitting together. Another group will be those persons sitting at the table (or within hearing distance) who are fully informed of their agreement and would also not be concerned that any impropriety will occur—and perhaps even commending their ethical conduct. Third, however, are those attendees who are aware of neither the only-seat-available circumstance nor the agreement, and who may well perceive a serious problem with their sitting together; thus, the "appearance" problem.[45]

And so it is, as with gossip versus truth: The problem turns on how much information people possess. As an old saying goes, "perception is reality." The definition of the situation—different parties' knowledge of the facts and the situation—will determine for each whether or not there is a serious ethical problem involved. See Exhibit 8.2 for an example of a situation that can be perceived differently depending on the information people possess.

EXHIBIT 8.2

JUDGE CENSURED FOR DISCHARGING A FIREARM IN CHAMBERS[46]

In hindsight, an upstate New York judge admitted that a courthouse is probably not the best place to repair a revolver with a faulty firing mechanism. The gun discharged while the judge was alone in his chambers, striking a wall and injuring no one. The state's Commission on Judicial Conduct censured the judge for the mishap—and for having approved his own gun permit, which it termed "an obvious conflict." Over a 4-year period the judge, who began carrying a weapon to court due to what he cited as several instances of threats on his life, made 14 amendments to his original gun permit, covering 17 other pistols. There were no administrative policies that prohibited judges from bringing firearms into their chambers.

▶ Judges as Court Managers

The Administrative Office of the U.S. Courts coordinates and administers the operations of the federal courts. In the states, judges assume three types of administrative roles: (1) statewide jurisdiction for state supreme court chief justices, (2) local jurisdiction—a trial judge is responsible for administering the operations of his or her individual court, and (3) *presiding* or *chief* judge—supervising several courts within a judicial district.

The practice of having a judge preside over several courts within a district developed as early as 1940, when Dean Roscoe Pound recommended that a chief or presiding judge of a district or a region be responsible for case and judge assignment.[47] Today, these judges assume "general administrative duties over the court and its divisions" and are typically granted authority over all judicial personnel and court officials.[48] The duties of the presiding judge are numerous and include personnel and docket management and case and judge assignments; coordination and development of all judicial budgets; the convening of *en banc* (judges meeting as a whole) court meetings; coordination of judicial schedules; creation and use of appropriate court committees to investigate problems and handle court business; interaction with outside agencies and the media; the drafting of local court rules and policies; the maintenance of the courts' facilities; and the issuing of orders for keeping, destroying, and transferring records.[49]

A basic flaw in this system is that the chief or presiding judge is actually a "first among equals" with his or her peers. The title of chief judge is often assigned by seniority; therefore, there is no guarantee that the chief judge will be interested in management or will be effective at it.[50]

From a court administrator's standpoint, the office of presiding judge and the person serving in that capacity are of the utmost importance. As one judge put it, "the single most determinative factor of the extent of the administrator's role, aside from his personal attributes, is probably the rate of turnover in the office of the presiding judge."[51]

While discussing the functions of the chief or presiding judges of this country, this is a good point at which to consider the duties of the chief justice of the United States; a few of those duties are listed in Exhibit 8.3.

EXHIBIT 8.3

DUTIES OF THE CHIEF JUSTICE OF THE UNITED STATES

Often incorrectly called the chief justice of the Supreme Court, the chief justice of the United States has 53 duties enumerated in the U.S. Code, the Constitution, and other sources. Following is a list of a few of those duties:

- Approve appointments and salaries of some court employees
- Direct the publication of Supreme Court opinions
- Approve rules for the Supreme Court library
- Select a company to handle the printing and binding of court opinions
- Send appeals back to lower courts if justices cannot agree on them
- Approve appointments of employees to care for the Supreme Court building and grounds as well as regulations for their protection

- Call and preside over an annual meeting of the Judicial Conference of the United States and report to Congress the conference's recommendations for legislation (the Judicial Conference is composed of 27 federal judges who represent all the levels and regions of the federal judiciary; the conference meets twice a year to discuss common problems and needed policies and to recommend to Congress measures for improving the operation of the federal courts)
- Report to Congress on changes in the Rules of Criminal Procedure
- Report to the president if certain judges have become unable to discharge their duties
- Designate a member of the Smithsonian Institution

Source: Based on The Federal Judicial Center, "History of the Federal Judiciary," http://www.fjc.gov/history/home.nsf/page/admin_04.html (accessed October 28, 2013).

► Court Clerks

Not to be overlooked in the administration of the courts is the **court clerk**, an officer of the court who is responsible for its clerical filings and recordkeeping, entering judgments and orders, and so on. The court clerk is also referred to as a *prothonotary*, *registrar of deeds*, *circuit clerk*, *registrar of probate*, and even *auditor*. Most courts have de facto court administrators in lieu of these clerks, even if they have appointed administrators. These are key individuals in the administration of local court systems. They also docket cases, collect fees and costs, oversee jury selection, and maintain court records. These local officials, elected in all but six states, can amass tremendous power.[52]

From the beginning of English settlement in North America, court clerks were vital members of the society. "Clerks of writs" or "clerks of the assize" existed in early Massachusetts, where people were litigious primarily about land boundaries. Hostility toward lawyers carried over from England, and the clerk was the intermediary between the litigants and the justice of the peace. During the late seventeenth century, American courts became more structured and formalized. Books were available that imposed English court practices in the colonies, and clerks, judges, and attorneys were provided proper forms that had to be used. In fact, some of the forms used by clerks 200 years ago are similar to those in use today.[53]

Clerks have traditionally competed with judges for control over local judicial administration. In fact, one study found that the majority (58.9%) of elected clerks perceived themselves as colleagues of and equal to the judges.[54]

► Trained Court Administrators

Development and Training

One of the most recent and innovative approaches to solving the courts' management problems has been the creation of the position of court administrator. This relatively new criminal justice position began to develop in earnest during the 1960s; since that time, the number of practicing trial court administrators has increased tenfold and continues to expand. Actually, this concept has its roots in early England, where, historically, judges abstained from any involvement in court administration. This fact has not been lost on contemporary court administrators and proponents of this position: "It seems to be a very valuable characteristic of the English system that the judges expect to *judge* when they are in the courthouse … it does not allow time for administrative distractions."[55]

The development of the position of court administrator has been sporadic. In the early 1960s, probably only 30 people in the United States worked as court administrators. By 1970, there were fewer than 50 such specially trained employees.[56] Estimates differ concerning the expansion of the administrator's role during the 1980s. One expert maintained that by 1982 between 2,000 and 3,000 people were in the ranks of court managers;[57] another argued that there were only about 500.[58] At any rate, most agree that more than twice as many of these positions were created between 1970 and 1980 than in the preceding six decades.[59]

By the 1980s, every state had a statewide court administrator, normally reporting to the state supreme court or the chief justice of the state supreme court. The four primary functions of state court administrators are preparing annual reports, summarizing caseload data, preparing budgets, and troubleshooting.[60] Figure 8-2 ■ summarizes the means by which state court administrators are selected as well as their requirements.

- The following states have the position of state court administrator established by constitution only: Alaska, Arizona, Illinois, Nebraska, New York, Pennsylvania, South Carolina, and South Dakota.
- These states rely on statutes only: Arkansas, Connecticut, Delaware, Hawaii, Idaho, Indiana, Iowa, Kansas, Kentucky, Maine, Maryland, Massachusetts, Minnesota, Mississippi, Montana, Nevada, New Mexico, Oregon, Rhode Island, Tennessee, Texas, Vermont, Virginia, Washington, and the District of Columbia.
- The following are a mix of constitution and statute: Alabama, California, Colorado, Michigan, New Jersey, North Carolina, Ohio, Oklahoma, and West Virginia.
- These states rely on constitution and rule: Florida, Missouri, and North Dakota.
- Other permutations:
  - Georgia: statute and order
  - Louisiana: constitution, statute, and rule
  - Wisconsin: rule

Educational Requirements for State Court Administrators

- Bachelor's degree: 6 states
- Law degree: 13 states
- Law or graduate degree: 2 states
- Degree in business or public administration: 3 states
- None specified: 23 states and District of Columbia

FIGURE 8-2 Establishing the Office of and Educational Requirements for State Court Administrators

Source: Excerpt from Creation of State Court Administrative Offices and Selection of State Court Administrators from Technical Assistance Report by David C Steelman; Anne E Skove. Copyright © 2007 by National Center for State Courts. Used by permission of National Center for State Courts.

Today, few, if any, metropolitan areas are without full-time court administrators[61] (the court organization chart shown in Figure 7-3 outlines the breadth of responsibilities held by court administrators). An underlying premise and justification for this role is that by having a trained person performing the tasks of court management, judges are left free to do what they do best: decide cases. Indeed, since the first trial-court administrative positions began to appear, "there was little doubt or confusion about their exact purpose."[62] (As will be seen later, however, there has been doubt and confusion concerning their proper role and functions.)

As court reformers have called for better-trained specialists (as opposed to political appointees) for administering court processes, the qualifications for this position have come under debate. The creation of the Institute for Court Management in 1970 was a landmark in the training for this role, legitimizing its standing in the legal profession. Many judges, however, still believe that a law degree is essential, whereas others prefer a background in business administration. There will probably never be total agreement concerning the skills and background necessary for this position, but the specialized training that is offered by the Institute and a few graduate programs in judicial administration across the country would seem ideal.

Court administrators are trained specifically to provide the courts with the expertise and talent they have historically lacked. This point was powerfully made by Bernadine Meyer:

> Management—like law—is a profession today. Few judges or lawyers with severe chest pains would attempt to treat themselves. Congested dockets and long delays are symptoms that court systems need the help of professionals. Those professionals are managers. If court administration is to be effective, judicial recognition that managerial skill and knowledge are necessary to efficient performance is vital.[63]

ADMINISTRATIVE ADVICE FROM THE FIELD

Kenneth J. Peak

Name: Maxine Cortes

Current Position/City/State: Court Administrator, District Court and Justice/Municipal Court, Carson City, Nevada

College attended/academic major/degree(s): University of Phoenix, Masters in Organization Management, BS degree in Business Management

My primary duties and responsibilities in this position include: court management, project management, budgeting, grant writing, development of procedures/protocol and programs, review of legislation, court technology and liaison between multiple agencies, the public and vendors.

Personal attributes/characteristics that have proven to be most helpful to me in this position are: analytical abilities, conflict resolution, management, and communication and time management skills.

My three greatest challenges in this administrative role include: lack of adequate funding for programs, positions and training for staff development, constant change in local government leadership, and changing the culture of the organization to enhance public service.

Personal accomplishments during my administrative career about which I am most proud are: grant awards to implement and sustain court programs, advancement of staff to managerial levels through mentorship, and improving the courts through the use of technology.

Advice for someone who is interested in occupying an administrative position such as mine would be: take time to job shadow a court administrator. Possess a solid background in personnel and project management, budgeting, grant writing, understand technology trends in the court system, courthouse security, and learn about courts by researching the National Center for State Courts website.

General Duties

Trial court administrators generally perform the following six major duties:

1. *Reports.* Administrators have primary responsibility for the preparation and submission to the judges of periodic reports on the activities and state of business of the court.

2. *Personnel administration.* Court administrators serve as personnel officers for the court's nonjudicial personnel.

3. *Research and evaluation.* This function is designed to improve court business methods.

4. *Equipment management.* Administrators are engaged in procurement, allocation, inventory control, and replacement of furniture and equipment.

5. *Preparation of the court budget*

6. *Training coordination.* Court administrators provide training for nonjudicial personnel.[64]

Other duties that are assumed by the trained court administrator include jury management, case flow or calendar management, public information, and management of automated data processing operations.[65]

Evaluating Court Administrators

Judges must determine whether or not their court administrator is performing competently and effectively. According to John Greacen,[66] following are several basic strategies in determining the quality of the work performed by their administrators:

1. *The judge looks for indications of good management.* A well-managed organization will have a number of plans and procedures in place, including personnel policies,

recruitment and selection procedures, an orientation program for new employees, performance evaluation procedures, a discipline and grievance process, case management policies, financial controls, and other administrative policies (such as for facilities and records management).

2. *The judge should be receiving regular information.* Critically important reports and data on the court's performance, plans, activities, and accomplishments should be provided to the judge on a routine basis. The judge should be notified of the number of case filings, terminations, and pending cases; financial information; staff performance; long- and short-range plans; and other statistical data.

3. *Judges must often ask others about the performance of the administrator.* This includes soliciting input from lawyers, other judges, and other court staff members.

▶ Jury Administration

The jury system has been in the forefront of the public's mind in recent years, primarily as a result of the jury nullification concept (the right of juries to nullify or refuse to apply law in criminal cases despite facts that leave no reasonable doubt that the law was violated).[67] Here, however, I focus on the responsibilities of the court administrator in **jury administration**, ensuring that a jury is properly composed and sustained prior to and during trials. Elements of the jury system that involve court administration include jury selection, sequestration, comfort, and notorious cases.

Regarding jury selection, the court administrator is responsible for compilation of a master jury list; this is a large pool of potential jurors compiled from voter registration, driver's license, or utility customer or telephone customer lists to produce a representative cross-section of the community. From that master list, a randomly selected smaller venire (or jury pool) is drawn; a summons is mailed out to citizens, asking them to appear at the courthouse for jury duty. There, they will be asked questions and either retained or removed as jury members.

Here is where juror comfort enters in. Unfortunately, many jurors experience great frustration in the process, being made to wait long hours, possibly in uncomfortable physical surroundings, while receiving minimal compensation and generally being inconvenienced. Courts in all states now have a juror call-in system, enabling jurors to dial a phone number to learn whether their attendance is needed on a particular day; in addition, many jurisdictions have reduced the number of days a juror remains in the pool.

Some trials involving extensive media coverage require jury sequestration—jurors remain in virtual quarantine, sometimes for many weeks, and are compelled to live in a hotel together. This can be a tiring experience for jurors and poses great logistical problems for court administrators. The court administrator must also consider security issues (protecting the jury from outside interference and providing for conjugal visits, room searches, transportation, and so on) as well as jurors' personal needs (such as entertainment and medical supplies).[68]

Notorious cases—local, regional, or national civil or criminal trials either involving celebrities or particularly egregious crimes, requiring attention to jury selection and trial procedures—can cause problems for judges and court administrators. As examples, the trials of celebrities such as Martha Stewart and Michael Jackson, athletes like O. J. Simpson and Mike Tyson, mafia don John Gotti, and child star Robert Blake were clearly "notorious."[69] Court administrators and other court staff members must deal with media requests; courtroom and courthouse logistics for handling crowds, the media, and security; and the management of the court's docket of other cases. A notorious trial may also require that a larger courtroom be used and many attorneys accommodated.[70] A number of other issues

jury administration
ensuring that a jury is properly composed and sustained prior to and during trials.

notorious cases
local, regional, or national civil or criminal trials either involving celebrities or particularly egregious crimes, requiring attention to jury selection and trial procedures.

must be considered: Are identification and press passes and entry screening devices needed? Do purses, briefcases, and other such items need to be searched? Perhaps the most important task in managing notorious cases is communication with the media, often by setting aside a certain time when reporters may discuss the case.[71]

Summary

Today, the functions of judges and court administrators are quite different from those of earlier times and involve policymaking as well. It is clear that, as one New York judge put it, "The 'grand tradition' judge, the aloof brooding charismatic figure in the Old Testament tradition, is hardly a real figure."[72]

In addition, judicial administrators, the nonlawyers who help judges to run the courts, now possess a basic body of practical knowledge, a rudimentary theoretical perspective, and a concern for professional ethics.

It was also shown that there are still several obstacles to the total acceptance of court administration as an integral part of the judiciary. Court administration in many ways is still a developing field. Still, it has come far from its roots and is evolving into a bona fide element of the American justice system.

Key Terms and Concepts

Appearance of impropriety *191*
Court clerk *194*
Courtroom civility *189*
Judicial (court) administration *182*

Judicial selection *185*
Jury administration *197*
Merit selection/Missouri Bar Plan *186*
Model Code of Judicial Conduct *190*

Notorious cases *197*
The National Judicial College
  (NJC) *187*

Questions for Review

1. Why is the term *judicial administration* multifaceted? What would be a good working definition for this term? For *court administration*?
2. What are the elements of the newly revised Model Code of Judicial Conduct for state and local judges?
3. What are the issues surrounding judges' use of electronic social networking sites? Do you believe that they should have unfettered ability to use such sites, or not? Explain your answer.
4. How do you define the appearance of impropriety in our courts? What is an example of such an "appearance" dilemma?

5. How might judges and court administrators receive training for their roles?
6. How have court clerks traditionally assumed and performed the role of court administrator?
7. What criteria may be employed by judges to evaluate the effectiveness of their administrators?
8. What are the court administrator's duties in general? What issues must the court administrator address in composing or sequestering a jury? In dealing with notorious cases?

Deliberate and Decide

The Case of the Jocular Jurist

In early 2013 a part-time South Hackensack, New Jersey, municipal court judge held a unique part-time job—as a stand-up comedian on a major network's hidden-camera program. But the judge was told his part-time job—which is his primary source of income—conflicts with his

judicial work and violates rules the state's judges are to follow. He pleaded his case to the state's supreme court.

One of the issues raised was whether or not the average person understands the difference between a character and an actor—as with movie actors, whether or not someone is seen as expressing their true selves or following a fictional script. A deputy attorney general argued that the judge's comedy program—which includes portraying racist and homophobic characters—may not know the judge is acting; in addition, the judge could meet defendants who are familiar with his comic routine and might not believe he is a serious judge. The state also argued that municipal court judges are the face of the judiciary for most citizens, and it is vital that such judges maintain the confidence of the public and the impartiality, dignity, and integrity of the court.[73] (The outcome of this matter is provided in the Notes section.)

Questions for Discussion

1. What do you think? If, as it is often said, judges must at all times "*appear* to do justice," should the judge be allowed to moonlight as a comedian on his own time?

2. Or, alternatively, do you agree with the state's arguments that judges are never actually "off-duty," and are thus obligated to avoid such activities?

3. What, if any, punishment do you believe would be appropriately meted out by the state bar association?

Learn by Doing

1. After many years of debate concerning its pros and cons, your state legislature appears to be edging closer to implementing the Missouri (or merit selection) Plan for judicial selection on the ballot. As a court administrator in your municipal court, you are asked by your local newspaper to prepare a position paper that presents both sides of the issues. What will you say are pros and cons, when compared with the current system of electing judges.

2. You are a court administrator and are currently attending a workshop that includes a section on ethical considerations. You are given the following case involving actual impeachment hearings against a federal judge in Texas (see, e.g., http://www.vanityfair.com/online/daily/2009/06/a-real-case-of-judicial-misconduct.html) who had served in that position for 18 years. The judge had long lied concerning an "atrocious pattern of sexual misconduct" toward his subordinates. For years, two female staff members were assaulted by the judge, who was frequently intoxicated while on duty. After pleading guilty, the judge was convicted and sentenced to 3 years in prison. Then, he also asked that he

- be allowed to retain his salary and benefits while he serves his sentence
- be allowed to tender his resignation effective in about 1 year, so as to retain his medical insurance for a little bit longer
- be shown mercy due to alcoholism and the death of his wife a few years earlier.

Assume that you are one of the members of the panel that is considering whether or not the judge should be granted the earlier-mentioned concessions, as well as whether or not he should be impeached. How will you respond or vote, and why?

Notes

1. Robert C. Harrall, "In Defense of Court Managers: The Critics Misconceive Our Role," *Court Management Journal* 14 (1982):52.

2. Russell Wheeler, *Judicial Administration: Its Relation to Judicial Independence* (Williamsburg, VA: National Center for State Courts, 1988), p. 19.

3. Roscoe Pound, "The Causes of Popular Dissatisfaction with the Administration of Justice," *Crime and Delinquency* 10 (1964):355–371 for a discussion of Pound's discourse; see also Judith Resnik, "Roscoe Pound Round-Table Discussion," Yale Law School, *Faculty Scholarship Series*. Paper 695 (2007), http://digitalcommons.law.yale.edu/cgi/viewcontent.cgi?article=1696&context=fss_papers (accessed October 28, 2014).

4. Pound, "The Causes of Popular Dissatisfaction with the Administration of Justice," p. 356.

5. Woodrow Wilson, "The Study of Administration," *Political Science Quarterly* 2 (1887):197; reprinted in *Political Science Quarterly* 56 (1941):481.

6. Quoted in Paul Nejelski and Russell Wheeler, *Wingspread Conference on Contemporary and Future Issues in the Field of Court Management* 4 (1980), Proceedings of the July 1979 Conference of the Institute for Court Management, July 9–11, 1979, Racine, Wisconsin.

7. National Advisory Commission on Criminal Justice Standards and Goals, *Courts* (Washington, DC: U.S. Government Printing Office, 1973), p. 171.

8. American Bar Association, Commission on Standards of Judicial Admission, *Standards Relating to Court Organization, Standard 1.41* (Chicago: Author, 1974).

9. Russell R. Wheeler and Howard R. Whitcomb, *Judicial Administration: Text and Readings* (Upper Saddle River, NJ: Prentice Hall, 1977), p. 8.

10. Ibid.

11. David W. Neubauer, *America's Courts and the Criminal Justice System,* 9th ed. (Belmont, CA: Thomson/Wadsworth, 2008), pp. 170–176.

12. U.S. Department of Justice, Bureau of Justice Statistics, *State Court Organization, 2004* (Washington, DC: Author, October 2006), p. 23.

13. Barbara Luck Graham, "Do Judicial Selection Systems Matter? A Study of Black Representation on State Courts," *American Politics Quarterly* 18 (1990):316–336.

14. Neubauer, *America's Courts and the Criminal Justice System,* p. 172.

15. Ibid., p. 173.

16. William Raftery, "Judicial Selection in the States," National Center for State Courts, http://www.ncsc.org/sitecore/content/microsites/future-trends-2013/home/Monthly-Trends-Articles/Judicial-Selection-in-the-States.aspx (accessed March 25, 2014).

17. Law.com, "O'Connor Says Judges Shouldn't Be Elected," http://www.law.com/jsp/article.jsp?id=900005558371&OConnor_Says_Judges_Shouldnt_Be_Elected&slreturn=20140928164023 (accessed October 28, 2014).

18. Ibid.

19. American Judicature Society, "Judicial Selection in the States," http://www.judicialselection.us/ (accessed October 28, 2014).

20. Abraham Blumberg, *Criminal Justice* (Chicago: Quadrangle Books, 1967).

21. Wheeler and Whitcomb, *Judicial Administration,* p. 370.

22. See generally the National Center for State Courts, "Education & Careers," http://www.ncsc.org/education-and-careers.aspx (accessed October 24, 2014).

23. Wheeler and Whitcomb, *Judicial Administration,* p. 372.

24. Ibid.

25. Ibid.

26. Ibid., p. 373.

27. William A. Batlitch, "Reflections on the Art and Craft of Judging," *The Judges Journal* 43(4) (Fall 2003):7–8.

28. Charles E. Patterson, "The Good Judge: A Trial Lawyer's Perspective," *The Judges Journal* 43(4) (Fall 2003):14–15.

29. See, for example, Allen K. Harris, "The Professionalism Crisis—The 'Z' Words and Other Rambo Tactics: The Conference of Chief Justices' Solution," 53 S.C. L. Rev. 549, 589 (2002).

30. *In re First City Bancorp of Tex., Inc.,* 282 F.3d 864 (5th Cir. 2002).

31. *People v. Williamson,* 172 Cal. App. 3d 737, 749 (1985).

32. *Landry v. State,* 620 So. 2d 1099, 1102-03 (Fla. Dist. Ct. App. 1993).

33. *Gaddy v. Cirbo,* 293 P.2d (Colo. 1956), at 962.

34. Marla N. Greenstein, "The Craft of Ethics," *The Judges Journal* 43(4) (Fall 2003):17–18.

35. Ty Tasker, "Sticks and Stones: Judicial Handling of Invective in Advocacy," *The Judges Journal* 43(4) (Fall 2003):17–18.

36. Collins T. Fitzpatrick, "Building a Better Bench: Informally Addressing Instances of Judicial Misconduct," *The Judges Journal* 44 (Winter 2005):16–20.

37. Ibid., pp. 18–20.

38. See American Bar Association, ABA Model Code of Judicial Conduct, "Preamble," p. 2, http://www.americanbar.org/content/dam/aba/migrated/judicialethics/ABA_MCJC_approved.authcheckdam.pdf (accessed October 28, 2014).

39. See *Domville v. Florida,* No. 4D12-556 (2014).

40. Tennessee State Courts, "Judicial Ethics Committee Advisory Opinion No. 12-01," http://www.tncourts.gov/sites/default/files/docs/advisory_opinion_12-01.pdf (accessed October 28, 2014).

41. Cynthia Gray, "ABA Social Media Advisory Opinion," *Judicature* 96 (5) (March/April 2014):245.

42. James Podgers, "ABA Opinion Cautions Judges to Avoid Ethics Pitfalls of Social Media," (May 1, 2014), http://www.abajournal.com/magazine/article/aba_opinion_cautions_judges_to_avoid_ethics_pitfalls_of_social_media/; also see Cynthia Gray, "ABA Social Media Advisory Opinion," *Judicature* 96 (5) (March/April 2014), https://www.ajs.org/judicature-journal/editorial/surviving-storm-2/ (accessed October 28, 2014).

43. Roy P. Basler (ed.), *The Collected Works of Abraham Lincoln* (Brunswick, NJ: Rutgers University Press, 1953), p. 41.

44. Ibid., remarks to a Pennsylvania Delegation (January 24, 1861), pp. 179–180.

45. For other examples of the appearance of impropriety, see Raymond J. McKoski, "Judicial Discipline and the Appearance of Impropriety: What the Public Sees Is What the Judge Gets," *Minnesota Law Review* 94 (6) (2010): 1914–1996.

46. James Barron, "Upstate Judge Is Censured for Accidentally Firing Gun in Chambers," *The New York Times,* August 27, 2012, http://www.nytimes.com/2012/08/28/nyregion/judge-vincent-sgueglia-censured-after-gun-mishap-in-chambers.html?_r=0 (accessed October 28, 2014).

47. Roscoe Pound, "Principles and Outlines of a Modern Unified Court Organization," *Journal of the American Judicature Society* 23 (April 1940):229.

48. See, for example, the Missouri Constitution, Article V, Sec. 15, paragraph 3.

49. Forest Hanna, "Delineating the Role of the Presiding Judge," *State Court Journal* 10 (Spring 1986):17–22.

50. Neubauer, *America's Courts and the Criminal Justice System,* p. 102.

51. Robert A. Wenke, "The Administrator in the Court," *Court Management Journal* 14 (1982):17–18, 29.

52. Marc Gertz, "Influence in the Court Systems: The Clerk as Interface," *Justice System Journal* 2 (1977):30–37

53. Robert B. Revere, "The Court Clerk in Early American History," *Court Management Journal* 10 (1978):12–13.

54. G. Larry Mays and William Taggart, "Court Clerks, Court Administrators, and Judges: Conflict in Managing the Courts," *Journal of Criminal Justice* 14 (1986):1–7.

55. Ernest C. Friesen and I. R. Scott, *English Criminal Justice* (Birmingham: University of Birmingham Institute of Judicial Administration, 1977), p. 12.

56. Harvey E. Solomon, "The Training of Court Managers," in Charles R. Swanson and Susette M. Talarico (eds.), *Court Administration: Issues and Responses* (Athens: University of Georgia Press, 1987), pp. 15–20.

57. Ernest C. Friesen, "Court Managers: Magnificently Successful or Merely Surviving?" *Court Management Journal* 14 (1982):21.

58. Solomon, "The Training of Court Managers," p. 16.

59. Harrall, "In Defense of Court Managers," p. 51.

60. Neubauer, *America's Courts and the Criminal Justice System,* p. 104.

61. Ibid.

62. Geoffrey A. Mort and Michael D. Hall, "The Trial Court Administrator: Court Executive or Administrative Aide?" *Court Management Journal* 12 (1980):12–16, 30.

63. Bernadine Meyer, "Court Administration: The Newest Profession," *Duquesne Law Review* 10 (Winter 1971):220–235.

64. Mort and Hall, "The Trial Court Administrator," p. 15.

65. Ibid.

66. John M. Greacen, "Has Your Court Administrator Retired? Without Telling You?" National Association for Court Management, Conference Papers from the Second National Conference on Court Management, Managing Courts in Changing Times, Phoenix, Ariz., September 9–14, 1990, pp. 1–20.

67. Darryl Brown, "Jury Nullification within the Rule of Law," *Minnesota Law Review* 81 (1997):1149–1200.

68. Timothy R. Murphy, Genevra Kay Loveland, and G. Thomas Munsterman, *A Manual for Managing Notorious Cases* (Washington, DC: National Center for State Courts, 1992), pp. 4–6. See also Timothy R. Murphy, Paul L. Hannaford, and Kay Genevra, *Managing Notorious Trials* (Williamsburg, VA: National Center for State Courts, 1998).

69. See Murphy et al., *A Manual for Managing Notorious Cases,* pp. 53, 73, for other notable celebrity cases.

70. Ibid., p. 23.

71. Ibid., pp. 27–30.

72. Blumberg, *Criminal Justice,* p. 120.

73. "Comedian Resigns as Hackensack Judge after Losing Appeal," *CBS New York,* September 19, 2014, http:// newyork.cbslocal.com/2014/09/19/nj-supreme-court-part-time-hackensack-judge-cant-also-be-comedian/ (accessed October 14, 2014).

Threatening or intimidating our judges cannot be tolerated in this country. The rise in threats against our judges puts the men and women who serve in our justice system at risk and is a repugnant assault on our independent judiciary.

—U.S. Senator Patrick Leahy, Chairman, Senate Judiciary Committee, 110th Congress

Justice is such a fine thing that we cannot pay too dearly for it.

—Alain Rene LeSage

9 Court Issues and Practices

LEARNING OBJECTIVES

After reading this chapter, the student will be able to:

1. distinguish the differences between the due process and crime control models

2. define the "CSI effect" as it relates to court operations and actors

3. describe courthouse violence, both actual and potential, and what must be done to assess and deal with threats to court actors

4. describe the growing trend toward problem-solving courts

5. review the problems and consequences of, and solutions for, trial delays

6. diagram and explain the two systems used in scheduling cases

7. relate the importance of alternative dispute resolution (ADR) for decreasing litigation

8. describe a recent major U.S. Supreme Court decision concerning federal sentencing guidelines

9. explain the courts' role in media relations

10. discuss such issues as juveniles being waived into adult criminal court jurisdiction, the exclusionary rule, and the use of cameras in the courtroom

▶ Introduction

Many of the topics discussed previously, primarily in Chapter 7—such as reforming court organization and unification, use of the adversary system, and alternative dispute resolution (ADR)—could have been included in this chapter. They are challenging areas. This chapter, however, examines additional contemporary issues and practices.

The chapter begins with a consideration of the so-called "CSI effect," and whether or not it has an impact on court operations and actors. Next, because history has shown that our courts—like the rest of our society—can be mean and brutish places, we review courthouse violence, its basic forms, and how to perform a threat assessment. We then discuss how problem-solving courts (focusing on drug, mental health, and veterans' courts) are expanding and using their authority and innovative techniques. Then, we examine the dilemma of delay (including its consequences, suggested solutions, and two systems of scheduling cases) and review how the spreading concept of ADR is used to decrease litigation and court backlogs. In a related vein, we look at two recent U.S. Supreme Court decisions concerning federal sentencing guidelines. Next, after a look at media relations and the courts, we briefly consider how courts have become more successful at grant writing in difficult financial times. Then the following issues are considered: whether juveniles should be waived and tried as adults, the exclusionary rule should be banned, cameras should be used during trials, and plea bargaining should be kept. The chapter concludes with review questions, "deliberate and decide" problems, and "learn by doing" exercises.

▶ Is There a "CSI Effect"?

Television programs focusing on criminal investigations and forensic techniques may not only be providing viewers with entertainment but also creating certain expectations about criminal cases in general and investigations in specific. This phenomenon—whereby television viewing influences peoples' perceptions, and is often referred to as cultivation theory—has been labeled the potential "**CSI effect**": the possibility that the administration of justice is affected by television programming that creates inaccurate expectations in the minds of jurors regarding the power and use of forensic evidence. Indeed, the creator of "CSI," Anthony E. Zuiker, observed, "'The CSI Effect' is, in my opinion, the most amazing thing that has ever come out of the series. For the first time in American history, you're not allowed to fool the jury anymore."[1]

Research findings on the CSI effect, which began to appear in 2003, have been mixed. What is known, however, is as follows: Overall, a majority of citizens did not have knowledge of the CS effect, but when provided with a definition, believe it exists. Furthermore, people who are watching crime shows are more likely to think crime shows are accurate and educational. Viewing forensic and crime dramas, specifically, appears to be influencing people's views of social reality can affect people's perceptions of crime investigation in the real world, which then affects their behavior during trial.[2] Studies of the legal field primarily indicate that many legal professionals believe it exists,[3] some prosecutors and defense attorneys arguing that the shows aid their opponents: Prosecutors believe that juries want to see all evidence subjected to substantial forensic examination, whether warranted in a specific case or not, while defense attorneys have indicated that juries believe that scientific evidence is perfect and thus trustworthy in establishing guilt. Finally, a recent study of 104 persons who had served as jurors supported the pro-defense argument, which states that if forensic evidence is absent, the jury who watches CSI type shows will be less likely to convict than the jury who does not watch CSI-type shows.[4]

To the extent the CSI effect exists, it may well be changing the manner in which many people in the criminal justice system approach their duties. Prosecutors might be using more

> **"CSI effect"** the belief that a trial may be affected by television programming that creates inaccurate expectations by jurors regarding the power and use of forensic evidence.

PowerPoint and video presentations and might take pains to explain to jurors that forensic evidence is not always collectible—or at the very least use experts to explain to jurors why they did not logically collect forensic evidence in a particular case. The *voir dire* process may also be altered to ensure that those jurors who are unduly influenced by shows like *CSI* are screened from jury service. Such adaptations might be resulting in longer trials and an increased use of expert witnesses to aid the jury in understanding the presence or absence of physical evidence.[5]

Finally, there are indications that the CSI effect could change the manner in which much of the criminal justice system functions; for example, a heightened view that forensic evidence will be required for a defendant's guilt can then lead to an increase in the amount of evidence that is collected from crime scenes (e.g., where a police officer or detective might have previously collected a dozen pieces of evidence in the past, they may now collect around one hundred pieces); the increased number of evidentiary items can, in turn, cause forensic labs to become backlogged, which can then create more strain on the entire process and those involved.[6] See Exhibit 9.1 for more information.

EXHIBIT 9.1

THE CSI EFFECT: "NOW PLAYING IN A COURTROOM NEAR YOU"

In a Delaware trial,[7] the defendant, having been indicted for murder, filed motions to exclude 10 pieces of state's evidence, including footwear impressions, voice identification, handwriting, fiber, DNA, fabric impressions, hair, video, and toolmarks. The defendant argued that tests for each piece of evidence were all inconclusive, exculpatory, or irrelevant.

In its response, the prosecution stated that the tests were necessary to show the jury that it had conducted a thorough criminal investigation. Noting the extent of crime show viewing by the public, the prosecution believed that it needed to produce such an amount of evidence in order to address jurors' heightened expectations of the prosecution to meet the burden of proof.

The judge admitted that, after reviewing the literature on the CSI effect, it would be naive to not believe the effect exists—especially having witnessed defendants taking advantage of the concept. The court also acknowledged that the defendant's objection had put the prosecution in a "Catch-22" position: On the one hand, the prosecution could be criticized for presenting too much irrelevant evidence, while on the other hand, it could be criticized for not presenting enough.

In the end, the court opted to not limit the prosecution's ability to thoroughly state its case, and found little harm in allowing the presentation of inconclusive evidence.

This is obviously an area of criminal justice that must be monitored and examined to determine whether or not knowledge of the CSI effect affects juror expectations and decision making (either pro-prosecution or pro-defense), and if so, whether or not steps can be taken to correct for that bias.

The "Deliberate and Decide" problem at chapter's end elaborates on this phenomenon, presenting related problems and approaches taken in two states and posing some questions for consideration.

▶ Courthouse Violence

Shooters in the Courthouses

It has been said that judges deal with "a segment of society that most people don't have to deal with—people who are violent, might be mentally unstable, are desperate because they don't have much more to lose."[8] That assessment is becoming increasingly true, especially when one considers some of the recent violent acts committed against the judiciary:

- A family court judge in Reno, Nevada, standing at a window in his chambers, is shot by a sniper.[9]

- A prisoner in Atlanta steals a deputy's gun and fatally shoots a judge, his court reporter, and a deputy sheriff.[10]

- A federal district court judge found her husband and mother shot dead in the basement of her Chicago home, less than a year after a white supremacist was convicted of trying to have her murdered for holding him in contempt of court.[11]

Recently, Etter and Swymeler conducted a study of **courthouse violence**, particularly shootings,[12] and determined that the problem of violent acts in courts has escalated in recent years. Following are the selected findings:

> **courthouse violence** where individuals perpetrate violent incidents against others in courthouses, both targeted and nontargeted in nature.

- Litigants (plaintiffs, defendants, witnesses, or lawyers) were the intended targets in about 60 percent of the shooting incidents, while judges and police officers were targeted in about 40 percent.

- About 40 percent of the shooters were shot either by the court's security forces or by their own hand (with 87% of the shooters dying as a result).

- The majority (61%) of the 114 courthouse shooting incidents that were identified occurred in about the past 25 years.

- The firearms used were brought in by the shooter (77%), taken from a deputy (19%), or smuggled into a defendant or prisoner (4%).

- Domestic violence or problems were the motive in one-third of the shootings, escape was the motive in one-fourth, and assassination or another reason was the motive in 35 percent.

- Victims of the shootings were judges (8%), police officers (about one-third), and litigants or other court officials (including plaintiffs, defendants, witnesses, and lawyers [59%]).

- The vast majority of the shooters were captured.

- While 91 percent of the respondents indicated that they have access to metal detectors, their usage varies widely; usage was often spotty or only for major trials.

General Types of Court Violence

Two types of courthouse violence can occur:

- Nontargeted courthouse violence involves an individual who has no specific preexisting intention of engaging in violence but who, either during, at the conclusion of, or sometime shortly after the court proceeding becomes incensed and defiant at some procedure or outcome and acts out in the courtroom or public corridors. If this person also has a weapon, it might be used against the source of the grievance—a judge, attorney, witness, court employee, defendant or plaintiff, or bystander. If there are no judicial security screening devices or patrols on the premises, the person may proceed to attack people within the courthouse.

- Targeted courthouse violence involves an individual who expressly intends to engage in courthouse violence. These persons often simmer and stew for long periods of time, so there is often some delay in responding to real or perceived affronts and insults. During this time, these people may or may not make threats and often create plans to circumvent security measures. They deliberately focus on specific individuals or the judiciary itself.[13]

Of the two groups, the nontargeting group has been responsible for most of the violent incidents in our nation's courthouses. With proper security precautions, many of these acts can be prevented or thwarted. This is a daunting task, however; each year, nearly 100 million cases are filed in the nation's 18,000 lower courts (61 million cases) and its 2,000 major trial courts (31 million cases),[14] which are presided over by more than 11,000 judges and quasi-judicial officers (e.g., masters, magistrates).[15] Because each filed case is potentially contentious, violence is also a potential outcome.

Other disturbing behaviors can affect the courts' functions as well. For example, judges can be sent inappropriate communications containing threats. Bombings of state and local government buildings have occurred as well.[16] Concerns about such acts of violence have spurred the implementation of enhanced security measures in many of our nation's courthouses, most of which have focused on the courts' physical environment, to detect weapons. Duress alarms and video surveillance cameras have been installed and separate prisoner, court staff, and public areas created.

One problem with enhancing courthouse security is its cost. In 1997, the cost to install 35 bullet-resistant windows in a Tacoma, Washington, federal courthouse following a shooting through a judge's window was $550,000. Today, the cost is still quite high: To install bullet-resistant glass would cost over $1,500 for the window frame and $120 per square foot for the glass. Another problem is that such glass can weigh up to 224 pounds a square foot; not all buildings can handle such weight.[17]

Following the sniper shooting of the judge in Reno,[18] mentioned earlier, several U.S. senators introduced a bill, The Court Security Improvement Act of 2006, which would have provided funds for both federal and state court security measures, but the bill was not passed before Congress adjourned.[19]

Making a Threat Assessment

threat assessment
a process of identifying, assessing, investigating, and managing a courthouse threat.

A good beginning point for enhancing courthouse security is to make a **threat assessment**, which involves, at a minimum, the following steps[20]:

1. *Identifying the Threat* First, determine if in fact there is a threat—an expression of intent to injure someone or damage something. Also, the suspect and who represents the potential target of the threat must be identified so as to understand the relationship, if any, between the two.

2. *Assessing the Threat* If a threat is identified, assess how serious the threat appears to be. Consider the suspect's commitment—intent, motive, opportunity, and ability—individually and in combination. For example, a suspect may be highly motivated but incapable of instigating an attack himself due to being incarcerated or some other limitation.

3. *Investigating the Threat* If a suspect does pose a serious threat, next, attempt to conduct an interview with the suspect at his home (by two trained investigators), observing the contents of the house, the suspect's demeanor, level of agitation, and so on. The presence of weapons and any other such items can indicate the suspect's resolve and ability to conduct the violence.

4. *Managing the Threat* When a suspect represents a bona fide risk, then put in place such measures as a simple warning to court personnel (so they may take precautions), placing the subject under surveillance, or even incarcerating him if warranted. Also, use of a mental health commitment and/or a temporary restraining order might be considered.

Obviously, the circumstances of the individual case will determine the strategies to be used (see Exhibit 9.2).

EXHIBIT 9.2

USING "BEST FRIENDS" TO ALLEVIATE ANXIETY IN COURT

French writer Milan Kundera wrote, "Dogs are our link to paradise. They don't know evil or jealousy or discontent."[21] Given that probably most people around the world agree with that assessment of our canine friends, it is probably not too surprising that dogs find their way into the criminal justice system in ways other than for their sense of smell. Because many crime victims find participation in the criminal justice process to be stressful (an experience sometimes termed "secondary victimization"), court actors and victim organizations are always looking for tools and strategies for reducing such stress and make their contribution to criminal justice one that does not inflict additional harm.

One such effort—a joint initiative by the National Crime Victim Law Institute and the Courthouse Dogs Foundation—uses courthouse facility dogs to provide such assistance to crime victims. Professionally trained dogs are currently working in the nation's prosecutors' offices and child advocacy centers to assist crime victims as they navigate various criminal justice proceedings. The dogs serve as companions for victims to assist them in participating in the criminal justice process, and thus to reduce or eliminate secondary victimization. The institute provides a webinar to prosecuting attorneys, victims' rights attorneys, victim advocates, and law enforcement officers to explain how these animals function and how they help to increase victims' satisfaction with the criminal justice process.[22]

▶ Problem-Solving Courts

Origin, Functions, and Rationale

The 1990s saw a wave of court reform across the United States as judges and other court actors experimented with new ways to deliver justice: Drug courts (discussed later) expanded into every state, and new mental health and veterans' courts began targeting different kinds of problems in different places, all with a desire to improve the results for victims, litigants, defendants, and communities.

Although **problem-solving courts**—special courts created to accommodate persons with specific needs and problems, such as drug, veteran, and mentally ill offenders—are still very much a work in progress, according to Robert V. Wolf[23] they share five principle aspects:

> **problem-solving courts** special courts created to accommodate persons with specific needs and problems, such as drug, veteran, and mentally ill offenders.

1. The proactive, problem-solving orientation of the judge
2. The integration of social services
3. The team-based, nonadversarial approach
4. Their interaction with the defendant/litigant; and
5. Their ongoing judicial supervision

These courts use their authority to forge new responses to chronic social, human, and legal problems, such as family dysfunction, addiction, delinquency, and domestic violence that have proven resistant to conventional solutions. Community courts, like those in New York City, target misdemeanor "quality-of-life" crimes (e.g., prostitution, shoplifting, and low-level drug possession) and have offenders pay back the community by performing service functions. Similar stories can be told about the genesis and spread of domestic violence courts, mental health courts (MHCs), and others.[24]

A New Role for the Courtroom Work Group

Problem-solving courts are presented as a judge-led and judge-centered movement; however, although it is true that judges are the public face of such courts, other members of the courtroom work group take on central roles as well. For example, probation officers (POs) spend the most time with problem-solving court participants and are charged with keeping other courtroom work group actors informed about the participant's progress and recommending incentives or sanctions for participants. POs may be said to act as the gate-keepers to the courts—recommending who should participate in these newly designed programs. POs maintain their traditional supervisory roles, overseeing the participants' progress in drug treatment, employment training, and prosocial skill development.[25]

Judges, who traditionally adjudicate the guilt or innocence of the defendants, still maintain a leadership role in the courtroom, but now lead a team focused on rehabilitative goals through collaborative processes. Judges in these courts base their interactions and decisions on information provided by other courtroom actors, often increasing their frequency of contact with participants while also limiting their contact with the criminal justice system. The presentation of information in problem-solving courts takes place behind closed doors in pre-court sessions. Participants no longer have a legally trained attorney to guide their decision making; instead, they now have a whole courtroom workgroup team (again, led by the judge) that is dedicated to their progress in a rehabilitative process. The team shares information as a whole before they interact with the participant.[26]

Drug, Mental Health, and Veterans' Courts

Extent and Effectiveness of Drug Courts

Drug courts are now proliferating. As of mid-2013, there were 2,383 drug court programs operating in the United States and another 198 programs were being planned; in sum, drug courts were operating or being planned in all 50 states, plus the District of Columbia, Guam, and Puerto Rico.[27] Drug court participants undergo long-term treatment and counseling, are given sanctions and incentives, and make frequent court appearances. Successful completion of the program results in dismissal of charges, reduced or set-aside sentences, lesser penalties, or a combination of these. Most important, graduating participants gain the necessary tools to rebuild their lives. The drug court model includes the following key components:

- Incorporating drug testing into case processing
- Creating a nonadversarial relationship between the defendant and the court
- Identifying defendants in need of treatment and referring them to treatment as soon as possible after arrest
- Providing access to a continuum of treatment and rehabilitation services
- Monitoring abstinence through frequent mandatory drug testing[28]

Do drug courts work? The National Institute of Justice has sponsored a number of research projects examining drug court outcomes and costs. The following findings are representative:

1. **Impact on Recidivism** Several studies have found that drug courts reduced recidivism among program participants as compared to comparable probationers. For example, one study found that within a 2-year follow-up period, the felony re-arrest rate decreased from 40 percent before the drug court to 12 percent after the drug court began in one county. Re-arrests were lower 5 years later when compared with re-arrests for similar drug offenders within the same county. In Oregon, using data

from 6,500 Oregon offenders, participation in a drug court treatment program also reduced recidivism.

2. ***Impact on Cost*** In a longitudinal study (over 10 years), the National Institute of Justice researchers found, using data from the same 6,500 Oregon offenders above, costs averaged $1,392 lower per drug court participant and resulted in public savings of $6,744 on average per participant (or $12,218 if victimization costs are included).[29]

Rationales and Methods of MHCs

The common-law standard used in the United States for determining one's competence to stand trial has generally been as follows: A defendant must be able to understand the proceedings against him, and assist in his defense. Then, in *Dusky v. United States* (1960),[30] the U.S. Supreme Court in essence affirmed this standard, as well as a defendant's right to have a competency evaluation prior to trial.

It is estimated that courts order 60,000 mental competency hearings per year; about 20 percent of such defendants are found unfit to stand trial.[31] As a result, MHCs are also beginning to spread as alternatives to traditional criminal court proceedings, and are in use for juveniles as well adults. Since the late 1990s, more than 175 such courts have been established and dozens more are being planned. Eligible participants typically have a misdemeanor or low-level felony charge and a diagnosis of schizophrenia, bipolar disorder, or major depression. Judges hold participants accountable to take their psychotropic medications, avoid taking illegal drugs, and attend hearings. Other characteristics of MHCs, according to the federal Bureau of Justice Assistance, are as follows:

- A specialized court docket, which employs a problem-solving approach in lieu of more traditional court procedures
- Judicially supervised, community-based treatment plans for each defendant participating in the court, designed and implemented by a team of court staff and mental health professionals
- Regular court hearings, where incentives are offered to reward adherence to court conditions and sanctions are imposed on participants who do not adhere to the conditions of participation[32]

The basic premise of these courts is that they increase public safety, facilitate participation in effective mental health and substance abuse treatment, improve the quality of life for people with mental illnesses charged with crimes, and make more effective use of limited criminal justice and mental health resources.[33] Exhibit 9.3 provides an example of a unique approach now associated with these courts.

EXHIBIT 9.3

MOCK HEARINGS AND TRIALS PREPARE MENTALLY ILL PATIENTS

Some mental health hospitals are using psychiatrists, treatment, and mock trials to prepare criminal defendants for actual trial. Mentally ill patients participate in make-believe hearings, assuming key courtroom roles, sitting on a "bench" and looking down at a fictitious courtroom (with tables marked as "prosecution" and "defense" and people sitting in a box marked "jury,"

while making "rulings") all of which is geared toward helping them to better understand real court proceedings. As a result, it is hoped that recidivism and public safety will be improved.[34]

Juvenile MHC services are being developed as well. Often, juveniles demonstrate mental health issues and behavioral problems because their families are going

(Continued)

through a period of dysfunction, and are perhaps desperate due to multiple crises, including unemployment, a serious accident, death of a close friend or family member, drug abuse, and so on. Most states provide expanded Medicaid services to all children under age 18 from low-income families. As with adult MHCs, juvenile MHCs have defined goals, such as weeks of sobriety, days of school attendance, and negative drug tests, in order to provide structure for moving through the program's various phases.[35]

Diverting Veterans into Treatment

Since the first veteran's court opened in Buffalo, New York, in 2008, veterans' courts have also been spreading across the United States. Certainly, the wars in Iraq and Afghanistan have created a nationwide push to help veterans who have troubling reintegrating into civilian life—20 percent of whom suffer from posttraumatic stress disorder (PTSD) and traumatic brain injuries (that percentage increases with the number of tours served).[36] Even Congressional legislation has been introduced that would establish a grant program to help develop such courts across the nation.[37] These courts are diversion programs where, in exchange for a guilty plea to crimes charged, the veteran consents to regular court visits, counseling, and random drug testing. Then, if successfully completing the treatment program, the criminal record is expunged (meaning it is erased or stricken from the record). This allows for better access to employment, housing, and educational opportunities while also avoiding the pains of prison and having a criminal record.[38]

Recently the federal Veterans Administration became involved in veterans' courts as well, teaming with state, and county organizations as well as the U.S. Department of Justice, Bureau of Justice Assistance (BJA), and the U.S. Department of Health and Human Services Substance Abuse and Mental Health Services Administration (SAMHSA). Veteran Justice Outreach (VJO) specialists work in veterans courts in 168 veterans' courts, dockets, and tracks, serving nearly 8,000 veterans who had been admitted to these courts by late 2012. The length of involvement with the courts ranges from 15 to 18 months, and data indicate that more than two-thirds of the veterans completed the court and healthcare treatment regime successfully.[39] See Exhibit 9.4 for a description of Veterans courts.

EXHIBIT 9.4

HOW VETERANS COURTS WORK[40]

When someone is arrested in Tulsa, Okla., officers ask if they are a military veteran. If so, those veterans who face criminal charges and are in need of mental health or substance use treatment may be eligible for the Veterans Treatment Court (VTC). VTCs were developed to help veterans avoid unnecessary incarceration if they have developed mental health problems. Although most courts work with veterans of all decades and wars, many such courts were initiated out of concern for veterans returning from Afghanistan and Iraq and encountering legal trouble.

VTCs connect vets with services at the earliest possible time and provide volunteer veteran mentors to provide nonclinical support. Their participation is voluntary, and those who choose to participate are first assessed by a mental health professional and their treatment needs are determined.

While the veteran remains in the community while undergoing treatment, a judge regularly checks on his or her progress. If not meeting the requirements of the program (e.g., failing a drug screening or disobeying court orders), the court will impose sanctions that may include community service, fines, jail time, or transfer out of veterans court and back into a traditional criminal court. Judges provide ongoing encouragement to participants as long as they continue on the path of recovery.

▶ The Dilemma of Delay

"Justice Delayed—"

There is no consensus on how long is too long with respect to bringing a criminal case to trial. Still, the principle that "justice delayed is justice denied" says much about the long-standing goal of processing court cases with due dispatch. Charles Dickens condemned the practice of slow litigation in nineteenth-century England, and Shakespeare mentioned "the law's delay" in *Hamlet*. Delay in processing cases is one of the oldest problems of U.S. courts. The public often hears of cases that have languished on court dockets for years. This can only erode public confidence in the judicial process.[41]

Case backlog and trial delay affect many of our country's courts. The magnitude of the backlog and the length of the delay vary greatly, however, depending on the court involved. It is best to view delay not as a problem but as a symptom of a problem.[42] Yet, some time is needed to prepare a case. What is a concern is *unnecessary* delay; however, there seems to be no agreed-on definition of unnecessary delay.

The Consequences

The consequences of delay can be severe. It can jeopardize the values and guarantees inherent in our justice system, and deprive defendants of their Sixth Amendment right to a speedy trial. Lengthy pretrial incarceration pressures can cause a defendant to plead guilty.[43] The reverse is also true: Delay can strengthen a defendant's bargaining position; prosecutors are more apt to accept pleas to a lesser charge when dockets are crowded. Delays cause pretrial detainees to clog the jails, police officers to appear in court on numerous occasions, and attorneys to spend unproductive time appearing on the same case. In sum, **case delay** in the courts is generally considered to be bad because it deprives defendants of a timely (speedy) trial. It may result in loss or deterioration of evidence, cause severe hardship to some parties (victims, witnesses), and bring about a loss of public confidence in the court system.

case delay an excessive amount of time passing prior to bringing a criminal case to trial.

One factor contributing to court delay is the lack of incentive to process cases speedily. Although at least 10 states require cases to be dismissed and defendants to be released if they are denied a speedy trial,[44] the U.S. Supreme Court has refused to give the rather vague concept of a "speedy trial" any precise time frame.[45] The problem with time frames, however, is twofold: First, more complex cases legitimately take a long time to prepare, and second, these time limits may be waived due to congested court dockets. In sum, there is no legally binding mechanism that works.

Suggested Solutions and Performance Standards

The best-known legislation addressing the problem is the Speedy Trial Act of 1974, amended in 1979. It provides firm time limits: 30 days from the time of arrest to indictment and 70 days from indictment to trial. Thus, federal prosecutors have a total of 100 days from the time of arrest until trial. This speedy trial law has proven effective over the years.

Unfortunately, however, laws that attempt to speed up trials at the state level have had less success than this federal law because most state laws fail to provide the courts with adequate and effective enforcement mechanisms. As a result, the time limits specified by speedy trial laws are seldom followed in practice.[46]

A number of proposals have emerged to alleviate state and local courts' logjams, ranging from judicial jury selection and limits on criminal appeals to six-person juries. The latter was actually suggested more than two decades ago as a means of relieving the congestion of court calendars and reducing court costs for jurors.[47] Thirty-three states have specifically authorized juries of fewer than 12, but most allow smaller juries only in misdemeanor cases. In federal courts, defendants are entitled to a 12-person jury unless the prosecuting and defense attorneys agree in writing to a smaller one.[48] Furthermore, the National Center for State Courts (NCSC) has developed a listing of *CourTools*,[49] which together provide a set of trial court performance measures that offer court administrators a perspective on their court's operations.

Case Scheduling: Two Systems

A key part of addressing case delay concerns the ability of the court administrator to set a date for trial. Scheduling trials is problematic because of forces outside the administrator's control: slow or inaccurate mail delivery, which can result in notices of court appearances arriving after the scheduled hearing; an illegible address that prevents a key witness or defendant from ever being contacted about a hearing or trial; or a jailer's inadvertent failure to include a defendant on a list for transportation. If just one key person fails to appear, the matter must be rescheduled. Furthermore, judges have limited ability to control the actions of personnel from law enforcement, probation, or the court reporter's offices, all of whom have scheduling problems of their own.[50]

The two primary methods by which cases are scheduled by the courts are the individual calendar and the master calendar.

Individual Calendar System

individual calendar system a system whereby cases are assigned to a single judge, who oversees all aspects of it from arraignment to pretrial motions and trial.

The simpler procedure for scheduling cases is the **individual calendar system**. A case is assigned to a single judge, who oversees all aspects of it from arraignment to pretrial motions and trial. The primary advantage is continuity; all parties to the case know that a single judge is responsible for its conclusion. There are other important advantages as well. Judge shopping (in which attorneys try to get their client's case on a particular judge's docket) is minimal, and administrative responsibility for each case is fixed. In addition, it is easier to pinpoint delays because one can easily compare judges' dockets to determine where cases are moving along and where they are not.

This system, however, is often affected by major differences in *case stacking* because judges work at different speeds. In addition, if a judge draws a difficult case, others must wait. Because most cases will be pleaded, however, case stacking is not normally a major problem unless a judge schedules too many cases for adjudication on a given day. Conversely, if a judge stacks too few cases for hearing or adjudication each day, delay will also result. If all cases settle, the judge has dead time, with a large backlog and nothing to do for the rest of the day.

Master Calendar System

master calendar system a system whereby judges is assigned to oversee all stages of a case (preliminary hearing, arraignment, trial).

The **master calendar system** is a more recent development. Here, judges oversee (usually on a rotating basis) given all stages of a case: preliminary hearings, arraignments, motions, bargaining, or trials. A judge is assigned a case from a central or master pool; once he or she has completed a specific phase of it, the case is returned to the pool. The primary advantage of this system is that judges who are good in one particular aspect of litigation (such as preliminary hearings) can be assigned to the job they do best. The disadvantage is that it is more difficult to pinpoint the location of or responsibility for delays. Judges also have less incentive to keep their docket current because when they dispose of one case, another appears. In addition, the distribution of work can be quite uneven. If, for example, three judges are responsible for preliminary hearings and one is much slower than the others, an unequal shifting of the workload will ensue; in other words, the two harder-working judges will be penalized by having to handle more cases.

Which System Is Better?

Each calendar system has advantages and disadvantages, and a debate has developed over which is better. The answer probably depends on the nature of the court. Small courts, such as U.S. district courts, use the individual calendar system more successfully. Largely because of their complex dockets, however, metropolitan and state courts almost uniformly use the master calendar system. Research indicates that courts using the master calendar experience greater difficulty. Typical problems include the following: (1) Some judges refuse to take their fair share of cases; (2) the administrative burden on the chief judge is often great; and (3) as a result of these two factors, a significant backlog of cases may develop. In those courts where the master calendar system was discontinued in favor of the individual system, delay was greatly reduced.[51]

► Decreasing Litigation: Alternative Dispute Resolution

Chapter 7 included information concerning annual caseloads of some of the nation's courts. Although these lawsuits—both criminal and civil—have arguably resulted in greater safety and a better quality of life in the United States, the fact remains that the weight of this litigation has imposed a tremendous workload on the nation's courts.

Several methods are now being proposed to reduce the number of lawsuits in this country. One is to limit punitive damages, with only the judge being allowed to levy them. Another is to force losers to pay the winners' legal fees. The process of discovery also warrants examination. This process involves exchange of information between prosecutors and defense attorneys to ensure that the adversary system does not give one side an unfair advantage over the other. Many knowledgeable people believe that the process of discovery wastes much time and could be revamped.[52]

Another procedure that is already in relatively widespread use is **alternative dispute resolution (ADR)**, or any means of settling disputes outside of court (and typically involving negotiation, conciliation, mediation, and arbitration). Realizing that the exploding backlog of both criminal and civil cases pushes business cases to the back of the queue, many private corporations are attempting to avoid courts and lawyers by using alternative means of resolving their legal conflicts. Some corporations have even opted out of litigation altogether; about 600 top corporations have signed pledges with other companies to consider negotiation and other forms of ADR prior to suing other corporate signers.[53]

ADR is appropriate when new law is not being created. ADR can provide the parties with a forum to reach a resolution that may benefit both sides. Litigation is adversarial; ADR can resolve disputes in a collaborative manner that allows parties' relationship to be maintained. Furthermore, ADR proceedings are normally confidential, with only the final agreement being made public. ADR is also much more expedient and less costly than a trial.[54]

The two most common forms of ADR used today are arbitration and mediation. Arbitration is similar to a trial, though less formal. An arbitrator is selected or appointed to a case; civil court rules generally apply. Parties are usually represented by counsel. The arbitrator listens to testimony by witnesses for both sides; then, after hearing closing remarks by counsel, the arbitrator renders a verdict. Arbitration may be mandatory and binding, meaning that the parties abandon their right to go to court once they agree to arbitrate. The arbitration award is usually appealable. Types of disputes commonly resolved through arbitration include collective bargaining agreements, construction and trademark disputes, sales contracts, warranties, and leases.[55]

Mediation is considerably less formal and more friendly than arbitration. Parties agree to negotiate with the aid of an impartial person who facilitates the settlement negotiations.

> **alternative dispute resolution (ADR)**
> settling disputes outside of court, typically by negotiation, conciliation, mediation, and arbitration.

A mediation session includes the mediator and both parties; each side presents his or her position and identifies the issues and areas of dispute. The mediator works with the parties until a settlement is reached or the negotiations become deadlocked; in the latter case, the matter may be continued in court. Mediation is not binding or adversarial; instead, it encourages the parties to resolve the dispute themselves. Mediation is commonly used when the parties in dispute have a continuing relationship, as in landlord–tenant disputes, long-term employment/labor disputes, and disputes between businesses.[56]

One of the oldest and leading ADR firms is Judicial Arbitration & Mediation Services, Inc. (JAMS), headquartered in Irvine, California, and started in 1979. It employs a panel of about 260 former judges. An Internet search will reveal a large number of other firms specializing in ADR as well, and there are even websites available to assist people in locating ADR firms to fit their specific needs. Fees for these private arbitration and mediation firms appear to range from $150 to $500 per hour *per party*, depending on the nature of the services provided and the mediator; this is still a huge savings given the $300 an hour that a battery of lawyers might each charge the litigants.[57]

Given the increasing number of lawsuits in this country, it appears that ADR is the wave of the future; as one law professor noted, "In the future, instead of walking into a building called a courthouse, you might walk into the Dispute Resolution Center."[58]

▶ Supreme Court Decisions on Federal Sentencing Guidelines

federal sentencing guidelines rules for computing uniform sentencing policy, they also provide classifications of offenses and offenders, severity of crimes, and suggested punishments.

The Sentencing Reform Act of 1984[59] created the U.S. Sentencing Commission, which in turn established **federal sentencing guidelines**—rules for computing uniform sentencing policy that also provide classifications of offenses and offenders, severity of crimes, and suggested punishments for the federal criminal justice system. Since that time, two notable U.S. Supreme Court decisions have been rendered concerning federal sentencing guidelines and federal judges' sentences using them.

First, in January 2005, the Court required federal courts to use the sentencing guidelines when determining the appropriate sentence for a crime, to ensure that similarly situated defendants were treated more or less alike rather than depending on the judge to whom their case happened to be assigned.[60] This Supreme Court's decision, in *U.S. v. Booker*,[61] involved a crack cocaine possession conviction where the Guidelines required a possible 210- to 262-month sentence; the trial judge, however, believed the defendant possessed a much larger amount of cocaine, and rendered a sentence that was almost 10 years longer than the one the Guidelines prescribed.[62] By a five-to-four vote, the U.S. Supreme Court also found that the U.S. Sentencing Guidelines violated the Sixth Amendment by allowing judicial, rather than jury, fact finding to form the basis for the sentence; in other words, letting in these judge-made facts is unconstitutional.[63] The Court did not discard the Guidelines entirely, however, saying the Guidelines are meant to be advisory and not mandatory. Thus, the Guidelines are a resource a judge can consider but may choose to ignore—although courts still must consider the Guidelines, they need not follow them. In addition, sentences for federal crimes will become subject to appellate review for "unreasonableness," allowing appeals courts to reduce particular sentences that seem far too harsh.

Then, in late 2007, the Supreme Court went further and explained what it meant in 2005 by "advisory" and "reasonableness," deciding two cases that together restored federal judges to their traditional central role in criminal sentencing. The Court found that district court judges do not have to justify their deviations from the federal sentencing Guidelines and have broad discretion to disagree with the Guidelines and to impose what they believe are reasonable sentences—even if the Guidelines call for different sentences.

Both cases—*Gall v. U.S.* and *Kimbrough v. U.S.*—were decided by the same 7–2 margin, and the Supreme Court chided federal appeals courts for failing to give district judges sufficient leeway.[64]

A related subject—the effect of the Prison Litigation Reform Act of 1996 on the filing of petitions by state prisoners—is discussed in Chapter 10.

▶ Courts' Media Relations

As with the police (see Chapter 6), good media relations can also be very important for the courts—particularly in high-profile cases. People often wonder why the courts act as they do with respect to public information. As an example, the lawyer defending singer Michael Jackson at his child molestation trial in 2005 caused a furor among the popular media when he asked the judge for a gag order in the case. The lawyer said he was not thinking about the First Amendment when he requested the order but rather about his client's best interests. The media, conversely, felt that the public had a right to know what was occurring in the case.

A debate between journalists and key players in high-profile legal cases occurred recently at one of many conferences sponsored by an organization that is a corollary to the National Judicial College, discussed in Chapter 8; this organization, the National Center for Courts and Media, also located in Reno, Nevada, was established to foster better communication and understanding between judges and lawyers on the one hand and between judges and journalists who serve the public on the other hand. The goal is to eliminate unnecessary friction between courts and the media, and bridge the gap between the two through workshops and conferences. The center helps judges to understand what a reporter is seeking and why; conversely, the workshops help journalists learn what records are open to the public, how the legal system works, who to go to for court information, how to gain access to documents, and what restrictions a judge works under.[65]

▶ Other Issues and Practices

Are "851 Notices" Being Overused and Abused?

There is growing criticism about a section of the **United States Code 21 U.S.C. §851**—that triggers enhanced penalties against drug dealers and is said to be the reason why "thousands of prisoners are serving life without parole for nonviolent crimes."[66]

Enacted by Congress in 1970, the original purpose of the law was straightforward and rational enough: to allow federal prosecutors to identify and more heavily punish (with sentencing enhancements, such as doubling the mandatory minimum sentences) those hardcore drug traffickers having prior drug felony convictions. However, many people now argue that the law is being used by prosecutors to coerce guilty pleas by routinely threatening, as one federal judge put it, "ultra-harsh, enhanced mandatory sentences that no one . . . thinks are appropriate."[67]

Writing "statements of reason" in October 2013—a means by which judges may express their views—Judge John Gleeson of the Eastern District of New York took strong issue with the use of "851 notices," citing one case in specific that had come before him.[68] Lulzim Kupa was convicted of distributing marijuana in 1999 and again in 2007. Kupa was paroled in 2010 but was soon caught trafficking cocaine, which carried a possible sentence of 10 years to life. Prosecutors offered Kupa 24 hours to accept or reject an offer—plead guilty and be sentenced to 110-137 months. Kupa rejected the offer, so prosecutors filed an "851 notice," citing his two prior marijuana convictions and threatening him with life without parole. Then, however, prosecutors gave Kupa 1 day to consider another proposal—plead guilty and receive a sentence of about 9 years (or, again, face a sentence of life without

> **United States Code 21 U.S.C. §851** a federal law allowing federal prosecutors to more heavily punish hard-core drug traffickers who have prior drug felony convictions.

parole). After taking too long to decide, prosecutors again increased their recommended sentence. At this point, Kupa gave in, telling Judge Gleeson, "I want to plead guilty, your honor, before things get worse."[69]

Alternatively, assume that Kupa—being 37 years of age in October 2013—had received the 851 notice and again declined to accept the prosecutors' offer, and was later convicted at trial. He would thus have died in prison for committing a nonviolent drug offense. Judge Gleeson added that, because there is no judicial oversight of the enhanced mandatory minimums prosecutors can inject into a case, they can put enormous pressure on defendants to plead guilty—using the threat of a life sentence as a "sledgehammer" to extort guilty pleas and in effect waive their right to trial.[70] Furthermore, because 97 percent of all federal convictions come without trials, the government is thus spared of the burden of proving guilt beyond a reasonable doubt—meaning that in 97 of 100 cases, the conviction is obtained with mere probable cause, which is all that is required of a grand jury indictment.[71]

Time to Rethink Juvenile Waivers?

Although crime in the United States peaked in the mid-1990s, there are yet about 1.6 million arrests of juveniles under age 18 each year, about 76,000 of which are arrests for murder and non-negligent manslaughter, forcible rape, robbery, and aggravated assault.[72]

Certainly there are some crimes committed by juveniles in our society that are so heinous or otherwise indicative that the youth is not amenable to the rehabilitative philosophy and protective shroud of the juvenile justice system. In such cases, nearly all states (45) have discretionary **juvenile waiver** provisions, allowing juvenile court judges to waive (transfer) jurisdiction over individual juvenile cases to *adult* criminal court for prosecution.[73]

There are three ways that a juvenile can be waived to adult criminal court: judicial, prosecutorial, and legislative:

> **juvenile waiver** a provision for juvenile court judges to transfer jurisdiction over individual juvenile cases to an adult criminal court for prosecution.

- *Judicial waivers* allow the juvenile court judge to determine if the juvenile meets minimum waiver criteria, including such variables as age, type of offense, previous criminal record, or a combination of the three. In some states, waivers are mandatory given certain specified criteria (age, offense, prior record).

- A *prosecutorial waiver* gives the decision making to the prosecutor who can decide whether to try a case in juvenile or adult court, depending on his or her assessment of the facts.

- A *legislative waiver* occurs when state laws require that certain offenses (such as murder) be automatically turned over to the adult criminal justice system—sometimes regardless of the youth's age.[74]

Statistically, juvenile waivers do not occur often, and the number of waivers has declined significantly since 1994 (when there were 13,800 such cases). Today, of about 1.5 million juvenile delinquency cases handled by the courts, about half (55%) are handled formally (i.e., a petition is filed requesting an adjudication or waiver hearing). Of those, an estimated 7,600 cases, or about 1 percent, results in judicial waiver. Most waivers involve crimes against persons (about 46%), property offenses (31%), and drug offenses (13%).[75]

Some researchers now argue that in recent years a movement has developed that militates against juvenile waivers and toward a less punitive philosophy. At the core of this argument are three U.S. Supreme Court decisions of the 2000s:

1. *Roper v. Simmons*,[76] in which the Court held that it is unconstitutional to impose a death sentence for a capital crime committed when one was under the age of 18;

2. *Graham v. Florida*,[77] where the Court decided that juvenile offenders cannot be sentenced to life imprisonment without parole (LWOP) for nonhomicide offenses; and

3. *Miller v. Alabama*,[78] which extended Graham and held that the Eighth Amendment forbids sentencing juvenile homicide offenders to LWOP.

In these cases, the Court relied heavily on social-science rationales to draw their conclusions: the tendency of juveniles toward immature and irresponsible behavior, juveniles being more susceptible to peer pressures and outside influences, and the fact that their personality or identity is not as well formed as an adult's. In sum, the young are very immature, impulsive, and easily manipulated or influenced. As a result, some authors have even questioned whether or not, under *Roper*, juvenile waiver is even constitutional.[79]

It is also argued that, for extralegal reasons, juveniles should not be waived: Such transfers discriminate against males, minorities, and the poor, and doing so does not reduce violent crime once juvenile offenders are released into the community as adults. Finally, it has been argued that the original purpose of the juvenile justice system was to operate with the juvenile's best interest in mind, to rehabilitate rather than employ retribution, and to view each juvenile offender on a case-by-case basis.[80] See Exhibit 9.5 for an example of a juvenile waiver.

EXHIBIT 9.5

AN EXAMPLE OF JUVENILE WAIVER

An example of juvenile waiver into adult court is a Florida case involving Lionel Tate, who, at age 12, was charged with first-degree murder of a 6-year-old girl. Tate declined a plea negotiation offer for second-degree murder that would have had him serving a term of 3 years in a juvenile facility, and then 10 years on probation. Under a prosecutorial waiver system, his case was then transferred to adult criminal court.

Over the defense's argument that Tate did not intend to harm the girl, and in view of medical reports showing the victim had suffered repeated violent blows, Tate was convicted of first-degree murder charge and sentenced to life in prison without parole (this case was decided in 2001, prior to the *Graham* or *Miller* decisions, above).

Both prosecuting and defense attorneys expressed the view that sentencing Tate to life in prison was not appropriate punishment for the 12-year-old Tate; however, the sentencing judge refused to overturn the conviction, believing that to do so would be disrespectful to the jury's discretion, and doing so would also have required him to disregard the evidence presented in the case.

In December 2003, Florida's appellate court granted Tate a retrial on the ground that his competency had not been evaluated prior to the conviction. In the end, after serving 3 years in prison, Tate finally agreed to accept the original plea offer and was released from prison that he had turned down earlier.[81]

Given the aforementioned Supreme Court decisions and their rationales, do you disagree that juveniles should be waived and tried/punished as adults? Or, conversely, do some crimes (particularly those against the person) committed by juveniles indicate such youths are beyond rehabilitation and thus warrant transfer to adult courts? Should the traditional rehabilitative philosophies and functions of the juvenile justice system be taken into account? These questions must be addressed not only in light of the hardened nature of today's violent juvenile offenders but also in terms of what the future holds for juvenile violence.

Should the Exclusionary Rule Be Banned?

The **exclusionary rule**—the Constitutional principle holding that evidence obtained illegally by law enforcement officers cannot be used against the suspect in a criminal prosecution— quickly became controversial for both crime control and due process advocates when it was adopted in 1961 by the U.S. Supreme Court in *Mapp v. Ohio*.[82] The view of the due process

exclusionary rule the Constitutional principle holding that evidence obtained illegally by law enforcement officers cannot be used against the suspect in a criminal prosecution.

model—as expressed by President Ronald Reagan in 1981—was, and is, that the rule "rests on the absurd proposition that a law enforcement error, no matter how technical, can be used to justify throwing an entire case out of court. The plain consequence is a grievous miscarriage of justice: the criminal goes free."[83]

For many legal experts who are inclined toward the due process model, however, illegal conduct by the police cannot be ignored. They believe that a court that admits tainted evidence tolerates the unconstitutional conduct that produced it and demonstrates an "insufficient commitment to the guarantee against unreasonable search and seizure."[84]

Although the exclusionary rule remains controversial, the nature of the debate has changed. Initially, critics called for complete abolition of the rule; now, they suggest modifications. Former Chief Justice Warren Burger urged an "egregious violation standard," whereby the police could be liable to civil suits when they were believed to be in error. Others support an exception for reasonable mistakes by the police. In fact, the U.S. Supreme Court recognized an "honest mistake" or "good faith" exception to the rule only in extremely narrow and limited circumstances.[85] Furthermore, the Rehnquist Court included six justices who publicly criticized *Mapp*. This majority, however, was not able to fashion a means of replacing *Mapp* while prohibiting truly bad-faith searches by the police. As a result, predicting the future of the exclusionary rule is difficult at best.

Should the exclusionary rule be abolished outright? Modified? Kept in its present form? These are compelling questions that our society and its courts may continue to ponder for many years to come.

Should Cameras Be Banned?

As the trial of actor Robert Blake (charged with murdering his wife, Bonny Lee Bakley) was being prepared in 2002, the controversy over whether cameras should be allowed in court—with a well-known actor playing himself in a real-life courtroom drama—was rekindled. The widely televised trial of O.J. Simpson clearly caused a reconsideration of this issue.

Perceptions that Simpson's lawyers played to the cameras apparently had an impact in several highly publicized cases that followed: A judge refused to allow broadcasts in the trial of Susan Smith, a South Carolina woman accused of drowning her two young sons in 1995,[86] and a California judge barred cameras in the trial of Richard Allen Davis, who kidnapped and killed Polly Klaas in 1993.

By the late 1990s, however, despite the Simpson trial backlash, opposition had cooled; a study found that four of every five television requests were approved by judges in California in 1998 and 1999.[87] Indeed, a judge allowed coverage of the trial of four police officers accused (and acquitted) of murdering Amadou Diallo in New York City in 2000.

The Blake trial once again put the spotlight on all of the concerns about televising high-publicity trials. Opponents of cameras in court—including due process advocates—complain that televising trials distorts the process by encouraging participants to play to the cameras, and that by covering only sensational trials and presenting only dramatic moments of testimony, television does not portray the trial process accurately.[88] They argue that in celebrity cases, even the witnesses "exaggerate things to give themselves a bigger role."[89] Supporters of the practice, conversely, maintain that televising trials has educational value, providing the public with a firsthand view of how courts operate. Indeed, studies have found that viewers of a television trial of moderate interest became more knowledgeable about the judicial process.[90]

The question of publicizing high-profile cases is not new. Cameras or recording devices were forbidden in the courthouse following the excessive press coverage of the trial of German immigrant Bruno Hauptman, who was accused of kidnapping and murdering the son of the famous aviator Charles Lindbergh in the 1930s. This case is the reason that television stations began to hire artists to provide sketches of courtroom participants.

Restrictions on cameras in the courtroom are changing, however. The Supreme Court unanimously held that electronic media and still-photographic coverage of public judicial proceedings does not violate a defendant's right to a fair trial; states are therefore free to set their own guidelines. Only 2 states prohibit all forms of electronic coverage of criminal trial proceedings; 35 states allow it.[91] The remaining states are still undecided.

To prevent disruption of the proceedings and to prohibit camera operators from moving about the courtroom while the trial is in session, states have limitations on electronic coverage. Furthermore, some states require the consent of the parties, meaning that either side can veto it. In others, the news media need only receive permission from the trial judge to broadcast the proceedings.[92]

The lingering question is whether cameras are an asset or a liability in the courtroom. To answer it, one must determine whether their education and publicity value exceeds their potential liabilities.

Summary

This chapter discussed several challenges involving the courts, generated from both internal and external sources, for today and for the future.

It is obvious that contemporary and future court issues and operations carry tremendous challenges for administrators. Those who serve as court leaders must be innovative, open to new ideas, accountable, well trained, and educated for the challenges that lie ahead. Legislators and policymakers must also become more aware of the difficulties confronting the courts and be prepared to provide additional resources for meeting the increasing caseloads, issues, and problems of the future.

Key Terms and Concepts

Alternative dispute resolution (ADR) *213*
Case delay *211*
Courthouse violence *205*
"CSI effect" *203*

Exclusionary rule *217*
Federal sentencing guidelines *214*
Individual calendar system *212*
Juvenile waiver *216*
Master calendar system *212*

Problem-solving courts *207*
Threat assessment *206*
United States Code
   21 U.S.C. §851 *215*

Questions for Review

1. What is the "CSI effect," and in what ways does research indicate it has affected court operations and court actors?

2. What are the characteristics of courthouse shootings, the differences between courthouse violence that is targeted and nontargeted, and means by which a threat assessment helps to determine whether someone poses a serious risk to court safety?

3. Give examples of some types and methods of problem-solving courts. How are they different in philosophy and function from traditional courts?

4. What are the possible consequences of delay in the courts, and what are some possible solutions to this problem?

5. What are the two primary methods of case scheduling employed by the courts? What are the advantages and disadvantages of each?

6. In what ways does ADR hold promise for reducing the current avalanche of lawsuits?

7. What did the U.S. Supreme Court recently decide concerning the application of federal sentencing guidelines?

8. What are the major considerations regarding the courts' relations with the media?

9. How have courts been successful in becoming grant-writers in recent hard times?

10. Should juveniles be waived into adult courts and tried as adults? Why or why not?

11. Should the exclusionary rule be banned? Why or why not?

12. Should courtroom cameras be kept or barred from our legal system? Why or why not?

Deliberate and Decide

The CSI Effect

Although the debate rages on concerning the "CSI effect," most "evidence" of this effect has been anecdotal in nature. But the fact remains that tens of millions of viewers watch television crime dramas each week, spawning a national obsession with forensic science.

A fundamental question is "Should prosecutors be permitted to question potential jurors concerning their views of forensics and to pose CSI-related questions to them—specifically, whether they would expect prosecutors to produce scientific evidence to prove their case beyond a reasonable doubt?"

States differ in this regard. For example, the Massachusetts Supreme Judicial Court recently ruled[93] that it was not an abuse of discretion for trial judges to pose CSI-related questions to potential jurors. The court gave judges wide discretion in jury selection and concluded that the trial judge had not abused his discretion and tilted the case toward the prosecution in attempting to seat jurors who were capable of deciding the case without bias and based on the evidence.

Conversely, Maryland's highest court[94] recently overturned two murder convictions because, during *voir dire* jury questioning, the trial judge asked people to stand up if they were "currently of the opinion or belief that you cannot convict a defendant without 'scientific evidence,' regardless of the other evidence in the case and regardless of the instructions that I will give you as to the law." The court, in ordering a new trial for the defendants, held that "the trial judge abused his discretion by essentially instructing the jury to convict the defendants 'on the non-scientific evidence of the case' . . . suggesting that the jury's only option was to convict, regardless of whether scientific evidence was adduced."

Questions for Discussion

1. Should trial judges be allowed to question potential jurors concerning their views of forensics and to pose CSI-related questions to them?

2. If you were a member of the jury, could you render a guilty verdict if there was no forensic evidence presented and yet it appeared from other evidence that the prosecutors proved their case beyond a reasonable doubt?

3. Do you believe, the lack of compelling evidence notwithstanding, there does in fact exist such an effect?

Learn by Doing

1. You are enrolled in a criminal justice internship with the district attorney's Victim Assistance Program. Recently there has been so much violence in the District Court's courtrooms directed toward members of the district attorney's staff that the level of concern has been greatly elevated—even more so because a high-profile case is scheduled for trial next week. The defendant has a lengthy criminal history, and the media have been full of phone calls and letters from citizens expressing outrage about the defendant and concerns about his being acquitted and eventually paroled back into the community. A reporter has also heard rumors of a planned attack against the defendant by some citizen-observers in court. What sort of threat assessment would be in order prior to the start of this trial?

2. Your criminal justice professor has been contacted by the local district court administrator seeking information concerning the methods and pitfalls involved in creating a veterans' court. You are to delineate what experts say are "do's and don'ts," relying on such resources as the Hamilton County, Ohio, Municipal Court's Veterans Treatment Court experience (see: http://www.hamilton-co.org/municipalcourt/Veterans/Veteran%20Project%20Handbook%20Final%20Municipal.htm). What will you write?

Notes

1. Brian Dakss, "The CSI Effect: Does the TV Crime Drama Influence How Jurors Think?" March 21, 2005, http://www.cbsnews.com/stories/2005/03/21/earlyshow/main681949.shtml (accessed November 1, 2014).
2. Rebecca Hayes-Smith and Lora M. Levett, "Community Members' Perceptions of the CSI Effect," *American Journal of Criminal Justice* 38(2) (June 2014): 216–235.
3. Rebecca Hayes-Smith and Lora M. Levett, "Jury's Still Out: How Television and Crime Show Viewing Influences Jurors' Evaluations of Evidence," *Applied Psychology in Criminal Justice* 7 (1) (2011): 29–46.
4. Hayes-Smith and Levett, "Community Members' Perceptions of the CSI Effect," p. 216.
5. Thomas Hughes and Megan Magers, "The Perceived Impact of Crime Scene Investigation Shows on the Administration of Justice," *Journal of Criminal Justice and Popular Culture* 14(3) (2007), http://www.albany.edu/scj/jcjpc/vol14is3/HughesMagers.pdf (accessed November 1, 2014).

6. Hayes-Smith and Levett, "Jury's Still Out," p. 46.

7. See *State v. Cooke*, 914 A.2d 1078 (2007).

8. Herbert L. Packer, *The Limits of the Criminal Sanction* (Stanford, CA: Stanford University Press, 1968).

9. Lee Sinclair, "Judicial Violence: Tipping the Scales," in Gary Hengstler (ed.), *Case in Point* (Reno, NV: The National Judicial College, 2006), p. 5.

10. Gary Hengstler, "Judicial Violence: Tipping the Scales," ibid., pp. 3–5.

11. Ibid., p. 3.

12. Gregg W. Etter and Warren G. Swymeler, "Research Note: Courthouse Shootings, 1907–2007," *Homicide Studies* 14(1) (2009):90–100, http://0-hsx.sagepub.com.innopac.library.unr.edu/content/14/1/90.full.pdf+html (accessed November 1, 2014).

13. Ibid.

14. Don Hardenbergh and Neil Alan Weiner, "Preface," in Don Hardenbergh and Neil Alan Weiner (eds.), *The Annals of the American Academy of Political and Social Science, Vol. 576: Courthouse Violence: Protecting the Judicial Workplace* (Thousand Oaks, CA: Author, 2001), p. 10.

15. David W. Neubauer, *America's Courts and the Criminal Justice System*, 9th ed. (Belmont, CA: Wadsworth, 2008), p. 402.

16. Ibid., p. 82.

17. Bryan Vossekuil, Randy Borum, Robert Fein, and Marisa Reddy, "Preventing Targeted Violence against Judicial Officials and Courts," in Hardenbergh and Weiner (eds.), *The Annals of the American Academy of Political and Social Science, Vol. 576: Courthouse Violence*, pp. 78–90.

18. Susan Voyles, "Shooting Sparks Worries about Safety," *Reno Gazette-Journal*, June 14, 2006, p. 1C.

19. See GovTrack.US, "H.R. 1751 [109th]: Court Security Improvement Act of 2006," http://www.govtrack.us/congress/bill.xpd?bill=h109-1751 (accessed November 1, 2014).

20. Conference of Chief Judges/Conference of State Court Administrators, *Court Security Handbook: Ten Essential Elements for Court Security and Emergency Preparedness* (September 2012), 5-1-5-5, http://ncsc.contentdm.oclc.org/cdm/singleitem/collection/facilities/id/165/rec/12 (accessed November 4, 2014).

21. Quoted in "Quotes about Dogs," Goodreads, "http://www.goodreads.com/quotes/tag/dogs?page=1 (accessed November 20, 2014).

22. Adapted from the National Crime Victim Law Institute, "Facilitating Access to Justice: Courthouse Dogs' Emerging Role in the Criminal Justice System," National Crime Victim Law Institute, November 21, 2014, http://law.lclark.edu/live/events/21239-facilitating-access-to-justice-courthouse-dogs (accessed November 26, 2014).

23. Robert V. Wolf, "Breaking with Tradition: Introducing Problem Solving in Conventional Courts," *International Review of Law Computers & Technology* 22(1–2) (2008):77–93.

24. Greg Berman and John Feinblatt, "Problem-Solving Courts: A Brief Primer," *Law & Policy* 23(2) (2001): 125–140.

25. Shannon Portillo, Danielle S. Rudes, Jill Viglione, and Matthew Nelson, "Front-Stage Stars and Backstage Producers: The Role of Judges in Problem-Solving Courts," *Victims & Offenders: An International Journal of Evidence-based Research, Policy, and Practice* 8(1) (2014), DOI: 10.1080/15564886.2012.685220 (accessed November 1, 2014).

26. Ibid.

27. DrugWarFacts.org, "Drug Courts & Treatment Alternatives to Incarceration," http://www.drugwarfacts.org/cms/Drug_Courts#sthash.oHdnuD1o.dpbs (accessed November 2, 2014).

28. U.S. Department of Justice, National Criminal Justice Reference Service, "In the Spotlight: Drug Courts," https://www.ncjrs.gov/spotlight/drug_courts/summary.html (accessed November 4, 2014).

29. National Institute of Justice, *Do Drug Courts Work? Findings from Drug Court Research*, http://www.nij.gov/topics/courts/drug-courts/work.htm (accessed November 1, 2014; many drug court evaluations may be found at: *NIJ's Multi-site Adult Drug Court Evaluation*, http://www.nij.gov/nij/topics/courts/drug-courts/madce.htm (accessed November 1, 2014).

30. *Dusky v. United States*, 362 U.S. 402 (1960).

31. Michael Brick, "Making Mentally Ill Defendants Ready for Trial," Associated Press, May 19, 2014, http://bigstory.ap.org/article/making-mentally-ill-defendants-ready-trial (accessed November 4, 2014).

32. U.S. Department of Justice, Bureau of Justice Assistance, *Improving Responses to People with Mental Illnesses*, 2007, p. vii, http://www.ojp.usdoj.gov/BJA/pdf/MHC_Essential_Elements.pdf (accessed December 2, 2014).

33. Ibid.

34. Brick, "Making Mentally Ill Defendants Ready for Trial," p. 1.

35. Lisa Callahan, Ph.D., Henry J. Steadman, Ph.D., and Lindsay Gerus "7 Common Characteristics of Juvenile Mental Health Courts," Substance Abuse and Mental Health Services Administration, http://gainscenter.samhsa.gov/cms-assets/documents/122718-887312.common-characteristics-jmhcs.pdf (accessed November 4, 2014).

36. Nicholas Riccardi, "These Courts Give Wayward Veterans a Chance," *Los Angeles Times*, March 30, 2009, http://articles.latimes.com/2009/mar/10/nation/na-veterans-court10 (accessed November 1, 2014).

37. Amanda Ruggeri, "New Courts Give Troubled Veterans a Second Chance," *US News and World Report*, April 3, 2009, http://politics.usnews.com/news/national/articles/2009/04/03/new-courts-give-troubled-veterans-a-second-chance.html (accessed November 1, 2014).

38. Disabled World, "Veterans Courts: A Second Chance for Those Who Have Served," http://www.disabled-world.com/disability/legal/veterans-court.php (accessed November 1, 2014).

39. Jim McGuire, Sean Clark, Jessica Blue-Howells, and Cedric Coe, "An Inventory of VA Involvement in Veterans Courts, Dockets and Tracks," VA Veterans Justice Programs (February 7, 2014),

http://www.justiceforvets.org/sites/default/files/files/An%20 Inventory%20of%20VA%20involvement%20in%20Veterans %20Courts.pdf (accessed November 4, 2014).

40. Adapted from Veterans Health Administration, "Vets in Crisis Get a Chance, Not a Cell," http://www.va.gov/health/ NewsFeatures/20120216a.asp (accessed November 4, 2014).

41. Neubauer, *America's Courts and the Criminal Justice System*, pp. 112–114.

42. Ibid.

43. Ibid.

44. See *Barker v. Wingo*, 407 U.S. 514 (1972).

45. Ibid., p. 522.

46. Neubauer, *America's Courts and the Criminal Justice System*, pp. 114–116.

47. National Advisory Commission on Criminal Justice Standards and Goals, *Courts* (Washington, DC: U.S. Government Printing Office, 1973), p. 12.

48. Neubauer, *America's Courts and the Criminal Justice System*, pp. 293–295.

49. Adapted from the National Center for State Courts, "CourTools: Trial Court Performance Standards," http://www .ncsconline.org/D_Research/CourTools/Images/CourTools OnlineBrochure.pdf (accessed November 17, 2010).

50. Steven Flanders, *Case Management and Court Management in the United States District Courts* (Washington, DC: Federal Judicial Center, 1977).

51. David W. Neubauer, Maria Lipetz, Mary Luskin, and John Paul Ryan, *Managing the Pace of Justice: An Evaluation of LEAA's Court Delay Reduction Programs* (Washington, DC: U.S. Government Printing Office, 1981).

52. Bob Cohn, "The Lawsuit Cha-Cha," *Newsweek* (August 26, 1991):59.

53. Michele Galen, Alice Cuneo, and David Greising, "Guilty!" *Business Week* (April 13, 1992):63.

54. American Bar Association, *Dispute Resolution: A 60-Minute Primer* (Washington, DC: Author, 1994), pp. 1–2

55. Ibid., p. 3.

56. Ibid., p. 4.

57. Quoted in American Bar Association, Dispute Resolution; also see Judicial Arbitration and Mediation Services, Inc., "About JAMS," http://www.jamsadr.com/aboutus_overview/ (accessed August 27, 2011).

58. ABA, Dispute Resolution, p. 64.

59. 18 U.S.C. Secs. 3551–3626 and 28 U.S.C. Secs. 991–998 (October 12, 1984).

60. Mark Allenbaugh, "The Supreme Court's New Blockbuster U.S. Sentencing Guidelines Decision," http://writ.news .findlaw.com/allenbaugh/20050114.html (accessed January 17, 2005).

61. *U.S. v. Booker*, 543 U.S.125 S.Ct. 738 (2005).

62. FindLaw Legal News, "*United States v. Booker*," http://caselaw. lp.findlaw.com/scripts/printer_friendly.pl?page=us/000/04-104. html (accessed January 17, 2005).

63. Allenbaugh, "The Supreme Court's New Blockbuster U.S. Sentencing Guidelines Decision," p. 2.

64. *San Francisco Chronicle*, SFGate.com, "High Court Gives U.S. Judges More Freedom in Sentencing," http://www. sfgate.com/cgi-bin/article.cgi?f=/c/a/2007/12/11/MNE-3TRS7O.DTL (accessed December 11, 2007). See *Gall v. U.S.*, 446 F3d 884 (cert. granted 6/11/2007), and *Kimbrough v. U.S*, 174 Fed. Appx. 798 (cert. granted 6/11/2007).

65. Martha Bellisle, "Bridging the Gap: Judges, Lawyers, and Members of the Media Learn to Understand One Another," *Reno Magazine* (September–October 2006):74.

66. George F. Will, "The Sledgehammer Justice of Mandatory Minimum Sentences," *The Washington Post*, December 25, 2013, http://www.washingtonpost.com/opinions/george-will-the-sledgehammer-justice-of-mandatory-minimum-sentences/2013/12/25/959e39de-6cb2-11e3-a523-fe73f0ff6b8d_story.html (accessed January 23, 2014).

67. Doug Berman, "Double Your Pleasure, Double Your Fun, with 21 U.S.C. § 851," *Simple Justice*, http://blog.simplejustice. us/2013/10/12/double-your-pleasure-double-your-fun-with-21-u-s-c-%C2%A7-851/; also see Drug Enforcement Administration, Office of Diversion Control, "Title 21 United States Code, Controlled Substances Act, Subchapter 1, Control and Enforcement, Proceedings to Establish Prior Convictions," at: http://www.deadiversion.usdoj.gov/21cfr/ 21usc/851.htm (accessed January 22, 2014).

68. *US v. Kupa*, No. 11-CR-345 (E.D.N.Y. Oct. 9, 2013).

69. John Gleeson, *U.S. v. Kupa*, Statement of Reason, 11-CR345, p. 23, http://sentencing.typepad.com/files/us-v-kupa-statement-of-reasons-final.pdf (accessed January 10, 2014).

70. Ibid., p. 32.

71. George F. Will, "The Sledgehammer Justice of Mandatory Minimum Sentences."

72. Bureau of Justice Statistics, *Arrests in the United States, 1990–2010* (October 2012), p. 2, http://www.bjs.gov/content/ pub/pdf/aus9010.pdf (accessed November 3, 2014).

73. Benjamin Adams and Sean Addie *Delinquency Cases Waived to Criminal Court, 2009* (Washington, DC: U.S. Department of Justice Office of Juvenile Justice and Delinquency Prevention, October 2012), p. 1, http://www.ojjdp. gov/pubs/239080.pdf (accessed November 2, 2014).

74. Maisha N. Cooper and Lynn S. Urban, "Factors Affecting Juvenile Waiver to Adult Court in a Large Midwestern Jurisdiction," *Journal of the Institute of Justice & International Studies* 12 (2012): 43–61.

75. Adams and Addie *Delinquency Cases Waived to Criminal Court, 2009*, p. 2

76. *Roper v. Simmons*, 543 U.S. 551 (2005).

77. *Graham v. Florida* 130 S.Ct. 2011 (2010).

78. *Miller v. Alabama*, 567 U.S. ___ (2012).

79. John Matthew Fabian, "Applying Roper v. Simmons in Juvenile Transfer and Waiver Proceedings: A Legal and Neuroscientific Inquiry," *International Journal of Offender Therapy and Comparative Criminology* 55 (August 2011): 732–755.

80. Cooper and Urban, "Factors Affecting Juvenile Waiver to Adult Court in a Large Midwestern Jurisdiction," p. 60.

81. Adapted from Daniel Mole and Dodd White, *Transfer and Waiver in the Juvenile Justice System* (Washington, DC: Child Welfare League of America, 2005), pp. 25–26,

http://www.cwla.org/programs/juvenilejustice/jjtransfer.pdf (accessed November 2, 2014).

82. 367 U.S. 643.

83. Quoted in Neubauer, *America's Courts and the Criminal Justice System*, p. 265.

84. Yale Kamisar, "Is the Exclusionary Rule an 'Illogical' or 'Unnatural' Interpretation of the Fourth Amendment?" *Judicature* 78 (1994):83–84.

85. See, for example, *U.S. v. Leon,* 486 U.S. 897 (1984), and *Illinois v. Krull,* 480 U.S. 340 (1987).

86. Jesse Holland, "Susan Smith Judge Bars TV Cameras from Murder Trial," *Times-Picayune,* June 25, 1995, p. 1A.

87. Zanto Peabody, "Blake Case Revives Issue of Cameras in Court," *Los Angeles Times,* May 27, 2002, p. 1A.

88. Paul Thaler, *The Watchful Eye: American Justice in the Age of the Television Trial* (Westport, CT: Praeger, 1994).

89. Peabody, "Blake Case Revives Issue of Cameras in Court," p. 1A.

90. S. L. Alexander, "Cameras in the Courtroom: A Case Study," *Judicature* 74 (1991):307–313; Paul Raymond, "The Impact of a Televised Trial on Individuals' Information and Attitudes," *Judicature* 57 (1992):204–209.

91. Alexander, "Cameras in the Courtroom."

92. Neubauer, *America's Courts and the Criminal Justice System*, pp. 312–313.

93. See *Commonwealth v. Perez*, 460 Mass. 683 (2011).

94. *Jamal Charles and Dwayne Drake v. Maryland*, 411 Md. 355, 983 A.2d 431 (2009).

PART 4

Corrections

This part includes three chapters that address corrections administration. Chapter 10 examines corrections organization and operation, including prisons, jails, and probation and parole agencies. Chapter 11 covers personnel roles and functions. Chapter 12 reviews corrections issues and practices. Specific chapter content is previewed in the introductory section of each chapter. Case studies relating to this part appear in Appendix I.

nobeastsofierce/shutterstock

10 Corrections Organization and Operation

LEARNING OBJECTIVES

After reading this chapter, the student will be able to:

1 *describe the general features of a correctional organization in the United States, including the levels of correctional incarceration, employment, expenditures, and several factors affecting prison and jail populations*

2 *delineate the personnel and divisions found in the state's central office as well as in individual prisons*

3 *describe supermax prisons, including their method of operation, alleged effects on inmates, constitutionality, and implications for corrections policy*

4 *explain the early* hands-off *era of the courts toward prisons, and selected constitutional rights afforded jail and prison inmates*

5 *describe what civil rights are held by institutionalized persons, under federal law*

6 *relate the nature and extent of litigation by prison and jail inmates, including the rationale, provisions, and impact of the Prison Litigation Reform Act (PLRA)*

7 *describe how direct supervision jails differ from the traditional model in design and functions*

8 *explain the U.S. Supreme Court's view of warrantless collection of DNA from pretrial arrestees*

9 *explain the means and rationale for accreditation of corrections facilities*

10 *generally describe how adult and juvenile probation and parole agencies are organizationally structured within their states, and whether or not their officers are armed and granted peace officer powers*

11 *relate the systems theory of probation and the six categories of probation systems, including their resources, activities, and outcomes*

12 *articulate the three services of parole agencies and the two models used for administering them*

13 *review the advantages of the independent and consolidated models of parole*

▶ Introduction

The organization and operation of prisons, jails, and probation and parole functions in our society are largely unknown and misunderstood. Indeed, most of what the public "knows" about the inner workings of these organizations is obtained through Hollywood's eyes and depictions—*The Shawshank Redemption, The Green Mile, The Longest Yard, Escape from Alcatraz,* and *Cool Hand Luke* are a few examples of such popular depictions that are frequently shown on television.

Unfortunately, however, because the movie industry is more concerned with box office sales than with depicting reality, liberties are taken and the portrayal of prisons in film is generally inaccurate. Furthermore, although problems certainly can and do arise in correctional institutions, movies often accentuate and exaggerate their negative aspects; therefore, it should be remembered that the reality of prison operations is often at considerable variance with what is projected on the big screen.

The opening of this chapter demonstrates that corrections is yet a booming industry in terms of both expenditures and employment, although correctional populations have been declining over the past few years. We look at some reasons for the decline. Then we focus on correctional agencies as organizations, including their mission and a view of the statewide central offices overseeing prison systems and their related functions as well as individual prisons. Next is a discussion of the relatively new supermax prisons, including their unique method of operation, alleged effects on inmates, constitutionality, and implications for corrections policy. After that is a consideration of selected constitutional and civil rights that federal courts and Congress have granted to jail and prison inmates; then we review prison litigation generally, including the rationale and impact of the PLRA.

Next, we examine local jails, including their organization, the unique structure and function of podular direct supervision jails, and, after briefly considering the accreditation of corrections facilities, we review probation and parole organizations, to include the organizational structure, arming, and peace officer status of adult and juvenile probation and parole agencies and their officers. The chapter concludes with review questions, "deliberate and decide" problems, and "learn by doing" exercises.

► Correctional Organizations

Employment and Expenditures

Today, prisons and jails at the federal, state, and local levels employ about 785,000 people (one-third of them at the local level and about 60% for state governments), and cost about $36 billion in annual payrolls[1] This figure excludes another $5.4 billion in annual prison costs arising from such expenditures as retiree health care, employee benefits, and taxes; capital costs; underfunded employee pensions; and health and hospital care for the prison population.[2]

Declining Prison Populations: Reasons and Some Caveats

As shown in Table 10-1 ■, U.S. prisons now hold about 1,484,000 adult prisoners—a number that has been declining since 2010 (while the table shows the number of jail inmates has remained fairly stable, averaging about 743,000, since 2005).[3]

Why a decline in prison populations? According to experts, the hard-nosed, punitive crime policies that began in the early 1980s—which included mass incarceration of nonviolent drug addicts, mandatory sentencing laws, and stiff sentences for repeat offenders, all of which brought a prison construction boom—are now being relaxed in many states. Indeed, marijuana is being increasingly decriminalized, and stiff sentences for repeat offenders that were in effect in a number of states are being eased. Another telling development is that six states have abolished the death penalty since 2007.[4]

Why this philosophical shift? Certainly dwindling public resources are a major reason: It costs all units of government about $80 billion per year to house these 2.2 million inmates in their jails and prisons. Also, experts increasingly see the fundamental question of fairness being raised; as David Kennedy of New York's John Jay College of Criminal Justice put it, the movement to ease mandatory minimum sentences and to reduce the use of solitary confinement is a result of "the basic recognition that the application of power without justice is brutal."[5] Even conservative politicians are admitting that the extreme punishment policies of the past several decades have largely failed. And this philosophical shift is literally paying off for the states. Since 2011, New York has closed 24 of its 93 adult and juvenile corrections facilities (thus saving about $221 million per year), and 16 other states have either closed or proposed prison closings of their own in a bid to slice about 30,000 beds.[6] See Exhibit 10.1 for a description of California's prison situation.

TABLE 10-1 Prison Populations in the United States

Year	Total correctional population	Community supervision			Incarcerated		
		Total	Probation	Parole	Total	Jail	Prison
2000	6,461,000	4,565,100	3,839,500	725,500	1,938,500	621,100	1,317,300
2005	7,050,400	4,946,800	4,162,500	784,400	2,195,000	747,500	1,447,400
2010	7,079,500	4,887,900	4,055,500	840,700	2,270,100	748,700	1,521,400
2011	6,978,500	4,814,200	3,971,300	853,900	2,240,600	735,600	1,505,000
2012	6,937,600	4,781,300	3,942,800	851,200	2,228,400	744,500	1,483,900
Average annual percent change, 2000–2011	0.7%	0.5%	0.3%	1.5%	1.3%	1.5%	1.2%
Percent change, 2011–2012	−0.7%	−0.8%	−1.0%	−0.1%	−0.5%	1.2%	−1.4%

Source: U.S. Department of Justice, Bureau of Justice Statistics, *Correctional Populations in the United States, 2012,* (December 2013)

AS CALIFORNIA GOES, SO GOES THE NATION . . .

It would probably not be inaccurate to say "As California goes, so too goes the nation" with respect to U.S. prison populations. In May 2011, the U.S. Supreme Court (in *Brown v. Plata*) upheld a lower court ruling mandating that within 2 years the state reduce its prison population to alleviate overcrowding (built to house approximately 85,000 inmates, at that time the prison system housed nearly twice that number, approximately 156,000 inmates).[7] Known as the Public Safety Realignment (PSR) policy, this approach should reduce the state's prison population through normal attrition of the existing population, releasing many nonviolent, nonserious, nonsexual offenders. Because California incarcerates more individuals than any other state except Texas (10.8% of the U.S. state prison population), these changes will have national implications.[8]

Another problem is that today's former prison inmates are less likely to have participated in prison rehabilitation and work programs, which also militates against their succeeding in the free world. At least a part of this lack of involvement in programming may be due to Robert Martinson's well-publicized finding of the mid-1970s that "almost nothing works"[9] in correctional treatment programs served to ignite a firestorm of debate that has lasted more than two decades.[10] Legislators and corrections administrators became unwilling to fund treatment programs from dwindling budgets, and academics such as Paul Louis and Jerry Sparger noted that "perhaps the most lasting effect of the 'nothing works' philosophy is the spread of cynicism and hopelessness" among prison administrators and staff members.[11]

General Mission and Features

Correctional organizations are complex hybrid organizations that utilize two distinct yet related management subsystems to achieve their goals: One is concerned primarily with managing correctional employees and the other is concerned primarily with delivering correctional services to a designated offender population. The correctional organization, therefore, employs one group of people (correctional personnel) to work with and control another group (offenders).

The mission of corrections agencies has changed little over time. It is as follows: to protect the citizens from crime by safely and securely handling criminal offenders while providing offenders some opportunities for self-improvement and increasing the chance that they will become productive and law-abiding citizens.[12]

An interesting feature of the correctional organization is that *every* correctional employee who exercises legal authority over offenders is a supervisor, even if the person is the lowest-ranking member in the agency or institution. Another feature of the correctional organization is that—as with the police—everything a correctional supervisor does may have civil or criminal ramifications, both for himself or herself and for the agency or institution. Therefore, the legal and ethical responsibility for the correctional (and police) supervisor is greater than it is for supervisors in other types of organizations.

▶ Prisons as Organizations

As noted earlier in this chapter, the mission of most prisons is to provide a safe and secure environment for staff and inmates, as well as programs for offenders that can assist them after release.[13] This section describes how prisons are organized to accomplish this mission. First, we look at the larger picture—the typical organization of the central office within the state government that oversees *all* prisons within its jurisdiction. Then we review the characteristic organization of an individual prison.

The Central Office

central office the state's central organization that oversees its prison system.

The state's central organization that oversees its prison system is often called the **central office**. Some of the personnel and functions typically found in a central office are discussed in the following subsections.

Office of the Director

prison director the person who sets policy for all wardens and prisons to follow in terms of management and inmate treatment.

Each state normally has a central department of corrections that is headed by a secretary (or someone with a similar title); in turn, the secretary appoints a person to direct the operation of all of the prisons in the state. The **prison director** sets policy for all wardens (discussed more thoroughly in Chapter 11) and prisons in terms of how the institutions should be managed and inmates cared for (with regard to both custody and treatment). In addition to the director, the staff within the office of the director includes public or media affairs coordinators, legislative liaisons, legal advisers, and internal affairs representatives.

As they are one of the largest state agencies, a tremendous demand for public information is made on correctional agencies. If a policy issue or a major incident is involved, the media will contact the director for a response. The office of public affairs also oversees the preparation of standard reports, such as an annual review of the department and its status or information on a high-profile program or project. In addition, because state correctional agencies use a large percentage of the state budget, the legislature is always interested in their operations. Therefore, there is usually within the department of corrections an office of legislative affairs, which responds to legislative requests and tries to build support for resources and programs.[14]

Legal divisions, typically composed of four to six attorneys, often report to the director as well. The work of the legal division includes responding to inmate lawsuits, reviewing policy for its legal impact, and offering general advice regarding the implementation of programs in terms of past legal decisions. These attorneys will predict how the courts are likely to respond to a new program in light of legal precedents.

Finally, the director's office usually has an inspector or internal affairs division. Ethics in government is a major priority; corrections staff may be enticed to bring contraband into a prison or may be physically abusive to inmates. Whenever there is a complaint of staff misconduct by anyone, the allegation needs to be investigated.

Administration Division

Two major areas of the administrative division of a corrections central office are budget development/auditing and new prison construction. The administrative division collects information from all of the state's prisons, other divisions, and the governor's office to create a budget that represents ongoing operations and desired programs and growth. Once it is approved by the governor's office, this division begins to explain the budget to the legislative budget committee, which reviews the request and makes a recommendation for funding to the full legislature. After a budget is approved, this division maintains accountability of funds and oversees the design and construction of new and renovated facilities.[15]

Correctional Programs Division

A central office will usually have a division that oversees the operation of correctional programs, such as security, education, religious services, mental health, and unit management. It is clear that:

> Offenders enter prison with a variety of deficits. Some are socially or morally inept, others are intellectually or vocationally handicapped, some have emotional hangups that stem from psychological problems, still others have a mixture of varying proportions of some or even all of these.[16]

Having to deal with inmates suffering from such serious and varied problems is a daunting task for correctional organizations. Prison culture makes the environment inhospitable to programs designed to rehabilitate or reform.

A major contemporary problem among persons entering prison is drug addiction. Drug-addicted offenders are subjected to one of three types of treatment programming that attempt to address the problem: punitive (largely involving withdrawal and punishment), medical (consisting of detoxification, rebuilding physical health, counseling, and social services), and the communal approach (using group encounters and seminars conducted by former addicts who serve as positive role models).[17] Chapter 12 discusses what prison administrators can do to interdict drugs coming into prisons and the kinds of treatment programs that are maintained in them.

Medical or Health Care Division

One of the most complicated and expensive functions within a prison is health care. As a result, this division develops policy, performs quality assurance, and looks for ways to make health care more efficient for inmates and less expensive for the prison. One of the best outcomes for a corrections health care program involved HIV/AIDS. A widespread epidemic of HIV/AIDS cases was initially feared in prisons (through homosexual acts and prior drug use) but such an outbreak never happened. Today, the problem persists, with about 20,100 prison inmates having HIV or AIDS, but the overall number has declined about three percent per year, from 194 cases per 10,000 inmates in 2001 to 146 per 10,000 at present.[18]

Human Resource Management Division

The usual personnel functions of recruitment, hiring, training, evaluation, and retirement are accomplished in the human resource management division. Affirmative action and labor relations (discussed in Chapter 14) may also be included. Workplace diversity is important for corrections agencies, particularly with the growing number of African American and Hispanic inmates. Most states have a unionized workforce, and negotiating and managing labor issues are time-consuming; therefore, this division has staff with expertise in labor relations.

Figure 10-1 ■ shows the organizational structure of a central office in a state of 3 million people.

Individual Prisons

Over time, prison organizational structure (See Figure 10-2 ■) has changed considerably to respond to external needs. Until the beginning of the twentieth century, prisons were administered by state boards of charities, boards composed of citizens, boards of inspectors, state prison commissions, or individual prison keepers. Most prisons were individual provinces; wardens who were given absolute control over their domain were appointed by governors through a system of political patronage. Individuals were attracted to the position of warden because it carried many fringe benefits, such as a lavish residence, unlimited inmate servants, food and supplies from institutional farms and warehouses, furnishings, and a personal automobile. Now most wardens or superintendents are civil service employees who have earned their position through seniority and merit.[19]

Attached to the warden's office are (possibly by some other title) an institutional services inspector and the institutional investigator who deal with inmate complaints against staff. As mentioned in the earlier section on the central office, prisons also need personnel who deal with labor contracts and the media, and who collect and provide this information to the central office. A computer services manager maintains the management information systems.

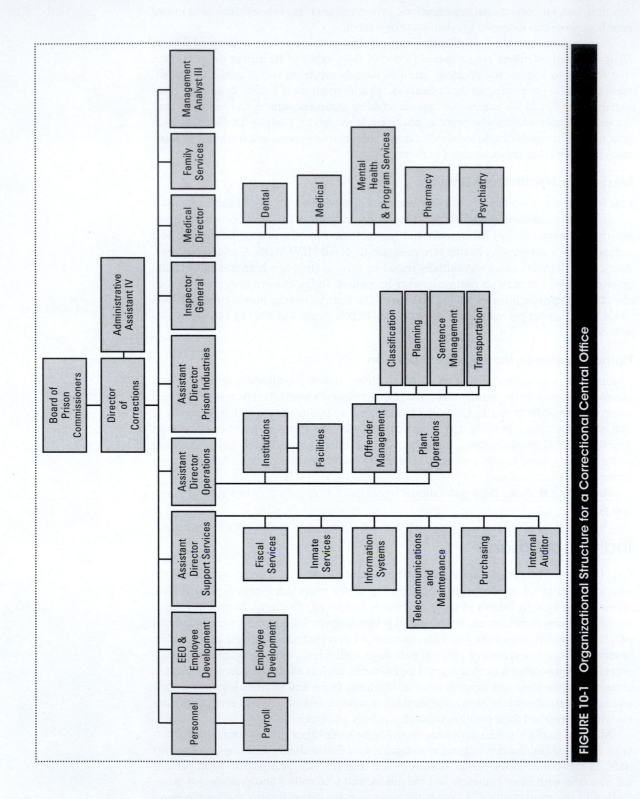

FIGURE 10-1 Organizational Structure for a Correctional Central Office

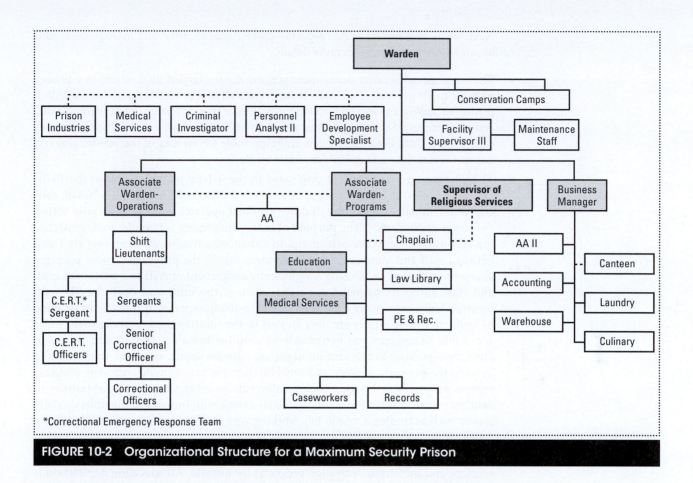

FIGURE 10-2 Organizational Structure for a Maximum Security Prison

Also reporting to the warden are deputy or associate wardens, each of whom supervises a department within the prison. The deputy warden for operations will normally oversee correctional security, unit management, the inmate disciplinary committee, and recreation. The deputy warden for special services will typically be responsible for functions that are more treatment oriented, including the library, mental health services, drug and alcohol recovery services, education, prison job assignments, religious services, and prison industries. Finally, the deputy warden for administration will manage the business office, prison maintenance, laundry, food service, medical services, prison farms, and the issuance of clothing.[20]

It is important to note that custody and treatment are not either/or in correctional organizations; rather, they are complementary. Although custody overshadows treatment in terms of operational priorities—treatment programs are unable to flourish if security is weak and staff and inmates work and live in chronic fear and danger—prisons without programming options for offenders are nothing more than warehouses, being amenable to violence, disruption, and the continuation of criminally deviant behavior. Correctional staff, regardless of their job function, does not support such volatile conditions. Most often, the overriding concern in a prison or jail is and should be security. Security must be maintained so that programs can be implemented. Programs are generally supported by staff, especially those that address inmate deficiencies such as lack of education and job skills as well as substance abuse. Prison administrators must decide which programs they will allow to be introduced into their facility; this is not often an easy task, especially when much of the public perceives that programs only "coddle" inmates.[21]

Next, we discuss several related aspects—correctional security, unit management, education, and penal industries—in more detail.

- The correctional security department is normally the largest department in a prison, with 50 to 70 percent of all staff. It supervises all of the security activities within a prison, including any special housing units, inmate transportation, and the inmate disciplinary process. Security staff wears military-style uniforms; a captain normally runs each 8-hour shift, lieutenants often are responsible for an area of the prison, and sergeants oversee the rank-and-file correctional staff.

- The *unit management* concept originated in the federal prison system in the 1970s and now is used in nearly every state to control prisons by providing a "small, self-contained, inmate living and staff office area that operates semiautonomously within the larger institution."[22] The purpose of unit management is twofold: to decentralize the administration of the prison and to enhance communication among staff and between staff and inmates. Unit management breaks the prison into more manageable sections based on housing assignments; assignment of staff to a particular unit; and staff authority to make decisions, manage the unit, and deal directly with inmates. Units are usually composed of 200 to 300 inmates; staff is not only assigned to units, but their offices are also located in the housing area, making them more accessible to inmates and better able to monitor inmate activities and behavior. Directly reporting to the unit manager are *case managers*, or social workers, who develop the program of work and rehabilitation for each inmate and write progress reports for parole authorities, classification (discussed in Chapter 12), or transfer to another prison. Correctional counselors also work with inmates in the units on daily issues, such as finding a prison job, working with their prison finances, and creating a visiting and telephone list.[23]

- The education department operates the academic teaching, vocational training, library services, and sometimes recreation programs for inmates. An education department is managed similarly to a conventional elementary or high school, with certified teachers for all subjects that are required by the state department of education or are part of the General Education Degree test. Vocational training can include carpentry, landscaping or horticulture, food service, and office skills.

prison industries
prison programs intended to provide productive work and skill development opportunities for offenders, to reduce recidivism and prepare offenders for re-entry into society.

Prison industries also exist—programs intended to provide productive work and skill development opportunities for offenders, to reduce recidivism and prepare offenders for re-entry into society.[24] They are typically legislatively chartered as separate government corporations and report directly to the warden because there is often a requirement that the industry be self-supporting or operate from funds generated from the sale of products. Generally, no tax dollars are used to run the programs, and there is strict accountability of funds.

Correctional administrators report that joint ventures provide meaningful, productive employment that helps to reduce inmate idleness and supplies companies with a readily available and dependable source of labor, as well as the partial return to society of inmate earnings to pay state and federal taxes, offset incarceration costs, contribute to the support of inmates' families, and compensate victims.

Several different types of business relationships exist—the personnel model, the employer model, and the customer model. In the personnel model, prisoners are employed by the state division of correctional industries, which in turn charges the companies a fixed rate for their labor. In the employer model, the company employs the inmates, and private companies own and operate their prison-based businesses, with prison officials providing the space in which the companies operate as well as a qualified labor pool from which the

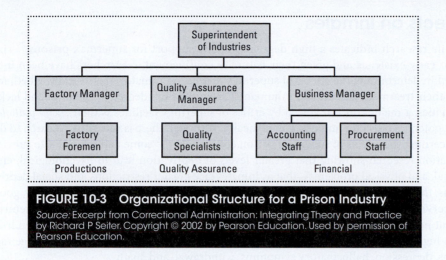

FIGURE 10-3 Organizational Structure for a Prison Industry

Source: Excerpt from *Correctional Administration: Integrating Theory and Practice* by Richard P Seiter. Copyright © 2002 by Pearson Education. Used by permission of Pearson Education.

companies hire employees. In the customer model, the company contracts with the prison to provide a finished product at an agreed-on price. The correctional institution owns and operates the business that employs the inmates. These joint ventures provide challenges and problems: absenteeism and rapid turnover of employees, limited opportunities for training, and logistical concerns. Still, many inmates who participate in these programs show up for their jobs on time, work hard during their shifts, and have been hired by companies after their release.[25]

A typical prison industry organizational structure is presented in Figure 10-3 ■.

▶ Rise of the Supermax Prisons

Definition and Operation

There are **supermax prisons** or their equivalent in more than 40 U.S. states; these institutions provide the most secure levels of custody in prisons, with long-term, segregated housing for inmates who represent the highest security risks.[26] Their method of operations and, as will be seen, the degree of controversy about them among academics justify some discussion about them specifically. To understand what supermax prisons are and how they operate, one can look at the Administrative Maximum prison, or ADX, located in Florence, Colorado.

ADX is the only federal supermax prison in the country (the others are state prisons). It is home to a Who's Who of criminals: "Unabomber" Ted Kaczynski; "Shoe Bomber" Richard Reid; Ramzi Yousef, who plotted the 1993 World Trade Center attack; Oklahoma City bomber Terry Nichols; and Olympic Park bomber Eric Rudolph. ADX is known as the "Alcatraz of the Rockies"; 95 percent of its prisoners are the most violent, disruptive, and escape-prone inmates from other federal prisons. Upon viewing its external aspect for the first time, one immediately sees that this is not the usual prison: Large cables are strung above the basketball courts and track; they are helicopter deterrents.[27]

The supermax prison is known variously in different states as a *special management unit*, *security housing unit (SHU)*, *high-security unit*, *intensive management unit*, or *special control unit*; its operations are quite different inside as well. Supermax inmates rarely leave their cells; in most cases, an hour a day of out-of-cell time is the norm. They eat all of their meals alone in the cells, and typically no group or social activity of any kind is permitted; they are generally denied access to vocational or educational training programs. Inmates can exist for many years separated from the natural world around them.[28]

> **supermax prison**
> institutions providing the most secure levels of custody in prisons, with long-term, segregated housing for inmates who represent the highest security risks.

Effects on Inmates

While research indicates a high degree of public support for supermax prisons,[29] since their early existence and given their nature of confinement, researchers have been interested in determining the effects of supermax prisons on inmates—specifically, whether or not their treatment is cruel and inhumane. Given the high degree of isolation and lack of activities, a major concern voiced by critics of supermax facilities is their *social pathology* and potential effect on inmates' mental health. Although there is very little research to date concerning the effects of supermax prison confinement,[30] some authors point to previous isolation research showing that greater levels of deprivation lead to psychological, emotional, and physical problems—that as inmates face greater restrictions and social deprivations, their level of social withdrawal increases; limiting human contact, autonomy, goods, or services is detrimental to inmates' health and rehabilitative prognoses, and tends to result in depression, hostility, severe anger, sleep disturbances, and anxiety. Women living in a high-security unit have been found to experience claustrophobia, chronic rage reactions, depression, hallucinatory symptoms, withdrawal, and apathy.[31]

Constitutionality

Because of their relatively recent origin, the constitutionality of supermax prisons—whether or not the conditions of confinement constitute cruel and unusual punishment (i.e., that the punishment either inflicts unnecessary or wanton pain or is grossly disproportionate to the severity of the crime)—has been tested in only a few cases. Not surprisingly, most of these challenges assess the harms done by extreme social isolation. The first, *Madrid v. Gomez*,[32] in 1995, addressed conditions of confinement in California's Pelican Bay SHU. The judge pointed to the "stark sterility and unremitting monotony" of the interior of the prison and noted that its image was "hauntingly similar to that of caged felines pacing in a zoo" (p. 1229; however, the judge concluded that he lacked any constitutional basis to close the prison).

In 1999, a federal district court in *Ruiz v. Johnson*[33] looked at Texas's high-security units and concluded that prisoners there "suffer actual psychological harm from the almost total deprivation of human contact, personal property, and human dignity" (p. 913). This judge also opined that such units are virtual incubators of psychoses and that long-term supermax confinement could result in mental illness.

In the most recent case, *Jones 'El v. Berge*,[34] in 2004, a federal district court in Wisconsin concluded that "extremely isolating conditions cause SHU syndrome in relatively healthy prisoners, as well as prisoners who have never suffered a breakdown; supermax is not appropriate for seriously mentally ill inmates." The judge ordered several prisoners to be removed from the supermax facility.

A Boon to Public Safety?

Pizarro et al.[35] examined whether supermax prisons, by housing the worst of the worst inmates, actually enhance public and prison safety. This claim, Pizarro et al. argue, has not been proven; they believe that the potential long-term, negative effects of supermax institutions (as discussed earlier) on inmates will contribute to future violence because the inmates begin to lose touch with reality and exhibit symptoms of psychiatric decomposition. Consequently, they believe that supermax prisons potentially endanger society, beyond regular imprisonment. They also bemoan that although most supermax inmates will one day return to society or to the general prison population, only a few supermax prisons provide inmates with a transitional program (e.g., moving inmates from supermax prison into a maximum-security prison, allowing inmates to participate in group activities, and placing inmates in institutional jobs).[36]

Policy Implications

Given the negative psychological effects of many forms of long-term supermax confinement, researchers such as Craig Haney[37] believe that there is a strong argument for limiting the use of supermax prisons:

> We should take steps to ensure that all such facilities implement the best and most humane of the available practices. Far more careful screening, monitoring, and removal policies should be implemented to ensure that psychologically vulnerable prisoners do not end up there in the first place, and that those who deteriorate once they are immediately identified and transferred. Strict time limits should be placed on the length of time that prisoners are housed in supermax. [T]here are very serious psychological, correctional, legal, and even moral issues at the core that are worthy of serious, continued debate.

▶ Constitutional Rights of Inmates

From Hands Off to Hands On: A Shift in Prisoners' Rights, Law, and Philosophy

Historically, the courts followed a **hands-off policy** regarding prisons, and prisoners' rights were virtually nonexistent as prisoners were deemed as "slaves of the state." Hands-off meant that the judiciary, believing it was neither trained in nor knowledgeable about penology, allowed wardens the freedom and discretion to operate their institutions without outside interference while being fearful of undermining the structure and discipline of the prison.

All that has changed, and the hands-on policy, beginning in the mid-1960s, brought about a change of philosophy in the courts regarding **prisoners' rights**—the collective body of Constitutional rights afforded jail and prison inmates relating to the fundamental human rights and civil liberties, to include the right to complain about prison conditions and treatment. In sum, prison inmates now retain all the rights of free citizens except those restrictions necessary for their orderly confinement or to provide safety in the prison community.

In subsequent sections, we discuss several U.S. Supreme Court decisions that spelled the demise of the hands-off era, in which it was established that no "iron curtain" was erected between the inmates and the Constitution and that they were not "wholly stripped of constitutional protections" (see the discussion of *Wolff v. McDonnell*). These decisions improved the everyday lives of prison and jail inmates and reformed correctional administration. Specifically, basic rights extended to inmates included greater access to the courts, to appeal their convictions and conditions of confinement; greater freedom of religion expression; restricting mail censorship by prison officials; and granting them due process for the purpose of inmate disciplinary proceedings.

> **hands-off policy** a practice by judges, in an era when they believed they had neither training nor knowledge concerning penology, allowing wardens the freedom to operate prisons as they saw fit.

> **prisoners' rights** the collective body of Constitutional rights afforded jail and prison inmates relating to the fundamental human rights and civil liberties.

A "Slave of the State"

Ruffin v. Commonwealth (1871)

An excellent beginning point for this overview of significant court decisions concerning inmates' rights is the 1871 case of *Ruffin v. Commonwealth*.[38] There, the Virginia Supreme Court held that a prisoner "had, as a consequence of his crime, not only forfeited his liberty, but also all his personal rights except those that the law in its humanity accords to him." The *Ruffin* court even declared inmates to be "slaves of the state," mentioned earlier, losing all their citizenship rights, including the right to complain about living conditions.

This view certainly does not reflect the law at present and may never have been entirely accurate. For example, in 1948, in *Price v. Johnston*,[39] the Supreme Court declared that "lawful incarceration brings about the necessary withdrawal or limitation of many privileges and rights," which indicated a much softer view than that stated in *Ruffin*; furthermore, "many" privileges indicate less than "all," and it was clear that the due process and equal protection clauses did apply to prisoners to some extent.

Prison Regulations and Laws Vis-à-vis Inmates' Constitutional Rights

Turner v. Safley[40] (1987)

Prison inmates brought a class action suit challenging the reasonableness of certain regulations of the Missouri Division of Corrections. Here, the Supreme Court took the opportunity to modify previous standards—such as "compelling state interest," "least restrictive means," and "rational relationship"—used to determine whether prison regulations and laws violate constitutional rights of inmates. In *Turner v. Safley*, the Court said that a prison regulation that impinges on inmates' constitutional rights is valid if it is reasonably related to *legitimate penological interests* (emphasis added). This decision gave prison authorities more power; all they must do is prove that a prison regulation is reasonably related to a legitimate penological interest in order for that regulation to be valid even if a constitutional right is infringed.

Legal Remedy and Access to the Courts

Cooper v. Pate[41] (1964)

One of the earliest prison cases, it is significant because the Supreme Court first recognized the use of Title 42 of the United States Code Section 1983 as a legal remedy for inmates. (Section 1983, discussed thoroughly in Chapter 14, concerns a public officer's violation of a prisoner's constitutional rights while acting "under color" of law.) Cooper, an inmate at the Illinois State Penitentiary, sued prison officials under Section 1983, alleging that he was unconstitutionally punished (i.e., placed in solitary confinement) and denied permission to purchase certain Muslim religious publications. Both the federal district court and the circuit court of appeals upheld Cooper's punishment but the Supreme Court reversed their ruling, finding that he was entitled to relief—and that he could use Section 1983.

Johnson v. Avery[42] (1969)

This was one of the first prison decisions that involved an alleged violation of a constitutional right—here, the right of access to the courts. Johnson, a Tennessee prisoner, was disciplined for violating a prison regulation that prohibited inmates from assisting other prisoners in preparing writs. The Supreme Court acknowledged that "writ writers" like Johnson are sometimes a menace to prison discipline, and their petitions are often so unskillful as to be a burden on the courts receiving them. However, because the State of Tennessee provided no "reasonable alternative" to assist illiterate or poorly educated inmates in preparing petitions for postconviction relief, the Supreme Court held that the state could not bar inmates from furnishing such assistance to other prisoners. However, what constituted "reasonable alternatives" to writ writers was not explained.

Bounds v. Smith[43] (1977)

This was another court-access decision, clarifying *Johnson v. Avery*. In *Bounds*—where North Carolina inmates alleged denial of reasonable access by having only one library in the prison (which was inadequate in nature)—the Court went further, saying that prisoners have a constitutional right to adequate law libraries or assistance from persons trained in the law. This case also listed several possible alternatives that prisons could use for providing inmates such access, including training inmates as paralegals to work under lawyers' supervision; using paraprofessionals and law students to advise inmates; hiring lawyers on a part-time consultant basis; and having voluntary programs through bar associations, whereby lawyers visit the prisons to consult with inmates.

First Amendment

Cruz v. Beto[44] (1972) (Religious Practices)

This landmark case clarified the right of inmates to exercise their religious beliefs, even if they did not belong to what are considered mainstream or traditional religions. Cruz, a Buddhist, was not allowed to use the prison chapel and was placed in solitary confinement on a diet of bread and water for sharing his religious material with other prisoners. He sued under Section 1983, alleging violations of the First Amendment right to freedom of religion. The Supreme Court held that inmates with unconventional religious beliefs must be given a reasonable opportunity to exercise those beliefs.

Procunier v. Martinez[45] (1974) (Mail Censorship)

Here, the Supreme Court invalidated prison mail censorship regulations that permitted authorities to hold back or to censor mail to and from prisoners whenever they thought that the letters "unduly complain[ed]," "express[ed] inflammatory views or beliefs," or were "defamatory" or "otherwise inappropriate." The Court based its ruling not on the rights of the prisoner but instead on the free-world recipient's right to communicate with the prisoner, either by sending or by receiving mail. The Court held that the regulation of mail must further an important interest unrelated to the suppression of expression; regulation must be shown to further the substantial interest of security, order, and rehabilitation; and it must not be utilized simply to censor opinions or other expressions. Furthermore, a prison's restriction on mail must be no greater than is necessary to the protection of the security interest involved.

Fourth Amendment

Bell v. Wolfish[46] (1979) (Searches of Body Cavities and Cells, Other Conditions of Confinement)

This is one of the few cases decided by the Supreme Court concerning the rights of *pretrial* detainees housed in local jails. Here, the Court in effect said that jail officials may run their institutions the same way prisons are managed. New York City's Metropolitan Correctional Center, within a short time of opening, experienced overcrowding and began double-bunking inmates in rooms built for single occupancy (later). Guards also conducted searches of inmates' cells in their absence, prohibited inmates from receiving hardcover books that were not mailed directly by publishers or bookstores, prohibited inmates' receipt of personal items from visitors, and employed body cavity searches of inmates following contact visits. Inmates sued and alleged several constitutional violations, but the Supreme Court held none of these practices to be unconstitutional "punishment," saying that these restrictions and practices were reasonable responses to legitimate security concerns and noting that they were of only limited duration. (Note that in a 1981 case specifically challenging the use of double bunking, *Rhodes v. Chapman*,[47] the Court held that double bunking of prisoners does not constitute cruel and unusual punishment as long as the conditions of confinement are not bad.)

Eighth Amendment

Estelle v. Gamble[48] (1976) (Medical Care)

Although Gamble lost in this case, it was the first major prison medical treatment case decided by the Supreme Court and set the standards by which such cases are determined. Here, the Court coined the term *deliberate indifference*, which occurs when the serious medical needs of prisoners involve the unnecessary and wanton infliction of pain. Examples the Court gave are injecting penicillin with the knowledge that the prisoner is allergic to it, refusing to administer a prescribed painkiller, and requiring a prisoner to stand despite the contrary instructions of a surgeon. Gamble, an inmate of the Texas Department of Corrections, claimed that he received cruel and unusual punishment because of inadequate treatment of a back injury sustained while he was engaged in prison work. The Court did not find a constitutional violation in his case, however, because medical personnel saw him on 17 occasions during a 3-month period, and treated his injury and other problems.

Fourteenth Amendment

Wolff v. McDonnell[49] (1974) (Due Process)

This case is significant because, for the first time, the Supreme Court acknowledged that inmates are entitled to certain due process rights—"fundamental fairness"—during prison disciplinary proceedings. McDonnell and other inmates at a Nebraska prison alleged, among other things, that disciplinary proceedings at the prison violated their due process rights. To establish misconduct, prison officials required a preliminary conference, where the prisoner was orally informed of the charge; a conduct report was prepared and a hearing was held before the prison's disciplinary body; and the inmate could ask questions of the charging party. The Court said, now rather famously, "There is no iron curtain drawn between the Constitution and the prisons of this country, a prisoner is not wholly stripped of constitutional protections, and prisoners must be given the following due process rights":

- Advance written notice of charges no less than 24 hours before appearing before the hearing committee.
- A written statement by the fact finders as to the evidence relied on and reasons for the disciplinary action.
- Ability to call witnesses and to present documentary evidence in the inmate's defense (if this did not jeopardize institutional safety or correctional goals).
- Use of counsel substitutes (e.g., a friend or staff member) when the inmate is illiterate or when complex issues require such assistance.
- An impartial prison disciplinary board.

See Exhibit 10.2 for a description of the world's worst prisons.

EXHIBIT 10.2

THE WORLD'S WORST PRISONS[50]

Certainly any attempt to catalogue the worst prisons in the world will be open to serious debate, and the following list of five such prisons is no exception; however, as will be seen, these are included (in no particular order) for very good reasons:

- **La Sant, France:** This, the last remaining prison in Paris, was established in 1867. Its mattresses are

infested with lice; because prisoners can only take two cold showers per week, skin diseases are common. Overcrowded cells, infestation of vermin, and inmate rape are also common. Its rate of suicide attempts each year is estimated to be almost five times higher than that of California's prison system. Its conditions have been condemned by the U.N. Human Rights Committee and the country's own minister of justice.

- **Black Beach Prison, Equatorial Guinea:** Amnesty International has described life in this prison as a slow, lingering death sentence. Torture, burning, beatings, and rape are systematic and brutal. Because food rations are minimal, with prisoners sometimes going up to 6 days without food, starving to death is common. Amnesty also reports that inmates are routinely denied access to medical treatment.

- **Vladimir Central Prison, Russia:** Constructed by Catherine the Great to house political prisoners, during the Soviet era the prison became synonymous with persecution of political dissidents. Today the prison also functions as a museum for the public. Visitors are not allowed into the penitentiary, where cells often contain six prisoners and reports of abuse by guards are common. HIV and tuberculosis are also rampant.

- **Camp 1391, Israel:** Officially, this prison does not exist, but descriptions of its conditions have been validated. Even the Red Cross is banned from visiting, and prisoners typically have no idea where they are being kept or when they might be released—a fact that former inmates say is the worst torture of all. Sexual humiliation and even rape are reportedly used as interrogation techniques.

- **The North Korean Gulag:** Up to 200,000 prisoners are held in these detention centers, and one houses more than 50,000 inmates. Entire families and even neighborhoods are sent here as punishment for the infraction of one member. In some camps, up to 25 percent of the prisoners die every year, only to be replaced by new inmates. Most of the camps are located along the North Korean border with China and Russia, and thus prisoners are forced to endure harsh weather conditions as well as inhumane treatment.

Again, any such list is debatable given harsh prison conditions in many places around the world; prisons and/or labor camps in China, Thailand, Cuba, Venezuela, Syria, Africa, and other foreign venues could easily have been included.[51]

▶ Civil Rights of Institutionalized Persons

The **Civil Rights of Institutionalized Persons Act** (CRIPA) of 1980 is a federal law[52] broadly enacted to protect the rights of people in state or local facilities who are mentally ill, disabled, or chronically ill or handicapped, and are residing in a jail, prison, or other correctional facility or pretrial detention facility. Juveniles are also covered, to be free from violent residents and abusive staff members and not be excessively isolated or unreasonably restrained. They must also receive medical and mental health care; be educated, and be granted access to legal counsel, family communication, recreation, and exercise.

> **Civil Rights of Institutionalized Persons Act** a federal law protecting the rights of people in state or local correctional facilities who are mentally ill, disabled, or handicapped.

The U.S. Department of Justice claims to now have open CRIPA matters in more than half the states.[53] Potential CRIPA laws violations are investigated and prosecuted by the U.S. Department of Justice Civil Rights Division (CRD). If a pattern of civil violations is uncovered, the facility will be informed of the alleged violations and the evidence supporting the findings, as well as what must minimally be done to correct the violations.

Following are three examples of recent jail- and treatment-related CRIPA investigations[54]:

- *Erie County, New York (agreement reached, June 2010):* A complaint was filed regarding conditions at several correctional facilities, alleging unconstitutional conditions that included: staff-on-inmate violence, inmate-on-inmate violence, sexual misconduct between staff and inmates, sexual misconduct among inmates, inadequate systems to prevent suicide and self-injurious behavior, inadequate medical and mental health care, and serious deficiencies in environmental health and safety. The agreement also addressed the County's inadequate system of suicide prevention and self-injurious behavior of holding center inmates, requiring officials to implement measures to ensure that holding center inmates are protected from suicide hazards.

- *Lake County, Indiana (agreement reached, December 2010):* Unlawful conditions of confinement were corrected after an investigation of the jail uncovered systemic deficiencies, including a suicide rate that was more than five times the national average. Conditions violated the constitutional rights of approximately 1,000 male and female inmates confined there, including failure to protect individuals from harm (particularly involving suicide risk); failure to identify and treat individuals' psychiatric disabilities; failure to provide adequate medical services and fire safety; and failure to adequately maintain the physical plant of the facility, thereby endangering both staff and inmates.

- *Delaware Mental Health (agreement reached, July 2011):* An investigation concluded that the state's mental health services system failed to provide services to individuals with serious mental illness in the most integrated setting appropriate to their needs, as required by the ADA. These failures were needlessly prolonging institutionalization of many individuals who could have been adequately served in community settings. Delaware will prevent unnecessary hospitalization by expanding and deepening its crisis intervention system and providing intensive community supports, such as assertive community treatment and intensive case management, rehabilitation services, and improved family and peer support systems.

▶ Inmate Litigation

Prior to the Twenty-First Century: "Hair-trigger" Suing

The volume of inmate litigation increased significantly following the aforementioned *Cooper v. Pate* decision in 1964. In 1980, inmates in state and federal correctional institutions filed 23,287 petitions alleging both civil and criminal violations of their rights and seeking compensatory damages, injunctions, and property claims.[55] By 1990, the number of such petitions had swollen to nearly 43,000, and more than 64,000 petitions were filed in 1996[56] (a more contemporary view of inmate filings, since the passage of the PLRA of 1995, is provided in the "Has PLRA Served its Purpose" section later).

Prisoners sued primarily because they were either unwilling to accept their conviction or wished to harass their keepers.[57] Inmate litigants tend to fall into one of two categories. First are those who file a single suit during their entire period of incarceration (usually requiring the assistance of others to do it); one study found that 71 percent of all litigants filed only one action but accounted for about half of all litigation.[58] The other group is composed of inmates who make law a prison career—the so-called jailhouse lawyers or writ writers.[59]

Although in past decades the media brought to light many abuses inside prisons, in the 1980s and 1990s media attention began turning in another direction: reports of trivial and **frivolous lawsuits**—those actions filed by parties or attorneys who are aware they are without merit, due to a lack of legal basis or argument for the alleged claim—by inmates. Following are some examples:

frivolous lawsuit
an action filed by a party or attorney who is aware it is without merit, due to a lack of legal basis or argument for the alleged claim.

- A death row inmate sued correction officials for taking away his Gameboy electronic game.
- A prisoner sued demanding L.A. Gear or Reebok "Pumps" instead of Converse.

- An inmate sued because he was served chunky instead of smooth peanut butter.

- An inmate claimed it was cruel and unusual punishment that he was forced to listen to his unit manager's country and Western music.

- An inmate claimed $1 million in damages because his ice cream melted (the judge ruled that the "right to eat ice cream was clearly not within the contemplation" of our nation's forefathers).[60]

Such examples of litigation caused an uproar over frivolous civil right lawsuits brought by inmates. Furthermore, the expense of defending against such lawsuits, coupled with the fact that the United States has the world's largest and costliest prison system,[61] combined to foster public resentment against prisons and prisoners.

Of course, not all lawsuits against prison administrators concerning inmate living conditions and treatment are frivolous. For example, in August 2006 Timothy Joe Souders, a 21-year-old mentally ill young man held in the Southern Michigan Correctional Facility in Jackson, died after 5 days of horrific abuse and neglect. He was held for 5 days in isolation, naked, shackled by his arms and legs to a concrete slab in temperatures exceeding 100 degrees, and forced to lie in his own urine. His family settled for $3.25 million.[62] A federal judge called Souders's death "predictable and preventable," and cited numerous documented and appalling instances of nontreatment, including an inmate who died of untreated cancer. He was found lying in excrement in his cell, after having lost 60 pounds from a "hunger strike."[63]

The Prison Litigation Reform Act

Four Main Parts

By the late 1980s, the courts were displaying more tolerance for minor violations of prisoners' constitutional rights, as exemplified by the following three cases:

1. *Turner v. Safley* (1987),[64] discussed earlier, in which the Supreme Court stated that when a prison regulation impinges on inmates' constitutional rights, "the regulation is valid if it is reasonably related to legitimate penological interests."

2. *Wilson v. Seiter* (1991),[65] which stated that when an inmate claims that the conditions of his or her confinement violate the Eighth Amendment, he or she must show a culpable state of mind on the part of prison officials.

3. *Sandin v. Conner* (1995),[66] which emphasized the Supreme Court's desire to give "deference and flexibility to state officials trying to maintain a volatile environment." This decision made it "more difficult to bring constitutional suits challenging prison management."[67]

Then, in April 1996, the **Prison Litigation Reform Act** of 1995 was enacted.[68] The PLRA has been praised by proponents as necessary "to provide for appropriate remedies for prison condition lawsuits, to discourage frivolous and abusive prison lawsuits, and for other purposes."[69]

The PLRA has four main parts[70]:

- **Exhaustion of administrative remedies.** Before inmates can file a lawsuit, they must try to resolve their complaint through the prison's grievance procedure, which usually includes giving a written description of their complaint to a prison official; if the prison requires additional steps, such as appealing to the warden, then the inmate must also follow those steps.

- **Filing fees.** All prisoners must pay court filing fees in full. If they do not have the money up front, they can pay the fee over time through monthly deductions from their prison

> **Prison Litigation Reform Act** a law providing remedies for prison condition lawsuits and to discourage frivolous and abusive prison lawsuits.

commissary account. A complex statutory formula requires the indigent prisoner to pay an initial fee of 20 percent of the greater of the prisoner's average balance or the average deposits to the account for the preceding 6 months.

- *Three-strikes provision.* Each lawsuit or appeal that an inmate files that is dismissed for being frivolous, malicious, or not stating a proper claim counts as a *strike*. After an inmate receives three strikes, he or she cannot file another lawsuit *in forma pauperis*; that is, he or she cannot file another lawsuit unless he or she pays the entire court filing fee up front (an exception is made if the inmate is at risk of suffering serious physical injury in the immediate future, described in the next point). An appeal of a dismissed action that is dismissed is a separate strike, and even dismissals that occurred prior to the effective date of the PLRA count as strikes.

- *Physical injury requirement.* An inmate cannot file a lawsuit for mental or emotional injury unless he or she can also show physical injury. (The courts differ in their evaluation of what constitutes sufficient harm to qualify as physical injury.)

Has PLRA Served Its Purpose?

According to data provided by the federal courts, in 1995—the year before implementation of the Act—there were 63,550 total prisoner petitions; in 1997, the first year following the implementation of the Act, there were 62,966 petitions, or 8 percent fewer.[71] Then, in 2009, there were 10,566 such petitions—an *83 percent* decrease since 1997.[72] Clearly, prisoner petitions to the U.S. District Courts have significantly diminished in number.

▶ Jails as Organizations

Across the United States, approximately 2,850 local jails are administered, which together will house about 745,000 inmates per year.[73] Their organization and hierarchical levels are determined by several factors: size, budget, level of crowding, local views on punishment and treatment, and even the levels of training and education of the jail administrator. An organizational structure for a jail serving a population of about 250,000 is suggested in Figure 10-4 ∎.

The administration of jails is frequently one of the major tasks of county sheriffs. Several writers have concluded that sheriffs and police personnel see themselves primarily as law enforcers first and view the responsibility of organizing and operating a jail as an unwelcome task.[74] Therefore, their approach is often said to be at odds with advanced corrections philosophy and trends.

Podular/Direct Supervision Jails

Rationale and Expanding Use

direct supervision jail a type of design where cells are arranged in podular fashion, have an open dayroom area, and correctional officers are close to and interact with the inmates.

As noted previously, in the past, the federal courts have at times become more willing to hear inmate allegations of constitutional violations ranging from inadequate heating, lighting, and ventilation to the censorship of mail. One of every five cases filed in federal courts was on behalf of prisoners,[75] and 20 percent of all jails were a party in a pending lawsuit.[76]

Court-ordered pressures to improve jail conditions afforded an opportunity for administrators to explore new ideas and designs; therefore, over the past several decades and in response to the deluge of lawsuits concerning jail conditions, many local jurisdictions constructed what is known as the **direct supervision jail**: where inmates' cells are arranged around a common area—in podular fashion, with no physical barriers between

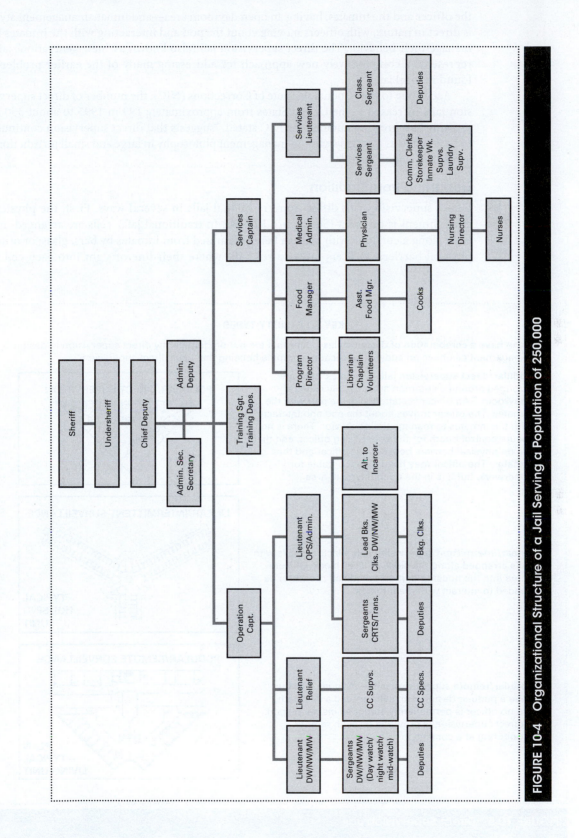

FIGURE 10-4 Organizational Structure of a Jail Serving a Population of 250,000

245

▼

the officer and the inmates, having an open dayroom area—and inmate management style is direct in nature, with officers moving about the pod and interacting with the inmates to manage their behavior. The direct supervision jail (also known as "new-generation" jail) represents a comparatively new approach for addressing many of the earlier problems found in local jails.[77]

According to the National Institute of Corrections (NIC), the number of direct supervision jails increased in the United States from approximately 199 in 1995 to about 350 at present. This growing number, the NIC stated, "suggests that direct supervision continues to be adopted as a design style and management philosophy in large and small jurisdictions across the United States."[78]

Departing from Tradition

Direct supervision jails differ from traditional jails in several ways. First, the physical environment is different (See Figure 10-5 ■). In traditional jails, cells are arranged linearly along a corridor, with officers being separated from inmates by bars, glass, or other physical barriers. Officers must patrol halls where their line of sight into each cell is

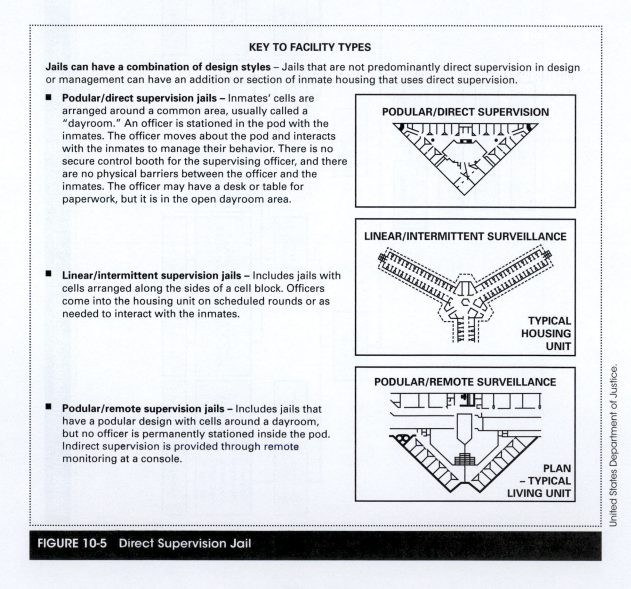

KEY TO FACILITY TYPES

Jails can have a combination of design styles – Jails that are not predominantly direct supervision in design or management can have an addition or section of inmate housing that uses direct supervision.

■ **Podular/direct supervision jails** – Inmates' cells are arranged around a common area, usually called a "dayroom." An officer is stationed in the pod with the inmates. The officer moves about the pod and interacts with the inmates to manage their behavior. There is no secure control booth for the supervising officer, and there are no physical barriers between the officer and the inmates. The officer may have a desk or table for paperwork, but it is in the open dayroom area.

PODULAR/DIRECT SUPERVISION

■ **Linear/intermittent supervision jails** – Includes jails with cells arranged along the sides of a cell block. Officers come into the housing unit on scheduled rounds or as needed to interact with the inmates.

LINEAR/INTERMITTENT SURVEILLANCE

TYPICAL HOUSING UNIT

■ **Podular/remote supervision jails** – Includes jails that have a podular design with cells around a dayroom, but no officer is permanently stationed inside the pod. Indirect supervision is provided through remote monitoring at a console.

PODULAR/REMOTE SURVEILLANCE

PLAN – TYPICAL LIVING UNIT

United States Department of Justice.

FIGURE 10-5 Direct Supervision Jail

severely restricted, and officers can observe what is happening inside a cell only when they are almost directly in front of it. In the direct supervision jail, inmates are separated into relatively small groups (usually 50 or fewer), housed in self-contained living units including several one- to two-person cells, a day room, and recreation space. These units, or "pods," usually are triangular or wedge shaped so that jail officers have a direct line of sight into all areas of the pod at all times. The furnishings in the living units also differ and generally include carpeting, porcelain lavatories, moveable furniture that may be padded or plastic, and other "soft" fixtures. The direct supervision philosophy has officers stationed within the living area with no physical barriers to separate them from inmates. In these units, officers maintain a constant physical presence, but they also interact extensively with inmates.[79]

Because of their constant physical and close presence, correctional officers (COs) in direct supervision jails must use active observation in order to gather information about what is occurring in the module, to gauge sources of conflict or tension, and to identify and react to situations before they escalate into serious problems. They must also develop a higher degree of interpersonal skills and creativity in managing inmates. Even minor conflicts and problems must be proactively addressed within the pod. The COs must also be fair with their discipline, and treat inmates with respect and dignity. Both formal and informal sanctions should be used so that punishment meted out is commensurate with the gravity of the infraction. Inmates should also be told the reason for their punishment.[80]

Most evaluations of direct supervision jails have been encouraging. Researchers and practitioners have reported reductions in inmate–inmate violence and assaults against jail officers and staff members[81]; inmates have also reported having more positive attitudes about the officers than inmates in more traditional facilities, and direct supervision officers have reported feeling less hostile toward the inmates.[82]

► A New Supreme Court Decree: Collecting DNA at Point of Arrest

Employees of local jails will be kept somewhat busier and have more responsibility after June 2013, when the U.S. Supreme Court held that a DNA swab may be taken from anyone arrested for a crime of violence. The Court's majority rationalized the decision on the grounds that, like fingerprinting and photographing, taking and analyzing a cheek swab of the arrestee's DNA is a legitimate police booking procedure under the Fourth Amendment.

Getting DNA swabs from arrestees was already a common practice in all 50 states; however, what set this decision apart was the Court's allowing DNA collection before conviction and without a judge issuing a warrant.[83]

► Corrections Accreditation

Like police organizations, as discussed in Chapter 4, corrections organizations may achieve the status of accreditation by meeting national standards through a series of reviews, evaluations, audits, and hearings. Since 1978, the American Correctional Association (ACA) has promulgated standards generally covering administrative and fiscal controls, staff training and development, physical plant, safety and emergency procedures, sanitation, food service, and rules and discipline. The ACA utilizes a 28-member private, nonprofit body, the Commission on Accreditation for Corrections, to render accreditation decisions.[84]

There are 21 different sets or manuals of accreditation standards covering all types of correctional facilities and programs, including state and federal adult institutions, juvenile facilities, probation and parole agencies, and health care and electronic monitoring programs. In order for a state or federal adult corrections institution to be accredited, it must meet 100 percent of 62 mandatory standards as well as 90 percent of 468 nonmandatory standards.[85]

As with the police, there are several benefits to be realized for corrections agencies wishing to become accredited: determining the facility or program's strengths and weaknesses, identifying obtainable goals, implementing state-of-the-art policies and procedures, establishing specific guidelines for daily operations, aiding in defending against frivolous lawsuits, and ensuring a higher level of staff professionalism and morale.[86]

▶ Probation and Parole Agencies as Organizations

Community corrections originated in the years following World War II, when returning veterans encountered adjustment problems as they attempted to re-enter civilian life.[87] It has also been stated that community corrections is "the last bastion of discretion in the criminal justice system."[88] Community corrections are typically viewed as a humane, logical, and effective approach for working with and changing criminal offenders.[89]

Today there are about 4.8 million adults under community supervision in the United States—3.97 million who are on probation (the lowest number since 2001) and about 850,000 on parole.[90]

Agency Organization, Armed and Sworn Status of Officers

What follows is a secondary analysis of a national survey by the American Probation and Parole Association. Specifically, the survey included questions concerning how adult/juvenile probation and parole agencies in the 50 states are organizationally structured (e.g., under which branch of government they function, to whom the administrators report), and whether or not the probation and parole officers are armed and possess **peace officer** powers (note: the definition of a "peace officer" can be quite broad, but normally includes those persons having arrest authority either with a warrant or based on probable cause).[91]

> **peace officer** those persons having arrest authority either with a warrant or based on probable cause.

- *Adult probation:* 32 (64%) of the state agencies are under the executive branch, and 13 (26%) are under the judicial branch; 5 (10%) are organized under an agency that is either a combination of these or a state or county agency.

- *Juvenile probation:* 21 (42%) of the state agencies are organized under the executive branch, and 19 (38%) are under the judicial branch; 10 (20%) are either a combination of these or under a state or county agency.

- *Adult parole:* 43 (86%) of the state agencies are organized under the executive branch, and 2 (4%) are under the judicial branch; 4 (8%) are either a combination of these or under a state or county agency; one state has abolished parole.

- *Juvenile parole* (generally, aftercare plans and activities for institutionalized juvenile offenders that assist them to transition back into the community): 39 (78%) of the state agencies are organized under the executive branch, and 6 (12%) are under the judicial branch; 5 (10%) are either a combination of these or under a state or county agency.

Regarding the arming of these officers, 18 states (36%) do not authorize their officers to carry arms, while 19 (38%) do so authorize; the remainder of the states are optional or allow being armed if approved by the governing body or supervisor. This continues to be an oft-debated topic in corrections. Traditionalists believe that carrying a firearm contributes to an atmosphere of distrust between the client and the officer; enforcement-oriented officers, conversely, view a firearm as an additional tool to protect themselves from the risk associated with violent, serious, or high-risk offenders.[92] The latter view is understandable, given that officers must make home and employment visits in the neighborhoods in which offenders live (some of which are very unsafe), and officers must often revoke offenders' freedom.

Some states classify probation and parole officers as peace officers and grant them the authority to carry a firearm both on and off duty.[93] Some authors believe that officers should not be required to carry a firearm if they are opposed to arming, and that providing an option allows for a better officer/assignment match.[94] In sum, it would seem that the administrator's decision concerning arming should focus on need, officer safety, and local laws and policies.

Probation and parole officers do not possess peace officer authority in 24 (48%) of the states, while they are authorized such powers in 26 (52%) states. Note, however, that in 8 (16%) of those states that grant officers such powers, it is granted only to *adult* probation and parole officers, not to those who work with juveniles.[95]

Probation Systems

Types of Systems

Figure 10-6 ■ depicts an organizational structure for a regional probation and parole organization. **Probation**—where a court places a person on supervision in the community, generally in lieu of incarceration—is the most frequently used sanction; it costs offenders their privacy and self-determination and usually includes some element of the other sanctions: jail time, fines, restitution, or community service.[96] Probation in the United States is administered by more than 2,000 different agencies. Its organization is a patchwork that defies simple explanation. In about three-fourths of the states, adult probation is part of the executive branch of state government.[97] In contrast, more than half of the agencies providing juvenile probation services are administered in juvenile courts on the local level.[98]

probation where a court places an offender on supervision in the community, generally in lieu of incarceration.

According to Howard Abadinsky, the administration of probation systems can be separated into six categories[99]:

1. *Juvenile.* Separate probation services for juveniles are administered on a county, municipal, or state level.

2. *Municipal.* Independent probation units are administered by the lower courts under state laws and guidelines.

3. *County.* Under laws and guidelines established by the state, a county operates its own probation agency.

4. *State.* One agency administers a central probation system, which provides services throughout the state.

5. *State combined.* Probation and parole services are administered on a statewide basis by one agency.

6. *Federal.* Probation is administered as an arm of the federal courts.

This patchwork nature of probation systems has raised two central organizational questions concerning the administration of probation services: Should probation be part of the

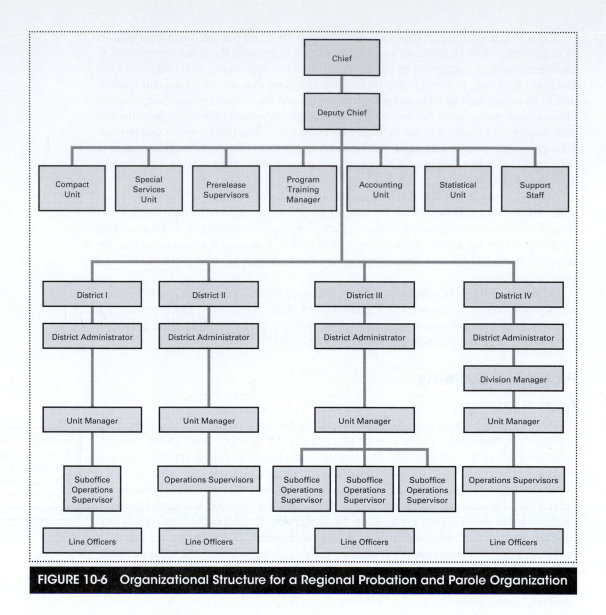

FIGURE 10-6 Organizational Structure for a Regional Probation and Parole Organization

judicial or the executive branch of government? Does the lack of uniformity in administering probation make justice less equitable statewide?[100] These important and lingering issues were first considered nearly 40 years ago by the President's Commission.[101]

Although it was shown previously that few probation/parole agencies are organized and governed at the county level, Abadinsky argued that probation administered by the judiciary on a county level promotes diversity:

> Innovative programming can be implemented more easily in a county agency because it has a shorter line of bureaucratic control than would a statewide agency. A county agency can more easily adapt to change, and the successful programs of one agency can more easily be adopted by other probation departments and unsuccessful programs avoided. Although the judiciary is nominally responsible for administering probation, the day-to-day operations are in the hands of a professional administrator—the chief probation officer.[102]

Systems Theory

As with the administration of police, court, or prison organizations, the probation department administrator's goals may affect the services provided to the client, which in turn may have an impact on the client's request for services. This systematic interaction between an organization's resources and structure and the community has been referred to as its "sociotechnical environment,"[103] meaning that the principles of the system are organized to execute the basic production technologies of the organization.

Each probation administrator needs to recognize that the organization is a system of inputs, processes, and outputs (discussed in Chapter 2). For probation, inputs are clients coming into the office for counseling and supervision (the processes); outputs are the probationer's obtaining employment, acquiring a skill, observing a curfew, and so on. This understanding of probation, using systems theory, provides a means of learning how probation departments function and interact with their environment and of examining the resources, activities, and outcomes in a way that can identify the goals, describe the day-to-day activities, and link the department's activities to resources and outcomes.

According to systems theory, probation may be conceptualized as a network of interwoven resources, activities, and outcomes.[104] According to Hardyman, resources include the probation department's funding level, goals, policies and procedures, organizational structure, and caseload; the probation staff's characteristics; the services available to probationers; and the rates of unemployment, poverty, and crime in the county. Activities are supervision techniques, rewards, leadership style, contacts, and direct and indirect services provided by the probation department. Outcomes, according to systems theory, are the number of probationers who were arrested, incarcerated, and/or cited for a technical violation during the follow-up period, as well as the needs of probationers that were considered.[105] See Exhibit 10.3 for a description of Hawaii's Project HOPE.

EXHIBIT 10.3

A "BEST PRACTICE" IN PROBATION: HAWAII'S PROJECT HOPE

A probation reform program developed in 2004 in Hawaii has resulted in an 80 percent drop in positive drug tests and in recidivism. The backbone of the program is simple: Rather than let small problems pile up, closely monitored probationers receive immediate punishment, usually a brief stint in jail. The Hawaii model, known as HOPE, or Hawaii's Opportunity Probation Enforcement, has now been implemented in five states, while also being established in cities in four states. The U.S. Department of Justice also is experimenting with HOPE.

According to program founder Judge Steve Alm, "This is Parenting 101, Personal Responsibility 101. One reason it works is because even the offenders think it's fair. They used to go along with infraction piling on top of infraction, over and over with no consequences.

Now there is some jail every time, though it's brief—it is swift, certain and proportionate. They get it."

HOPE's stated goals are reductions in drug use, new crimes, and incarceration. The National Institute of Justice commissioned a study to determine whether or not those goals were met. According to the study's authors:

Those goals have been achieved. Probationers assigned to HOPE had large reductions in positive drug tests and missed appointments, and were significantly less likely to be arrested during follow-up at 3 months, 6 months, and 12 months. They averaged approximately the same number of days in jail for probation violations, serving more but shorter terms. They spent about one-third as many days in prison on revocations or new convictions.[106]

Parole Systems

Models for Providing Services

parole where an offender is conditionally released from prison to serve the remaining portion of a criminal sentence in the community.

The administration of **parole**—for offenders who are conditionally released from prison to serve the remaining portion of their sentence in the community—is much less complex than that of probation because parole services are administered centrally on a statewide basis.[107] (It should also be noted that in about 20 states, probation officers also serve as parole officers; thus, much of the information presented in the previous section applies to parole as well.) One state agency administers the parole function on a statewide basis, except that in a number of states, parolees from a local jail come under the supervision of a county probation and parole department.[108]

A parole agency can provide three basic services: parole release, parole supervision, and executive clemency. In a number of states that have abolished parole release (such as California), parole officers continue to supervise offenders released by the prison on good time (reduction of sentence through good behavior).

The National Advisory Commission on Criminal Justice Standards and Goals delineated two basic models for administering parole services:

1. *The independent model.* A parole board is responsible for making release (parole) determinations as well as supervising persons released on parole (or good time). It is independent of any other state agency and reports directly to the governor.

2. *The consolidated model.* The parole board is a semiautonomous agency within a large department that also administers correctional institutions. Supervision of persons released on parole (or good time) is under the direction of the commissioner of corrections, not the parole board.[109]

Both models sometimes combine probation services with parole services in a single statewide agency.

The President's Commission summarized the advantages of the *independent* model[110]:

1. The parole board is in the best position to promote the idea of parole and to generate public support and acceptance of it. Because the board is accountable for parole failures, it should be responsible for supervising parolees.

2. The parole board that is in direct control of administering parole services can evaluate and adjust the system more effectively.

3. Supervision by the parole board and its officers properly divorces parole release and parolees from the correctional institution.

4. An independent parole board in charge of its own services is in the best position to present its own budget request to the legislature.

Conversely, the Commission summarized the advantages of including both parole services and institutions in a *consolidated* department of corrections as follows[111]:

1. The correctional process is a continuum; all staff, both institutional and parole, are under a single administration rather than divided, which avoids competition for public funds and friction in policies.

2. A consolidated correctional department has consistent administration, including staff selection and supervision.

3. Parole boards are ineffective in performing administrative functions; their major focus should be on case decision, not on day-to-day field operations.

4. Community-based programs that fall between institutions and parole, such as work release, can best be handled by a single centralized administration.

Clearly, the trend in this country, beginning in the late 1960s, has been in the direction of consolidation.

Summary

This chapter presented an overview of corrections as a booming industry; it discussed prison and jail organization; the rise of, and controversies surrounding, supermax prisons; selected inmate rights under the First, Fourth, Eighth, and Fourteenth Amendments as set forth by the U.S. Supreme Court; inmate litigation; and the organization of probation and parole agencies.

The chapter also demonstrated how times have changed with respect to the manner in which correctional facilities are organized, while providing a glimpse into some of the issues and problems that challenge administrators, some of which are further examined in the following chapter.

Key Terms and Concepts

Central office 230
Civil Rights of Institutionalized
  Persons Act 241
Direct supervision jail 244
Frivolous lawsuits 242

Hands-off policy 237
Parole 252
Peace officer 248
Prison director 230
Prison industries 234

Prison Litigation Reform Act
  (PLRA) 243
Prisoners' rights 237
Probation 249
Supermax prison 235

Questions for Review

1. What factors contribute to the recent decline in correctional populations? What impact do drug laws have on them? How do California's prison populations affect that of the nation?
2. What are some of the major administrative positions within a prison system?
3. How do supermax prisons differ from other prisons? What concerns have been raised concerning their alleged effects on inmates, constitutionality, and public safety?
4. What are at least five of the major U.S. Supreme Court decisions affording rights to prisoners? When and how did such decisions serve to end the hands-off doctrine?
5. What is a direct supervision jail, and how does it differ in design and function from traditional jails?
6. Why was the Prison Litigation Reform Act enacted, and has it made an impact?

7. In what major ways do jails differ from prisons in their organization and administration?
8. What did the U.S. Supreme Court hold recently concerning the warrantless collection of DNA from pretrial arrestees?
9. What advantages accrue to a corrections facility if it is accredited?
10. What is the profile of state adult and juvenile probation and parole agencies in terms of their organizational structure as well as the arming and peace officer status of their officers?
11. What are the various types of probation systems administered in the United States? Describe each.
12. Should probation services be placed within the judicial or the executive branch of government? Defend your answer.
13. What are the two basic models of parole administration?

Deliberate and Decide

Prison Policy Options

Your state's prison population has risen dramatically since the early 1990s, with much of the growth being attributable to changes in criminal justice policy during the previous

three decades. As a result, your state is now experiencing a rapid rise in per capita cost of incarceration, making it very expensive to operate and maintain the prison system; increasingly crowded conditions (which can negatively affect inmate misconduct) have resulted, and there has been an increase in the inmate-to-staff ratio (increasing from 4.1

to 5.2 inmates per staff member in the past few years). Furthermore, crowding takes a toll on the prison system's infrastructure, further exacerbating maintenance costs. Your governor has chosen to consider a variety of policy options to address the issues resulting from this growth.

Consider what types of data and program information you would need if asked to investigate the following policy options, as well as how you might measure any outcomes. Where possible, determine which, if any, policy options you would endorse, and *why* or *why not.*

Questions for Discussion

1. *Expanding the capacity of your prison system* (to include construction of new facilities and adding staffing): Can you "sell" the construction costs to relevant politicians and the public?

2. *Investing in more in rehabilitative programs:* Can academic and vocational education, work programs, and substance abuse treatment programs reduce recidivism?

3. *Placing some inmates in private prisons:* Can private facilities incarcerate inmates at a lower cost and provide adequate services?

4. *Changing the state's existing sentencing policies:* Will some or all mandatory minimum penalties be repealed?

5. *Greater use of alternatives to incarceration:* Do house arrest, electronic monitoring, intensive supervision, boot camps, day reporting centers, fines, and community service work?

6. *Expanding use of residential reentry centers:* Can more inmates with short sentences who are deemed to be low security risks be placed into such transitional halfway houses?

7. *Expanding good time credits:* To slow or reduce prison growth, can you use such approaches as reducing a nonviolent inmate's sentence by up to 1 year if the inmate participates in residential substance abuse treatment and other rehabilitative programs? What do current laws allow?[112]

Learn by Doing

1. As part of a criminal justice honor society paper to be presented at a national conference, you are examining the role of local jails. Considering the diagram of the flow of the justice system process in the front matter of this book, as well as this chapter's discussion about jails, at which point(s) would you argue that jails become involved and contribute to the overall functions of the criminal justice system? How does the direct supervision jail concept apply to these functions?

2. Your criminal justice professor has assigned a class debate wherein class members are to determine which court decision within *each* of three amendments—the Fourth, Fifth, and Sixth—is the most important right therein granted to inmates. You are to analyze those three amendments and explain and defend your decision.

3. Your criminal justice professor is concerned because it seems that students know relatively little about the general functions and organizational attributes of probation and parole agencies. As an upper-division criminal justice student, she asks you to prepare a short presentation on that topic for the coming "Career Day" program offered each year by the faculty. What will you say?

Notes

1. Bureau of Justice Statistics, "Percent Distribution of Employment and Payrolls for the Justice System by Level of Government," Table 2, jeeus1002.csv (July 1, 2014), http://www.bjs.gov/index.cfm?ty=pbdetail&iid=4679 (accessed November 4, 2014)

2. For a cost breakdown, see Vera Institute of Justice, *The Price of Prisons: What Incarceration Costs Taxpayers*, January 2012, p. 6, http://www.vera.org/sites/default/files/resources/downloads/Price_of_Prisons_updated_version_072512.pdf (accessed November 4, 2014).

3. Bureau of Justice Statistics, *Correctional Populations in the United States, 2012* (December 2013), p. 2 (accessed November 4, 2014).

4. Kevin Johnson, "Toughness on Crime Gives Way to Fairness, Cost Reality," *USA Today* (March 30, 2014), http://www.usatoday.com/story/news/nation/2014/03/30/tough-crime-fairness-cost/6836605/ (accessed November 5, 2014).

5. Ibid.

6. Ibid.

7. See William J. Newman and Charles L. Scott, "*Brown v. Plata*: Prison Overcrowding in California," *Journal of the American Academy of Psychiatry Law* 40(4) (December 2012):547–552, http://www.jaapl.org/content/40/4/547.full (accessed May 31, 2014).

8. U.S. Department of Justice, Bureau of Justice Statistics, *Prisoners in 2011*, p. 4.

9. Robert Martinson, "What Works? Questions and Answers about Prison Reform," *The Public Interest*, 35(1974):22–54.

10. T. Paul Louis and Jerry R. Sparger, "Treatment Modalities within Prison," in John W. Murphy and Jack E. Dison (eds.), *Are Prisons Any Better? Twenty Years of Correctional Reform* (Newbury Park, CA: Sage, 1990), p. 148.

11. Ibid., p. 149.

12. Richard P. Seiter, *Correctional Administration: Integrating Theory and Practice* (Upper Saddle River, NJ: Prentice Hall, 2002), p. 11.

13. Ibid., p. 192.

14. Ibid., p. 189.

15. Ibid., pp. 190–191.

16. Robert Levinson, "Try Softer," in Robert Johnson and Hans Toch (eds.), *The Pains of Imprisonment* (Beverly Hills, CA: Sage, 1982), p. 246.

17. Louis and Sparger, "Treatment Modalities within Prison," pp. 147–162.

18. Bureau of Justice Statistics, *HIV in Prisons, 2001–2010* (September 2012), pp. 1–2, http://www.bjs.gov/content/pub/pdf/hivp10.pdf (accessed November 6, 2014).

19. James A. Inciardi, *Criminal Justice*, 7th ed. (Fort Worth, TX: Harcourt Brace, 2001), p. 454.

20. Ibid., p. 194.

21. Mary Ellen Mastrorilli, personal communication, September 1, 2010.

22. United States Bureau of Prisons, *Unit Management Manual* (Washington, DC: Author, 1977), p. 6.

23. Seiter, *Correctional Administration*, p. 196.

24. See, for example, a description of prison industries as operated by the California Prison Industry Authority, at http://pia.ca.gov/About_PIA/mission.aspx (accessed March 25, 2014).

25. U.S. Department of Justice, National Institute of Justice, *Work in American Prisons: Joint Ventures with the Private Sector* (Washington, DC: U.S. Government Printing Office, 1995), pp. 2–3.

26. ABCNews.go.com, "How to Survive a Supermax Prison," http://abcnews.go.com/TheLaw/Story?id=3435989&page=1 (accessed November 5, 2014).

27. CNN.com/U.S., "Reporters Get First Look inside Mysterious Supermax Prison," http://www.cnn.com/2007/US/09/13/supermax.btsc/index.html (accessed November 5, 2014).

28. Craig Haney, "Mental Health Issues in Long-term Solitary and 'Supermax' Confinement," *Crime & Delinquency* 49(1) (January 2003):124–156.

29. See Daniel P. Mears, Christina Mancini, Kevin M. Beaver, and Marc Gertz, "Housing for the 'Worst of the Worst' Inmates: Public Support for Supermax Prisons," *Crime & Delinquency* 59(4) (June 2014):587–615. This survey of about 1,300 adults in Florida found that more than 80 percent of respondents supported supermax prisons; however, the support declined to 60 percent when there was no expectation of public-safety benefit; furthermore, 70 percent did not believe supermaxes are inhumane.

30. See, however, ibid.

31. Sharon Shalev, "Solitary Confinement and Supermax Prisons: A Human Rights and Ethical Analysis," *Journal of Forensic Psychology Practice* 11(2/3) (2011):151–183; also see Jesenia Pizarro and Vanja M. K. Stenius, "Supermax Prisons: Their Rise, Current Practices, and Effect on Inmates," *The Prison Journal* 84(2) (June 2004):248–264.

32. *Madrid v. Gomez*, 889 F. Supp. 1146 (1995).

33. 37 F. Supp. 1265 (1980).

34. 374 F.3d 541 (7th Cir. 2004), p. 1118.

35. Jesenia M. Pizarro, Vanja M. K. Stenius, and Travis C. Pratt, "Supermax Prisons: Myths, Realities, and the Politics of Punishment in American Society," *Criminal Justice Policy Review* 17(1) (March 2006):6–21.

36. Ibid.

37. Haney, "Mental Health Issues in Long-term Solitary and 'Supermax' Confinement," p. 150.

38. *Ruffin v. Commonwealth*, 62 Va. 790 (1871).

39. *Price v. Johnston*, 334 U.S. 266, 144 F.2d 260 (1948).

40. *Turner v. Safley*, 482 U.S. 78 (1987).

41. *Cooper v. Pate*, 378 U.S. 546, 384 S. Ct. 1733 (1964).

42. *Johnson v. Avery*, 393 U.S. 483, 89 S. Ct. 747 (1969).

43. *Bounds v. Smith*, 430 U.S. 817, 97 S. Ct. 1491 (1977).

44. *Cruz v. Beto*, 405 U.S. 319, 92 S. Ct. 1079 (1972).

45. *Procunier v. Martinez*, 416 U.S. 396, 94 S. Ct. 1800 (1974).

46. *Bell v. Wolfish*, 441 US 520, 99 S. Ct. 1861 (1979).

47. *Rhodes v. Chapman*, 452 U.S. 337 (1981).

48. *Estelle v. Gamble*, 429 U.S. 974, 97 S. Ct. 285 (1976).

49. *Wolff v. McDonnell*, 418 U.S. 539, 394 S. Ct. 296 (1974).

50. Greg Shtraks, "The List: The World's Most Notorious Prisons," *Foreign Policy*, January 21, 2009, http://www.foreignpolicy.com/articles/2009/01/20/the_list_the_worlds_most_notorious_prisons (accessed March 10, 2014).

51. "The Ten Worst Prisons in the World," http://www.thetoptenworld.com/violent_prisons.html (accessed November 10, 2014).

52. See 42 U.S.C. § 1997)

53. U.S. Department of Justice Office, "Rights of Persons Confined to Jails and Prisons: Overview," http://www.justice.gov/crt/about/spl/corrections.php (accessed November 6, 2014).

54. U.S. Department of Justice Office of Legislative Affairs, *Department of Justice Activities Under the Civil Rights of Institutionalized Persons Act, Fiscal Year 2011* (March 28, 2012), pp. 4–9, http://www.justice.gov/crt/about/spl/documents/split_cripa11.pdf (accessed November 2, 2014).

55. Timothy J. Flanagan and Kathleen Maguire (eds.), *Sourcebook of Criminal Justice Statistics 1991* (Washington, DC: U.S. Government Printing Office, 1992), p. 555.

56. Ibid. Also see Kathleen Maguire and Ann L. Pastore (eds.), *Sourcebook of Criminal Justice Statistics 1995* (Washington, DC: U.S. Government Printing Office, 1996), p. 177.

57. Jim Thomas, Kathy Harris, and Devin Keeler, "Issues and Misconceptions in Prisoner Litigation," *Criminology* 24 (1987):901–919.

58. Jim Thomas, "Repackaging the Data: The 'Reality' of Prisoner Litigation," *New England Journal of Criminal and Civil Confinement* 15 (1989):195–230.

59. Ibid., p. 50.

60. Jennifer A. Puplava, "Peanut Butter and the Prison Litigation Reform Act," http://www.law.indiana.edu/ilj.v73/no1/puplava.html (accessed November 12, 2004).

61. Francis X. Cline, "Prisons Run Out of Cells, Money and Choices," *New York Times,* May 28, 1993, p. B7.

62. Associated Press, "Lawsuit over Michigan Inmate Death Settled for $3.25 Million," http://blog.mlive.com/grpress/2008/07/lawsuit_over_michigan_inmate_d.html (accessed November 20, 2010).

63. Libby Sander, "Inmate's Death in Solitary Cell Prompts Judge to Ban Restraints," *The New York Times,* http://www.nytimes.com/2006/11/15/us/15prison.html (accessed November 20, 2014).

64. 107 S. Ct. 2254 (1987), at 2254.

65. 111 S. Ct. 2321 (1991).

66. 115 S. Ct. 2321 (1995), at 2293.

67. Linda Greenhouse, "High Court Makes It Harder for Prisoners to Sue," *New York Times,* June 20, 1995, p. A11.

68. Public Law No. 104-134, 110 Stat. 1321 [codified as amended in scattered sections of 18 U.S.C., 28 U.S.C., and 42 U.S.C.] (1996).

69. See 141 *Congressional Record* S14,413 (daily ed., September 27, 1995), Senator Robert Dole's statement in his introduction of the PLRA as a bill to the Senate. Senator Dole provided other examples of the frivolous litigation that he felt the PLRA was needed to cure: "insufficient storage locker space, a defective haircut by a prison barber, [and] the failure of prison officials to invite a prisoner to a pizza party for a departing prison employee."

70. American Civil Liberties Union, "The Prison Litigation Reform Act (PLRA)," http://www.aclu.org/Prisons/Prisons.cfm?ID=14379&=26 (accessed September 16, 2005)

71. Administrative Office of the U.S. Courts, "1997 Judicial Business of the United States Courts," http://www.uscourts.gov/Statistics/JudicialBusiness/JudicialBusiness1997.aspx (accessed November, 2014).

72. United States Courts, "Caseload Statistics, 2009," Table C3, http://www.uscourts.gov/Statistics/FederalJudicialCaseloadStatistics/FederalJudicialCaseloadStatistics2009.aspx (accessed November 2, 2014).

73. Bureau of Justice Statistics, *Jail Inmates at Midyear 2012—Statistical Tables* (May 2014), pp. 1–2, http://www.bjs.gov/content/pub/pdf/jim12st.pdf (accessed November 4, 2014).

74. For example, see James M. Moynahan and Earle K. Stewart, *The American Jail: Its Development and Growth* (Chicago: Nelson-Hall, 1980), p. 100; Clemens Bartollas, Stuart J. Miller, and Paul B. Wice, *Participants in American Criminal Justice: The Promise and the Performance* (Upper Saddle River, NJ: Prentice Hall, 1983), p. 59.

75. J. Moore, "Prison Litigation and the States: A Case Law Review," *State Legislative Report* 8 (1981):1.

76. National Sheriffs' Association, *The State of Our Nation's Jails, 1982* (Washington, DC: Author, 1982), p. 55.

77. Linda L. Zupan, *Jails: Reform and the New Generation Philosophy* (Cincinnati, OH: Anderson, 1991), p. 71.

78. U.S. Department of Justice, National Institute of Justice, *Direct Supervision Jails: 2006 Yearbook* (Longmont, CO: National Institute of Corrections Information Center, 2006), p. viii.

79. G. J. Bayens, J. J. Williams, and J. O. Smykla, "Jail Type Makes a Difference: Evaluating the Transition from a Traditional to a Podular, Direct Supervision Jail across Ten Years," *American Jails* 11(2) (1997):32–39.

80. Ibid.

81. Ibid.

82. R. Yocum, J. Anderson, T. DaVigo, and S. Lee, "Direct-supervision and Remote-supervision Jails: A Comparative Study of Psychosocial Factors," *Journal of Applied Social Psychology* 36(7) (2006):1790–1812.

83. See *Maryland v. King,* 12-207 (2014).

84. American Correctional Association, "Standards & Accreditation," http://www.aca.org/standards.faq.asp (accessed May 29, 2008).

85. Ibid.

86. Ibid.

87. Belinda McCarthy and Bernard McCarthy, quoted in Howard Abadinsky, *Probation and Parole: Theory and Practice,* 7th ed. (Upper Saddle River, NJ: Prentice Hall, 2000), p. 196.

88. Todd R. Clear, "Punishment and Control in Community Supervision," in Clayton A. Hartjen and Edward E. Rhine (eds.), *Correctional Theory and Practice* (Chicago: Nelson-Hall, 1992), pp. 31–42.

89. See the President's Commission on Law Enforcement and Administration of Justice, *Task Force Report: Corrections* (Washington, DC: U.S. Government Printing Office, 1967), p. 7

90. Bureau of Justice Statistics, *Probation and Parole in the United States, 2011* (November 2012), pp. 1–2, http://www.bjs.gov/content/pub/pdf/ppus11.pdf (accessed November 4, 2014).

91. See, for example, the State of California Model Penal Code Section 830-832.17, which defines the following persons as peace officers: the office of attorney general special agents and investigators, deputy sheriffs, certain corrections employees (e.g., jail, prison, probation and parole), highway patrol troopers, campus police, fish and game employees, forestry and alcoholic beverage control agents, and state fair marshals; at: http://www.leginfo.ca.gov/cgi-bin/displaycode?section=pen&group=00001-01000&file=830-832.17 (accessed November 6, 2014).

92. Shawn E. Small and Sam Torres, "Arming Probation Officers: Enhancing Public Confidence and Officer Safety," *Federal Probation* 65(3) (2001):24–28.

93. Seiter, *Correctional Administration,* p. 387.

94. Small and Torres, "Arming Probation Officers," p. 27.

95. American Probation and Parole Association, *Adult and Juvenile Probation and Parole National Firearm Survey,* 2nd ed. (October 2006), http://www.appanet.org/eweb/Resources/Surveys/National_Firearms/docs/NFS_2006.pdf (accessed November 5, 2014).

96. Barry J. Nidorf, "Community Corrections: Turning the Crowding Crisis into Opportunities," *Corrections Today* (October 1989):82–88.

97. Howard Abadinsky, *Probation and Parole: Theory and Practice*, 5th ed. (Englewood Cliffs, NJ: Prentice Hall, 1994), p. 104.

98. Ibid., p. 57.

99. Ibid., pp. 104–105.

100. Ibid., pp. 106–107.

101. See President's Commission, *Task Force Report*, pp. 35–37.

102. Abadinsky, *Probation and Parole*, p. 107.

103. Eric Trist, "On Socio-Technical Systems," in Kenneth Benne and Robert Chin (eds.), *The Planning of Change*, 2nd ed. (New York: Holt, Rinehart and Winston, 1969), pp. 269–281.

104. Daniel Katz and Robert I. Kahn, *The Social Psychology of Organizations* (New York: John Wiley & Sons, 1966).

105. Patricia L. Hardyman, "Management Styles in Probation: Policy Implications Derived from Systems Theory," in Hartjen and Rhine (eds.), *Correctional Theory and Practice*, p. 68.

106. Angela Hawken and Mark Kleiman, "Managing Drug Involved Probationers with Swift and Certain Sanctions: Evaluating Hawaii's HOPE National Institute of Justice," December 2, 2009, p. 4, https://www.ncjrs.gov/pdffiles1/nij/grants/229023.pdf; also see Steve Lopez, "Hawaii Finds Success with Tough-Love Approach to Repeat Offenders," *Los Angeles Times*, December 1, 2012, http://hopehawaii.net/assets/la-times-total.pdf (accessed December 4, 2014).

107. Abadinsky, *Probation and Parole*, p. 223.

108. Ibid.

109. National Advisory Commission on Criminal Justice Standards and Goals, *Corrections* (Washington, DC: U.S. Government Printing Office, 1973), pp. 396–397.

110. President's Commission, *Task Force Report*, p. 71.

111. Ibid.

112. Adapted from Nathan James, *The Federal Prison Population Buildup: Overview, Policy Changes, Issues, and Options*, Congressional Research Service, January 22, 2014 (accessed October 2, 2014).

The mood and temper of the public in regard to the treatment of crime and criminals is one of the most unfailing tests of the civilization of any country.

—*Winston Churchill*

11 Corrections Personnel Roles and Functions

LEARNING OBJECTIVES

After reading this chapter, the student will be able to:

1 *describe in general the duties of prison, jail, and probation and parole administrators and their employees*

2 *review the type of training that is available to new wardens to help them be successful, and the principles of good prison leadership*

3 *review the basic responsibilities of prison wardens in carrying out executions*

4 *describe the responsibilities of middle managers and supervisors*

5 *relate the duties and types of correctional officers*

6 *delineate and describe several key issues for, and practices of prison administrators, to include achieving racial balance, managing staff deviance, and maintaining appropriate staff-inmate relationships*

7 *explain how jail administrators can motivate and retain jail employees*

8 *review probation administrators' management styles*

9 *discuss the kinds of organizational stressors that can occur and cause depression, low job satisfaction, and high attrition among corrections employees, and some measures to be taken to deal with it*

▶ Introduction

This chapter focuses on the role and functions of personnel who work within correctional institutions and in probation and parole agencies. Presented first is a profile of prison wardens, including means of preparing new wardens for the position, principles of good prison leadership, and the administrator's role in carrying out death sentences. Then, we cover the roles of correctional middle managers and supervisors, and following that we examine the front-line personnel in prisons: correctional officers (COs). This section includes a typology of the types of COs in terms of their overall job performance. Then, we consider the "cousins" of prisons, the local jails: the functions of the jail administrator, motivating and retaining jail personnel, and some problems in selecting and keeping people who will want detention work to be their career. Next, we consider administrative functions and management styles as they relate to probation and parole. The chapter concludes with review questions, "deliberate and decide" problems, and "learn by doing" exercises.

Before examining these personnel who work within corrections, it is important to bear in mind that correctional facilities constitute a society within a society; as such, a wide range of personnel are employed therein. As examples, a typical prison employs food service workers, skilled tradesmen (e.g., carpenters and electricians), teachers, secretaries, chaplains, nurses, mental health clinicians, computer technicians, and recreation personnel.

Even more importantly, remember that whether or not one wears a correction officer's uniform, *everyone's* job is to be security oriented. As former corrections administrator Mary Ellen Mastrorilli puts it:

> Nurses must double and triple check their syringe counts to ensure that syringes do not end up in the hands of an inmate. Catholic priests must substitute grape juice for wine when saying Mass, as alcohol is prohibited inside prison walls. Carpenters must carefully account for each and every one of their tools during the work day. A hacksaw in the hands of an inmate can mean a future escape or a deadly assault. Every secretary's desk is home to a pair of scissors or a letter opener, but not so in a prison. A prison chef must keep track of all kitchen utensils, especially cutlery, because metal objects can be easily fashioned into shanks (homemade prison knives).[1]

Finally, before discussing corrections administration, we need to mention two basic principles that undergird corrections administration: First, whatever the reasons for which a person is incarcerated, he or she is not to suffer pains beyond the deprivation of liberty—confinement itself is the punishment. Second, regardless of the crime, the prisoner must be treated humanely and in accordance with his or her behavior. Even the most heinous offender is to be treated with respect and dignity and given privileges if institutional behavior warrants it.[2] Our analysis of institutional management is predicated on these two principles.

▶ Prisons

The Warden: A Profile

Several guest corrections speakers in the author's criminal justice administration classes have argued that the prison **warden**—that person who is responsible for all activities, safety, and security of the staff and inmates within the prison, to include establishing prison policies and carrying out financial and programming goals—has the most difficult position of all in the corrections field.[3] This assessment is arguably true because the warden must also take the central office and prison director's general policies and put them into effect

> **warden** the person responsible for all activities, safety, and security of the staff and inmates within a prison.

throughout the prison, while being responsible for the smooth day-to-day operation of the institution. These correctional executives also oversee the fastest-growing agencies in state government; administer increasingly visible operations; and are held accountable by politicians, auditors, the press, organized labor, and numerous other stakeholders.[4] Wardens work within a field that has become more demanding, consumes an increasing share of public funds, and involves responsibility for the lives and safety of others.

IN THEIR OWN WORDS

ADMINISTRATIVE ADVICE FROM THE FIELD

Name: Robert Bayer, Ph.D.

Current Position/City/State: Former Director of Corrections/Warden/Inspector General, other related positions, State of Nevada

College attended/academic major/degree(s): University of Nevada, Reno: Ph.D., political science/public administration; master of public administration (MPA); master of arts, English literature. University of New York, College at Oswego, bachelor of arts in liberal arts.

My primary duties and responsibilities in this position include: functioning as the CEO of a very large public organization. Unlike a warden, who administers departmental policy, the director is responsible for the actual promulgation and oversight of the department's policies and procedures. It is important to operate a constitutional prison within the budget provided by the legislature and the policies and procedures are the lynchpin to accomplish this duty. The director is responsible for the overall departmental budget development, legislative passage, and ongoing implementation throughout the budget calendar. The director also provides testimony during the legislative session, presentations to the Board of Prison Commissioners, and provides key testimony on policies, procedures, and actions of the department in state and federal court as required. As one of the senior cabinet members for the Governor, an essential responsibility is to function as part of the Governor's cabinet and insure that there is an efficient and effective flow of information between the Governor and the department. The director must be an effective communicator and this takes up much of the average working day at every level including inmates, inmate families, victims and victim groups, interested stakeholder groups, legislators, staff and staff organizations, the courts, and the media. One of the

key divisions reporting directly to the director is the human resources division, which recognizes the critical importance of every level of staff recruitment, hiring, training, and benefits. The inspector general of the system reports directly to the director to ensure that all levels of staff and inmate investigations are being properly conducted and brought to a timely conclusion. It is important to develop a span of control that is practical and provides you with the proper level of control and oversight over the entire system in order to accomplish all of these duties and responsibilities.

Personal attributes/characteristics that have proven to be most helpful to me in this position are:

Top Ten:

1. Intelligence. It may be a trait we are born with, but it is essential at this level because of the constant multitasking and complexity of decisions that must be made.

2. Integrity. Demonstrate a strong moral ethic. Always do the right thing, even when no one is looking. Staff looks to you as true north on their compass even though they may not say it.

3. A sense of fairness to everyone, the public, legislators, staff, and inmates alike.

4. Commitment to the position. Demonstrate a strong work ethic that includes reliability, willingness to take on more important assignments, and the stamina to work long hours.

5. Develop a reputation for loyalty and trust.

6. Assertiveness and tenacity while remaining open to criticism and new ideas.

7. An absolute passion for the field of corrections. This attitude is infectious with staff. Love every assignment and learn as much as you can from every position you work. It all goes into a valuable data base in your brain that you will rely on during critical times and emergency situations.

8. Be honest, approachable, and always tell the truth to staff, politicians, and even the inmate population. Your reputation for diligence and honesty will really help develop a solid rapport with the inmate population, which is always important.

9. Cooperate with all stakeholders in this field. Ensure that they all feel welcomed at the discussion table, even if their constituency holds opposite opinions.

10. A sense of humor is critical in a field like this that is rife with tensions and life altering decisions.

My three greatest challenges in this administrative role include: (1) the operation of a constitutional prison system in the face of dwindling and scarce fiscal resources; (2) the nurturing, maintaining, and developing good political relationships with all legislative and executive branch stakeholders; (3) the hiring, training, and retention of sufficient professional and law enforcement staff to ensure the seamless operation of a state prison system.

Personal accomplishments during my administrative career about which I am most proud are:

- The first privatization of a prison in Nevada: the women's correctional center in Las Vegas. It stood for years as one of the best examples of a privatization contract in the nation.

- The appointment by first a Democratic governor and then a Republican governor.

- The first Director of Corrections ever promoted from within the Nevada system and subsequent to retirement, three of my top level staff were appointed to Director in succession. Nevada has not had to look outside the system for talented, well-trained, and well-qualified administrative appointments.

- No staff ever died or sustained serious life altering injury while on duty during my watch. Staff safety was always a paramount concern. The Department experienced a steady decline in industrial injury claims and expenditures from the first year to the last year of my employment as Director.

- The longest serving Director in Nevada's 150 year history.

Advice for someone who is interested in occupying an administrative position such as mine would be: to take a long-term view of a position such as this. Corrections is a field that takes a lot of actual experience in a wide variety of positions, to gain the necessary experience to make good decisions, especially in emergency situations. I would urge anyone interested in becoming a Director or Commissioner of Corrections to become a "triple threat" in these areas: operations, programming, and budget. In addition, here are some milestones to accomplish:

- Develop a mentor relationship with a top level role model who will take an active interest in your education and advancement through the system.

- Obtain an advanced education, because that is a characteristic that is found in most current Directors. A master's degree should be considered a minimal criterion. Never forget, however, that this is an experience-based field and it is critical to develop a thorough operational knowledge of the laws, policies, and procedures of the system. Remember that when you attain the position of director, "the buck stops here," and it is important to make final decisions with the confidence of a complete experience-based background.

- Study the budget and learn in great detail how to build and execute a budget within appropriations.

- Develop excellent written and verbal skills. Again, be a good communicator.

- Be a student of politics and develop the political connections needed for support when a Governor begins to search for the next Director of Corrections.

- Develop your leadership skills throughout your career. They should improve with every promotion that you receive. Although there are certain characteristics of leadership that a person is born with, leadership is a skill that can be learned and one should read and study management and leadership throughout their career.

Of course, both staff and inmates are sensitive to the warden's granting of what each side perceives to be a strengthened position for the other side. For example, if a policy is enacted that gives the staff more power over inmates, the inmates will be unhappy, perhaps even rebellious; conversely, if a policy is put into practice that the staff thinks affords too much additional freedom to inmates, the staff will feel sold out. Furthermore, the prison director, typically appointed by and serving at the pleasure of the state's governor, can exert on the warden all manner of political influences at any time.

▼

A national survey by Kim et al.[5] of more than 600 male and female prison wardens at adult state prisons provided the following demographic and ideological information: Regional differences account for a great degree of gender difference; in fact, the South employed 21,862 female corrections officers, fully half of the female correctional population in the United States. Of the prison wardens, 85.9 percent were men and 14.1 percent were women. The mean age of all wardens was 47 years, about 47.6 years for men and 44.9 years for women. The majority (81.3%) was white, with 70.8 percent being white men; African American men made up 11.8 percent. White women made up 10.4 percent and African American women 3.0 percent. A large proportion of the respondents had experience as COs (57.6%) or treatment officers (62.6%). Almost half of the male wardens (49.1%) had some military experience, compared with only 7.5 percent of the female wardens. Almost half of the wardens had a graduate degree, a law degree, or some graduate work; female wardens were more likely to have done such postbaccalaureate work (61.1% compared with 47.8% of the men).

Regarding the goals of imprisonment, male wardens ranked their four preferred goals as follows: incapacitation, deterrence, rehabilitation, and retribution. Female wardens, however, ranked them thus: incapacitation, rehabilitation, deterrence, and retribution. A greater proportion of female wardens (89.9%) than male wardens (83.3%) strongly or very strongly agreed that rehabilitation programs had an important place in their institutions. A majority of the wardens thought that the following amenities should be reduced or eliminated in prisons: martial arts instruction, conjugal visitation, cosmetic surgery and dentistry, condom distribution, disability benefits, sexually oriented reading material, and nonregulation clothing. Male wardens were more likely than female wardens to support the reduction of college education, copy privileges, condom distribution, a full-time recreation director, musical instruments, and special diets. In contrast, female wardens were more likely to support reduction of organ transplants, weight lifting, boxing, and tobacco smoking. Generally, data support the findings that female wardens seem more likely to reduce amenities that can potentially promote violence in prison and are more interested than male wardens in the health conditions of inmates.

Overall, Kim et al. concluded that although the differences between male and female wardens are somewhat noticeable, the roles of corrections administrators are becoming more gender neutral.[6]

Preparing New Wardens for Success

The growth of the nation's incarcerated population, discussed in Chapter 10, has increased the need for competent correctional administrators to ensure public safety, ensure that staff and inmates are safe, and spend tax dollars effectively. They must also understand and appreciate the importance of culture (the sum total of the organization's history, staff, inmates, community, and past leadership) as they begin their tenure at an institution. Today's correctional administrator must excel in more than just correctional operations and not rely on the all-powerful, autocratic working style and strong paramilitary organization of decades past.[7]

New wardens who were surveyed by McCampbell indicated that they would have been better prepared for these challenges had they had job experience or skills in business administration/fiscal management, personnel and labor relations, legislative issues, and media and public relations.[8] Unfortunately, however, a large majority (90%) of new wardens also reported in this survey that they did not receive any special training or orientation for their new responsibilities prior to, or just after, they received their assignment. Since 1994, there has been a 36-hour training program for new wardens, as well as related publications and other resources, available through the National Institute of Corrections (NIC). Participants of **NIC Executive Training Program for New Wardens** enhance their

NIC Executive Training Program for New Wardens training for new wardens to help grasp such areas as institutional culture, budget management, decision making, and media relations.

understanding in such areas as institutional culture, central office relationships, budget management strategies, decision making, and media relations.[9]

Principles of Good Prison Leadership

Throughout the nineteenth century and the early twentieth century, studies of prisons generally focused on the administrators rather than the inmates. Beginning in the 1940s, however, an ideological shift from studying prison administrators to studying inmates occurred. The central reason for the shift seems to have been that prisons were poorly managed or were what prison researcher John J. DiIulio Jr. referred to as "ineffective prisons."[10] Many writers expressed grave doubts about the efficacy of correctional administrators and stated that prison managers could do nothing to improve conditions behind bars.

It is not surprising that when contemporary researchers attempt to relate prison management practices to the quality of life behind bars, the results are normally quite negative: Prisons that are managed in a tight, authoritarian fashion are plagued with disorder and inadequate programs; those that are managed in a loose, participative fashion are equally troubled; and those with a mixture of these two styles are no better.[11]

In a 3-year study of prison management in Texas, Michigan, and California, however, DiIulio found that levels of disorder (rates of individual and collective violence and other forms of misconduct), amenities (availability of clean cells, decent food, and so on), and service (availability of work opportunities and educational programs) did not vary with any of the following factors: a higher socioeconomic class of inmates, higher per capita spending, lower levels of crowding, lower inmate/staff ratios, greater officer training, more modern plant and equipment, and more routine use of repressive measures. DiIulio concluded that "all roads, it seemed, led to the conclusion that the quality of prison life depended mainly on the quality of prison management."[12]

DiIulio also found that prisons managed by a stable team of like-minded executives, structured in a paramilitary, security-driven, bureaucratic fashion, had better order, amenities, and service than those managed in other ways *even when* the former institutions were more crowded, spent less per capita, and had higher inmate/staff ratios: "The only finding of this study that, to me at least, seems indispensable is that *prison management matters*" (emphasis in the original).[13]

Studies analyzing the causes of major prison riots found that they were the result of a breakdown in security procedures—the daily routine of numbering, counting, frisking, locking, contraband control, and cell searches—that are the heart of administration in most prisons.[14] Problems such as crowding, underfunding, festering inmate/staff relations, and racial animosities may make a riot more *likely*, but poor security management will make a riot *inevitable*.[15]

DiIulio offered six general **principles of good prison leadership**[16]:

1. Successful leaders focus, and inspire their subordinates to focus, on results rather than process, on performance rather than procedures, on ends rather than means. In short, managers are judged on results, not excuses.

2. Professional staff members—doctors, psychiatrists, accountants, nurses, and other nonuniformed staff—receive some basic prison training and come to think of themselves as COs first.

3. Leaders of successful institutions follow the *management by walking around* principle. These managers are not strangers to the cellblocks and are always on the scene when trouble erupts.

4. Successful leaders make close alliances with key politicians, judges, journalists, reformers, and other outsiders.

principles of good prison leadership DiIulio's six principles for success in corrections management.

5. Successful leaders rarely innovate, but the innovations they implement are far reaching and the reasons for them are explained to staff and inmates well in advance. Line staff are notoriously sensitive to what administrators do "for inmates" versus "what they do for us." Thus, leaders must be careful not to upset the balance and erode staff loyalty.

6. Successful leaders are in office long enough to understand and, as necessary, modify the organization's internal operations and external relations. DiIulio used the terms *flies, fatalists, foot soldiers,* and *founders.* The flies come and go unnoticed and are inconsequential. Fatalists also serve brief terms, always complaining about the futility of incarceration and the hopelessness of correctional reform. The foot soldiers serve long terms, often inheriting their job from a fly or fatalist, and make consequential improvements whenever they can. Founders either create an agency or reorganize it in a major and positive way.

new old penology
DiIulio's term for a shift of attention from the society of captives to the government of keepers

To summarize, to "old" penologists, prison administrators were admirable public servants, inmates were to be restricted, and any form of self-government was eschewed. To "new" penologists, prison administrators are loathsome and evil, inmates are responsible victims, and complete self-government is the ideal. DiIulio called for a **new old penology**, or a shift of attention from the society of captives to the government of keepers. He asserted that tight administrative control is more conducive than loose administrative control to decent prison conditions. This approach, he added, will "push administrators back to the bar of attention," treating them at least as well as their charges.[17]

Administering the Death Penalty

One of the major responsibilities of prison administrators, in 32 states (three states abolishing capital punishment since 2009) and in federal prisons, is to carry out the death penalty. By law, the warden or a representative presides over the execution.

To minimize the possibility of error, executions are carried out by highly trained teams. The mechanics of the process have been broken down into several discrete tasks and are practiced repeatedly. During the actual death watch—the 24-hour period that ends with the prisoner's execution—a member of the execution team is with the prisoner at all times. During the last 5 or 6 hours, two officers are assigned to guard the prisoner. The prisoner then showers, dons a fresh set of clothes, and is placed in an empty tomb-like death cell. The warden reads the court order or death warrant. Meanwhile, official witnesses—normally 6 to 12 citizens—are prepared for their role. The steps that are taken from this point to perform the execution depend on the method of execution that is used.[18]

Today state prisons and the Federal Bureau of Prisons hold about 3,100 inmates under sentence of death; lethal injection is the predominant method of execution in use; it is employed in all death-penalty states and in the federal system. In addition to lethal injection, 16 states authorize an alternative method of execution: Eight states also use electrocution; three states, lethal gas; three states, hanging; and two states, firing squad.[19] See Exhibit 11.1 for a description of capital puinishment.

In the new millennium, the U.S. Supreme Court has rendered two significant decisions concerning the administration of the death penalty: In *Roper v. Simmons* (March 2005), the Court abolished the death penalty for convicted murderers who were less than 18 years of age when they committed their crimes; this decision ended a practice used in 19 states and affected about 70 death-row inmates who were juveniles when they committed murder.

THE FEDERAL GOVERNMENT AND CAPITAL PUNISHMENT: COMPLICATED AND CONTROVERSIAL

It might appear, on its face, that a conviction and execution of Boston Marathon bomber Dzhokhar Tsarnaev are all but a foregone conclusion. After all, a majority of Americans favor capital punishment and have little or no sympathy toward terrorists since 9/11; furthermore, the case against him is strong—photos allegedly showing him perpetrating (and being charged with) 30 criminal counts in connection with the April 2013 blasts that killed 3 persons and wounded more than 260.[20]

However, the federal government's history of carrying out capital punishment makes Tsarnaev's and other federal executions doubtful at best. Since 1988, when the federal government's death penalty law was reinstated, only three condemned persons have actually been executed; no one has been put to death in the past 10 years.

In Tsarnaev's case, a litany of factors could militate against his execution, even though his has been certified as a death penalty case: First, although a poll conducted in May 2013 by *The Washington Post* found that 70 percent of respondents favored Tsarnaev's execution, Massachusetts jurors have long opposed death penalty[21]; then there is Tsarnaev's youthfulness—and the question of whether or not Tsarnaev's participation may have been the result of duress or influence by his older brother, Tamerlan (who was killed during the incident by police). Finally, the federal government has an extensive appeals process and is also coping with challenges to its lethal injection protocol.[22]

For all of these reasons, Tsarnaev may well be allowed to live out his natural life rather than be put to death by a combination of lethal drugs.

In *Atkins v. Virginia* (June 2002), the Court held that the execution of mentally retarded persons—which was permissible in 20 states—constituted cruel and unusual punishment.[23]

Achieving Racial Balance

The rapid growth of the inmate population, increased oversight by the federal courts, increased demands from the public, and a change in the demographic composition of the inmate population (more African American and Hispanic prisoners) all have presented wardens with a new set of challenges. As a result, half of all wardens in maximum-security prisons now have a policy on racially integrating male inmates within prison cells to try to achieve racial balance. Similarly, about 40 percent of these wardens do not allow their inmates to object to their cell assignments.[24]

Middle Managers and Supervisors

Chapter 5 examined in detail the roles of *police* supervisors and managers. It would be repetitious to dwell at length here on those roles and functions because most of them apply to *corrections* supervisors and managers as well.

Custodial staff at most prisons is typically divided into four ranks: captain, lieutenant, sergeant, and officer. Captains typically work closely with the prison administration in policymaking and disciplinary matters, lieutenants are even more closely involved with the security and disciplinary aspects of the institution, and sergeants oversee a specified number of rank-and-file correctional officers who work in their assigned cell blocks or workplaces.

Middle managers, although not on the front lines, are also in challenging and important positions. They are responsible for organizing their departments, planning and developing goals and objectives, overseeing the efficient use of resources, and developing effective communication networks throughout the organization.

Clearly, supervisors have one of the most demanding positions in correctional institutions. They must direct work activities, assign tasks, provide employee feedback, and serve as technical experts for the staff reporting to them. They serve as boss, adviser, counselor, mentor, coach, trainer, and motivator.

"Thy Brother's Keeper": Evolving Roles and Types of COs

Subordinate to the institutional administrator, middle managers, and supervisors is the correctional staff itself—those who, in the words of Gordon Hawkins, are "the other prisoners."[25] Their role is particularly important and challenging, given that they provide the front-line supervision and control of inmates and constitute the level from which correctional administrators may be chosen. Certainly one of the most challenging positions in prisons is that of front-line **correctional officer** (CO), who is generally responsible for: the custody, safety, security, and supervision of inmates; ensuring that inmates adhere to the relevant rules, regulations, and policies; maintaining discipline, peace, and order in prison; conducting searches for contraband; transporting inmates as needed; and tactically responding to riots and other emergency situations. Their duties may be further categorized as follows:

1. *Work detail supervisors:* Many prisons have inmates working in various positions, such as the prison cafeteria, laundry, and other such locations; officers must supervise them during such activities.

2. *Industrial shop and educational programs:* Prison industries have inmates producing everything from license plates, state-use paint, and mattresses to computer parts; correctional officers ensure that inmates do not create any problems during their work day and do not misappropriate any related tools that may be fashioned into weapons.

3. *Yard officers:* While inmates are outdoors and engaged in physical exercise and socialization, there is the potential for problems, such as fights between different racial or ethnic groups; officers must be alert for breaches of security and order.

4. *Tower guards:* Officers observe inmates who are in the prison yard while encased in an isolated, silent post high above the prison property and being vigilant for any outbreaks of violence or attempts to escape while inmates are outdoors.

5. *Administrative building assignments:* Officers are responsible for providing security at all prison gates, places where inmates' families come to visit, clerical work that involves inmate transfer, and so on.[26]

Mary Ann Farkas[27] also categorized COs into five types based on their approach to, and philosophy regarding their role, as follows:

1. *Rule enforcers* (about 43% of COs) are the most common type in Farkas's sample. They are characterized as rule bound and inflexible in discipline. They are likely to be less than 25 years old and to have a baccalaureate degree; they tend to have less work experience and to work the evening or night shift. They are more likely to have entered corrections for extrinsic reasons, including job security, benefits, and job availability, and to have a militaristic approach to inmates, expecting deference to their authority and obedience to their orders. Generally, they are not willing to negotiate or use exchange as a strategy to gain inmate compliance.[28]

2. The *hard liners* (14%) are actually an extreme version of the rule enforcers, being hard, aggressive, power hungry, and inflexible in applying rules. These officers are also more likely to be men, with a high school education or GED, and between the ages of 26 and

36 years. They also tend to work in maximum-security or segregation units, and to endorse militaristic values and distinction and deference to rank and the chain of command. At times, they may become abusive and aggressive toward inmates and perceive acting tough as the way a CO is supposed to act to maintain control and order.[29]

3. *People workers* (22% of COs) have a more comfortable style with inmates, are more flexible in rule enforcement and disciplinary measures, use their own informal reward and punishment system, and believe that the way to gain inmate compliance is through interpersonal communication and personalized relations. They regard over-reliance on conduct reports as an indication of one's inability to resolve difficult situations. They often discuss issues privately with inmates instead of embarrassing them in front of peers. They often rely on verbal skills in defusing situations, enjoy the challenge of working with inmates, and prefer the posts with more inmate contact.[30]

4. The *synthetic officers* (14% of COs), according to Farkas, are essentially a synthesis of the rule enforcer and the people worker types. They are typically older (37 years of age or more), more experienced officers who work in regular inmate housing units on the day shift. These officers follow rules and regulations closely, yet they try to consider the circumstances. They are careful not to deviate too far from procedure, however, which might cause sanctions for themselves. Strict enforcement of rules and flexibility in enforcement are juggled in their interactions with inmates.[31]

5. *Loners* (about 8% of COs) are also similar to rule enforcers but differ in the motivation behind their policy of strict enforcement. Loners closely follow rules and regulations because they fear criticism of their performance. Farkas believes that female and black officers are more likely to be of this type. Loners are likely to be between the ages of 26 and 36 years, to be less experienced COs, and to work on solitary posts. They feel a need to constantly prove themselves, and neither feel accepted by other officers nor identify with them. They are wary of inmates. There is a basic mistrust, even fear, of working with inmates.[32]

To summarize, age and seniority are associated with officer types. Rule enforcers and hard liners tend to be younger, less experienced COs, whereas older, more experienced officers belong to the people worker or synthetic officer categories. Generally, as officers mature, they become more interested in service delivery. Educational attainment is also a factor: Farkas also found that rule enforcers were more likely to hold baccalaureate or master's degrees.[33] Considerable evidence also suggests that higher education may lead to lower job satisfaction.[34] Other studies have determined that as officers' educational level increased, the less likely they are to feel a sense of accomplishment working as COs, or to want to make a career of corrections, and the less willing they are to engage in rehabilitation activities.[35]

Managing Staff Deviance

In Chapter 14, we will discuss examples of deviant behavior and ethical misconduct in corrections. Here we focus more on what to do to manage it.

Certainly most COs are honest, hard-working people; however, as with any occupation, there will be a few individuals who come into this work and engage in deviant behavior; such behavior may be simply defined as that CO conduct performed while on duty that violates either statutory law or agency policies and procedures.

Prison and jail corruption differs from other forms of public corruption because of the uniqueness of the environment, function, opportunities, and patterns of relationships of correctional institutions. Prison and jail personnel must control a reluctant, resistant, and sometimes hostile inmate population whose welfare—and comfortable lifestyle, by their standards—may seem better served by corruption than by honest compliance with prison rules; a culture of manipulation and violence may ensue.

To counter the existence of such acts, there are three types of approaches that administrators can take in terms of one's career phase: preservice, in-service, and continuous. Following are activities relating to all three phases that, per criminal justice ethicist Sam Souryal, correctional administrators can implement:

1. *Upgrade the quality of correctional personnel.* The entry-level pay for COs must be competitive. Correctional administrators should ensure that their hiring standards are competitive enough to attract qualified applicants yet high enough to keep high-risk applicants away from employment. Certainly included are thorough background investigations and certification. Psychological testing should also be used to check the character of those who are selected, and interviews should be conducted by a hiring board prior to appointment.

2. *Establish quality-based supervisory techniques.* Supervisors should realize that loyalty to moral principles is more durable than loyalty to individuals, and understand that although trivial and insignificant policy violations can be justified, serious transgressions must be earnestly reported. Quality-based supervisors are expected to possess the professional wisdom to be able to know which matter is trivial and which is serious, without being told. They should also see that employees are properly evaluated, subjected to random drug tests, and credit checks,

3. *Strengthen fiscal controls.* Most acts of prison corruption involve the illegal acquisition of money; therefore, establishing financial controls is an effective tool for checking corruption in correctional institutions and involves the proper conduct of preaudit and postaudit controls. Experienced internal auditors can determine whether bidding procedures are followed, expenditure ceilings are observed, and purchase vouchers are issued for the exact objects.

4. *Emphasize true ethical training.* If correctional leaders truly want their subordinates to act professionally, to pursue integrity, fidelity, and obligation and to shun corruption, they should support and increase such training—to include cultural awareness, diversity, and gender sensitivity training. Doing otherwise would signal that the subject is unimportant.[36]

Staff–Inmate Relationships

Despite formal policies prohibiting familiarity between inmates and prison staff employees, infractions occur that range from serious (e.g., romantic affairs—sometimes leading to childbearing) to minor (e.g., giving or receiving candy or soft drinks to/from an inmate). Many contemporary prisons are no longer sexually segregated, with female security officers working in male institutions. Such situations—and adding as well the fact that many inmates are quite manipulative—can foment different types of **inappropriate staff-inmate relationships** to develop. These relationships can involve behavior that is not only sexual in nature but also other transgressions such as staff performing special favors for inmates, or smuggling in contraband. Such wrongdoing by staff typically results in both staff and inmates being placed at risk and undermining the overall safety of the prison.

Worley et al.[37] found three types of "turners"—offenders identified as developing inappropriate relationships with staff members:

1. *Heartbreakers.* They seek to form an emotional bond with a staff member, which can even lead to marriage; they generally act alone and may spend several months courting a staff member.

2. *Exploiters.* They use an employee as a means of obtaining contraband or fun and excitement; they usually act with the help of other inmates, are very manipulative, and are likely to use a "lever" (intimidation) on prison employees.

inappropriate staff-inmate relationships such correctional staff behaviors as sexual relations with inmates, providing special favors for inmates, or smuggling in contraband.

3. **Hell raisers.** These inmates engage in a unique kind of psychological warfare, and simply want to cause trouble and create hell for the prison system. They often have a long history of personal involvement and form relationships as a way to create problems or disruptions. They thrive on putting staff members in situations wherein their jobs are compromised and enjoy the notoriety that follows the exposure of their relationship. They focus on staff members (e.g., secretaries; trustees have even become involved with staff members' spouses) rather than security officers.

Worley et al. point out that such behaviors are not the norm in penal environments; nevertheless, prison administrators must understand that offenders are very persistent in initiating interactions with employees for a variety of reasons.[38]

▶ Jail Personnel

About 730,000 individuals are incarcerated in local jails in the United States, either awaiting trial or serving a sentence;[39] furthermore, about 266,000 people are employed in local jails.[40] Jails represent the point of entry into the criminal justice system. Although prisons hold persons who have committed felonies and have been sentenced to at least 1 year in prison, jails hold persons who are arrested and booked for criminal activity or are waiting for a court appearance if they cannot arrange bail, as well as those who are serving sentences of up to 1 year for misdemeanors. Jails also temporarily hold felons whose convictions are on appeal or who are awaiting transfer to a state prison.

Perhaps one of the most neglected areas in criminal justice research concerns individuals who are employed in local jails; what limited studies have been performed generally focus on the conditions of confinement. Jail personnel—such as police and prison employees—often must work in an environment that is potentially unstable, uncertain, and unsafe. Therefore, it would be beneficial for jail administrators to become knowledgeable about why people choose to work in local jails, as well as jail employee job satisfaction and turnover, discussed later.

Jail Administrators' Functions

Because of their responsibilities, changes in structure and function, and shifts in inmate populations (as discussed in Chapter 10), today's jails warrant being recognized and operated as professional institutions—rather than an adjunct to, or an *ad hoc* appendage (most of them being administered by a county sheriff, in the sheriff's department). The jail administrator should be a full-time professional, capable of handling multiple roles internal and external to the jail; therefore, according to a federal report, jail administrators must function as the jail's *leader*, as the *manager* of its operations and resources, and as its *supervisor*.[41] Exhibit 11.2 discusses these three roles in more depth.

A Few Comments on "Jail First" Policies and Detention as a Career Path

A "jail first" policy is where sheriffs' offices require that recruits first work in the jail—often for several years—before they can become eligible for patrol duties. Such policies can result in jail administrators having considerable difficulty in recruiting and keeping people for jail duties, and can also result in high employee attrition due to low job satisfaction (deputies going elsewhere to do "real" police work out on patrol). Jail administrators may wish to re-examine this policy and try to create a culture that values detention work. In addition to

EXHIBIT 11.2

THE SHERIFF'S ROLES IN EFFECTIVE JAIL OPERATIONS

As a *leader,* the sheriff:
- helps define the jail's mission and the goals that must be met to achieve that mission.
- creates a sheriff's office executive management team that includes the jail administrator as an equal member.
- builds a culture within the jail division that supports the attainment of desired outcomes.
- serves as liaison to the external environment (i.e., the local criminal justice system, special interest groups, stakeholders, the community, and the media).
- influences and develops public policy supporting the agency mission.
- creates and maintains a competent and diverse workforce.

As a *manager,* the sheriff:
- mentors and coaches the jail administrator and other staff to elicit desired behaviors and develop talent.
- ensures that policies and procedures that meet professional standards are established to guide the staff and the organization in day-to-day operations.

- motivates the jail administrator and other staff to align their personal goals with those of the jail.
- provides thorough written directives and training on those directives.
- monitors activities and assesses results by collecting and analyzing performance data on a regular basis.
- manages and allocates budgets, staff, and other resources.
- manages the organization's preparation for and response to crisis situations and emergencies.

As a supervisor, the sheriff:
- stays informed about day-to-day operations in the jail and is visible and available to assist when necessary.
- monitors compliance with policies, standards, and legal requirements through the establishment of a systematic internal inspection and review process.
- supports and facilitates the jail administrator's efforts to redirect underperformers and address misconduct of jail staff.
- monitors the jail administrator's performance through regular reviews and quality assessment.

Source: Based on Mark D. Martin and Paul Katsampes, *Sheriff's Guide to Effective Jail Operations* (Washington, DC: U.S. Department of Justice, National Institute of Corrections, 2006), pp. 5–6.

thus establishing *detention as a career path*—where one can choose to remain in detention, be promoted within it, and, it is hoped, eventually retire from it—jail administrators can encourage their recruiters to emphasize the "big picture," for example, that only about 20 percent of a deputy's 20-year career would be spent working in detention, with the remaining 80 percent being spent as a road deputy.

Employee Training

Jail administrators and employees need to be thoroughly trained in all aspects of their job. Jail workers have been criticized for being untrained and apathetic, although most are highly effective and dedicated. One observer wrote that:

> Personnel is still the number one problem of jails. Start paying decent salaries and developing decent training and you can start to attract bright young people to jobs in jails. If you don't do this, you'll continue to see the issue of personnel as the number one problem for the next 100 years.[42]

Training should be provided on the booking process; inmate management and security; general liability issues; policies related to AIDS; problems of inmates addicted to alcohol and other drugs; communication and security technology; and issues concerning suicide, mental health problems, and medication.

▶ Probation and Parole Officers

How many probation and parole officers are employed in the United States today? Unfortunately, that question is impossible to answer, due to the diverse nature of organization and functions of the community corrections field. For example, does one count only those officers who supervise a caseload? What about supervisory staff, with no direct supervisory duties? Furthermore, some staff members only write presentencing reports or work in an agency's pretrial division, and larger agencies may also have treatment staff. The problem of "headcounts" thus becomes obvious, so even the national American Probation and Parole Association does not venture to estimate the numbers of officers.[43] What is known, however, is that these persons directly or indirectly supervise 4.8 million adults who are either on parole or probationary status.[44] This chapter section discusses their primary duties, supervisory styles (over their probationers and parolees), and sources of stress.

IN THEIR OWN WORDS

ADMINISTRATIVE ADVICE FROM THE FIELD

Kenneth J. Peak

Name: Jolene R. Whitten

Current Position/City/State: Chief United States Probation and Pretrial Services Officer, Northern District of Texas, Dallas, Texas

College attended/academic major/degree(s): Bachelor of Science in Education (major in Political Science, minor in English), Midwestern State University, Wichita Falls, Texas; Master of Arts, Humanities (coursework in history, literature, art, music, and philosophy), California State University at Dominguez Hills.

My primary duties and responsibilities in this position include: serving as the court unit executive for the United States Probation and Pretrial Services Office in the Northern District of Texas, which covers a geographical area that includes 100 counties. I am responsible for the oversight of our mission and staff, as well as for the budgetary and personnel decisions,

implementation of policy, and communicating with our judges, including the Chief U.S. District Judge. I also represent our office when meeting with leaders of other agencies and community organizations. As the chief probation and pretrial services officer, I am also a law enforcement officer.

Personal attributes/characteristics that have proven to be most helpful to me in this position are: optimism, resilience, innovation, integrity, the ability and desire to interact with people from diverse backgrounds, written and verbal communications skills, organizational skills, confidence, compassion, a high energy level, and knowledge about and a strong belief in our mission. A sense of humor also helps!

My three greatest challenges in this administrative role include:

1. **Budgeting:** Over the past 2 years, the federal courts have not been funded adequately to achieve our mission. Sequestration has hit us hard. Our work does not decrease when we have limited resources, so we've had to be very innovative in order to be effective and also protect our employees' jobs.

(Continued)

2. **Communication:** Because our district is so large, it's not possible to communicate face-to-face with all employees. Learning how and when to communicate information has been challenging but is critical. Effective communication can prevent problems and ensure success.

3. **Personnel issues:** Even in the best of organizations, personnel issues will arise. Learning how to respond appropriately for all concerned can be challenging.

Personal accomplishments during my administrative career about which I am most proud are: managing our limited resources innovatively so our agency did not have to furlough staff during sequestration, while maintaining our ability to meet our mission. Working with others to implement strengths-based leadership and evidence based practices in our district. Having the first mobile officer team in the system and expanding the mobile concept in order to greatly reduce rental costs for the judiciary by closing three field offices. Ensuring quality to serve our courts, protect our communities, and assist clients in making positive changes in their lives.

Advice for someone who is interested in occupying an administrative position such as mine would be: first—work hard! If you are successful in your current position, others will recognize your efforts. Furthermore, developing a strong work ethic will serve you well, regardless of your position. Be willing to take on additional responsibilities and volunteer for projects and initiatives that will benefit your organization. Be a "servant leader," in whatever position you occupy. You don't have to have a title to be a leader. Be innovative and always continue learning. Learn to work with others, rather than trying to do it all yourself. Find good mentors, and be a mentor to others. Take care of your health and don't forget your personal priorities, such as family. In this type of position, one never really escapes the responsibilities of the job. During vacations, I've responded to e-mails, taken calls, and made some difficult work-related decisions. Over time, it can be draining. So, it's important to find ways to make time for yourself and to live a healthy, balanced lifestyle. Have a few people you can trust and call for advice or just to listen. Always remember the "why" of what you do—I can't imagine doing this job if I didn't believe in the purpose of the organization.

Duties and Orientation

Probation officers supervise convicted offenders whom the courts have allowed to remain at liberty in the community, while being subject to certain conditions and restrictions on their activities. Parole officers, conversely, supervise inmates who have been conditionally released from prison and returned to their community. These officers report violations of the conditions of offenders' release to the body that authorized their community placement and placed conditions on their behavior (the court for probation and the parole board for parole).[45]

Because a number of agencies are often organized under a state's department of public safety umbrella—probation and parole, state police/highway patrol, capitol police, state bureau of investigations, and even fire marshals—probation and parole officer recruits often go through the same background, physical, polygraph, drug testing, and psychiatric exam regardless of which division they wish to work in.

Probation and parole officers must possess important skills similar to those of a prison caseworker, such as good interpersonal communication, decision making, and writing skills. They operate independently, with less supervision than most prison staff. These officers are trained in the techniques for supervising offenders and then assigned a caseload. Probation and parole officers supervise inmates at the two ends of the sentencing continuum (incarceration being in the middle).

Whom do we want to be supervising probationers and parolees—officers who are more grounded in enforcement or treatment in their orientation? In some jurisdictions, probation and parole officers are given, to the extent possible, a far different role or job description from those agencies having much more of an enforcement-oriented mission. As one Western probation and parole administrator put it:

> Although we arrest people, conduct investigations, conduct surveillance, and so on, a huge part of our job is trying to help people. The biggest hat we wear here is social worker. The law enforcement officer hat is much smaller for the most part. I think that is the most unique situation P&P has to offer. Our officers find themselves being social workers, disciplinarians, officers, mentors, coaches, etc. given the offender and his/her specific set of needs.[46]

There are means of determining one's orientation when he or she is being screened for a probation and parole position—whether tending more toward an authoritarian attitude (emphasis placed on monitoring and controlling of offenders, and enforcing the restrictions and general conditions of their parole or probation) or one that tends more toward being an advisor, friend, and willing to reward offenders who are successful in achieving their supervision-related goals.[47]

One approach to determining such orientation—although no doubt considerably more costly, time-intensive, and laborious—is for the agency to hire a for-profit human resources firm that has developed a reliable and valid survey instrument for this purpose. Such questions as the following might be included in such a survey: "Most offenders should receive strict and harsh discipline," "Most offenders are lazy and do not wish to work," "Most offenders cannot be trusted," "Most offenders want to better themselves," "Most offenders are not better or worse than other people," "Most offenders are victims of unfortunate circumstances," and "In general, rehabilitation of criminal offenders is not possible."

In reality, most probation and parole agencies probably cannot afford to employ an outside entity to test prospective officers in terms of their attitudes; however, once an extensive background investigation has been completed, applicants can then be sent to a contracted psychiatrist for an evaluation. In addition, as indicated above, because some parole and probation agencies are part of their state's larger department of public safety or corrections, all prospective officers can be subjected to the same hiring process as other state employees.

Research has shown, not surprisingly, that probation and parole officers' attitudes will largely influence and can even predict their supervisory practices toward their offender clients. The message for parole and probation administrators is that they may wish to consider applicants' attitudes when making hiring decisions. See Exhibit 11.3 for a parole decision-making exercise.

EXHIBIT 11.3

PAROLE DECISION MAKING FOR A NOTORIOUS KILLER[48]

Assume that you are a parole officer who is to make a recommendation to your state's parole board in the following matter: Charles Manson, age 77, is serving a life sentence for a 1969 killing spree in Los Angeles (his "family" brutally murdered seven people). Manson has not been a model inmate, recently caught possessing a weapon, threatening a peace officer, and being caught twice with contraband cell phones. Given his age, this could be Manson's final appearance before the state parole board. Debra Tate, a victim's sister (murdered actress Sharon Tate), is attending the hearing, and attorneys from both sides are prepared to give presentations, read documents by victims' relatives or other interested parties, and examine Manson's prison records. Manson, as is his custom, is not attending the parole hearing.

- Will you recommend that the board grant or deny Manson's parole at this time?
- If not, do you believe there programs or redeeming actions or qualities Manson might undertake or possess to secure his freedom in the future?

(The outcome of Manson's 2012 parole hearing is provided in the Notes section at chapter's end.)

Probation Management Styles

Patricia Hardyman's study of probation administrators focused on their *probation management style*—this style being the fundamental determinant of the nature of the probation organization—and was instructive in describing the impact of this style on the department's operation. Few departments, even those with a hierarchical organizational structure, had a pure management style; administrators vacillated among a variety of styles, including laissez faire, democratic, and authoritarian. The degree to which administrators included the probation officers in the decision-making process and communicated with officers varied. Authoritarian administrators created emotional and physical distance between the officers and themselves. Surprisingly, the most common management style used by probation administrators was laissez faire.[49]

Hardyman found that many probation administrators simply did not participate in the day-to-day activities and supervision strategies of the staff. They remained remote but made final decisions on critical policies and procedures.[50] Hardyman also found that few probation administrators across the country operated with the democratic style. Those who did, of course, listened more to the concerns and suggestions of the line supervisors and officers. The administrator still made the final decisions, but information was generally sought from the line staff and their opinions were considered. Officers working under administrators with this style had a greater sense that their opinions mattered and that the administrator valued their input. An additional benefit of the democratic style was that the administrators had power by virtue of both their position and their charisma, which inspired teamwork and task accomplishment.[51]

▶ Addressing Stress, Burnout, and Attrition

As with the other components of the criminal justice system, anyone working in corrections—either with clients behind bars or in an office, often in antiquated facilities, and surrounded by clients who possess all forms of social and behavioral problems—can find themselves to be severely stressed. Certainly administrators must realize that such stress can have a direct bearing on the quality of one's work productivity, job satisfaction, and even retention on the job; therefore, this is a topic that merits closer examination.

Stressful Prisons

As regards COs in prisons, one recent study of 500 officers in a Southern prison system found that, while race, marital status, and education did not appear to significantly affect CO's job stress or satisfaction, their gender and generation did. Specifically, female COs often feel that some characteristics they can bring to the job—compassion and a family orientation, for example—might be undervalued in a correctional environment that emphasizes toughness and physical strength. Furthermore, individuals who are part of the younger X and Y generations were found to be far more likely to be dissatisfied with their job as correctional officers than older generations. As indicated in Chapter 2, as younger people enter the correctional workforce, it will be important to understand what motivates them, and for correctional administrators to consider the needs of workers of every generation, for developing retention strategies and increasing job satisfaction. Allowing for individual preferences in such areas as compressed work schedules and a more participatory style of leadership and management, to the extent that doing so is viable, may help to improve generation X and Y workers' needs and job satisfaction.[52]

Prison crowding has also been correlated with stress, fear of inmates, and health issues. Although, as was shown in Chapter 10, U.S. prison populations have declined a bit in the past few years, many if not most remain crowded due to the tough sentencing policies and War on Drugs of past decades. A study of three Alabama prisons for men found that *all* responding officers identified crowding as negatively affecting officer safety, job performance, and health, while leading to violence at their facility. Specifically, crowding foments mental and physical health problems among officers, causing chronic health problems involving headaches, alcoholism, hypertension, obesity, heart attacks, diabetes, and weak immune systems. The study concluded that such issues will likely persist unless state and federal policy makers begin to address prison crowding, especially with regard to greater use of diversion programs (e.g., drug courts) and alternative sentencing (discussed in Chapter 12), as well as U.S. crime and sentencing laws.[53]

Stressors in Jails

Recent studies have also looked at generational differences in jails in order to assess job satisfaction and hopefully stem turnover rates. Jail administrators also need to realize that, like in prison, when employees from different generations come together in the same workplace, they are not likely to be motivated or rewarded in the same manner, or responsive to the same supervisory techniques. And, as Abraham Maslow taught us in the 1950s in his hierarchy of needs (see Chapter 2), what satisfies employees' needs can also vary depending on one's priorities and even location in the organizational hierarchy: Extrinsic motivators as paychecks, fringe benefits, and other economic incentives are generally sufficient only at the lowest levels, where salaries are lower and working conditions possibly more demanding; conversely, individuals functioning at higher levels are more likely to be motivated intrinsically, deriving satisfaction from receiving respect and appreciation from subordinates, and given more and more responsibility. As was also indicated in Chapter 2, the younger generations are more positively influenced by having input into decisions that affect them, control over how they complete their assignments, and a say in how things are done. They are more motivated by being recognized for good work and feeling appreciated by the community for the work they do, and seek opportunities for personal development and upward advancement. They also value such extrinsic benefits as college tuition, child care, and a fitness center. Although there will always be some aspects of the workplace that agency officials can do nothing about—e.g., civil service rules and bargaining contracts regarding tenure and seniority, legislative control over compensation and retirement plans—there are a number of intrinsic types of rewards that administrators can attempt to use to positively influence job satisfaction and reduce turnover—e.g., reducing paperwork, treating people fairly, maintaining a positive work climate, and allowing employees to have input and to be recognized and appreciated.[54]

But keeping people happily working in the nation's jails may not be as daunting as it might appear: A national survey by Jeanne Stinchcomb of more than 2,000 line staff and nearly 600 administrators[55] found, for example, that:

- Jail employment was not the job of "last resort"—only 13 percent of staff said they had no other employment options when they accepted the jail's offer.

- Most staff rated their jail as a good (45%) or an excellent (20%) place to work.

- Fifty-nine percent of jail staff described themselves as "very committed" to the agency where they work, and this finding held among various generations of employees.

- Nearly 7 in 10 (69%) staff members felt appreciated by their supervisor, and believed that they are recognized when they do good work (64%).[56]

Still, Stinchcomb's survey underscored the need for jail administrators to strengthen the jail as a workplace, by providing some of the intrinsic and extrinsic rewards that are discussed above.

Stress in Probation and Parole

Finally, with regard to probation and parole officers, studies indicate that their job stress and clinical depression are closely related to organizational climate. In specific, a study of nearly 900 probation and parole officers found that they tend to characterize their work environments as having high levels of role ambiguity (i.e., they are unclear about the objectives and goals of their position—see the discussion of enforcement versus assistance orientations, above), role conflict (i.e., having a general feeling that one cannot satisfy the conflicting demands of their administrators, managers, and supervisors), role overload (e.g., feeling under heavy job pressure at all times), and emotional exhaustion/burnout. Of particular note, researchers found that emotional exhaustion/burnout and role conflict contribute to, and can even predict, depression. This is obviously a complex undertaking for probation and parole administrators—i.e., untangling the web of complex work roles and organizational environment in order to identify those aspects of work that contribute to burnout and depression. Clearly, administrators must do what they can to investigate and identify such stressors (perhaps being manifested by employees' resignations, interpersonal problems, poor work productivity, and so on), and then develop strategies for ameliorating their negative effects. Such strategies may include knowing how and when to refer such officers to professional counseling, given that many officers may well lack adequate coping skills with high levels of stress, role conflict, and burnout associated with their jobs.[57]

Summary

This chapter examined the criminal justice employees who work in correctional institutions and probation and parole agencies, with particular emphasis placed on administrators. Certainly, as noted in this chapter, substantial pressures are now placed on these administrators by the external and internal environments. They must maintain a secure environment while attempting to offer some treatment to their clients, who should not leave incarceration or probation/parole in a much worse condition than when they entered. At the same time, another increasingly difficult challenge is that these administrators must constantly strive to maintain a competent, dedicated, noncorrupt workforce—as well as an organizational climate that will maintain a desirable level of job satisfaction for employees and minimize attrition—that will also uphold the primary tenets of incarceration: providing a secure environment while ensuring that inmates are treated with respect and dignity.

Key Terms and Concepts

Correctional officer 266
Inappropriate staff–inmate
    relationships 268
New old penology 264

NIC Executive Training Program
    for New Wardens 262
Principles of good prison
    leadership 263

Stressors
Warden 259

Questions for Review

1. What is meant by the term *new old penology*?
2. What are the different responsibilities of the warden and other prison administrators?
3. According to DiIulio, what are some major principles of successful prison administration?

4. What are some of the major problems encountered by prison or jail employees?
5. What are the types of COs, per Farkas? How do age, length of service, type of assignment, and education affect where one fits in this typology?

6. What are the means by which corrections personnel can become corrupted, and what can their administrators do to address and prevent it?
7. What are the three types of inmates who engage in inappropriate relationships with correctional staff members?
8. What are the functions of middle managers and supervisors in jails and prisons (see Chapter 3 if necessary)?
9. How would you describe the prison warden and his or her role? What kinds of training and education are necessary for a new warden to succeed?
10. What are the primary roles of the jail administrator?

11. Why are advantages and disadvantages of having, in effect, two career tracks in jails: a detention track and a patrol track? What can jail administrators do to foster careers and improve job satisfaction in the jail or detention side?
12. What are the primary duties and orientation of probation and parole officers, and what are the arguments for and against their carrying firearms?
13. What are some organizational stressors that can occur and cause depression, low job satisfaction, and high attrition among corrections employees, and what kinds of measures can be taken to attempt to minimize it?

Deliberate and Decide

Probation Decision Making

After a jury acquitted 25-year-old Casey Anthony in July 2011 on charges of first-degree murder, aggravated child abuse, and aggravated manslaughter of her 2-year-old daughter Caylee, the only convictions that remained were for lying to detectives seeking to find out what happened to the child. The task then facing Orlando, Florida, Judge Belvin Perry was to determine whether and how Anthony would serve a term of probation. Complicating Judge Perry's decision was a survey that found Anthony was the most hated person in America—and a high probability that many people would like to do her harm. Anthony's attorneys argued that she had already served her probation while in jail awaiting the

murder trial. On the other side, prosecutors maintained that probation should be continued, because the purpose of probation is to help offenders after they are released back into the community. Meanwhile, Anthony's parents stated that she would not be returning to their home (wishing to avoid media and traffic problems there). Other possibilities included having her serve probation out of state or giving her administrative probation—being able to travel anywhere but contacting her probation officer each month. (The judge's decision is provided in the Notes section at chapter's end.[58])

Questions for Discussion

1. Should the judge order Casey Anthony to serve probation?
2. If so, where, how, and for what length of time would you recommend it be served?

Learn by Doing

1. Most, if not all, of us has had to work in a position where we were supervised. Using DiIulio's "Six Principles of Good Prison Leadership," identify a supervisor you either worked for directly or were able to observe and discuss how this person measured up in his/her leadership skills. Also, discuss one of DiIulio's traits of leadership you would implement were you in a leadership position.
2. Your criminal justice honor society is planning a noon forum/debate concerning capital punishment. Your role will be to discuss the problems that exist with prison wardens administering the death penalty, as well as whether or not the recruitment of wardens is limited if one of their position requirements is the ability to supervise use of the death penalty.
3. You are a well-known jail consultant and have been hired by a medium-sized county to examine its jail

operations. One observation you quickly make concerns its pattern of recruitment and hiring of personnel: A newly hired deputy, upon completion of required academy training, is automatically assigned to work in the jail. Then, perhaps several years later, as he or she gains seniority and a position becomes available, application may be made for a transfer to the patrol division. What would seem to be the advantages of such an arrangement? Disadvantages? What would you recommend is needed in order to establish a career path for correctional workers in the jail?
4. As part of your criminal justice department's annual "Career Day" program, you are to discuss the general roles of prison COs and jailers as well as the primary differences between probation and parole officers. What will be in your oral report?

Notes

1. Mary Ellen Mastrorilli, personal communication, September 11, 2010.

2. John J. DiIulio, Jr., *Governing Prisons: A Comparative Study of Correctional Management* (New York: Free Press, 1987), p. 167.

3. Personal communication, Ron Angelone, Director, Nevada Department of Prisons, April 27, 1992.

4. F. T. Cullen, E. J. Latessa, R. Kopache, L. X. Lombardo, and V. S. Burton, Jr., "Prison Wardens' Job Satisfaction," *The Prison Journal* 73 (1993):141–161.

5. Ahn-Shik Kim, Michael DeValve, Elizabeth Quinn DeValve, and W. Wesley Johnson, "Female Wardens: Results from a National Survey of State Correctional Executives," *The Prison Journal* 83(4) (December 2003):406–425.

6. Ibid.

7. Susan W. McCampbell, "Making Successful New Wardens," *Corrections Today* 64(6) (October 2002):130–134. Also see the National Institute of Corrections website, http://nicic.org.

8. Ibid.

9. Ibid.

10. John J. DiIulio, Jr., "Well Governed Prisons Are Possible," in George F. Cole, Marc C. Gertz, and Amy Bunger (eds.), *The Criminal Justice System: Politics and Policies,* 8th ed. (Belmont, CA: Wadsworth, 2002), pp. 411–420.

11. Ibid., p. 449.

12. DiIulio, *Governing Prisons*, p. 256.

13. Ibid.

14. Bert Useem, *States of Siege: U.S. Prison Riots, 1971–1986* (New York: Oxford University Press, 1988).

15. DiIulio, "Well Governed Prisons Are Possible," p. 413.

16. John J. DiIulio, Jr., *No Escape: The Future of American Corrections* (New York: Basic Books, 1991), Chapter 1.

17. DiIulio, "Well Governed Prisons Are Possible," p. 456.

18. See Robert Johnson, *Death Work: A Study of the Modern Execution Process,* 2nd ed. (Belmont, CA: West/Wadsworth, 1998); Robert Johnson, "This Man Has Expired," *Commonweal* (January 13, 1989):9–15.

19. Tracy L. Snell, *Capital Punishment, 2011: Statistical Tables* (U.S. Department of Justice, *Bureau of Justice Statistics* (July 2014), http://www.bjs.gov/content/pub/pdf/cp11st.pdf (accessed November 18, 2014), pp. 1–4.

20. See, for example, Kevin Johnson, "Death Penalty for Boston Bomber a Complicated Question," *USA Today,* December 1, 2014, http://www.usatoday.com/story/news/nation/2014/12/01/boston-marathon-bomber-tsarnaev/3760253/ (accessed December 6, 2014).

21. Sebastian Murdock, "Dzhokhar Tsarnaev, Boston Bombing Suspect, Has Life or Death Resting in Attorney General," *Huffington Post*, December 1, 2014, http://www.huffingtonpost.com/2014/12/01/boston-bombing-death-penalty_n_4367908.html (accessed December 6, 2014).

22. Kevin Johnson, "Death Penalty for Boston Bomber a Complicated Question,"

23. *Roper v. Simmons,* No. 03-633 (2005); *Atkins v. Virginia,* 536 U.S. 304 (2002).

24. Barbara Sims, "Surveying the Correctional Environment: A Review of the Literature," *Corrections Management Quarterly* 5(2) (Spring 2001):1–12.

25. Gordon Hawkins, *The Prison* (Chicago: University of Chicago Press, 1976).

26. Adapted from Lucien X. Lombardo, *Guards Imprisoned: Correctional Officers at Work* (Cincinnati: Anderson, 1989), pp. 51–71.

27. Mary Ann Farkas, "A Typology of Correctional Officers," *International Journal of Offender Therapy and Comparative Criminology* 44 (2000):431–449.

28. Ibid., pp. 438–439.

29. Ibid., pp. 439–440.

30. Ibid., pp. 440–441.

31. Ibid., p. 442.

32. Ibid., pp. 442–443.

33. Ibid.

34. Susan Philliber, "Thy Brother's Keeper: A Review of the Literature on Correctional Officers," *Justice Quarterly* 4 (1987): 9–37.

35. David Robinson, Frank J. Porporino, and Linda Simourd, "The Influence of Educational Attainment on the Attitudes and Job Performance of Correctional Officers," *Crime and Delinquency* 43 (1997):60–77.

36. Adapted from ibid., pp. 41–43.

37. Robert Worley, James W. Marquart, and Janet L. Mullings, "Prison Guard Predators: An Analysis of Inmates Who Established Inappropriate Relationships with Prison Staff, 1995–1998," *Deviant Behavior: An Interdisciplinary Journal* 24 (2003):175–194.

38. Ibid., p. 93.

39. U.S. Department of Justice, Bureau of Justice Statistics, *Jail Inmates at Midyear 2013 - Statistical Tables* (August 2014), p. 1 (accessed November 22, 2014).

40. U.S. Department of Justice, Bureau of Justice Statistics, *Justice Expenditure and Employment Abtracts* (see spreadsheet at: *C:\Documents and Settings\Ken Peak\Local Settings\Temporary Internet Files\Content.IE5\MGKYODXY\cjee07[1].zip* (accessed November 15, 2014).

41. Mark D. Martin Paul Katsampes, *Sheriff's Guide to Effective Jail Operations* (Washington, DC: U.S. Department of Justice, National Institute of Corrections, 2006), pp. 5–6.

42. Quoted in Advisory Commission on Intergovernmental Relations, *Jails: Intergovernmental Dimensions of a Local Problem* (Washington, DC: Author, 1984), p. 1.

43. Personal communication, Diane Kincaid, Deputy Director/Information Specialist American Probation and Parole Association, November 21, 2014.

44. Bureau of Justice Statistics, *Probation and Parole in the United States, 2011* (November 2012), pp. 1–2, http://www.bjs.gov/content/pub/pdf/ppus11.pdf (accessed November 4, 2014).

45. Richard P. Seiter, *Correctional Administration: Integrating Theory and Practice* (Upper Saddle River, NJ: Prentice Hall, 2002), pp. 387–388.

46. Anonymous personal communication, November 12, 2014.

47. See Benjamin Steiner, Lawrence F. Travis III, Matthew D. Makarios, and Taylor Brickley, "The Influence of Parole Officers' Attitudes on Supervision Practices," *Justice Quarterly* 28 (6) (December 2011):903–930.

48. Manson was denied parole for the 12th time in April 2012. The parole board duly noted that he had recently bragged to a prison psychologist, "I'm special. I'm not like the average inmate. I have spent my life in prison. I have put five people in the grave. I am a very dangerous man." The board stated: "This panel can find nothing good as far as suitability factors go," See Christina Ng, "Charles Manson Denied Parole after Saying He is a "Very Dangerous Man,'" *ABC News*, April 11, 2012, http://abcnews.go.com/US/charles-manson-denied-parole-dangerous-man/story?id=16111128 (accessed November 16, 2014).

49. Patricia L. Hardyman, "Management Styles in Probation: Policy Implications Derived from Systems Theory," in Clayton A. Hartjen and Edward E. Rhine (eds.), *Correctional Theory and Practice* (Chicago: Nelson-Hall, 1992), pp. 61–81.

50. Ibid.

51. Ibid., p. 71.

52. Kelly Ann Cheeseman and Ragan A. Downey, "Talking 'Bout My Generation: The Effect of 'Generation' on Correctional Employee Perceptions of Work Stress and Job Satisfaction," *The Prison Journal* 92 (1): 24–44.

53. Joseph L. Martin, Bronwen Lichtenstein, Robert B. Jenkot, and David R. Forde, "'They Can Take Us Over Any Time They Want': Correctional Officers' Responses to Prison Crowding," *The Prison Journal* 92(1) (2012):88–105.

54. Jeanne B. Stinchcomb and Leslie Ann Leip, "Turning Off Jail Turnover: Do Generational Differences Matter?" *Criminal Justice Studies* 26(26) (March 2014):67–83; also see Jeanne B. Stinchcomb and Leslie A. Leip, "Retaining Desirable Workers in a Less-Than-Desirable Workplace: Perspectives of Line Staff and Jail Administrators," *Corrections Compendium* 37 (2) (Summer 2014): 1–8. Matthew D. Gayman and Mindy S. Bradley, "Organizational Climate, Work Stress, and Depressive Symptoms among Probation and Parole Officers," *Criminal Justice Review* 26 (3) (September 2014):326–346.

55. See Jeanne B. Stinchcomb, *The National Jail Workforce Survey: Methodological Challenges*, April 1, 2010, http://www.faqs.org/periodicals/201004/2041517401.html (accessed November 17, 2014).

56. Ibid.

57. Jeanne B. Stinchcomb and Leslie Ann Leip, "Turning Off Jail Turnover: Do Generational Differences Matter?" *Criminal Justice Studies* 26(26) (March 2014):67–83; also see Jeanne B. Stinchcomb and Leslie A. Leip, "Retaining Desirable Workers in a Less-Than-Desirable Workplace: Perspectives of Line Staff and Jail Administrators," *Corrections Compendium* 37 (2) (Summer 2014):1–8.

58. Adapted from Michael Muskal, "Two of Casey Anthony's Four Convictions Overturned by Appeals Court," http://www.latimes.com/news/nation/nationnow/la-na-nn-casey-anthony-appeals-court-20140125,0,3022534.story (accessed February 16, 2014); "Judge Perry Rules on Casey Probation," November 12, 2011, http://www.wesh.com/news/casey-anthony-extended-coverage/Judge-Perry-Rules-On-Casey-Probation/-/13479888/13130886/-/item/0/-/po7t4vz/-/index.html (accessed November 16, 2014). Judge Perry ruled that Anthony must serve a year of supervised probation, with the Florida Department of Corrections to keep Anthony's residential information confidential. Perry said in the order he did not want any information released that could lead to the discovery of her location.

[Correctional administrators] undoubtedly must take into account the very real threats unrest presents to inmates and officials alike, in addition to the possible harms to inmates.

—*United States Supreme Court, in Whitley v. Albers, 475 U.S. 312 (1986), at 320–321*

Boredom is beautiful.

—*Former Nevada Prison Warden*

12 Corrections Issues and Practices

LEARNING OBJECTIVES

After reading this chapter, the student will be able to:

1 *explain the Supreme Court's rationales for ending juvenile life without parole sentences*

2 *delineate several issues and problems concerning inmate populations: sexual and physical violence, issuing condoms to inmates, hostage taking, and dealing with mentally ill and geriatric inmates*

3 *discuss the rationale and major administrative considerations regarding inmate classification*

4 *describe the problem and possible solutions of drugs in prisons and jails*

5 *articulate the general approach used to drug abuse by a therapeutic community, and kind of approaches that seem to work best*

6 *discuss the pros, cons, and efficacy of privatizing correctional operations and programs*

7 *explain the types and effects of intermediate sanctions that stop short of incarceration*

▶ Introduction

The preceding two chapters in this Part addressed some of the organizational and personnel issues and functions related to correctional institutions (i.e., prisons and jails) and community corrections (probation and parole). This chapter discusses additional issues for correctional administrators regarding their operations.

First, we briefly examine several selected issues in the institutional setting that concern certain offender populations: new developments concerning juvenile offenders and life sentences, sexual and physical violence in prisons (and the Prison Rape Elimination Act of 2003 or PREA), whether or not inmates should be issued condoms, hostage taking in detention facilities, mentally ill and geriatric inmates, the rationale and methods for using inmate classification, and an overview of the drug problem in prisons (to include some treatment efforts). The move to privatize prisons is then examined, including purported advantages, disadvantages, and evaluations of such attempts. After discussions of several intermediate sanctions—punishments that are more severe than mere probation but less than prison—including intensive probation/parole, house arrest (HA), electronic monitoring (EM), shock probation and parole, shock incarceration, and day reporting—the chapter concludes with review questions, "deliberate and decide" problems, and "learn by doing" exercises.

▶ Issues Concerning Inmate Populations

Correctional administrators not only must deal with issues such as institutional population and design, budgets, politics, and the Eighth Amendmenz's proscription against cruel and unusual punishment but also cope with problems relating to the types of inmates who are under their supervision. Next, we consider several selected administrative issues and problems.

Juvenile Justice: An End to Death and Life without Parole Sentences

Over the past 10–15 years, juvenile offenders have received considerable attention from the U.S. Supreme Court, and have seen a more benevolent justice system as a result. First, having ruled in 2005 that it is unconstitutional to execute a person who committed a capital crime while younger than 18 years (see *Roper v. Simmons*, 543 U.S. 551), in May 2010, the U.S. Supreme Court decided *Graham v. Florida*,[1] which held that the Eighth Amendment's ban on cruel and unusual punishment prohibits juveniles who commit nonhomicide crimes from being sentenced to **life without parole (LWOP)** (however, this type of sentence can still be applied to convicted adult offenders, who must spend the remainder of their natural life in prison). Although 37 states, the District of Columbia, and the federal government had laws allowing LWOP sentences for youthful offenders, the justices stated that such sentences had been "rejected the world over," and that only the United States and perhaps Israel had imposed such punishment even for *homicides* committed by juveniles.

Then, in 2012 the Court, combining two cases, ruled that the Eighth Amendment also prohibits sentencing any juvenile offender who commits a murder to serve a term of LWOP sentence (see *Miller v. Alabama* and *Jackson v. Hobbs*).[2] The Court noted that such sentences do not take into account the possibility that an adolescent's personality and judgment are still developing, and that criminal tendencies can be outgrown.

> **life without parole (LWOP)** a type of sentence that can be applied to convicted adult (not juvenile) offenders, requiring that they spend the remainder of their natural life in prison.

Sexual and Physical Violence: Facts of Institutional Life

People who live and work in correctional institutions obviously do not leave their libido at the institution's front gate when they enter. Physical violence is a constant possibility, and **sexual violence**—termed "the plague that persists"[3]—must also be addressed. Sexual violence is defined by the World Health Organization as:

> any sexual act, attempt to obtain a sexual act, unwanted sexual comments or advances, or acts to traffic, or otherwise directed, against a person's sexuality using coercion, by any person regardless of their relationship to the victim, in any setting, including but not limited to home and work.[4]

Persons entering prisons and jails express their sexuality in many forms, with solitary or mutual masturbation at one end of the continuum, consensual homosexual behavior in the middle, and gang rapes at the other end. Factors that appear to increase sexual coercion rates include large population size (more than 1,000 inmates), understaffed workforces, racial conflict, barracks-type housing, inadequate security, and a high percentage of inmates incarcerated for crimes against persons.[5] Furthermore, inmates who are young, physically small or weak, suffering from mental illness, known to be "snitches," not gang affiliated, or convicted of sexual crimes, are at increased risk of sexual victimization.[6]

Wolff and Shi[7] examined physical and sexual victimizations that were reported by nearly 7,000 male inmates. They found that during the period under study, nearly one-third (32%) of inmates had been *physically* assaulted at least once, and approximately 3 percent reported at least one *sexual* assault. On an average, regardless of the type of assault, the victims were typically in their early 30s, African American, had spent 2 years at their prison, had 4 to 5 years left on their current sentences, and had spent roughly 8 years in prison since turning 18. Mental health problems were more frequently reported by victims of sexual assault. The most common forms of physical assault reported were being threatened with a weapon and being hit. Inmate-on-inmate sexual assault most often involved forced, attempted, or coerced anal or oral sex. Physical assaults were most likely to occur between noon and midnight (primarily between noon and 6 P.M.) and in the inmate's cell or yard. For sexual assaults, the inmate's cell was also the most likely place of occurrence, and inmates were at greatest risk of sexual assault by other inmates between 6 P.M. and midnight.[8]

Wolff and Shi also found that inmate-on-inmate physical and sexual assault incidents most often involved attackers with a gang affiliation and with whom the victim was acquainted, and roughly half of the incidents involved the use of a weapon, typically a knife or shank. The victims typically did not know why they were attacked. Episodes of inmate-on-inmate sexual assault were more likely to be committed by a repeat perpetrator, and physical injuries were more likely from inmate-on-inmate sexual assaults; injuries typically involved bruises, cuts, and scratches. One-third of the physical and sexual assaults resulted in medical attention, and about one-fifth of the incidents involving medical attention required hospitalization outside the prison.[9]

Several policy issues arise from these findings. Wolff and Shi[10] suggest that, at a minimum, an intervention plan be employed that is selectively targeted to prison areas and times of day, and to inmates who are most at risk (e.g., those with mental illness; mental disabilities; or bisexual, transsexual, or homosexual orientations); these at-risk individuals should be placed in single cells or protective units. Prison administrators must attempt to prevent and prosecute sexual assaults, as well as increase surveillance in vulnerable areas, such as transportation vans, holding tanks, shower rooms, stairways, and storage areas. Finally, new inmates should be informed of the potential for being sexually assaulted while incarcerated and be told about prevention and what medical, legal, and psychological help is available if they are targeted.[11]

The Prison Rape Elimination Act of 2003

Until recently, there were very little current data or information on the extent of sexual coercion in prisons. Fortunately, however, federal legislation has indirectly provided some enlightenment. As part of the **Prison Rape Elimination Act of 2003** (P.L. 108-79), the U.S. Department of Justice's Bureau of Justice Statistics (BJS) was mandated to develop a new national data collection effort on the incidence and prevalence of sexual assault in correctional facilities. The law also required that public hearings be held concerning the prisons having the highest and lowest rates in order to determine what they are doing, that is, right and wrong; ultimately, a commission is to develop national standards for preventing prison rape.[12]

A BJS survey of federal and state prisons and local jails found that the number of allegations of sexual violence actually *increased* by 21 percent following enactment of the PREA; some of this increase, BJS states, may be the result of new definitions being adopted as well as improved reporting by correctional authorities. In fact, a more recent BJS survey found that, while the problem of sexual violence still exists, it is at least consistent with patterns over the previous 6 years.[13] Following are some of the BJS findings:

- An estimated 4 percent of state and federal prison inmates and 3.2 percent of jail inmates experienced one or more incidents of sexual victimization in the past 12 months.

- Among state and federal prison inmates, 2 percent reported an incident involving another inmate, 2.4 percent reported an incident involving facility staff, and 0.4% reported both an incident by another inmate and staff.

- About 1.6 percent of jail inmates reported an incident with another inmate, 1.8% reported an incident with staff, and 0.2% reported both an incident by another inmate and staff.[14]

> **Prison Rape Elimination Act of 2003** a law mandating national data collection on the incidence and prevalence of sexual assault in correctional facilities.

Should Inmates Be Issued Condoms?

An issue related to the earlier discussion of sexual violence in prisons is whether or not inmates should be given condoms. Given that prison inmates have unprotected sexual contact, both forced and consensual—and often leading to the spread of HIV and other diseases in the prisons as well as in communities where felons are paroled—the question is raised about the possible wisdom of offering inmates condoms.

In mid-2013, California lawmakers began considering just that—a proposal to do so in five prisons by 2015 and expand the program to each of the state's 33 adult prisons no later than 2020. To date, the Vermont Department of Corrections is the only state making condoms available throughout its prison system; it has been doing so since 1992, and the state's 2,200 inmates can request one condom at a time from a nurse. Canada, most of the European Union, Australia, Brazil, Indonesia, and South Africa already offer condoms to inmates. Mississippi has provided condoms to inmates for at least 20 years, but only to the few (about 10%) of inmates who are married and qualify for conjugal visits.[15]

Public health officials have found few problems and recommended the program be expanded. Similarly, the Center for Health Justice has found no related security problems in cities where condoms are being issued.[16] On the other hand, critics believe that handing out condoms would result in increased levels of voluntary or forced sexual activity, and that the condoms could be used to smuggle or hide drugs and other contraband.

From a policy standpoint, what must be recognized is that illicit relations by inmates have always been, and will likely always be an ongoing problem, and no state law barring inmate sex alone will solve the problem. Perhaps what might serve to convince both camps—those pros and cons—is an estimate by the University of California, San Francisco, that the rate of HIV infection among state prison inmates is 10 times higher than in the population at large; in addition, California's prison officials estimate that more than 1,000 prisoners are HIV-infected, or about 1 percent of the state's inmate population.[17]

But prison and jail administrators take another tack: Issuing condoms sends the wrong message, it encourages consensual or coercive sex (and prison rapists might use condoms to avoid leaving DNA evidence after their assaults), and condoms can be used to conceal drugs. In late 2007, California Governor Arnold Schwarzenegger agreed and vetoed a bill that would have provided condoms in penal institutions statewide. This issue is difficult for proponents to promote, and may or may not remain on the table for discussion. As the policy director of the Center for Health Justice says, "People don't like to think about prisoners having sex, even though everybody knows it goes on."[18]

Hostage Taking in Detention Facilities: An Overview

Nature of the Problem

Riots and hostage taking are probably as old as corrections itself, and are the jail and prison administrator's worst nightmare. They can occur at any time; even the most safety-concerned staff cannot always avoid such crises. Inmates will be inmates, and they do not want to be where they are.[19] A corrections **hostage-taking** event occurs when any person—staff, visitor, or inmate—is held against his or her will by an inmate seeking to escape, gain concessions, or achieve other goals such as publicizing a particular cause. It may also be a planned or an impulsive act. When they occur, jail and prison rioting and hostage taking are potentially explosive and perilous situations from beginning to end; hostages are always directly in harm's way.[20] Following are some examples of such incidents:

- At the Morey Unit of the Lewis Prison Complex in Buckeye, Arizona, two inmates took two correctional officers (COs) hostage and seized the unit's tower, triggering a 15-day standoff—the longest prison hostage situation in the nation's history.[21]

- Approximately 450 prisoners rioted in the Southern Ohio Correctional Facility, in Lucasville, Ohio; nine inmates and one officer were murdered and six officers taken hostage during the 10-day siege.[22]

- Jail inmates in a Louisiana parish held the warden and two corrections officers hostage at knifepoint, demanding a helicopter to escape to Cuba or anywhere else.[23]

- A SWAT team stormed the Bay County Jail in Florida after inmates threatened to rape and cut off the body parts of a fourth hostage, a nurse; four inmates overpowered the only officer on the floor, leading to an 11-hour standoff.[24]

Also permanently seared in the annals of corrections rioting are the horrific incidents at the Attica Correctional Facility in Attica, New York, in 1971 (39 inmates and staff killed), and at the New Mexico State Prison in Santa Fe, in 1980 (33 inmates dead), where inmates took over most of these institutions.[25]

Local jails are included in this discussion because such incidents certainly occur in them, and are even more common in jails in foreign venues. U.S. jails—such as prisons—can become quite dangerous because of their overcrowded conditions and the nature of their clientele, which will include arrestees awaiting trial for felony offenses, mentally ill persons awaiting movement to health facilities, convicted felons awaiting transport to a state or federal institution, military offenders, and many violent, often mentally unstable or sociopathic offenders with histories of substance abuse; certainly such individuals are capable of hostage taking. Indeed, 4 of 10 jail inmates have a violent arrest record.[26] Because 85 percent of local jails are operated by sheriff's offices or municipal police departments,[27] local sheriffs and police chiefs with lockup responsibilities must shoulder the burden of preparing for such emergencies.

hostage taking when any person—staff, visitor, or inmate—is held against his or her will by an inmate seeking to escape, gain concessions, or achieve other goals.

Administrative Considerations: Using Force and Negotiation

Before correctional administrators can begin to plan for emergencies within their facilities, the following three broad elements are especially important: command, planning, and training (subsequently). Successful resolution also requires a controlled, measured response, clear lines of authority, and effective communication. Unity of command—the principle that members of an organization are accountable to a single superior—is also a paramount consideration.[28] Also, staffing levels must be established—traditional crisis response teams (CRTs), armed CRTs, and tactical teams—all of which can employ less lethal intervention options and even the use of deadly force:

1. *Traditional CRTs.* The first, primary level of response is the traditional CRT, which is composed of staff from all job specialties who train in riot control formations and use of defensive equipment (e.g., batons, stun guns, chemical agents, control, and containment).

2. *Armed CRTs.* This level of response provides managers with an option for dealing with the emergency situation if it escalates to the point where staff members' or inmates' lives are in imminent danger; it involves a specially trained team that can respond with deadly force when necessary.

3. *Tactical teams.* These are the most highly trained and skilled emergency response staff. They must be trained in advanced skills such as barricade breaching; hostage rescue; and precision marksmanship with pistols, rifles, and assault rifles.[29]

Another critical element of emergency planning is a use-of-force policy. Which staff members are authorized to order the use of force, and what weapons and less lethal munitions are appropriate? The riot plan should also include contact names and phone numbers and an outline of existing agreements between agencies.[30] Training is another indispensable facet of emergency planning. It does little good to have an emergency plan if staff and supervisors are not trained to activate it; people must clearly understand their own functions as well as those of people in other components; indeed, negotiators and personnel from tactical teams should train together regularly.[31]

The goals of hostage negotiation are to open communication lines, reduce stress and tension, build rapport, obtain intelligence, stall for time, allow hostage takers to express emotion and ventilate, and establish a problem-solving atmosphere.[32] Jail/prison records will provide valuable intelligence information on the hostage taker, including prior criminal, educational, work, psychological, and family history. Studies of hostage negotiations indicate that they tend to follow a common cycle: Initially, both parties make exaggerated demands. This is followed by a period of withdrawal and a return to negotiations with more moderate demands.

The passage of time can be a very important ally during such incidents and is a major element of the negotiator's role. Often, the preferred strategy for negotiating is to wait it out. The advantages of time's passing include that hostage takers may develop sympathy for their hostages, develop rapport with negotiators, or just get tired of doing what they are doing.[33] The question "How long is too long?" cannot be easily answered because every incident is different. Generally, negotiations may continue if no one is being injured and if no major damage or destruction to the facility is occurring

Certain demands by hostage takers are nonnegotiable: Allowing release or escape, weapons, an exchange of hostages, and pardon or parole are not on the table. A number of other demands are open to negotiation. A maxim of negotiations is "Always get something for something." Negotiators should never cede to a demand without obtaining a concession in return.[34] Nor should they engage in trickery such as trying to drug hostage takers' food or drink (it might backfire) or have face-to-face contact (unless, as in rare instances, the decision is made that it is advantageous to do so).[35]

When negotiations deadlock, commanders may decide to employ ultimatums regarding use of force and issues. A *use-of-force ultimatum* can be given in the expectation that inmates, given a clear choice between surrender and an armed assault, will choose surrender.[36]

Aftermath: A Return to Normalcy

In the aftermath of hostage incidents, it is critical to learn whether or not there were contributing factors such as lax inmate search activities, contraband, contractors and visitors coming and going, inmate familiarity with staff work routines, unlocked doors or gates, or other contributing factors; if so, new policies and procedures must be enacted covering those exigencies. The administration must also consider any damages, renovations, repairs, and remodeling that need to be addressed, and continuing control of the inmates while these are attended to.[37]

Mentally Ill Offenders

While in solitary confinement in a Massachusetts prison, an inmate cut his legs and arms, tried to hang himself with tubing from a breathing machine, smashed the machine to get a sharp fragment to slice his neck, and ate pieces of it, hoping to cause internal bleeding; he eventually hanged himself. Such inmates, with histories of mental illness and depression, often try suicide. In fact, this was one of 18 suicides or attempted suicides since 2004; a federal lawsuit filed by advocates for inmates and the mentally ill is seeking to prevent the state from placing mentally ill inmates in such segregated cells.[38]

Several other states have faced similar lawsuits and other challenges in attempting to address the problem of **mentally ill inmates**. These are prisoners who meet a specified definition based on the diagnostic system of the American Psychiatric Association, and can include schizophrenia, bipolar disorders, and major depression, among others.[39]

Following are some related developments:

- In 2007, Indiana agreed to stop putting some mentally ill inmates in isolation cells.

- In California, after a record number of prison suicides—44—in 2005, a special master appointed by a federal judge reported that inmates "in overcrowded and understaffed segregation units are killing themselves in unprecedented numbers." The judge also ordered the governor to spend more than $600 million to improve mental health services.

- In New York, the legislature passed a law in 2007 to remove mentally ill inmates from solitary cells, but the governor vetoed it.[40]

- All states are struggling with what to do about inmates who are very violent, out of control, need to be segregated from other inmates, and also mentally ill. Such segregated inmates are typically locked up for 23 hours per day, allowed out only to shower or get outdoor exercise in a small caged space. A national expert in prison suicide argues that confining suicidal inmates under such circumstances only enhances their feeling of isolation and is antitherapeutic.[41]

Owing to several causes—the closing or downsizing of state psychiatric hospitals, the lack of adequate community support programs, chronic underfunding of public services, the poverty and transient lifestyles of many people with serious mental illness, and substance abuse disorders—the number of criminal offenders and inmates suffering from mental illness has been increasing.[42] In prison, these individuals pose a dual dilemma for administrators. They are often violent and may be serving a long sentence; therefore, they require a high level of security and are housed with other offenders who have committed equally serious offenses and who are serving equally long sentences. The presence of potentially violent, mentally ill prisoners in high-security and probably overcrowded institutions is a dangerous situation. Mental illness must be treated while inmates are incarcerated.

mentally ill inmate one who meets the definition and has a significant mental disorder(s), which can include schizophrenia, bipolar disorders, and major depression, among others.

A related problem concerns the release of mentally ill convicts back into the community. These inmates must be tracked and supervised to ensure that they receive proper case management and stay on their medications. This approach goes far beyond the traditional "$25 in gate money and a bus ticket" for the inmate, and not only protects the public but also helps to hold the prison population down. To provide these follow-up services, many states have developed written agreements between the state and local correctional agencies and between the state and local mental health services agencies. Local mental health agencies can be used to provide counseling and support to probationers. The challenge for correctional administrators is to maintain a viable program to treat and control a difficult group of offenders. The treatment of this group requires resources, trained staff, and appropriate facilities.

Geriatric Inmates: Problems and Approaches

Rich, violent, or otherwise celebrated convicts who are in the sunset of their lives often receive the most public attention; recent examples include:

- Bernie Madoff, age 71 at the time he received a sentence of 150 years for Ponzi schemes in 2009.[43]

- James "Whitey" Bulger, Boston's most notorious gangster, was convicted in 2013 at age 84 for 11 murders and 31 counts of racketeering, extortion, money laundering, trafficking in cocaine and marijuana, and weapons possession; he was sentenced in November 2013 to two life sentences plus 5 years after evading capture for 16 years.[44]

- Anthony Marshall, an 89-year-old heir to one of America's first mega-fortunes (he is the son of late New York writer and philanthropist Brooke Astor), was taken to prison in a wheelchair in 2013 to serve a 1-to-3-year sentence for taking advantage of his aged mother's slipping mind and looting her millions.[45]

However, those inmates are only the tip of the iceberg in what has become a significant national problem: the special needs of **geriatric inmates**. According to the Vera Institute of Justice, there is no national consensus or definition concerning when an inmate qualifies as "old" or "elderly." While the U.S. Census Bureau defines the general "elderly" population as those 65 and older, the 27 states that have definitions for who is an "older prisoner" include 15 states that used age 50 as the cutoff, 5 states using age 55, 4 states 60, 2 states 65, and 1 used age 70.[46]

What is known, however, is that prisoners older than 55 make up the single fastest-growing segment of the U.S. prison community—indeed, approximately 245,000 inmates are now above age 50 and are raising medical costs dramatically (see Exhibit 12.1). Unforeseen consequences of legislative enactments—tougher mandatory sentencing laws, "truth in sentencing" laws, three-strikes laws, and the abolition of parole for certain violent offenders (with concurrent reductions in early release)—have combined to put people in prison longer and create this situation.[47]

Certainly prison administrators are already confronted with an aging inmate population, seeing increasing numbers of prisoners who need wheelchairs, walkers, canes, oxygen bottles, and hearing aids; many cannot even dress or go to the bathroom by themselves and are incontinent, suffering from dementia and chronic illnesses, extremely ill, or dying. They also see the high costs of caring for these inmates: Estimates by the National Institute of Corrections are that states spend about $70,000 a year to incarcerate someone age 50 or older—about triple the cost to house a younger prisoner; this gap is largely due to higher health care costs.[48]

Some states now contract with private or private providers to establish and operate skilled nursing facilities to incarcerate and care for inmates who (1) have limited ability to

geriatric inmates while there is no standard definition concerning what age an inmate becomes "elderly," it is known that the aging inmate population is growing rapidly, raising medical costs and requiring special needs be met.

perform activities of daily living and (2) need skilled nursing services. Others contract with physicians to assess and diagnose all inmates who are limited in performing activities of daily living; the physicians then develop a service plan to meet the individual inmate's medical and mental health needs, and to see they are housed consistent with their custody level and medical status. Other states have developed special units to work with the cognitively impaired (dementia).[49] Finally, one state has a dedicated structured living program just for such inmates (see Exhibit 12.1).

There are some relatively easy, short-term responses and accommodations that can be adopted for this growing population: assigning them to a bottom bunk, installing grab bars near the toilets and in showers, housing them closer to the dining hall, and giving them more time to report to prison counts.[50] However, policy decisions and recommendations for a more long-term timeframe are more challenging; in short, the policy question that requires more thought and attention concerns what to do, as a society, with inmates who suffer from dementia or have become nearly or totally paralyzed—in short, how to make society safe but also be as humanitarian as possible.

NEVADA'S PROGRAM FOR GERIATRIC INMATES

Only about 5.8 percent of Nevada's 13,000 prison inmates are age 60 and older, but they consume 20 percent of the medical budget. The state now has 14 inmates in their 80s, and until recently, 1 inmate was in his 90s.[51]

A unique—and increasingly publicized—program at the Northern Nevada Correctional Center in Carson City, Nevada, called the Senior Structured Living Program (SSLP), is designed to work with such inmates. The program provides physical fitness, diversion therapy (arts, crafts, games, reading, poetry), music (a choir and band), wellness and life skills training, individual and group therapy, and community involvement (involving area social services, veterans', Alcoholics Anonymous, and other groups). Volunteers also provide psychological, spiritual, and social support to the men. To enter the program, inmates must sign a contract obligating them to maintain certain standards of conduct, be at least 60 years of age, and not be engaged in a full-time job or educational program. Today 170 men are enrolled in the program (with a waiting list of 50); although an extensive evaluation of the program is under way, it is known that the prison medical department has witnessed a significant reduction in the men's overall medical complaints, overutilization of medical care, and the use of psychotropic medications.[52]

---

classification the placing of inmates into the proper levels of security, housing, programming, and other aspects of their incarceration.

unit management a corrections management approach with the larger prison population being subdivided into smaller units, felt to be more effective and to improve inmate classification.

Inmate Classification: Cornerstone of Security and Treatment

Although it may not seem to be so on its face, the **classification** of inmates into the proper levels of security, housing, programming, and other aspects of their incarceration will have major influence on their behavior, treatment, and progress while in custody as well as the general safety of inmates and staff.

Corrections staff must make classification decisions in at least two areas: the inmate's level of *physical restraint* or "security level" and the inmate's level of supervision or *custody grade*.

These two concepts are not well understood and are often confused, but they significantly impact a prisoner's housing and program assignments[53] as well as an institution's overall security level.

The most recent development in classification is **unit management**, in which a large prison population is subdivided into several mini-institutions analogous to a city and its neighborhoods.

Unit management is felt to be a more humane, effective, and efficient approach than the former, centralized approach. A unit can include a unit manager, case manager(s), counselor(s), full- or part-time psychologist(s) and education representative, and correctional officers whose offices are on the living unit; this approach also enables classification decisions to be made by personnel who are in daily contact with their inmates and know them fairly well.[54]

Robert Levinson delineated four categories into which corrections agencies classify new inmates: security, custody, housing, and programs[55]:

1. *Security* needs are classified in terms of the number and types of architectural barriers that must be placed between the inmates and the outside world to ensure that they will not escape and can be controlled. Most correctional systems have four security levels: supermax (highest), maximum (high), medium (low), and minimum (lowest).

2. *Custody* assignments determine the level of supervision and types of privileges an inmate will have. A basic consideration is whether or not an inmate will be allowed to go outside the facility's secure perimeter, so some systems have adopted four custody grades—two inside the fence (one more restrictive than the other) and two outside the fence (one more closely supervised than the other).

3. *Housing* needs were historically determined by an "assign to the next empty bed" system, which could place the new, weak inmate in the same cell with the most hardened inmate; a more sophisticated approach is known as *internal classification*, in which inmates are assigned to live with prisoners who are similar to themselves. This approach can involve the grouping of inmates into three broad categories: heavy (victimizers), light (victims), and moderate (neither intimidated by the first group nor abusers of the second).

4. *Program* classification involves using interview and testing data to determine where the newly arrived inmate should be placed in work, training, and treatment programs; these are designed to help the prisoner make a successful return to society.

In the past, most prison systems used a highly subjective system of classifying inmates that involved a review of records pertaining to the inmate's prior social and criminal history, test scores, school and work performance, and staff impressions developed from interviews. Today, however, administrators employ a much-preferred objective system that is more rational, efficient, and equitable. Factors used in making classification decisions are measurable and valid and are applied to all inmates in the same way. Criteria most often used are escape history, detainers, prior commitments, criminal history, prior institutional adjustment, history of violence, and length of sentence.[56]

Drug Use in Prisons: Interdiction and Treatment

More than half of all adult arrestees test positive for drug use at the time of their apprehension; their drug use prior to incarceration is typically chronic. Indeed, 50 percent of federal prisoners and 56 percent of state prison inmates used drugs during the month before the arrest for which they were incarcerated.[57] Furthermore, offenders still manage to obtain illicit drugs during their incarceration, threatening the safety of inmates and staff while undermining the authority of correctional administrators, contradicting rehabilitative goals, and reducing public confidence.[58]

Next, we discuss Pennsylvania's approach to **drug interdiction**, which may be defined as a continuum of efforts to reduce the supply and demand for drugs in the prison, and includes focusing on visitors, staff, mail, warehouses, gates, volunteers, and contractors. Then, we look at what can be done to treat offenders' substance abuse problems inside the institution.

drug interdiction
efforts to reduce the supply and demand for drugs in prison, to include focusing on visitors, staff, mail, warehouses, gates, volunteers, and contractors.

The Pennsylvania Plan

The state of Pennsylvania was compelled to acknowledge that drug use was pervasive in several of its prisons. Six inmates had died from overdoses in a 2-year period, and assaults on COs and inmates had increased. To combat the problem, the state first adopted a zero-tolerance drug policy, the so-called Pennsylvania plan for drug interdiction: Inmates caught with drugs were to be criminally prosecuted, and those who tested positive (using hair testing) were to serve disciplinary custody time. Highly sensitive drug detection equipment was employed to detect drugs that visitors might try to smuggle into the prison, to inspect packages arriving in the mail, and to detect drugs that correctional staff might try to bring in. New policies were issued for inmate movement and visitation, and a new phone system was installed to randomly monitor inmates' calls.[59]

The results were impressive. The state's 24 prisons became 99 percent drug free. The number of drug finds during cell searches dropped 41 percent, assaults on staff decreased 57 percent, inmate-on-inmate assaults declined 70 percent, and the number of weapons seized during searches dropped from 220 to 76. Marijuana use dropped from 6.5 percent before interdiction to 0.3 percent, and there was a significant decline in the use of other types of drugs. Pennsylvania now believes that the foundation has been laid for inmates to abstain from drug use during service of their sentences—a necessary first step toward long-term abstinence and becoming a better citizen for their families and communities.[60]

Treating the Problem

During the past several years, a number of aggressive federal and state initiatives have been undertaken to expand substance abuse treatment within correctional settings. These initiatives have been fueled by the high rates of substance abuse among offenders and the view that intensive prison-based treatment efforts can significantly reduce postprison substance use and recidivism.[61]

Several barriers remain for correctional administrators in implementing substance abuse treatment programs, however. First, institutions tend to use limited criteria (such as any lifetime drug use, possession, drug sales, trafficking) to determine the need for treatment, leading to a lack of treatment of a large portion of the prison population that has abused substances; conversely, many inmates who legitimately need treatment may be excluded for reasons unrelated to their substance abuse problems (gang affiliation or the commission of a sexual or violent offense). Treatment staff should be involved in the selection of candidates to ensure the appropriateness of the program population.[62]

Second, it is difficult to find and recruit qualified and experienced staff in the remote areas where prisons are often located. In addition, counselors who are well suited for community-based treatment programs will not necessarily be effective in the prison setting. They often resist the rigid custody regulations that are common in institutional settings. For these reasons, limited human resources and high turnover rates for drug abuse treatment counselors make staffing an ongoing problem for prison administrators.[63]

Possible solutions to this staffing problem include offering sufficient wages and other amenities to induce counselors to move to and stay with the prison, recruiting and training "lifers" as inmate counselors and mentors, and professionalizing treatment positions for COs. With the use of counselors, certification and financial incentives would help to retain staff, as well as enhance their professional development for the treatment setting.[64]

Can a "Therapeutic Community" Work?

As indicated earlier, drug use is not unknown to most prison inmates, with more than half of all adult arrestees testing positive for drug use at the time of their apprehension and using drugs during the month before the arrest for which they were incarcerated. Several treatment modalities have been attempted in the past to deal with such offenders, to include individual and group counseling, methadone maintenance, shock incarceration (or boot camp), drug education, and 12-step programs.[65]

One of the most widely used treatment models, however, is the **therapeutic community** (TC). Existing for more than a half-century, TCs are typically drug-free residential settings relying heavily on peer influence and group processes to promote drug-free behavior. At the root of TCs is the provision of an environment in which drug abusers seek and receive support from individuals with similar problems. Also extremely important for drug-abusing inmates' success is aftercare upon release.

Evaluations of TCs with prison inmates have been mostly positive, finding that TCs that include aftercare are both effective and cost-effective in reducing drug use and recidivism. However, the use of boot camps (or shock incarceration) and group counseling have not been found to be effective in these regards. Most studies of TCs have been based on short-term outcomes, typically 1 to 2 years following release.[66]

A more long-term study, using 5 years of data with about 400 California inmates, contradicted these studies; however, it found that TCs as implemented there failed to reduce reincarceration and rearrest over time. Researchers believed that this was a result of the prison TC program failing to optimize its aftercare-phase treatment. Furthermore, because most aftercare programs are voluntary, it appears that inmates there fell short of the levels of participation needed, and thus successful reintegration into the community.[67]

The implications are obvious: Because few prison drug programs are available, and yet the demand for such programming remains high, there needs to be rigorous research into what seems to work best for the TC as a treatment strategy.

> **therapeutic community** drug-free residential settings relying heavily on peer influence and group processes to promote drug-free behavior.

▶ The Move Toward Privatization

Emergence of the Concept

Perhaps one of the most controversial and rapidly growing aspects of corrections has been the outsourcing or **privatization** of prisons: a term that includes either the operation of existing prison facilities, or the building and operation of new prisons by for-profit companies. In 1995, there were fewer than 30 adult confinement facilities operated by private contractors. Within 5 years, private prisons had increased to more than 100.[68] Now, the BJS reports that about 130,000 state and federal inmates (8.2% of all such inmates) are being held in private correctional facilities.[69] Taken together, private facilities would be the third largest state-level prison system, following only Texas and California.[70]

The two largest companies, the Corrections Corporation of America (CCA) and the Geo Group, reported combined revenues of $2.9 billion in 2010. The CCA houses about 80,000 prisoners; of the more than 60 facilities it operates, it owns 44.[71]

Historically, strong arguments have been put forth, both pro and con, regarding the privatizing of prisons; and today there is no dearth of differing points of view on the matter. Proponents, such as the Reason Foundation, argue that private prisons:

> **privatization** either the operation of existing prison facilities, or the building and operation of new prisons by for-profit companies.

provide an effective, cost-saving alternative for governments seeking to address significant capacity needs while taking pressure off their corrections budgets. Studies have consistently shown that privately run correctional facilities typically save a conservative range of 5 to 15% over staterun prisons while offering the same level of security and service and easing overcrowding in staterun prisons.[72]

Opponents, on the other hand, maintain that there is no guarantee that standards will be upheld, no one will maintain security if employees go on strike, the public will have regular access to the facility, there will be different inmate disciplinary procedures, the company will be able to refuse certain inmates or could go bankrupt, and the company can increase its fees to the state.[73]

Evaluation: Seven "Domains"

Which is better—public or private prisons? First, while perhaps inevitably, there is a tendency to compare public and private institutions in terms of their inmates' recidivism rates; some observers, however,[74] argue that this is an unfair comparison, as prison administrators are not responsible for what occurs outside of their prison's walls.

What might stand as a much better and comprehensive standard to use for comparison is that which was developed originally in 1992 by Charles H. Logan,[75] and refined in 2003 by Dina Perrone and Travis C. Pratt,[76] which are termed the "seven domains" of prison quality and include the following:

- *Condition*, which refers to the physical environment in which the inmates are held. Indications of a poorly kept prison such as crowding, noise, food, and sanitation have been used as measures.
- *Management*, which refers to the ability of the prison administrators to effectively and efficiently run their institution; it can be measured by comparing staff turnover and stress rates.
- *Activity*, which refers to the ability of prison administrators to keep their inmate population involved and active in prison life; this domain is commonly measured in terms of the number of educational, treatment, and work programs available to and used by inmates.
- *Care*, referring to the extent and quality of medical care afforded to inmates.
- *Security* measures how well the prison is able to keep its inmates securely incapacitated from the outside world; it can be evaluated by measuring the number of escapes, while some studies have also taken into account the amount of contraband entering the prison.
- *Safety* refers to the ability to keep both inmates and prison staff from being assaulted or killed; and
- *Order*, which refers to the overall ability of an institution to control its population; often considered is the number of disciplinary actions and disturbances that occur.

No single study has examined all seven domains; however, a number of studies have examined the quality of private prisons by examining some of the domains. The results have tended to be mixed in all such studies, with most comparing only a small number of private institutions (usually one or two) to a public institution(s); therefore, generalizing these findings to other institutions is problematic. Another shortcoming is that custody level, size, crowding, age, and architecture can all have a strong influence on such measures of quality.

Makarios and Maahs sought, in 2012, to address these shortcomings by examining a larger sample of private and public prisons. Specifically, they looked at 1,129 institutions—105 of which were private, 80, federal; and 944, state-operated.[77] They found a significant difference in one regard: State prisons were much more likely to be under a court order for the conditions of confinement than private prisons. Therefore, private prisons are less crowded than those that are publicly operated. Given the negative effects of crowding, this is a significant finding and most likely a result of public facilities having much less control over the level and nature of new admissions.

Overall, however, Makarios and Maahs generally found a fair degree of similarity between private and public prisons. Consistent with prior research, they find that "the differences between private and public prisons become relatively small."[78]

► Alternatives to Incarceration: Intermediate Sanctions

The United States is not soft on crime, but because prisons are not in a position to effect great change,[79] the search for solutions must include correctional programs in the community. The demand for prison space has created a reaction throughout the corrections industry.[80] With the cost of prison construction now exceeding $250,000 per cell in maximum-security institutions, cost-saving alternatives are becoming more attractive, if not essential.

An **alternative to incarceration** can be any form of punishment or treatment other than prison or jail time given to a convicted person. It must have three elements to be effective—it must incapacitate offenders enough so that it is possible to interfere with their lives and activities to make committing a new offense extremely difficult, it must be unpleasant enough to deter offenders from wanting to commit new crimes, and it has to provide real and credible protection for the community.[81]

The aforementioned realities of prison construction and crowding have led to a search for an intermediate range of punishments.[82] This, in turn, has brought about the emergence of a new generation of programs, making community-based corrections, according to Barry Nidorf, a "strong, full partner in the fight against crime and a leader in confronting the crowding crisis."[83] Economic reality dictates that cost-effective measures be developed, and this is motivating the development of **intermediate sanctions**[84]: a range of sentencing options designed to fill the gap between probation and confinement, reduce institutional crowding, and reduce correctional costs. In the past, they have included such punishments as intensive supervision probation (ISP), problem-solving courts, fines, community service, day reporting centers, home detention/electronic monitoring, and boot camps.

A recent survey by the BJS found that, of all persons being supervised outside a jail facility, 25 percent were engaged in some form of community service and 17 percent were involved in EM; fewer than 1 percent were undergoing home detention only.[85] Table 12-1 ■ shows these findings as well as the number of persons under jail supervision and involved with other types of programs.

> **alternatives to incarceration** any form of punishment or treatment other than prison or jail time given to a convicted person.

> **intermediate sanctions** a range of sentencing options designed to fill the gap between probation and confinement, reduce institutional crowding, and reduce correctional costs.

TABLE 12.1 Persons under jail supervision, by confinement status and type of program, midyear 2000 and 2006–2012

Confinement status and type of program	2000	2006	2007	2008	2009	2010	2011	2012
Total	687,033	826,041	848,419	858,385	837,647	809,360	798,417	808,622
Held in jail	621,149	765,819	780,174	785,533	767,434	748,728	735,601	744,524
Supervised outside of a jail facility	65,884	60,222	68,245	72,852	70,213	60,632	62,816	64,098
Weekend programs	14,523	11,421	10,473	12,325	11,212	9,871	11,369	10,351
Electronic monitoring	10,782	10,999	13,121	13,539	11,834	12,319	11,950	13,779
Home detention	332	807	512	498	738	736	809	2,129
Day reporting	3,969	4,841	6,163	5,758	6,492	5,552	5,200	3,890
Community service	13,592	14,667	15,327	18,475	17,738	14,646	11,680	14,761
Other pretrial supervision	6,279	6,409	11,148	12,452	12,439	9,375	10,464	7,738
Other work programs	8,011	8,319	7,369	5,808	5,912	4,351	7,165	7,137
Treatment programs	5,714	1,486	2,276	2,259	2,082	1,799	2,449	2,164
Other	2,682	1,273	1,857	1,739	1,766	1,983	1,731	2,149

Intensive Probation or Parole

Intensive supervision—tight control and supervision of offenders in the community through strict enforcement of conditions and frequent reporting to a probation officer—has become a popular program in probation and parole. Early versions were based on the premise that increased client contact would enhance rehabilitation while affording greater client control. Current programs are simply a means of easing the burden of prison crowding.[86]

Intensive supervision can be classified into two types: those stressing diversion and those stressing enhancement. A diversion program is commonly known as a *front door* program because its goal is to limit the number of generally low-risk offenders who enter prison. Enhancement programs generally select already sentenced probationers and parolees and subject them to closer supervision in the community than they receive under regular probation or parole.[87]

As of 1990, jurisdictions in all 50 states had instituted ISP. Persons placed on ISP are supposedly those offenders who, in the absence of intensive supervision, would have been sentenced to imprisonment. In parole, intensive supervision is viewed as risk management—allowing a high-risk inmate to be paroled but under the most restrictive circumstances. In either case, intensive supervision is a response to crowding; although ISP is invariably more costly than regular supervision, the costs "are compared not with the costs of normal supervision but rather with the costs of incarceration."[88]

ISP is demanding for probationers and parolees and does not represent freedom; in fact, it may stress and isolate repeat offenders more than imprisonment does. Given the option of serving prison terms or participating in ISPs, many offenders have chosen prison.[89] Many offenders may prefer to serve a short prison term rather than spend five times as long a period in ISP. Consider the alternatives now facing offenders in one western state:

> **ISP.** The offender serves 2 years under this alternative. During that time, a probation officer visits the offender two or three times per week and phones on the other days. The offender is subject to unannounced searches of his or her home for drugs and has his or her urine tested regularly for alcohol and drugs. The offender must strictly abide by other conditions set by the court: not carrying a weapon, not socializing with certain persons, performing community service, and being employed or participating in training or education. In addition, he or she is strongly encouraged to attend counseling and/or other treatment, particularly if he or she is a drug offender.

> **Prison.** The alternative is a sentence of 2 to 4 years, of which the offender will serve only about 3 to 6 months. During this term, the offender is not required to work or to participate in any training or treatment but may do so voluntarily. Once released, the offender is placed on 2-year routine parole supervision and must visit his or her parole officer about once a month.[90]

Although compelling evidence of the effectiveness of ISP is lacking, it has been deemed a public relations success.[91] Intensive supervision is usually accomplished by greatly reducing the caseload size per probation or parole officer, leading to increased contact between officers and clients or their significant others (such as the client's spouse or parents). It is hoped that this increased contact will improve service delivery and control and thus reduce recidivism.[92]

House Arrest

Although **house arrest** (or home detention)—typically court-ordered punishment where convicted or accused offenders must remain in their home, usually while being monitored electronically, and can leave only for work, community service, or medical attention—has also become increasingly common, BJS data provided in Table 12-1 show only about 2,100 of 64,000 offenders (3%) who were supervised outside of a jail facility were on home detention only. It is seen that many more (about 14,000, or about 22%) were being monitored electronically—many of them being monitored in their homes. The primary motivation for using this intermediate sanction is a financial one: the conservation of scarce resources. It is also hoped, of course, that HA is more effective in preventing recidivism than traditional probation alone or incarceration.

Many people apparently feel that HA is not effective or punitive enough. Indeed, one study reported that nearly half (44%) of the public feels that HA is not very effective or not effective at all.[93]

Does HA work? Jeffery Ulmer[94] found that the sentencing combination associated with the least likelihood of rearrest was HA/probation. The combinations of HA/work release and HA/incarceration were also significantly associated with decreased chances of rearrest compared with traditional probation. Furthermore, whenever any other sentence option was paired with HA, that sentence combination significantly reduced the chances and frequency of rearrest.[95] Clearly, HA works when used in tandem with other forms of sentencing options.

What is it about HA that might explain its success? It puts the offender in touch with opportunities and resources for rehabilitative services (such as substance abuse or sex offender counseling, anger management classes, and so on), which supports the contention that for intermediate sanctions of any type to reduce recidivism, they must include a rehabilitative emphasis.[96]

Electronic Monitoring

The use of EM (**electronic monitoring**)—the use of technologies by probation and parole officers to monitor remotely the physical location of an offender—is accelerating rapidly (see Table 12-1), with HA and EM programs being combined for use with new categories of offenders.[97] It is far cheaper to keep an offender at home on EM than to incarcerate him or her in prison—which runs about $62 per day compared with EM's cost of about $5.00 per day. Even a higher-level system where an e-mail is sent or a beep goes off if an offender goes past set boundaries or active monitoring (an offender's movement is tracked on a computer screen) costs only about $12 a day.[98]

Martin et al.[99] examined offenders' perceptions of HA/EM. The typical respondent in their survey spent approximately 1 month on HA/EM, paid $3,578.00 in fines, and provided 17 hours of community service. Respondents indicated that while being sentenced to HA was preferable to being incarcerated, it is a punitive sanction. These punitive aspects are manifested in at least two ways:

- The restrictive nature of personal freedoms: Offenders reported that this was the most troublesome aspect of their experience with EM. Although employed offenders were permitted to go to and from work, they are generally prohibited from leaving their homes to run errands or to complete outdoor tasks without permission from their probation officer.

- The degree to which this sanction causes embarrassment/shame for the offender: Respondents reported that EM had a shaming effect for them or their family members, and that the supervision associated with EM was intrusive. Wearing a visible ankle bracelet and having a device attached to their telephone caused embarrassment, as well as having to tell other people that they could not leave the house.

Despite the loss of freedom and embarrassment of serving time on EM, the survey respondents indicated that they preferred EM to incarceration. The majority (about 70%) of the respondents in this study indicated that they would rather be sentenced to HA than to jail.[100]

Although the public is generally supportive of alternatives to incarceration, it is clear that there is an expectation that these alternatives serve as a punishment. So, although HA with EM is a less costly option than incarceration, the question remains—Is it effective punishment?

Shock Probation/Parole

shock probation/ parole where a judge sends a convicted offender to prison for a short time and then suspends the remainder of the sentence, granting probation.

Shock probation/parole—where a judge sends a convicted offender to prison for a short time and then suspends the remainder of the sentence, granting probation—has as its goal the hope that the "shock" of a short stay in prison will give the offender a taste of institutional life and make such an indelible impression that he or she will be deterred from future crime and thus avoid the negative effects (and costs) of lengthy confinement.[101] Typically, the sentencing judge will reconsider the original sentence to prison and, upon a motion, recall the inmate after a few months in prison and place him or her on probation under conditions deemed appropriate.

In many states, each candidate for shock probation/parole must obtain a community sponsor who will be responsible for the applicant's actions while in the community. The sponsor serves as an adjunct to and a resource for the probation officer. Specific activities for the sponsor can include providing transportation to work, checking on compliance with curfew and other restrictions, assisting with housing and employment problems, and maintaining contact with the probation officer. The offender may also be required to perform community service, usually physical labor.[102]

Boot Camps/Shock Incarceration

shock incarceration/ boot camp a short-term program where offenders experience rigorous military drill and ceremony, physical training and labor, and treatment and education to reduce recidivism and develop personal responsibility.

Correctional **boot camps**, also called **shock incarceration**, were first implemented as an intermediate sanction in 1983.[103] This approach is usually of a few months' duration, where (typically) young, nonviolent offenders experience rigorous military drill and ceremony, strenuous physical training and labor, and treatment and education to promote their reintegration into the community as law-abiding citizens and the development of personal responsibility. Their goal is to reduce recidivism, prison and jail populations, and operating costs. To be eligible, inmates generally had to be young, nonviolent offenders.

Unfortunately, early evaluations of boot camps generally found that participants did no better than other offenders without this experience.[104] Only boot camps that were carefully designed, targeted the right offenders, and provided rehabilitative services and aftercare were deemed likely to save the state money and reduce recidivism.[105] As a result of these findings, the number of boot camps declined; by the year 2000, only 51 prison boot camps remained.[106] Boot camps have evolved over time, however, and are now in their third generation. The first-generation camps were those just discussed, with military discipline and physical training being stressed. Second-generation camps emphasized rehabilitation by adding components such as alcohol and drug treatment and social skills training (some even including postrelease EM, HA, and random urine tests). Recently, in the third generation, some boot camps have substituted an emphasis on educational and vocational skills for the military components.[107]

A U.S. Department of Justice report, coauthored by former U.S. Attorney General John Ashcroft, stated that correctional administrators and planners might learn from boot camps' failures to reduce recidivism or prison populations by considering the following[108]:

1. Building reintegration into the community into an inmate's program may improve the likelihood that he or she will not recidivate.

2. Programs that offer substantial reductions in time served to boot camp "graduates" and that choose for participation inmates with longer sentences are the most successful in reducing prison populations.

3. Chances of reducing recidivism increase when boot camps last longer and offer more intensive treatment and postrelease supervision.

Day Reporting Centers

Another intermediate sanction is the **day reporting center**—a site where selected offenders report while under probation or parole supervision to receive an array of educational, vocational, treatment, and other services in order to reduce the risk factors that are linked with recidivism. The needs of each offender are assessed so that case workers and employment specialists may provide positive problem-solving, coping, and social skills. Also used for offenders returning from incarceration, the centers also assist in their reintegration back into society.[109]

Exhibit 12.2 discusses some of the benefits one jurisdiction has realized by opening day reporting centers—rather than by expanding their existing jails. Table 12-1 shows only about 6 percent (roughly 3,900 of 64,000) of persons being supervised outside of jail were involved with day reporting.

> **day reporting center** a site where offenders report to receive an array of educational, vocational, treatment, and other services, to reduce the risk factors associated with recidivism.

EXHIBIT 12.2

FIVE YEARS OF SUCCESS FOR WAUKESHA COUNTY DAY REPORT CENTER

In 2012 Waukesha County, Wisconsin, officials celebrated 5 years of successes for its Day Report Center. Praise for the program's contribution to public safety and prisoner rehabilitation came with the realization that many offenders don't need to be locked up; they can be held accountable in other ways while being given a chance and support to change their behavior.

A Waukesha County Circuit Judge called its establishment and success his proudest accomplishment in 6 years with the council. According to program statistics, the Day Report Center has had nearly 1,000 participants since opening in April 2007. Of those, 85 percent have successfully completed requirements that may include drug and alcohol testing, electronic monitoring, job searches, community service, and regular meetings with case managers (who connect with, monitor, advise, encourage, and support the clients).

The program, first established in an open hallway area of a jail, now has several offices and a group meeting room, so participants can meet with staff. The caseload is 55 participants—many of whom have been convicted of drunken driving, but also include those convicted of other nonviolent misdemeanors and felonies.

Judges order center reporting as an addition to or condition of sentences, while the sheriff uses it to supplement some Huber inmates released on electronic monitoring. Officials say it appears to be reducing crowding in jails and changing clients' behavior. The Day Report Center saved 13,739 jail bed days in 2011—each the equivalent of one prisoner a day—and 38,969 days over 5 years.[110]

Studies of day reporting centers generally indicate success. As an example, a 2011 study of day centers in Pennsylvania found that 95 percent of offenders completed the treatment programs without recidivating and the results translated to cost savings for the county—about $970,000 over 3 years.[111]

Summary

This chapter has examined several major contemporary and future issues confronting correctional administrators. It is clear that many, if not all, of these issues do not have easy or quick solutions and will continue to pose challenges to correctional administrators for many years. Included in this discussion were several new forms of diversion termed *intermediate sanctions*.

Corrections agencies bear the brunt of the combined effects of increased crime, tough mandatory sentencing laws leading to increased incarceration of offenders, a get-tough public and justice system attitude toward crime that permeates the country, overcrowded prisons, and large probation and parole caseloads. As a result, and as this chapter has shown, they must develop new ways to deal with offenders.

Key Terms and Concepts

Alternatives to incarceration *293*
Classification *288*
Day reporting center *297*
Drug interdiction *289*
Electronic monitoring *294*
Geriatric inmates *287*
Hostage taking *284*

House arrest *294*
Intensive supervision *294*
Intermediate sanctions *293*
Life without parole (LWOP) *281*
Mentally ill inmate *286*
Prison Rape Elimination
    Act of 2003 *283*

Privatization *291*
Sexual violence *282*
Shock incarceration/boot camp *296*
Shock probation/parole *296*
Therapeutic community *291*
Unit management *288*

Questions for Review

1. What was the Supreme Court's decision concerning capital punishment for someone who committed a capital crime while younger than the age of 18 years? Life without parole sentences? What was the Court's reasoning in both?

2. What do studies show concerning the nature and extent of physical and sexual victimizations in prisons? What policy issues arise from those findings?

3. Has the Prison Rape Elimination Act of 2003 worked?

4. How would you delineate the major arguments for and against inmates being issued condoms?

5. What administrative considerations apply to the potential problem of hostage taking in detention facilities?

6. What unique problems are involved with mentally ill and geriatric inmates?

7. How would you describe the importance of inmate classification, as well as the four categories into which new inmates are classified?

8. How can prison administrators interdict and treat the drug problem? What role can therapeutic communities play in this effort?

9. What are some stated advantages and disadvantages of privatization, what criteria can be used to evaluate them, and what do available studies report concerning their efficacy?

10. How would you define and describe the underlying philosophy of intermediate sanctions? Why are they so widely used, and what does research tell us about their efficacy?

11. How can shock probation further the goals of corrections? Boot camps/shock incarceration? What successes and problems have been found with these practices?

Deliberate and Decide

The Controlling Convict

You are the warden at a medium-security prison of approximately 1,000 inmates. One of your inmates is serving a life sentence for killing a highway patrol trooper in your state.

The determined inmate wants to take control of his life and situation either by escaping or by ending his life—and thus, either way, "leaving" prison. He has, therefore, hatched a plot: He plans to take a hostage, and then either use that person to escape or die trying. Another major component of his plan is for it to occur on his own terms—either to escape or to die *tomorrow*, on the tenth anniversary of his killing the state trooper.

At 4 P.M. today, he manages to feign illness and is escorted to the infirmary to see the prison doctor, a female

around age 40. Once inside the small room serving as an infirmary, he manages to obtain a sharp instrument, and does in fact take the doctor hostage. (*Note*: This real-life scenario, occurring in a Western prison, was resolved without use of a highly trained crisis response team. However, you may assume you have such a team in your institution, and can also request that another institution—with probably 12 hours' delay in travel and preparation time—send you its team.)

Questions for Discussion

1. The walls of the infirmary are solid concrete block; there is only one door leading in and out. What will you do to attempt to safely defuse this situation, and what other trained teams of experts might you call in to assist?

Learn by Doing

1. As a state criminal justice agency employee, your duties include working as a legislative liaison for your agency. You have been contacted by a state senator and asked to summarize the problem of sexual assaults in correctional institutions, and specifically what the Prison Rape Elimination Act has added to our knowledge of sexual assaults—and whether it has contributed to its diminution—in correctional institutions. What will be the content of your report?

2. You are engaging in a class discussion about the potential problem of hostage taking in correctional institutions. Your criminal justice professor asks that, after reading the accounts of two such incidents in the 1970s and 1980s in which hostages were taken, you consider whether, in the long run, these tragedies had positive or negative effects for the administration of prisons. What is your response, and why?

3. While your criminal justice professor is away from campus attending a conference, you, her Teaching Assistant, are assigned to present a lecture on privatization of prisons in her introductory corrections course. You are to focus on what are the "domains" used to evaluate them, and what studies do in fact reveal about their efficacy. What will you say?

4. You have been invited to appear at a luncheon meeting of a local civic group. During your luncheon speech, the topic of discussion turns to the high cost of incarceration, and then questions segue to using alternatives to incarceration. What will you say concerning the types—and the efficacy—of these intermediate sanctions?

Notes

1. *Graham v. Florida,* No. 08-7412 (May 17, 2010); also see Adam Liptak, "Justices Limit Life Sentences for Juveniles," *The New York Times,* May 17, 2010, http://www.nytimes.com/2010/05/18/us/politics/18court.html?pagewanted=print (accessed November 24, 2014).

2. *Miller v. Alabama,* 132 S. Ct. 2455 (2012; *Jackson v. Hobbs,* No. 10–9647 (2012).

3. Robert W. Dumond, "Inmate Sexual Assault: The Plague That Persists," *The Prison Journal* 80 (December 2000): 407–414; see also Human Rights Watch, *No Escape: Male Rape in U.S. Prisons* (New York: Author, 2001).

4. World Health Organization, *World Report on Violence and Health,* 2002, p. 149, http://www.who.int/violence_injury_prevention/violence/world_report/chapters/en/ (accessed March 26, 2014).

5. Cindy Struckman-Johnson and David Struckman-Johnson, "Sexual Coercion Rates in Seven Midwestern Prison Facilities for Men," *The Prison Journal* 80 (December 2000):379–390. See also Christopher Hensley, Robert W. Dumond, Richard Tewksbury, and Doris A. Dumond, "Possible Solutions for Preventing Inmate Sexual Assault: Examining Wardens' Beliefs," *American Journal of Criminal Justice* 27(1) (2002):19–33.

6. Dumond, "Inmate Sexual Assault," p. 408.

7. N. Wolff and J. Shi, "Contextualization of Physical and Sexual Assault in Male Prisons: Incidents and Their Aftermath," *Journal of Correctional Health Care* 15(1) (2009), http://www.ncbi.nlm.nih.gov/pmc/articles/PMC2811042/ (accessed November 27, 2014).

8. Ibid.

9. Ibid.

10. Ibid.

11. Leanne Fiftal Alarid, "Sexual Assault and Coercion among Incarcerated Women Prisoners: Excerpts from Prison Letters," *The Prison Journal* 80 (December 2000):391–406.

12. U.S. Department of Justice, *Bureau of Justice Statistics Status Report, Data Collections for the Prison Rape Elimination Act of 2003* (Washington, DC: Author, 2004), pp. 1–2.

13. Bureau of Justice Statistics, *Sexual Victimization in Prisons and Jails Reported by Inmates, 2011–12* (May 2014), p. 6, http://www.bjs.gov/content/pub/pdf/svpjri1112.pdf (accessed November 27, 2014).

14. Bureau of Justice Statistics, PREA Data Collection Activities, 2014 (June 2014), p. 1, http://www.bjs.gov/content/pub/pdf/pdca13.pdf (accessed November 27, 2014).

15. CBS Los Angeles, "To Cut STD Rate, Calif. Considers Condoms in Prison," July 17, 2014, http://losangeles.cbslocal.com/2014/07/07/to-cut-std-rate-calif-considers-condoms-in-prison/ (accessed November 27, 2014).

16. *Chicago Tribune News,* "Condom Debate Targets Prisons," March 18, 2007, http://articles.chicagotribune.com/2007-03-18/news/0703180058_1_prisons-state-inmates-condoms (accessed March 27, 2014).

17. CBS Los Angeles, "To Cut STD Rate, Calif. Considers Condoms in Prison."

18. Ibid.

19. Earnest A. Stepp, "Preparing for Chaos: Emergency Management," in Peter M. Carlson and Judith Simon Garrett (eds.), *Prison and Jail Administration: Practice and Theory* (Boston: Jones and Barlett Publishers, 2006), p. 367.

20. Thomas A. Zlaket, personal communication to Hon. Janet Napolitano, governor of Arizona, October 25, 2004, p. 2.

21. State of Arizona, Office of the Governor, *The Morey Unit Hostage Incident: Preliminary Findings and Recommendations* (Phoenix, AZ: Author, 2004), p. 1.

22. Ohio History Central, "Lucasville Prison Riot," http://www.ohiohistorycentral.org/entry.php?rec=1634 (accessed March 25, 2014).

23. "Meet Captors' Demands, Hostages Urge," *Chicago Tribune News*, December 7, 1999, http://articles.chicagotribune.com/1999-12-17/news/9912170075_1_warden-todd-louvierre-jolie-sonnier-female-guard (accessed March 27, 2014).

24. *St. Petersburg Times,* "Officials: Inmates Talked of Killing Jail Hostage," September 8, 2004, http://www.sptimes.com/2004/09/08/State/Officials_Inmates_ta.shtml (accessed March 27, 2014).

25. For an excellent examination and comparison of these two extremely violent prison riots, see Sue Mahan, "An 'Orgy of Brutality' at Attica and the 'Killing Ground' at Santa Fe: A Comparison of Prison Riots," in Michael C. Braswell, Reid H. Montgomery, Jr., and Lucien X. Lombardo (eds.), *Prison Violence in America*, 2nd ed. (Cincinnati: Anderson, 1994), pp. 253–264.

26. U.S. Department of Justice, Bureau of Justice Statistics, *Profile of Jail Inmates* (Washington, DC: Author, 2004), pp. 1–4.

27. U.S. Department of Justice, Bureau of Justice Statistics, *Local Police Departments, 2003* (Washington, DC: Author, 2006), p. iii; U.S. Department of Justice, Bureau of Justice Statistics, *Sheriff's Offices, 2003* (Washington, DC: Author, 2006), p. iii.

28. U.S. Department of Justice, National Institute of Justice, *Resolution of Prison Riots* (Washington, DC: Author, October 1995), pp. 2–5.

29. Adapted from Stepp, "Preparing for Chaos: Emergency Management," pp. 367–368.

30. U.S. Department of Justice, *Resolution of Prison Riots*, pp. 2–5.

31. B. Wind, "A Guide to Crisis Negotiations," *FBI Law Enforcement Bulletin* (October 1995):1–7.

32. Gabriel Lafleur, Louis Stender, and Jim Lyons, "Hostage Situations in Correctional Facilities," in Peter M. Carlson and Judith Simon Garrett (eds.), *Prison and Jail Administration: Practice and Theory* (Boston: Jones and Bartlett, 2006), p. 376.

33. U.S. Department of Justice, *Resolution of Prison Riots*, p. 13.

34. Ibid., p. 292.

35. National Institute of Justice Information Center, *Prison Hostage Situations*, (Boulder, CO: Author, 1983), pp. 16–17.

36. U.S. Department of Justice, *Resolution of Prison Riots*, p. 14.

37. Ibid, p. 21.

38. Pam Belluck, "Mentally Ill Inmates Are at Risk Isolated, Suit Says," *The New York Times*, March 9, 2007, p. A10.

39. Steven C. Norton, "Successfully Managing Mentally Ill Offenders: Thoughts and Recommendations," *Corrections Today* 67 (1) (February 2005), pp. 28–29, 37.

40. Ibid.

41. Ibid.

42. U.S. Department of Justice, National Institute of Corrections, *Effective Prison Mental Health Services* (Washington, DC: Author, May 2004), p. 1.

43. Diana B. Henriques, "Madoff Is Sentenced to 150 Years for Ponzi Scheme," *The New York Times*, June 29, 2009, http://www.nytimes.com/2009/06/30/business/30madoff.html?ref=bernardlmadoff (accessed October 20, 2014).

44. Katherine Q. Seelye, "Crime Boss Bulger Gets 2 Life Terms and Is Assailed by Judge for His 'Depravity,'" *The New York Times*, November 14, 2014, http://www.nytimes.com/2014/11/15/us/bulger-sentenced-to-life-in-prison.html?_r=0 (accessed October 4, 2014).

45. Jennifer Peltz, "Anthony Marshall, 89-Year-Old Heir to Brooke Astor's Fortune, Goes to Prison," *Huff Post New York* (June 21, 2014), http://www.huffingtonpost.com/2014/06/21/anthony-marshall_n_3479633.html (accessed October 20, 2014).

46. Vera Institute of Justice, *It's about Time Aging Prisoners, Increasing Costs, and Geriatric Release* (New York, NY: Author, 2010), p. 4.

47. Kevin E. McCarthy and Carrie Rose, "State Initiatives to Address Aging Prisoners," Connecticut General Assembly, March 4, 2014, http://www.cga.ct.gov/2014/rpt/2014-R-0166.htm (accessed October 14, 2014).

48. Ibid.

49. Ibid.

50. Brie Williams, "Geriatric Inmates Face Challenges Unique to Prison," March 10, 2006, http://www.ucsf.edu/news/2006/03/5398/geriatric-inmates-face-challenges-unique-prison (accessed October 14, 2014).

51. Geoff Dornan, "Aging Prisoners Boost Costs," NevadaAppeal.com (October 13, 2014), http://www.nevadaappeal.com/news/8481490-113/inmates-population-medical-older (accessed October 6, 2014).

52. Mary Harrison, *True Grit Notes* 5(3) (Summer 2009); Terence P. Hubert, Mary T. Harrison, and William O. Harrison, "True Grit: An Innovative Humanistic Living Program for a Geriatric Population." Carson City, NV: Nevada Department of Corrections, n.d.

53. Robert B. Levinson, "Classification: The Cornerstone of Corrections," in Peter M. Carlson and Judith Simon Garrett (eds.), *Prison and Jail Administration: Practice and Theory* (Boston: Jones and Bartlett, 2006), pp. 261–267.

54. Ibid., p. 262.

55. Ibid., pp. 262–263.

56. James Austin and Patricia L. Hardyman, *Objective Prison Classification: A Guide for Correctional Agencies* (Washington, DC: National Institute of Corrections, July 2004); also see R. Buchanan, "National Evaluation of Objective Prison Classification Systems: The Current State of the Art," *Crime and Delinquency* 32(3) (1986):272–290.

57. U.S. Department of Justice, Bureau of Justice Statistics, *Drug Use and Dependence, State and Federal Prisoners, 2004* (January 2007), p. 3, http://www.bjs.gov/content/dcf/duc.cfm (accessed March 27, 2014).

58. Thomas E. Feucht and Andrew Keyser, *Reducing Drug Use in Prisons: Pennsylvania's Approach* (Washington, DC: National Institute of Justice Journal, October 1999), p. 11.

59. Ibid., pp. 11–12.

60. Ibid., pp. 14–15.
61. David Farabee, Michael Prendergast, Jerome Cartier, Harry Wexler, Kevin Knight, and M. Douglas Anglin, "Barriers to Implementing Effective Correctional Drug Treatment Programs," *The Prison Journal* 79 (June 1999):150–162.
62. Ibid., p. 152.
63. Ibid., p. 153.
64. Ibid., pp. 154–155.
65. Sheldon X. Zhang, Robert E. L. Roberts, and Kathryn E. McCollister, "Therapeutic Community in a California Prison: Treatment Outcomes after 5 Years," *Crime & Delinquency* 57(1) (2011):82–101.
66. Ibid.
67. Ibid.
68. J. J. Stephan and J. C. Karlberg, *Census of State and Federal Correctional Facilities, 2000*. Washington, DC: U.S. Department of Justice, Bureau of Justice Statistics, 2003, http://www.bjs.gov/index.cfm?ty=pbdetail&iid=533 (accessed October 4, 2014).
69. Bureau of Justice Statistics, *Prisoners in 2011* (December 2012), p. 32, http://www.bjs.gov/content/pub/pdf/p11.pdf (accessed December 4, 2014).
70. W. D. Bales, L. E. Bedard, S. T. Quinn, D. T. Ensley, and G. P. Holley, "Recidivism of Public and Private State Prison Inmates in Florida." *Criminology & Public Policy* 4(2005): 57–82.
71. Matthew D. Makarios and Jeff Maahs, "Is Private Time Quality Time? A National Private–Public Comparison of Prison Quality," *Prison Journal* 92(3) (September 2012): 336–357.
72. Leonard C. Gilroy, Adam B. Summers, Anthony Randazzo and Harris Kenny, *Public-Private Partnerships for Corrections in California: Bridging the Gap between Crisis and Reform*, Reason Foundation (April 2011), p. 3, http://reason.org/files/private_prisons_california.pdf (accessed December 5, 2014).
73. O'Connor, "The Debate over Prison Privatization," p. 1.
74. C. Thomas, "Recidivism of Public and Private State Prison Inmates in Florida: Issues and Unanswered Questions," *Criminology and Public Policy* 4 (2005):89–100.
75. Charles H. Logan "Well Kept: Comparing Quality of Confinement of Private and Public Prisons," *Journal of Criminal Law and Criminology* 83 (1992):577–603.
76. Dina Perrone and Travis C. Pratt, "Comparing the Quality of Confinement and Cost Effectiveness of Public Versus Private Prisons: What We Know, Why We Do Not Know More, and Where to Go from Here," *The Prison Journal* 83 (2003):301–322.
77. Makarios and Maahs, "Is Private Time Quality Time? A National Private–Public Comparison of Prison Quality," p. 336.
78. Ibid.
79. John P. Conrad, "The Redefinition of Probation: Drastic Proposals to Solve an Urgent Problem," in Patrick McAnany, Doug Thomson, and David Fogel (eds.), *Probation and Justice: Reconsideration of Mission* (Cambridge, MA: Oelgeschlager, Gunn, and Hain, 1984), p. 258.
80. Peter J. Benekos, "Beyond Reintegration: Community Corrections in a Retributive Era," *Federal Probation* 54 (March 1990):53.
81. Ibid.
82. Belinda R. McCarthy, *Intermediate Punishments: Intensive Supervision, Home Confinement, and Electronic Surveillance* (Monsey, NY: Criminal Justice Press, 1987), p. 3.
83. Barry J. Nidorf, "Community Corrections: Turning the Crowding Crisis into Opportunities," *Corrections Today* (October 1989):85.
84. Benekos, "Beyond Reintegration," p. 54.
85. U.S. Department of Justice, Bureau of Justice Statistics, *Jail Inmates at Midyear 2012: Statistical Tables*, p. 9 (May 2014), http://www.bjs.gov/content/pub/pdf/jim12st.pdf) (accessed March 23, 2014).
86. Howard Abadinsky, *Probation and Parole: Theory and Practice*, 7th ed. (Upper Saddle River, NJ: Prentice Hall, 2000), p. 410.
87. Joan Petersilia and Susan Turner, *Evaluating Intensive Supervision Probation/Parole: Results of a Nationwide Experiment* (Washington, DC: National Institute of Justice, 1993).
88. Lawrence A. Bennett, "Practice in Search of a Theory: The Case of Intensive Supervision—An Extension of an Old Practice," *American Journal of Criminal Justice* 12 (1988):293–310.
89. Ibid., p. 293.
90. This information was compiled from ISP brochures and information from the Oregon Department of Correction by Joan Petersilia.
91. Todd R. Clear and Patricia R. Hardyman, "The New Intensive Supervision Movement," *Crime and Delinquency* 36 (January 1990):42–60.
92. Ibid., p. 44.
93. Barbara A. Sims, "Questions of Corrections: Public Attitudes toward Prison and Community-Based Programs," *Corrections Management Quarterly* 1(1) (1997):54.
94. Jeffery T. Ulner, "Intermediate Sanctions: A Comparative Analysis of the Probability and Severity of Recidivism," *Sociological Inquiry* 71(2) (Spring 2001):164–193.
95. Ibid., p. 184.
96. Ibid., p. 185.
97. R. Gable and R. Gable, "Electronic monitoring: Positive intervention strategies," Federal Probation, 69(1) (2005):21–25; also see A. Crowe, L. Sydney, P. Bancroft, and B. Lawrence, *Offender Supervision with Electronic Technology: A User's Guide* (Washington, DC: U.S. Department of Justice, 2002).
98. Sandra Norman-Eady, "Electronic Monitoring of Probationers and Parolees," OLR Research Report, January 2007, http://www.cga.ct.gov/2007/rpt/2007-R-0096.htm (accessed March 27, 2014).
99. Jamie S. Martin, Kate Hanrahan, and James H. Bowers, Jr., "Offenders' Perceptions of House Arrest and Electronic Monitoring," *Journal of Offender Rehabilitation* 48 (2009): 547–570.
100. Ibid.
101. Jeanne B. Stinchcomb and Vernon B. Fox, *Introduction to Corrections*, 5th ed. (Upper Saddle River, NJ: Prentice Hall, 1999), p. 165.

102. Abadinsky, *Probation and Parole,* p. 434.

103. Gaylene Styve Armstrong, Angela R. Gover, and Doris Layton MacKenzie, "The Development and Diversity of Correctional Boot Camps," in Rosemary L. Gido and Ted Alleman (eds.), *Turnstile Justice: Issues in American Corrections* (Upper Saddle River, NJ: Prentice Hall, 2002), pp. 115–130.

104. Doris Layton MacKenzie, "Boot Camp Prisons and Recidivism in Eight States," *Criminology* 33(3) (1995):327–358.

105. Doris Layton MacKenzie and Alex Piquero, "The Impact of Shock Incarceration Programs on Prison Crowding," *Crime and Delinquency* 40(2) (April 1994):222–249.

106. John Ashcroft, Deborah J. Daniels, and Sarah V. Hart, *Correctional Boot Camps: Lessons from a Decade of Research* (Washington, DC: U.S. Department of Justice, Office of Justice Programs, June 2003), p. 2.

107. Ibid.

108. Ibid., p. 9.

109. Dale G. Parent, "Day Reporting Centers: An Evolving Intermediate Sanction," *Federal Probation* 60 (December 1996):51–54.

110. Excerpt from Officials laud success of Waukesha County Day Report Center by Laurel Walker. Copyright © 2012 by Journal Sentinel. Used by permission of Journal Sentinel.

111. David R. Champion, Patrick J. Harvey, and Youngyol Yim Schanz, "Day Reporting Center and Recidivism: Comparing Offender Groups in a Western Pennsylvania County Study," *Journal of Offender Rehabilitation* 50(7) (October 2011):433–446.

PART 5

Issues Spanning the Justice System
Administrative Challenges and Practices

The four chapters in this part focus on administrative problems or methods spanning the entire justice system. Chapter 13 examines ethical considerations that relate to police, courts, and corrections administration. Chapter 14 discusses several challenges involving human resources (employee discipline, labor relations, and liability). Chapter 15 discusses financial administration, and Chapter 16 reviews the latest technological hardware and software now in use in criminal justice agencies. With the exception of Chapter 16, case studies are provided in Appendix I relating to each chapter in this part.

In the fall of 1959, I spoke at one of the country's most respected law schools. The professor in charge of teaching ethics told me the big question up for discussion among his students was whether, as a lawyer, you could lie to a judge. I told the professor that I thought we had all been taught the answer to that question when we were six years old.

—*Robert F. Kennedy*[1]

13 Ethical Considerations

LEARNING OBJECTIVES

After reading this chapter, the student will be able to:

1. *distinguish and explain absolute and relative ethics, the utilitarian approach to ethics, and the meaning of noble cause corruption*

2. *distinguish the issues surrounding the acceptance of gratuities and a proposed model for determining whether or not such acceptance is corrupt*

3. *describe ethics among criminal justice employees, including potentially career-ending Brady materials*

4. *review employees' role in the ethics of the court system*

5. *review the different tests for the justice system recruitment*

6. *explain types of workplace loyalties, and why loyalty to one's superiors can be problematic*

7. *review how the concept of ethics applies in corrections agencies*

8. *delineate some helpful guidelines for making ethical decisions*

► Introduction

As the late U.S. Attorney General and U.S. Senator Robert Kennedy implied, by the time one reaches the point of being a college or university student, hopefully he or she (and, it might be added, everyone who is studying the field of criminal justice) will have deeply ingrained the desire to practice exemplary and ethical behavior. Ethical behavior is often emphasized in postsecondary education in the form of instructors explaining the need for academic honesty. Later, at some point in your life, it will likely be emphasized in terms of how you are to conduct yourself in terms of dealing with others as well as perhaps with the property and responsibility that has been entrusted to you.

"Character," it might be said, "is who we are when no one is watching." Unfortunately, character cannot be trained at the police or corrections academy, or in law school, or given to someone intravenously, or in a pill. Character and ethical conduct, for criminal justice personnel, mean that they would never betray their oath of office, their public trust, or their badge. Indeed, as is indicated by several practitioners in boxed exhibits throughout this book, character and ethics are *sine qua non* for these persons—without those attributes, nothing else matters. These qualities constitute the foundation of their occupation and will certainly affect the manner in which they carry out their public safety duties.

At its root, then, criminal justice administration is about people and activities; in the end, the primary responsibilities of administrators involve monitoring subordinates' activities to ensure that they act correctly relative to their tasks and responsibilities and that these duties and responsibilities are carried out in an acceptable and effective manner. Therefore, this chapter is essentially concerned with what constitutes correct behavior in the administration of criminal justice. Individuals and organizations have standards of conduct. To understand organizations, it is important to comprehend these standards and their etiology.

The chapter opens with a glimpse into the kinds of ethical situations criminal justice employees experience, providing three scenarios based on actual cases. Then, we discuss ethics in general, reviewing philosophical foundations and types of ethics. Next, we examine ethics in policing. Because of the nature of their contacts with the public and the unique kinds of vices, crimes, and temptations to which they are directly exposed, the police are given a high degree of attention; included here are problems such as the "slippery slope," lying and deception, the receipt of gratuities, and greed and temptation. Also emphasized and examined here is a relatively new and powerful—and possibly career-ending—area of police ethics, which is an outgrowth of the U.S. Supreme Court's decision in *Brady v. Maryland*. We then also examine ethical considerations as they apply to courts and corrections organizations.

Although justice administrators are mentioned throughout the chapter, next we consider some specific challenges they face, guidelines they must issue, some ethical tests for justice professionals, and a consideration of the value of organizational loyalty. The chapter concludes with review questions, "deliberate and decide" problems, and "learn by doing" exercises.

► Food for Thought: Three Ethical Dilemmas

To frame the concept of ethics, I begin this chapter with three true scenarios:

> **Police.** Seeing a vehicle weaving across the center line of the highway, Officer A stops the car, approaches the driver's door, and immediately detects a strong odor of alcohol. The motorist is removed from the car and joins Officer A and a backup, Officer B, on the roadside. Officer A decides to use a portable breath test device to confirm his suspicions of driving under the influence (DUI) of drugs or alcohol, and he gives a sterile plastic mouthpiece to the driver to blow into. The driver attempts to thwart the test by appearing (but failing) to blow into the mouthpiece. Irritated by this attempt, Officer A

yanks the mouthpiece away, throws it on the ground, and arrests the driver for DUI. At trial, the driver claims that the mouthpiece was flawed (blocked), so he was unable to blow into it; Officer A testifies under oath that it was not blocked and as "evidence," he takes a mouthpiece out of his pocket, stating that it was the mouthpiece he had used for the test that night. Officer B, sitting in the room, hears this testimony and knows differently, having seen Officer A impatiently throw the mouthpiece on the ground.[2]

Courts. For several weeks, a wealthy divorcee receives menacing telephone calls that demand dates and sexual favors. The caller's voice is electronically disguised. The suspect also begins stalking the woman. After following some clues and tailing a suspect, a federal agent finally makes contact with a suspect, determining that he is the Chief Judge of the state's supreme court. Upon confronting him, the agent is told by the judge to "forget about it, or you'll be checking passports in a remote embassy."[3]

Corrections. A corrections officer in a minimum-security facility for young offenders is working in the night shift when a youth is admitted. The youth is frightened because this is his first time in custody, and the officer places him in isolation because the youth told the staff that he is feeling suicidal. Over the next several days, the officer develops a friendship with the youth. Looking through the youth's file, the officer learns that the boy does not wish to remain male; rather, he wants to be a female. One day while doing a routine cell search, the officer observes the youth stuffing women's panties into his pillowcase. With a terrified and pleading look, the youth explains that he prefers them to boxer shorts and begs the officer not to mention this to other staff or youths in the facility. The officer ponders what to do; surely, the boy would be severely ridiculed if others knew of the panties, and it does not seem to be important; on the contrary, if the officer does not report the action and the boy's choice of underwear is revealed later, the officer knows he will lose credibility with other staff and the administration.[4]

Each of these reality-based scenarios poses an ethical dilemma for the criminal justice employee involved. In each case, the officer or agent had to determine the best course of action. In making this determination, the employee had to draw on his or her ethical foundation and training and even on the organization's subculture.

These scenarios should be kept in mind as this chapter examines ethics and many related dilemmas.

► Ethics, Generally

Philosophical Foundations

ethics moral principles governing individual and group behavior, based on ideas concerning what is morally good and bad.

The term **ethics** is rooted in the ancient Greek idea of *character*. Ethics involves moral principles and behavior, based on ideas about what is morally good and bad, doing what is right or correct, and how people should behave in their professional capacity.

A central problem with understanding ethics is the question of "whose ethics" or "which right." This becomes evident when one examines controversial issues, such as the death penalty, abortion, use of deadly force, and gun control. How individuals view a particular controversy largely depends on their values, character, or ethics. Both sides on controversies such as these believe that they are morally right. These issues demonstrate that to understand behavior, the most basic values must be examined and understood.

deontological ethics a branch of ethics that focuses on the duty to act and the rightness or wrongness of actions, rather than rightness or wrongness of the consequences of those actions.

Another area for examination is that of **deontological ethics**, which does not consider consequences, but instead examines one's duty to act. The word *deontology* comes from two Greek roots: *deos*, meaning duty, and *logos*, meaning study. Thus, deontology means the study of duty. When police officers observe a violation of law, they have a duty to act.

Officers frequently use this as an excuse when they issue traffic citations that appear to have little utility and do not produce any great benefit for the rest of society. For example, when an officer writes a traffic citation for a prohibited left turn made at 2 o'clock in the morning when no traffic is around, the officer is fulfilling a departmental duty to enforce the law. From a utilitarian standpoint (where we judge an action by its consequences), however, little, if any, good was achieved. Here, duty and not good consequence was the primary motivator.

Immanuel Kant, an eighteenth-century philosopher, expanded the ethics of duty by including the idea of *good will*. People's actions must be guided by good intent. In the previous example, the officer who wrote the traffic citation for an improper left turn would be acting unethically if the ticket was a response to a quota or some irrelevant motive. On the contrary, if the citation was issued because the officer truly believed that it would result in something good, it would have been an ethical action.

Some people have expanded this argument even further. Richard Kania[5] argued that police officers should be allowed to accept gratuities because such actions would constitute the building blocks of positive social relationships between the police and the public. In this case, duty is used to justify what under normal circumstances would be considered unethical. Conversely, if officers take gratuities for self-gratification rather than to form positive community relationships, then the action would be considered unethical by many.

Types of Ethics

Ethics usually involves standards of fair and honest conduct—what we call conscience, the ability to recognize right from wrong—and actions that are good and proper. There are absolute ethics and relative ethics. **Absolute ethics** has only two sides: something is good or bad, black or white; in other words, certain acts are inherently right or wrong in themselves, irrespective of one's culture. Some examples in police ethics would be unethical behaviors such as bribery, extortion, excessive force, and perjury, which nearly everyone would agree are unacceptable behaviors by the police.

Relative ethics is more complicated because here, judgments of what acts are good and bad are relative to the individual or culture and thus can depend on the end or outcome of an action or one's culture; here, what is considered ethical behavior by one person or culture may be deemed highly unethical by someone else. Not all ethical issues are clear-cut, however, and communities *do* seem willing at times to tolerate extralegal behavior if a greater public good is served, especially in dealing with problems such as gangs and the homeless. This willingness on the part of the community can be conveyed to the police. A community's acceptance of relative ethics as part of criminal justice may send the wrong message: that there are few boundaries placed on justice system employees' behaviors and that, at times, "anything goes" in their fight against crime. As John Kleinig[6] pointed out, giving false testimony to ensure that a public menace is "put away" or the illegal wiretapping of an organized crime figure's telephone might sometimes be viewed as necessary and justified, though illegal. Another example is that many police officers believe they are compelled to skirt the edges of the law—or even violate it—to arrest drug traffickers. The ethical problem here is that even if the action could be justified as morally proper, it remains illegal. For many persons, however, the protection of society overrides other concerns.

This viewpoint—the *principle of double effect*—holds that when one commits an act to achieve a good end and an inevitable but intended effect is negative, the act might be justified. A long-standing debate has raged about balancing the rights of individuals against the community's interest in calm and order.

These special areas of ethics can become problematic and controversial when police officers use deadly force or lie and deceive others in their work. Police can justify a whole range of activities that others may deem unethical simply because the consequences result

absolute ethics a belief that something is good or bad, black or white, and that certain acts are inherently right or wrong in themselves, irrespective of one's culture.

relative ethics a belief that determining what is good or bad is relative to the individual or culture and can depend on the end or outcome of an action.

in the greatest good for the greatest number—the *utilitarian* approach. If the ends justified the means, perjury would be ethical when committed to prevent a serial killer from being set free to prey on society. In our democratic society, however, the means are just as important as, if not more important than, the desired end.

The community—and criminal justice administrators—cannot tolerate completely unethical behavior, but they may seemingly tolerate extralegal behavior if it serves a greater public good.

It is no less important today than in the past for criminal justice employees to appreciate and come to grips with ethical considerations. Indeed, ethical issues in policing have been affected by three critical factors[7]: (1) growing level of temptation stemming from illicit drug trade, (2) potentially compromising nature of the organizational culture—a culture that can exalt loyalty over integrity, with a "code of silence" that protects unethical employees, and (3) challenges posed by decentralization (flattening the organization and pushing decision making downward) through the advent of community-oriented policing and problem solving (COPPS; discussed later).

Noble Cause Corruption

Bending the Rules

noble cause corruption corruption committed in the name of good ends; when an act is committed to achieve a good end, it might still be justified.

When relative ethics and the principle of double effect, described above, are given life and practiced in overt fashion by the police, the situation is known as **noble cause corruption**—what Thomas Martinelli[8] defined as "corruption committed in the name of good ends, corruption that happens when police officers care too much about their work." This viewpoint is also known as the principle of double effect. As noted above, it holds that when an act is committed to achieve a good end (such as an illegal search) and an inevitable but intended effect is negative (the person who is searched eventually goes to prison), the act might still be justified.

Although noble cause corruption can occur anywhere in the criminal justice system, we might look at the police for examples. Officers might bend the rules, such as not reading a drunk person his rights or performing a field sobriety test; planting evidence; issuing "sewer" tickets—writing a ticket but not giving it to the person, resulting in a warrant issued for failure to appear in court; "testilying"; or "using the magic pencil," where police officers write up an incident in a way that criminalizes a suspect (this is a powerful tool for punishment). Noble cause corruption involves a different way of thinking about the police relationship with the law; here, officers operate on a standard that places personal morality above the law, become legislators *of* the law, and act as if they *are* the law.[9]

Such activities can be rationalized by some officers; however, as a Philadelphia police officer put it, "When you are shoveling society's garbage, you gotta be indulged a little bit."[10]

Nonetheless, when officers participate in such activities and believe that the ends justify the means, they corrupt their own system.

Challenges for Administrators, Managers, and Supervisors

Obviously, the kinds of ends-justify-means noble cause behaviors that are mentioned above often involve arrogance on the part of the police and ignore the basic constitutional guidelines their occupation demands. Administrators and middle managers must be careful to take a hard-line view that their subordinates always tell the truth and follow the law. For their part, when red flags surface, supervisors must look deep for reasons behind this sudden turn of events and make reasonable inquiries into the cause.[11] They must not fail to act, lest noble cause corruption be reinforced and entrenched; their inability to make the tough decisions that relate to subordinate misconduct can be catastrophic.

A supervisory philosophy of discipline based on due process, fairness, and equity, combined with intelligent, informed, and comprehensive decision making, is best for the department, its employees, and the community. This supervisory philosophy demonstrates the moral commitment employees look for in their leaders and the type that is expected in police service.[12]

Having defined the types of ethics and some dilemmas, we will now discuss in greater detail some of the ethical issues faced by police leaders and their subordinates.

▶ Ethics in Policing

The Root of the Problem: Greed and Temptation

Edward Tully[13] underscored a vast amount of temptation that confronts today's police officers and what police leaders must do to combat it:

> Socrates, Mother Teresa, or other revered individuals in our society never had to face the constant stream of ethical problems of a busy cop on the beat. One of the roles of police leaders is to create an environment that will help an officer resist the temptations that may lead to misconduct, corruption, or abuse of power. The executive cannot construct a work environment that will completely insulate the officers from the forces that lead to misconduct. The ultimate responsibility for an officer's ethical and moral welfare rests squarely with the officer.

Most citizens have no way of comprehending the amount of temptation that confronts today's police officers. They frequently find themselves alone inside retail business stores after normal business hours, clearing the building after finding an open door or window. A swing or graveyard shift officer can easily obtain considerable plunder on these occasions, acquiring everything from clothing to tires for his or her personal vehicle. At the other end of the spectrum is the potential for huge payoffs from drug traffickers or other big-money offenders who will gladly pay the officer to look away from their crimes. Some officers, of course, find this temptation impossible to overcome.

A Primer: The Oral Interview

During oral interviews for a position in policing, applicants are often placed in a hypothetical situation that tests their ethical beliefs and character. For example, they are asked to assume the role of a police officer who is checking on foot an office supplies retail store that was found to have an unlocked door during early morning hours. On leaving the building, the officer observes another officer, Smith, removing a $200 writing pen from a display case and placing it in his uniform pocket. What should the officer do?

This kind of question commonly befuddles the applicant: "Should I 'rat' on my fellow officer? Overlook the matter? Merely tell Smith never to do that again?" Unfortunately, applicants may do a lot of "how am I *supposed* to respond" soul-searching and second-guessing with these kinds of questions.

Bear in mind that criminal justice agencies do not wish to hire someone who possesses ethical shortcomings; it is simply too potentially dangerous and expensive, from both the perspectives of potential litigation and morality, to take the chance of bringing someone who is corrupt into an agency. That is the reason for such questioning and a thorough background investigation of applicants.

Before responding to a scenario like the one concerning Officer Smith, the applicant should consider the following issues: Is this likely to be the first time that

Smith has stolen something? Don't the police arrest and jail people for this same kind of behavior?

In short, police administrators should *never* want an applicant to respond that it is acceptable for an officer to steal. Furthermore, it would be incorrect for an applicant to believe that police do not want an officer to "rat out" another officer. Applicants should never acknowledge that stealing or other such activities are to be overlooked.

Accepted and Deviant Lying

In many cases, no clear line separates acceptable and unacceptable behavior. The two are separated by an expansive gray area that comes under relative ethics. Some observers have referred to such illegal behavior as a *slippery slope*. People tread on solid or legal ground, but at some point slip beyond the acceptable into illegal or unacceptable behavior.

lying (accepted/deviant) lying that serves legitimate purposes and lying that conceals or promotes crimes or illegitimate ends.

Criminal justice employees lie or deceive for different purposes and under varying circumstances. In some cases, their misrepresentations are accepted as an integral part of a criminal investigation; in other cases, they are viewed as violations of law. David Carter[14] examined police **lying** and perjury and developed a taxonomy that centered on a distinction between accepted lying and deviant lying. *Accepted lying* includes police activities intended to apprehend or entrap suspects. This type of lying is generally considered to be trickery. *Deviant lying*, on the contrary, refers to officers committing perjury to convict suspects or being deceptive about some activity that is illegal or unacceptable to the department or the public in general.

Deception has long been practiced by the police to ensnare violators and suspects. For many years, it was the principal method used by detectives and police officers to secure confessions and convictions. Accepted lying is that allowed by law and, to a great extent, is expected by the public. Gary Marx[15] identified three methods used by police to trick a suspect: (1) performing an illegal action as part of a larger, socially acceptable, and legal goal; (2) disguising the illegal action so that the suspect does not know it is illegal; and (3) morally weakening the suspect so that the suspect voluntarily becomes involved. The courts have long accepted deception as an investigative tool. For example, in *Illinois v. Perkins*,[16] the U.S. Supreme Court ruled that police undercover agents are not required to administer the *Miranda* warning to incarcerated inmates when investigating crimes. Lying, although acceptable by the courts and the public in certain circumstances, results in an ethical dilemma. It is a dirty means to accomplish a good end; the police use untruths to gain the truth relative to some event.

In their taxonomy of lying, Barker and Carter[17] identified two types of deviant lying: lying that serves legitimate purposes and lying that conceals or promotes crimes or illegitimate ends. Lying that serves legitimate goals occurs when officers lie to secure a conviction, obtain a search warrant, or conceal omissions during an investigation. Barker[18] found that police officers believe that almost one-fourth of their agency would commit perjury to secure a conviction or to obtain a search warrant. Lying becomes an effective, routine way to sidestep legal impediments. When left unchecked by supervisors, managers, and administrators, lying can become organizationally accepted as an effective means to nullify legal entanglements and remove obstacles that stand in the way of convictions. Examples include using the services of nonexistent confidential informants to secure search warrants, concealing that an interrogator went too far, coercing a confession, or perjuring oneself to gain a conviction.

Lying to conceal or promote criminality is the most distressing form of deception. Examples range from lying by the police to conceal their use of excessive force when arresting a suspect to obscuring the commission of a criminal act.

"*Brady* Material"

Consider the following scenario:

> At the end of his duty shift, Officer Jones acknowledges a dispatch to assist an animal control unit that is struggling to pick up a large, vicious dog. Because he has social plans after work and believes the incident to be minor in nature, Jones opts instead to drive to the police station and leave for home. The animal control officer, thus acting alone, incurs a number of severe dog bites, $10,000 in medical costs (she has medical insurance), the loss of 2 week's work, and potential long-term injuries. As a result, Jones is contacted by his supervisor to justify his lack of response; he explains that he was enroute to the call, but was diverted by seeing what he felt was a robbery in progress that needed "checking out" (no robberies were reported). Largely owing to the animal control officer's injuries, the matter is referred to the department's Internal Affairs (IA) office for investigation. Upon being questioned, Jones initially lies to IA investigators, but when pressed for specifics concerning the alleged robbery, Jones finally admits that he thought the dog call was a minor problem and opted to ignore it. He is given 2 weeks' leave without pay, and placed on a performance review for 6 months.

To Officer Jones, this matter may seem to be ended, a lesson learned for the future. In truth, however, Jones has possibly opened a can of worms from which his career may never recover. Jones lied to both his supervisor and the IA investigators. Police officers are first and foremost required to tell the truth; to do any less can be career-ending. An officer with credibility issues is unable to make cases because he or she can no longer testify effectively in court from that point forward. His or her department is required to advise the prosecutor's office of this issue—and the prosecutor is required to disclose it to the defense—in every criminal case in which Jones will testify during the remainder of his career. Furthermore, Jones may well have to endure the following type of cross examination and/or closing argument by the defense attorney:

> Ladies and gentlemen of the jury, as you consider the testimony of Officer Jones, whom the prosecution has called as its witness, it is my duty to inform you that you are being asked to believe the testimony of an officer who will lie in his reports.

To further sully Jones' reputation, the prosecutor's office may also inform the chief of police or sheriff that they will not take any future cases in which Jones was a witness.[19]

Questions for you to consider:

1. What *internal* (department-level, per agency policies and procedures) punishment, if any, would you deem appropriate for Jones in this incident?
2. (Looking ahead at information presented in Chapter 9, on civil liability): Assume the animal control officer files a civil suit against the city and Jones for his negligence, seeking (1) compensatory damages (medical costs, pain and suffering, loss of wages, etc.) and (2) punitive damages (money due to Jones' acting in a wanton, malicious, vindictive, or oppressive manner). How much is the animal control officer due?

Such is the current status of policing, a result of *Brady v. Maryland* (1963),[20] with one large Western police agency recently discovering more than 135 of its officers having potential *Brady* problems in a disciplinary case.[21] *Brady* was convicted of first-degree murder and sentenced to death. He testified at trial about his participation in the crime, but also stated that his companion, Boblit, was the actual murderer. Before trial, Brady's attorney had requested to see Boblit's statements. The government provided some of his statements, but did not turn over those in which Boblit actually admitted to the murder. Brady was convicted, and later his attorney, then knowing of Boblit's statement admitting guilt, filed an appeal. The U. S. Supreme Court stated that Brady was entitled to obtain and use Boblit's statement, and that the government's failure to provide the statement amounted to a denial of his right to due process.

Brady thus established that in a criminal case the accused has a right to any exculpatory evidence (sometimes termed "**Brady material**," i.e., any evidence in the government's possession that is favorable to the accused and is material to either guilt or punishment). Prosecutors must, therefore, disclose to the defense all exculpatory evidence.[22]

Today many police agencies take the "Brady officer" matter quite seriously, training officers about its existence, sanctions, and ramifications. They are generating policies and procedures that address this issue, explaining that the agency may be placed in a position where the officer's termination is the only appropriate outcome.

Finally, agencies are encouraged to review all officers' personnel files to determine if any of them has a disciplinary history that would seriously impeach his or her credibility as a witness. Any such information should also be made available to the prosecutor before such officers are allowed to testify in a criminal prosecution.[23]

Gratuities: A Model for Gauging Degrees of Corruption

Gratuities are complimentary gifts of money, services, or something of other value given by one party to another. In policing, on-duty officers are often provided free or reduced-price meals and drinks by restaurants and convenience stores, and some businesses offer officers discounts on services or merchandise. While some agencies consider the offer of gratuities to be simple gestures to reward officers for their (often thankless) tasks, other departments prohibit all such gifts and discounts. In either case, agencies must spell out clearly—and enforce—what its views and practices will be regarding the receipt of gratuities.

There are two basic arguments *against* police acceptance of gratuities. First is the slippery slope argument, discussed earlier, which proposes that gratuities are the first step in police corruption. This argument holds that once gratuities are received, police officers' ethics are subverted and they are open to additional breaches of their integrity. In addition, officers who accept minor gifts or gratuities are then obligated to provide the donors with some special service or accommodation. Furthermore, some propose that receiving a gratuity is wrong because officers are receiving rewards for services that, as a result of their employment, they are obligated to provide. That is, officers have no legitimate right to accept compensation in the form of a gratuity. If the police ever hope to be accepted as members of a full-fledged profession, then they must decide whether accepting gratuities is a professional behavior or not.

Police officers who solicit and receive free gifts were categorized by the Knapp Commission in New York City as either "grass-eaters" or "meat-eaters."[24] *Grass-eaters* are officers who freely accept gratuities and sometimes solicit minor payments and gifts. *Meat-eaters*, on the contrary, spend a significant portion of the workday aggressively seeking out situations that can be exploited for financial gain. These officers are corrupt and are involved in thefts, drugs, gambling, prostitution, and other criminal activities.

At least in some cases, it seems that taking gratuities may be the first step toward corruption. Gratuities do indeed provide a slippery slope from which officers can easily slide into corruption. The problem is that many officers fail to understand when and where to draw the line. In a different light, one writer[25] argues that retail store and restaurant owners often feel indebted to the police and that gratuities provide an avenue of repayment. Thus, gratuities result in social cohesion between the police and business owners, and the acceptance of gratuities does not necessarily lead to the solicitation of additional gratuities and gifts or corruption.

Withrow and Dailey[26] recently offered a uniquely different viewpoint on gratuities. They propose a **model of circumstantial corruptibility**, stating that the exchange of a gift is influenced

Brady material evidence in the government's possession that is favorable to the accused, material to either guilt or punishment, and must, therefore, be disclosed to the defense.

gratuities complimentary gifts of money, services, or something of other value.

model of circumstantial corruptibility a view regarding acceptance of gratuities, holding that the exchange of a gift is influenced by two elements: the roles of the giver and the receiver.

by two elements: the role of the giver and the role of the receiver. The role of the giver determines the level of corruptibility; in this model, the giver is either taking a position as a:

- *presenter,* who offers a gift voluntarily without any expectation of a return from the receiver;
- *contributor,* who furnishes something and expects something in return;
- *capitulator,* who involuntarily responds to the demands of the receiver.

The role of the receiver of the gift is obviously very important as well in the model; the receiver can act as:

- an *acceptor,* who receives the gift humbly and without any residual feelings of reciprocity;
- an *expector,* who looks forward to the gift and regards it as likely to be given, and will be annoyed by the absence of the gift;
- a *conqueror,* who assumes total control over the exchange and influence over the giver.

The function of the model, Withrow and Dailey argue, is centered on the intersection of the giver and the receiver; for example, when the giver assumes the role of the presenter and the receiver is the acceptor, the result is a giving exchange and corruption does not occur. However, if the giver and the receiver occupy other roles, corruptibility can progress to higher levels of social harm, which they term *hierarchy of wickedness.* Bribery results when something of value is given and the giver expects something in return, while the receiver agrees to make his or her behavior conform to the desires of the giver. This model is not clear-cut, however, because the confusion of roles between givers and receivers is inevitable.[27]

Withrow and Dailey's model is distinguishable from Kania's view, discussed above, that the police should be encouraged to accept minor gratuities to foster good relations; rather, Withrow and Dailey encourage the police to consider the role of the giver as well as their own intentions when deciding whether or not to accept a gratuity. In certain circumstances, the exchange of *any* gratuity is ethical or unethical regardless of its value.[28]

Figure 13-1 ■ is an example of a policy developed by a sheriff's office concerning gratuities.

1. Without the express permission of the Sheriff, members shall not solicit or accept any gift, gratuity, loan, present, or fee where there is any direct or indirect connection between this solicitation or acceptance of such gift and their employment by this office.
2. Members shall not accept, either directly or indirectly, any gift, gratuity, loan, fee or thing of value, the acceptance of which might tend to improperly influence their actions, or that of any other member, in any matter of police business, or which might tend to cast an adverse reflection on the Sheriff's Office.
3. Any unauthorized gift, gratuity, loan, fee, reward or other thing falling into any of these categories coming into the possession of any member shall be forwarded to the member's commander, together with a written report explaining the circumstances connected therewith. The commander will decide the disposition of the gift.

—Washoe County (Nevada) Sheriff's Office

FIGURE 13-1   Washoe County Sheriff's Office gratuities policy
Source: Excerpt from Washoe County Sheriff's Office Gratuities Policy. Copyright by Washoe County, NV Sheriff Office. Used by permission of Washoe County, NV Sheriff Office.

Training, Supervision, and Values

Another key element of ethics in policing is the recruitment and training of police personnel. Formal training programs in ethics can help to ensure that officers understand their department's code of ethics, elevate the importance of ethics throughout the agency, and underscore top management's support. It is imperative that police administrators see that applicants are thoroughly tested, trained, and exposed to an anticorruption environment by proper role modeling.

No supervision of police officers, no matter how thorough and conscientious, can keep bad cops from doing bad things. There are simply too many police officers and too few supervisors. If there is not enough supervision, then the bad cop will not be afraid. As Marcus Aurelius said, "A man should be upright, not be kept upright." There must be leadership at every level. Line officers are sincere and hard-working; their leaders need to ensure that core values are part of the department's operations and become the basis of the subordinates' behavior.

The organization's culture is also important in this regard. The police culture often exalts loyalty over integrity. Given the stress usually generated more from within the organization than from outside and the nature of life-and-death decisions they must make daily, even the best officers who simply want to catch criminals may become frustrated and vulnerable to bending the rules for what they view as the greater good of society.

Police agencies must also attempt to shape the standards of professional behavior. Many begin to do so by articulating their values such as "we believe in the sanctity of life" and "we believe that providing superior service to the citizens is our primary responsibility." Other rules try to guide officers' behavior such as not lying or drinking in excess in a public place.

▶ Ethics in the Courts

Evolution of Standards of Conduct

The first call during the twentieth century for formalized standards of conduct in the legal profession came in 1906 with Roscoe Pound's speech "The Causes of Popular Dissatisfaction with the Administration of Justice,"[29] discussed in Chapter 7. The American Bar Association (ABA) quickly responded by formulating and approving the Canons of Professional Ethics in 1908 governing lawyers. No separate rules were provided for judges, however.

The first Canons of Judicial Ethics probably grew out of baseball's 1919 scandal, in which the World Series was "thrown" by the Chicago White Sox to the Cincinnati Reds. Baseball officials turned to the judiciary for leadership and hired U.S. District Court Judge Kenesaw Mountain Landis as baseball commissioner—a position for which Landis was paid $42,500 compared with his $7,500 earnings per year as a judge. This affair prompted the 1921 ABA convention to pass a resolution of censure against the judge and appoint a committee to propose standards of judicial ethics.[30]

In 1924, the ABA approved the Canons of Judicial Ethics under the leadership of Chief Justice William Howard Taft, and in 1972 the ABA approved a new **Model Code of Judicial Conduct**—rules governing the conduct of judges while acting in their professional capacity; in 1990, the same body adopted a revised Model Code. Nearly all states and the District of Columbia have promulgated standards based on the code. In 1974, the U.S. Judicial Conference adopted a Code of Conduct for Federal Judges, and Congress has, over the years, enacted legislation regulating judicial conduct, including the Ethics Reform Act of 1989. Finally, in October 1977, the American Judicature Society (AJS) established the Center for Judicial Conduct Organizations. The Center compiles materials involving judicial

Model Code of Judicial Conduct rules governing the conduct of judges while acting in their professional capacity.

discipline, advisory opinions, disciplinary procedures, codes of judicial conduct, and related court decisions, and is probably best known in judicial circles for its publication, Judicial Conduct Reporter.[31]

The Judge

Ideally, our judges are flawless. They do not allow emotion or personal biases to creep into their work, treat all cases and individual litigants with an even hand, and employ "justice tempered with mercy." The perfect judge would be like the one described by the eminent Italian legal philosopher Pierro Calamandrei:

> The good judge takes equal pains with every case, no matter how humble; he knows that important cases and unimportant cases do not exist, for injustice is not one of those poisons, which when taken in small doses may produce a salutary effect. Injustice is a dangerous poison even in doses of homeopathic proportions.[32]

Not all judges, of course, can attain this lofty status. Recognizing this fact, nearly 800 years ago, King John of England met with his barons on the field of Runnymede and, in the Magna Carta, promised that henceforth he would not "make men justices, unless they are such as know the law of the realm and are minded to observe it rightly."[33] See Exhibit 13.1 for information about the "Cash for Kids" Scandal.

The subject of judicial ethics seemed to arouse little interest until relatively recently. Indeed, from 1890 to 1904, an era of trusts and political corruption, only a few articles were published on the subject of judicial ethics. In contrast, since 1975, more than 900 articles have appeared in magazines and newspapers on the topic of judges and judicial ethics.

Judges can engage in improper conduct or overstep their bounds in many ways: abuse of judicial power (against attorneys or litigants), inappropriate sanctions and dispositions (including showing favoritism or bias), not meeting the standards of impartiality and competence (discourteous behavior, gender bias and harassment, and incompetence),

---

EXHIBIT 13.1

THE "CASH FOR KIDS" SCANDAL

A former county juvenile court judge in Pennsylvania was sentenced to prison for 28 years after being convicted on federal racketeering charges—specifically, sentencing juveniles to a detention facility for minor crimes while accepting more than $1 million in kickbacks from the private company that built and maintained the facility.[34]

One-fourth of this judge's juvenile defendants were sentenced to detention centers, as he routinely ignored requests for leniency made by prosecutors and probation officers. Some of the nearly 5,000 sentenced juveniles were as young as 10. One girl, who described the experience as a "surreal nightmare," was sentenced to 3 months of "hard time" for posting spoofs about an assistant school principal on the Internet. Some juveniles even committed suicide

following their commitment.[35] The judge was said to have maintained a culture of intimidation in which no one was willing to speak up about the sentences he was handing down. Although he pleaded guilty to the charges, he denied sentencing juveniles who did not deserve it or receiving remuneration from the detention centers.[36]

The matter—termed "Cash for Kids"[37]—also raised concerns about whether juveniles should be required to have counsel either before or during their appearances in court: It was revealed that more than 500 juveniles had appeared before the judge without representation. Although juveniles have long had a right to counsel,[38] Pennsylvania, like at least 20 other states, allows children to waive counsel, and about half of these Pennsylvania youths had chosen to do so.[39]

conflict of interest (bias, conflicting financial interests or business, social, or family relationships), and personal conduct (criminal or sexual misconduct, prejudice, or statements of opinion).[40]

Following are examples of some true-to-life ethical dilemmas involving the courts[41]:

1. A judge convinces jailers to release his son on a nonbondable offense.

2. A judge is indicted on charges that he used his office for a racketeering enterprise.

3. Two judges attend the governor's $500-per-person inaugural ball.

4. A judge's allegedly intemperate treatment of lawyers in the courtroom is spurred by a lawyer's earlier complaints against the judge.

5. A judge is accused of acting with bias in giving a convicted murderer a less severe sentence because the victims were homosexual.

6. A judge whose car bears a bumper sticker reading "I am a pro-life democrat" acquits six pro-life demonstrators of trespassing at an abortion clinic on the ground of necessity to protect human life.

These incidents do little to bolster public confidence in the justice system. People expect more from judges, who are "the most highly visible symbol of justice."[42] The quality of the judges determines the quality of justice.

Many judges recoil at the need for a code of judicial conduct or an independent commission to investigate complaints. They dislike being considered suspect and put under regulation. No one likes to be watched, but judges must heed Thomas Jefferson's admonition that everyone in public life should be answerable to someone.[43]

Unfortunately, codes of ethical conduct have not served to eradicate the problems or allay the concerns about judges' behavior. Indeed, as three professors of law put it, "The public and the bar appear at times to be more interested in judicial ethics and accountability than the judges are."[44] One judge who teaches judicial ethics at the National Judicial College in Reno, Nevada, stated that most judges attending the college admit never having read the ABA's Model Code of Judicial Conduct before seeking judicial office.[45] Some judges also dismiss the need for a judicial conduct code because they believe that it governs aberrant behavior, which, they also believe, is rare among the judiciary. According to the American Judicature Society, however, during one year, 25 judges were suspended from office and more than 80 judges resigned or retired either before or after formal charges were filed against them; 120 judges also received private censure, admonition, or reprimand.[46]

The Code of Judicial Conduct strives to strike a balance between allowing judges to participate in social and public discourse and prohibiting conduct that would threaten a judge's independence. The essence of judicial independence is that judges' minds, according to John Adams, "should not be distracted with jarring interests; they should not be dependent upon any man, or body of men."[47]

Living by the code is challenging; the key to judicial ethics is to identify the troublesome issues and to sharpen one's sensitivity to them, that is, to create an "ethical alarm system" that responds.[48] Perhaps the most important tenet in the code, and the one that is most difficult to apply, is that judges should avoid the appearance of impropriety.

By adhering to ethical principles, judges can maintain their independence and follow the ancient charge Moses gave to his judges in Deuteronomy:

Hear the causes between your brethren, and judge righteously. Ye shall not respect persons in judgment; but ye shall hear the small as well as the great; ye shall not be afraid of the face of man; for the judgment is God's; and for the cause that is too hard for you, bring it unto me, and I will hear it.[49]

See Exhibit 13.2 for information about ethics training for federal judges.

ETHICS TRAINING FOR FEDERAL JUDGES

According to the Code of Conduct for U.S. Judges, Canon 1 commentary, "Deference to the judgments and rulings of courts depends upon public confidence in the integrity and independence of judges."

To further those goals, the Federal Judicial Center—the education agency for the federal courts—works closely with the Judicial Conference to provide orientation programs for new judges. By regularly covering ethics, the goal is to heighten judges' sensitivity to ethical issues and to interpret the sources of ethical rules: statutes and the *Code of Conduct for United States Judges*. Together they have developed curricula for in-class programs, online formats, and television programs.

An overview is provided of the seven canons of the Code of Conduct. Other specific ethical areas that are covered include conflicts of interest, relationships with a former law firm, and outside activities such as teaching, membership in legal or social organizations, fund-raising prohibitions, and political activities. Greatest attention is devoted to conflicts of interest—particularly financial conflicts—because mistakes seem to occur more commonly here. There is also a detailed discussion of how to fill out the financial-disclosure report. Examples are provided concerning judges who did not, or allegedly did not, follow the rules.

Source: Based on John S. Cooke, Judicial Ethics in the Federal Courts," *Justice System Journal* 28(3) (2007): 385–393.

Lawyers for the Defense

Defense attorneys, too, must be legally and morally bound to ethical principles as agents of the courts. Elliot Cohen[50] suggested the following moral principles for defense attorneys:

1. Treat others as ends in themselves and not as mere means to winning cases.

2. Treat clients and other professional relations in a similar fashion.

3. Do not deliberately engage in a behavior apt to deceive the court as to truth.

4. Be willing, if necessary, to make reasonable personal sacrifices of time, money, and popularity for what you believe to be a morally good cause.

5. Do not give money to, or accept money from, clients for wrongful purposes or in wrongful amounts.

6. Avoid harming others in the course of representing your client.

7. Be loyal to your client and do not betray his or her confidence.

Prosecutors

Prosecutors can also improve their ethical behavior. Contrary, perhaps, to what is popularly believed, it was decided over a half century ago that the primary duty of a prosecutor is "not that he shall win a case, but that justice shall be done."[51]

Instances of prosecutorial misconduct were reported as early as 1897[52] and are still reported today. One of the leading examples of unethical conduct by a prosecutor was *Miller v. Pate*,[53] in which the prosecutor concealed from the jury in a murder trial the fact that a pair of undershorts with red stains on it were stained not by blood but by paint.

If similar (though not so egregious) kinds of misconduct occur today, one must ask why. According to Cohen,[54] the answer is simple: Misconduct works. Oral advocacy is important in the courtroom and can have a powerful effect. Another significant reason for such conduct is the *harmless error doctrine*, in which an appellate court can affirm a conviction despite the presence of serious misconduct during the trial. Only when appellate courts take a stricter, more consistent approach to this problem, will it end.[55]

Other Court Employees

Other court employees have ethical responsibilities as well. Primarily known as *confidential employees*, these are justice-system functionaries who have a special role in the court system and work closely with a judge or judges. These individuals have a special responsibility to maintain the confidentiality of the court system and, thus, have a high standard of trust. For example, an appellate court judge's secretary is asked by a good friend, who is a lawyer, whether the judge will be writing the opinion in a certain case. The lawyer may wish to attempt to influence the judge through his secretary, renegotiate with an opposing party, or engage in some other improper activity designed to alter the case outcome.[56] Bailiffs, court administrators, court reporters, courtroom clerks, and law clerks all fit into this category. The judge's secretary, of course, must use his or her own ethical standard in deciding whether to answer the lawyer's question.

It would be improper for a bailiff who is accompanying jurors back from a break in a criminal trial to mention that the judge "sure seems annoyed at the defense attorney" or for a law clerk to tell an attorney friend that the judge she works for prefers reading short bench memos.[57]

▶ Ethics in Corrections

By virtue of their association with offenders, corrections personnel confront many of the same ethical dilemmas as police personnel. Thus, prison and jail administrators, like their counterparts in the police realm, would do well to understand their occupational subculture and its effect on ethical decision making.

Worley and Worley studied correctional officer (CO) misconduct and deviance (which they defined as "behavior that is either against policy or illegal, performed during a CO's employment")[58] using surveys administered to COs in the Texas prison system. They found that an overwhelming number of COs perceived that their fellow staff members were involved in inappropriate and, in some cases, illegal types of behavior. One of the most often-reported types of deviance was that "some employees have inappropriate relationships with inmates." Also heavily reported was that "some employees allow inmates to break the rules."[59] The researchers also observed that "every year there are some correctional officers who end their careers in disgrace by engaging in activities that are deemed illegal and/or at the very least highly unethical."[60]

According to noted criminal justice ethicist Sam Souryal,[61] public corruption is ostensibly a learned behavior—no one is born corrupt, and assuming correctional applicants are carefully scrutinized prior to employment, the logical explanation must be that COs learn corruption in the course of performing their job. Ensuring a work environment that is conducive to an ethical work culture is essential.

In very broad terms, there are two major types of CO deviance: the abuse of power and corruption.[62] More specifically, Souryal described the following three general categories of prison corruption:

> **misfeasance** illegitimate acts likely committed by high-ranking officials who knowingly allow indiscretions that undermine the public interest and benefit them personally.

1. *Acts of* **misfeasance**. These acts are illegitimate acts more likely committed by high-ranking officials who knowingly allow contractual indiscretions that would undermine the public interest and benefit them personally. Misfeasance can also involve outsiders—a building firm, a group of consultants, a planning and research agency, and a law firm hired to defend the agency—who are associated with the correctional facility through a political or professional appointment.

> **malfeasance** crimes or misconduct that officials knowingly commit in violation of state laws and/or agency rules and regulations.

2. *Acts of* **malfeasance**. These acts involve crimes or misconduct that officials knowingly commit in violation of state laws and/or agency rules and regulations. Acts of

malfeasance are usually committed by officials at the lower or middle management levels. Acts that might fall in this category include theft; embezzlement; trafficking in contraband; extortion; official oppression; and the exploitation of inmates or their families for money, goods, or services.

3. *Acts of* **nonfeasance.** These are acts of omission or avoidance knowingly committed by officials who are responsible for carrying out such acts. Examples of nonfeasance would include looking the other way when narcotics are smuggled into a prison by inmates or visitors, and failure to report misconduct by other officers out of personal loyalty.[63]

> **nonfeasance** acts of omission or avoidance knowingly committed by officials who are responsible for carrying out such acts.

The strength of the corrections subculture is correlated with the security level of a correctional facility and is strongest in maximum-security institutions. Powerful forces within the correctional system have a stronger influence over the behavior of COs than the administrators of the institution, legislative decrees, or agency policies.[64] Indeed, it has been known for several decades that exposure to external danger in the workplace creates a remarkable increase in group solidarity.[65]

Some of the job-related stressors for COs are similar to those the police face: the ever-present potential for physical danger, hostility directed at officers by inmates and even by the public, unreasonable role demands, a tedious and unrewarding work environment, and dependence on one another to work effectively and safely in their environment.[66] For these reasons, several norms of corrections work have been identified—always go to the aid of an officer in distress, do not "rat," never make another officer look bad in front of inmates, always support an officer in a dispute with an inmate, always support officer sanctions against inmates, and do not wear a "white hat" (participate in behavior that suggests sympathy or identification with inmates).[67]

Security issues and the way in which COs have to rely on each other for their safety make loyalty to one another a key norm. The proscription against ratting out a colleague is strong. In one documented instance, two officers in the Corcoran, California, State Prison blew the whistle on what they considered to be unethical conduct by their colleagues: Officers were alleged to have staged a gladiator-style fight among inmates from different groups in a small exercise yard. The two officers claimed that their colleagues would even place bets on the outcome of the fights, and when the fights got out of hand, the officers would fire shots at the inmates. Since the institution had opened in 1988, eight inmates had been shot dead by officers and numerous others had been wounded. The two officers who reported these activities were labeled by colleagues as "rats" and "no-goods" and had their lives threatened; even though they were transferred to other institutions, the labels traveled with them. Four COs were indicted for their alleged involvement in these activities, and all were acquitted in a state prosecution in 2001.[68]

In another case, a female CO at a medium-security institution reported some of her colleagues for sleeping during the night shift. She had first approached them and expressed concern for her safety when they were asleep, and told them that if they did not refrain from sleeping, she would have to report them to the superintendent. They continued sleeping and she reported them. The consequences were severe: Graffiti was written about her on the walls, she received harassing phone calls and letters, her car was vandalized, and bricks were thrown through the windows of her home.[69]

It would be unfair to suggest that the kind of behavior depicted here reflects the behavior of COs in all places and at all times. The case studies demonstrate, however, the power and loyalty of the group, and correctional administrators must be cognizant of that power. It is also noteworthy that the corrections subculture, like its police counterpart, has several positive qualities, particularly in crisis situations, including mutual support and protection, which is essential to the emotional and psychological health of the officers involved; the "family" is always there to support you.

▶ Guiding Decision Making

One of the primary purposes of ethics is to guide decision making.[70] Ethics provides more comprehensive guidelines than law and operational procedures, and answers questions that might otherwise go unanswered. When in doubt, justice administrators and employees should be able to consider the ethical consequences of their actions or potential actions to determine how they should proceed. Guidelines must be in place to assist employees in making operational decisions. Criminal justice leaders obviously play a key role in ethics. Not only must they enforce and uphold ethical standards, they must also set an example and see that employees are instructed in the ethical conduct of police business.

Some experts in police ethics lay problems involving employees' ethics, and their lapses in good conduct, squarely at the feet of their leaders; for example, Edward Tully[71] stated the following:

> Show me an agency with a serious problem of officer misconduct and I will show you a department staffed with too many sergeants not doing their job. Leaders must recognize the vital and influential role sergeants play within an organization. They should be selected with care, given as much supervisory training as possible, and included in the decision-making process. Sergeants are the custodians of the culture, the leaders and informal disciplinarians of the department, and the individual most officers look to for advice.

Stephen Vicchio[72] added another caveat. Even in communities where all seems to be going well with respect to ethical behavior, trouble may be lurking beneath the surface:

> In departments where corruption appears to be low and citizen complaints are minimal, we assume that the officers are people of integrity. Sometimes this is a faulty assumption, particularly if the motivation to do the right thing comes from fear of punishment.

Most efforts to control justice system employees' behavior are rooted in statutes and departmental orders and policies. These written directives spell out inappropriate behavior and, in some cases, behavior or actions that are expected in specific situations. Written directives cannot address every contingency, however, and employees must often use their discretion. These discretionary decisions should be guided by ethics and values. When there is an ethics or policy failure, the resulting behavior is generally considered to be illegal or inappropriate.

▶ Ethics Tests for Justice Professionals

Following are some tests to help guide the criminal justice employee in deciding what is and is not an ethical behavior:[73]

- *Test of common sense.* Does the act make sense, or would someone look askance at it?
- *Test of publicity.* Would you be willing to see what you did highlighted on the front page of the local newspaper?
- *Test of one's best self.* Will the act fit the concept of oneself at one's best?
- *Test of one's most admired personality.* What would one's parents or minister do in this situation?
- *Test of hurting someone else.* Will it cause pain for someone?
- *Test of foresight.* What is the long-term likely result?

Other questions that the officer might ask are: Is it worth my job and career? Is my decision legal?

Another tool is that of "the bell, the book, and the candle": Do bells or warning buzzers go off as I consider my choice of actions? Does it violate any laws or codes in the statute or ordinance books? Will my decision withstand the light of day or the spotlight of publicity (the candle)?[74]

In sum, all we can do is try to make the best decisions we can and be good persons and good justice system employees, who are consistent and fair. We need to apply the law, the policy, the guidelines, or whatever it is we dispense in our occupation without bias or fear and to the best of our ability, being mindful along the way that others around us may have lost their moral compass and attempt to drag us down with them. To paraphrase Franklin Delano Roosevelt, "Be the best you can, wherever you are, with what you have."

▶ Is Workplace Loyalty Always Good?

Loyalty

If you work for someone, in heaven's name, work for him!

Speak well of him and stand by the institution he represents.

Remember, an ounce of loyalty is worth a pound of cleverness.

If you must growl, condemn, and eternally find fault, resign your position. And when you are on the outside, damn to your heart's content; but as long as you are part of the institution, do not condemn it. If you do, the first high wind that comes along will blow you away, and probably you will never know why.

—Author Unknown

This quote leaves no doubt that loyalty to the organization, and to one's superior, is highly desired. But is such unequivocal loyalty always a good thing, especially in criminal justice organizations? Certainly, one would think that justice system administrators would view loyalty as a very positive attribute for their employees. There are some, however, who have serious doubts about whether loyalty is indeed an asset.

Sam S. Souryal and Deanna L. Diamond, for example, believe that criminal justice employees often suffer from a "**personal loyalty syndrome**," which can be defined as loyalty that is given by subordinates to their unworthy peers or superiors—even when resulting in violations of constitutional provisions, legal requirements, or the public good.

They are often compelled to offer unwavering personal loyalty to their superiors and, as a result, can violate constitutional provisions, legal requirements, or the public good; therefore, in extreme cases, practitioners may find themselves justifying untruth, impeding justice, supporting cover-ups, and lying under oath.[75]

Souryal and Diamond argued that there are several paradoxes involving the expectation and practice of personal loyalty to superiors in criminal justice agencies:

> **personal loyalty syndrome** loyalty that can be given to unworthy peers or superiors, even when resulting in violations of constitutional provisions, legal requirements, or the public good.

- Despite the emotional support for the practice, there is no mention of it in agency rules and regulations. If loyalty is such a great virtue, why are agency rules and regulations silent about it?

- Superiors usually make demands for loyalty when the agency is under attack, not when the agency is stable and business is conducted "as usual."

- Personal loyalty to superiors ignores the fact that some superiors are not worthy of loyalty; hundreds of supervisors and administrators are fired or disciplined each year for violating agency rules.
- Loyalty is a one-way street (superiors need not return the loyalty).[76]

In sum, there are three types of loyalty for justice practitioners to follow and to think about before offering their loyalties unconditionally; ranked from most important to least important, they are as follows:

First is *integrated* loyalty, the highest and most virtuous level of loyalty at the workplace. It is the genuine concern of each worker for the values and ideals of the profession, honoring the ideals of accountability, rationality, fairness, and good will. This is the cornerstone of all workplace loyalties and is pursued before any institutional loyalty.

Second is *institutional* loyalty; it is the obligation of each agency member, including subordinates and superiors, to support the agency's mission. Examples include the obligation of police, court, and probation and parole officers to be loyal to agency policies, rules, and regulations. This form of loyalty is the most supportive and durable, and should be positioned ahead of loyalty to superiors.

Finally, there is *personal* loyalty, the lowest level of loyalty in the workplace because it is mechanical in nature. Examples include the obligation of deputy sheriffs to be loyal to their sheriff. This form of loyalty is the most volatile and temporal, and should never replace institutional loyalty.[77]

In the final analysis, criminal justice administrators need to educate themselves in the exercise of workplace loyalties—both as an asset and as a detriment—as it relates to ethics, public service, and public good. They must act in good faith and, at a minimum, must be certain that the loyalties of their subordinates are legally and morally justified.

Summary

This chapter has examined criminal justice employee behavior from an ethical standpoint. Ethics form the foundation for behavior. It is important that police, courts, and corrections administrators and subordinates understand ethics and the role ethics plays in the performance of their duties. It is also important that these leaders understand the incipient and dangerous nature of noble cause corruption, in which their employees (and the community) may support unethical actions if they are deemed worthwhile to accomplish a good end.

Corruption has few easy remedies. Although not discussed, given civil service regulations, union rules, and other forms of job protection, it can be very difficult to remove even the worst employees. To avoid rotten apples, criminal justice administrators need to maintain high standards for recruitment and training. And to avoid rotten structures, these kinds of agencies need leaders who will not tolerate corruption, institutional procedures for accountability, and systematic investigation of complaints and of suspicious circumstances.[78]

Key Terms and Concepts

Absolute ethics *307*
Brady material *312*
Deontological ethics *306*
Ethics *306*
Gratuities *312*
Lying (accepted/deviant) *310*

Malfeasance *318*
Misfeasance *318*
Model Code of Judicial Conduct *314*
Model of circumstantial corruptibility *312*

Noble cause corruption *308*
Nonfeasance *319*
Personal loyalty syndrome *321*
Relative ethics *307*

Questions for Review

1. How would you define *ethics*? What are examples of relative and absolute ethics?
2. What is the meaning of *noble cause corruption*, and how does it apply to policing?
3. Should police accept minor gratuities? Explain why doing so might be permitted, per Withrow and Dailey's model of circumstantial corruptibility.
4. How has *Brady v. Maryland* affected both police and prosecutors, and how might one's career be ruined if *Brady's* provisions are violated?

5. In what ways can judges, defense attorneys, and prosecutors engage in unethical behavior?
6. In what substantive ways do the police and corrections subcultures resemble each other?
7. How may corrections officers in prisons be unethical?
8. Which do you believe are the most difficult ethical dilemmas presented in the case studies in Appendix I? Consider the issues presented in each.

Deliberate and Decide

Confronting Ethical Dilemmas

The following scenarios are based on actual cases and pose a possible ethical dilemma for the criminal justice employee (and, by extension, the agency's leadership or governing body):

1. A deputy sheriff has been using a variety of problem-solving approaches to address problems at a shopping mall where juveniles have been loitering, engaging in acts of vandalism, dumping trash, and generally causing traffic problems after hours in the parking lot. Now the mall manager, Mr. Chang, feels morally obligated to express his appreciation to the deputy. Mr. Chang has made arrangements for the deputy and family to receive a 15 percent discount while shopping at any store in the mall. Also, as part-owner of a children's toy store in the mall, Mr. Chang offers the deputy a bicycle for his young daughter. Knowing that the agency policy requires that such offers be declined, the deputy is also aware that Mr. Chang will be very hurt or upset if the proffered gifts are refused.

2. A municipal court judge borrows money from court employees, publicly endorses and campaigns for a candidate for judicial office, conducts personal business from chambers (displaying and selling antiques),

directs other court employees to perform personal errands for him during court hours, suggests that persons appearing before him contribute to certain charities in lieu of paying fines, and uses court employees to perform translating services at his mother's nursery business.

3. A.   An associate warden and "rising star" in a state's prison system has just been stopped and arrested for driving while intoxicated while off-duty and in his personal vehicle. There are no damages or injuries involved, he is very remorseful, and he has just been released from jail. You, as warden, must determine whether or not the individual should receive agency discipline for this action.

   B.   One week later, this same associate warden stops at a local convenience store after work; as he leaves the store, a clerk stops him and summons the police—the individual has just been caught shoplifting a package of cigarettes. You have just been informed of this latest arrest.

Questions for Discussion

1. For each scenario, determine the available options and select what you believe is the best course of action, drawing on information presented in this chapter as well as from your own moral compass.

Learn by Doing

1. As a criminal justice student and friend of the president of your local Citizens' Police Academy, you are asked to speak at the group's training session concerning police ethics. Specifically, you are to discuss ethical dilemmas in policing—providing several examples—and explain how the police must deal with such dilemmas. What would your presentation address?

2. You are a court administrator in County District Court, supervised by Chief Judge Williams. While walking through staff office area today, you believe you overhear a court reporter say that on two occasions that week, Judge Williams smelled like he had alcohol on his breath. They stifle their conversation when they see you walk by. Later that day, you send

your administrative assistant to Judge Williams' chambers to borrow a budget sheet. When he returns, he tells you that the judge appeared to smell of alcohol. A week later, while working late, the judge summons you to his office. There he explains that he is awaiting a jury verdict, and while casually chatting, he makes himself a cocktail. In fact, he eventually consumes several of these drinks (and appears to be more than "tipsy"). When word comes that the jury has returned with its verdict, he quickly leaves his office to return to the bench.

a. What, if anything, are you ethically bound to do regarding Judge Williams?

b. Do you draw a distinction between his drinking, which occurred while he was in his office versus while he is in the court chamber and sitting on the bench?

c. Do you draw a distinction between someone merely smelling alcohol versus actually seeing him drink alcohol? The number of occasions people have smelled alcohol on his breath? Whether he only smelled of alcohol, as opposed to appearing to be intoxicated? Whether he acted inappropriately, unprofessionally, or incompetently while in the observed condition or after drinking alcohol?

d. Would you feel any differently if, instead of a judge, the same situation involved a prosecutor or defense attorney? Why or why not?

3. You are a final candidate for a staff position at a newly constructed state prison in your community. An oral board member asks you the following questions: You discover that a fellow staff member routinely accepts free food, candy, and other gifts of small value from inmates/clients. These items are not solicited from inmates, nor is special treatment given to the gift-givers. (1) How serious do you consider this behavior to be? (2) Do you believe such behavior should be prohibited under official policy in your organization? (3) What, if any, disciplinary measures do you believe to be appropriate in this case? (4) Would you report a fellow staff member to a supervisor for engaging in this behavior? How do you respond to each?

Notes

1. Robert F. Kennedy, *The Enemy Within: The McClellan Committee's Crusade against Jimmy Hoffa and Corrupt Labor Unions* (Jackson, TN: Perseus Books, 1994), p. 324.

2. Adapted from John R. Jones and Daniel P. Carlson, *Reputable Conduct: Ethical Issues in Policing and Corrections,* 2nd ed. (Upper Saddle River, NJ: Prentice Hall, 2001), p. 14.

3. This scenario is loosely based on David Gelman, Susan Miller, and Bob Cohn, "The Strange Case of Judge Wachtler," *Newsweek* (November 23, 1992):34–35. Wachtler was later arraigned on charges of attempting to extort money from the woman and threatening her 14-year-old daughter (it was later determined that the judge had been having an affair with the woman, who had recently ended the relationship). After being placed under house arrest with an electronic monitoring bracelet, the judge resigned from the court, which he had served with distinction for two decades.

4. Adapted from Jones and Carlson, *Reputable Conduct,* pp. 162–163.

5. Richard Kania, "Police Acceptance of Gratuities," *Criminal Justice Ethics* 7 (1988):37–49.

6. John Kleinig, *The Ethics of Policing* (New York: Cambridge University Press, 1996).

7. T. J. O'Malley, "Managing for Ethics: A Mandate for Administrators," *FBI Law Enforcement Bulletin* (April 1997):20–25.

8. Thomas J. Martinelli, "Unconstitutional Policing: The Ethical Challenges in Dealing with Noble Cause Corruption," *The Police Chief* (October 2006):150.

9. John P. Crank and Michael A. Caldero, *Police Ethics: The Corruption of Noble Cause* (Cincinnati: Anderson, 2000), p. 75.

10. U.S. Department of Justice, National Institute of Justice, Office of Community Oriented Policing Services, *Police Integrity: Public Service with Honor* (Washington, DC: U.S. Government Printing Office, 1997), p. 62.

11. Ibid.

12. Ibid.

13. Edward Tully, "Misconduct, Corruption, Abuse of Power: What Can the Chief Do?" http://www.neiassociates.org/-misconduct-corruption-abuse-i/ (accessed September 16, 2014).

14. David Carter, "Theoretical Dimensions in the Abuse of Authority," in Thomas Barker and David Carter (eds.), *Police Deviance* (Cincinnati: Anderson, 1994), pp. 269–290; also see Thomas Barker and David Carter, "Fluffing Up the Evidence and 'Covering Your Ass': Some Conceptual Notes on Police Lying," *Deviant Behavior* 11 (1990):61–73.

15. Gary T. Marx, "Who Really Gets Stung? Some Issues Raised by the New Police Undercover Work," *Crime & Delinquency* (1982):165–193.

16. *Illinois v. Perkins,* 110 S.Ct. 2394 (1990).

17. Barker and Carter, *Police Deviance.*

18. Thomas Barker, "An Empirical Study of Police Deviance Other Than Corruption," in Barker and Carter (eds.), *Police Deviance* (Cincinnati, OH: 1994), pp. 123–138.

19. Jaxon Van Derbeken, "Police with Problems Are a Problem for the D.A.," *San Francisco Chronicle*, May 16, 2010, http://www.sfgate.com/cgi-bin/article.cgi?f=/c/a/2010/05/15/MNKC1DB57E.DTL (accessed November 14, 2014).

20. *Brady v. Maryland*, 373 U.S. 83 (1963).

21. See Richard Lisko, "Agency Policies Imperative to Disclose *Brady v. Maryland* Material to Prosecutors," *The Police Chief* 77(3) (March 2011), http://www.policechiefmagazine.org/magazine/index.cfm?fuseaction=display_arch&article_id=2329&issue_id=32011 (accessed November 14, 2014).

22. Lisko, "Agency Policies Imperative to Disclose *Brady v. Maryland* Material to Prosecutors," also see Val Van Brocklin, "Brady v. Md Can Get You Fired," Officer.com (August 16, 2010), http://www.officer.com/article/10232477/brady-v-md-can-get-you-fired (accessed November 14, 2014).

23. Jack Ryan, "Police Officers May Be Liable for Failure to Disclose Exculpatory Information under the Brady Rule Managing Risks," Policelink (n.d.), http://policelink.monster.com/training/articles/2123-police-officers-may-be-liable-for-failure-to-disclose-exculpatory-information-under-the-brady-rulemanaging-risks- (accessed November 14, 2014).

24. New York City Commission to Investigate Allegations of Police Corruption and the City's Anti-Corruption Procedures, *The Knapp Commission Report on Police Corruption* (New York: George Braziller, 1972), p. 4.

25. Kania, "Police Acceptance of Gratuities," p. 40. For an excellent analysis of how the acceptance of gratuities can become endemic to an organization and pose ethical dilemmas for new officers, see Jim Ruiz and Christine Bono, "At What Price a 'Freebie'? The Real Cost of Police Gratuities," *Criminal Justice Ethics* (Winter–Spring 2004):44–54. The authors also demonstrate through detailed calculations how the amount of gratuities accepted can reach up to 40 percent of an annual officer's income—and is therefore no minor or inconsequential infraction of rules that can be left ignored or unenforced.

26. Brian L. Withrow and Jeffrey D. Dailey, "When Strings Are Attached," in Quint C. Thurman and Jihong Zhao (eds.), *Contemporary Policing: Controversies, Challenges, and Solutions* (Los Angeles: Roxbury, 2004), pp. 319–326.

27. Ibid.

28. Ibid.

29. See *Crime Delinquency* 10 (1964):355–371; American Bar Association, 29 *A.B.A. Report* 29, part I (1906):395–417.

30. John P. MacKenzie, *The Appearance of Justice* (New York: Scribner's, 1974). See also Eliot Asimof, *Eight Men Out: The Black Sox and the 1919 World Series* (New York: Henry Holt, 1963); a movie by the same name was released in 1988.

31. Cynthia Gray, "The Center for Judicial Ethics," *Judicature* 96(6) (May/June 2014):305–313. https://www.ajs.org/index.php/judicial-ethics/judicial-conduct-reporter For more information about Judicial Conduct Reporter, see its website at: https://www.ajs.org/index.php/judicial-ethics/judicial-conduct-reporter (accessed November 26, 2014).

32. Quoted in Frank Greenberg, "The Task of Judging the Judges," *Judicature* 59 (May 1976):464.

33. Ibid., p. 460; direct quote from the original.

34. Walter Pavlo, "Pennsylvania Judge Gets 'Life Sentence' for Prison Kickback Scheme," http://www.forbes.com/sites/walterpavlo/2011/08/12/pennsylvania-judge-gets-life-sentence-for-prison-kickback-scheme/ (accessed November 25, 2014).

35. Ian Urbina and Sean D. Hamill, "Judges Plead Guilty in Scheme to Jail Youths for Profit," *The New York Times*, February 12, 2009, http://www.nytimes.com/2009/02/13/us/13judge.html?pagewanted=all&_r=0 (accessed November 22, 2014).

36. Ibid.

37. Cynthia Gray, "Top Judicial Ethics Stories of 2010," *Judicature* 94 (4) (Jan/Feb 2011):187–191.

38. See *In re Gault*, 387 U.S. 1 (1967).

39. Urbina and Hamill, "Judges Plead Guilty in Scheme to Jail Youths for Profit."

40. For thorough discussions and examples of these areas of potential ethical shortcomings, see Jeffrey M. Shaman, Steven Lubet, and James J. Alfini, *Judicial Conduct and Ethics*, 3rd ed. (San Francisco: Matthew Bender & Co., 2000).

41. Ibid.

42. Ibid., p. vi.

43. Ibid.

44. Ibid., p. vi.

45. Tim Murphy, "Test Your Ethical Acumen," *Judges' Journal* 8 (1998):34.

46. American Judicature Society, *Judicial Conduct Reporter* 16 (1994):2–3.

47. John Adams, "On Government," quoted in Russell Wheeler, *Judicial Administration: Its Relation to Judicial Independence* (Alexandria, VA: National Center for State Courts, 1988), p. 112.

48. Shaman et al., *Judicial Conduct and Ethics*, p. viii.

49. Deut. 1:16–17.

50. Elliot D. Cohen, "Pure Legal Advocates and Moral Agents: Two Concepts of a Lawyer in an Adversary System," in Michael C. Braswell, Belinda R. McCarthy, and Bernard J. McCarthy (eds.), *Justice, Crime and Ethics*, 2nd ed. (Cincinnati: Anderson, 1996), pp. 131–167.

51. *Berger v. United States*, 295 U.S. 78 (1935).

52. See *Dunlop v. United States,* 165 U.S. 486 (1897), involving a prosecutor's inflammatory statements to the jury.

53. 386 U.S. 1 (1967). In this case, the Supreme Court overturned the defendant's conviction after determining that the prosecutor "deliberately misrepresented the truth."

54. Cohen, "Pure Legal Advocates and Moral Agents," p. 168.

55. Ibid.

56. Cynthia Kelly Conlon and Lisa L. Milord, *The Ethics Fieldbook: Tools for Trainers* (Chicago: American Judicature Society, n.d.), pp. 23–25.

57. Ibid., p. 28.

58. Robert M. Worley and Vidisha Barua Worley, "Guards Gone Wild: A Self-report Study of Correctional Officer Misconduct and the Effect of Institutional Deviance on "Care" Within the Texas Prison System," *Deviant Behavior* 32(4) (April 2011):293–319.

59. Ibid.
60. Ibid.
61. Sam Souryal, "Deterring Corruption by Prison Personnel: A Principle-Based Perspective," *The Prison Journal* 89(1) (March 2009):21–45.
62. Jeffrey Ian Ross," "Deconstructing Correctional Officer Deviance: Toward Typologies of Actions and Controls," *Criminal Justice Review* 38 (1) (March 2014):110–126.
63. Ibid., p. 36.
64. Elizabeth L. Grossi and Bruce L. Berg, "Stress and Job Dissatisfaction Among Correctional Officers: An Unexpected Finding," *International Journal of Offender Therapy and Comparative Criminology* 35 (1991):79.
65. Irving L. Janis, "Group Dynamics under Conditions of External Danger," in Darwin Cartwright and Alvin Zander (eds.), *Group Dynamics: Research and Theory* (New York: Harper & Row, 1968).
66. Ibid.
67. Ibid., p. 85.
68. *CBS News*, March 30, 1977; see Jones and Carlson, *Reputable Conduct*, p. 76.
69. Jones and Carlson, *Reputable Conduct,* p. 77.
70. F. K. Fair and W. D. Pilcher, "Morality on the Line: The Role of Ethics in Police Decision-Making," *American Journal of Police* 10(2) (1991):23–38.
71. Tully, "Misconduct, Corruption, Abuse of Power."
72. Stephen J. Vicchio, "Ethics and Police Integrity," *FBI Law Enforcement Bulletin* (July 1997):8–12.
73. Kleinig, *The Ethics of Policing.*
74. Ibid.
75. Sam S. Souryal and Deanna L. Diamond, "The Rhetoric of Personal Loyalty to Superiors in Criminal Justice Agencies," *Journal of Criminal Justice* 29(2001):543–554.
76. Ibid., p. 548.
77. Ibid., p. 549
78. Delattre, *Character and Cops,* p. 84.

DOC RABE Media/Fotolia

No man is fit to command another that cannot command himself.

—*William Penn*

14 Special Challenges
Labor Relations, Liability, and Discipline

LEARNING OBJECTIVES

After reading this chapter, the student will be able to:

1 *define collective bargaining and labor negotiations generally, as well as the recent political backlash in several states against collective bargaining and workers' wage and benefits packages*

2 *describe the three models used in collective bargaining*

3 *delineate the four types of job actions employees can use to express their displeasure with working conditions*

4 *explain how administrators must "navigate the waters" of unionism*

5 *describe the nature of civil liability, the kinds of actions that can lead to a determination of negligence, and different types of lawsuits filed against criminal justice practitioners*

6 *discuss the due process requirements concerning the discharge of public employees*

7 *describe the kinds of disciplinary actions and approaches (including the positive discipline approach) that may be used by agencies in an investigation of a criminal justice employee*

8 *articulate why and how a disciplinary matrix is being used in increasing numbers of police agencies*

9 *delineate the steps taken when a citizen's complaint is filed*

10 *review the grievance process*

11 *explain how one can appeal disciplinary measures, as well as the system for identifying problem officers who receive complaints from both internal and external sources*

▶ Introduction

Those who administer criminal justice agencies are confronted with, and must successfully address, countless challenges in the course of performing their daily duties; therefore, because they provide criminal justice administrators with nearly endless challenges—as well as trials, tribulations, and often a very large proportion of their workload—we discuss three broad topics concerning personnel.

This chapter opens by discussing labor relations/collective bargaining. In the past 50 years, probably no factor has had a greater impact on the administration of criminal justice agencies, with the possible exception of civil liability, which is also discussed in this chapter. Indeed, the decade of the 2010s witnessed unprecedented battles between politicians (who are trying to address huge budget deficits, union powers, and what they perceive to be runaway wages and benefits packages) and labor unions (who are trying to protect their members' wages and benefits—and their sphere of influence). This chapter discusses those recent battles, including how the unionization movement developed in criminal justice, contemporary collective bargaining practices, and a primer on "navigating the waters" of unionization.

Next, we examine criminal justice employees visà-vis potential civil liability. This discussion includes several legal concepts (such as negligence and torts), court decisions, and legislation that serve to hold criminal justice practitioners accountable, both civilly and criminally, for acts of misconduct and negligence.

Then we look at employee discipline, including the tradition of problems in policing, due process requirements that must be afforded such employees, what is being done to identify and deal with problem officers, how the agency might employ a positive discipline program, use of the disciplinary matrix, some proper means of dealing with citizen complaints, and the need to account for violations of *internal* departmental standards. The chapter concludes with review questions, "deliberate and decide" problems, and "learn by doing" exercises. Three exhibits will elaborate on liability, corruption, and discipline.

▶ Collective Bargaining, Generally: Nature, Extent—and Recent Political Backlash

The Nature and Principles of Shared Governance

Three Models

collective bargaining See "negotiation".

Each state is free to decide whether and which public sector employees will have **collective bargaining** rights and under what terms; therefore, there is considerable variety in collective bargaining arrangements across the nation. In states with comprehensive public sector bargaining laws, the administration of the statute is the responsibility of a state agency such as a public employee relations board (PERB) or a public employee relations commission (PERC). There are three basic models used in the states: binding arbitration, meet-and-confer, and bargaining-not-required.[1] Table 14-1 ■ shows the use of these models in the various states.

TABLE 14-1 State Collective Bargaining Laws Governing Law Enforcement Officers

State	Binding Arbitration Model	Meet-and-Confer Model	Bargaining-Not-Required Model
Alabama			X
Alaska	X		
Arizona			X
Arkansas			X
California	X		
Colorado			X
Connecticut	X		
Delaware	X		
District of Columbia	X		
Florida		X	
Georgia			X
Hawaii	X		
Idaho			X
Illinois	X		
Indiana		X	
Iowa	X		
Kansas	X		
Kentucky		X	
Louisiana			X
Maine	X		
Maryland		X	
Massachusetts	X		
Michigan	X		
Minnesota	X		
Mississippi			X
Missouri		X	
Montana	X		
Nebraska		X	
Nevada		X	
New Hampshire	X		
New Jersey	X		
New Mexico		X	
New York	X		
North Carolina			X
North Dakota		X	
Ohio	X		
Oklahoma	X		
Oregon	X		
Pennsylvania	X		

(continued)

TABLE 14-1 (*continued*)

State	Binding Arbitration Model	Meet-and-Confer Model	Bargaining-Not-Required Model
Rhode Island	X		
South Carolina		X	
South Dakota		X	
Tennessee			X
Texas			X
Utah			X
Vermont	X		
Virginia			X
Washington	X		
West Virginia			X
Wisconsin	X		
Wyoming			X

Source: Excerpt from The Rights of Law Enforcement Officers by Will Aitchison. Copyright © 2009 by Labor Relations Information System. Used by permission of Labor Relations Information System.

The binding arbitration model is used in 25 states and the District of Columbia. Public employees are given the right to bargain with their employers. If the bargaining reaches an impasse, the matter is submitted to a neutral arbitrator who decides what the terms and conditions of the new collective bargaining agreement will be.[2]

Only eleven states use the **meet-and-confer** model, which grants very few rights to public employees. As with the binding arbitration model, criminal justice employees in meet-and-confer states have the right to organize and to select their own bargaining representatives.[3] When an impasse is reached, however, employees are at a distinct disadvantage. Their only legal choices are to accept the employer's best offer, try to influence the offer through political tactics (such as appeals for public support), or take some permissible job action.[4]

The fifteen states that follow the *bargaining-not-required* model either do not statutorily require or do not allow collective bargaining by public employees.[5] In the majority of these states, laws permitting public employees to engage in collective bargaining have not been passed.

States with collective bargaining must also address the issue of whether an individual employee must be a member of a union that represents his or her class of employees in a particular organization. In a "closed shop," employees must be dues-paying members or they will be terminated by the employer. "Open" shops, conversely, allow employees a choice of whether to join, even though the union has an obligation to represent them.

> **meet-and-confer**
> a comparatively weak bargaining system where employees may organize and select bargaining representatives; but if an impasse occurs, their options are limited.

Organizing for Collective Bargaining

If collective bargaining is legally established, the process of setting up a bargaining relationship is as follows: First, a union will begin an organizing drive seeking to get a majority of the class(es) of employees it wants to represent to sign authorization cards. At this point, agency administrators may attempt to convince employees that they are better off without the union. Questions may also arise, such as whether certain employees (e.g., police or prison lieutenants) are part of management and therefore ineligible for union representation.

Once a majority ("50% plus 1" of the eligible employees) have signed cards, the union notifies the criminal justice agency. If management believes that the union has obtained a majority legitimately, it will recognize the union as the bargaining agent of the employees it has sought to represent. Once recognized by the employer, the union will petition the PERB or other body responsible for administering the legislation for certification.

Negotiation

Labor **negotiation** typically involves a dialogue between labor and management that is intended to develop a written agreement that will bind both parties during the life of the agreement concerning such issues as working conditions, salaries, and benefits. Negotiations at times are also used to prevent or to resolve disputes concerning same.

Management normally prefers a narrow scope of negotiations because it means less shared power; conversely, the union will opt for the widest possible scope. The number of negotiating sessions may run from one to several dozen, lasting from a few minutes to 10 or more hours, depending on how close or far apart union and management are when they begin to meet face to face.

Figure 14-1 ■ depicts a typical configuration of the union and management bargaining teams. Positions shown in the broken-line boxes typically serve in a support role and may or may not actually partake in the bargaining. Management's labor relations manager (lead negotiator) is often an attorney assigned to the human resources department, reporting to the city manager or assistant city manager and representing the city in grievances and arbitration matters; management's chief negotiator may also be the director of labor relations or human resources director for the unit of government involved or a professional labor relations specialist. Similarly, the union's chief negotiator normally is not a member of the organization involved; rather, he or she will be a specialist who is brought in to represent the union's position and to provide greater experience, expertise, objectivity, and autonomy. The union's chief negotiator may be accompanied by some people who have conducted surveys on wages and benefits, trends in the consumer price index, and so on.[6]

In the minds of many chief executives, the agency administrator should NOT appear at the bargaining table; it is difficult for the chief executive to represent management one day and then return to work among the employees the next. Rather, management is represented by a key member of the command staff having the executive's confidence.

> **negotiation** a dialogue between labor and management for developing a written agreement that concerning such issues as working conditions, salaries, and benefits.

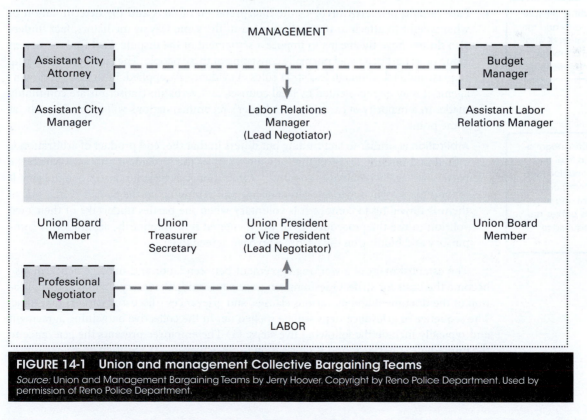

FIGURE 14-1   Union and management Collective Bargaining Teams
Source: Union and Management Bargaining Teams by Jerry Hoover. Copyright by Reno Police Department. Used by permission of Reno Police Department.

The issues, and the way in which they are presented, will impact how the negotiations will go. In the initial session, the chief negotiator for each party will make an opening statement. Management's representative will often go first, touching on general themes such as the need for patience and the obligation to bargain in good faith. The union's negotiator will generally follow, outlining what the union seeks to achieve under the terms of the new contract. Ground rules for the bargaining may then be reviewed, modified, or developed. The attention then shifts to the terms of the contract that the union is proposing. Both sides need to understand what it is they are attempting to commit each other to. Ultimately, unless a total impasse is reached, agreement will be obtained on the terms of a new contract. The union's membership will vote on the contract as whole. If approved by the membership, the contract then goes before the necessary government officials and bodies for approval.[7]

In the Event of an Impasse . . .

Even parties bargaining in good faith may not be able to resolve their differences by themselves, and an impasse may result. In such cases, a neutral third party may be introduced to facilitate, suggest, or compel an agreement. Three major forms of impasse resolution are mediation, fact finding, and arbitration.

mediation a third party who comes in to help opposing parties to settle their negotiations.

- **Mediation** occurs when a third party, called the mediator, comes in to help the opposing parties to settle their negotiations.[8] This person may be a professional mediator or someone else in whom both parties have confidence. In most states, mediation may be requested by either labor or management. The mediator's task is to build agreement about the issues involved by reopening communications between the two sides. The mediator cannot compel an agreement, so an advantage of the process is that it preserves collective bargaining by maintaining the decision-making power in the hands of the involved parties.[9]

fact finding interpretation of facts and the determination of what weight to attach to them in negotiations.

- **Fact finding** primarily involves the interpretation of facts and the determination of what weight to attach to them. Appointed in the same way as mediators, fact finders also do not have the means to impose a settlement of the dispute. Fact finders may sit alone or as part of a panel normally consisting of three people. The fact-finding hearing is quasi-judicial, although less strict rules of evidence are applied. Both labor and management may be represented by legal counsel, and verbatim transcripts are commonly made. In a majority of cases, the fact finder's recommendations will be made public at some point.[10]

arbitration negotiation with a final and binding decision that sets the terms of the settlement and with which the parties are legally required to comply.

- **Arbitration** is similar to fact finding but differs in that the "end product of arbitration is a final and binding decision that sets the terms of the settlement and with which the parties are legally required to comply."[11] Arbitration may be voluntary or compulsory. It is compulsory when mandated by state law and is binding on the parties even if one of them is unwilling to comply. It is voluntary when the parties undertake of their own volition to use the procedure. Even when entered into voluntarily, arbitration is compulsory and binding on the parties who have agreed to it.

The establishment of a working agreement between labor and management can also become the basis for strife. Questions can arise concerning the interpretation and application of the document and its various clauses, and grievances (discussed earlier) may arise. The sequence of grievance steps will be spelled out in the collective bargaining agreement and typically include the following five steps: (1) The employee presents the grievance to the immediate supervisor, and if satisfaction is not achieved, (2) a written grievance is presented to the division commander, then (3) to the chief executive officer, then (4) to the city or county manager, and, finally, (5) to an arbiter, selected according to the rules of the American Arbitration Association.[12]

The burden of proof is on the grieving party, except in disciplinary cases, when it is always on the employer. The parties may be represented by counsel at the hearing, and the format will include opening statements by each side, examination and cross-examination of any witnesses, and closing arguments in the reverse order of which opening arguments were made.[13]

Job Actions

A **job action** is an activity by employees to express their dissatisfaction with a particular person, event, or condition or to attempt to influence the outcome of some matter pending before decision makers. Employees seek to create pressure that may shift the course of events to a position more favorable or acceptable to them.[14] Job actions are of four types: the vote of confidence, work slowdowns, work speedups, and work stoppages.

- *Vote of confidence.* This job action is used sparingly; a vote of no confidence signals employees' collective displeasure with the chief administrator of the agency. Although such votes have no legal standing, they may have high impact as a result of the resulting publicity.

- *Work slowdowns.* Employees continue to work during a slowdown, but they do so at a leisurely pace, causing productivity to fall. As productivity declines, the unit of government is pressured to resume normal work production; for example, a police department may urge officers to issue more citations so that revenues are not lost. Citizens may complain to politicians to "get this thing settled."[15]

- *Work speedups.* These involve accelerated activity in the level of services and can foster considerable public resentment. For example, a police department may conduct a "ticket blizzard" to protest a low pay increase, pressure governmental leaders to make more concessions at the bargaining table, or abandon some policy change that affects their working conditions.

- *Work stoppages.* When a bargaining impasse occurs, a work stoppage—or strike—can constitute the most severe job action employees can undertake. Because it involves the withholding of all employees' services in an attempt to force management back to the bargaining table, public employees are generally forbidden by state law to strike. For example, New York's "Taylor Law" makes it a crime for public employees and their unions to "cause, instigate, encourage or condone a strike" (however, the law also granted public employees the right to unionize and to bargain collectively).[16] Work stoppages involving public employees are rare, but they do occur and often involve educational systems; an example is the 2012 strike involving the Chicago Public Schools and the Chicago Teachers Union, with 26,500 workers accounting for 185,500 days idle.[17] Criminal justice employee strikes are now rare. Short of a strike by all employees are briefer work stoppages, known in policing as "blue flu," which typically last only a few days.

> **job action** an activity by employees to express their dissatisfaction with a particular person, event, or condition relating to their work.

▶ Labor Relations in Criminal Justice

In 1971, Tucson police legal advisor John H. Burpo authored a book entitled *The Police Labor Movement: Problems and Perspectives*,[18] In the book's Preface, Burpo stated, "Police labor problems, of which unionization is but one facet, will be the major administrative headache facing the police service during the next decade."[19]

Burpo was certainly correct in that assessment. However, many of today's police, courts, and corrections administrators would argue that he was off by nearly a half century in his view of unionization as posing an "administrative headache" for a decade. Unions obviously are here to stay—and have become involved in all manner of issues, including not only wages and benefits but also working conditions, promotions, staffing levels, bans on smoking in public, even the kinds of vehicles officers drive. And they have contributed much to the rights and privileges that criminal justice employees enjoy and were discussed in Chapter 13.

In this chapter section, we discuss the history, nature, and principles of collective bargaining in criminal justice organizations. Included is a discussion of how criminal justice administrators must "navigate the waters" of unionization in order to coexist with them in today's criminal-justice environment.

The Movement Begins: Policing Then and Now

Early Campaigns

The first campaign to organize the police started shortly after World War I, when the American Federation of Labor (AFL) reversed a long-standing policy and issued charters to police unions in Boston, Washington, DC, and about 30 other cities. Many police officers were suffering from the rapid inflation following the outbreak of the war and believed that unions could obtain long-overdue pay raises for them. Capitalizing on their sentiments, the fledgling unions signed up about 60 percent of all officers in Washington, DC, 75 percent in Boston, and a similar proportion in other cities.[20]

The unions' success was short-lived, however. The Boston police commissioner refused to recognize the union, forbade officers to join it, and filed charges against several union officials. Shortly thereafter, on September 9, 1919, the Boston police initiated their now-famous 3-day strike, leading to major riots and a furor against the police all across the nation; 9 rioters were killed and 23 were seriously injured. During the strike, Massachusetts Governor Calvin Coolidge stated, "There is no right to strike against the public safety by anybody, anywhere, anytime."

During World War II, however, the unionization effort was reignited. Unions issued charters to a few dozen locals all over the country and sent in organizers to help enlist the rank and file. Most police chiefs continued speaking out against unionization, but their subordinates were moved by the thousands to join, sensing the advantage in having unions press for higher wages and benefits.[21] In a series of rulings, however, the courts upheld the right of police authorities to ban police unions.

The unions were survived in the early 1950s by many benevolent and fraternal organizations of police. Some were patrolmen's benevolent associations (PBAs), like those formed in New York City, Chicago, and Washington, DC; others were fraternal orders of police (FOPs). During the late 1950s and early 1960s, a new group of rank-and-file association leaders came into power that was more vocal in articulating their demands. Soon, a majority of the rank-and-file vocally supported higher salaries and pensions, free legal aid, low-cost insurance, and other services and benefits. Beginning with the granting of public-sector collective bargaining rights in Wisconsin in 1959, rank-and-file organizations were legally able to insist that their administrators sit down at the bargaining table.[22]

Today labor relations remain a critical topic in policing, and these relations have a significant impact on the administration of police departments and individual units. A virtual maze of affiliations dots the police labor landscape, with the two largest unions—the Fraternal Order of Police and the National Association of Police Organizations—reporting a combined membership of nearly 570,000 sworn officers.[23] Police unions are strongest in the Northeast, Midwest, and West and tend to play a greater role in larger departments. Unions in larger departments tend to have larger staffs working full-time to advance union causes; they often have lobbyists who work the political system for union purposes; and they frequently are politically active, often supporting particular candidates and contributing to campaigns. Thus, police unions in many jurisdictions are a formidable force with which to be reckoned.

Once unions are recognized in a jurisdiction, the relationship between the department and the governmental entity is codified in a contract or memorandum of understanding.

The contract specifies the rights and privileges of employees, and it places restrictions on the political entity and police administrators. In effect, the contract has the force of law. The contract can only be changed via renegotiations, which occur generally on a 3-year cycle or by mutual agreement on the part of the union and police management. When there is a dispute over the interpretation of the contract or its administration, the question is sorted out by an arbitrator or sometimes in the courts.[24]

Unions can obviously have a major impact on police departments. Their activities and the contract not only affect police administrators but also place limitations or restrictions on supervisors and managers. Thus, it is important for supervisors and managers to understand the collective bargaining process, the implications of the contract, and how supervisors and managers negotiate tasks and responsibilities within the confines of the contract.

Corrections Follows the Precedent

Correctional officers (COs) were probably the last group of public workers to organize. After authorization of collective bargaining in the 1960s and 1970s, correctional administrators feared that unionization would diminish management authority and undermine staff discipline and prison security. Over the years that collective bargaining has been in place for correctional agencies, however, the early fears have not materialized, and the benefits of shared governance by line staff and management have led to better decisions and higher morale. As with the police, negotiations usually involve pay and benefits for correctional employees, including seniority rights, how staff members are selected for overtime, the type of clothing provided to staff by the agency, educational programs, and so on. After a contract is negotiated, each prison or community corrections office must implement and administer it. When disputes about the true meaning of a contract arise, management can make a decision, and the union can file a grievance to argue against it.[25]

Collective bargaining is now well entrenched in prison and other correctional agency operations, and it will continue to have an impact on policy and practice. There remains some disagreement, however, concerning its implications. Some argue that sharing of power in a correctional setting benefits all parties, and that unions are a powerful voice to the legislature for increases in staffing and budgets. Others maintain that collective bargaining has resulted in a clear distinction between line staff and management, with managers no longer looking out for subordinates because union leadership promotes an adversarial relationship. As James Jacobs and Norma Crotty suggested, collective bargaining "has redefined the prison organization in adversary terms so that wardens are bosses and complaints are grievances."[26]

A major issue with corrections unions involves the right to strike. One can only imagine the chaos that would occur if COs strike. Such unlawful strikes have occurred. The most infamous strike action was in New York State in 1979, when 7,000 correctional workers simultaneously struck the state's 33 prisons. A court found the union in violation of the law, heavily fined the union for the failure of its members to return to work, and jailed union leaders for contempt of court.[27] The strike ended 17 days after it began; the corrections officers gained very few concessions, and the salary gains did not offset the fines imposed on the strikers.[28]

Finally, another concern regarding collective bargaining is its impact on rehabilitation. Some argue that prison unions, stressing staff safety issues, may impede the institution's efforts toward rehabilitation, while also pointing out that rehabilitative programs that improve inmate morale, reduce idleness, and enhance security result in benefits to the staff who work in prison.[29]

Overall, much like the unionization of the police, it is the attitude of agency administrators and union leaders and the relationships that develop that set the direction of the impact. If both parties communicate with and listen to each other, show mutual respect, and are reasonable in their positions, collective bargaining can benefit corrections.

If, however, the parties let issues get personal and become overly adversarial, corrections and collective bargaining will experience many negative outcomes.[30]

Unionization in the Courts

The movement to exercise the right to bargain collectively, especially when compared with law enforcement and corrections, has been rare in the courts, occurring on a random, localized basis; however, unified court systems exist in which court personnel are organized statewide, as in Hawaii. Many states adhere generally to model legislation on public employee relation commissions, which provide mediation and fact-finding services and make determinations of unfair labor practices. On occasion, these commissions make decisions that greatly affect the management authority of the judiciary over its personnel.

When a collective bargaining unit exists in a court system, the process has all the basic elements found in other systems: (1) recognition (the employing court recognizes that henceforth employees will be represented by their chosen agent); (2) negotiation (there are established methods for arriving at collective bargaining agreements, breaking deadlocks, ratifying contracts, and so on); and (3) contract administration (the day-to-day management of a court is accomplished within the framework of the labor contract).[31]

▶ In Sum: "Navigating the Waters" of Unionization

It should now be evident from the foregoing discussions that collective bargaining is now under close scrutiny and that there is inherent conflict between labor and management. Government officials expect management to represent its interests well; conversely, there is an expectation by labor that the union will be a strong advocate for its membership. However, when their relationship becomes antagonistic, everyone suffers; the challenge is to keep that conflict within a healthy range.[32] Therefore, the four principles of collective bargaining—communication, cooperation, trust, and respect—are of utmost importance. As a general rule, administrators who actively engage the union will accomplish far more than those who employ hostile isolation.[33] Furthermore, it is generally *not* fruitful for the following to occur:

- Meetings being held in the administrator's office, with management sitting at the head of the table. Rather, informal settings—or, at the very least, a generic conference room setting—communicates a great deal.
- "Secret deals" being struck. Perhaps such an arrangement might occasionally be struck, but it certainly should be done very carefully, and only rarely.
- Blending issues concerning economics with agency management. Management should not be involved in negotiations that concern limits on wages and benefits. Management's position should simply be a neutral one, that "My employees deserve as much money as the jurisdiction can possibly afford to give them." Management needs to excuse themselves when the management team caucuses on economic issues.[34]

Following are some other potential pitfalls to avoid, especially when conflicts, crises, or controversies occur, per Ronald G. DeLord[35]:

1. *Assuming traditional labor-management roles:* Management should avoid entering every contract negotiation fighting to gain control over discipline and working conditions; nor should the union seek only higher pay and benefits. Rather, they should develop a shared vision of community safety—and then realize that the methods used to gain that vision are negotiable.

2. *Rushing to judgment:* If an employee is, say, being investigated for an alleged brutality complaint caught on video, both sides should be patient and let the criminal and internal affairs investigators complete their jobs. The media always wants an immediate response from management and the union. There is no requirement that either party respond to questions quickly; sometimes a "no comment until all the facts are in" statement will suffice.

3. *Ignoring or not recognizing the pressures on management or union leaders during a crisis or controversy:* During a high-profile incident, there may be pressure from union members to take certain public positions that may appear confrontational to management, or vice versa. Although some statements or actions are required as a part of the role each has to play, communication, cooperation, respect, and trust become valuable to avoiding unnecessary conflicts.

4. *Defending the indefensible:* Assume that a high-ranking criminal justice official is caught drinking while driving and the agency administrator deems a minor suspension to be appropriate. Or, an employee is arrested for the same offense and the union defends his or her actions as caused by "stress of the job." When such occurrences arise, union and management must be truthful—and be aware that the public might see such "discipline" as too lenient and preferential.

5. *Forgetting that elected officials do not like to make waves, and all battles are won and lost in the court of public opinion:* Just about everything that happens in a criminal justice agency is open to the public, and any conflict between management and the union during a crisis or controversy will be played out the media. Information leaks occur during high-profile incidents, and management and unions need to realize that all of their words and actions will be brought to light. Efforts by management and the union to resolve conflicts before they escalate will go a long way toward preventing a public collision.

6. *Making an end run:* When management goes around the union to communicate with or to encourage the rank-and-file to support or oppose an issue, a union backlash is sure to come. The union has a role to play, and its leadership was elected to speak for the members on labor-related issues. The same holds true for the union when it decides to make an end run to the city manager or to elected officials.

▶ Civil Liability: A Primer

Definitions and Legal Foundation

Criminal justice administrators, particularly those working in law enforcement and corrections, certainly understand the potential and actual existence of **civil liability**—i.e., blame assigned to a person or organization because its employees committed negligent or other acts resulting in some type of harm. These administrators very likely reflect their experiences and concerns with litigation in their training, policies and procedures, general orders, and so on.

They also understand that, with the possible exception of professionals working in the medical field, no group of workers is more susceptible to litigation and liability than police and corrections employees. Frequently thrust into confrontational situations, and given the complex nature of their work and its requisite training needs, they will from time to time act in a manner that evokes public scrutiny and complaints. As we will see, the price of failure among public servants can be quite high in both human and financial terms. In addition, some police officers and COs are overzealous and even brutal in their work; they may intentionally or otherwise violate the rights of the citizens they are sworn to protect, detain, or supervise. For these inappropriate actions, the public has become quick to file suit for damages for what are perceived to be egregious actions.

> **civil liability** blame assigned to a person or organization because its employees committed negligent or other acts resulting in some type of harm.

Next, we examine the kinds of inappropriate and negligent behaviors that can lead to civil liability and even incarceration for police and corrections personnel in the justice system; included is a discussion of a major legislative tool that citizens used to seek redress when such activities occur: Title 42, U.S. Code, Section 1983.

Torts and Negligence

It is important to have a basic understanding of tort liability. A **tort** is the infliction of some injury on one person by another. Three categories of torts generally cover most of the lawsuits filed against criminal justice practitioners: negligence, intentional torts, and constitutional torts.

Negligence can arise when a criminal justice employee's conduct creates a danger to others. In other words, the employee did not conduct his or her affairs in a manner that avoids subjecting others to a risk of harm and may be held liable for the injuries caused to others.[36]

Intentional torts occur when an employee engages in a voluntary act that is quite likely to result in injury to another; examples are assault and battery, false arrest and imprisonment, malicious prosecution, and abuse of process.

Constitutional torts involve employees' duty to recognize and uphold the constitutional rights, privileges, and immunities of others; violations of these guarantees may subject the employee to a civil suit, most frequently brought in federal court under 42 U.S. Code Section 1983, discussed in the next section.[37]

Assault, battery, false imprisonment, false arrest, invasion of privacy, negligence, defamation, and malicious prosecution are examples of torts that are commonly brought against police officers.[38] False arrest is the arrest of a person without probable cause. False imprisonment is the intentional illegal detention of a person not only in jail but also in any confinement to a specified area. For example, the police may fail to release an arrested person after a proper bail or bond has been posted, may delay the arraignment of an arrested person unreasonably, or may fail to release a prisoner after they no longer have authority to hold him or her.[39]

A single act may also be a crime as well as a tort. If Officer Smith, in an unprovoked attack, injures Jones, the state will attempt to punish Smith in a *criminal* action by sending him to jail or prison, fining him, or both. The state would have the burden of proof at a criminal trial, having to prove Smith guilty "beyond a reasonable doubt." Furthermore, Jones may sue Smith for money damages in a *civil* action for the personal injury he suffered. In this civil suit, Jones would have the burden of proving that Smith's acts were tortious by a "preponderance of the evidence"—a lower standard than that in a criminal court and thus easier to satisfy.

Section 1983 Legislation

Following the Civil War and in reaction to the activities of the Ku Klux Klan, Congress enacted the Ku Klux Klan Act of 1871, later codified as **Title 42, U.S. Code, Section 1983**. It states:

> Every person who, under color of any statute, ordinance, regulation, custom, or usage of any State or Territory, subjects, or causes to be subjected, any citizen of the United States or any other person within the jurisdiction thereof to the deprivation of any rights, privileges, or immunities secured by the Constitution and laws, shall be liable to the party injured in an action at law, suit in equity, or other proper proceeding for redress.

This legislation was intended to provide civil rights protection to all "persons" protected under the act when a defendant acted "under color of law" (misused power of office) and provided an avenue to the federal courts for relief of alleged civil rights violations. We will see how Section 1983 can be used against the police.

Lawsuits against the Police Generally

A police executive once commented to the author, "The decision-making process is not directed so much by the question 'Is it right or wrong?' but rather 'How much will it cost us if we're sued?'"

While that may be a bit overstated, the specter of lawsuits certainly looms large over police executives, their supervisors and officers, and their unit of government. Next, we focus on this omnipresent facet of contemporary police administration.

The police are not irrationally paranoid when it comes to their being sued: Between 1980 and 2005, federal court decisions involving lawsuits against the police nearly tripled; and, according to one study, the police are currently faced with more than 30,000 civil actions annually.[40]

The cost of civil suits against police can be quite high. For example, according to one study, from 1990 to 1999, the City of Los Angeles paid more than $67.8 million in judgments and settlements in 80 lawsuits involving the use of excessive force and police officer involvement in sexual assault, sexual abuse, molestation, and domestic violence; this amount does not include the millions of dollars the city spent in defending against these civil suits, nor does it cover lawsuits stemming from the Rampart Division scandal of the late 1990s[41] (where a former LAPD officer testified that he and other officers routinely lied in court, stole and resold drugs, beat handcuffed suspects in the police station, and killed unarmed people and then planted guns and drugs on them; dozens of lawsuits were filed).[42] Facing potential judgments amounting to millions of dollars, municipalities are forced to secure liability insurance to protect against civil litigation—insurance that is very expensive. But such expenditures are necessary; the cost of an average jury award of liability against a municipality is reported to be about $2 million.[43] To prevent such large judgments, many cities and their insurers attempt to settle many claims of police misconduct out of court, as opposed to having a jury give the plaintiff(s) a large award.

Such litigation—although costly in terms of both money and police morale—may have beneficial effects, however. Proponents of civil liabilities argue that these lawsuits keep the police accountable, give real meaning to citizens' rights, foster better police training, and force the police agencies to correct any deficiencies and review all policies, practices, and customs.[44]

Liability of Police Leadership

Another trend is for such litigants to cast a wide net in their lawsuits, suing not only the principal actors in the incident but also agency administrators and supervisors as well; this breadth of suing represents the notion of *vicarious liability* or the doctrine of *respondeat superior,* an old legal maxim meaning "let the master answer." In sum, an employer can be found liable in certain instances for wrongful acts of the employee.

Using Section 1983, litigants often allege inadequate hiring and/or training of personnel by police leadership, or that they knew, or should have known, of the misconduct of their officers yet failed to take corrective action and prevent future harm. An example is the case of *Brandon v. Allen,*[45] in which two teenagers parked in a lovers' lane were approached by an off-duty police officer, Allen, who showed his police identification and demanded that the male exit the car. Allen struck the young man with his fist, stabbed him with a knife, and then attempted to break into the car where the young woman was seated. The young man was able to reenter the car and manage an escape. As the two teenagers sped off, Allen fired a shot at them with his revolver. The shattered windshield glass severely injured the youths to the point that they required plastic surgery. Allen was convicted of criminal charges, and the police chief was also sued under Section 1983. The plaintiffs charged that the chief and others knew of Allen's reputation as an unstable officer; none of the other police officers wished to ride in a patrol car with him. At least two formal charges of misconduct had been filed previously, yet the chief failed to take any remedial action or even to review the disciplinary records of officers when he became chief. The court called this behavior "unjustified inaction," held the police department liable, and allowed the plaintiffs damages. The U.S. Supreme Court upheld this judgment.[46]

Police supervisors have also been found liable for injuries arising out of an official policy or custom of their department. Injuries resulting from a chief's verbal or written support of heavy-handed behavior resulting in the use of excessive force by officers have resulted in such liability.[47]

Whereas Section 1983 is a civil action, **Title 18, *U.S. Code*, Section 242**, makes it a *criminal* offense for any person acting under color of law to violate another person's civil rights. Section 242 applies not only to police officers but also to the misconduct of public officials and to the prosecution of judges, bail bond agents, public defenders, and even prosecutors. An example of the use of Section 242 with law enforcement officers is the murder of a drug courier by two U.S. customs agents while the agents were assigned to the San Juan International Airport. The courier flew to Puerto Rico to deposit approximately $700,000 in cash and checks. He was last seen being interviewed by the two customs agents in the airport; 10 days later, his body was discovered in a Puerto Rican rain forest. An investigation revealed that the agents had lured the victim away from the airport and had murdered him for his money, later disposing of the body. They were convicted under Section 242 and related federal statutes, and each agent was sentenced to a prison term of 120 years.[48]

Duty of Care and Failure to Protect

The *public duty doctrine* is derived from common law and holds that police have a duty to protect the general public where they have a "special relationship"; this exists, for example, where the officer knows or has reason to know the likelihood of harm to someone if he or she fails to do his or her duty, and is thus defined by the circumstances surrounding an injury or damage. A special relationship can be based on:

1. whether the officer could have foreseen that he or she was expected to take action in a given situation to prevent injury[49] (such as where a police officer released from his custody an intoxicated pedestrian near a busy highway)

2. departmental policy or guidelines that prohibit a certain course of action[50] (such as a case where an officer released a drunk driver who then killed another driver, and the police department had a standard operating procedure manual that mandated that an intoxicated individual likely to do physical injury to himself or others "*will* be taken into protective custody")

3. the spatial and temporal proximity of the defendant–officer behavior to the injury damage[51] (an example is where an individual was arrested for drunk driving, taken into custody, found to have a high blood alcohol level, was released 3 hours later, and then had a fatal car accident)

Under the general heading of **duty of care** are three related concepts: proximate cause, persons in custody, and safe facilities.

a. **Proximate cause** is established by asking the question "But for the officer's conduct, would the plaintiff have sustained the injury or damage?" If the answer to this question is no, then proximate cause is established, and the officer can be held liable for the damage or injury. An example is where an officer is involved in a high-speed chase and the offending driver strikes an innocent third party. Generally, if the officer was not acting in a negligent fashion and did not cause the injury, there would be no liability on the officer's part.[52] Proximate cause may also be found in such cases as one where an officer leaves the scene of an accident aware of dangerous conditions (e.g., spilled oil, smoke, vehicle debris, stray animals) without giving proper warning to motorists.[53]

b. Courts generally confer on police executives a duty of care for *persons in their custody*[54] to ensure that reasonable precautions are taken to keep detainees free from harm, to render medical assistance when necessary, and to treat detainees humanely.[55] A duty is also owed to persons in custody and while outside a jail setting, such as when arresting or transporting prisoners and mental patients, as well as in booking or interrogation areas.[56] Courts have also held that if a prisoner's suicide is "reasonably foreseeable," the jailer owes the prisoner a duty of care to help prevent that suicide.

c. A related area concerns administrators' *need to provide safe facilities*. For example, a Detroit jail's holding cell was constructed so that it did not allow officers to observe detainees' movements; there were no electronic monitoring devices for observing detainees or detoxification cells, as required under state policy. Therefore, following a suicide in this facility, the court concluded that these conditions constituted building defects and were the proximate cause of the decedent's death.[57]

Failure to protect as a form of negligence may occur if a police officer fails to protect a person from a known and foreseeable danger. These claims most often involve battered women, but other circumstances can also create a duty to protect people from crime. Informants, witnesses, and other people who are dependent on the police can be a source of police liability if officers fail to take reasonable action to prevent victimization. The officer's conduct cannot place a person in peril or demonstrate deliberate indifference to his or her safety. In one case, for example, a man became seriously ill on his porch and two police officers arrived, cancelled the request for paramedics, broke the lock and door jam on the front door of his residence, moved him inside the house, locked the door, and left. The next day, family members found the man dead inside the house as a result of respiratory failure. His mother sued under Section 1983, and the court found that the officers' conduct clearly had placed him in a more dangerous position than the one in which they found him.[58] Another example is where the Green Bay, Wisconsin, police department released the tape of a phone call from an informant, which led to the informant's death.[59] See Exhibit 14.1 for an exercise on failure to protect.

> **failure to protect** a form of negligence where a police officer fails to protect a person from a known and foreseeable danger.

EXHIBIT 14.1

LIABILITY FOR FAILURE TO PROTECT?[60]

What, if any, legal obligation is held by the police to protect someone from their estranged spouse who has been served with a legal restraining order? That question was at the crux of a lawsuit from Castle Rock, Colorado, which was ultimately heard by the U.S. Supreme Court. Jessica Gonzales' restraining order required her husband to remain at least 100 yards from her and their three daughters except during specified visitation times. One evening the husband took possession of the three children in violation of the order; Mrs. Gonzalez repeatedly urged the police to search for and arrest her husband, but they took no immediate action (due to Jessica's allowing her husband to take the children at various hours). At approximately 3:20 A.M., the husband appeared at the city police station and instigated a shoot-out with the police (he died). A search of his vehicle revealed the corpses of the three daughters, whom the husband had killed. U.S. cities are generally immune from lawsuits, so in this case the Supreme Court was asked to decide whether Jessica Gonzales could sue the city because of inaction by its police officers.

1. Were the police *morally* responsible for the deaths of the three girls?

2. Were the police *legally* responsible for their deaths?

3. If you believe Jessica should be allowed to sue the city, and the police were liable, how much financial compensation should Jessica receive?

[See the Notes section at chapter's end for the outcome and whether or not the city was deemed to be liable for its police department's actions.]

Vehicle Pursuits

Basically, with regard to operation of their vehicles, officers are afforded *no* special privileges or immunities.[61] While driving in nonemergency situations, officers do not have immunity for their negligence or recklessness and are held to the same standard of conduct as private citizens. When responding to emergency situations, however, officers are governed by statutes covering emergency vehicles.[62] In such circumstances, most jurisdictions afford the police limited immunity for violations of traffic laws; in other words, they are accorded some protections and privileges not given to private citizens, and are permitted to take greater risks that would amount to negligence if taken by citizens.[63]

In 2007, the U.S. Supreme Court issued a major decision concerning the proper amount of force the police may use during a high-speed **vehicle pursuit**—when one or more law enforcement officers attempting to apprehend a suspect who is evading arrest while operating a motor vehicle, usually at high speed or using other elusive means. The issue was whether or not the serious danger created by the fleeing motorist and high-speed pursuers justifies the use of deadly force to eliminate the threat; in other words, was the level of force used proportionate to the threat of reckless and dangerous driving? Victor Harris, a 19-year-old Georgia youth, drove at speeds of up to 90 miles per hour and covered 9 miles in 6 minutes with a deputy sheriff in pursuit. The chase ended in a violent crash that left Harris a quadriplegic; his lawyers argued that the Fourth Amendment protects against the use of such excessive force and high-speed drivers having their cars rammed by police (by intentionally stopping a fleeing vehicle in such a manner, a "seizure" occurs for Fourth Amendment purposes). Conversely, the deputy sheriff's lawyers argued that such drivers pose an escalating danger to the public and must be stopped to defuse the danger (the deputy's supervisor had authorized the use of the Precision Immobilization Technique [PIT], whereby the officer uses the patrol vehicle to cause the speeder's car to spin out. PIT was not used in the Harris chase, however). The Court's 8–1 opinion held that "A police officer's attempt to terminate a dangerous high-speed car chase that threatens the lives of innocent bystanders does not violate the Fourth Amendment, even when it places the fleeing motorist at risk of serious injury or death."[64]

Liability of Corrections Personnel

The liability of corrections workers often centers on their lack of due care for persons in their custody. This responsibility concerns primarily police officers and civilians responsible for inmates in local jails.

When an inmate commits suicide while in custody, police agencies are frequently—and often successfully—sued in state court under negligence and wrongful death claims. The standard used by the courts is whether the agency's act or failure to act created an unusual risk to an inmate. A "special duty" of care exists for police officers to protect inmates suffering from mental disorders and those who are impaired by drugs or alcohol. Foreseeability—the reasonable anticipation that injury or damage may occur—may be found when inmates make statements of intent to commit suicide, have a history of mental illness, are in a vulnerable emotional state, or are at a high level of intoxication or drug dependence.[65]

Suicides are not uncommon among jail inmates; each year, more than 300 jail inmates take their own lives.[66] Inmate suicide rates have also been found to be higher in small jails and highest in small jails with lower population densities.[67] State courts generally recognize that police officials have a duty of care for persons in their custody.[68] Thus, jail administrators are ultimately responsible for taking reasonable precautions to ensure the health and safety of persons in their custody; they must protect inmates from harm, render medical assistance when necessary, and treat inmates humanely.[69]

vehicular pursuit where one or more law enforcement officers is attempting to apprehend a suspect who is evading arrest while operating a motor vehicle, usually at high speed or using other elusive means.

Several court decisions have helped to establish the duties and guidelines for jail employees concerning the care of their charges. An intoxicated inmate in possession of cigarettes and matches started a fire that resulted in his death; the court stated that "the prisoner may have been voluntarily drunk, but he was not in the cell voluntarily . . . [he] was helpless and the officer knew there was a means of harm on his person." The court concluded that the police administration owed a greater duty of care to such an arrestee.[70] Emotionally disturbed arrestees can also create a greater duty for jail personnel. In an Alaskan case, a woman had been arrested for intoxication in a hotel and had trouble talking, standing, and walking; her blood alcohol content was 0.26 percent. Two and a half hours after her incarceration, officers found her hanging by her sweater from mesh wiring in the cell. The Alaska Supreme Court said that the officers knew she was depressed and that in the past few months, one of her sons had been burned to death, another son had been stabbed to death, and her mother had died. Thus, the court believed that the officers should have anticipated her suicide.[71]

In New Mexico, a 17-year-old boy was arrested for armed robbery; he later told his mother that he would kill himself rather than go to prison and subsequently tried to cut his wrists with an aluminum can top. The assistant chief executive ordered the officers to watch him, but he was found dead by hanging the following morning. The state supreme court held that the knowledge officers possess is an important factor in determining liability and negligence in such cases.[72] In a New Jersey case in which a young man arrested for intoxication was put in a holding cell but officers failed to remove the leather belt that he used to take his life, the court found that the officers' conduct could have been a "substantial" factor in his death.[73]

As mentioned earlier, courts have also found the design of detention facilities to be a source of negligence—where a Detroit holding cell limited officers' ability to observe inmates' movements, and no detoxification cell or electronic monitoring devices were used; a suicide in such circumstances may constitute a "building defect" and a finding of proximate cause.[74] In another incident, an intoxicated college student was placed in a holding cell at the school's public safety building. Forty minutes later, officers found him hanging from an overhead heating device by a noose fashioned from his socks and belt. The court found the university liable for operating a defective building and awarded his parents $650,000.[75]

The behavior of jail personnel *after* a suicide or attempted suicide may also indicate a breach of duty. Officers are expected to give all possible aid to an inmate who is injured or has attempted suicide. Thus, when officers found an inmate slumped in a chair with his belt around his neck and left him in that position instead of trying to revive him or call for medical assistance, the court ruled that this behavior established a causal link between the officers' inaction and the boy's death.[76]

It is clear that correctional administrators must ensure that their organizations are cognizant of their legal responsibilities and their expanded custodial role in dealing with their detainees.

▶ Disciplinary Policies and Practices

By virtue of their relatively high numbers and frequent contacts with the general public, a great majority of complaints and disciplinary actions in criminal justice will involve law enforcement personnel, and thus the following discussion centers on police behaviors. However, occasionally, as seen in Exhibit 14.2, the taint of corruption and abuse can also involve corrections personnel.

The public's trust and respect are precious commodities and can be quickly lost with improper behavior by criminal justice employees and the improper handling of an allegation

EXHIBIT 14.2

DEPUTIES INDICTED IN CORRUPTION PROBE

Nearly 20 current and former Los Angeles County sheriff's deputies were arrested in December 2013 following a 2-year federal probe into corruption and inmate abuse in the county jail system. Several grand jury indictments and criminal complaints alleged the unjustified beating of inmates, unjustified detention, and a conspiracy to obstruct a federal investigation. Included were civil rights violations that included excessive force and unlawful arrests.

The investigation revealed that the jailers' behavior had become institutionalized to the point that some employees of the Sheriff's Department considering themselves to be above the law. Deputies also attempted to conceal an informant who was providing photos and information to the FBI while locked up, leading to additional charges of conspiracy to obstruct justice. Two sergeants also allegedly confronted an FBI agent at her home in an attempt to intimidate her into revealing details concerning the investigation.[77]

of misconduct. The public expects that criminal justice agencies will have sound disciplinary policies, and make every effort to respond to citizens' complaints in a judicious, consistent, fair, and equitable manner.

Employee misconduct and violations of departmental policy are the two principal areas in which discipline is involved.[78] Employee misconduct includes those acts that harm the public, including corruption, harassment, brutality, and civil rights violations. Violations of policy may involve a broad range of issues, including substance abuse and insubordination, as well as minor violations of dress and lack of punctuality.

Due Process Requirements

The well-established, minimum due process requirements for discharging public employees include that employees must:

1. Be afforded a public hearing.

2. Be present during the presentation of evidence against them and have an opportunity to cross-examine their superiors.

3. Have an opportunity to present witnesses and other evidence concerning their side of the controversy.

4. Be permitted to be represented by counsel.

5. Have an impartial referee or hearing officer presiding.

6. Have a decision made based on the weight of the evidence introduced during the hearing.

Such protections apply to any disciplinary action that can significantly affect a criminal justice employee's reputation and/or future chances for special assignment or promotion. A disciplinary hearing that might result in only a reprimand or short suspension may involve fewer procedural protections than one that could result in more severe sanctions.[79]

When a particular disciplinary action does not include termination or suspension, however, it may still be subject to due process considerations. An example is a Chicago case involving a police officer who was transferred from the Neighborhood Relations Division to less desirable working conditions in the patrol division, with no loss in pay or benefits. The court found that the officer's First Amendment free speech rights were violated because his de facto demotion was in retaliation for his political activities (inviting political opponents of the mayor to a civic function and in retaliation for a speech given there that criticized the police department) and that he was thus entitled to civil damages. The court stated, "Certainly a demotion can be as detrimental to an employee as denial of a promotion."[80]

On the contrary, no due process protection may be required when the property interest (one's job) was fraudulently obtained. Thus, a deputy sheriff was not deprived of due process when he was summarily discharged for lying on his application about a juvenile felony charge, which would have barred him from employment in the first place.[81]

In sum, agency rules and policies should state which due process procedures will be utilized under certain disciplinary situations; the key questions regarding due process are whether the employer follows established agency guidelines and, if not, whether the employer has a compelling reason not to do so.

At times, the administrator will determine that an employee must be disciplined or terminated. What are adequate grounds for discipline or discharge? Grounds can vary widely from agency to agency. Certainly, the agency's formal policies and procedures should specify and control what constitutes proper and improper behavior. Normally, agency practice and custom enter into these decisions. Sometimes administrators will "wink" at the formal policies and procedures, overlooking or only occasionally enforcing certain provisions contained in them. But the failure of the agency to enforce a rule or policy for a long period of time may provide "implied consent" by the employer that such behavior, although officially prohibited, is permissible. (In other words, don't allow an employee to violate the agency's lateness policy for 3 months and then decide one day to summarily fire him.) Attempts to fire employees for behavior that has been ignored or enforced only infrequently at best may give rise to a defense by the employee.

Hiring minority employees to meet state hiring goals and then attempting to terminate them as quickly and often as possible violate the employees' Title VII rights. Such a situation occurred in an Indiana case in which it was alleged that black prison COs were hired to fulfill an affirmative action program, only to be fired for disciplinary reasons for which white officers were not discharged.[82]

Generally, violations of an employee's rights in discharge and discipline occur (1) in violation of a protected interest, (2) in retaliation for the exercise of protected conduct, (3) with a discriminatory motive, and (4) with malice.[83]

A Tradition of Problems in Policing

Throughout its history, policing has experienced problems involving misconduct and corruption. Incidents such as the beating of Rodney King in Los Angeles as well as major corruption scandals in several big-city police departments have led many people to believe that police misbehavior is greater today than ever before.

Without question, police administrators need to pay close attention to signs of police misconduct, respond quickly, and enact policies to guide supervisors in handling disciplinary issues. Such policies should ensure that there is certainty, swiftness, fairness, and consistency of punishment when it is warranted.

Automated Records Systems

A number of police agencies have automated their personnel processes in an effort to establish a better system for tracking and sanctioning personnel actions.[84] Specifically, an **automated records system** involves use of technologies to assist police administrators to more equitably receive, investigate, and arrive at proper dispositions concerning employee complaints and commendations (see Exhibit 14.3). Within minutes, the database provides supervisors with 5 years of history about standards of discipline for any category of violation. A variety of reports can be produced, showing patterns of incidents for the supervisor.

automated records system technologies that assist police administrators in receiving, investigating, and arriving at proper dispositions employee complaints and commendations.

AURORA, COLORADO: USING TECHNOLOGY TO TRACK COMPLAINTS AND COMMENDATIONS

The Aurora, Colorado, Police Department created the Automated Complaint and Commendation System in 2006 to record all complaints and commendations received concerning its sworn officers. All complaints and commendations—regardless of whether they are received through the city's website, via the telephone, or in written form—are entered into the system. Once entered, the complaint or commendation remains open until closed by some means of disposition. In addition, the system directs the complaint or commendation to the officer's immediate supervisor for action; the supervisor then reports his or her findings to his or her supervisor, who must approve or disapprove the investigation. That process continues until the officer's Division Chief has reviewed all decisions in the chain of command and approves the investigation and resulting actions. Certain safeguards are built into the system; as examples, no one can delete the complaint or commendation, and only one supervisor can work on the complaint at a time; supervisors can add information but cannot remove it; and supervisors can search the system to determine if the officer has other similar complaints or commendations. The system also produces statistical information, which police managers can use to determine future training needs as well as an appropriate level of discipline.[85]

Determining the Level and Nature of Action

When an investigation against an employee is sustained, the sanctions and level of discipline must be decided. Management must be careful when recommending and imposing discipline because of its impact on the morale of the agency's employees. If the recommended discipline is viewed by employees as too lenient, it may send the wrong message that the misconduct was insignificant. On the other hand, discipline that is viewed as too harsh may have a demoralizing effect on the officer(s) involved and other agency employees and result in allegations that the leadership is unfair. This alone can have significant impact on the esprit de corps or morale of the agency.

In addition to having a disciplinary process that is viewed by employees as fair and consistent, it is important that discipline be progressive and that more serious sanctions be invoked when repeated violations occur. For example, a third substantiated instance of rude behavior may result in a recommendation for a 1-day suspension without pay, but a first offense may be handled by documented oral counseling or a letter of reprimand. The following list shows disciplinary actions commonly used by agencies in increasing order of severity.

Counseling. This is usually a conversation between the supervisor and employee about a specific aspect of the employee's performance or conduct; it is warranted when an employee has committed a relatively minor infraction or the nature of the offense is such that oral counseling is all that is necessary. For example, an employee who is usually punctual but arrives at a briefing 10 minutes late 2 days in a row may require nothing more than a reminder and a warning to correct the problem.

Documented oral counseling. This is usually the first step in a progressive disciplinary process and is intended to address relatively minor infractions. It occurs when there are no previous reprimands or more severe disciplinary action of the same or a similar nature.

Letter of reprimand. This is a formal written notice regarding significant misconduct, more serious performance violations, or repeated offenses. It is usually the second step in the formal disciplinary process and is intended to provide the employee and agency with a written record of the violation of behavior; it identifies what specific corrective action must be taken to avoid subsequent, more serious disciplinary steps.

Suspension. This is a severe disciplinary action that results in an employee being relieved of duty, often without pay. It is usually administered when an employee commits a serious violation of established rules or after written reprimands have been given and no change in behavior or performance has resulted.

Demotion. In this situation, an employee is placed in a position of lower responsibility and pay. It is normally used when an otherwise capable employee is unable to meet the standards required for the higher position, or when the employee has committed a serious act requiring that he or she be removed from a position of management or supervision.

Transfer. Many agencies use the disciplinary transfer to deal with problem employees; they can be transferred to a different location or assignment, and this action is often seen as an effective disciplinary tool.

Termination. This is the most severe disciplinary action that can be taken. It usually occurs when previous serious discipline has been imposed and there has been inadequate or no improvement in behavior or performance. It may also occur when an employee commits an offense so serious that continued employment would be inappropriate.

Positive and Negative Discipline

When policies and procedures are violated, positive or negative disciplinary measures may be imposed. Although different in their philosophy, both seek to accomplish the same purpose: to correct negative behavior and promote the employee's voluntary compliance with departmental policies and procedures.

A **positive discipline** program (also known as *positive counseling*) attempts to change poor employee behavior without invoking punishment. An example of positive discipline or counseling is when an employee ("John") has been nonproductive and nonpunctual, has caused interpersonal problems with coworkers, and/or has other problems on the job. To this point, John has been in control of the situation—on the offensive, one might say— whereas the supervisor ("Jane") and his coworkers have been on the defensive. John is jeopardizing the morale and productivity of the workplace, but the preferred approach is to try to salvage him because of the agency's investment in time, funds, and training.

Finally, Jane calls John into her office. She might begin with a compliment to him (if indeed she can find one) and then proceed to outline all of his workplace shortcomings; this demonstrates to John that Jane "has his number" and is aware of his various problems. Jane explains to him why it is important that he improve (for reasons related to productivity, morale, and so on) and the benefits he might realize from improvement (promotions, pay raises, bonuses). She also outlines what can happen if he does *not* show adequate improvement (demotion, transfer, termination). Now having gained John's attention, she gives him a certain time period (say, 30, 60, or 90 days) in which to improve; she emphasizes, however, that she will be constantly monitoring his progress. She might even ask John to sign a counseling statement form that sets forth all they have discussed, indicating that John has received counseling and understands the situation.

Note that Jane is now on the offensive, thereby putting John on the defensive and in control of his destiny; if he fails to perform, Jane would probably give him a warning, and if the situation continues, he will be terminated. If he sues or files a grievance, Jane has proof that every effort was made to allow John to salvage his position. This is an effective means of giving subordinates an incentive to improve their behavior while at the same time making the department less vulnerable to successful lawsuits.

Negative discipline is some form of punishment. It is generally used when positive efforts fail or the violation is so serious that punishment is required. Negative discipline varies in its severity and involves documented oral counseling, a letter of reprimand, demotion, days off without pay, or even termination.

> **positive discipline** a formal program that attempts to change poor employee behavior without invoking punishment.

> **negative discipline** that which involves some form of punishment.

Use of a Discipline Matrix

discipline matrix intended to provide disciplinary actions against police officers that are consistent and fair, taking into account several variables and circumstances.

Recently there has been a growing movement to create a **discipline matrix**, similar to sentencing guideline grids used by criminal courts across the United States. Such matrices represent an effort to provide disciplinary actions against police officers that are consistent and fair, rather than arbitrary, biased, or inappropriate. They generally are intended to take into account the seriousness of the infraction, the prior disciplinary history of the officer involved, and any aggravating and mitigating circumstances.[86]

Although the adoption of such matrices has been slow, they have been implemented by the Los Angeles County Sheriff's Office, state police in Washington State, and police departments in Las Vegas, Nevada; Phoenix and Tucson, Arizona; Oakland, California; Providence, Rhode Island; Baltimore, Maryland; and Denver, Colorado; one is also under consideration in Portland, Oregon, and other cities.[87] Their use has also been favorably regarded by collective bargaining units; for example, the Las Vegas unit's legal counsel stated in a newsletter that the agency can "enact fairer discipline via the Matrix."[88] And, according to police accountability expert Samuel Walker, the matrix can be a potentially useful tool and, if properly designed, ensure greater consistency in discipline.[89]

Such matrices are too lengthy and complex to be reproduced and examined here, as they generally include numerous penalty levels, infractions, and sentencing presumptions; however, several examples are available for viewing (see notes section).[90]

Dealing with Complaints

Complaint Origin

personnel complaint an allegation of misconduct or illegal behavior against an employee by anyone inside or outside the organization.

A **personnel complaint** is an allegation of misconduct or illegal behavior against an employee by anyone inside or outside the organization. **Internal complaints** (discussed later) may come from supervisors who observe officer misconduct, officers who complain about supervisors, supervisors who complain about other supervisors, civilian personnel who complain about officers, and so on. External complaints originate from sources outside the organization and usually involve the public.

internal complaints complaints filed against employees by persons within the organization, either by one's peers or supervisors.

Complaints may be received from primary, secondary, and anonymous sources. A victim is a primary source. A secondary source is someone who makes the complaint on behalf of the victim, such as an attorney, a school counselor, or a parent of a juvenile. An anonymous source complaint derives from an unknown source and may be delivered to the police station via a telephone call or an unsigned letter.

Every complaint, regardless of the source, must be accepted and investigated in accordance with established policies and procedures. Anonymous complaints are the most difficult to investigate because there is no opportunity to obtain further information or question the complainant about the allegation. Such complaints can have a negative impact on employee morale because officers may view them as unjust and frivolous.

Types and Causes

Complaints may be handled informally or formally, depending on the seriousness of the allegation and the preference of the complainant. A formal complaint occurs when a written and signed and/or tape-recorded statement of the allegation is made and the complainant asks to be informed of the investigation's disposition. Figure 14-2 ■ provides an example of a complaint form used to initiate a personnel investigation.

An informal complaint is an allegation of minor misconduct made for informational purposes that can usually be resolved without the need for more formal processes. When a citizen calls the watch commander to complain about the rude behavior of a dispatcher but does not wish to make a formal complaint, the supervisor may simply discuss the incident with the dispatcher and resolve it through informal counseling as

```
****ⓐⓐ*******************************************************************************************
                                                                    Control Number_____
                                                       Interview
Date & Time Reported      Location of Interview
_____         _____      _____Verbal _____Written _____Taped

Type of Complaint:        _____Force _____Procedural _____Conduct
                          _____Other (Specify) _____

Source of Complaint:      _____In Person _____Mail _____Telephone
                          _____Other (Specify) _____

Complaint originally      _____Supervisor     _____On Duty Watch Commander     _____Chief
Received by:              _____IAU             _____Other (Specify) _____

Notifications made:       _____Division Commander      _____Chief of Police
Received by:              _____On-Call Command Personnel
                          _____Watch Commander          _____Other (Specify) _____

Copy of formal personnel complaint given to complainant?     _____Yes _____No

**********************************************************************************************
Complainant's name:                          Address:
_____               _____ Zip_____
Residence Phone:                             Business Phone:
_____               _____

DOB:              Race:                       Sex:              Occupation:
_____         _____                 _____        _____

**********************************************************************************************
Location of Occurrence:                       Date & Time of Occurrence:
_____                  _____
Member(s) Involved:                           Member(s) Involved:
(1) _____                  (2)_____
(3) _____                  (4)_____
Witness(es) Involved:                         Witness(es) Involved:
(1) _____                  (2)_____
(3) _____                  (4)_____
**********************************************************************************************
(1) _____  Complainant wishes to make a formal statement and has requested an investigation into the
           matter with a report back to him/her on the findings and actions.
(2) _____  Complainant wishes to advise the Police Department of a problem, understand that some type of
           action will be taken, but does not request a report back to him/her on the findings and actions.
**********************************************************************************************
                              CITIZEN ADVISEMENTS
(1)   If you have not yet provided the department with a signed written statement or a videotaped or
      tape-recorded statement, one may be required in order to pursue the investigation of this matter.
(2)   The complainant(s) and/or witness(es) may be required to take a polygraph examination in order to
      determine the credibility concerning the allegations made.
(3)   Should the allegations prove to be false, the complainant(s) and/or witness(es) may be liable for
      criminal and/or civil prosecution.   _____      _____
                                              Signature of Complainant      Date & Time

_____
Signature of Member Receiving Complaint
```

FIGURE 14-2 Police Department Formal Personnel Complaint Report Form

long as more serious problems are not discovered and the dispatcher does not have a history of similar complaints.

Few complaints involve acts of physical violence, excessive force, or corruption. Rojek et al.[91] found that complaints against officers also fall under the general categories of verbal abuse, discourtesy, harassment, improper attitude, and ethnic slurs.[92] Another study[93] found that 42 percent of complaints involved the "verbal conduct" of officers; verbal conduct also accounted for 47 percent of all sustained complaints. The majority of repeated offenses also fell into this category. It is clear that officers' verbal actions generate a significant number of complaints. Finally, minority citizens, and those with less power and fewer resources, are more likely than persons with greater power and more resources to file complaints of misconduct and to allege more serious forms of misconduct.[94]

Receipt and Referral

Administrators should have in place a process for receiving complaints that is clearly delineated by departmental policy and procedures. Generally, a complaint will be made at a police facility and referred to a senior officer in charge to determine its seriousness and the need for immediate intervention.

In most cases, the senior officer will determine the nature of the complaint and the employee involved; the matter will be referred to the employee's supervisor to conduct an initial investigation. The supervisor completes the investigation, recommends any discipline, and sends the matter to the Internal Affairs Unit (IAU) and the agency head for finalization of the disciplinary process. This method of review ensures that consistent and fair standards of discipline are applied.

The Investigative Process

D. W. Perez[95] indicated that all but a small percentage of the 17,000 police agencies in the United States have a process for investigation of police misconduct. Generally, the employee's supervisor will conduct a preliminary inquiry of the complaint, commonly known as fact finding. Once it is determined that further investigation is necessary, the supervisor may conduct additional questioning of employees and witnesses, obtain written statements from those persons immediately involved in the incident, and gather any evidence that may be necessary for the case, including photographs. Care must be taken to ensure that the accused employee's rights are not violated. The initial investigation is sent to an appropriate division commander and forwarded to IAU for review.

Making a Determination and Disposition

Categories

Once an investigation is completed, the supervisor or IAU officer must make a determination as to the culpability of the accused employee and report this to the administrator. Each allegation should receive a separate adjudication. Following are the categories of dispositions that are commonly used:

- *Unfounded.* The alleged act(s) did not occur.
- *Exonerated.* The act occurred, but it is lawful, proper, justified, and/or in accordance with departmental policies, procedures, rules, and regulations.
- *Not sustained.* There is insufficient evidence to prove or disprove the allegations made.
- *Misconduct not based on the complaint.* Sustainable misconduct was determined but is not a part of the original complaint. For example, a supervisor investigating an allegation of excessive force against an officer may find that the force used was within departmental policy but that the officer made an unlawful arrest.
- *Closed.* An investigation may be halted if the complainant fails to cooperate or if it is determined that the action does not fall within the administrative jurisdiction of the police agency.
- *Sustained.* The act did occur, and it was a violation of departmental rules and procedures. Sustained allegations include misconduct that falls within the broad outlines of the original allegation(s).

▼

Once a determination of culpability has been made, the complainant should be notified of the department's findings. Details of the investigation or recommended punishment will not be included in the correspondence. As shown in Figure 14-3 ■, the complainant will normally receive only information concerning the outcome of the complaint, including a short explanation of the finding along with an invitation to call the agency if further information is needed.

Grievances

Criminal justice employees may complain—have a **grievance**, which is a real or imagined wrong or other cause for complaint about job-related matters. Following is an overview of the general process that exists for handling grievances.

Grievance procedures establish a fair and expeditious process for handling employee disputes that are not disciplinary in nature. Grievance procedures involve collective bargaining issues, conditions of employment, and employer–employee relations. More specifically, grievances may cover a broad range of issues, including salaries, overtime, leave, hours of work, allowances, retirement, opportunities for advancement, performance evaluations, workplace conditions, tenure, disciplinary actions, supervisory methods, and administrative practices. Grievance procedures are often established as a part of the collective bargaining process.

> **grievance** a real or imagined wrong or other cause for complaint by an employee concerning job-related matters.

Police Department
3300 Main Street
Downtown Plaza
Anywhere, USA. 99999
June 20, 2000

Mr. John Doe
2200 Main Avenue
Anywhere, USA.

Re: Internal affairs #000666-98
   Case Closure

Dear Mr. Doe:

Our investigation into your allegations against Officer Smith has been completed. It has been determined that your complaint is SUSTAINED and the appropriate disciplinary action has been taken.

Our department appreciates your bringing this matter to our attention. It is our position that when a problem is identified, it should be corrected as soon as possible. It is our goal to be responsive to the concerns expressed by citizens so as to provide more efficient and effective services.

Your information regarding this incident was helpful and of value in our efforts to attain that goal. Should you have any further questions about this matter, please contact Sergeant Jane Alexander, Internal Affairs, at 555-9999.

Sincerely,

I.M. Boss
Lieutenant
Internal Affairs Unit

FIGURE 14-3   Citizens' Notification-of-Discipline Letter

```
                        Police Department
                        Formal Grievance Form

        Grievance #_____

        Employee Name: _____  Work Phone: _____
        Department Assigned: _____
        Date of Occurrence: _____
        Location of Occurrence: _____

        Name of:   1.   Department Head:_____

                   2.   Division Head:_____

                   3.   Immediate Supervisor:_____

        Statement of Grievance: _____
        _____
        _____
        _____
        _____

        Witnesses:_____
        _____
        _____

        What article(s) and or section(s) of the labor agreement of rules and regulations do
        you believe have been violated? _____
        _____
        _____
        _____

        What remedy are you requesting?_____
        _____
        _____


        _____       _____
        Employee signature                   Signature of labor representative
```

FIGURE 14-4 Employee Grievance Form

The preferred method for settling employees' grievances is through informal discussion, in which the employee explains his or her grievance to the immediate supervisor. Most complaints can be handled through this process. Complaints that cannot be dealt with informally are usually handled through a more formal grievance process, as described next. A formal grievance begins with the employee submitting the grievance in writing to the immediate supervisor, as illustrated in Figure 14-4 ■.

The process for formally handling grievances will vary among agencies and may involve as many as three to six different levels of action. Following is an example of how a grievance may proceed:

Level I. An employee's grievance is submitted in writing to a supervisor. The supervisor will be given 5 days to respond. If the employee is dissatisfied with the response, the grievance moves to the next level.

Level II. At this level, the grievance proceeds to the chief executive, who will be given a specified time (usually 5 days) to render a decision.

Level III. If the employee is not satisfied with the chief's decision, the grievance may proceed to the city or county manager, as appropriate. The manager will usually meet with the employee and/or representatives from the bargaining association and attempt to resolve the matter. An additional 5–10 days is usually allowed for the manager to render a decision.

Level IV. If the grievance is still not resolved, either party may request that the matter be submitted to arbitration. Arbitration involves a neutral outside person, often selected from a list of arbitrators from the Federal Mediation and Conciliation Service. An arbitrator will conduct a hearing, listen to both parties, and usually render a decision within 20–30 days. The decision of the arbitrator can be final and binding. This does not prohibit the employee from appealing the decision to a state court.

Failure to act on grievances quickly may result in serious morale problems within an agency.

Appealing Disciplinary Measures

Appeals processes—frequently outlined in civil service rules and regulations, labor agreements, and departmental policies and procedures—normally follow an officer's chain of command. For example, if an officer disagrees with a supervisor's recommendation for discipline, the first step of an appeal may involve a hearing before the division commander, usually of the rank of captain or deputy chief. The accused employee may be allowed labor representation or an attorney to assist in asking questions of the investigating supervisor, clarifying issues, and presenting new or mitigating evidence. The division commander has 5 days to review the recommendation and respond in writing to the employee.

If the employee is still not satisfied, an appeal hearing before the chief executive is granted. This is usually the final step in appeals within the agency. The chief or sheriff communicates a decision in writing to the employee within 5 to 10 days. Depending on labor agreements and civil service rules and regulations, some agencies extend their appeals of discipline beyond the department. For example, employees may bring their issue before the civil service commission or city or county manager for a final review. Employees may also have the right to an independent arbitrator's review of the discipline. The arbitrator's decision is usually binding.

The Early Warning System

Early identification of and intervention in employee misconduct or performance problems are vital to preventing ongoing and repeated incidents. An **early warning system (EWS)** is designed to identify officers whose behavior is problematic, usually involving citizen complaints and improper use of force; more comprehensive systems can include such indicators (e.g., sick leave usage, involvement in civil litigation, and resisting arrest reports)[96] and provide a form of intervention. The system alerts the department to these individuals and warns the officers while providing counseling or training to help them change their problematic behavior. Many EWSs have a "three-strikes rule," with three complaints in a given time frame (normally a 12-month period) causing intervention to be initiated. The EWS thus helps agencies to respond proactively to patterns of behavior that may lead to more serious problems. The EWS may require that the officer's supervisor intervene with early prevention methods such as counseling or training.

In some cases, repeated incidents of violent behavior may require that officers attend anger training or verbal judo sessions to learn how to deescalate confrontational situations. Some preventive measures, such as counseling, remedial training, or temporary change of assignment, may also be used. A referral to an employee assistance program (EAP) to deal with more serious psychological or substance abuse problems is another possible outcome.

early warning system (EWS) a means of identifying officers whose behavior is problematic, usually involving citizen complaints and improper use of force.

Not to Be Overlooked: Internal Complaints and Problems

Generally when looking to identify problem, police and corrections officers, administrators, and supervisors focus on citizens' excessive force complaints and related actions. However, there are some officers who might interact well with citizens but fail to meet internal departmental standards, generating internal complaints—as indicated earlier, those complaints filed against employees by persons within the organization, either peers or supervisors. Or, there may be officers who are rude to citizens and generate the most use of force complaints—and who also generate internal complaints by neglecting their duties, being insubordinate to their supervisors, failing to be at work punctually, and so on. Therefore, agency administrators and supervisors should also seek to determine the extent of *internal* complaints, relationship between internal complaints and citizen complaints.[97]

Indeed, research indicates that officers demonstrating behavioral problems with citizens are also those officers who are identified by their peers or supervisors. In addition, while complaints generated by citizens generally peak early in one's career and then decline thereafter, internal complaints (although at lower rates than citizen complaints) quickly peak but then maintain a steady level across one's career[98]—indicating that misbehavior that involves internal departmental standards can be a problem that lasts many years.

Summary

This chapter has examined three aspects of criminal justice administration that pose exceptionally serious challenges for them: discipline, liability, and labor relations. It is clear from this triad of issues that administrators need to understand the current and developing laws that serve to make criminal justice practitioners legally accountable; this need cannot be overstated. It is far better to learn the proper means of discipline, areas of liability, and effective collective bargaining methods through education and training than to learn about these issues by virtue of serving in the role of a defendant in a lawsuit. Better to learn "in house," rather than to learn "in the courthouse."

Criminal justice executives need to be proactive and learn as well as follow appropriate laws and guidelines as they recruit, hire, train, supervise, and negotiate with their subordinates in order to avoid legal difficulties; for administrators not to do so could place them and their jurisdiction at serious financial, legal, and moral risk. As Edmund Burke observed in the eighteenth century, "Example is the school of mankind," and the many examples provided in this chapter lay bare that kinds of outcomes that can arise when discipline, liability, and labor relations laws are not adhered to. There is certainly merit in looking at what some agencies have done to address these complex problems.

Key Terms and Concepts

Arbitration *332*

Automated records system *345*

Civil liability *337*

Collective bargaining *328*

Discipline matrix *348*

Duty of care *340*

Early warning system (EWS) *353*

Fact finding *332*

Failure to protect *341*

Grievance *351*

Internal complaints *348*

Job action *333*

Mediation *332*

Meet-and-confer *330*

Negative discipline *347*

Negligence *338*

Negotiation *331*

Personnel complaint *348*

Positive discipline *347*

Proximate cause *340*

Title 18, *U.S. Code*, Section 242 *340*

Title 42, *U.S. Code*, Section 1983 *338*

Tort *338*

Vehicle pursuit *342*

Questions for Review

1. How and why did unionization begin, what is its contemporary status in policing, and how does it influence courts and corrections organizations?
2. What are the three models of collective bargaining, as well as the process that comes into play when an impasse is reached?
3. What are some of the primary suggestions concerning how an administrator should "navigate the waters" of unionization?
4. What are the seven forms of disciplinary action that may be taken against police officers?
5. How would you define the following: *tort, Section 1983,* and *respondeat superior*?
6. How can the doctrines of duty of care and failure to protect, as well as laws covering vehicular pursuits, lead to police liability?
7. For what kinds of actions (and lack of action) can corrections agencies be held liable?
8. How would you delineate the minimum due process requirements for discharging public employees?
9. How would you explain the differences between positive and negative discipline?
10. How would you describe the nature of, and rationale for a police disciplinary matrix?
11. What are the categories of dispositions that are commonly used with complaints?
12. What is an example of how a grievance may proceed through its various levels?
13. What are the benefits and functions of an early warning system (EWS) for identifying problem officers? How might it work effectively with internal complaints (those involving violations of departmental standards)?

Deliberate and Decide

Liability for Failure to Protect?

On a cold winter night with a chill factor of minus 25 degrees, two municipal police officers ejected an individual (Munger) from a bar who had become extremely intoxicated. The individual was not permitted to drive home; rather, he was left by the officers to walk away from the bar clothed in only a T-shirt and jeans; he then died in an alley due to hypothermia.

Questions for discussion

1. Were the officers *morally* responsible to see that Munger was delivered safely to his home? Explain.
2. Were the officers (and thus the agency) *legally* responsible for his death? If so, on what legal grounds?

See notes section for the outcome of this case.[99]

Learn by Doing

1. You are enrolled in an internship with a small county sheriff's office, and after several weeks you begin to develop close friendships with some of the deputies. Eventually you learn that nearly all of the deputies are very disgruntled—and some are even irate—due to what they perceive as a lack of parity with other intra-county offices and intercounty sheriff's offices in wages and benefits, and general apathy by the county commission. They perceive a danger exists because low salaries lead to high turnover, which causes too few deputies—and too many inexperienced ones—to normally be on duty per shift. A deputy asks you if it is legally possible in your state for them to align themselves with a labor union, as well as your overall opinion concerning the pros and cons of collective bargaining and whether or not a "peaceful protest" by

sheriff's personnel and their families and supporters at the county commission offices might help. What is your response?

2. Donna King has been a CO in your jail for 6 years, and one of your subordinates for 2 years. Her productivity, both in terms of quality and quantity as well as interactions with the staff and inmates, has generally been at or above standard; her performance evaluations are normally above average. In recent weeks, however, there have been rumors concerning her work; although no formal complaints have been filed, there are rumors concerning abusive treatment of inmates, not responding in a timely manner to calls by other jail staff for assistance, general lack of compliance with policies and procedures, and other matters. Today another CO contacts you to complain

about her rough treatment of an inmate during booking. You decide it is time to call her into your office to discuss these matters. How will you address this situation?

3. Sergeant Tom Gresham is newly promoted and assigned to patrol on the graveyard shift; he knows each officer on his shift and several of them are his close friends. Gresham was an excellent patrol officer and prides himself on his reputation as a "cop's cop" and his ability to get along with his peers; in fact, he frequently socializes with them after work. He believes his officers perform very well, particularly as they generate the highest number of arrest and citation statistics in the entire department. Unfortunately, his shift is also generating the highest number of citizen complaints for abusive language and improper use of force, and you—his shift lieutenant—have learned in conversations with the city attorney's office that some citizens are contem-

plating legal action. When questioned, Gresham tells you that such complaints are "the price of doing business." You outline for him several examples of use-of-force complaints lodged against his officers during the past few weeks while he was away on vacation. However, it is clear that Gresham still fails to grasp the seriousness of the complaints and how his supervisory style may have contributed to them.

a. What do you believe are some of Sergeant Gresham's problems as a new supervisor? Could anything have been done *before* he assumed his new position to help him understand his role better?

b. As Gresham's superior officer, what advice would you give to him? Are there any other supervisory or command officers who you should ask to be involved in dealing with the situation?

c. What corrective action(s), if any, might Sergeant Gresham immediately take with his shift of officers?

Notes

1. Will Aitchison, *The Rights of Police Officers,* 3rd ed. (Portland, OR: Labor Relations Information System, 1996), p. 7.
2. Ibid.
3. Ibid.
4. Ibid., p. 8.
5. Ibid., p. 9.
6. Charles R. Swanson, Leonard Territo, and Robert W. Taylor, *Police Administration: Structures, Processes, and Behavior,* 6th ed. (Upper Saddle River, NJ: Prentice Hall, 2005), p. 517.
7. Ibid., p. 522.
8. Arnold Zack, *Understanding Fact-Finding and Arbitration in the Public Sector* (Washington, DC: U.S. Government Printing Office, 1974), p. 1.
9. Thomas P. Gilroy and Anthony V. Sinicropi, "Impasse Resolution in Public Employment," *Industrial and Labor Relations Review* 25 (July 1971–1972): 499.
10. Robert G. Howlett, "Fact Finding: Its Values and Limitations—Comment, Arbitration and the Expanded Role of Neutrals," in *Proceedings of the Twenty-Third Annual Meeting of the National Academy of Arbitrators* (Washington, DC: Bureau of National Affairs, 1970), p. 156.
11. Zack, *Understanding Fact-Finding,* p. 1.
12. Swanson, Territo, and Taylor, *Police Administration,* p. 530.
13. Ibid.
14. Ibid., p. 532.
15. Ibid., p. 534.
16. Codified at Civ. Serv. Law § 201(9); also see United Federation of Teachers, "The History of the Taylor Law," http://www.uft.org/labor-spotlight/history-taylor-law (accessed January 24, 2014). The Taylor Law also provides a dispute resolution procedure, which begins with mediation.

Unions comprising police officers, firefighters, and certain other law enforcement personnel are then entitled to compulsory and binding arbitration.

17. U.S. Department of Labor, Bureau of Labor Statistics, "Major Work Stoppages in 2012," http://www.bls.gov/news.release/archives/wkstp_02082013.pdf (accessed January 24, 2014).
18. John H. Burpo, *The Police Labor Movement: Problems and Perspectives* (Springfield, IL: Charles C Thomas, 1971).
19. Ibid., p. xi.
20. W. Clinton Terry III, *Policing Society: An Occupational View* (New York: Wiley, 1985), p. 168.
21. Ibid., p. 168
22. Ibid., pp. 170–171.
23. See Fraternal Order of Police, "Frequently Asked Questions," http://www.fop.net/about/faq/index.shtml (accessed November 7, 2014); National Association of Police Organizations, "Welcome to NAPO," http://www.napo.org/ (accessed November 7, 2014).
24. Kenneth J. Peak, Larry K. Gaines, and Ronald W. Glensor, *Police Supervision and Management: In an Era of Community Policing,* 3rd ed. (Upper Saddle River, NJ: Prentice Hall, 2010), p. 282.
25. Richard P. Seiter, *Correctional Administration: Integrating Theory and Practice* (Upper Saddle River, NJ: Prentice Hall, 2002), pp. 333–334.
26. James B. Jacobs and Norma Meacham Crotty, *Guard Unions and the Future of Prisons* (Ithaca, NY: Institute of Public Employment, 1978), p. 41.
27. James B. Jacobs, *New Perspectives on Prisons and Imprisonment* (Ithaca, NY: Cornell University Press, 1983), p. 153.
28. Ibid., pp. 154–155.

29. Seiter, *Correctional Administration*, p. 337.

30. Ibid.

31. U.S. Department of Justice, National Institute of Law Enforcement and Criminal Justice, *Trial Court Management Series, Personnel Management* (Washington, DC: U.S. Government Printing Office, 1979), pp. 42–47.

32. Larry T. Hoover, Jerry L. Dowling, and Gene Blair, "Management and Labor in Community Policing: Charting a Course," in U.S. Department of Justice, Office of Community Oriented Policing Services, *Police Labor-Management Relations (Vol. I): Perspectives and Practical Solutions for Implementing Change Making Reforms, and Handling Crises for Managers and Union Leaders,* August 2006, pp. 19–20, http://www.cops.usdoj.gov/files/ric/Publications/e07063417.pdf (accessed September 29, 2010).

33. Ibid., p. 20.

34. Ibid., p. 21.

35. Based on Ronald G. DeLord, "Ten Things That Law Enforcement Unions and Managers Do to Run Aground," in U.S. Department of Justice, Office of Community Oriented Policing Services, *Police Labor-Management Relations (Vol. I): Perspectives and Practical Solutions for Implementing Change Making Reforms, and Handling Crises for Managers and Union Leaders,* August 2006, pp. 153–157, http://www.cops.usdoj.gov/files/ric/Publications/e07063417.pdf (accessed September 29, 2014).

36. H. E. Barrineau III, *Civil Liability in Criminal Justice* (Cincinnati, OH: Pilgrimage, 1987), p. 58.

37. Ibid., p. 5.

38. Swanson et al., *Police Administration*, p. 549.

39. Ibid.

40. Isidore Silver, *Police Civil Liability* (New York: Matthew Bender, 2005), p. 4.

41. The Feminist Majority Foundation and the National Center for Women and Policing, "Gender Differences in the Cost of Police Brutality and Misconduct: A Content Analysis of LAPD Civil Liability Cases: 1990–1999," http://www.womenandpolicing.org/ExcessiveForce.asp?id=4516 (accessed October 14, 2014).

42. CNN.com, "LAPD Officers Take Stand in Rampart Scandal Trial," http://edition.cnn.com/2000/LAW/10/16/lapd.corruption.tria/ (accessed October 14, 2014).

43. Victor E. Kappeler, *Critical Issues in Police Civil Liability,* 4th ed. (Long Grove, IL: Waveland, 2005), p. 4.

44. G. P. Alpert, R. G. Dunham, and M. S. Stroshine, *Policing: Continuity and Change* (Long Grove, IL: Waveland, 2006).

45. 516 F.Supp. 1355 (W.D. Tenn., 1981).

46. *Brandon v. Holt,* 469 U.S. 464, 105 S.Ct. 873 (1985).

47. See, for example, *Black v. Stephens,* 662 F.2d 181 (1991).

48. On appeal, the Section 242 convictions were vacated, as the victim was not an inhabitant of Puerto Rico; therefore, he enjoyed no protection under the U.S. Constitution. On resentencing, in January 1991, the agents each received 50 years in prison for convictions of several other federal crimes under Title 18.

49. *Irwin v. Ware,* 467 N.E.2d 1292 (1984).

50. *Fudge v. City of Kansas City,* 239 Kan. 369, 720 P.2d 1093 (1986), at 373.

51. *Kendrick v. City of Lake Charles,* 500 So.2d 866 (La. App. 1 Cir. 1986).

52. *Fielder v. Jenkins,* 833 A.2d 906 (N.J. Super. A.D. 1993).

53. Silver, *Police Civil Liability,* p. 4; also see *Coco v. State,* 474 N.Y.S.2d 397 (Ct.Cl. 1984).; *Duvernay v. State* 433 So.2d 254 (La.App. 1983).

54. *Joseph v. State of Alaska,* 26 P.3d 459 (2001).

55. *Thomas v. Williams,* 124 S.E.2d 409 (Ga. App. 1962).

56. *Morris v. Blake,* 552 A.2d 844 (Del. Super. 1988).

57. *Davis v. City of Detroit,* 386 N.W.2d 169 (Mich. App. 1986).

58. *Penilla v. City of Huntington Park,* 115 F.3d 707 (9th Cir., 1997).

59. *Monfils v. Taylor,* 165 F.3d 511 (7th Cir. 1998), cert. denied, 528 U.S. 810 (1999).

60. The U.S. Supreme Court said, in a 7–2 decision, that Gonzales could not sue the city and claim the police had violated her rights to due process. Furthermore, it held she had no constitutionally protected interest in the enforcement of the restraining order. The opinion also established that the holder of a restraining order is not entitled to any specific mandatory action by the police; rather, restraining orders only provide grounds for *arresting* the person restrained by order. See: *Castle Rock v. Gonzales,* 545 U.S. 748 (2005).

61. *Seide v. State of Rhode Island,* 875 A.2d 1259 (2005).

62. Silver, *Police Civil Liability,* p. 8.

63. *Seide v. State of Rhode Island,* 875 A.2d 1259 (2005).

64. *Scott v. Harris,* 550 U.S._(2007), Docket #05-1631, at p. 13.

65. Kappeler, *Critical Issues in Police Civil Liability,* pp. 177–178.

66. U.S. Department of Justice, Bureau of Justice Statistics, "Jail Suicide Rates 64 Percent Lower Than in Early 1980s," http://www.bjs.gov/content/pub/press/shspljpr.cfm (accessed October 14, 2014).

67. Ibid., p. 9.

68. Victor E. Kappeler and Rolando V. del Carmen, "Avoiding Police Liability for Negligent Failure to Prevent Suicide," *The Police Chief* (August 1991):53–59.

69. Ibid., p. 53.

70. *Thomas v. Williams,* 124 S.E.2d 409 (Ga. App. 1962).

71. *Kanayurak v. North Slope Borough,* 677 P.2d 892 (Alaska 1984).

72. *City of Belen v. Harrell,* 603 P.2d 711 (NM: 1979).

73. *Hake v. Manchester Township,* 486 A.2d 836 (NJ: 1985).

74. *Davis v. City of Detroit,* 386 N.W.2d 169 (Mich. App. 1986).

75. *Hickey v. Zezulka,* 443 N.W.2d 180 (Mich. App. 1989).

76. *Hake v. Manchester Township,* 486 A.2d 836 (NJ: 1985).

77. Andrew Blankstein, "Nearly 20 LA Sheriff's Deputies to be Charged in Corruption, Inmate Abuse Probe," NBC News Investigations, December 9, 2013, http://investigations.nbcnews.com/_news/2013/12/09/21835238-nearly-20-la-sheriffs-deputies-to-be-charged-in-corruption-inmate-abuse-probe?lite (accessed January 29, 2014).

78. V. McLaughlin and R. Bing, "Law Enforcement Personnel Selection," *Journal of Police Science and Administration* 15 (1987):271–276.

79. Ibid.

80. *McNamara v. City of Chicago,* 700 F.Supp. 917 (ND Ill., 1988), at 919.

81. *White v. Thomas,* 660 F.2d 680 (5th Cir. 1981).

82. *Yarber v. Indiana State Prison,* 713 F.Supp. 271 (ND Ind., 1988).

83. Robert H. Chaires and Susan A. Lentz, "Criminal Justice Employee Rights: An Overview," *American Journal of Criminal Justice* 13 (April 1995):273–274.

84. M. Guthrie, "Using Automation to Apply Discipline Fairly," *FBI Law Enforcement Bulletin* 5 (1996):18–21.

85. Aurora, Colorado, Police Department, *2011 Awards, Commendations, Complaints, and Discipline Report* (Aurora, CO: Author, 2012), pp. 1–2.

86. See "Employee Disciplinary Matrix: A Search for Fairness in the Disciplinary Process," *The Police Chief* 73(10) (October 2006), http://www.policechiefmagazine.org/magazine/index.cfm?fuseaction=display_arch&article_id=1024&issue_id=102006 (accessed January 23, 2014).

87. Peter Korn, "City Police Watchdog Wants More bite," *Portland Tribune,* November 13, 2013, http://portlandtribune.com/pt/9-news/200942-city-police-watchdog-wants-more-bite%20; also see Maxine Bernstein, "Disciplining Portland Police Proves Challenging Task, The Oregonian, July 14, 2012, http://www.oregonlive.com/portland/index.ssf/2012/07/disciplining_portland_police_p.html (accessed January 30, 2014).

88. John Dean Harper, "Ten Years with the PPA and Counting," *LVPPA Vegas Beat* 3(2) (July/August 2008), p. 11, http://lvppa.com/docs/vegas-beat/2008/july-august-2008.pdf (accessed January 22, 2014).

89. Samuel Walker, *The Discipline Matrix: An Effective Police Accountability Tool?* Police Professionalism Initiative, University of Nebraska at Omaha, January 2003, p. 14, http://www.unomaha.edu/criminaljustice/PDF/matrixreport.pdf (accessed January 27, 2014).

90. For examples of discipline matrices, see Jon M. Shane, "Police Employee Disciplinary Matrix: An Emerging Concept," *Police Quarterly* 15(1) (March 2012):62–91; *Denver Police Department Discipline Handbook: Conduct Principles and Disciplinary Guidelines,* October 1, 2008, http://www.denvergov.org/Portals/744/documents/handbooks/DPD_Handbook_Final_6-4-2008_with_appendix.pdf; Tucson, Arizona, Police Department, October 2009, http://www.portlandonline.com/auditor/index.cfm?a=368332&c=56523 (accessed January 25, 2014).

91. Jeff Rojek, Allen E. Wagner, and Scott H. Decker, "Evaluating Citizen Complaints against the Police," in R. G. Dunham and G. P. Alpert (eds.), *Critical Issues in Policing: Contemporary Readings,* 4th ed. (Prospect Heights, IL: Waveland, 2001), pp. 317–337.

92. Ibid., p. 318.

93. J. R. Dugan and D. R. Breda, "Complaints about Police Officers: A Comparison among Types and Agencies," *Journal of Criminal Justice* 19 (1991):165–171.

94. Kim Michelle Lersch, "Police Misconduct and Malpractice: A Critical Analysis of Citizens' Complaints," *Policing* 21 (1998): 80–96.

95. D. W. Perez, *Police Review Systems* (Washington, DC: Management Information Service, 1992).

96. Christopher Harris, "The Relationship between Career Pathways of Internal and Citizen Complaints," *Police Quarterly* 14(2) (June 2011):142–165.

97. Ibid.

98. Ibid.

99. In *Munger v. City of Glasgow Police Dept.* (227 F. 3d 1082, 1086-1087 (9th Cir. 2000), the court held that the officers created a danger to Munger by ejecting him and then not allowing him to return or go to his car on such a frigid night. The court also found that the officers had thus placed Munger in a position of danger. The court also found that the police agency had a policy of taking such intoxicated individuals to their home, but that it had failed to train officers in this policy and thus was liable.

15 Financial Administration

LEARNING OBJECTIVES

After reading this chapter, the student will be able to:

1. review specific ways in which the Great Recession affected the United States in general, and police, courts, and corrections budgets and operations in specific

2. explain several measures agencies have taken to cope with the Great Recession, including more grant writing and shifting their philosophies and practices

3. define the term budget

4. delineate the concepts of the budget cycle's four steps

5. distinguish among the three different budget formats and know the advantages and disadvantages of each

6. delineate potential pitfalls and common waste problems involved in budgets

> How pleasant it is to have money, heigh ho! How pleasant it is to have money.
> —*Arthur Hugh Clough*

> It's a recession when your neighbor loses his job; it's a depression when you lose yours.
> —*Harry S. Truman*

▶ Introduction

The importance of financial administration for criminal justice administrators is unquestioned. Money is the key to just about everything these agencies do, and the ability to obtain and expend necessary financial resources is the key to an organization's short- and long-term success. Indeed, if unlimited funds were available, planning would not be needed. As Frederick Mosher observed, "Not least among the qualifications of an administrator is one's ability as a tactician and gladiator in the budget process."[1]

Certainly the recent Great Recession created many problems and challenges for contemporary criminal justice administrators, and that is a primary topic to be addressed in our discussion later of financial administration. As will be seen, unprecedented actions have been taken within criminal justice agencies to cope with the economic downturn—in a field long considered to be the stalwart of job security and stable revenues. Another major purpose of this chapter, however, is to convey the fundamental elements of controlling fiscal resources through formulating and executing a budget. And although this chapter is not intended to prepare the reader to be an expert on the more intricate aspects of financial administration, it will provide a foundation for and insight concerning some of its basic methods and issues.

After looking at various ways in which the recent Great Recession affected state government budgets in general, and criminal justice agencies in specific, we then look at the broader issue of financial *stewardship* (a word that generally refers to the responsibility of taking care of something that is owned by someone else). Of the four components of financial administration—budgeting, auditing, accounting, and purchasing—budgeting is the primary focus here. Included are discussions of budget definitions and uses; the influence of politics and fiscal realities in budgeting, which often lead to budget cuts for the organization; the several elements of the budget process, including formulation, approval, execution, and audit; and budget formats. Also presented is an examination of some of the budget pitfalls and waste problems that units of government are now experiencing. The chapter includes a career profile written by a budget analyst, and concludes with review questions, "deliberate and decide" problems, and "learn by doing" exercises.

▶ Effects of the Great Recession, Generally

Great Recession the severe, prolonged economic downturn lasting from December 2007 to June 2009.

The **Great Recession**—a severe, prolonged economic downturn that is said to have officially lasted from December 2007 to June 2009[2]—is certainly still being felt by many Americans and most particularly by state and local governments. Prior to the onset of the recession, for three decades the states had enjoyed average revenue growth of 6 percent per year—and state expenditures grew in transportation and other infrastructure, law enforcement and general public safety, K-12 education through higher education, health care, and social welfare policy. But trouble was looming on the horizon: 43 states had a personal income tax, generating one-third of their revenues, and 45 percent had a sales tax (generating 32% of revenues). In sum, this heavy reliance on personal income tax and from personal spending would not put the states in good stead when workers saw their hours cut or lost their jobs and the economy nosedived—and causing more individuals to become eligible for social programs such as Medicaid. Many states thus witnessed firsthand the inadequacies of their fiscal foundations.[3]

As a result, the recession wreaked havoc with governmental budgets. According to the Center on Budget and Policy Priorities, by mid-2010, 46 state governments faced budget deficits:

- Eighteen states had shortfalls of over 20 percent;
- Ten states had budgets that were short between 10 percent and 20 percent; and
- Eighteen state budgets had shortfalls between 1 percent and 10 percent.[4]

TABLE 15-1 **Largest State Budget Shortfalls on Record**

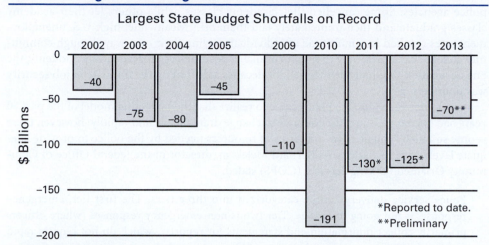

Largest State Budget Shortfalls on Record

Source: Created by using data from "Table, Largest State Budget Shortfalls on Record from Reshaping the Face of Justice: The Economic Tsunami Continues" by National Center for State Courts.

Table 15-1 ■ depicts how the Great Recession affected state budgets.

Decreasing state revenues and increasing demands for social assistance combined to create state budget shortfalls never before witnessed. Concurrently, balanced-budget requirements in nearly all states forced cuts to spending along with increases in taxes—strategies that further hampered the economic recovery.[5]

While some people see indications that the previously described fiscal malaise is beginning to dissipate nationally, most experts agree that local jurisdictions are still in decline and will continue to be so, at least in the short term. Local government budgets tend to lag behind the general economy as it recovers, and certainly the continuing housing foreclosures are holding down property taxes—a staple of local agency revenues.

▶ Impact on Police, Courts, and Corrections

Police: Budgets—and Job Security—Wane

Prior to the onset of the Great Recession, there was a steady increase in the number of full-time, sworn officers employed by state and local law enforcement agencies. Specifically, from 1986 (with 514,494 such officers) to 2008 (724,413), the number swelled by 41 percent. An even greater increase was seen in civilian personnel—91 percent—between 1986 and 2008.[6]

This steady rise began to deteriorate soon thereafter, however; the Bureau of Justice Statistics (BJS) reported in 2011 that 15 of the 50 largest local police departments experienced a decrease in number of officers employed, compared with 20 of 50 between 2000 and 2004. The decline was small for some departments, such as the NYPD, which had 95 (0.3%) fewer officers in 2008 than 2004. In other departments, however, the loss was more substantial: As seen later, 4 of the 50 largest departments experienced a drop of more than 10% in the number of full-time officers:

- Detroit Police (35.9% fewer officers)
- Memphis Police (23.2%)
- New Orleans Police (13.4%)
- San Francisco Police (10.5%)[7]

The Great Recession also inspired some cost-cutting measures seldom if ever seen in police agencies: Some cancelled their academy classes, while others let their academy classes graduate and then immediately laid them off.[8] Meanwhile, high U.S. unemployment rates resulted in a multitude of individuals paying their own way through community college academies, only to find no available positions upon graduating. Suddenly, the one occupation that had been viewed for decades as affording the ultimate in job security was floundering.

Given these declines, the police came to realize that the budgeting model of the past 50 years had to change, and must continue to change dramatically and rapidly; however, there is only so much "wiggle room" in terms of resources needed by the police to provide adequate levels of public safety. As Bernard Melekian, director of the federal Office of Community Oriented Policing Services (COPS) stated:

> Police service delivery can be categorized into three tiers. The first tier, emergency response, is not going to change. Tier two is non-emergency responses [where officers primarily collect information and statements for reports...which do not require rapid response]. Tier three deals with quality of life issues, such as crime prevention efforts or traffic management duties. They help make our communities better places to live, but they are proactive and ongoing activities. The second and third tiers of police service delivery have always competed for staffing and financial resources, but as local budgets constrict, that competition becomes fiercer. The public expects that both tiers are addressed, and agencies with shrinking payrolls are faced with finding new ways to make sure that can happen.[9]

What this says is that the police do not have the luxury of "doing more with less." The public expects a certain, minimal level of service, and agencies must develop ways to do things *differently*, using their resources in the most efficient and effective ways possible.

Effects on the Courts: A "Tragedy"

Because of their constitutional role—to include providing due process, speedy and public trial, trial by jury, effective counsel, due process, and other protections afforded for all under our rule of law—it may seem at first blush that the nation's state courts would be spared from the budget axe that came down on so many criminal justice agencies during the Great Recession. However, that is not the case, and as a board member of the National Center for State Courts (NCSC) described the fiscal situation, "We have a tragedy taking place in our courts."[10] This situation continues: The NCSC reported that 47 states have experienced funding reductions since 2010, resulting in widespread service reductions (reduced hours, furloughs, less time spent by judges on the bench, judges' vacancies going unfilled, and trial postponed).[11]

To help to weather this storm and prepare for the uncertain future, NCSC and American Bar Association (ABA) have been busy forming task forces, preparing written documents for legislators, and developing "toolkits" for judges and court administrators toward addressing the problem.[12] Furthermore, NCSC either has worked with or currently is working with nearly 40 states to re-engineer their court systems; this can involve evaluating and adjusting a court's structure as well as its use of technology and its processes.[13]

Corrections: Cost-Prohibitive Beds

By 2010, 31 states had made reductions to their corrections budgets.[14] It had become clear that corrections would not, at least temporarily, be given all the funding it needed to incarcerate inmates; as one observer put it, the "political monopoly" of incarceration had been undermined by the economic conditions.[15]

These fiscal challenges to corrections are particularly daunting; as Marie Gottschalk stated, "Most prison costs are fixed and not easily cut. The only way to substantially reduce spending is to send fewer people to jail or prison and shut down penal facilities."[16] Some short-term, stopgap measures adopted in some jurisdictions included charging inmates fees for services, such as meals, lodging, and visits to the doctor.

Legislators in a number of states found themselves unable to afford to build their way out of prison overcrowding problems. As examples:

- Texas lawmakers were told they needed to add 17,000 new beds over 5 years to keep up with the pace of incarceration at a cost of $2.6 billion.

- Ohio found that about 57 percent of its inmates were low-level felony offenders who averaged less than 1 year in prison but whose intake and transportation costs were about *$21 million per month*.[17]

With little or no money to build new prisons, and no political support to keep increasing corrections budgets, it became clear that new policies and approaches were needed. Several states turned to the Pew Center on the States and the Council of State Governments Justice Center to obtain information on sentencing policy.

▶ The System Reacts: Confronting the Great Recession

Given these fiscal straits, police, courts, and corrections agencies were compelled to think "outside of the silo" and develop means of surviving their fiscal cutbacks. Following are some examples of the methods employed.

Police Responses: Some Services Lost, Some Technologies Gained

Police agencies, according to national surveys, rose to the challenge in the following ways:

- Eight percent of departments surveyed no longer respond to all motor vehicle thefts.
- Nine percent of departments no longer respond to all burglar alarms.
- Fourteen percent of departments no longer respond to all noninjury motor vehicle accidents.
- Seventeen percent of respondents stopped responding to some calls for service.
- Forty-three percent increased their use of telephone reporting, along with 30 percent who had increased the use of online reporting.
- Twenty-six percent reduced investigative follow-ups, specifically those relating to property crimes, fugitive tracking, nonfelony domestic assaults, financial crimes, computer crimes, narcotics, and traffic cases.

Police policies and practices have also undergone a transformation in order to adapt to the economic changes. For example, two-thirds of the agencies reported that they had reduced or discontinued training programs because of their limited budgets. More than half stated that they had cut back or even eliminated plans to obtain new technology; however, while some agencies were cutting back on expenditures for technology, others found that expanding the use of technology systems can serve as a 'force multiplier;' specifically, using closed-circuit televisions (CCTVs) and light-based intervention systems (LBIS, which uses CCTV cameras with a powerful stream of light targeted on suspicious activity; see an example of its use in East Orange, New Jersey, at http://www. youtube.com/watch?v=AvSbYIqgxr4). Such technologies can allow police opportunities for incident intervention and crime prevention, without requiring the immediate presence of an officer.

Furthermore, one-fourth of agencies indicated that their county had consolidated services with another county government in response to economic conditions; another 31 percent said that their county has participated in discussions regarding the consolidation of services. Innovative multi-jurisdictional operations that are cost-effective in providing service delivery include:

joint task forces, combinations that include police, sheriffs, state police, and constables.

sharing of services/functions, such as crime scene technicians, dispatch, SWAT, hazardous materials (hazmat), laboratories, and training.

The Courts Respond: Turning to Grants

grant writing preparing and submitting required documents and information for making application to funding bodies that award monies to assist eligible businesses and government agencies.

To help weather the financial storm and become more fiscally solvent and independent, judges and court administrators have increasingly become more involved in **grant writing**— i.e., the preparing and submitting of required documents and information in order to apply to agencies and foundations that award monies to assist governments, businesses, or other eligible organizations. There are a surprising number of funding sources available to the enterprising grant writer. Following is an overview:

- *Justice Assistance Grants (JAG) program.* Administered by the federal Bureau of Justice Assistance (BJA), JAG is a broad-based, competitive program with 29 funding areas; its funding is intended as "seed money" to start new programs, and funding ranges from 1 to 3 years. JAG also offers an online Grant Writing and Management Academy, a five-module course that includes such topics as BJA funding opportunities, rules associated with grant funding, managing grants, strategic planning, and budgeting.[18]

- *Bureau of Justice Assistance.* BJA has funding opportunities for treatment programs and specialty courts, drug testing and equipment, and intensive outpatient programs. Annual funding for adult drug court funding alone has ranged from $35 million to $45 million since 2009.[19]

- *Office of Justice Programs.* OJA provides a variety of types of grants geared toward implementing strategies that involve identifying the most pressing crime-related challenges and to provide information, training, and coordination for addressing these challenges.[20]

- *The Violence Against Women Reauthorization Act of 2013.*[21] Known as VAWA 2013, this is an improved and expanded grant programs addressing domestic violence, dating violence, sexual assault, and stalking; it also establishes new programs.[22]

- *The Office of Juvenile Justice and Delinquency Prevention (OJJDP).* OJJDP is dedicated to being the national leader for "the future, safety, and well-being of children and youth in, or at risk of entering, the juvenile justice system." Toward that end, it provides a variety of grants for research, training, and technical assistance; funding of new projects; and dissemination of information.[23]

In addition, most states have an administrative office, department of public safety, and other entities that can provide courts with funding for a variety of purposes, including the

▼

aforementioned functions, specialty court improvement, court technologies, interpreters, security, equipment, and so on.

Corrections Answers: A Shift in Philosophy and Practice

The Great Recession probably placed corrections administrators—in conjunction with legislators, judges, and others—in a position of having to consider the most broad, sweeping changes of all three criminal justice components. Certainly the recession served as a catalyst for reducing funds spent on incarceration and to improve public safety, both of which involve changes in such major areas as sentencing, inmate treatment, paroling, and prisoner re-entry into the community.

As mentioned earlier, several states turned to such organizations as the Pew Center and the Council of State Governments for suggestions. Following are some of the results:

- In Texas, lawmakers—rather than spend $2.6 billion on new beds—opted to allocate $241 million to enhance treatment programs for nonviolent offenders and to hire re-entry coordinators. As a result, Texas's crime rate has steadily dropped, along with its prison population and recidivism of parolees.

- Ohio increased funding to community corrections diversions, raising the felony theft threshold, creating sentencing alternatives for non-payment of child support, and reinstating the good-time credit program.

- Indiana also bolstered its use of diversionary programs (e.g., drug courts, veterans' courts, and community transition for low-level or first-time offenders), increased the number of nonviolent offenders on probation and parole, and focused on re-entry services.[24]

- Michigan opted to focus on providing inmates with counselling and skills to use upon leaving prison earlier, and the creation of an entirely new program (the Michigan Prisoner Reentry Initiative). The MPRI educated staff, prisoners, and the communities, while developing risk and need indicators and building partnerships for service delivery in 18 sites. The net result was a 29 percent reduction in its prison return rate.[25]

Succinctly, after four decades of tough-on-crime policies, some states used the recession to consider sentence reform and, at least temporarily, a shift from confinement to rehabilitation, as well as emphases on cost-effectiveness, evidence-based programming, and measureable outcomes.[26] In addition, the U.S. Supreme Court's 2011 decision in *Brown v. Plata* (discussed in Chapter 10) will play a role in prison policy, serve as a precedent for other states to reduce prison overcrowding, and affect prison budgets.

▶ The Budget

In this chapter section, we leave the effects of fiscal exigency, and focus on the more intricate parts of budgeting, to include elements, types (with several examples provided), formulation, and execution. Included is a brief explanation of the role of auditing.

> **budget** a plan, in financial terms, estimating future expenditures and indicating agency plans and policy regarding financial resources and the appropriation and expenditure of funds.

A Working Definition

The word **budget** is derived from the old French word *bougette*, meaning a small leather bag or wallet. Initially, it referred to the leather bag in which the Chancellor of the Exchequer carried documents stating the government's needs and resources given to the English

Parliament.[27] Later, it came to mean the documents themselves. More recently, *budget* has been defined as a plan stated in financial terms, an estimate of future expenditures, a policy statement, the translation of financial resources into human purposes, and a contract between those who appropriate the funds and those who spend them.[28] To some extent, all of these definitions are valid.

In addition, the budget is a management tool, a process, and a political instrument. It is a comprehensive plan, expressed in financial terms, by which a program is operated for a given period. It includes (1) the services, activities, and projects comprising the program; (2) the resultant expenditure requirements; and (3) the resources available for their support.[29]

It is "a plan or schedule adjusting expenses during a certain period to the estimated income for that period."[30] Lester Bittel added:

A budget is, literally, a financial standard for a particular operation, activity, program, or department. Its data are presented in numerical form, mainly in dollars—to be spent for a particular purpose—over a specified period of time. Budgets are derived from planning goals and forecasts.[31]

Although these descriptions are certainly apt, one writer warns that budgets involve an inherently irrational process: "Budgets are based on little more than the past and some guesses."[32]

Financial management of governmental agencies is clearly political. Anything the government does entails the expenditure of public funds.[33] Thus, the most important political statement that any unit of government makes in a given year is its budget. Essentially, the budget causes administrators to follow the gambler's adage and "put their money where their mouth is."[34] When demands placed on government increase while funds are stable or decline, the competition for funds is keener than usual, forcing justice agencies to make the best case for their budgets. The heads of all departments, if they are doing their jobs well, are also vying for appropriations. Special-interest groups, the media, politicians, and the public, with their own views and priorities, often engage in arm twisting during the budgeting process.

► Elements of a Budget

The Budget Cycle

budget cycle a time frame that determines how long a budget lasts, that can vary from agency to agency.

Administrators must think in terms of a **budget cycle**—simply put, how long a budget lasts, which is a time frame that can vary from agency to agency. In government (and, therefore, all public criminal justice agencies) the budget cycle is typically set on a fiscal-year basis. Some states have a biennial budget cycle; their legislatures, such as those in Kentucky and Nevada, budget for a 2-year period. Normally, however, the fiscal year is a 12-month period that may coincide with a calendar year or, more commonly, will run from July 1 through June 30 of the following year. The federal government's fiscal year is October 1 through September 30. The budget cycle is important because it drives the development of the budget and determines when new monies become available.

The budget cycle consists of four sequential steps, repeated every year at about the same point in time: (1) budget formulation, (2) budget approval, (3) budget execution, and (4) budget audit.

▼

Budget Formulation

Depending on the size and complexity of the organization and the financial condition of the jurisdiction, **budget formulation**—which involves the preparation of a budget so as to be able to allocate funds in accordance with agency priorities, plans, and programs, and to deliver necessary services—can be a relatively simple or an exceedingly difficult task; in either case, it is likely to be the most complicated stage of the budgeting process. The administrator must anticipate all types of **expenditures**—i.e., payment for goods or services, to settle a financial obligation indicated by an invoice, contract, or other such document—and predict expenses related to major incidents or events that might arise. Certain assumptions based on the previous year's budget can be made, but they are not necessarily accurate. One observer noted that "every expense you budget should be fully supported with the proper and most logical assumptions you can develop. Avoid simply estimating, which is the least supportable form of budgeting."[35] Another criminal justice administrator, discussing budget formulation, added:

> The most important ingredient for any budgeting process is planning. Administrators should approach the budget process from the planning standpoint of "How can I best reconcile the [criminal justice] needs of the community with the ability of my jurisdiction to finance them, and then relate those plans in a convincing manner to my governing body for proper financing and execution of programs?" After all, as budget review occurs, the document is taken apart and scrutinized piece by piece or line by line. This fragmentation approach contributes significantly to our inability to defend interrelated programs in an overall budget package.[36]

To illustrate, let us assume that a police department budget is being prepared in a city having a manager form of government. Long before a criminal justice agency (or any other unit of local government) begins to prepare its annual budget, the city manager and/or the staff of the city have made revenue forecasts, considered how much (if any) of the current operating budget will be carried over into the next fiscal year, analyzed how the population of the jurisdiction will grow or shift (affecting demand for public services), and examined other priorities for the coming year. The city manager may also appear before the governing board to obtain information about its fiscal priorities, spending levels, pay raises, new positions, programs, and so on. The city manager may then send department heads a memorandum outlining the general fiscal guidelines to be followed in preparing their budgets.

On receipt of the city's guidelines for preparing its budget, the heads of functional areas, such as the chief of police, have a planning and research unit (assuming a city large enough to have this level of specialization) prepare an internal budget calendar and an internal fiscal policy memorandum (Table 15-2 ■ shows an internal budget calendar for a large municipal police department). This memo may include input from unions and lower supervisory personnel. Each bureau is then given the responsibility for preparing its individual budget request.

In small police departments with little or no functional specialization, the chief may prepare the budget alone or with input from other officers or the city finance officer. In some small agencies, chiefs and sheriffs may not even see their budget or assist in its preparation. Because of tradition, politics, or even laziness, the administrator may have abdicated control over the budget. This puts the agency in a precarious position indeed; it will have difficulty engaging in long-term planning and spending money productively for personnel and programs when the executive has to get prior approval from the governing body to buy items such as office supplies.

The planning and research unit then reviews the bureau's budget request for compliance with the budgeting instructions and the chief's and city manager's priorities.

budget formulation the preparation of a budget to allocate funds in accordance with agency priorities, plans, and programs, and to deliver necessary services.

expenditure a payment for goods or services, to settle a financial obligation indicated by an invoice, contract, or other such document.

TABLE 15-2 Budget Preparation Calendar for a Large Police Department

What Should Be Done	By Whom	On This Date
Issue budget instructions and applicable forms	City administrator	November 1
Prepare and issue budget message, with instructions and applicable forms, to unit commanders	Chief of police	November 15
Develop unit budgets with appropriate justification and forward recommended budgets to planning and research unit	Unit commanders	February 1
Review unit budget	Planning and research staff with unit commanders	March 1
Consolidate unit budgets for presentation to chief of police	Planning and research unit	March 15
Review consolidated recommended budget	Chief of police, planning and research staff, and unit commanders	March 30
Obtain department approval of budget	Chief of police	April 15
Forward recommended budget to city administrator	Chief of police	April 20
Review recommended budget by administration	City administrator and chief of police	April 30
Approve revised budget	City administrator	May 5
Forward budget document to city council	City administrator	May 10
Review budget	Budget officer of city council	May 20
Present to council	City administrator and chief of police	June 1
Report back to city administrator	City council	June 5
Review and resubmit to city council	City administrator and chief of police	June 10
Take final action on police budget	City council	June 20

Source: U.S. Department of Justice, National Advisory Commission on Criminal Justice Standards and Goals, *Police* (Washington, DC: U.S. Government Printing Office, 1973), p. 137.

Eventually, a consolidated budget is developed for the entire police department and submitted to the chief, who may meet with the planning and research unit and bureau commanders to discuss it. Personalities, politics, priorities, personal agendas, and other issues may need to be addressed; the chief may have to mediate disagreements concerning these matters, sometimes rewarding the loyal and sometimes reducing allotments to the disloyal.[37] Requests for programs, equipment, travel expenses, personnel, or anything else in the draft budget may be deleted, reduced, or enhanced. The budget is then presented to the city manager. At this point, the chief executive's reputation as a budget framer becomes a factor. If the chief is known to pad the budget heavily, the city manager is far more likely to cut the department's request than if the chief is known to be reasonable in making budget requests, engages in innovative planning, and has a flexible approach to budget negotiations.

The city manager consolidates the police budget request with those from other municipal department heads and then meets with them individually to discuss their requests further. The city manager directs the city finance officer to make any necessary additions or cuts and then to prepare a budget proposal for presentation to the governing body. The general steps in budget development are shown in Exhibit 15.1.

The courts have a similar budgetary process. In a large court, the process may include five major procedures: (1) developing an internal budgetary policy, (2) reviewing budget submissions, (3) developing a financial strategy, (4) presenting the budget, and (5) monitoring the budget. Figure 15-1 ■ illustrates the relationship of the steps in the judicial budget process.

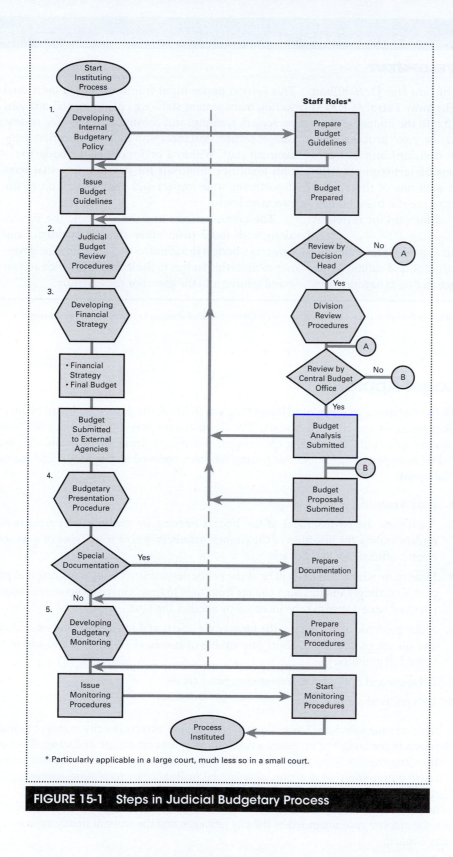

Start
Instituting
Process

1. Developing Internal Budgetary Policy

Issue Budget Guidelines

2. Judicial Budget Review Procedures

3. Developing Financial Strategy

• Financial Strategy
• Final Budget

Budget Submitted to External Agencies

4. Budgetary Presentation Procedure

Special Documentation

No

5. Developing Budgetary Monitoring

Issue Monitoring Procedures

Staff Roles*

Prepare Budget Guidelines

Budget Prepared

Review by Decision Head — No — A

Yes

Division Review Procedures — A

Review by Central Budget Office — No — B

Yes

Budget Analysis Submitted

B

Budget Proposals Submitted

Yes — Prepare Documentation

Prepare Monitoring Procedures

Start Monitoring Procedures

Process Instituted

* Particularly applicable in a large court, much less so in a small court.

FIGURE 15-1 Steps in Judicial Budgetary Process

EXHIBIT 15.1

STEPS IN BUDGET DEVELOPMENT

Following is a description of how the $1.96 billion budget for the California Highway Patrol (CHP) is typically developed. According to the budget section, "It is an all-year and year-on-year process" that begins at the level of the 8 divisions and 103 area offices/dispatch centers, where budget requests originate. The requests are dealt with one of three ways: (1) funded within the department's base budget, (2) disapproved, or (3) carried forward for review by CHP personnel.

At the division level, managers review the area requests, make needed adjustments, and submit a consolidated request to the budget section at headquarters.

This section passes input from the field to individual section management staff (e.g., planning and analysis, personnel, training, and communications) for review. Budget section staff meet with individual section management staff. Within 2 or 3 months, the budget section identifies proposals for new funding that have department-wide impact and passes them on to the executive level.

The commissioner and aides review the figures along with those from other state departments and agree on a budget to submit to the governor. The governor submits this budget to the legislature, which acts on it and returns it to the governor for signature.

Source: Excerpt from Working Out a Budget by Hal Rubin from Law and Order. Copyright © 1989 by Hendon Publishing Company. Used by permission of Hendon Publishing Company.

Budget Approval

With the city manager's proposed budget request in hand, the governing board begins its deliberations on the citywide budget. The city manager may appear before the board to answer questions concerning the budget; individual department heads also may be asked to appear. Suggestions for getting monies approved and appropriated include the following:

1. Have a carefully justified budget.
2. Anticipate the environment of the budget hearing by reading news reports and understanding the priorities of the council members. Know what types of questions elected officials are likely to ask.
3. Determine which "public" will be at the police department's budget hearing and prepare accordingly. Public issues change from time to time; citizens who were outraged over one issue 1 year may be incensed by another the next.
4. Make good use of graphics in the form of pie charts and histograms, but be selective and do not go overboard. Short case studies of successes are normal and add to the impact of graphics.
5. Rehearse and critique the presentation many times.
6. Be a political realist.[38]

After everyone scheduled has spoken, the city council directs the city manager to make further cuts in the budget or to reinstate funds or programs cut earlier, and so on. The budget is then approved. It is fair to say that at this stage, budgeting is largely a legislative function that requires some legal action, as a special ordinance or resolution approving the budget is passed each year by the governing board.

The columns in Table 15-3 ■ indicate the budget amount requested by the chief of police, the amount recommended by the city manager, and the amount finally approved by the city council.

▼

TABLE 15-3 Police Operating Budget ($) in a Community of 100,000 Population

Description	FY 2013–2014 Expenses	FY 2014–2015 Expenses	FY 2015–2016 Police Request	City Manager	City Council
Salaries/wages					
Regular salaries	28,315,764	28,392,639	32,221,148	32,221,148	32,221,148
Overtime	1,976,165	1,564,421	1,902,875	1,902,875	1,422,875
Severence pay	456,712	452,465	454,936	-0-	-0-
Holiday pay	790,952	1,182,158	1,396,958	1,396,958	1,396,958
Callback pay	1,205,947	1,326,534	1,476,925	1,395,241	1,395,241
Subtotals	32,745,540	32,918,217	36,916,222	36,916,222	36,436,222
Employee benefits					
Retirement	6,345,566	6,485,888	8,069,521	8,069,521	8,069,521
Group insurance	2,256,663	2,467,406	2,752,718	2,752,718	2,752,718
Life insurance	86,797	106,164	234,590	234,396	234,396
Disability insurance	1,452,885	1,588,686	2,346,909	2,346,038	2,024,398
Uniform allowance	376,079	386,827	392,750	392,750	392,750
Medicare	154,730	160,868	200,058	198,739	198,739
Long-term disability	22,583	42,974	96,517	96,517	96,517
Subtotals	10,695,303	11,238,813	14,093,063	14,090,679	13,769,039
Services and supplies					
Office supplies	124,357	98,292	102,485	102,485	102,485
Operating supplies	454,563	296,569	540,661	540,661	540,661
Repair/maintenance	496,922	390,941	466,118	466,118	466,118
Small tools	98,508	1,576	24,175	24,175	24,175
Professional services	674,263	580,359	668,765	668,765	668,765
Communications	574,757	446,200	784,906	784,906	784,906
Services and supplies					
Public utilities	222,935	232,773	242,008	242,008	242,008
Rentals	162,840	192,294	226,071	226,071	226,071
Vehicle rentals	1,668,416	2,193,926	2,363,278	2,363,278	2,169,278
Extradition	40,955	44,411	40,000	40,000	40,000
Other travel	8,649	10,123	46,500	46,500	46,500
Advertising	4,662	4,570	8,100	8,100	8,100
Insurance	656,360	1,190,257	1,884,921	1,884,921	1,884,921
Books/manuals	32,285	24,813	24,404	24,404	24,404
Employee training	94,029	60,851	-0-	-0-	-0-
Aircraft expenses	-0-	-0-	30,000	30,000	30,000
Special inventory	22,527	26,465	30,000	30,000	30,000
Other services and supplies	2,386,201	2,039,651	2,386,201	2,386,201	2,386,201
Subtotals	7,723,229	7,834,071	9,868,593	9,868,593	9,868,593
Capital outlay					
Machinery and equipment	1,144,301	204,964	-0-	-0-	-0-
Totals	52,308,373	52,196,065	60,877,878	60,875,494	60,073,854

Budget Execution

The third stage of the process, **budget execution**, has several objectives: (1) to carry out the organization's budgeted objectives for the fiscal year in an orderly manner, (2) to ensure that the department undertakes no financial obligations or commitments other than those

TABLE 15-4 A Police Department's Budget Status Report ($)

Line Item	Amount Budgeted	Expenses to Date	Amount Encumbered	Balance to Date	Percentage Used
Salaries	16,221,148	8,427,062.00	-0-	7,794,086.00	52.0
Professional services	334,765	187,219.61	8,014.22	139,531.17	58.3
Office supplies	51,485	16,942.22	3,476.19	31,066.59	39.7
Repair/ maintenance	49,317	20,962.53	1,111.13	27,243.34	44.8
Communications	392,906	212,099.11	1,560.03	179,246.86	54.4
Utilities	121,008	50,006.15	10,952.42	60,049.43	51.4
Vehicle rentals	1,169,278	492,616.22	103,066.19	573,595.59	51.9
Travel	23,500	6,119.22	2,044.63	15,336.15	34.7
Extraditions	20,000	12,042.19	262.22	7,695.59	61.5
Printing/binding	36,765	15,114.14	2,662.67	18,988.19	48.4
Books/manuals	12,404	5,444.11	614.11	6,345.78	48.8
Training/education	35,695	19,661.54	119.14	15,914.32	55.4
Aircraft expenses	15,000	8,112.15	579.22	6,308.63	57.9
Special investigations	15,000	6,115.75	960.50	7,922.75	47.2
Machinery	1,000	275.27	27.50	697.23	30.3
Advertising	4,100	1,119.17	142.50	2,838.33	30.8

---

budget execution carrying out the organization's budgeted responsibilities in a proper manner, and providing an accounting of the administrator's actions with same.

funded by the city council, and (3) to provide a periodic accounting of the administrator's stewardship over the department's funds.[39]

Supervision of the budget execution phase is an executive function that requires some type of fiscal control system, usually directed by the city or county manager. Periodic reports on accounts are an important element of budget control; they serve to reduce the likelihood of overspending by identifying areas in which deficits are likely to occur as a result of change in gasoline prices, extensive overtime, natural disasters, and unplanned emergencies (such as riots). A periodic budget status report tells the administrator what percentage of the total budget has been expended to date (Table 15-4 ■).

Prudent administrators normally attempt to manage the budget conservatively for the first 8 or 9 months of the budget year, holding the line on spending until most fiscal crises have been averted. Because unplanned incidents and natural disasters can wreak havoc with any budget, this conservatism is normally the best course. Then the administrator can plan the most efficient way to allocate funds if emergency funds have not been spent.

The Audit

audit an objective examination of the financial statements of an organization, either by its employees or an outside firm.

The word *audit* means "to verify something independently."[40] The basic rationale for an **audit** of a budget—which is an objective examination of the financial statements of an organization, either by its employees or by an outside firm—was described by the controller general of the United States as follows:

Governments and agencies entrusted with public resources and the authority for applying them have a responsibility to render a full accounting of their activities. This accountability is inherent in the governmental process and is not always specifically identified by legislative provision. This governmental accountability should identify not only the object for which the public resources have been devoted but also the manner and effect of their application.[41]

After the close of each budget year, the year's expenditures are audited to ensure that the agency spent its funds properly. Budget audits are designed to investigate three broad areas of accountability: financial accountability (focusing on proper fiscal operations and reports of the justice agency), management accountability (determining whether funds were utilized efficiently and economically), and program accountability (determining whether the unit of government's goals and objectives were accomplished).[42]

Financial audits determine whether funds were spent legally, the budgeted amount was exceeded, and the financial process proceeded in a legal manner. For example, auditors investigate whether funds transferred between accounts were authorized, grant funds were used properly, computations were made accurately, disbursements were documented, financial transactions followed established procedures, and established competitive bidding procedures were employed.[43] Justice administrators should welcome auditors' help to identify weaknesses and deficiencies and correct them.

▶ Budget Formats

The three types of budgets primarily in use today are the **line-item budget** (or object-of-expenditure) budget, the **performance budget**, and the program (or results or outcomes) budget. Two additional types, the **planning–programming–budgeting system (PPBS)** and the **zero-based budget (ZBB)**, are also discussed in the literature but are used to a lesser extent.

The Line-Item Budget

Line-item budgeting (or *item budgeting*) is the most commonly used budget format. It is the basic system on which all other systems rely because it affords control. It is so named because it breaks down the budget into the major categories commonly used in government (e.g., personnel, equipment, contractual services, commodities, and capital outlay items); every amount of money requested, recommended, appropriated, and expended is associated with a particular item or class of items.[44] In addition, large budget categories are broken down into smaller line-item budgets (in a police department, examples include patrol, investigation, communications, and jail function). The line-item format fosters budgetary control because no item escapes scrutiny.[45] Table 15-3, shown earlier, demonstrates a line-item budget for police, as do Tables 15-5 ■ for a court, 15-6 for probation and parole, and 15-7 for a state prison organization. Each demonstrates the range of activities and funding needs of each agency. Note in Tables 15-3, 15-6 ■, and 15-7 ■ how a recession affected budgets and requests from year to year in many categories, resulting in severe cuts and even total elimination of items previously funded. Also note some of the ways in which administrators deviated from their usual practices to save money (e.g., the police budget shows that the department found it to be less expensive to lease patrol vehicles than to buy a huge fleet).

The line-item budget has several strengths and weaknesses. Its strengths include ease of control, development, comprehension (especially by elected and other executive branch officials), and administration. Weaknesses are its neglect of long-range planning and its limited ability to evaluate performance. Furthermore, the line-item budget tends to maintain the status quo; ongoing programs are seldom challenged. Line-item budgets are based on history: This year's allocation is based on last year's. Although that allows an inexperienced manager to prepare a budget more easily, it often precludes the reform-minded chief's careful deliberation and planning for the future.

line-item budget a budget format that breaks down its components into major categories, such as personnel, equipment, contractual services, commodities, and capital outlay items.

performance budget a budget format that is input-output oriented and relates the volume of work to be done to the amount of money spent.

planning–programming–budgeting system (PPBS) a budgeting tool that links program to the ways and means of facilitating the program - and better informing decision makers of outcomes of their actions.

zero-based budget (ZBB) a budget format that requires managers to justify their entire budget request in detail, rather than simply using budget amounts established in previous years.

The line-item budget provides ease of control because it clearly indicates the amount budgeted for each item, the amount expended as of a specific date, and the amount still available at that date (See, e.g., Table 15-4).

TABLE 15-5 Operating Budget for a District Court in a County of 100,000 Population

Category	Amount ($)
Salaries and wages	
Regular salaries	3,180,792
Part-time temporary	19,749
Incentive/longevity	70,850
Subtotal	3,271,391
Employee benefits	
Group insurance	270,100
Worker compensation	18,470
Unemployment compensation	33,220
Retirement	612,211
Social security	15,605
Medicare	23,503
Subtotal	973,109
Services and supplies	
Computers and office equipment	62,865
Service contracts	5,000
Minor furniture/equipment	2,000
Computer supplies	15,000
Continuous forms	8,000
Office supplies	86,066
Advertising	8550
Copy machine expenses	80,000
Dues and registration	8,000
Printing	64,000
Telephone	106,000
Training	12,000
Court reporter/transcript	535,000
Court reporter per diem	465,000
Law books/supplements	19,000
Jury trials	575,000
Medical examinations	180,000
Computerized legal research	120,000
Travel	4,500
Subtotal	2,423,981
Child support	
Attorneys and other personnel	266,480
Court-appointed attorneys	1,656,000
Grand juries	88,600
Family court services	1,762,841
Total	8,974,823

**TABLE 15-6 Probation and Parole Budget ($) for a State Serving
1 Million Population**

Description	FY 2013–2014 Actual	FY 2014–2015 Agency Request	FY 2015–2016 Governor's Recommendation	Legislature Approved
Personnel	26,741,104	28,290,523	26,620,991	26,540,222
Travel	824,588	824,588	824,588	802,689
Operating expenses	2,307,020	2,395,484	2,307,020	2,256,787
Equipment	20,569	8,379	8,379	8,379
Loans to parolees	8,500	8,500	8,500	8,500
Training	18,073	18,073	18,073	18,073
Extraditions	400,000	400,000	400,000	285,000
Client drug tests	224,962	224,962	224,962	224,962
Home arrest fees	224,005	224,005	224,005	228,005
Community programs	100,000	100,000	100,000	87,500
Residential confinement	896,709	1,000,709	896,709	887,663
Utilities (paid by building lessors) Totals	31,765,530	33,495,223	31,633,227	31,347,780

**TABLE 15-7 Operating Budget ($) for a State Medium Security
Prison with 500 Inmates**

Description	FY 2013–2014 Actual	FY 2014–2015 Agency Request	FY 2015–2016 Governor's Recommendation	Legislature Approved
Personnel				
Salaries	10,051,095	10,370,979	10,186,421	10,105,533
Worker's compensation	284,362	243,462	401,198	298,016
Retirement	2,142,010	2,174,968	2,215,674	2,196,028
Recruit tests	89,447	101,528	85,692	84,972
Insurance	874,330	888,250	1,013,000	1,000,175
Retirement insurance	60,963	61,872	65,917	65,349
Unemployment compensation	12,003	12,383	12,162	12,065
Overtime	265,856	-0-	-0-	-0-
Holiday pay	250,519	258,500	254,643	251,936
Medicare	69,965	85,140	82,225	80,948
Shift differential	185,925	201,011	188,553	186,828
Standby pay	12,465	12,807	12,641	12,526
Longevity pay	28,095	28,095	28,095	28,095
Subtotals	14,327,035	14,438,995	14,546,221	14,322,471
Services and supplies				
Operating supplies	280,672	477,495	280,647	414,859
Communications/freight	8,877	10,314	10,023	10,023
Printing/copying	40,900	87,222	29,016	41,527
Equipment repair	24,385	23,542	24,817	24,817
Vehicle operation	40,405	41,601	41,016	41,016

(*continued*)

▼

TABLE 15-7 (*continued*)

Description	FY 2013–2014 Actual	FY 2014–2015 Agency Request	FY 2015–2016 Governor's Recommendation	Legislature Approved
Uniforms—custody	218,122	205,976	203,237	213,856
Inmate clothing	142,436	284,790	142,430	166,167
Equipment issued	40,403	23,236	25,451	27,086
Inmate wages	66,645	102,815	65,572	82,309
Food	1,695,897	2,299,838	1,695,759	2,065,403
Postage	14,738	16,793	14,036	14,738
Telephone	44,808	43,802	42,130	44,808
Subscriptions	682	801	1,425	801
Hand tools	210	486	213	213
Subtotals	2,619,180	3,618,711	2,575,772	3,147,623
Special equipment	216,863	64,088	22,557	23,661
Grounds maintenance	250,098	409,003	238,560	285,843
Inmate law library	28,564	40,115	26,419	41,836
Special projects	103,237	16,887	16,887	16,887
Gas and power	1,054,478	1,086,604	1,005,823	1,204,335
Water	120,390	129,377	102,266	127,171
Garbage	160,035	201,240	162,436	162,436
Canine unit	23,936	4,521	8,260	4,543
Total	18,903,816	20,009,541	18,705,201	19,336,833

Virtually all criminal justice agencies are automated to some extent, whether the financial officer prepares his or her budget using a computerized spreadsheet or a clerk enters information into a database that will be uploaded to a state's mainframe computer. Some justice agencies use an automated budgeting system that can store budget figures, make all necessary calculations for generating a budget request, monitor expenditures from budgets (similar to that shown in Table 15-7), and even generate some reports.

The Performance Budget

The key characteristic of a performance budget is that it relates the volume of work to be done to the amount of money spent.[46] It is input–output oriented, and it increases the responsibility and accountability of the manager for output as opposed to input.[47] This format specifies an organization's activities, using a format similar to that of the line-item budget. It normally measures activities that are easily quantified such as the number of traffic citations issued, crimes solved, property recovered, cases heard in the courtroom, and caseloads of probation officers. These activities are then compared with those of the unit that performs at the highest level. The ranking according to activity attempts to allocate funds fairly. Following is an example from a police department: The commander of the traffic accident investigation unit requests an additional three investigators, which the chief approves. Later, the chief might compare the unit's output and costs to these measures before the three investigators were added to determine how this change affected productivity.[48] An example of a police performance budget is provided in Table 15-8 ∎

▼

TABLE 15-8 Example of a Police Performance Budget

Category		Amount
Units/activities		
Administration (chief)	Subtotal	$
Strategic planning		$
Normative planning		$
Policies and procedures formulation, etc.		$
Patrol	Subtotal	$
Calls for service		$
Citizen contacts		$
Special details, etc.		$
Criminal investigation	Subtotal	$
Suspect apprehension		$
Recovery of stolen property		$
Transportation of fugitives, etc.		$
Traffic services	Subtotal	$
Accident investigation		$
Issuance of citations		$
Public safety speeches, etc.		$
Juvenile services	Subtotal	$
Locate runaways/missing juveniles		$
Arrest of offenders		$
Referrals and liaison, etc.		$
Research and development	Subtotal	$
Perform crime analysis		$
Prepare annual budget		$
Prepare annual reports, etc.		$

The performance budget format could be used in other justice system components as well. The courts could use performance measures, such as filing cases, writing opinions, disposing of cases, and accuracy of presentence investigations.

Advantages of the performance budget include a consideration of outputs, the establishment of the costs of various justice agency efforts, improved evaluation of programs and managers, an emphasis on efficiency, increased availability of information for decision making, and the enhancement of budget justification and explanation.[49] The performance budget works best for an assembly line or other organization where work is easily quantifiable, such as paving streets. Its disadvantages include its expense to develop, implement, and operate because of the extensive use of cost accounting techniques and the need for additional staff (Figure 15-2 ■ illustrates the elements used to determine the cost of providing police services); the controversy surrounding attempts to determine appropriate workload and unit cost measures (in criminal justice, although many functions are quantifiable, such reduction of duties to numbers often translates into quotas, which are anathema to many people); its emphasis on efficiency rather than effectiveness; and the failure to lend itself to long-range planning.[50]

Determining which functions in criminal justice are more important (and should receive more financial support) is difficult; therefore, in terms of criminal justice

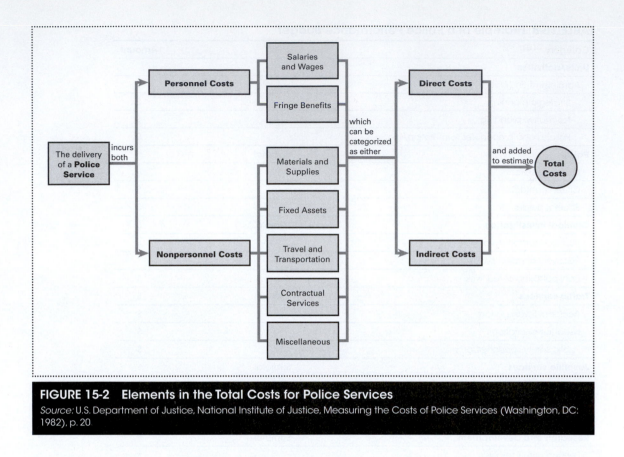

FIGURE 15-2 Elements in the Total Costs for Police Services
Source: U.S. Department of Justice, National Institute of Justice, Measuring the Costs of Police Services (Washington, DC: 1982), p. 20.

agency budgets, the selection of meaningful work units is difficult and sometimes irrational. How can a justice agency measure its successes? How can it count what does not happen?

The Program Budget

The best-known type of budget for monitoring the activities of an organization is the **program budget**, developed by the RAND Corporation for the U.S. Department of Defense. This format examines cost units as units of activity rather than as units and subunits within the organization. This budget becomes a planning tool; it demands justification for expenditures for new programs and for deleting old ones that have not met their objectives.

Police agencies probably have greater opportunities for creating new community-based programs than do the courts or corrections agencies. Some of these include crime prevention and investigation, drug abuse education, home security, selective enforcement (e.g., drunk driving) programs, and career development for personnel. Each of these endeavors requires instructional materials or special equipment, all of which must be budgeted. For example, traffic crash investigations (TCI) may be a cost area. The program budget emphasizes output measures. Outputs for TCI include the number of accidents handled and enforcement measures taken (such as citations issued, driving under the influence of alcohol and/or drugs (DUI) and other types of arrests made, and public safety speeches given). If the budget for these programs were divided by the units of output, the administrator could determine the relative cost for each unit of output or productivity. The cost of TCI, however, entails more than just the TCI unit; patrol and other support units also engage in this program.

Thus, the program budget is an extremely difficult form to execute and administer because it requires tracking the time of all personnel by activity as well as figuring in the cost of all support services and supplies. For this reason, criminal justice agencies rarely use the program budget.[51] Some advantages of the program budget, however, include its emphasis on the social utility of programs conducted by the agency; its clear relationship between policy objectives and expenditures; its ability to provide justification for and explanation of the budget; its establishment of a high degree of accountability; and its format and the wide involvement in formulating objectives, which lead employees at all levels of the organization to understand more thoroughly the importance of their roles and actions.[52]

Examples of police and court program budgets are presented in Tables 15-9 ■ and 15-10 ■, respectively.

TABLE 15-9 Example of a Police Program Budget

Program Area		Amount
Crime prevention	Subtotal	$
Salaries and benefits		$
Operating expenses		$
Capital outlay		$
Miscellaneous		$
Traffic crash investigation	Subtotal	$
Salaries and benefits		$
Operating expenses		$
Capital outlay		$
Miscellaneous		$
Traffic crash prevention	Subtotal	$
Salaries and benefits		$
Operating expenses		$
Capital outlay		$
Miscellaneous		$
Criminal investigation	Subtotal	$
Salaries and benefits		$
Operating expenses		$
Capital outlay		$
Miscellaneous		$
Juvenile delinquency prevention	Subtotal	$
Salaries and benefits		$
Operating expenses		$
Capital outlay		$
Miscellaneous		$
Special investigations	Subtotal	$
Salaries and benefits		$
Operating expenses		$
Capital outlay		$
Miscellaneous, Etc.		$

TABLE 15-10 Example of a Court's Program Budget

Program Area		Amount
Adjudicate criminal cases	Subtotal	$
Adjudicate felony cases	Total	$
Adjudicate misdemeanor appeals	Total	$
Adjudicate civil cases	Subtotal	$
Adjudicate major civil cases	Total	$
Adjudicate minor civil cases	Total	$
Adjudicate domestic relations cases	Total	$
Adjudicate juvenile cases	Subtotal	$
Adjudicate delinquency and dependent and neglect cases	Total	$
Adjudicate crimes against juveniles	Total	$
Provide alternatives to adjudication	Subtotal	$
Divert adult offenders	Total	$
Divert juvenile offenders	Total	$
Provide security	Subtotal	$
Handle prisoner transport	Total	$
Provide courtroom security	Total	$

Source: U.S. Department of Justice, National Institute of Law Enforcement and Criminal Justice, *Financial Management* (Washington, DC: The American University, 1979), p. 41.

PPBS and ZBB Formats

General Motors used the PPBS as early as in 1924,[53] and the RAND Corporation contributed to its development in a series of studies dating from 1949.[54] By the mid-1950s, several states were using it, and Secretary Robert McNamara introduced PPBS into the Defense Department in the mid-1960s.[55] By 1971, a survey revealed, however, that only 28 percent of the cities and 21 percent of the counties contacted had implemented PPBS or significant elements of it,[56] and in 1971 the federal government announced that it was discontinuing its use.

PPBS is a decision-making tool that links the program under consideration to the ways and means of facilitating the program. It is thus "a long-term planning tool, better informing decision makers of the future implications of their actions, and is typically most useful in capital projects."[57] PPBS treats the three basic budget processes—planning, management, and control—as coequals. It was predicated on the primacy of planning.[58] This future orientation transformed budgeting from an annual ritual into a "formulation of future goals and policies."[59] The PPBS budget featured a program structure, ZBB, the use of cost-budget analysis to distinguish among alternatives, and a budgetary horizon, often 5 years.[60]

Associated with PPBS, the zero-based planning and budgeting process requires managers to justify their entire budget request in detail rather than simply to refer to budget amounts established in previous years.[61] That is, each year, all budgets begin at zero and must justify any funding. Following Peter Phyrr's use of ZBB at Texas Instruments, Governor Jimmy Carter adopted it in Georgia in the early 1970s and then as president implemented it in the federal government for fiscal year 1979. An analysis of this experience at the Department of Agriculture indicates that although its use saved $200,000 in the department's budget, it costs at least 180,000 labor hours of effort to develop.[62]

It is important to note that few organizations have budgets that are purely one format or another; therefore, it is not unusual to find that because of time, tradition, and personal preferences, a combination of several formats is used.

IN THEIR OWN WORDS

ADMINISTRATIVE ADVICE FROM THE FIELD

Name: Terri Genin

Current Position/City/State: Finance Manager, Madison Police Department/Madison/WI

College attended/academic major/degree(s): University of Illinois/Nursing/B.S.N.

My primary duties and responsibilities in this position include: development, analysis, and management of the $63,500,000 annual police operating budget, oversight of payroll and purchasing functions, and management of multiple state and federal grants. Responsibilities also include serving on the Department's Management Team and providing professional analytical expertise in the Department's strategic planning efforts.

Personal attributes/characteristics that have proven to be most helpful to me in this position are: creativity combined with the ability to breakdown plans into small components that are more readily funded than large initiatives.

My three greatest challenges in this administrative role include:

1. Police organizations rotate command level employees on a regular basis. This rotation often results in commanders with limited financial skills that have responsibility for obtaining and managing various resources, including finances. The end result is a constant need to be training police command staff in how to be successful in managing money and obtaining support for their initiatives.

2. Elected officials often have an extremely unrealistic point of view in regards to what a Police Department can do to adapt to dwindling financial resources. It is very challenging to clearly explain what is realistically possible without creating barriers for future needs. In addition, the constant focus of elected officials on "boots on the street" often

results in lack of resources for critical support areas, such as technology, which are necessary for officers to be effective in their work.

3. The ongoing environment of annual budget cuts has created considerable challenges in all aspects of policing. Officers and other police employees are continually being asked to provide more service with less resource options. This can often result in competition for resources and an increased level of frustration as highly motivated employees are limited in providing optimal service by a lack of funds.

Personal accomplishments during my administrative career about which I am most proud are: (1) coordinating the transition of payroll and scheduling from paper to a computerized system; (2) developing clear, concise reporting systems to effectively provide information to elected officials so that they have developed confidence in, and an understanding of, how police overtime is utilized. This has eliminated considerable acrimony and provided a framework for authorization to implement new initiatives; (3) updating grant tracking systems so that numerous federal and state grants are coordinated across several disciplines and audit reviews have resulted in positive feedback.

Advice for someone who is interested in occupying an administrative position such as mine would be: get to know rank and file employees, as they often have great information about potential improvements and/or new possibilities. Listen well and ask a lot of questions so that you are well prepared to explain thoroughly when others raise questions of you. Be creative. There is often more than one way to obtain resources and/or needed support for programs and initiatives, so explore a wide variety of options and timelines to obtain resources. Sometimes very simple "fixes" are more helpful to an officer than complex programs and/or purchases. Take the time and effort to educate rank-and-file officers on process and limitations as they relate to administrative functions, as this will result in greater "buy in" and reduced frustration.

▶ Potential Pitfalls in Budgeting

The Need for Budgeting Flexibility

Ancient Greek mythology tells of a highwayman named Procrustes who had an iron bedstead. He measured all who fell into his hands on the bed. If they were too long, their legs were lopped off to fit it. If they were too short, they were stretched to fit the bed. Few criminal justice administrators have not seen their monies and programs laid out on the Procrustean bed of a state or municipal budget officer and lopped off.

It, therefore, becomes imperative to build as much flexibility into the planned program and budget as possible. One technique is to make up three budgets: an optimistic one, reflecting the ideal level of service to the jurisdiction and organization; an expected one, giving the most likely level of service that will be funded; and finally, one that will provide a minimum level of service.[63]

To maximize the benefits of using budgets, managers must be able to avoid major pitfalls, which, according to Samuel Certo,[64] include the following:

1. Placing too much emphasis on relatively insignificant organizational expenses. In preparing and implementing a budget, managers should allocate more time to deal with significant organizational expenses and less time for relatively insignificant ones. For example, the amount of time spent on developing and implementing a budget for labor costs typically should be more than the amount of time spent on developing and implementing a budget for office supplies.

2. Increasing budgeted expenses year after year without adequate information. Perhaps the best-known method developed to overcome this potential pitfall is ZBB.[65]

3. Ignoring the fact that budgets must be changed periodically. Administrators must recognize that factors such as the cost of materials, new technology, and demands for services are constantly changing and that budgets should reflect that by being reviewed and modified periodically. The performance budget (discussed earlier) is designed to assist in determining the level of resources to be allocated for each organizational activity.

Common Cost and Waste Problems

Now more than ever, given the challenges posed by the recent economic downturn, it is imperative that administrators must be able to identify areas where waste and costs might be controlled. Louise Tagliaferri[66] identified 14 common cost factors that can be found in most organizations. Note that some costs are uncontrollable, but others can be reduced or at least maintained within a reasonable range:

absenteeism and turnover

accident loss

direct and indirect labor

energy

maintenance

materials and supplies

overtime

paperwork

▼

planning and scheduling

product quality

productivity

tools and equipment

transportation

waste

Tagliaferri also noted that "literally billions of dollars are lost to industry (and criminal justice!) each year through carelessness, inattention, inefficiency, and other cost problems."[67]

Summary

This chapter focused on the very important area of financial administration, primarily budgeting, and included its elements, formats, and potential pitfalls. Emphases were placed on the effects of the recent Great Recession besetting all states, as well as the need for administrators to develop new means of cutting costs (while maintaining public safety) as well as skill in budget formulation and execution.

This chapter also discussed the budget process and different types of budgets. No single budgeting format is best; through tradition and personal preference, a hybrid format normally evolves in an organization. Nor should an administrator, under normal circumstances, surrender control of the organization's budget to another individual or body; the budget is integral to planning, organizing, and directing programs and operations.

Clearly, in these times of fiscal exigency, the justice administrator should attempt to become knowledgeable about, and recommend, sound means for reducing expenditures through changes in policy.

Key Terms and Concepts

Audit 372
Budget 365
Budget cycle 366
Budget execution 372
Budget formulation 367

Expenditure 367
Fiscal year 366
Grant writing 364
Great Recession 360
Line-item budget 373

Performance budget 373
Planning–programming–budgeting system (PPBS) 373
Program budget 378
Zero-based budget (ZBB) 373

Questions for Review

1. In what major ways did the recent financial crisis that blanketed this country affect the United States? Police agencies? Courts? Corrections organizations?
2. What measures have these three criminal justice components taken to cope with budget shortfalls?
3. What is a budget? How is it used?
4. What is a budget cycle? What is its importance in budgeting?
5. What is involved in formulating a budget? In its approval and execution?
6. List four budget formats used in the past. Which type is used most frequently? What are its major advantages and component parts?

▼

Deliberate and Decide

Brainstorming the Budget

Your city of 650,000 people and nearly 7,000 employees is in dire financial straits, with no end in sight unless bold actions are taken. The city council has held several public hearings to consider alternative courses of action to get out of the fiscal doldrums, but most such meetings result in very little agreement on how to resolve the problems.

Look at the following options that have been proposed and debated, and *determine the pros and cons and possible ramifications of each*, as well as the numbers of citizens who would be positively or negatively affected if implemented.

Questions for Discussion

1. Whether or not to lease 150 traffic speed cameras in school zones, which could generate $29 million in the first year alone.

2. Whether or not to terminate 350 city employees—about 5 percent of the total—from the city's payroll for a savings of about $25 million; or, alternatively, lay off 100 employees and offer voluntary buyouts for 300 employees for a total cost of $14 million; or simply let them leave or retire on their own terms, which would save $15 million.

3. Whether or not to restore a 4.6 percent pay cut taken from city employees 2 years ago, which would cost about $20 million.

4. Whether or not to eliminate vacant, nonpublic-safety positions ($2.6 million savings), reduce the materials and supplies budgets for all city divisions ($3.3 million savings), and reduce some health care expenses ($3.4 million).

5. Whether or not to raise property tax rates for all citizens.

6. Whether or not, as suggested by one council member, to discontinue other non-state mandated responsibilities, such as eliminating the police department and turn over those duties to the county sheriff's office.[68]

Learn by Doing

1. You are in the research and planning division of your state department of corrections. Fiscal issues are becoming a great concern as more state funding has been diverted to homeland security and court initiatives. Your director asks for some general ideas concerning what sorts of sentencing, treatment, parole, and prisoner re-entry programs are being developed in similarly strapped states. What kinds of information and examples will you provide?

2. You are an assistant sheriff and thus jail administrator in a county that has only raised the tax rate in recent years to pay for jail improvements required by state and federal authorities. However, your county now finds itself in dire financial straits, primarily because the fragile "no new taxes" and a "lock 'em up" mentality have finally combined to make fiscal matters extremely tenuous. Your judges are generally sympathetic, using a Jail Alternatives Program (intensive probation, a drug court and other options) for misdemeanants to the extent possible in order to save the cost of incarcerating and transporting jail inmates. It is estimated that these programs have reduced your jail population by more than 200 people. Now, however, one of the local judges seems bent on sentencing to jail anyone who is behind on child support payments—which accounts for around 150 people in the program. It becomes clear that this policy will soon cause the jail population to explode and break the county's jail budget. You know the judge personally. What will you do to save the county's jail budget?

Notes

1. Quoted in Charles R. Swanson, Leonard Territo, and Robert W. Taylor, *Police Administration: Structures, Processes, and Behavior,* 6th ed. (Upper Saddle River, NJ: Prentice Hall, 2005), p. 682.
2. Bureau of Labor Statistics, *The Great Recession of 2007–2009,* http://www.bls.gov/spotlight/2012/recession/pdf/recession_bls_spotlight.pdf (accessed November 26, 2014).
3. Andrea Louise Campbell and Michael W. Sances, "State Fiscal Policy during the Great Recession: Budgetary Impacts and Policy Responses," *Annals of the American Academy of Political & Social Science* 650(1) (November 2014):252–273.
4. Daniel J. Hall, "Reshaping the Face of Justice: The Economic Tsunami Continues," National Center for State Courts, http://www.ncsc.org/Information-and-Resources/Budget-Resource-Center/Analysis_Strategy/~/media/Files/PDF/Information%20and%20Resources/Budget%20Resource%20Center/Hall.ashx (accessed December 7, 2014).

5. Campbell and Sances, "State Fiscal Policy during the Great Recession: Budgetary Impacts and Policy Responses."

6. *U.S. Department of Justice, Office of Community Oriented Policing Services, The Impact of the Economic Downturn on American Police Agencie*s, October 2011, pp. 7, 9, http://www.cops.usdoj.gov/files/RIC/Publications/e101113406_Economic%20Impact.pdf (accessed December 8, 2014).

7. Bureau of Justice Statistics, *Census of State and Local Law Enforcement Agencies, 2008*, p. 4, http://www.bjs.gov/content/pub/pdf/csllea08.pdf (accessed December 8, 2014).

8. Joe Spurrier, "Police Academies Still Thriving despite Recession," Policeone.com, http://www.policeone.com/patrol-issues/articles/1961137-Police-academies-still-thriving-despite-recession/ (accessed December 8, 2014).

9. U.S. Department of Justice, Office of Community Oriented Policing Services, *The Impact of the Economic Downturn on American Police Agencie*s, p. 2.

10. Ted Olson, quoted in National Center for State Courts, "Budget Resource Center," http://www.ncsc.org/information-and-resources/budget-resource-center.aspx; also see National Center for State Courts, *Crisis in the Courts: Reconnaissance and Recommendations*, 2012, http://www.ncsc.org/sitecore/content/microsites/future-trends-2012/home/Better-Courts/1-2-Crisis-in-the-Courts.aspx (accessed November 8, 2014).

11. James Podgers, "End of Round Two: Progress in Raising Awareness about Funding Crisis in State Courts," *ABA Journal* 98(8) (August 2012), http://0-search.proquest.com.innopac.library.unr.edu/docview/1032541397/fulltext/14234C8D47E7BBB9086/26?accountid=452; also see Marie Gottschalk, "Cell Blocks & Red Ink: Mass Incarceration, the Great Recession & Penal Reform," *Daedalus* (Summer 2010):62 (accessed December 8, 2014).

12. American Bar Association, *Task Force on Preservation of the Justice System: Report to the House of Delegates* (2011) http://www.micronomics.com/articles/aba_report_to_the_house_of_delegates.pdf (accessed November 8, 2014).

13. National Center for State Courts, "As Budget Woes Persist, NCSC Helps Courts Redesign to Save Money," http://www.ncsc.org/services-and-experts/court-reengineering.aspx (accessed November 11, 2014).

14. Carl Nink, Stephen MacDonald, and Robert T. Jones, "New Correctional Models: How the Budget Crisis is Reshaping Corrections," *Criminal Justice Research Review* 13(3) (January/February 2012):38–44.

15. F.R. Baumgartner and B. D. Jones, *Agendas and Instability in American Politics* (Chicago, IL: University of Chicago Press, 2009).

16. Gottschalk, "Cell Blocks & Red Ink: Mass Incarceration."

17. Randall T. Shepard, "The Great Recession as a Catalyst for More Effective Sentencing," *Federal Sentencing Reporter* 23(2) (December 2010):146–149.

18. See Bureau of Justice Assistance, "The BJA Grant Writing and Management Academy," https://www.bja.gov/gwma/index.html (accessed November 8, 2014).

19. Bureau of Justice Assistance, "Drug Court Discretionary Grant Program for United States Substance Abusers," https://www.bja.gov/Publications/2014NADCP-BJApresentation.pdf; also see: http://grants.ojp.usdoj.gov:85/selector/awardDetail?awardNumber=2010-DD-BX-0537&fiscalYear=2010&applicationNumber=2010-H8086-NJ-D1&programOffice=BJA&po=BJA; ibid., "Drug Court Discretionary Grant Program," https://www.bja.gov/ProgramDetails.aspx?Program_ID=58 (accessed November 7, 2014).

20. Office of Justice Programs, "About Us," http://www.ojp.gov/about/about.htm (accessed November 7, 2014).

21. Pubic Law No. 113-4.

22. Office on Violence Against Women, "VAWA 2014 Summary: Changes to OVW-Administered Grant Programs," http://www.ovw.usdoj.gov/docs/vawa-2014-sum.pdf (accessed November 8, 2014).

23. *Federal Register* 76 (8) (January 12, 2011):2136, http://www.ojjdp.gov/funding/FY11OJJDPProposedPlan.pdf (accessed November 8, 2014).

24. Shepard, "The Great Recession as a Catalyst for More Effective Sentencing," p. 148.

25. Patricia Caruso, "Operating a Corrections System in a Depressed Economy: How Michigan Copes," *Corrections Today* 72(1) (February 2010):36–39.

26. Nink, et al., "New Correctional Models: How the Budget Crisis Is Reshaping Corrections," p. 40.

27. James C. Snyder, "Financial Management and Planning in Local Government," *Atlanta Economic Review* (November–December 1973):43–47.

28. Aaron Wildavsky, *The Politics of the Budgetary Process,* 2nd ed. (Boston: Little, Brown, 1974), pp. 1–4.

29. Orin K. Cope, "Operation Analysis—The Basis for Performance Budgeting," in *Performance Budgeting and Unit Cost Accounting for Governmental Units* (Chicago: Municipal Finance Officers Association, 1954), p. 8.

30. Lester R. Bittel, *The McGraw-Hill 36-Hour Management Course* (New York: McGraw-Hill, 1989).

31. Ibid., p. 187.

32. Robert Townsend, *Further Up the Organization: How to Stop Management from Stifling People and Strangling Productivity* (New York: Alfred A. Knopf, 1984), p. 2.

33. Roland N. McKean, *Public Spending* (New York: McGraw-Hill, 1968), p. 1

34. S. Kenneth Howard, *Changing State Budgeting* (Lexington, KY: Council of State Governments, 1973), p. 13.

35. Michael C. Thomsett, *The Little Black Book of Budgets and Forecasts* (New York: AMACOM, American Management Association, 1988), p. 38.

36. Quoted in V. A. Leonard and Harry W. More, *Police Organization and Management,* 7th ed. (Mineola, NY: Foundation Press, 1987), p. 212.

37. Swanson et al., *Police Administration*, p. 693.

38. Adapted, with some changes, from Wildavsky, *Politics of the Budgetary Process,* pp. 63–123.

39. Lennox L. Moak and Kathryn W. Killian, *A Manual of Techniques for the Preparation, Consideration, Adoption, and Administration of Operating Budgets* (Chicago: Municipal Finance Officers Association, 1973), p. 5, with changes.

40. Lennis M. Knighton, "Four Keys to Audit Effectiveness," *Governmental Finance* 8 (September 1979):3.

41. The Comptroller General of the United States, *Standards for Audit of Governmental Organizations, Programs, Activities, and Functions* (Washington, DC: General Accounting Office, 1972), p. 1.

42. Ibid.

43. Peter F. Rousmaniere (ed.), *Local Government Auditing* (New York: Council on Municipal Performance, 1979), Tables 1 and 2, pp. 10, 14.

44. Swanson et al., *Police Administration,* p. 707.

45. Allen Schick, *Budget Innovation in the States* (Washington, DC: Brookings Institution, 1971), pp. 14–15. Schick offers 10 ways in which the line-item budget fosters control.

46. Malchus L. Watlington and Susan G. Dankel, "New Approaches to Budgeting: Are They Worth the Cost?" *Popular Government* 43 (Spring 1978):1.

47. Jesse Burkhead, *Government Budgeting* (New York: Wiley, 1956), p. 11.

48. Larry K. Gaines, John L. Worrall, Mittie D. Southerland, and John E. Angell, *Police Administration,* 2nd ed. (New York: McGraw-Hill, 2003), p. 519.

49. Swanson et al., *Police Administration,* p. 710.

50. Ibid, p. 711.

51. Gaines et al., *Police Administration,* p. 519.

52. Ibid.

53. David Novick (ed.), *Program Budgeting* (New York: Holt, Rinehart and Winston, 1969), p. xxvi.

54. Ibid., p. xxiv.

55. Council of State Governments, *State Reports on Five-Five-Five* (Chicago: Author, 1968).

56. International City Management Association, *Local Government Budgeting, Program Planning and Evaluation* (Washington, DC: Author, 1972), p. 7.

57. Democracy Arsenal, "Increasing Our Security by Cutting Military Spending," http://www.democracyarsenal. org/2010/05/increasing-our-security-by-cutting-military-spending.html (accessed April, 2014).

58. Allen Schick, "The Road to PPBS: The Stages of Budget Reform," *Public Administration Review* 26 (December 1966):244.

59. Ibid.

60. Swanson et al., *Police Administration,* p. 712.

61. Peter A. Phyrr, "Zero-Base Budgeting," *Harvard Business Review* (November–December 1970):111–121; see also E. A. Kurbis, "The Case for Zero-Base Budgeting," *CA Magazine* (April 1986):104–105.

62. Joseph S. Wholey, *Zero-Base Budgeting and Program Evaluation* (Lexington, MA: Lexington Books, 1978), p. 8.

63. Donald F. Facteau and Joseph E. Gillespie, *Modern Police Administration* (Upper Saddle River, NJ: Prentice Hall, 1978), p. 204.

64. Samuel C. Certo, *Principles of Modern Management: Functions and Systems,* 4th ed. (Boston: Allyn & Bacon, 1989), pp. 484–485.

65. George S. Minmier, "Zero-Base Budgeting: A New Budgeting Technique for Discretionary Costs," *Mid-South Quarterly Business Review* 14 (October 1976):2–8.

66. Louise E. Tagliaferri, *Creative Cost Improvement for Managers* (New York: Wiley, 1981), p. 7.

67. Ibid., p. 8.

68. Adapted from Toby Sells, "City Council Budget Meeting: Lots of Ideas, No Easy Solutions," Scripps International Paper Group–Online, June 18, 2014, http://www.commercialappeal.com/news/2014/jun/18/city-council-budget-meeting-lots-of-ideas-no/ (accessed October 2, 2014); also see Linda Moore, "Memphis' Financial Woes Impact All of Shelby County," Scripps International Paper Group – Online, June 18, 2014, https://www.commercialappeal.com/news/2014/jun/18/memphis-financial-woes-impact-all-of-shelby/?print=1 (accessed October 14, 2014).

Maksim Kabakou/shutterstock

16   Technologies and Tools: In an Era of Big Data and "The Cloud"

LEARNING OBJECTIVES

After reading this chapter, the student will be able to:

❶ *describe what is meant by "big data" and "cloud computing"*

❷ *discuss uses of new databases in criminal justice agencies*

❸ *explain new police technologies, to include what the Federal Bureau of Investigation and other agencies are doing with criminal justice information systems*

❹ *explain the nature of electronic court records*

❺ *review how video and tracking devices, mobile electronics, telemedicine, and other technologies are assisting in correctional facilities*

❻ *delineate dangers may be looming on the horizon with 3-D printers*

A popular government without popular information or the means of acquiring it, is but a prologue to a farce, or a tragedy, or perhaps both.
—*James Madison*

However far modern science and technics [sic] have fallen short of their inherent possibilities, they have taught mankind at least one lesson: Nothing is impossible.
—*Lewis Mumford*

▶ Introduction

It is almost impossible to comprehend the extent to which the power of computers and the Internet have developed over time—and are predicted to continue to advance in only a few years. As examples: by 2020 the number of Internet users will reach almost 5 billion—equal to the entire world's population in 1987 (compared with 1.7 billion users in 2010 and only 360 million in 2000). Memory cards have shrunk in size to where it is now possible to store 32 gigabytes of data on a small device weighing 0.5 grams; soon the ability of such cards to store memory will even exceed that of the human brain. In sum, Moore's law—stating that the number of transistors that can be placed inexpensively on an integrated circuit doubles approximately every 2 years—has continued in an even and predictable curve for about half a century, and is expected to continue beyond 2020.[1] Computers that can see, hear, smell, taste, and translate are here, or soon will be here; just over the horizon is the day they will be capable of predicting colds, creating healthy food recipes, translating baby talk, and duplicating the feel of textures. IBM's supercomputer and "Jeopardy" champion, Watson, even demonstrated that computers are capable of learning from interactions with data and humans.[2]

The affordability, implementation, application, and training in uses of new technologies will be challenging for many criminal justice agencies. And certainly their use and related policy considerations will have to be consistent with the agency's overall goals and philosophy.

This chapter discusses many of those technologies, as well as some of those policy issues and other concerns. To begin, we briefly examine the relatively new concepts of "big data" and "cloud computing," including how they apply and what they bode for criminal justice administration. Following those discussions is an overview of new databases that have been developed for a variety of justice-related purposes.

Then we begin examining a number of technological developments in the three criminal justice subsystems *per se*. Because policing is where the bulk of technological research, development, use, and policy application and management has occurred, we will largely focus on that component and begin by examining selected developments in this field (e.g., license plate readers, body-worn video cameras, "hot buttons" in schools, bait cars). Also included are related developments and/or concerns with drones, robotics, and smartphones. Next we review what appears to be the major impetus in the courts: the movement toward electronic court records. Finally, the field of corrections is examined, including what is being done with inmate management using video cameras and tracking devices, how inmates can benefit from mobile devices, corrections' use of social media, and the expanding field of telemedicine.

After a brief "warning shot" concerning the imminent uses of plastic guns due to 3D printers, the chapter concludes with review questions, "deliberate and decide" problems, and "learn by doing" exercises. Six exhibits in this chapter expand on this chapter's technologies and their uses.

▶ Big Data: Definition and Application

big data applying tremendous computing power to massive and often highly complex sets of information.

Criminal justice now finds itself in the era of what has been termed "**big data**." There is considerable confusion about how the term is defined, but Microsoft deems it as being "the process of applying serious computing power—the latest in machine learning and artificial intelligence—to seriously massive and often highly complex sets of information."[3] What does seem abundantly clear is that we live in a world that is highly connected where people are deluged with data, and everything involving technology—from social media, all manner of infrastructure, and private and governmental operations and transactions—moves with the speed of light. The world has become overwhelmed by data, and we have only touched the proverbial tip of the iceberg. Studies indicate that 90 percent of the data in the world today were acquired in the past 18 months, and that we will double this vast store every 18 months for the foreseeable future. It is also estimated that we generate 2.5 quintillion bytes of data each day.[4] Perhaps the essence of big data lies therein: i.e., with this much information and knowledge, we must seek to find patterns, make predictions, and be better informed criminal justice administrators and managers so that our organizations can function more effectively, efficiently, and equitably.

One way to view the use of Big Data as it is applied to law enforcement is to consider the Law Enforcement National Data Exchange (**N-DEx**)—a service launched after 9/11 and provided free of charge by the Federal Bureau of Investigation (FBI) to assist agencies in making data correlations and in predictive policing.

Specifically, N-DEx is a 10-terabyte data warehouse and a cloud service, capable of processing criminal information and returning results in fractions of a second over secure Internet links. It comprises roughly 200 million law enforcement records and more than 1.5 billion data points. N-DEx uses a simple traffic light model to specify permissions—green indicates anyone on N-DEx is allowed to see the information, yellow indicates a point of contact at the agency for accessing relevant information, and red means the information is not available to N-DEx users.[5]

Users mine N-DEx data in two ways. First, using a web interface that the FBI provides, agencies can search records to scour information. The second N-DEx search engine performs correlation and resolution analysis. Within each record are what are termed entities—people, places, things, or events—that are tagged by the originating agency; algorithms are used to find relationships among entities. In other words, N-DEx provides the agency with the ability to tell whether a person identified in an offense report by a law enforcement (Agency A) is really the same person who was encountered 2 years ago by Agency B. Police personnel can basically press a button and get a composite biography, a geographical view of where certain incidents occurred, a link to all the person's relationships, and a link to a timeline of the person's different encounters.[6]

> **N-DEx** a service launched after 9/11 by the Federal Bureau of Investigation to assist agencies in making data correlations and in predictive policing.

▶ Cloud Computing

Today it is quite costly to keep all employees technologically up-to-date, especially given the rapid advances in computer hardware. In addition, the costs of software, licenses, and other related needs are daunting. Imagine, however, rather than installing all that is needed for every employee's computer, only having to load one application that allows employees to log into a web-based service that contains all of the programs needed to perform for his or her job. In addition, remote machines owned by another company operate everything from e-mail to word processing to complex data analysis programs.

This is now happening in what is called cloud computing—an industry that involves computer networking. It is estimated to grow at an annual rate of about 30 percent, reaching $270 billion by 2020, and predicted to change the entire computer industry.[7]

How It Works

Most people have probably had experience working with the cloud; indeed, anyone who has an e-mail account with a web-based e-mail service (e.g., Hotmail, Yahoo!, or Gmail) has been involved with cloud computing.[8]

Cloud computing—which, like big data, can be difficult to define—is basically the use of a network of remote servers hosted on the Internet to store, manage, and process data,

> **cloud computing** using a network of remote servers hosted on the Internet to store, manage, and process data, rather than a local server or a personal computer.

rather than a local server or a personal computer.[9] In fact, all that is required of the user's computer is the ability to run the cloud computing system's interface software, and the cloud's network takes care of the rest. The applications of cloud computing are thus practically limitless. Imagine, for example, a terrorist attack, where the need for computing resources skyrockets. The cloud is capable of providing this kind of service within minutes, while prioritizing the most urgent tasks and performing a tenfold increase in computing processes.[10] Some agencies will also employ cloud computing for such administrative functions as personnel management, training, customer relations, and vehicle maintenance. Interestingly, the greatest benefits of the cloud may be to smaller agencies, which typically cannot afford to acquire and maintain their own computer systems; for them, the concept of cloud computing may be quite attractive.[11]

Rationales for Its Use

Why would anyone want to rely on another computer system to run programs and store data? Following are several reasons:

1. Users can access their applications and data from anywhere, at any time: Users are not limited to doing work that is confined to a hard drive on one's own computer.

2. Hardware and software costs are reduced: No longer does one require a fast computer with huge memory, because the cloud system takes care of those needs.

3. Space is saved: Cloud computing allows individuals, government agencies, and corporations the ability to store data on someone else's hardware, thereby removing the need for physical space on the front end.

4. Costs of IT support are reduced: With streamlined, heterogeneous hardware, there are fewer problems.

5. Greater processing power is realized: The client sends an application to the cloud for processing, and the cloud system uses all the processing power of all available computers, significantly speeding up the calculation.[12]

There are about 10 major corporations that have invested in cloud computing and offer individuals and businesses a range of cloud-based solutions.[13] [For a list of the top 150 players in cloud computing, see the Cloud Computing Journal website, at: http://cloudcomputing.sys-con.com/node/770174.]

Some Concerns

Certainly cloud computing technologies offer a number of potential benefits to criminal justice and other government agencies (with 54% of police agencies reporting that they had implemented or were planning or considering implementing cloud-based solutions by 2015 for records storage and crime analysis, reporting, and mapping).[14] At its essence, however, cloud computing involves those same agencies handing over important data to another company for storage. This raises concerns among many people in terms of the company's security and privacy. Therefore, given the delicate nature of criminal justice data and information, in 2013 the International Association of Chiefs of Police (IACP) issued the following guidelines:

- Services provided by a cloud service provider must comply with the requirements of the Federal Bureau of Investigation's Criminal Justice Information Services (CJIS) Security Policy. [This policy may be viewed in its entirety at: http://www.fbi.gov/about-us/cjis/cjis-security-policy-resource-center/view; in August 2012, the FBI also published a technical report, *Recommendations for Implementation of Cloud Computing Solutions,* available at: http://www.fbi.gov/about-us/cjis/CJIS%20Cloud%20Computing%20 Report_20121214.pdf].

- Law enforcement agencies should ensure that they retain ownership of all data; this includes all text, numerical data, database records, media files, demographic information, search history, geo-location information, meta data, or any other data and information. No such data should be released to any third party without proper and timely notification made to the data owner.

- Law enforcement agencies should ensure that the cloud service provider does not mine or otherwise process or analyze data for any purpose not explicitly authorized by the agency (to include advertising, product improvement, or other commercial purposes).

- Upon request, the cloud service provider should conduct, or allow the law enforcement agency to conduct audits of the cloud service provider's performance.

- The cloud service provider must maintain the physical or logical integrity of law enforcement data, and any data used for evidentiary purposes must be maintained so as to allow the law enforcement agency to establish a clear and precise chain of custody.[15]

▶ New Databases: Criminal Justice Assets

In a related vein, discussed next are a number of relatively new databases that exist to serve the criminal justice system in various capacities.

- At the National Center for Missing and Exploited Children (NCMEC), forensic imaging specialists are re-creating images of what a child may have looked like based on skull and bone remains. NCMEC then assists law enforcement investigators by using the bones and skulls as a template for re-creating the image of the deceased's face. A 3D picture of what the deceased may have looked like enhances the chances of someone's recognizing and identifying the individual.[16]

- More than 80 police agencies in the Courts and Law Enforcement Management Information Systems (CLEMIS) Consortium are better able to analyze crime trends and deploy resources with a new system that acts as a mobile workstation. The system includes seven data sets, including: arrestees, citations, crashes, incidents, offenses, parolees, and sex offenders. The system can warn officers of prior incidents at a particular address, quickly run license plate numbers, or match a set of fingerprints to a mug shot; officers can thus make more warrant arrests, recover more stolen vehicles, and improve the quality and accuracy of field reports.[17]

Exhibit 16.1 discusses predictive analytics.

EXHIBIT 16.1

PREDICTIVE ANALYTICS

Police at Arlington Cemetery in northern Virginia stopped a suspicious individual as he wandered among the veterans' white gravestones. The man was actually a highly sought-after sniper who had recently fired multiple rounds at the Pentagon, the Marine Corps Museum, and Marine Corps and Coast Guard recruiting stations.

The police encounter with this man was no accident: His behavioral profile had been mapped using predictive analytics—data concerning his previous shootings were analyzed with a special software model, so that night in Arlington, the police were able to catch the sniper in exactly the kind of location the model had

(Continued)

predicted: near a place of military significance, with long lines of sight, and close to a major highway.

Predictive analytics of this sort have a long history in crime prevention, tracing back to New York City's CompStat program. Computing power has doubled every 40 months since the 1980s—and so, too, the ability to analyze vast quantities of data and predict future behavior. Such data analytics now provide a management solution that allows the police to do more, and to do more with less. In sum, deploying resources more efficiently, anticipating the behavior of criminals, and estimating where crimes will occur before they do.[18]

In similar fashion, some agencies can predict where crimes are likely to occur in a geographic prediction box as small as 500 feet by 500 feet. For example, the Santa Cruz Police Department, beginning in 2011, reported a 27 percent reduction in burglaries that year and a 19 percent reduction in property theft by 2012. In Los Angeles, crimes were down 13 percent, compared with an increase of 0.4 percent elsewhere in the city.[19]

- In late 2012, Louisiana became the first state to initiate a ballistics database that allows investigators to match shell casings with a national database in order to solve crimes. As of late 2013, the database—called the National Integrated Ballistic Information Network (or NIBIN)—had linked 600 shootings using the database. At times, a criminal may use the same handgun in multiple crimes involving shootings; this database allows police to make such connections.[20]

- A new California database replaces pen-and-paper logs maintained by pawn shop owners and metal recyclers for tracking metal sales and thefts of copper wire from construction sites or vacant buildings. Pawn shop owners and recycled metal dealers will pay a yearly fee of $300 to be a licensed user, but the program will be cost-effective for those business owners by not having to maintain and store paper logs.[21]

- The FBI has begun collaborating with academia, private industry, and police agencies toward creating a tattoo database. Working with Michigan State University to develop biometric tattoo recognition technology, individuals will be matched with their tattoo images in a database. In many crimes, police do not have fingerprints or facial images of a suspect. However, if a robbery occurs, authorities can then develop a list of possible suspects based on the tattoo image to determine if the tattoo connected to a gang. Such a database could also help to identify possible terrorists and hate group organizations that have unique tattoos representing their organization.[22]

- Alabama prisons require all prison visitors to have their fingerprint scanned before entering, in order to verify they are who they say they are. These fingerprints are not stored in a database, but only used to verify identity at the door.[23]

- Police in Pennsylvania can access the state's Justice Network (JNET) for several purposes, including its facial recognition system, which allows police to compare images from sources such as surveillance footage and social media sites against a statewide criminal database containing 3.5 million photos. To broaden its facial recognition capabilities, JNET is also integrated with the state's department of transportation, which stores 36 million driver's license and identification photo images in a photo repository.[24]

- Many crime scenes involve the perpetrator's leaving behind shoe prints; however, even if located, lifted, and preserved, searching through images and catalogs to find a match and identify a footprint can take several days if not weeks or months. Now, however, software exists that contains about 24,000 types of shoes in its database and can reduce that time frame to 20 minutes.[25]

► Other Policing Technologies: Selected Examples

Certainly because of the nature of their work—and the ever-present specter of terrorism—the police have experienced the lion's share of criminal justice technological research and development. Following are some examples:

- Police departments are using cameras on patrol cars to scan and track the license plates of each vehicle they pass. Although such systems have been in use for at least a decade (primarily for locating stolen vehicles), they are now deployed for other purposes. As an example, patrol vehicles in the Greenwich, Connecticut, Police Department can scan up to 3,600 license plates per minute on all vehicles they pass; officers manually upload a list of local outstanding parking ticket warrants; expired, canceled, and suspended license plates; and a directory of wanted people.[26] [Note, however, that such expanded uses of license plate readers are being challenged in the courts; e.g., Wisconsin is considering a bill that would limit the technology's use by local and state agencies to only active criminal investigations of a suspect. Lawsuits against their use have been filed as well.][27]

- Arresting officers are now better equipped than ever to respond to citizens' complaints using videos of their own (and, indeed, sales of body cameras have increased dramatically since the August 2014 police shooting of Michael Brown, an unarmed, black teenager in Ferguson, Missouri); today's officer carries a video system on his or her body that can help keep them safer and more accountable while protecting them and their employing agencies from frivolous lawsuits. Some agencies are using ear-mounted video cameras that capture an officers' view of traffic stops and other incidents, which are activated when officers are on a call for service or at an incident. The video files must be stored, tracked, managed, and shared with prosecutors and defense attorneys during the discovery process if used as evidence; however, private companies now offer cloud-based storage as a solution to all of these needs.[28]

- A device is being tested that shoots a small GPS-equipped dart that attaches itself to a suspect's vehicle during a high-speed pursuit. The device—mounted on the front of the patrol car that includes a sighting device, a targeting device, and a deployment device inside the patrol car—allows officers to use a laser pointer to aim and shoot the dart, which attaches itself to the suspect's vehicle. Officers then track the vehicle's movement, while dispatchers monitor the vehicle's speed and location on a computer screen. Thus officers can follow pursued vehicles from a safer distance, and dispatchers can more safely deploy officers around the suspect's location once the vehicle stops.[29]

- Sending the police a crime tip via text message might seem "old news" at this point, but in reality it is still a relatively new practice. Residents in several states can now anonymously report a crime through an online system that accepts text messages. In Utah, for example, more than 50 police agencies utilize a program that allows the public to submit anonymous crime tips via texting through a smartphone app or online at the program's website. One of 14 such tips results in an arrest. Dallas, Texas, police launched a similar program to allow citizens to report crimes or suspicious behavior that could possibly be linked to terrorism.[30]

- Strip searches conducted at jails for drugs and other contraband typically require about 15 minutes' time; furthermore, some states require a court order before a body-cavity search can be performed. Strip searches now, however, use full-body scanning technology and require only that arrestees remove their shoes and about seven seconds' time to identify any metallic or organic materials. The system, using a light beam, informs jail staff if anything looks out of place.[31]

- A simulated training program that monitors real-time decision making during critical incident drills is now used in 60 cities. It provides training for high-level, command staff officers in everything from crimes and terrorist attacks to natural disasters, press briefings, meeting with victims' families, and community forums. Trainees are divided into incident management teams, which are given a stream of information. Once the exercise is ended, everyone is brought in for debriefing and the team's decisions are discussed.[32]

- QR (for "Quick Response") codes are gaining in use and utility round the world. Similar to the barcodes used by retailers, QR codes are two-dimensional and can hold thousands of alphanumeric characters of information. When a QR code is scanned with a camera-enabled smartphone, the user can link to digital content on the web and activate a number of other functions. Police in Vancouver, Canada, are using QR codes obtain crime clues, tips, and leads. Some cities in Texas are seeking to reduce drunk driving, display posters with QR codes that can be scanned by a smartphone, and then direct the user to a mobile site called "Choose Your Ride."[33]

- A baited cell phone and/or tablet is placed inside a vehicle in an "armed" mode and communicates with a cloud server, and police receive a text alert if the sensor on the phone detects motion. The bait captures a series of photos of the suspect and provides updated mapping information to the officer, who can begin tracking the suspect. Once an arrest is made, the prosecution and defense have access to the baited device's serial number, the date and time of the theft, GPS movement of the bait, and the photos captured. In Dayton, Ohio, after individuals who stole electronic bait were arrested, theft from vehicles in the precinct dropped by 75 percent, thus showing this tool also functions as a crime deterrent.

- Madison, Wisconsin, police understand that cellphones often contain information relevant to investigations (particularly those involving stalking, homicide, and drug trafficking and use). They use special equipment to extract data from cellphones, including text messages, call history, photos, or other data. Then, the MPD uses software to analyze the data. (Note, however, that the department only extracted such data if the cellphone or other device was obtained with a search warrant, or if a witness gave consent to have his or her cellphone information used for investigative purposes.)[34]

- The December 2012 shooting tragedy in Newtown, Connecticut, which resulted in the deaths of 26 elementary school students and staff members, launched serious discussion of a "hot button" policy in schools. The buttons, which cost about $5,000, are now ready to use and operate on a dedicated, direct line to police dispatchers. When the dispatcher receives a signal, all available units are sent to the school. The buttons will also make it easier for school staff to get in touch with the police when a 911 phone call might not be feasible. Police departments have conducted extensive training with school staff on proper usage of the buttons.

One potentially helpful tool once used by the police has been curtailed, however. In 2012 the U.S. Supreme Court[35] held that police attaching a Global Positioning System (GPS) device to a suspect's vehicle without a search warrant violates the Fourth Amendment. This decision will likely have its greatest effect on major narcotics investigations.

▶ Drones: Old Tech, New Concerns with Use and Privacy

In early 2014, the Federal Aviation Administration (FAA) announced that six states (Alaska, Nevada, New York, North Dakota, Texas, and Virginia) had been selected to develop test sites for drones (also termed unmanned aerial vehicles, or UAVs, which were discussed in

Chapter 6), representing a major step toward the development of unmanned aircraft in U.S. skies.[36] Certainly the potential abilities and uses of drones are well-known, expanding, and limited only by our imagination; however, related legal and policy questions remain that warrant national attention.

First, although the FAA currently forbids the operation of such aircraft in national air space, that will likely change soon: In early 2012 the Obama Administration began considering legislation that would require the FAA to devise ways to allow drones to share airspace with passenger planes within 3 years. In fact, it is predicted that 15,000 flying robots will be in the skies by 2020, and that number will double by 2030. Certainly as their costs continue to decline, more police agencies will be adopting drones, and state and local officials will have to draft ordinances and statutes for their use.[37]

Second, regarding privacy concerns, civil libertarians have raised questions about the potential for UAV use to violate citizens' rights, and at least 10 states are attempting to limit the use of the camera-equipped aircraft.[38] Advocates, however, argue that people have become accustomed to such monitoring, given the widespread use of cellphone cameras, parking lot videos, convenience store taping devices, and cameras mounted on street lights.[39] See Exhibit 16.2 for an example of a drone used to potentially commit a crime.

EXHIBIT 16.2

THE "DROPPING DRUGS FROM A DRONE" CAPER

Four people were arrested in Morgan, Georgia, in late 2013 after a prison corrections officer at Calhoun State Prison observed a small, six-rotor drone hovering over the prison yard, in what was apparently an attempt to drop contraband items to inmates. Soon after the officer's sighting, a vehicle was searched, with owner's consent, and found to contain a small helicopter-like device. Inside the device was approximately 2 pounds of a tobacco-like substance wrapped in plastic. Prison officials believe the suspects planned to call their intended inmates and arrange for a drop of the plastic-wrapped bundles.[40]

In late 2012, the IACP issued a national advisory for the use of drones, recommending that drones not be armed for purposes relating to domestic law enforcement (some drones use stun-gun projectiles, tear gas, and rubber balls from as high up as 300 feet). The IACP also recommends that police secure a search warrant prior to launching them for investigative purposes.[41]

▶ Robotics

Recent advances in **robotics**—a term for the branch of technology involving the design, construction, and function of robots—have allowed policing (and military service) to become much safer. Robots are now fitted with odor sensors, video capability, including night vision; a camera (also useful for photographing crime scenes); an electronic control device; and even the ability to engage in two-way communications.[42] Robots with 7-foot arms (that scan the inside and undercarriage of vehicles for bombs), lights, video cameras (that zoom and swivel), obstacle-hurling flippers, and jointed arms (that have hand-like grippers to disable or destroy bombs) are even relatively commonplace.

A recent application of such a robot for policing—which, it will be seen, may well have saved a number of lives—is discussed in Exhibit 16.3.

> **robotics** a branch of technology involving the design, construction, and function of robots.

POLICE USES OF ROBOTS

James Eagan Holmes stands accused of one of the worst mass shootings in American history for killing 12 people and wounding 58 at an Aurora, Colorado, movie theater on July 20, 2012 (during a late-night screening of a Batman movie). Holmes faces 141 felony charges.

After being arrested for the shootings, Holmes informed police that his apartment was booby-trapped, so local, state, and federal police officers, firefighters, and bomb-squad experts converged on Holmes's apartment to evacuate neighbors and search for additional evidence.

The officers' first action was to send in a bomb-removal robot to disarm a tripwire guarding the apartment's front door. The robot then neutralized potential explosive devices, incendiary devices and fuel found near the door. Next, the robot's camera—which revealed numerous containers with accelerants and trigger mechanisms—searched for computers or any other evidence to be removed before attempting to disarm additional explosives. Eventually, 30 aerial shells filled with gunpowder, 2 containers filled with liquid accelerants, and numerous bullets left to explode in the resulting fire were found in the apartment, which was obviously designed to kill whoever entered it. Evidence was collected and sent to the FBI laboratory's Terrorist Explosive Device Analytical Center in Quantico, Virginia. Later, another bomb-disposal robot was sent to a potentially related threat on the University of Colorado-Denver's medical campus in Aurora, where Holmes could have shipped some of the items used in the attack.[43]

▶ Smartphones: The Good and the Bad

Unquestionably, the spread and increasing sophistication of smartphones have been felt in policing. As examples, today's officers can point their phone at a particular location and, using the phone's GPS, check the arrest history or officer safety hazard information of the address in question. When looking for a missing child, an icon appears if any sex offenders are living nearby. The app can also track the location of police units, allowing the officer to determine distances of backup units.[44]

However, few police agencies can afford to buy all of their officers' smartphones or other mobile devices. Therefore, many agencies now have a **"bring your own device" (BYOD)** policy—one that allows employees to bring their personal mobile devices (laptops, tablets, and smart phones) to the workplace for accessing privileged agency information. In addition to the obvious cost savings, BYOD avoids the need to train employees in their use, enabling employees to use the devices that they are already comfortable in using. Added benefits include that BYOD can result in officers spending more time on the streets and less time in the office, giving them greater access to resources and communication when in the field.

However, there are several potential problems with BYOD, which have led to lawsuits and created a need for new policies. For example, a lawsuit filed against the city of Chicago could result in hundreds of thousands of dollars in overtime pay for the 200 officers in the class action suit, should they prevail. The officers claim the police department violated the Fair Labor Standards Act (FLSA, discussed in Chapter 3) by refusing to pay them for time they incurred due to working on their own time, checking work-related e-mails, voice mails, and text messages on their smartphones.[45] The officers/plaintiffs argue that, if the city wanted them to work while they were off-duty, then they should have been compensated for it.

This is where the need for new policies comes into play. According to human resources experts, following are some key elements that should be incorporated into such a policy, in order to prevent such as those alleged in the Chicago lawsuit:

- Provide information concerning what the agency considers to be acceptable business use of personal devices.

bring your own device (BYOD) a policy whereby employees may bring their personal mobile devices to their workplace and use those devices to access privileged agency information.

- Bar supervisors from sending messages to their subordinates after-hours (unless there is an urgent need to do so).

- Require that employees not perform after-hours work without their supervisor's approval.

- Have employees inform their supervisors of any off-hours work they perform (and ensure that the supervisors properly track that time).

- Make clear that employees are not to check for, or respond to work e-mail, voice mail, and texts after hours.

- Provide disciplinary measures that will be taken if the BYOD policy is violated.[46]

See Exhibit 16.4 for a case involving smartphones.

EXHIBIT 16.4

SMARTPHONES, INVESTIGATIONS, AND THE STORED COMMUNICATIONS ACT

In February 2001 a businessman was gunned down in Fort Lauderdale, Florida. The ensuing police investigation found no witnesses or physical evidence, but 4 years later the prosecutor charged three men with the murder. Evidence against the three suspects focused on the admissibility of two of the suspects' cell phone records—specifically, the location data contained in them (which placed two of the men within 500 feet of where the murder occurred). The defense argued that the use of such evidence violated the defendants' constitutional rights; however, the judge refused to suppress the cell phone records, citing federal law saying that cell phone users have no reasonable expectation of privacy in location information gathered by the police.[47]

This case points out the legal dilemmas and debates that are now posed by cell site location information (CSLI). The potential for assisting police investigations is undeniable. At issue, however, is whether or not, as smartphones have become more sophisticated, law enforcement, phone manufacturers, cell carriers, and software makers are exploiting users' personal privacy data without their knowledge.[48] At present, the Stored Communications Act,[49] enacted in 1986 as part (Title II) of the Electronic Communications Privacy Act of 1986, allows law enforcement access to electronic messages greater than 180 days old without a warrant (or, with a court order or subpoena, such access may be obtained for messages that are more than 180 days old). The government does not need to establish probable cause, but must only offer facts showing that the information sought is material to an ongoing criminal investigation.[50]

▶ Courts Technologies

The Problems: Paper, Space, and Time

Problems of paper, space, and time have always plagued the courts, being a major source of stress, cost, and inaccuracies. A typical case file—composed of documents from litigants, attorneys, judges, court staff, the clerk's office, and other officials—makes up the "official record" that governs everything that happens. Imagine thousands of such files being generated and filed per day in a single court. In the past, only one copy of the file would be available at a given time, and it would be needed for use by many people at the same time. In addition, paper records are subject to being lost, misfiled, and even defaced or stolen.

The Solution: Electronic Court Records

All of the above has led to **electronic court records** (ECR), where incoming documents are scanned and then processed using images rather than paper; then they are stored in an

> **electronic court records** where incoming documents are scanned, processed (using images rather than paper), and stored in an electronic document management system.

electronic document management system. Since the 1990s, "electronic filing" has been a primary topic for court conferences, product information, and publications. Many of today's courts have thus begun to do the following:

- Court support, with judges and court staff having access to the images, from the bench, chambers, and desktop.

- Connectivity, with this same electronic access being granted to prosecutors, defenders, and law enforcement.

- Electronic filing, with digital documents going directly to the clerk's electronic filing manager system, bypassing the need to scan them.

- Electronic records also being accessible to litigants and the public remotely via the Internet.

Exhibit 16.5 discusses benefits of electronic file sharing of court documents.

EXHIBIT 16.5

BENEFITS OF ELECTRONIC FILING OF COURT DOCUMENTS

Certainly electronic court records have revolutionized the way courts conduct business. For example, Manatee County, Florida, revealed a cost saving of almost $1,000,000 by e-filing their 2.3 million documents per year. Multiple users can simultaneously view documents from their workstations. King County (Washington), Oregon, Missouri, Colorado, and Orange County (California) have been trendsetters in this area, while large projects are underway in Iowa, Massachusetts, and Alabama, just to name a few. Following are some benefits that are being realized:

- Physical space savings. No longer is hundreds if not thousands of square feet of expensive courthouse floor space consumed by the storage of paper documents.

- Speed and ease of access to the electronic court documents. Files can potentially be accessed remotely from anywhere in the world, any time of day; literally thousands of pages of electronic copies can be downloaded to users' laptops for instant use and reference.

- Ease of maintenance and organization of the electronic files. Court staff no longer needs to roam through file rooms with carts to gather and organize file folders. Lost files are generally a thing of the past.

- Secure environment for court information. Documents are no longer stolen from the public viewing area. Electronic files can be encrypted with a password or more advanced security measures to limit their use.

- Environmentally friendly. Courts converting to electronic documents eliminate the need for literally tons of paper annually. Remote access to court documents also eliminates the need for users to physically drive to the courthouse, saving fuel and reducing carbon emissions.

- Built-in calendaring and scheduling capabilities. CA side benefit of electronic filing is that case tracking is automatically provided for stored documents, making justice much better served in a timely fashion.

- Data-entry time savings. With electronic documents being read by the computer system, a great deal of data-entry time is saved.

In a few years, simplified case summaries, judicial opinions, and audio recordings from all federal appellate and state supreme courts could be accessible at the touch of a button.

The Oyez Project at IIT Chicago-Kent College of Law will spearhead the effort, aggregating documents and media from courts in California, Florida, Illinois, New York, and Texas. When the project is complete, content will be more accessible to non-legal audiences, such as to journalists and the general public.

► Corrections Technologies

More Sophisticated Video Cameras and Tracking Devices

Advancements in video surveillance systems, along with **radio-frequency identification tracking (RFID)** devices that both inmates and correctional officers now wear for tracking purposes (discussed more later), combine to make prisons safer and require fewer correctional personnel for surveillance. Next these two developments are discussed briefly.

Today, many of the cameras used to monitor inmates are more sophisticated than those used by gas stations and shopping malls. These modern prison cameras are even bullet resistant and able to withstand both a beating by a sledgehammer and attempts by inmates to disable them during a fight or escape.[51]

In one such instance, in late 2013 the Los Angeles Sheriff's Office deployed 2,500 new, high-definition systems at eight correctional institutions and concurrently expanded its video surveillance and data storage system. When an incident occurs, officers can quickly identify all inmates who are involved and better understand what really happened. To store the large amounts of data collected by the video surveillance cameras, the department implemented a storage engine that can hold more than 3 petabytes and allows for rapid retrieval of the footage to help resolve both frivolous and legitimate claims.[52]

Regarding RFID devices, if an inmate wearing such a bracelet enters a prohibited area, an alarm will sound. RFID tracking also makes it easier to count prisoners, and prison staff can react quicker when inmates try to escape. They can also provide information on prisoners' movements and to alert staff if there is an unusual concentration of inmates in a certain area; such movement information can be stored for later analysis, and be helpful in investigations to determine which inmate was present in a specific part of a building at a particular time. Furthermore, officers wearing an RFID device on their belts find it can assist in determining which one of several hundred officers is closest in the event of an emergency.

A study of RFID devices by the RAND Corporation underscored the need for staff to be trained in the many uses of these devices; RAND concluded that:

> When used in its most basic capacity as a perimeter-control device, RFID technology does not deter inmates from committing violent or nonviolent acts of misconduct and may indeed increase violence in the short run. If, however, the system is used in its full capacity, RFID technology may well reduce sexual assault, related violence, and other prohibited acts in prison settings by increasing inmates' perceived risks of detection.[53]

Although more advanced tracking mechanisms exist, such as biometric devices that scan an inmate's iris or fingerprints, their cost is often prohibitive.

Inmates Benefit from Mobile Devices

Although mobile devices such as cell phones can get—and have increasingly gotten—into the hands of jail and prison inmates, allowing inmates to contact people outside of prison to organize crimes, commit illegal acts, and harass lawmakers and their victims' families,[54] positive uses for such devices are now being realized. For example, in mid-2013 Ohio began allowing jail inmates to purchase and use mini-tablet computers, to better connect them with their families and friends on the outside. At least six other states permit the practice. Proponents of the concept say it will deepen prisoners' ties to their communities while keep them up to speed with modern technology, while connecting them with educational opportunities—affording opportunities to do homework, study for their GED, learn to read

English, improve their math, and so on, as well as get access to such resources as anger management lessons.[55]

Generally, inmates or their family members purchase a cheap (around $50) mini-tablet that they use to send e-mails and listen to music (e-mails and any attachments can be monitored by the facility staff). It is also hoped that the program will help inmates transition into their communities by keeping them in contact with family and potential employers. Of course, tablets, like cellphones, can also breed criminal activity. In a case in early 2013, Baltimore City Detention Center guards were indicted for allegedly smuggling in cellphones to help the Black Guerrilla Family operate a drug gang.

Use of Telemedicine

telemedicine the use of telecommunications technology to remotely diagnosis and treat inmates.

Employing **telemedicine** in correctional facilities, which is the use of telecommunications technology to remotely diagnosis and treat inmates, has provided tremendous benefits. First, by providing remote inmate health consultations and treatment, the cost of transporting them to a medical facility is avoided. As state budgets contract and prisons become more crowded and older in nature, telemedicine is only expected to expand.

In June 2013 the Colorado Department of Corrections teamed with a Denver medical center to launch a pilot program using video conferencing for inmates who needed consultation. In Wyoming, where much of the state's population is remote and distant from medical facilities, telemedicine for prison inmates helps to address challenges of distance and distribution of doctors. Approximately 2,000 physician visits are conducted annually via remote connection. Similarly, the corrections department in Louisiana signed a contract to provide 17,000 annual checkups to thousands of inmates, increasing telemedicine by nearly 600 percent.[56]

Mental health services can also be provided to prisoners via mobile devices. Estimates are that a state can save $30,000 to $40,000 a month with such a system, which includes a voice platform, video software, and special videophones.

A program developed in Palm Bay, Florida, involving the police department and a trauma center, has even partnered to provide SWAT officers the ability to communicate virtually with trauma surgeons during high-risk incidents. Using a laptop or some other mobile device and a webcam, officers connect with the trauma center's secure servers. Trauma surgeons can rapidly look at the trauma injuries and give assistance to the tactical team, thus "seeing" the patient within minutes of when the injury occurred. Exhibit 16.6 discusses the benefits of telemedicine.

EXHIBIT 16.6

BENEFITS OF TELEMEDICINE

A study found that a telemedicine program led to nearly $1 billion in savings over a 10-year period, while also cutting back on emergency-room and doctor office visits by 70 percent, and reducing unnecessary medical tests by 45 percent. The program also significantly cut back on prison transports, which are expensive and dangerous, while allowing staff to see patients more often, including specialists (including at remote sites all across the state of Texas). Meanwhile, costs for the program have been reduced dramatically, from $1.2 million to $600 thousand per year, while the technology has been improved. The program has been expanded to include mental health screenings, hepatitis C screenings, orthopedic and urology care, and pain management. In addition, the system is linked to an electronic medical record system, which documents the complete patient medical chart information including lab results and physician notes.[57]

Another Use of Social Media

Police use of social media is fairly widely known; for example, if the police are looking for a suspect or wishing to put out a sort of community alert, they can easily send a message to their community followers via Facebook podcasts, blogs, and Twitter. Such abilities have not been lost on corrections, however. For example, in late 2013 the state of Kansas began using Facebook to arrest people who skip out on court-mandated parole. Each Monday, the Department of Corrections posts information about an offender who has failed to maintain contact with his or her parole officer. In addition, such individuals (known as absconders) have warrants issued for their arrest.[58]

▶ A Coming Conundrum: Plastic Guns

Any discussion of new and developing technologies must include mention of **3D printing**— the process whereby practically any 3D solid object can be made from a digital model, as layers of material are laid down in different shapes. Of greatest concern to criminal justice agencies is that the applications of this technology include the ability to make plastic guns and other illegal materials that can slip through metal detectors. The capabilities of such printers are now well-known: In May 2013 a Texas law student fired a plastic gun he had created with a 3D printer; he then posted the plans on a website, which received more than 100,000 hits before federal authorities were able to get the plans removed.

> **3D printing** a process whereby a solid object – including guns and other weapons - can be made from a digital model, as layers of material are laid down in different shapes.

On December 9, 2013, President Obama signed into law a bill that extends the ban on plastic firearms for another 10 years. The Undetectable Firearms Act makes illegal the "manufacture, import, selling, shipment, delivery, possession, transfer, or reception of any firearm that is not detectable by walk-through metal detectors, or has major components that do not generate an accurate image by airport X-ray machines."[59] However, 3D printing technology might soon render even these provisions as obsolete.

3D printing technology can create firearms that use digital blueprints and are made with polymers that are able to be brought into even the most restricted areas. 3D printing can also allow amateurs and virtually anyone with access to a printer to make guns in the privacy of their own home without requiring any components that can be detected by metal detectors.

One means of attempting to stem the tide of such guns is to require them to have at least one metal piece in order to fire. Any laws covering the manufacture of plastic guns without such a provision could render the legislation useless.

Certainly our society is only in the early phases of a 3D printing revolution, as there seems to be a new use for such printing every week. This technology bears close scrutiny, however, as we become more and more aware of its dark side; surely the criminals among us will be willing and able to devise new and dangerous applications for 3D-printed materials.

Summary

"Everything we do is driven by data." This is the new mantra of many criminal justice administrators, managers, and supervisors.

This relatively new state of affairs began in policing, which was long denigrated for its resistance to alter tradition (as some used to put it, like "bending granite") but is now (and will likely continue to be) engaged in rapid, dynamic change. Since 9/11 and the subsequent emphases on homeland security, the creation of Fusion Centers, and the inception of CompStat in the New York Police Department in 1995—as well as the Great Recession, enhanced accountability, the expansion and affordability of technologies, and the need to "do more with less"—change is now the norm.

Therefore, intelligence-led policing, predictive policing, and "smart policing" have become the order of the day. We are also seeing these same approaches spreading and in use in courts and corrections agencies—both of which, like neighborhoods, have "hot spots" where problems are frequent and predictable.

Certainly all of the technological advances described in this chapter have made advances in problem solving possible. And this is really a no-brainer: In order to address crime and disorder with limited resources, various uses of technological assets and analytics must be directed to the time, places, hot spots, and people where they are most sorely needed.

This is, therefore, a very exciting and challenging time to be employed in the criminal justice field; however, such entities as political governing boards, the taxpaying public, and institutions of higher education owe it to their practitioners, stakeholders, and students to keep abreast of these changing times and to have the technological capability to analyze data, perform crime analyses, understand the basics of mapping, perform trend analysis, and so on. To not do so, in the midst of this widespread sea change in crime fighting, would be to do them a great disservice.

Key Terms and Concepts

3D printing *401*	Electronic court records *397*	Robotics *395*
Big data *388*	N-DEx *389*	Telemedicine *400*
"Bring your own device" (BYOD) *396*	Radio-frequency identification	
Cloud computing *389*	tracking (RFID) *399*	

Questions for Review

1. How would you define big data? Cloud computing? What are their applications?
2. What are some new types of databases that now exist for criminal justice agency use?
3. What concerns exist with drone, in terms of both their use and citizens' privacy?
4. How would you describe some of the advances regarding police use of robotics?
5. What are some of the good and bad applications and considerations with smartphones?

6. Regarding court technologies, what are the primary problems courts have, and what is the solution?
7. What advances have been made in corrections regarding inmate control? Use of mobile devices?
8. What advantages are offered through the use of telemedicine?
9. How does the eminent manufacture of plastic guns threaten Americans?

Deliberate and Decide

"The Turned-down Texter"

A female officer comes to you alleging that her direct supervisor in the Drug Suppression Unit, who is a former lover, began sending explicit text messages to her a few weeks ago, including "I must lick you" and "I am just a man. Never satisfied always wanting more."

Now, however, the sergeant is phoning her repeatedly at work to discuss personal matters and sometimes calls her offensive names. If she doesn't answer the phone, he angrily confronts her at the police station, yelling and using abusive language.

Today, she agreed to meet him in a parking lot while they were both on duty. He became angry when she

refused to date him again, and he again sent her harassing text messages soon afterward. She indicates that he obviously uses GPS to track her while doing drug interdiction work, because he showed up twice yesterday where she was on a stakeout with a colleague. She claims she has brought these matters to the attention of her shift lieutenant, but so far he ignores her complaints.

Questions for Discussion

1. Is the sergeant's behavior in violation of any law? If so, specifically what?
2. What are the issues involved?
3. As her captain, what will you do about the matter?

Learn by Doing

1. As head of the research and development unit of your law enforcement agency, you are tasked to "bring the agency into the new millennium" by making recommendations concerning new technologies to be acquired. Using information provided in this chapter, select and prioritize *five* new technologies that you believe your city/county agency should obtain, including a justification for each in terms of its crime-fighting, predictive, and preventive capabilities.

2. You occasionally consult on justice system planning and operations, and have been contacted by a nearby county to examine its court functions. Apparently the former court administrator (Jameson) was very popular and considered efficient because he always operated within his rather meager budget. You discover, however, that those low operating costs were due to his notion that the court did not need any "fancy gizmos," and thus the court's staff struggles to perform the court's daily functions with outmoded equipment. With Jameson now retired, the county manager (learning how antiquated the court's functions really are), supports a major upgrade, and contacts you to learn of the available court technologies. What will you report?

3. As warden of a small minimum custody prison facility in a remote part of the state and having an unusually high geriatric inmate population, your secretary of corrections has learned that fully one-third of your total budget is now consumed by medical and related costs (e.g., transportation to clinics and hospitals). You are ordered to come up with alternatives. What will you propose?

Notes

1. Future Timeline.net, "Computers and the Internet," http://www.futuretimeline.net/subject/computers-internet.htm (accessed March 23, 2014).

2. Ted Samson, "IBM's Next Revolution: Computers That See, Smell, Hear, and Taste," *Infoworld*, March 17, 2012, http://www.infoworld.com/t/big-data/ibms-next-revolution-computers-see-smell-hear-and-taste-209396 (accessed March 23, 2014).

3. "The Big Data Conundrum: How to Define It?" *MIT Technology Review*, October 3, 2013, http://www.technologyreview.com/view/519851/the-big-data-conundrum-how-to-define-it/ (accesse°d March 30, 2014).

4. "The Promise of Big Data in Public Safety and Justice," 2014, http://www.ijis.org/EDblog/2012/09/the-promise-of-big-data-in-public-safety-and-justice/ (accessed March 24, 2014).

5. Brad Grimes, "Big Data Is Taking a Byte out of Crime," October 13, 2014, *FedTech*, http://www.fedtechmagazine.com/article/2014/10/big-data-taking-byte-out-crime (accessed March 20, 2014).

6. Ibid.

7. Market Research Media, "Global Cloud Computing Market Forecast 2015–2020," http://www.marketresearchmedia.com/?p=839 (accessed March 23, 2014).

8. Jonathan Strickland, "How Cloud Computing Works," http://computer.howstuffworks.com/cloud-computing/cloud-computing.htm (accessed March 23, 2014).

9. See, for example, PC News, "Definition of: Cloud," http://www.pcmag.com/encyclopedia/term/39847/cloud (accessed March 28, 2014).

10. Paul Wormeli, *Mitigating Risks in the Application of Cloud Computing in Law Enforcement,* IBM Center for the Business of Government (2012), p. 10, http://www.cjisgroup.com/sites/www.cjisgroup.com/files/publications/Mitigating%20Risks%20in%20the%20Application%20of%20Cloud%20Computing%20%20in%20Law%20Enforcement%202012.pdf (accessed March 24, 2014).

11. Ibid., p. 14.

12. University of North Carolina School of Law, "Examples of Cloud Computing Services," http://www.unc.edu/courses/2010spring/law/357c/001/cloudcomputing/examples.html (accessed March 23, 2014).

13. Strickland, "How Cloud Computing Works."

14. International Association of Chiefs of Police, "Guiding Principles for Law Enforcement's Transition to Cloud Services," http://www.safegov.org/2014/1/31/guiding-principles-for-law-enforcement%E2%80%99s-transition-to-cloud-services (accessed March 23, 2014).

15. International Association of Chiefs of Police, *Guiding Principles on Cloud Computing in Law Enforcement* (January 31, 2014), http://www.theiacp.org/portals/0/pdfs/GuidingPrinciplesonCloudComputinginLawEnforcement.pdf (accessed March 23, 2014).

16. Sarah Rich, "Facial Reconstruction Tech Helps Identify Skeletal Remains," *Government Technology*, June 26, 2014, http://www.govtech.com/public-safety/Facial-Reconstruction-Tech-Helps-Identify-Skeletal-Remains.html (accessed March 23, 2014).

17. "CLEMIS Deploys MW810 Mobile Workstations to Enable 'Virtual Office' in Squad Cars," Motorola Solutions,

http://www.motorolasolutions.com/web/Business/_Documents/Case%20studies/_Static%20files/MW810-CLEMIS-Case-Study.pdf (accessed March 23, 2014).

18. Steven Goldsmith, "To Catch a Sniper: How Data Analytics Are Transforming Police Work and Taking Criminals Off the Streets," *Government Technology*, May 22, 2014, http://www.govtech.com/public-safety/To-Catch-A-Sniper.html (accessed March 23, 2014).

19. Ibid.

20. "Louisiana First to Launch Ballistic Information Network," *Government Technology,* October 19, 2012, http://www.govtech.com/Louisiana-First-to-Launch-Ballistic-Information-Network.html (accessed March 23, 2014).

21. "California Law Enforcement Forges Metal Database," *Government Technology*, August 22, 2012, http://www.govtech.com/public-safety/California-Law-Enforcement-Forges-Metal-Database.html

22. "FBI Wants a Tattoo Database," *Government Technology*, July 19, 2012, http://www.govtech.com/public-safety/FBI-Tattoo-Database.html (accessed March 23, 2014).

23. "Report: Alabama Starts Scanning Prison Visitor Fingerprints," *Government Technology,* June 6, 2012, http://www.govtech.com/public-safety/Alabama-Starts-Scanning-Prison-Visitor-Fingerprints.html (accessed March 23, 2014).

24. Sarah Rich, "Pennsylvania Facial Recognition Systems Integrate to Widen Search for Criminals," September 3, 2014, http://www.govtech.com/public-safety/Pennsylvania-Facial-Recognition-Systems-Integrate-to-Widen-Search-for-Criminals.html (accessed March 23, 2014).

25. Elaine Pittman, "Sole Searcher," *Government Technology*, July 2011, http://www.govtech.com/public-safety/Shoe-Print-Databases-Catch-Up-to-CSI-Fiction.html (accessed March 28, 2014).

26. Pittman, "Real-Life Police Technology Catches up with Science Fiction," *Government Technology*, April 29, 2010, http://www.govtech.com/featured/Real-Life-Police-Technology-Catches-up-With.html (accessed March 23, 2014).

27. Ibid. In other litigation, the ACLU of Southern California and the Electronic Frontier Foundation (EFF) sued the Los Angeles Police Department and the Los Angeles County Sheriff's Department in November 2014 over records collected by license plate readers over the past several years.

28. Pittman, "Real-Life Police Technology Catches up with Science Fiction,"

29. Brian Heaton, "5 Tech Policy Issues to Watch in 2014," *Government Technology*, March 19, 2014, http://www.govtech.com/data/5-Tech-Policy-Issues-to-Watch-in-2014.html?elq=275ab7d7af4e45e9a4f3daa36669b5a5&elqCampaignId=6127 (accessed March 19, 2014).

30. Sara Rich, "Utah Police Taking Anonymous Crime Tips Online," August 2, 2011, http://www.govtech.com/public-safety/Utah-Police-Anonymous-Crime-Tips-Online.html?elq=7128333f79404469b86b4ad6716f0ddd (accessed March 28, 2014).

31. Pittman, "Inside Out," *Government Technology* (May 2011), pp. 36–37.

32. Pittman, "Incident Immersion," *Government Technology*, October 2010, pp. 30–31.

33. Hilton Collins, "QR Codes Aim to Curb Drunken Driving in Texas," *Government Technology*, June 6, 2011, http://www.govtech.com/health/QR-Codes-Curb-Drunken-Driving-Texas.html (accessed November 28, 2012); also see BeQRious, "QR Codes Against Drunk Driving," http://beqrious.com/qr-codes-against-drunk-driving/(accessed March 28, 2014).

34. Sarah Rich, "Madison Police Extract Forensic Evidence from Cellphones," August 28, 2014, http://www.govtech.com/data/Madison-Police-Extract-Forensic-Evidence-from-Cellphones.html (accessed March 23, 2014).

35. *U.S. v. Jones*, 565 US ___, 132 S.Ct. 945 (2012).

36. "FAA Announces Drone Testing Sites in Six States," *The Associated Press* (December 31, 2013), http://www.cbsnews.com/news/faa-announces-drone-testing-sites-in-six-states/ (accessed August 29, 2014).

37. Christina Hernandez Sherwood, "Are You Ready for Civilian Drones?" *Government Technology*, August 2, 2012, http://www.govtech.com/public-safety/Are-You-Ready-for-Civilian-Drones.html?elq=117d5398aecb45709a0c398ae05092d8&elqCampaignId=1626 (accessed March 28, 2014).

38. Judy Keen, "Citing Privacy, Critics Target Drones Buzzing over USA," *USA TODAY* (January 10, 2014), http://www.usatoday.com/story/news/politics/2014/01/10/domestic-drones-backlash/1566212/ (accessed March 11, 2014).

39. Sherwood, "Are You Ready for Civilian Drones?" http://www.govtech.com/public-safety/Are-You-Ready-for-Civilian-Drones.html?elq=117d5398aecb45709a0c398ae05092d8&elqCampaignId=1626 (accessed March 28, 2014).

40. Adapted from Lindsay Perez, "Drone Tries to Sneak Contraband into Georgia Prison," NBC News Investigations, November 27, 2013, http://investigations.nbcnews.com/_news/2013/11/27/21645567-drone-tries-to-sneak-contraband-into-georgia-prison?lite (accessed January 27, 2013).

41. Kevin Johnson, "Police Chiefs Urge Limits on Use of Drones," *USA Today*, September 7, 2012, http://usatoday30.usatoday.com/news/nation/story/2012-09-06/cop-drones/57639048/1 (accessed November 28, 2014).

42. Brian Huber, "Wis. Police Get Robo-Cop's Help," *PoliceOne.com*, November 14, 2006, www.policeone.com/police-technology/robots/articles/1190983 (accessed March 5, 2014).

43. See John Ingold, "James Holmes Faces 142 Counts, Including 24 of First-degree Murder," *The Denver Post*, July 30, 2012, http://www.denverpost.com/breakingnews/ci_21191265/hearing-underway-man-suspected-killing-12-aurora-theater; also see Larry Greenmeier, "Bomb-Disarming Robot Was First to Enter Alleged Aurora Shooter's Apartment," July 25, 2012, http://blogs.scientificamerican.com/observations/2012/07/25/bomb-disarming-robot-was-first-to-enter-alleged-aurora-shooters-apartment/; Miranda Leitsinger and Miguel Llanos, "Colorado Shooting Suspect's Apartment Was 'Designed to Kill,' Police Say," *U.S. News*, http://usnews.nbcnews.com/_news/2012/07/21/12875178-colorado-shooting-suspects-apartment-was-designed-to-kill-police-say?lite (accessed March 23, 2014).

44. Lauren Katims, "Crime Scan," *Government Technology* (April 2011), p. 38.

45. See Susanna Kim, "Lawsuit against Chicago Police for Blackberry Overtime," *ABC News.com*, February 7, 2014, http://abcnews.go.com/Business/chicago-police-officer-sues-hoping-overtime-pay-blackberry/story?id=18432865 (accessed March 23, 2014).

46. Christian Schappel, "6 Must-Haves for BYOD Policies," *HRMorning.com*, March 18, 2014, http://www.hrmorning.com/6-must-haves-for-byod-policies/ (accessed March 23, 2014).

47. Kyle Malone, "The Fourth Amendment and the Stored Communications Act: Why the Warrantless Gathering of Historical Cell Site Location Information Poses No Threat to Privacy," *Pepperdine Law Review* 39(3) (September 8, 2014), http://digitalcommons.pepperdine.edu/cgi/viewcontent.cgi?article=1368&context=plr&sei-redir=1&referer=http%3A%2F%2Fwww.google.com%2Furl%3Fsa%3Dt%26rct%3Dj%26q%3D1986%2520stored%2520communications%2520act%2520warrantless%2520searches%26source%3Dweb%26cd%3D7%26ved%3D0CFgQFjAG%26url%3Dhttp%253A%252F%252Fdigitalcommons.pepperdine.edu%252Fcgi%252Fviewcontent.cgi%253Fartic le%253D1368%2526context%253Dplr%26ei%3D3jO9UNDsOMbmiwLDsoC4Aw%26usg%3DAFQjCNEsKOZHRJZkkCfue0F_QKYroFrfxQ#search=%221986%20stored%20communications%20act%20warrantless%20searches%22 (accessed March 3, 2014).

48. Massimo Calabresi, "The Phone Knows All," *Time* (August 27, 2012), http://www.time.com/time/magazine/article/0,9171,2122241,00.html (accessed March 3, 2014).

49. See 18 U.S.C. Chapter 121 §§ 2701–2712.

50. 18 U.S.C. § 2703(b) (2006).

51. South University, "Prison Security Goes High Tech," June 2014, http://source.southuniversity.edu/prison-security-goes-hightech-24647.aspx (accessed March 23, 2014).

52. Sarah Rich, "Expanded Video Surveillance for LA County Correctional Facilities," Government Technology, September 27, 2014, http://www.govtech.com/public-safety/Expanded-Video-Surveillance-for-LA-County-Correctional-Facilities.html (accessed March 23, 2014).

53. Laura Hickman, "Prison RFID Study Finds Planning Is Critical," *RFID Journal*, http://www.rfidjournal.com/articles/view?7862/4#sthash.4yXxmsVY.dpuf (accessed March 23, 2014).

54. Tom McNichol, "Prison Cell-Phone Use a Growing Problem," *Time.com*, May 26, 2009, http://www.time.com/time/nation/article/0,8599,1900859,00.html (accessed March 30, 2014).

55. Anne Field, "Can Tablets Help Educate Prisoners—and Keep Them from Returning to Jail?" *Forbes*, June 29, 2014, http://www.forbes.com/sites/annefield/2014/06/29/can-tablets-help-educate-prisoners-and-keep-them-from-returning-to-jail/ (accessed March 23, 2014).

56. Susan Miller, "Prisons Turn to Telemedicine for Treating Inmates," GCN, May 21, 2014, http://gcn.com/blogs/pulse/2014/05/prisons-telemedicine-treating-inmates.aspx (accessed March 23, 2014).

57. Gabriel Perna, "Under the Microscope: Telemedicine Care in Texas Prisons," *Healthcare Infomatics*, June 21, 2014, http://www.healthcare-informatics.com/article/under-microscope-telemedicine-care-texas-prisons (accessed March 23, 2014).

58. "Kansas Using Facebook to Nab Parole Absconders," *Kansas City Star*, September 25, 2014, http://www.kansascity.com/2014/09/25/4506637/kansas-using-facebook-to-nab-parole.html (accessed March 23, 2014).

59. Chloe Albanesius, "Obama Signs Bill to Extend Ban on Plastic Guns," *PCMag.com*, December 10, 2013, http://www.pcmag.com/article2/0,2817,2428186,00.asp; also see David Daw, "Criminals Find New Uses for 3D Printing," *PC World*, October 10, 2014, http://www.pcworld.com/article/241605/criminals_find_new_uses_for_3d_printing.html (accessed March 23, 2014).

Appendix I Case Studies

Following are 28 case studies involving problems and issues in police, courts, and agencies that students are invited to address.

▶ Part 1 Justice Administration: An Introduction

Chapter 2 Organization and Administration: Principles and Practices

I. Targeting Tattoos

You are a police chief in a medium-sized city and have just received information from a captain that one of your officers, Newton, has recently had a swastika tattooed on one arm and a naked woman on the other. The captain says that both tattoos are visible in the summer uniform and, as news is spreading about these adornments, an increasing number of officers are becoming offended and some are even saying that they will refuse to respond to any calls for service with Newton. Based on this information, you believe that the tattoo may violate the city's policy against workplace harassment and quickly call Newton into your office. He admits having the tattoos but rather sarcastically states that he has a "liberty" interest under the Fourteenth Amendment and a right to "expression" under the First Amendment. He adds that for you to try to control such activity would constitute a "hostile" work environment. You know that there is currently no policy that prohibits the displaying of any tattoos, let alone any that are offensive.

Questions for Discussion

1. Can you take any action in response to the complaint?
2. Do you have the right to reasonably regulate the appearance of employees and require a professional appearance?
3. If you implement a policy against such tattoos, does the rule impermissibly discriminate against Newton?
4. Can you use to advantage any U.S. Supreme Court decisions in response to this matter?

Chapter 3 Rights of Criminal Justice Employees

I. A Neanderthal Lives!

You are an administrator in a small minimum-security facility where the day shift is composed of four veteran male officers and one new female officer. The woman is a member of a minority, has a college degree from a reputable out-of-state university, and is married to a member of the armed forces. There have been recent reports from your supervisors of obscene and racially offensive remarks and drawings turning up in the female officer's mailbox, but you have not seen any such materials, nor has the woman complained to you about such occurrences. Today, however, your day shift sergeant storms into your office with a piece of paper he says was just removed from a locker room wall. It shows a "stick figure" woman and contains several racial slurs and comments to the effect that "women do not belong in this man's business, and you should go back where you came from." The woman saw this material, and the sergeant says she is now in the conference room, crying, and distraught.

Questions for Discussion

1. What would you do about this situation? Should you ignore it? Call the female officer to your office?
2. If you bring her in and she says that you should just leave the matter alone, should you pursue it?
3. If you determine which officer is responsible for these materials, what disciplinary action (if any) would you deem warranted? On what grounds?

▶ Part 2   The Police

Chapter 4   Police Organization and Operation

I. Malfunction Junction

Junction City, a rapidly growing community of 150,000 residents, is an agriculturally based area located in the center of the state, about 20 miles from the ocean. The city gains a population of 10,000 to 20,000 visitors a day during the summer months, when ocean recreation is a popular activity. Owing to local growth in the meat-packing industry, the city's demographics are changing rapidly, especially its blue-collar population. The down-town area of the city has slowly deteriorated over the past few years, resulting in increased crime and disorder. A property tax cap has resulted in reduced revenues to local jurisdictions, and the recent recession has taken a substantial toll on the city's budget; the result has been significant reductions in staffing. The police department now has 100 sworn and 35 nonsworn personnel, and has experienced its share of budget cuts and staff reductions. The chief of police of 10 years' duration retired recently, leaving an agency that is still very traditional in nature and has a growing number of desk-bound administrative personnel and degree of rank structure (corporal, sergeant, lieutenant, captain, deputy chief, commander, and chief). The morale of the department is poor because of the increases in workload resulting from tourism and agricultural expansion. You have been hired as the new police chief. As a result of the current situation, the city manager

and council are calling for an emergency meeting with you to discuss the future of the department. They explain that at a recent council retreat, they heard a consultant's presentation on the implementation and operation of community policing and problem solving. They are now seeking your views on this strategy, its potential for Junction City, and how you might approach its implementation. (*Note:* They emphasize that you have to explain how you might reorganize the police department to move away from its current traditional organization, with only one police facility and its administration- and rank-laden status.)

Questions for Discussion

1. Do you envision any problems with traditional-thinking officers and supervisors still working in the organization? If so, how will you handle their concerns?
2. Using the seven elements of police organizational structure described in this chapter, where does it appear that you would need to reorganize the agency, especially to accommodate Community Oriented Policing and Problem Solving (COPPS)?
3. Would you anticipate that the officers' workload would be reduced or increased under the COPPS strategy?
4. What types of information would you use to evaluate the progress of your community policing initiative?

II. Sins and the City

Officers assigned to your district have been responding to a number of noise complaints, reckless driving incidents, and fight calls in the area of 7500 Commercial Row. This area contains a number of restaurants, bars, and several strip malls that attract juveniles and young adults. Within the past week, there have also been three gang-related drive-by shootings and seven gas drive-offs. A majority of the underage adults are attracted to the area by a dance club located in one of the strip mall centers and two all-night fast food restaurants. All

three locations attract large crowds that loiter and drink alcohol in their parking lots. The owners of the shopping centers and restaurants have also complained about thousands of dollars in vandalism caused by the loitering youths.

Question for Discussion

1. How would you use the S.A.R.A. (scanning, analysis, response, and assessment) process to address this problem?

Chapter 5   Police Personnel Roles and Functions

You are to assume the role of Sergeant Doe in the Gotham City Police Department. After working as a patrol officer for 6 years and then spending 2 years in the detective section, you were promoted to sergeant 4 weeks ago. This is your first shift since completing a supervisory course; the date is June 10.

You are in charge of a 12-person patrol team and work swing (evening) shift. Due to the increased activities that occur during the summer months, it is the policy of your department to not allow more than two officers to take vacation or training leave at a time. You have two senior officers off on vacation for the entire month of June.

Your task is to respond to the items below exactly as you would if this were an actual situation. If a letter or memorandum is to be sent, briefly describe the contents. If you intend to attend a meeting, briefly describe the agenda. Indicate (and justify) any action(s) you choose to defer. You cannot use a telephone, and there is no clerical assistance available for dictation.

Memorandum, June 6

To: Sergeant Doe

From: Lieutenant Gruff

Subject: **Emergency Leave**

On this date I was advised of a death in my family. Due to the urgency of the situation, I will be out of town the week of June 8–14, and you will be the watch commander. Please clear my in-basket, as some urgent matters are pending.

Memorandum: June 3

To: Sergeant Doe

From: Officer Smith, #202

Subject: Time-Off Request

I am respectfully requesting to take off on the night of Friday and Saturday, June 13–14, as I have just learned that my wife and I have won a trip to Disneyland through a local radio station. The trip is three fully paid days, but I have to go on June 13–15 in order to be eligible. I realize that I have exhausted all of my leave time, but this would be our honeymoon. Also, I have to know by 10 June so I can take care of the arrangements.

Memorandum, June 4

To: Lieutenant Gruff, Patrol Bureau

From: Sergeant Kidd, Community Affairs Section

Subject: Southside Community Center Activities

The director of the Southside Community Center has scheduled a Battle of the Bands Concert on Friday, June 13, from 2000–2400 hrs. You will recall that the last concert at that location resulted in a huge fiasco, with numerous arrests and injuries to three officers. I am trying to provide you with enough advanced notice of this event that you can be prepared. They expect more than 1,000 people to attend. I will not be able to spare any assistance from my Section, because my three officers and I will be out of town at a child abuse seminar. We are taking our wives and have already paid for the trip.

Memorandum, June 9

To: Lt. Gruff

From: Chief Harrington

Subject: Officer Race

At a recent Otters Club meeting, I was advised by a prominent member of the northside area that Officer Race is not getting along well with the citizens. He is too aggressive and not understanding of their problems. It is also my understanding that he has had several accidents with his patrol vehicle this year. What is his problem? I want you to look into this matter and provide me a response by June 16th.

Memorandum, June 5

Police Department

To: Lt. Gruff

From: Officer Bland, #336

Subject: Personal Problems

As you are probably aware, my wife and I recently separated and I have made every attempt to reconcile with her. However, so far I have had no success. I am having difficulty sleeping and that is why I have been late to work so much recently. I would love very much to talk with you about this situation. I do not know Sergeant Doe very well, and am not sure I would want to discuss my personal problems with him.

June 4

Dear Chief Harrington:

Last night my 17-year-old daughter, Denise, was stopped by one of your officers for speeding. I do not know the officer's name, but his badge number is 336. This officer apparently got very sarcastic with my daughter and said some things that weren't very nice. He even told her that if she would go out with him on a date, he wouldn't give her a ticket. When she told him that she would not go out with him, he gave her a ticket. I think this officer should be disciplined. If I don't hear from you by Friday, June 13, I am going to take my complaint to the City Council.

Sincerely,

Mrs. RuthBrown

Memorandum, May 30

To: All Command Officers

From: Chief Harrington

Subject: Overtime Budget

I was contacted by the City Manager and the Finance Director on this date and advised that the police overtime budget for this fiscal year has been totally exhausted. Therefore, no overtime shall be approved for any reason during the month of June. Court overtime will be taken from the equipment and supplies budget. This will be the only exception.

Chapter 6 Police Issues and Practices

I. Bias-Based Policing or Good Police Work?

Officer James and Sergeant Drummond are on surveillance in a strip mall. A detective received an anonymous tip that a credit union might be robbed at 3:00 P.M. The detective also told the patrol division that the person providing the tip is a known drug addict and not at all reliable, but as there has been a string of credit union robberies during the past 2 months, Drummond decides to surveil the area with Officer James. The main suspects in the robberies are Asians, and the officers have stopped and talked with several Asian people in the area, taking their names and other identifying information. At approximately 2:45 P.M., Drummond and James are notified by Communications that a security officer reported hearing a gunshot in the parking lot of a nearby grocery store where he was working. Because they are nearby and there might be a connection to the credit union robberies, Drummond and James decide to take the call. On arrival at the scene, the security officer meets the two officers and informs them that he "might have" heard a small-caliber pistol shot in the parking lot; he also believes that a young African American man who walked into the grocery store a few minutes ago might be carrying a gun under his coat. About 10 minutes later, a 30-year-old African American man comes walking out of the store. The officers draw their guns and order him to get down on the asphalt and to their vehicle. At that time, an Asian woman carrying a child approaches the officers, yelling at them that the man is her husband and demanding to know what they are doing to him. The officers order her to go her car, whereupon she faints while suffering an epileptic seizure. The African American man, seeing his wife and child on the ground, now becomes very agitated; as a result, the officers use considerable force to subdue and handcuff him. He is arrested for resisting arrest and a host of other offenses; later, he sues for violation of his civil rights.

Questions for Discussion

1. Did the officers have reasonable cause to be engaged in the initial (credit union) surveillance? To question Asian people in the area? Defend your answer.

2. Did the officers violate the African American man's civil rights? Why or why not? If you answer "yes," would you support (as the chief of police) some form of disciplinary action against them?

3. Should the woman be entitled to collect damages? Why or why not?

4. In which (if any) aspects of this scenario do you believe the officers are guilty of engaging in racial profiling? Explain your answer.

5. Assume that this case led to a public outcry for a citizen review board to examine questionable police activities and recommend disciplinary and policy actions. Would you support the creation of such a board? Why or why not?

II. Adapting to the Responsibilities of the Role

Sergeant Tom Gresham was newly promoted and assigned to patrol on the graveyard shift; he knew each officer on his shift, and several were close friends. Gresham was an excellent patrol officer, and prided himself on his reputation and his ability to get along with his peers. He also believed this trait would benefit him as a supervisor. From the beginning, Gresham believed that he could get more work from his officers by relating to them at their level. He made an effort to socialize with them after work and took pride in giving his team the liberty of referring to him by his first name. Gresham also believed that it was a supervisor's job to not get in the way of good police work. In his view, his team responded magnificently, generating the highest number of arrest and citation statistics in the entire department. Unfortunately, his shift also generated the highest number of citizen complaints for abusive language and improper use of force, but few complaints were sustained by Internal Affairs. It was

Gresham's opinion that complaints are the product of good, aggressive police work. He had quickly developed the reputation among subordinates of being "a cop's cop."

One Monday morning, Gresham is surprised when called in to see you, his patrol captain. The Internal Affairs lieutenant is also present. You show Gresham a number of use-of-force complaints against his team over the past week, while Gresham was on vacation. Despite your efforts to describe the gravity of the situation, Gresham fails to grasp the seriousness of the complaints and how his supervisory style may have contributed to them.

Questions for Discussion

1. What do you believe are some of Sergeant Gresham's problems as a new supervisor?
2. As his captain, what advice would you give Gresham?
3. What corrective action must Gresham take immediately with his team of officers?

▶ Part 3   The Courts

Chapter 7   Court Organization and Operation

I. Chief Judge Cortez's Embattled Court

You have just been hired as the new court administrator for a medium-sized court with approximately 90 employees. Once on the job, you discover that you have been preceded by two heavy-handed court administrators who together lasted less than 1 year on the job because of their inability to handle employee conflicts and to achieve a minimal level of productivity. They were more or less forced to resign because of a lack of employee cooperation and increasing talk of unionization. There is general turmoil and distrust throughout the organization. Employees do not trust each other, and as a group, they do not trust management. The courthouse runs on gossip and inertia. There is very little official communication throughout the organization. Prior court administrators made no attempt to solicit employees' opinions or ideas. The judges are all aware of the problem, but they have formed no clear consensus on how to respond to it. In fact, there is turmoil and conflict among the judges themselves. They engage in "turf protection" with operating funds and the court's cases and often take sides in office

squabbles. As a result, they are unable to achieve a clear consensus or to provide the court administrator with any guidance. The chief judge, Dolores Cortez, has served in that capacity for 10 years and is known to be exceedingly fair, compassionate, and competent; however, she is approaching retirement (in 6 months) and appears unwilling to take a firm stand on, or a strong interest in, addressing intraoffice disputes and difficulties. In fact, she is not altogether convinced that there is a problem. Furthermore, in past years, she has been quite reluctant to intervene in arguments between individual judges.

Questions for Discussion

1. As the "new kid on the block," how would you respond to this organizational problem? What is the first issue you would address, and how would you address it? What additional problems require your attention?
2. As court administrator, how would you respond to the inability of the judges to develop a consensus? How could the decision-making process be improved?

3. What techniques could be employed to improve communication throughout the organization, lessen tension and strife, and generally create a more harmonious work environment?

4. What would be your general approach to Judge Cortez? To her successor?

II. What Action, Which Court? A Quiz[1]

1. Melvin entered a federally insured bank and robbed money from the safe. In which level of court will this case most likely be filed?

   Your Answer: federal   state   either

2. Two weeks later, Melvin robbed a man who had just taken money out of an ATM machine in a grocery store. Where will this case most likely be filed?

   Your Answer: federal   state   either

3. Mary works for a local criminal justice agency; she claims that her supervisor refused to promote her because she is related to his ex-wife. Where will Mary file this case?

   Your Answer: federal   state   either

4. True or false? There are two kinds of courts in the federal court system: the trial court and the Supreme Court.

   Your Answer: True   False

5. True or false? A person accused of a crime is generally charged in a formal accusation. The name of this accusation for a misdemeanor is called an indictment.

   Your Answer: True   False

Answers

1. The correct answer is "federal." Because this crime was committed within the bank and is a theft of the bank's money, which is insured by the federal government, it is a federal crime and would be filed in federal court.

2. The correct answer is "state." Because the money had already come out of the ATM machine and was in the man's possession, the victim was the man and not the bank. Thus, it is a state crime and it would be tried in state court.

3. The correct answer is "either." Both federal and state laws prohibit gender discrimination, and plaintiffs in employment discrimination cases may sue in either federal or state court.

4. The correct answer is "false." The federal system is composed of trial courts and appellate courts. The Supreme Court is the highest appellate court but not the only appeals court.

5. The correct answer is "false." The document charging a person with a misdemeanor is called an information. An indictment is used for felonies or serious crimes.

Chapter 8   Court Personnel Roles and Functions

I. The Court Administrator and the Prudent Police Chief

You are the court administrator in a system that has the following procedure for handling traffic matters:

1. All persons who are given a traffic citation are to appear in court at 9:00 A.M. either on Monday or on Wednesday within 2 weeks of their citation date. They are given a specific date to appear.

2. Persons cited are not required to appear; they have the option of staying home and simply forfeiting their bond, which has been posted in advance of their initial appearance.

3. At the initial appearance, the arresting agency is represented by a court officer who has previously filed copies of all the citations with the clerk of the court.

4. The clerk, prior to the return date on the citation, prepares a file for each citation.

5. The clerk calls each case, and those persons appearing are requested by the court to enter a plea; if the plea is "not guilty," the matter is set for trial at a future date.

6. One case is scheduled per hour. On the trial date, the prosecutor and arresting officer are required to appear, ready for trial.

7. Statistics show that 75 percent of those persons pleading not guilty in this jurisdiction fail to appear for trial.

The chief of police in the court's jurisdiction is concerned about overtime for officers. He communicates with you, the court administrator, about this issue and explains that all police officers who appear in court for trial are entitled to the minimum 2 hours of overtime when they are not appearing during their regular shift. He views this as a tremendous and unnecessary expense to the city in view of the fact that most of the officers are not needed because the defendants do not appear and wishes to devise some system to save the city this high overtime cost.

Questions for Discussion

1. What system would you propose for solving the problem—within the existing law, with no changes in statutes or ordinances?
2. After you have finished designing a system, including how you would obtain the cooperation of the judges, prosecuting and defense attorneys, clerk's office, and other law enforcement agencies, discuss any proposed changes in the law that you think might improve the system further.
3. How would you go about making other significant, ongoing changes to improve the procedures and operation of this system?

Chapter 9 Court Issues and Practices

I. Carol's Construct for Court Chaos

Carol Smith, a divorced mother of one, employed as an assistant manager at a large discount center, was denied custody of her 10-year-old son following a bitter divorce (in which her husband accused her of neglect and inattentive behavior toward the child). In July, she filed several actions against the county and other parties, alleging violations of her civil rights. When these petitions were denied, she petitioned the state Supreme Court, writing a letter about her case that stated in part, "This county's courts and social services do not have a bit of compassion for anyone, and cared nothing about protecting my rights or administering due process to me. I should not have to be paying all of these lawyer's fees and losing so much sleep about getting my son back. No one should have to turn to such actions as the World Trade Center to get some proper attention, but that is the only thing some people will listen to." Smith later told former coworkers at a grocery store that if the state Supreme Court would not hear her case, she would go to the state capital "and shoot up the place." Then, when that court did decline to review her case, she became distraught. A number of her neighbors were very alarmed as she kept ranting about her violent

intentions. One day she left her home and traveled to the state capital, where she went to the Supreme Court building. While there, she called a relative back home and stated that she had "found her purpose in life" that she "planned to shoot the top judge" and had bought a gun. The relative contacted the police, who arrested her for making threats against the judge's life.

Questions for Discussion

Looking at this case from a threat perspective:

1. What potential motives for her behavior first brought Carol Smith to official attention?
2. What events represented significant losses to her, which she found quite stressful?
3. What elements of the case point to her having a reasonable level of cognitive ability that would allow her to formulate and execute a plan if she chose to do so?
4. What communications and arrangements did she make that indicated that she planned to carry out her threat?
5. What events might have increased or decreased the likelihood of an attack?
6. Taken together, which events suggest that she was on a path toward a violent attack?

II. An Unmanageable Case-Management Quandary

You are the administrator for a court with 50 employees. This court, which used to dispose of about 700 cases per month, now hears an average of 100 criminal and 400 civil cases per month. Case filings have doubled in the past 7 years. The present "hybrid" combination of the individual and master case-management systems has evolved over a long period of time through tradition and expediency. A growing caseload and increasing difficulties in avoiding a backlog, however, have prompted the judges to rethink their present system. Criminal cases that formerly reached final disposition in 1 month now require 2 to 3 months. The situation shows no signs of improving in the foreseeable future. Again, the court has a mixed calendar system. Two judges are assigned to hear criminal cases and motions for a 1-month period, whereas the remaining four judges hear all manner of civil cases on a random basis on the filing of civil complaints. The judges are responsible for the management of these cases until final disposition. At the end of the 1-month period, the two judges hearing criminal cases return to the civil division and two other judges rotate onto the criminal bench; any pending criminal cases or motions are then heard by these two incoming criminal judges. One of the judges hears all juvenile-related cases in addition to any assignment in the criminal and civil divisions. The court collects statistics on the number of court filings and motions filed in each division on a month-to-month basis.

Questions for Discussion

1. In a general way, discuss both the merits and difficulties of this case-management approach. What are the general advantages and disadvantages of the individual and master calendar systems?
2. What specific problems could arise in the criminal division? Why?
3. What specific problems could be created by the permanent assignment of a judge to the juvenile division? What advantages might there be?
4. What changes would you recommend with regard to the court's statistical report? Are other data needed for management purposes? If so, what kind?

▶ Part 4 Corrections

Chapter 10 Corrections Organization and Operation

1. As Bad as It Can Get

You are the deputy warden for operations in a comparatively small (500 inmates) maximum-security prison for adults. As is typical, you oversee correctional security, unit management, the inmate disciplinary committee, and recreation. One Wednesday at about 2:00 A.M., an inmate who is a minority group member with a history of mental health problems and violent behavior begins destroying his cell and injures himself by ramming into the walls. The supervisor in charge collects a group of four correctional officers with the intention of removing the inmate from his cell and isolating, medicating, and checking him for injuries. The group of four—all fairly new on the job, untrained in cell extraction or self-defense, and with no specialized extraction equipment—prepares to enter the cell. When the officers open the cell door, the inmate charges them, knocking two of them down. They finally wrestle the inmate to the floor, although he is still struggling. One officer attempts to subdue him by wrapping his arm around the inmate's neck, pressing on his carotid artery. Finally, the inmate quiets down and is restrained and removed to another, larger cell. After 15 minutes, however, the inmate has failed to regain consciousness. A medical staff person rushes to the cell, sees the inmate in an unconscious state, and has him taken to a local hospital. After the inmate has remained comatose for 2 months and has been classified as brain dead, the family decides to remove the life-support system that has sustained him.

Questions for Discussion

1. What, if any, inmate rights are involved in this case?
2. Which, if any, of the inmate's rights were violated?
3. To what extent does the prison system's central office become involved? What kinds of policies need to be developed to cover similar occurrences in the future?
4. As deputy warden, what disciplinary action would you consider against the officers? Did the officers intend to harm the inmate?
5. What needs and problems require new policies? Facilities for mentally ill inmates? Officer training? Equipment?

II. When Politics Trumps Policy

For 2 years, you have been director of a prison system for adults in a medium-sized state. As a result of revenue shortfalls for several years, it has been a constant struggle to keep a full labor force in your state's 10 prisons and to lure professional staff members to work and live in the more rural areas where they are located. During the past 6 months, however, you have managed to assemble a fine staff of wardens and other subordinates in the prisons and have implemented a number of policies that provide for educational, vocational, and treatment opportunities, which have been gaining national attention for their effectiveness. Recidivism has been reduced to 30 percent, and your policies are beginning to be accepted by staff and citizens alike. Running a "Take Back the Streets" anti-crime campaign, a politically inexperienced person (formerly a popular college quarterback playing at a state university) was recently elected governor. The new governor has just sent you a letter stating in effect that your institution is not the "Ritz" and demanding that all "frivolous, namby-pamby programs teaching the ABCs and where cons learn how to hammer nails" cease immediately. He asks for your written response, a plan for tightening security, and the implementation of tougher inmate programs within 1 month.

Questions for Discussion

1. How would you respond? Would you just capitulate and end some or all of these programs? Explain your answer.
2. Is there any room to negotiate with the governor? As a trade-off, would you offer to put in place some programs that are known to be tough on inmates? If so, what kind?
3. Before dismantling your policies and programs, would you attempt to see how much internal and external support you have for them? If yes, whom would you contact and how?
4. How might you go about demonstrating how successful your policies have been?

III. "Out-of-Town Brown" and the Besieged Probation Supervisor

Joan Casey is a career probation officer. She majored in criminal justice as an undergraduate, holds memberships in several national correctional organizations, attends training conferences, and does a lot of reading on her own time to stay current in the field. Casey began working for the Collier County Probation Department soon after she graduated from college and was promoted to a supervisory position, where she supervises an adult probation unit consisting of eight seasoned probation officers. The unit is responsible for investigating approximately 80 offenders a month and preparing presentence investigation (PSI) reports on them. Collier County's Probation Department made the front page of the local newspapers twice in the past month. Both times it was a nightmare for the chief probation officer, Jack Brown, and the entire agency. "Northside Stalker Gets Probation!" screamed the first headline, and then, just a week later, "Collier County Soft on Crime!" Brown called a management team meeting: "Better PSIs," he said, "or heads are gonna roll!" Everybody got the point. This week Brown is on annual leave and Casey is the designated officer in charge. One of Casey's probation officers has recommended intermediate sanctions for a 23-year-old man who murdered his stepfather with a knife after suffering many years of physical and mental abuse. The young man had no prior record and had been an incest victim since he was 5 years old; he is considered an otherwise nonviolent person, a low recidivism risk. Casey is aware of the probation officer's recommendation and agrees with it. However, she receives a call from a well-known veteran local television anchor—a strong crusader in the local war against crime. He knows the young man will be sentenced tomorrow.

Questions for Discussion

1. What should Casey's response be to the reporter (other than hanging up or telling him to call back) concerning the agency's recommendation?
2. If Casey elects to discuss her officer's recommendation for some form of intermediate sanction, how can she justify such sanctions in general and in this case specifically?
3. Do you feel that the probation officer's recommendation based on these facts is correct? Why or why not?
4. Which form of intermediate sanction would appear to hold the most promise for the offender in this case?

Chapter 11 Corrections Personnel Roles and Functions

I. The Wright Way

Lieutenant Bea Wright has been in her current position in the state prison for 1 year and is the shift supervisor on the swing (evening) shift, which consists of 20 officers. There is also a recreation and development lieutenant who oversees the yard, commissary, and other high-use areas during the shift. Wright begins at 4:00 P.M. by holding a roll call for officers, briefing them on the activities of the day, any unusual inmate problems or tensions in progress, and special functions (such as Bible study groups) that will be happening during the evening. Soon after roll call, Wright has the staff conduct the very important evening count—important because inmates have not been counted since the morning. At about 5:00 P.M., Wright determines that there are only four COs in the dining room with 1,000 inmates, so she contacts other units (such as education, library, and recreation) and asks them to send available staff to the dining hall for support. After dinner, Wright finds a memo from the warden asking her to recommend ways of improving procedures for having violent inmates in the Special Housing Unit (SHU) taken to the recreation area in the evening. Wright asks two of her top COs who work in the SHU to provide her with some preliminary information concerning the system in place and any recommendations they might have. While walking the yard, Wright observes what appears to be an unusual amount of clustering and whispering by inmates by race; she asks a sergeant to quietly survey the COs to determine whether there have also been unusual periods of loud music or large amounts of long-lasting foodstuffs purchased in the commissary (together, these activities by inmates might indicate that a race war is brewing or an escape plan is being developed). Furthermore, as she is on the way to her office, an inmate stops her, saying that a group of inmates is pressuring him to arrange to have drugs brought into the prison and he fears for his safety. Wright arranges for him to be called out of the general population the next day under the guise of being transported to a prison law library, at which time he can meet privately with an investigator and thus not draw suspicion to himself for talking to the staff. At about 9:00 P.M., Anderson, a CO, comes to her office to report that he overheard another CO, Jones, making disparaging remarks to other staff members concerning Anderson's desire to go to graduate school and to become a warden some day. Anderson acknowledges that he does not get along with Jones and is tired of his "sniping," and he asks Wright to intercede. She also knows that Jones has been argumentative with other staff members and inmates of late and makes a mental note to visit with him later in the shift to see if he is having personal problems.

Questions for Discussion

1. Does it appear that Lieutenant Wright, although fairly new in her position, has a firm grasp of her role and performs well in it?
2. In what ways is it shown that Wright seeks input from her subordinates?
3. How does she delegate to and empower her subordinates?
4. Is there any indication that Wright is interested in her COs' training and professional development?
5. In which instances does Wright engage in mediation? In management by walking around?

II. "Cheerless Chuck" and the Parole Officer's Orientation Day

"So, you are the new parole officer with a criminal justice degree from the university? Well, I hope you last longer than the last recruit I had. She meant well, but I guess her idealistic ideas about the job of parole officer could not handle the realities of the work. In a way, I understand what she went through. Same thing happened to me 12 years ago when I started this job. There, I was fresh out of college with a brand new diploma. It did not take me long to realize that the real world was different from what I had learned in college. The crises we deal with here make it darned difficult to do the work we all see needs to be done. Years ago, when I first started with the parole department, things were a lot better than they are now. Caseloads were lower, fewer people were getting parole who did not deserve it, and the rest of the criminal justice system was in a lot better shape, which made our jobs a lot easier to do.

Think about it. We vote in politicians who promise the public that they are going to 'get tough' on crime, and the first thing they do is allot more money for law enforcement stuff: beat cops, car computers, helicopters, and so on. These things are great, but all they do is add more people to a system that is already overloaded. No one gets elected by promising to build more courts or add jail and prison space or hire more probation and parole officers. Eventually, these added police officers arrest more people than the system can handle. The courts back up, which in turn messes up the prisons and the jails. The inmates stuck in these crowded places get tired of living like sardines, so they sue the prisons and jails. Remember, the Constitution prohibits cruel and unusual punishment. A lot of times inmates' complaints are legitimate, and they win. The judge orders the prison to lower its population to a reasonable level, which forces the parole board to consider more inmates for early release. Nobody mentions giving the parole department more officers or a bigger budget for added administrative help. No, the bucks go to the flashy, visible things such as cops and cars.

Meanwhile, in the past 10 years, our average caseload for a parole officer has increased 75 percent. We have more people who need supervision, and we are doing it on a budget that has not kept pace with the remainder of the criminal justice system. This would not be so bad if the system was at least adding things to other areas such as the jail or the courts. The problem here is that we depend on the jail to hold our parolees who have violated their conditions. We catch some of them using booze or drugs, and we are supposed to bring them into the county jail to wait for a hearing to decide whether they are going back to prison or back on the street. But the jail has its own set of problems. A couple of years ago, the U.S. district court slapped a population cap on our jail. If it goes over that population, the jail will not accept our violators. So we send them home. If they get into more serious trouble, we call it a new crime, the police arrest them, and the jail has to take them. Then, they have to sit and wait for the court to catch up because the courts are not in

much better shape than the jail. I guess the job would be easier if the prisons were doing their jobs, too. I cannot really blame them because the prisons are funded in much the same way that parole is. We are not 'glamorous' places to send your tax dollars, but if the prisons were getting more money, they might be able to improve the quality of inmate they send to us. Maybe a little more vocational training and substance abuse counseling, so that they could stay off the booze and drugs. Possibly then fewer of these parolees would wind up back behind bars a few years later.

The worst part about the job is the caseload. We presently have so many on parole that I am lucky if I can get a phone call to each of them once a week and maybe a home visit once a month. The sad part about it is that with the proper budget and staff, we could really make a difference. We spend so much time bailing water out of the boat that we do not realize that there is no one steering and we are just drifting in circles.

By the way, my name is Charlie Matthews, but everyone calls me Chuck. I am a supervisor here as well as the designated new-employee orientation specialist and all-round public relations person. Welcome aboard."

Questions for Discussion

1. Should Chuck be retained as orientation coordinator? Why or why not?
2. How would changes in politics affect the parole system directly and indirectly?
3. How does an old criminal justice planning adage that "you cannot rock one end of the boat" seem to be applicable to what Chuck says about new police positions and the subsequent impact on the courts and corrections components?
4. What administrative problems and practices might be responsible for this agency's situation?
5. Why do crowded jails and prisons make the job of parole officers more difficult?
6. How could practices of the jails and prisons change the success of the parole system?

Chapter 12   Corrections Issues and Practices

I. Double, Double, Toil, and Trouble

There seems to be trouble brewing in a nearby medium-level adult prison. Inmate informers have noted several conditions indicating that a riot may be imminent:

Inmates are stocking up on long-term items (e.g., canned goods) in the commissary and banding together more throughout the institution by racial groupings;

furthermore, inmates are seen standing in or near doorways, as if preparing for a quick exit. Over the past several months, the inmates have become increasingly unhappy with their conditions of confinement—not only with the usual bland food, but also with the increasing number of assaults and gang attacks—and many are either very young, nonviolent offenders or very old and frail. The staff has also become increasingly unhappy, particularly, with their low salaries and benefits, perceived unsafe working conditions and attacks on officers, institutional overcrowding, the increasing number of sexual attacks among inmates, and greater amounts of drugs and other forms of contraband found in the cellblocks. They demand that the prison administration ask the courts to give more consideration to house arrest and other intermediate sanctions. They also want the legislature to consider privatization of the prison.

You are the state's prison system director. The governor's office has asked that you prepare an immediate position paper for the chief executive setting forth a plan for dealing with this prison's current situation.

Questions for Discussion

1. What are the critical issues that should be dealt with immediately?
2. How would you proceed to defuse the potential for a riot?
3. What would be your response to the suggestions for prison privatization and the use of intermediate sanctions?
4. What, if anything, might be done to address the concerns of the inmates? The staff?

II. A Corrections Futures Forum

Assume that your jurisdiction is planning a new week-long futures-oriented program, "Leadership Forum for 2015," which will bring together professionals from the business and governmental sectors. Topics to be discussed at the forum include a wide array of area issues, challenges, methods, and concerns. Assume further that you are a prison or probation/parole administrator. After applying for and being selected to attend this program, you are advised that you are to make a 60-minute presentation concerning your profession generally, as well as the future challenges facing your local corrections organization.

Questions for Discussion

1. Using some of the materials discussed in this book, how would you briefly explain your role as a chief executive of your agency to this group?
2. What are some of the important *current* themes and issues that you would take to the forum concerning a corrections administrator's job to indicate its complexities and challenges?
3. How would you describe the changing nature of the corrections administrator's role and the *future* issues and challenges of this position?

▶ Part 5   Issues Spanning the Justice System
Chapter 13   Ethical Considerations

I. Setting Up Mr. Smith

Assume that the police have multiple leads that implicate Smith as a pedophile, but they have failed in every attempt to obtain a warrant to search Smith's car and home, where evidence might be present. Officer Jones feels frustrated and, early one morning, takes his baton and breaks a rear taillight on Smith's car. The next day he stops Smith for operating his vehicle with a broken taillight; he impounds and inventories the vehicle and finds evidence leading to Smith's conviction on 25 counts of child molestation and possession of pornography. Jones receives accolades for the apprehension.

3. What if he argues that he is correct in using this approach because he was molested as a child?
4. What constitutional issues are involved?

II. Burns Goes Ballistic

Officer Burns is known to have extreme difficulty relating to persons of color and others who are socially different from himself. This officer never received any sensitivity or diversity training at the police academy or within the department. His supervisor fails to understand the magnitude of the problem and has little patience with Burns. So, to correct the problem, the supervisor decides to assign Burns to a minority section of town so that he will improve his ability to relate to diverse groups. Within a week, Burns responds to a disturbance at a housing project where residents are partying noisily. He immediately begins yelling at the residents to quiet down; they fail to respond, so Burns draws his baton and begins poking residents and

ordering them to obey his orders. The crowd immediately turns against Burns, who then has to radio for backup assistance. After the other officers arrive, a fight ensues between them and the residents. Several members of both sides are injured, and numerous arrests are made.

Questions for Discussion

1. How could the supervisor have dealt better with Burns's lack of sensitivity?
2. What should the supervisor/administration do with Burns?
3. Are any liability or negligence issues present in this situation?

III. Justice in Jeopardy?

A municipal court judge borrows money from court employees, publicly endorses and campaigns for a candidate for judicial office, conducts personal business from chambers (displaying and selling antiques), directs other court employees to perform personal errands for him during court hours, suggests that persons appearing before him contribute to certain charities in lieu of paying

fines, and requires court employees to act as translators for his mother's nursery business.

Questions for Discussion

1. Which, if any, of these activities is unethical? Why?
2. Taken together, would these activities warrant the judge's being disciplined? Removed from office?

IV. Malice over Manners

You have been employed for 2 months as a corrections officer at a detention center with about 15 young offenders, most of whom have psychological problems. You are beginning to fit in well and to be invited to other staff members' social functions. During today's lunchtime, you are in the dining room and notice eight of the youths sitting at one table. One of them is an immature 18 years old whose table manners are disgusting. Today, he decides to pour mounds of ketchup over his meal, swirling it around his plate and then slurping it into his mouth. He then eats

with his mouth open and spits the food across the table while talking. You, the other officers, and even other inmates are sickened by his behavior. A fellow officer, Tom, gets up and tugs the boy away from the table by his shirt collar. The officer sets the boy's tray of food on the floor and orders him to get down on all fours next to it. "Your manners are disgusting," Tom says. "If you are going to eat like a dog, you may as well get down on all fours like a dog; get down there and lick the food off the plate till it is clean." Tom later tells you that he acted out of frustration and the desire to use a "shock tactic" to change the boy's behavior.

Questions for Discussion

1. What, if anything, should you do in this situation?
2. Did Tom act professionally? Ethically?

3. Should you have intervened on the boy's behalf?
4. What would you do about this incident if you were the superintendent of this institution and it was reported to you?

Chapter 14 Special Challenges: Labor Relations, Liability, and Discipline

I. Lost Love—and a Lost Laborer?

A police officer, Blake, is dispatched to a domestic violence call; on his arrival, a woman runs out of the house screaming, "Help me! He is going to kill me!" Her right eye is swollen. She also tells the officer, "I have had it with his drinking and womanizing and told him to pack up his things and go. That is when he began beating me."

You, a lieutenant, heard the call go out to Blake from Communications, but at shift's end you cannot find any offense report concerning the matter submitted by Blake. You ask Blake about the report, and he tells you that on entering the home he observed another officer, Carter, who works in your agency, who commented, "Thanks for coming out here, but things are cool now. She slapped me once, and I dealt with it. I admit I got a little out of hand, but it is under control. She is nothing but a cheating, money-grubbing louse." Blake admits that he purposely avoided

completing a report, deciding to consider it "like an offsetting penalty in football" and to overlook the matter.

Questions for Discussion

1. What would you, as the lieutenant and shift commander, do about this situation?
2. Should you call the female victim, or Officer Carter, into your office for an interview?
3. What action should you take if you do bring them both in, separately, and they deny that the incident occurred?
4. Suppose that you bring the woman in and she indicates that she wants to drop the matter because "it has happened before"; do you pursue it?
5. If you determine that Blake is in fact culpable for not reporting the incident, what actions (if any) should you take? On what grounds?

II. Bicycle Blues in Baskerville

Baskerville has a population of about 100,000, with an ethnic composition of 52 percent Anglo, 38 percent African American, and 10 percent Latino. The police force, however, composed of 200 sworn officers, has only about 20 percent women and minority officers. The city's central business district has deteriorated since the opening of a new shopping mall on the outskirts of the city, and the chief of police is receiving pressure from the mayor and the governing board to reduce crime in the central business district—where the largest percentage of minorities and lower-income residents in the city resides. The chief of police receives a federal grant to implement a bicycle patrol unit composed of one sergeant and five patrol officers in the central business district. The Baskerville Police Association (BPA) is the certified collective bargaining agent for all police officers and police sergeants. The

collective bargaining agreement has a seniority bidding clause for all shifts and certain designated job assignments, but the agreement does not include a bike unit. Therefore, the city attorney has advised the chief of police that he can select the five officers and one sergeant without complying with the collective bargaining agreement. The chief—under pressure from the city manager, mayor, and council to ensure that women and minority officers are given preference for these new assignments—knows that if he follows the collective bargaining agreement, only the most senior officers and sergeants, all older white males, have a chance of getting the assignments. The chief posts a notice stating that officers can apply for the new bike patrol unit but he will ultimately make the selection without regard to seniority. Several senior officers and sergeants then file a grievance with the BPA alleging that the chief has violated the agreement's seniority bidding provisions. Next, several female and minority officers approach the BPA president and say that the association betrayed them by not upholding their right to gain these high-profile assignments. The local newspaper editorializes that the chief has made the right decision, if not legally, at least morally. If the dispute heightens, the chief of police knows that his job might be in jeopardy; conversely, the BPA president may face a recall election if he is perceived as letting the chief get away with violating the agreement—and also faces a divided

membership if the BPA is perceived as fighting only for its older white male members.

Questions for Discussion

1. What are the key issues in this case?
2. What steps should be taken by the police chief and union leadership in response to this crisis?
3. Who are the key stakeholders in the situation, and what are their interests?
4. What options are available to the police leadership?

Chapter 15   Financial Administration

I. The Emptying Horn of Plenty

The chief of police in a small (20,000 population) city has seen nearly one-third of the agency's officers leave in the last year. Budget cuts, attrition, and better salaries in other regional agencies have been the impetus for the departures. Furthermore, the city council is proposing a 15 percent cut in the police budget for the coming year. Citizens are already complaining about delays in police responses and about having to drive to the police department to make complaints or to file reports. The county sheriff has offered in the local newspaper to provide backup for the city when needed, but the chief of police believes the sheriff to be power hungry and primarily motivated by a desire to absorb the city's police force into his agency. Severe cutbacks have already been made in the Drug Abuse and Resistance Education and gang prevention programs, and other nonessential services have been terminated. A number of concerts, political rallies, and outdoor events—all of which are normally peaceful—will be held soon during the summer months, requiring considerable overtime; the chief's view is that

"it is better to have us there and not be needed than vice-versa." Federal grants have run out.

One of the chief's staff suggests that the chief propose to the city council a drastic reduction in the city's parks, streets, or fire department budget, those monies being transferred to the police budget. The council, in turn, already wants to explore the possibility of hiring private security services for some events. Exacerbating the situation is the fact that violent crimes are increasing in the jurisdiction.

Questions for Discussion

1. What measures could the chief implement or propose to the council to slow or eliminate the resignations of sworn personnel?
2. How might the chief obtain more revenues or, alternatively, realize some savings for the department?
3. Should the chief go public with the idea of reducing budgets in the parks or other city departments?
4. How should the chief deal with the local sheriff's offer?

II. The Tourist Trap

You are a veteran in a medium-sized police department, with the rank of major, and are often asked to consult with and assist in writing grants for smaller police agencies that are experiencing problems. The City of White Springs is a rural community of about 3,000 year-round residents. However, given that it is both a prime skiing and shopping location, during the summertime and

Christmas holidays, the tourist population easily doubles that number on any given day. Normally, there are few crime or traffic problems, but during the past few years the growing number of local beer taverns and nightclubs has increased the incidence of alcohol-related problems—fighting, domestic violence, drunk driving, and so on. A small military base about 40 miles away has increasingly contributed to these problems. Your force of seven full-time and four part-time reserve officers is becoming strained and burned out during these peak times. More and more time is also spent with false burglar alarms, starting dead batteries, unlocking vehicles, and so on. There is no more money in the budget for additional hires, and the department's $50,000 overtime budget has been exceeded the past 2 years, causing unhappy council members to dip into other municipal budgets to bail you out. The town's charter requires that all members of the police force be graduates of the state police academy or trained by the department (for reserve officers).

Questions for Discussion

1. What are the major issues involved?
2. What are some possible solutions to the problems?

Chapter 16   Technologies and Tools: In an Era of Big Data and "the Cloud"

Although law enforcement technologies have become very advanced, many people working with those technologies believe the bigger, related obstacles that remain to be solved involve organizational inertia. In fact, some of those people argue that the technology side of police operations is *easy*; rather, it is the *people* side of the equation that makes progress more difficult to attain.

Consider the following arguments that have been offered as reasons for this inertia:

1. Cultural differences between federal, state, and local agencies as well as turf protection and communications barriers among law enforcement personnel cause far more "technical difficulties" and shortcomings than infrastructure, software, and database platforms.

2. There is a technology mindset and a culture—one that poses a hurdle to information-sharing at every level—that states information is not to be shared except to thos e having the proper classification and/ or on a "need-to-know" basis.

3. Agency bureaucracies and politics also may impede information sharing and interagency communications.

4. Some people simply do not wish to devote the time necessary to learn to use technologies correctly.[2]

Given the aforementioned issues, assume the following:

Your police agency is attempting to implement a new software system to estimate crime and predict future hot spots. The system uses confirmed crime data to predict future offenses in 500-square-foot locations, and requires between 1,200 and 2,000 data points, including burglaries, batteries, assaults, or other crimes, to obtain the most accuracy. Employees must transfer the data on designated crime types from the records management system to the secure Web-based system. The system processes the information through the algorithm and combines it with historical crime data to make predictions. After staff members log in to the system, it generates hot spot maps.

As with any new program, however, employees resist change; they are now raising questions and concerns that indicate resistance to implementing this new system. Your agency's research division is attempting to work with officers and detectives to develop maps and solicit feedback before implementation of the program.[3]

Questions for Discussion

1. What steps would you take in order to (1) ameliorate the employees' concerns, questions, and overall resistance, in order to (2) implement the new system smoothly and thus maximize its efficiency and effectiveness?

Notes

1. Adapted from the Federal Judicial Center, "Inside the Federal Courts: What the Federal Courts Do," http://www.fjc. gov/federal/courts.nsf/autoframe!openform&nav=menu1& page=/federal/courts.nsf/page/172 (accessed May 2, 2014).

2. Adapted from Doug Wyllie, "Technology Isn't the (Biggest) Problem for Information Sharing in Law Enforcement," *PoliceOne.com*, April 30, 2009, http://www.policeone.com/police-products/communications/articles/1816539-Technology-isn-t-the-biggest-problem-for-information-sharing-in-law-enforcement/ (accessed May 2, 2014).

3. To see how the Santa Cruz, California, Police Department implemented this new system, see: Zach Friend, "Predictive Policing: Using Technology to Reduce Crime," *FBI Law Enforcement Bulletin*, http://www.fbi.gov/stats-services/publications/law-enforcement-bulletin/2013/April/predictive-policing-using-technology-to-reduce-crime (accessed May 2, 2014).

Appendix II   Writings of Confucius, Machiavelli, and Lao-Tzu

The writings of certain major figures have stood the test of time. The analects of Confucius (551–479 B.C.E.) and the teachings of Machiavelli (1469–1527) are still quite popular today. Many graduate and undergraduate students in a variety of academic disciplines analyze the writings of both, especially Machiavelli's *The Prince*. Both men tend to agree on many points regarding the means of governance, as the following will demonstrate. After presenting some comments from each philosopher, I will consider their application to justice administration.

Confucius often emphasized the connection between morality and leadership, saying, for example:

> He who rules by moral force is like the pole star, which remains in its place while all the lesser stars do homage to it. Govern the people by regulations, keep order among them by chastisements, and they will flee from you, and lose all self-respect. Govern them by moral force, keep order among them and they will come to you of their own accord. If the ruler is upright, all will go well even though he does not give orders. But if he himself is not upright, even though he gives orders, they will not be obeyed.[1]

Confucius also commented on the leader's treatment of subordinates: "Promote those who are worthy, train those who are incompetent; that is the best form of encouragement."[2] He also felt that leaders should learn from and emulate good administrators:

> In the presence of a good man, think all the time how you may learn to equal him. In the presence of a bad man, turn your gaze within! Even when I am walking in a party of no more than three I can always be certain of learning from those I am with. There will be good qualities that I can select for imitation and bad ones that will teach me what requires correction in myself.[3]

Unlike Confucius, Machiavelli is often maligned for being cruel; the "end justifies the means" philosophy imputed to him has cast a pall over his writings. However, although he often seems as biting as the "point of a stiletto"[4] and at times ruthless ("Men ought either to be caressed or destroyed, since they will seek revenge for minor hurts but will not be able to revenge major ones,"[5] and "If you have to make a choice, to be feared is much safer than to be loved"[6]), he, like Confucius, often spoke of the leader's need to possess character and compassion. For all of his blunt, management-oriented notions of administration, Machiavelli was prudent and pragmatic.

Like Confucius, Machiavelli felt that administrators would do well to follow examples set by other great leaders:

> Men almost always prefer to walk in paths marked out by others and pattern their actions through imitation. A prudent man should always follow the footsteps of the great and imitate those who have been supreme. A prince should read history and reflect on the actions of great men.[7]

Machiavelli's counsel also agreed with that of Confucius with regard to the need for leaders to surround themselves with persons both knowledgeable and devoted: "The first notion one gets of a prince's intelligence comes from the men around him."[8]

But, again, like Confucius, Machiavelli believed that administrators should be careful of their subordinates' ambition and greed:

A new prince must always harm those over whom he assumes authority. You cannot stay friends with those who put you in power, because you can never satisfy them as they expected. The man who makes another powerful ruins himself. The reason is that he gets power either by shrewdness or by strength, and both qualities are suspect to the man who has been given the power.[9]

On the need for developing and maintaining good relations with subordinates, he wrote:

If a prince puts his trust in the people, knows how to command, is a man of courage and doesn't lose his head in adversity, and can rouse his people to action by his own example and orders, he will never find himself betrayed, and his foundations will prove to have been well laid. The best fortress of all consists in not being hated by your people. Every prince should prefer to be considered merciful rather than cruel. The prince must have people well disposed toward him; otherwise in times of adversity there's no hope.[10]

In this era of collective bargaining and a rapidly changing workforce, contemporary criminal justice administrators might do well to heed the comments of Confucius and Machiavelli.

Perhaps a leader, in the purest sense, also influences others by example. This characteristic of leadership was recognized in the sixth century B.C.E. by Lao-Tzu, who wrote:

The superior leader gets things done

With very little motion.

He imparts instruction not through many words

But through a few deeds.

He keeps informed about everything

But interferes hardly at all.

He is a catalyst.

And although things wouldn't get done as well

If he weren't there.

When they succeed he takes no credit.

And because he takes no credit

Credit never leaves him.[11]

Notes

1. Confucius, *The Analects of Confucius*, Arthur Waley (trans.) (London: George Allen and Unwin, 1938), pp. 88, 173
2. Ibid., p. 92.
3. Ibid., pp. 105, 127
4. Niccolo Machiavelli, *The Prince,* Robert M. Adams (trans.) (New York: W. W. Norton, 1992), p. xvii.
5. Ibid., p. 7.
6. Ibid., p. 46

7. Ibid., pp. 15, 41
8. Ibid., p. 63.
9. Ibid., pp. 5, 11
10. Ibid., pp. 29, 60
11. Quoted in Wayne W. Bennett and Karen M. Hess, *Management and Supervision in Law Enforcement*, 3rd ed. (Belmont, CA: Wadsworth, 2001), p. 63.

3D printing: a process whereby a solid object, including guns and other weapons, can be made from a digital model, as layers of material are laid down in different shapes

Absolute ethics: a belief that something is good or bad, black or white, and that certain acts are inherently right or wrong in themselves, irrespective of one's culture

Accreditation: a voluntary effort by a criminal justice agency where it seeks to meet national standards in its field and thus be officially designated as accredited

Active shooter: an individual who is actively engaged in killing or attempting to kill people in a confined and populated area

Administrator: the person whose focus is on the overall organization, its mission, acquisition and use of resources, and agency relationship with external organizations and groups

Adversarial system: the legal system whereby two opposing sides present their arguments in court

Affirmative action: actions or policies that favor persons or groups who have suffered from discrimination, particularly in employment or education

Alternative dispute resolution (ADR): settling disputes outside of court, typically by negotiation, conciliation, mediation, and arbitration

Alternatives to incarceration: any form of punishment or treatment other than prison or jail time given to a convicted person

Americans with Disabilities Act: legislation making it illegal to discriminate against persons with disabilities in their recruitment, hiring, and promotion practices and then focusing on reducing forces of resistance

Appearance of impropriety: where someone creates a circumstance or situation that appears to raise questions of ethics

Arbitration: negotiation with a final and binding decision that sets the terms of the settlement and with which the parties are legally required to comply

Assessment center: a process used for promoting and hiring personnel that may include oral interviews, psychological tests, group and in-basket exercises, and writing and role-playing exercises

Audit: an objective examination of the financial statements of an organization, either by its employees or by an outside firm

Autocratic leader: leaders who are primarily authoritarian in nature and prefer to give orders rather than invite group participation

Automated records system: technologies that assist police administrators in receiving, investigating, and arriving at proper dispositions employee complaints and commendations

Big data: applying tremendous computing power to massive and often highly complex sets of information

Bona fide occupational qualifier (BFOQ): in certain situations, a rationale for discriminating on the basis of a business necessity

Brady material: evidence in the government's possession that is favorable to the accused, material to either guilt or punishment, and must therefore be disclosed to the defense; also, because of Brady, prosecutors must inform the defense whenever a police officer involved in their case has knowingly lied in his reports in the past

Bring your own device (BYOD): a policy whereby employees may bring their personal mobile devices to their workplace and use those devices to access privileged agency information

Budget: a plan, in financial terms, estimating future expenditures and indicating agency plans and policy regarding financial resources and the appropriation and expenditure of funds

Budget cycle: a time frame that determines how long a budget lasts, which can vary from agency to agency

Budget execution: carrying out the organization's budgeted responsibilities in a proper manner, and providing an accounting of the administrator's actions with the same

Budget formulation: the preparation of a budget to allocate funds in accordance with agency priorities, plans, and programs, and to deliver necessary services

Bureaucracy: structuring of an organization so as to function efficiently; it includes rules, division of labor, hierarchy of authority, and expertise among its members

Case delay: an excessive amount of time passing prior to bringing a criminal case to trial

Central office: the state's central organization that oversees its prison system

Chief executive officer (CEO): the highest-ranking executive or administrator in an organization, who is in charge of its overall operation

Chief of police: the title given to the top official in the chain of command of a municipal police department

Civil liability: blame assigned to a person or organization because its employees committed negligent or other acts resulting in some type of harm.

Civil Rights of Institutionalized Persons Act: a federal law protecting the rights of people in state or local correctional facilities who are mentally ill, disabled, or handicapped

Classification: the placing of inmates into the proper levels of security, housing, programming, and other aspects of their incarceration

Cloud computing: using a network of remote servers hosted on the Internet to store, manage, and process data, rather than a local server or a personal computer

Collective bargaining: See "negotiation"

Communication: use of words, sounds, signs, bodily cues, or other actions to convey or exchange information, or to express ideas, to another person or group

Conflict model: holds that actors within the criminal justice system are self-serving, with pressures for success, promotion, and general accountability and resulting in fragmented efforts

Consensus model: the view of the criminal justice system in which it is assumed that all parts of the system work toward a common goal

Consolidation: the merging of two or more city and/or county law-enforcement agencies into a single entity

Contingency theory: an effort to determine the fit between the organization's characteristics and its tasks and the motivations of individuals

Contract policing: where a (usually smaller) community contracts with an outside unit of government to provide its policing services

COPPS: community-oriented policing and problem solving, which has emerged as the dominant philosophy and strategy of policing

Correctional officer: the person responsible for the custody, safety, security, and supervision of inmates in a prison or other correctional facility

Court clerk: an officer of a court who is responsible for its clerical filing and recordkeeping, entering judgments and orders, and so on.

Court of last resort: that court in a given state that has its highest and final appellate authority

Court unification: reorganizing a trial court's structure, procedures, funding, and administration so streamline operations, better deploy personnel, and improve trial and appellate processes

Courthouse violence: where individuals perpetrate violent incidents against others in courthouses, both targeted and nontargeted in nature

Courtroom civility: judges, litigants, and court actors conducting themselves appropriately so that all parties are afforded a fair opportunity to present their case

Crime control model: a philosophy that states crime must be repressed, the accused presumed guilty, legal loopholes eliminated, offenders swiftly punished, and police and prosecutors given a high degree of discretion

Criminal justice network: a view that the justice system's components cooperate and share similar goals but operate independently and competing for funding.

Criminal justice nonsystem: the view that police, courts, and corrections agencies do not function harmoniously, are not a coordinated structure, and are neither efficient nor fair enough to create fear of punishment nor respect for its values

Criminal justice process: the decisions and actions by an institution, offender, victim, or society that influence the offender's movement into, through, or out of the justice system

"CSI effect": the belief that a trial may be affected by television programming that creates inaccurate expectations by jurors regarding the power and use of forensic evidence

Day reporting center: a site where offenders report to receive an array of educational, vocational, treatment, and other services, to reduce the risk factors associated with recidivism

Décor: the physical or decorative style of a setting

Decorum: correct or proper behavior indicating respect and politeness

Democratic leader: leaders who stress working within the group and strive to attain cooperation from group members by eliciting their ideas and support

Deontological ethics: a branch of ethics that focuses on the duty to act and the rightness or wrongness of actions, rather than rightness or wrongness of the consequences of those actions

Direct supervision jail: a type of design where cells are arranged in podular fashion, have an open dayroom area, and correctional officers are close to and interact with the inmates

Discipline matrix: intended to provide disciplinary actions against police officers who are consistent and fair, taking into account several variables and circumstances

Disparate treatment: treating people differently because of their age, gender, sex, or other protected status

Division of labor: a basic feature of traditional organizational theory, where specialization produces different groups of functional responsibilities

Dress code: a set of rules, usually written as policy, specifying the required manner of dress and appearance for employees in an organization

Drug interdiction: efforts to reduce the supply and demand for drugs in prison, to include focusing on visitors, staff, mail, warehouses, gates, volunteers, and contractors

Dual court system: an organizational distinction between courts, with a federal court system and 50 individual state court systems

Due process model: the ideal that the accused should be presumed innocent and have their rights protected, while police must act only in accordance with the Constitution

Duty of care: a doctrine holding that police have a duty to protect the general public where a "special relationship" exists

Early warning system (EWS): a means of identifying officers whose behavior is problematic, usually involving citizen complaints and improper use of force

Electronic court records: where incoming documents are scanned, processed (using images rather than paper), and stored in an electronic document management system

Ethics: moral principles governing individual and group behavior, based on ideas concerning what is morally good and bad

Exclusionary rule: the Constitutional principle holding that evidence obtained illegally by law enforcement officers cannot be used against the suspect in a criminal prosecution

Expectancy theory: a theory that certain beliefs can influence effort and performance

Expenditure: a payment for goods or services, to settle a financial obligation indicated by an invoice, contract, or other such document

Fact finding: interpretation of facts and the determination of what weight to attach to them in negotiations

Failure to protect: a form of negligence where a police officer fails to protect a person from a known and foreseeable danger

Fair Labor Standards Act (FLSA): a federal law establishing minimum wages and requiring overtime compensation in the private sector as well as state and local governmental employees

Family and Medical Leave Act (FMLA): legislation that entitles eligible employees to take unpaid, job-protected leave for specified family and medical reasons

Federal sentencing guidelines: rules for computing uniform sentencing policy, they also provide classifications of offenses and offenders, severity of crimes, and suggested punishments

Federalization: the notion that local police are being overly co-opted by federal law enforcement agencies, directing too many resources toward protecting the nation's borders and other federal duties

Field training officer (FTO): a program designed to help new officers to transition smoothly from the recruit academy phase of their career, with a veteran officer observing and evaluating their performance in the field

First-line supervisor: the lowest yet a very important level of leadership, the supervisor directs, controls, and evaluates the work of field personnel, ensures that agency policies and procedures are followed, counsels and places employees where resources are most needed, resolves employee conflicts, and performs related duties

Force-field analysis: a process of identifying forces in support of change, those resisting change

Frivolous lawsuit: an action filed by a party or attorney who is aware it is without merit, due to a lack of legal basis or argument for the alleged claim

Fusion center: coordination of all counter-terrorism elements within a jurisdiction by receiving and analyzing terrorist threat or activity information

Generation Y: sometimes termed the millennials, persons born between 1980 and 2000

Geriatric inmates: while there is no standard definition concerning what age an inmate becomes "elderly," it is known that the aging inmate population is growing rapidly, raising medical costs and requiring special needs be met

Grant writing: preparing and submitting required documents and information for making application to funding bodies that award monies to assist eligible businesses and government agencies

Grapevine: an informal means of circulating and communicating information or gossip

Gratuities: complimentary gifts of money, services, or something of other value

Great Recession: the severe, prolonged economic downturn lasting from December 2007 to June 2009

Grievance: a real or imagined wrong or other cause for complaint by an employee concerning job-related matters

Hands-off policy: a practice by judges, in an era when they believed they had neither training nor knowledge concerning penology, allowing wardens the freedom to operate prisons as they saw fit

Hatch Acts: legislation that limits partisan political activities by governmental employees

Hawthorne effect: a theory meaning that employees' behavior may be altered if they believe they are being studied—and that management *cares*

Hierarchy of needs: Maslow's belief that people's basic and primary needs or drives are physiological (survival), safety or security, social, ego (self-esteem), and self-realization or actualization

Hostage taking: when any person—staff, visitor, or inmate—is held against his or her will by an inmate seeking to escape, gain concessions, or achieve other goals

House arrest/electronic monitoring: court-ordered punishment where a convicted or accused offender must remain in his home, usually while being remotely monitored electronically

Humanistic school: a school of psychological thought that stressed the importance of growth and self-actualization and argued that people are innately good

Inappropriate staff–inmate relationships: such correctional staff behaviors as sexual relations with inmates, providing special favors for inmates, or smuggling in contraband

Individual calendar system: a system whereby cases are assigned to a single judge who oversees all aspects of it from arraignment to pretrial motions and trial

Inferior courts: the lowest level of state courts, normally trial courts of limited jurisdiction

Inputs: an organization's committing such resources as funds, personnel/labor, and equipment toward accomplishing a goal or mission

Intelligence-led policing: a style of policing that combines crime analysis (where the "who, what, when, and where" of crime is analyzed) with intelligence analysis (which looks at the "who" of crime—the crime networks and individuals)

Intensive supervision: tight control and supervision of offenders in the community through strict enforcement of conditions and frequent reporting to a probation officer

Intermediate courts of appeals (ICAs): courts in the federal and state court systems that hear appeals, organizationally situated between the trial courts and the court of last resort

Intermediate sanctions: a range of sentencing options designed to fill the gap between probation and confinement, reduce institutional crowding, and reduce correctional costs

Internal complaints: complaints filed against employees by persons within the organization, either by one's peers or by supervisors

Job action: an activity by employees to express their dissatisfaction with a particular person, event, or condition relating to their work

Judicial (court) administration: the day-to-day and long-range activities of those persons who are responsible for the activities and functions of a court

Judicial Conference of the United States: the administrative policymaking organization of the federal judicial system

Judicial selection: the method used to nominate, select, or elect and install judges into office

Jurisdiction: the power or authority given to a court by law to hear certain kinds of cases

Jury administration: ensuring that a jury is properly composed and sustained prior to and during trials

Juvenile waiver: a provision for juvenile court judges to transfer jurisdiction over individual juvenile cases to an adult criminal court for prosecution

Laissez-faire leader: a hands-off approach to leadership, in which the organization essentially runs itself

Leadership: influencing and working with and through individuals or a group to generate activities that will accomplish organizational goals

Learning organization: an organizational culture that looks to the future to continually experiment, improve, and adapt so as to meet the challenges of a more complex role

Life without parole (LWOP): a type of sentence that can be applied to convicted adult (not juvenile) offenders, requiring that they spend the remainder of their natural life in prison

Line-item budget: a budget format that breaks down its components into major categories, such as personnel, equipment, contractual services, commodities, and capital outlay items

Lying (accepted/deviant): lying that serves legitimate purposes and lying that conceals or promotes crimes or illegitimate ends

Maintenance and hygiene factors: elements of one's career that provide one with their need to avoid pain (e.g., adequate pay, benefits, job security, decent working conditions, supervision, interpersonal relations)

Malfeasance: crimes or misconduct that officials knowingly commit in violation of state laws and/or agency rules and regulations

Manager: a person in the intermediate level of management, responsible for carrying out the policies and directives of upper-level administrators and supervising subordinate managers and employees

Master calendar system: a system whereby judges are assigned to oversee all stages of a case (preliminary hearing, arraignment, trial)

Mediation: a third party comes in to help opposing parties to settle their negotiations

Meet and confer: a comparatively weak bargaining system where employees may organize and select bargaining representatives; but if an impasse occurs, their options are limited

Mentally ill inmate: one who meets the definition and has a significant mental disorder(s), which can include schizophrenia, bipolar disorders, and major depression, among others

Merit selection/Missouri Bar Plan: a nonpartisan method of selecting judges; a nominating commission provides names of qualified persons to the governor, who chooses one person to serve

Middle manager: typically a captain or lieutenant, one who coordinates agency units' activities and sees that the administrative strategies and overall mission are carried out

Militarization: a belief held by some that local police—using military-style weapons, tactics, training, uniforms, and even heavy equipment—are becoming too militaristic in nature

Military model: where, for example, police and many correctional officers wear uniforms, use rank designations, and have a hierarchical command structure much as the military services

Mintzberg model for CEOs: a model that delineates and defines the primary roles of a chief executive officer

Misfeasance: illegitimate acts likely committed by high-ranking officials who knowingly allow indiscretions that undermine the public interest and benefit them personally

Model Code of Judicial Conduct: (1) rules governing the conduct of judges while acting in their professional capacity; (2) standards written by the ABA to assist judges in maintaining the highest standards of judicial and personal conduct

Model of circumstantial corruptibility: a view regarding acceptance of gratuities, holding that the exchange of a gift is influenced by two elements: the roles of the giver and the receiver

Motivational factors: those psychosocial factors providing intrinsic satisfaction on the job, serving as an incentive to devote more of their time, energy, and expertise in productive behavior

N-DEx: a service launched after 9/11 by the Federal Bureau of Investigation to assist agencies in making data correlations and in predictive policing

National Incident Management System: a nationwide system providing for levels of governments to work together to address domestic incidents

National Judicial College, The: an institute of learning in Reno, Nevada, that trains judges how to be better arbiters of justice

Negative discipline: discipline that involves some form of punishment

Negligence: when someone's conduct creates a danger to others, often by subjecting others to a risk of harm and resulting in some form of injury

Negotiation: a dialogue between labor and management for developing a written agreement concerning such issues as working conditions, salaries, and benefits

New old penology: Dilulio's term for a shift of attention from the society of captives to the government of keepers

NIC Executive Training Program for New Wardens: training for new wardens to help grasp such areas as institutional culture, budget management, decision making, and media relations

Noble cause corruption: corruption committed in the name of good ends; when an act is committed to achieve a good end, it might still be justified

Nonfeasance: acts of omission or avoidance knowingly committed by officials who are responsible for carrying out such acts

Notorious cases: local, regional, or national civil or criminal trials either involving celebrities or particularly egregious crimes, requiring attention to jury selection and trial procedures

Organization: entities of two or more people who cooperate to achieve an objective(s)

Organizational structure: how an organization divides up its work and establishes lines of authority and communication

Organizational theory: the study of organizational designs and structures that includes the behavior of administrators and managers within organizations

Outputs: an organization's desired outcome, goods, or services

Parole: where an offender is conditionally released from prison to serve the remaining portion of a criminal sentence in the community

Peace officer: those persons having arrest authority either with a warrant or based on probable cause

Peace Officers Bill of Rights (POBR): legislation mandating due process rights for peace officers who are the subject of internal investigations that could lead to disciplinary action

Performance budget: a budget format that is input-output oriented and relates the volume of work to be done to the amount of money spent

Personal loyalty syndrome: loyalty that can be given to unworthy peers or superiors, even when resulting in violations of constitutional provisions, legal requirements, or the public good

Personnel complaint: an allegation of misconduct or illegal behavior against an employee by anyone inside or outside the organization

Planned change: rational approach to criminal justice planning that involves problem analysis, setting goals and objectives, program and policy design, developing an action plan, and monitoring and evaluation

Planning–programming–budgeting system (PPBS): a budgeting tool that links program to the ways and means of facilitating the program and better informing decision makers of outcomes of their actions

Police training officer (PTO): a relatively new program where new officer are evaluated on their application of community policing and problem-solving principles, using adult- and problem-based learning principles

Policies: written guidelines that are general in nature and serve to further the organization's philosophy and mission and help in interpreting their elements to the officers

Policymaking: (1) developing plans that are then used by an organization or government as a basis for making decisions; (2) establishing rules, principles, or guidelines to govern actions by ordinary citizens and persons in positions of authority

POSDCORB: an acronym for planning, organizing, staffing, directing, coordinating, reporting, and budgeting; this philosophy was emphasized in police management for many years

Positive discipline: a formal program that attempts to change poor employee behavior without invoking punishment

Predictive policing: a policing strategy that integrates crime analysis, technology, intelligence-led policing, and other tactics to inform forward thinking crime prevention strategies

Principles of good prison leadership: Dilulio's six principles for success in corrections management

Prison director: the person who sets policy for all wardens and prisons to follow in terms of management and inmate treatment

Prison industries: prison programs intended to provide productive work and skill development opportunities for offenders, to reduce recidivism and prepare offenders for re-entry into society

Prison Litigation Reform Act: a law providing remedies for prison condition lawsuits and to discourage frivolous and abusive prison lawsuits

Prison Rape Elimination Act of 2003: a law mandating national data collection on the incidence and prevalence of sexual assault in correctional facilities

Prisoners' rights: the collective body of Constitutional rights afforded jail and prison inmates relating to the fundamental human rights and civil liberties

Privatization: either the operation of existing prison facilities, or the building and operation of new prisons by for-profit companies

Probation: where a court places an offender on supervision in the community, generally in lieu of incarceration

Problem-solving courts: special courts created to accommodate persons with specific needs and problems, such as drug, veteran, and mentally ill offenders

Procedures: specific guidelines that serve to direct employee actions, such as how to prepare investigations and conduct patrol, bookings, radio communications, and prepare reports

Program budget: a budget format that examines cost units as units of activity rather than as units and subunits within the organization

Proximate cause: due to someone's conduct, a person sustained injury or damage

Radio-frequency identification tracking (RFID): a device worn by both inmates and correctional officers for tracking purposes

Relative ethics: a belief that determining what is good or bad is relative to the individual or culture and can depend on the end or outcome of an action

Relatively identifiable boundary: an organization's goals and the public it is intended to serve

Reverse discrimination: the argument that affirmative action policies have resulted in unfair treatment for members of majority groups

Robotics: a branch of technology involving the design, construction, and function of robots

Rules and regulations: specific managerial guidelines for officers, such not smoking in public, types of weapons to be carried on duty, and so on

S.A.R.A.: for scanning, analysis, response, assessment—the logical framework for officers to respond to crime and neighborhood disorder

Scientific management: a school of management thought that is concerned primarily with the efficiency and output of an individual worker

Social entity: an organization composed of people who interact with one another and with other people

Sexual violence: any sexual act or attempted sexual act, unwanted sexual comments or advances, or acts to traffic, against a person's sexuality using coercion

Sheriff: the title given to the top official in the chain of command of a county law enforcement agency

Shock incarceration/boot camp: a short-term program where offenders experience rigorous military drill and ceremony, physical training and labor, and treatment and education to reduce recidivism and develop personal responsibility

Shock probation/parole: where a judge sends a convicted offender to prison for a short time and then suspends the remainder of the sentence, granting probation

Smart policing: a policing approach that emphasizes the use of data and analytics as well as improved crime analysis, performance measurement, and evaluation research

Social contract: a belief that people are essentially irrational and selfish, but have enough rationality to come together to form governments for self-protection

Social media: forms of electronic communication for social networking, to share information, ideas, personal messages

Span of control: the number of subordinates a chief executive, manager, or supervisor in a criminal justice organization can effectively supervise

Style theory: a theory that focuses on what leaders do, and arguing that leaders engage in two distinct types of behaviors: those relating to task and relationships

Succession planning: identifying and developing employees who have the potential to fill key leadership positions in the organization

Supermax prison: institutions providing the most secure levels of custody in prisons, with long-term, segregated housing for inmates who represent the highest security risks

Supervisor: typically the lowest position of leadership in an organization, one who plans, organizes, and directs staff members in their daily activities

System fragmentation: the view that members of police, courts, and corrections agencies have tremendous discretion and their own perception of the offender, resulting in goal conflict

Telemedicine: the use of telecommunications technology to remotely diagnosis and treat inmates

Terrorism: the unlawful use of force against persons or property to intimidate or coerce a government or its population, so as to further political or social objectives

Theory X: the management view holding that people inherently dislike work and will avoid it, and thus negative reinforcements (punishments) and other "drivers" must be used as motivators

Theory Y: the management view holding that people inherently like to work, seek greater responsibility, and are inherently motivated rather than by punishment

Therapeutic community: drug-free residential settings relying heavily on peer influence and group processes to promote drug-free behavior

Threat assessment: a process of identifying, assessing, investigating, and managing a courthouse threat

Title 18, *U.S. Code*, Section 242: a law making it a criminal offense for any person acting under color of law to violate another person's civil rights

Title 42, *U.S. Code*, Section 1983: a law making it a civil offense for any person acting under color of law to violate another person's civil rights

Tort: the infliction of some injury on one person *by* another

Trait theory: a theory based on the notion that good leaders possess certain character traits that poor leaders do not

Trial courts: courts of original jurisdiction (or "first instance") where evidence and testimony are first introduced and findings of fact and law are made

Unit management: a corrections management approach with the larger prison population being subdivided into smaller units, felt to be more effective and to improve inmate classification

***United States Code* 21 U.S.C. §851:** a federal law allowing federal prosecutors to more heavily punish hard-core drug traffickers who have prior drug felony convictions

Unity of command: the principle holding that only one person should be in command or control of a situation or an employee

Unmanned aerial vehicles: ground-operated, powered aerial vehicles that are designed to carry nonlethal payloads for reconnaissance, command and control, and deception

Use of force: the amount of effort required by police or other criminal justice functionary to compel compliance by an unwilling subject

Use-of-force continuum: a graphic depiction of levels of force used by police to determine the type of force that is appropriate for certain types of citizen resistance

Vehicular pursuit: (1) where one or more law enforcement officers is attempting to apprehend a suspect who is evading arrest while operating a motor vehicle, usually at high speed or using other elusive means; (2) police attempts to apprehend someone in a fleeing vehicle who has indicated he or she does not intend to stop or yield

Warden: the person responsible for all activities, safety, and security of the staff and inmates within a prison

Workplace harassment: unwelcome verbal or physical conduct (whether or not of a sexual nature) that creates a hostile work environment, or a change in an employment status or benefits

Zero-based budget (ZBB): a budget format that requires managers to justify their entire budget request in detail, rather than simply using budget amounts established in previous years

Index